JOE CELKO'S

SQL FOR SMARTIES: ADVANCED SQL PROGRAMMING

THIRD EDITION

The Morgan Kaufmann Series in Data Management Systems

Series Editor: Jim Gray, Microsoft Research

- *Joe Celko's SQL for Smarties: Advanced SQL Programming*, Third Edition, Joe Celko
- *Moving Objects Databases*, Ralf Güting and Markus Schneider
- *Foundations of Multidimensional and Metric Data Structures*, Hanan Samet
- *Joe Celko's SQL Programming Style*, Joe Celko
- *Data Mining, Second Edition: Concepts and Techniques*, Ian Witten and Eibe Frank
- *Fuzzy Modeling and Genetic Algorithms for Data Mining and Exploration*, Earl Cox
- *Data Modeling Essentials*, Third Edition, Graeme C. Simsion and Graham C. Witt
- *Location-Based Services*, Jochen Schiller and Agnès Voisard
- *Database Modeling with Microsft® Visio for Enterprise Architects,* Terry Halpin, Ken Evans, Patrick Hallock, Bill Maclean
- *Designing Data-Intensive Web Applications*, Stephano Ceri, Piero Fraternali, Aldo Bongio, Marco Brambilla, Sara Comai, and Maristella Matera
- *Mining the Web: Discovering Knowledge from Hypertext Data*, Soumen Chakrabarti
- *Advanced SQL: 1999—Understanding Object-Relational and Other Advanced Features*, Jim Melton
- *Database Tuning: Principles, Experiments, and Troubleshooting Techniques*, Dennis Shasha and Philippe Bonnet
- *SQL:1999—Understanding Relational Language Components*, Jim Melton and Alan R. Simon
- *Information Visualization in Data Mining and Knowledge Discovery*, Edited by Usama Fayyad, Georges G. Grinstein, and Andreas Wierse
- *Transactional Information Systems: Theory, Algorithms, and Practice of Concurrency Control and Recovery*, Gerhard Weikum and Gottfried Vossen
- *Spatial Databases: With Application to GIS*, Philippe Rigaux, Michel Scholl, and Agnes Voisard
- *Information Modeling and Relational Databases: From Conceptual Analysis to Logical Design*, Terry Halpin
- *Component Database Systems*, Edited by Klaus R. Dittrich and Andreas Geppert
- *Managing Reference Data in Enterprise Databases: Binding Corporate Data to the Wider World*, Malcolm Chisholm
- *Data Mining: Concepts and Techniques*, Jiawei Han and Micheline Kamber
- *Understanding SQL and Java Together: A Guide to SQLJ, JDBC, and Related Technologies*, Jim Melton and Andrew Eisenberg
- *Database: Principles, Programming, and Performance, Second Edition*, Patrick and Elizabeth O'Neil
- *The Object Data Standard: ODMG 3.0*, Edited by R. G. G. Cattell and Douglas K. Barry
- *Data on the Web: From Relations to Semistructured Data and XML*, Serge Abiteboul, Peter Buneman, and Dan Suciu
- *Data Mining: Practical Machine Learning Tools and Techniques with Java Implementations*, Ian Witten and Eibe Frank
- *Joe Celko's SQL for Smarties: Advanced SQL Programming*, Second Edition, Joe Celko
- *Joe Celko's Data and Databases: Concepts in Practice*, Joe Celko

- *Developing Time-Oriented Database Applications in SQL*, Richard T. Snodgrass
- *Web Farming for the Data Warehouse*, Richard D. Hackathorn
- *Database Modeling & Design, Third Edition*, Toby J. Teorey
- *Management of Heterogeneous and Autonomous Database Systems*, Edited by Ahmed Elmagarmid, Marek Rusinkiewicz, and Amit Sheth
- *Object-Relational DBMSs: Tracking the Next Great Wave*, Second Edition, Michael Stonebraker and Paul Brown,with Dorothy Moore
- *A Complete Guide to DB2 Universal Database*, Don Chamberlin
- *Universal Database Management: A Guide to Object/Relational Technology*, Cynthia Maro Saracco
- *Readings in Database Systems*, Third Edition, Edited by Michael Stonebraker and Joseph M. Hellerstein
- *Understanding SQL's Stored Procedures: A Complete Guide to SQL/PSM*, Jim Melton
- *Principles of Multimedia Database Systems*, V. S. Subrahmanian
- *Principles of Database Query Processing for Advanced Applications*, Clement T. Yu and Weiyi Meng
- *Advanced Database Systems*, Carlo Zaniolo, Stefano Ceri, Christos Faloutsos, Richard T. Snodgrass, V. S. Subrahmanian, and Roberto Zicari
- *Principles of Transaction Processing*, Philip A. Bernstein and Eric Newcomer
- *Using the New DB2: IBMs Object-Relational Database System*, Don Chamberlin
- *Distributed Algorithms*, Nancy A. Lynch
- *Active Database Systems: Triggers and Rules For Advanced Database Processing*, Edited by Jennifer Widom and Stefano Ceri
- *Migrating Legacy Systems: Gateways, Interfaces, & the Incremental Approach*, Michael L. Brodie and Michael Stonebraker
- *Atomic Transactions, Nancy Lynch, Michael Merritt*, William Weihl, and Alan Fekete
- *Query Processing for Advanced Database Systems*, Edited by Johann Christoph Freytag, David Maier, and Gottfried Vossen
- *Transaction Processing: Concepts and Techniques*, Jim Gray and Andreas Reuter
- *Building an Object-Oriented Database System: The Story of* O_2, Edited by François Bancilhon, Claude Delobel, and Paris Kanellakis
- *Database Transaction Models for Advanced Applications*, Edited by Ahmed K. Elmagarmid
- *A Guide to Developing Client/Server SQL Applications*, Setrag Khoshafian, Arvola Chan, Anna Wong, and Harry K. T. Wong
- *The Benchmark Handbook for Database and Transaction Processing Systems*, Second Edition, Edited by Jim Gray
- *Camelot and Avalon: A Distributed Transaction Facility*, Edited by Jeffrey L. Eppinger, Lily B. Mummert, and Alfred Z. Spector
- *Readings in Object-Oriented Database Systems*, Edited by Stanley B. Zdonik and David Maier

JOE CELKO'S
SQL FOR SMARTIES: ADVANCED SQL PROGRAMMING
THIRD EDITION

Joe Celko

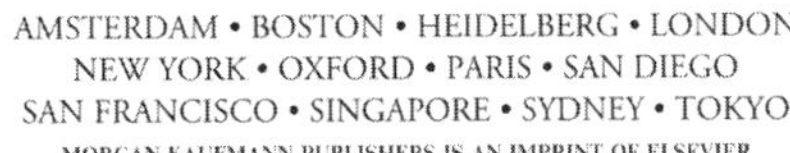

Publishing Director	Michael Forster
Publisher	Diane Cerra
Publishing Services Manager	Andre Cuello
Senior Project Manager	George Morrison
Editorial Assistant	Asma Stephan
Cover Design	Side by Side Studios
Cover Image	Side by Side Studios
Composition	Multiscience Press, Inc.
Copyeditor	Multiscience Press, Inc.
Proofreader	Multiscience Press, Inc.
Indexer	Multiscience Press, Inc.
Interior printer	The Maple-Vail Book Manufacturing Group
Cover printer	Phoenix Color Corp.

Morgan Kaufmann Publishers is an imprint of Elsevier.
500 Sansome Street, Suite 400, San Francisco, CA 94111

This book is printed on acid-free paper.

Library of Congress Cataloging-in-Publication Data

Application submitted.

ISBN-13: 978-0-12-369379-2
ISBN-10: 0-12-369379-9

For information on all Morgan Kaufmann publications,
visit our Web site at www.mkp.com or www.books.elsevier.com

Printed in the United States of America
06 07 08 5 4 3

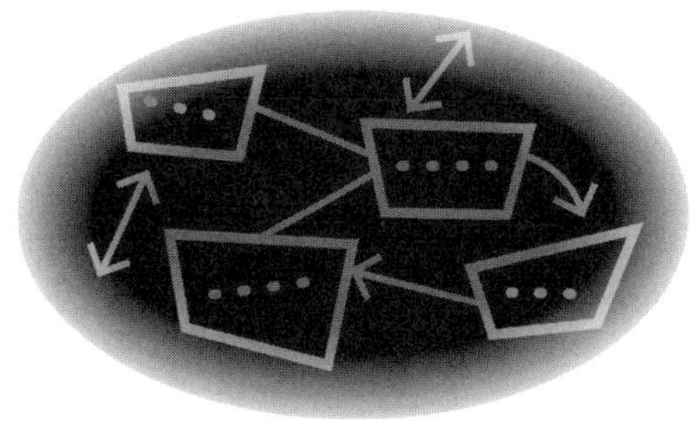

To Ann and Jackers

CONTENTS

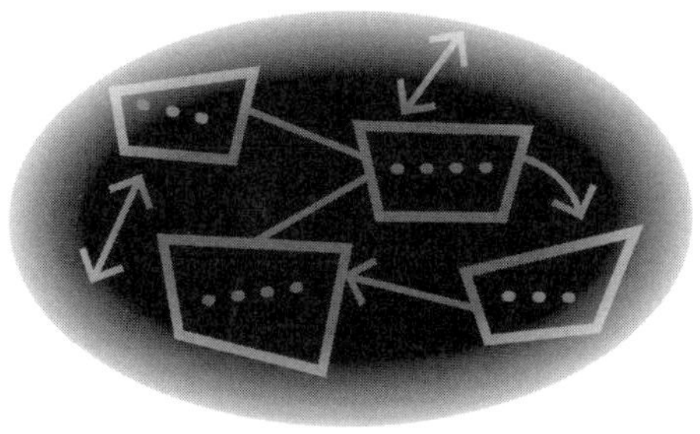

Introduction to the Third Edition

THIS BOOK, LIKE THE first and second editions before it, is for the working SQL programmer who wants to pick up some advanced programming tips and techniques. It assumes that the reader is an SQL programmer with a year or more of experience. It is not an introductory book, so let's not have any gripes in the Amazon.com reviews about that, as we did with the prior editions.

The first edition was published ten years ago and became a minor classic among working SQL programmers. I have seen copies of this book on the desks of real programmers in real programming shops almost everywhere I have been. The true compliment is the Post-it® notes sticking out of the top. People really use it often enough to put stickies in it! Wow!

1.1 What Changed in Ten Years

Hierarchical and network databases still run vital legacy systems in major corporations. SQL people do not like to admit that Fortune 500 companies have more data in IMS files than in SQL tables. But SQL people can live with that, because we have all the new applications and all the important smaller databases.

Object and object-relational databases found niche markets, but never caught on with the mainstream. But OO programming is firmly in place, so object-oriented people can live with that.

XML has become the popular data tool *du jour* as of this writing in 2005. Technically, XML is syntax for describing and moving data from one platform to another, but its support tools allow searching and reformatting. It seems to be lasting longer and finding more users than DIF, EDI, and other earlier attempts at a "Data Esperanto" did in the past. An SQL/XML subcommittee in INCITS H2 (the current name of the original ANSI X3H2 Database Standards Committee) is making sure they can work together.

Data warehousing is no longer an exotic luxury reserved for major corporations. Thanks to the declining prices of hardware and software, medium-sized companies now use the technology. Writing OLAP queries is different from writing OLTP queries, and OLAP probably needs its own *Smarties* book now.

Small "pseudo-SQL" products have appeared in the open source arena. Languages such as MySQL are very different in syntax and semantics from Standard SQL, often being little more than a file system interface with borrowed reserved words. However, their small footprint and low cost have made them popular with Web developers.

At the same time, full scale, serious SQL databases have become open source.

Firebird (http://firebird.sourceforge.net/) has most ANSI SQL-92 features, and it runs on Linux, Microsoft Windows, and a variety of UNIX platforms. Firebird offers optimistic concurrency and language support for stored procedures and triggers. It has been used in production systems (under a variety of names) since 1981, and became open source in 2000. Firebird is the open source version of Borland Software Corporation's (*nèe* Inprise Corporation) InterBase product.

CA-Ingres became open source in 2004, and Computer Associates offered one million dollars in prize money to anyone who would develop software that would convert existing database code to Ingres. Ingres is one of the best database products ever written, but was a commercial failure due to poor marketing.

Postgres is the open-source descendent of the original Ingres project at UC-Berkeley. It has commercial support from Pervasive Software, which also has a proprietary SQL product that evolved from their Btrieve products.

The SQL standard has changed over time, but not always for the best. Parts of the standard have become more relational and set-oriented, while other parts have added things that clearly are procedural, deal with nonrelational data and are based on file system models. To quote David McGoveran, "A committee never met a feature it did not like." In this case, he seems to be quite right.

But strangely enough, even with all the turmoil, the ANSI/ISO Standard SQL-92 is still the common subset that will port across various SQL products to do useful work. In fact, the U.S. Government described the SQL-99 standard as "a standard in progress" and required SQL-92 conformance for federal contracts.

The reason for the loyalty to SQL-92 is simple. The FIPS-127 conformance test suite was in place during the development of SQL-92, so all the vendors could move in the same direction. Unfortunately, the Clinton administration canceled the program, and conformity began to drift. Michael M. Gorman, the President of Whitemarsh Information Systems Corporation and secretary of INCITS H2 for more than 20 years, has a great essay on this and other political aspects of SQL's history at www.wiscorp.com; it is worth reading.

1.2 What Is New in This Edition

Ten years ago, in the first edition, I tried to stick to the SQL-89 standard and to use only the SQL-92 features that are already used in most implementations. Five years ago, in the second edition, I wrote that it would be years before any vendor had a full implementation of SQL-92, but all products were moving toward that goal. This is still true today, as I write the third edition, but now we are much closer to universal implementations of intermediate and full SQL-92. I now feel brave enough to use some of the SQL-99 features found in current products, while doing most of the work in SQL-92.

In the second edition, I dropped some of the theory from the book and moved it to *Joe Celko's Data and Databases: Concepts in Practice* (ISBN 1-55860-432-4). I find no reason to add it back into this edition.

I have moved and greatly expanded techniques for trees and hierarchies into a separate book (*Joe Celko's Trees and Hierarchies in SQL for Smarties*, ISBN 1-55860-920-2) because there was enough material to justify it. I have included a short mention of some techniques here, but not at the detailed level offered in the other book.

I put programming tips for newbies into a separate book (*Joe Celko's SQL Programming Style*, ISBN 1-12088-797-5).

This book is an advanced programmer's book, and I assume that the reader is writing real SQL, not some dialect or his native programming language in a thin disguise. I also assume that he or she can translate Standard SQL into their local dialect without much effort.

I have tried to provide comments with the solutions to explain why they work. I hope this will help the reader see underlying principles that can be used in other situations.

A lot of people have contributed material, either directly or via newsgroups, and I cannot thank all of them. But I made a real effort to put names in the text next to the code. In case I missed anyone, I got material or ideas from Aaron Bertrand, Alejandro Mesa, Anith Sen, Craig Mullins, Daniel A. Morgan, David Portas, David Cressey, Dawn M. Wolthuis, Don Burleson, Erland Sommarskog, Itzik Ben-Gan, John Gilson, Knut Stolze, Louis Davidson, Michael L. Gonzales of HandsOn-BI LLC, Dan Guzman, Hugo Kornelis, Richard Romley, Serge Rielau, Steve Kass, Tom Moreau, Troels Arvin, and probably a dozen others I am forgetting.

1.3 Corrections and Additions

Please send any corrections, additions, suggestions, improvements, or alternative solutions to me or to the publisher.

Morgan-Kaufmann Publishers

500 Sansome Street, Suite 400

San Francisco, CA 94111-3211

Database Design

THIS CHAPTER DISCUSSES THE DDL (Data Definition Language), which is used to create a database schema. It is related to the next chapter on the theory of database normalization. Most bad queries start with a bad schema. To get data out of the bad schema, you have to write convoluted code, and you are never sure if it did what it was meant to do.

One of the major advantages of databases, relational and otherwise, was that the data could be shared among programs so that an enterprise could use one trusted source for information. Once the data was separated from the programs, we could build tools to maintain, back up, and validate the data in one place, without worrying about hundreds or even thousands of application programs possibly working against each other.

SQL has spawned a whole branch of data modeling tools devoted to designing its schemas and tables. Most of these tools use a graphic or text description of the rules and the constraints on the data to produce a schema declaration statement that can be used directly in a particular SQL product. It is often assumed that a CASE tool will automatically prevent you from creating a bad design. This is simply not true.

Bad schema design leads to weird queries that are trying to work around the flaws. These flaws can include picking the wrong data

types, denormalization, and missing or incorrect constraints. As Elbert Hubbard (American author, 1856-1915) put it: "Genius may have its limitations, but stupidity is not thus handicapped."

1.1 Schema and Table Creation

The major problem in learning SQL is that programmers are used to thinking in terms of files rather than tables.

Programming languages are usually based on some underlying model; if you understand the model, the language makes much more sense. For example, FORTRAN is based on algebra. This does not mean that FORTRAN is exactly like algebra. But if you know algebra, FORTRAN does not look all that strange to you. You can write an expression in an assignment statement or make a good guess as to the names of library functions you have never seen before.

Programmers are used to working with files in almost every other programming language. The design of files was derived from paper forms; they are very physical and very dependent on the host programming language. A COBOL file could not easily be read by a FORTRAN program, and vice versa. In fact, it was hard to share files even among programs written in the same programming language!

The most primitive form of a file is a sequence of records, ordered within the file and referenced by physical position. You open a file, then read a first record, followed by a series of next records until you come to the last record to raise the end-of-file condition. You navigate among these records and perform actions one record at a time. The actions you take on one file have no effect on other files that are not in the same program. Only programs can change files.

The model for SQL is data kept in sets, not in physical files. The "unit of work" in SQL is the whole schema, not individual tables.

Sets are those mathematical abstractions you studied in school. Sets are not ordered, and the members of a set are all of the same type. When you perform an operation on a set, the action happens "all at once" to the entire membership of the set. That is, if I ask for the subset of odd numbers from the set of positive integers, I get all of them back as a single set. I do not build the set of odd numbers by sequentially inspecting one element at a time. I define odd numbers with a rule "If the remainder is 1 when you divide the number by 2, it is odd" that could test any integer and classify it. Parallel processing is one of many, many advantages of having a set-oriented model.

SQL is not a perfect set language any more than FORTRAN is a perfect algebraic language, as we will see. But if you are in doubt about something in SQL, ask yourself how you would specify it in terms of sets, and you will probably get the right answer.

1.1.1 CREATE SCHEMA Statement

A `CREATE SCHEMA` statement, defined in the SQL Standard, brings an entire schema into existence all at once. In practice, each product has very different utility programs to allocate physical storage and define a schema. Much of the proprietary syntax is concerned with physical storage allocations.

A schema must have a name and a default character set, usually ASCII or a simple Latin alphabet as defined in the ISO Standards. There is an optional `AUTHORIZATION` clause that holds a `<schema authorization identifier>` for security. After that the schema is a list of schema elements:

```
<schema element> ::=
   <domain definition> | <table definition> | <view definition>
 | <grant statement> | <assertion definition>
 | <character set definition>
 | <collation definition> | <translation definition>
```

A schema is the skeleton of an SQL database; it defines the structures of the schema objects and the rules under which they operate. The data is the meat on that skeleton.

The only data structure in SQL is the table. Tables can be persistent (base tables), used for working storage (temporary tables), or virtual (`VIEW`s, common table expressions, and derived tables). The differences among these types are in implementation, not performance. One advantage of having only one data structure is that the results of all operations are also tables, you never have to convert structures, write special operators, or deal with any irregularity in the language.

The `<grant statement>` has to do with limiting user access to certain schema elements. The `<assertion definition>` is not widely implemented yet, but it works as a constraint that applies to the schema as a whole. Finally, the `<character set definition>`, `<collation definition>`, and `<translation definition>` deal with the display of data. We are not really concerned with any of these schema objects; they are usually set in place by the DBA (database

administrator) for the users, and we mere programmers do not get to change them.

Conceptually, a table is a set of zero or more rows, and a row is a set of one or more columns. Each column has a specific data type and constraints that make up an implementation of an abstract domain. The way a table is physically implemented does not matter, because you only access it with SQL. The database engine handles all the details for you and you never worry about the internals, as you would with a physical file.

In fact, almost no two SQL products use the same internal structures. SQL Server uses physically contiguous storage accessed by two kinds of indexes; Teradata uses hashing; Nucleus (SAND Technology) uses compressed bit vector; Informix and CA-Ingres use more than a dozen different kinds of indexes.

There are two common conceptual errors made by programmers who are accustomed to file systems or PCs. The first is thinking that a table is a file; the second is thinking that a table is a spreadsheet. Tables do not behave like either, and you will get surprises if you do not understand the basic concepts.

It is easy to imagine that a table is a file, a row is a record, and a column is a field. This concept is familiar, and when data moves from SQL to the host language, it must be converted into host language data types and data structures to be displayed and used.

The big differences between working with a file system and working with SQL are in the way SQL fits into a host program. If you are using a file system, your programs must open and close files individually. In SQL, the whole schema is connected to or disconnected from the program as a single unit. The host program might not be authorized to see or manipulate all of the tables and other schema objects, but that is established as part of the connection.

The program defines fields within a file, whereas SQL defines its columns in the schema. FORTRAN uses the `FORMAT` and `READ` statements to get data from a file. Likewise, a COBOL program uses a Data Division to define the fields and a `READ` to fetch it. And so it goes for every 3GL's programming; the concept is the same, though the syntax and options vary.

A file system lets you reference the same data by a different name in each program. If a file's layout changes, you must rewrite all the programs that use that file. When a file is empty, it looks exactly like all other empty files. When you try to read an empty file, the `EOF` (end of file) flag pops up and the program takes some action. Column names and data types in a table are defined within the database schema. Within reasonable limits, the tables can be changed without the knowledge of the host program.

The host program only worries about transferring the values to its own variables from the database. Remember the empty set from your high school math class? It is still a valid set. When a table is empty, it still has columns, but has zero rows. There is no `EOF` flag to signal an exception, because there is no final record.

Another major difference is that tables and columns can have constraints attached to them. A constraint is a rule that defines what must be true about the database after each transaction. In this sense, a database is more like a collection of objects than a traditional passive file system.

A table is not a spreadsheet, even though they look very similar when you view them on a screen or in a printout. In a spreadsheet you can access a row, a column, a cell, or a collection of cells by navigating with a cursor. A table has no concept of navigation. Cells in a spreadsheet can store instructions, not just data. There is no real difference between a row and column in a spreadsheet; you could flip them around completely and still get valid results. This is not true for an SQL table.

1.1.2 Manipulating Tables

The three basic table statements in the SQL DDL are `CREATE TABLE`, `DROP TABLE`, and `ALTER TABLE`. They pretty much do what you would think they do from their names: they bring a table into existence, remove a table, and change the structure of an existing table in the schema, respectively. We will explain them in detail shortly. Here is a simple list of rules for creating and naming a table.

1. The table name must be unique in the schema, and the column names must be unique within a table. SQL can handle a table and a column with the same name, but it is a good practice to name tables differently from their columns. (See items 4 and 6 in this list.)

2. The names in SQL can consist of letters, underscores, and digits. Vendors commonly allow other printing characters, but it is a good idea to avoid using anything except letters, underscores, and digits. Special characters are not portable and will not sort the same way in different products.

3. Standard SQL allows you to use spaces, reserved words, and special characters in a name if you enclose them in double quotation marks, but this should be avoided as much as possible.
4. The use of collective, class, or plural names for tables helps you think of them as sets. For example, do not name a table "Employee" unless there really is only one employee; use something like "Employees" or (better) "Personnel," for the table name.
5. Use the same name for the same attribute everywhere in the schema. That is, do not name a column in one table "sex" and a column in another table "gender" when they refer to the same property. You should have a data dictionary that enforces this on your developers.
6. Use singular attribute names for columns and other scalar schema objects.

I have a separate book on SQL programming style that goes into more detail about this, so I will not mention it again.

A table must have at least one column. Though it is not required, it is also a good idea to place related columns in their conventional order in the table. By default, the columns will print out in the order in which they appear in the table. That means you should put name, address, city, state, and ZIP code in that order, so that you can read them easily in a display.

The conventions in this book are that keywords are in `UPPERCASE`, table names are Capitalized, and column names are in lowercase. I also use capital letter(s) followed by digit(s) for correlation names (e.g., the table Personnel would have correlation names P0, P1, . . ., P*n*), where the digit shows the occurrence.

DROP TABLE <table name>

The `DROP TABLE` statement removes a table from the database. This is not the same as making the table an empty table. When a schema object is dropped, it is gone forever. The syntax of the statement is:

```
<drop table statement> ::= DROP TABLE <table name> [<drop
behavior>]
<drop behavior> ::= RESTRICT | CASCADE
```

The <drop behavior> clause has two options. If RESTRICT is specified, the table cannot be referenced in the query expression of any view or the search condition of any constraint. This clause is supposed to prevent the unpleasant surprise of having other things fail because they depended on this particular table for their own definitions. If CASCADE is specified, then such referencing objects will also be dropped along with the table.

Either the particular SQL product would post an error message, and in effect do a RESTRICT, or you would find out about any dependencies by having your database blow up when it ran into constructs that needed the missing table.

The DROP keyword and <drop behavior> clause are also used in other statements that remove schema objects, such as DROP VIEW, DROP SCHEMA, DROP CONSTRAINT, and so forth.

This is usually a "DBA-only" statement that, for obvious reasons, programmers are not typically allowed to use.

ALTER TABLE

The ALTER TABLE statement adds, removes, or changes columns and constraints within a table. This statement is in Standard SQL; it existed in most SQL products before it was standardized. It is still implemented in many different ways, so you should see your product for details. Again, your DBA will not want you to use this statement without permission. The Standard SQL syntax looks like this:

```
ALTER TABLE <table name> <alter table action>

<alter table action> ::=
  | DROP [COLUMN] <column name> <drop behavior>
  | ADD [COLUMN] <column definition>
  | ALTER [COLUMN] <column name> <alter column action>
  | ADD <table constraint definition>
  | DROP CONSTRAINT <constraint name> <drop behavior>
```

The DROP COLUMN clause removes the column from the table. Standard SQL gives you the option of setting the drop behavior, which most current products do not. The two options are RESTRICT and CASCADE. RESTRICT will not allow the column to disappear if it is referenced in another schema object. CASCADE will also delete any schema object that references the dropped column.

When this statement is available in your SQL product, I strongly advise that you first use the RESTRICT option to see if there are references before you use the CASCADE option.

As you might expect, the ADD COLUMN clause extends the existing table by putting another column on it. The new column must have a name that is unique within the table and that follows the other rules for a valid column declaration. The location of the new column is usually at the end of the list of the existing columns in the table.

The ALTER COLUMN clause can change a column and its definition. Exactly what is allowed will vary from product to product, but usually the data type can be changed to a compatible data type [e.g., you can make a CHAR(n) column longer, but not shorter; change an INTEGER to a REAL; and so forth].

The ADD <table constraint definition> clause lets you put a constraint on a table. Be careful, though, and find out whether your SQL product will check the existing data to be sure that it can pass the new constraint. It is possible in some older SQL products to leave bad data in the tables, and then you will have to clean them out with special routines to get to the actual physical storage.

The DROP CONSTRAINT clause requires that the constraint be given a name, so naming constraints is a good habit to get into. If the constraint to be dropped was given no name, you will have to find what name the SQL engine assigned to it in the schema information tables and use that name. The Standard does not say how such names are to be constructed, only that they must be unique within a schema. Actual products usually pick a long random string of digits and preface it with some letters to make a valid name that is so absurd no human being would think of it. A constraint name will also appear in warnings and error messages, making debugging much easier. The <drop behavior> option behaves as it did for the DROP COLUMN clause.

CREATE TABLE

The CREATE TABLE statement does all the hard work. The basic syntax looks like the following, but there are actually more options we will discuss later.

```
CREATE TABLE <table name> (<table element list>)

<table element list> ::=
  <table element> | <table element>, <table element list>
```

```
<table element> ::=
  <column definition> | <table constraint definition>
```

The table definition includes data in the column definitions and rules for handling that data in the table constraint definitions. As a result, a table acts more like an object (with its data and methods) than like a simple, passive file.

Column Definitions

Beginning SQL programmers often fail to take full advantage of the options available to them, and they pay for it with errors or extra work in their applications. A column is not like a simple passive field in a file system. It has more than just a data type associated with it.

```
<column definition> ::=
  <column name> <data type>
   [<default clause>]
   [<column constraint>...]

<column constraint> ::= NOT NULL
 | <check constraint definition>
 | <unique specification>
 | <references specification>
```

The first important thing to notice here is that each column must have a data type, which it keeps unless you ALTER the table. The SQL Standard offers many data types, because SQL must work with many different host languages. The data types fall into three major categories: numeric, character, and temporal data types. We will discuss the data types and their rules of operation in other sections; they are fairly obvious, so not knowing the details will not stop you from reading the examples that follow.

DEFAULT Clause

The default clause is an underused feature, whose syntax is:

```
<default clause> ::=
  [CONSTRAINT <constraint name>] DEFAULT <default option>

<default option> ::= <literal> | <system value> | NULL
```

```
<system value> ::= CURRENT_DATE | CURRENT_TIME |
CURRENT_TIMESTAMP | SYSTEM_USER | SESSION_USER | CURRENT_USER
```

The SQL 2003 Standard also added `CURRENT_PATH` and `<implicitly typed value specification>`.

Whenever the SQL engine does not have an explicit value to put into this column during an insertion, it will look for a `DEFAULT` clause and insert that value. The default option can be a literal value of the relevant data type, the current timestamp, the current date, the current user identifier, or so forth. If you do not provide a `DEFAULT` clause and the column is `NULL`-able, the system will provide a `NULL` as the default. If all that fails, you will get an error message about missing data.

This approach is a good way to make the database do a lot of work that you would otherwise have to code into all the application programs. The most common tricks are to use a zero in numeric columns; a string to encode a missing value ('{{unknown}}') or a true default ("same address") in character columns; and the system timestamp to mark transactions.

1.1.3 Column Constraints

Column constraints are rules attached to a table. All the rows in the table are validated against them. File systems have nothing like this, since validation is done in the application programs. Column constraints are also one of the most underused features of SQL, so you will look like a real wizard if you can master them.

Constraints can be given a name and some attributes. The SQL engine will use the constraint name to alter the column and to display error messages.

```
<constraint name definition> ::= CONSTRAINT <constraint name>

<constraint attributes> ::=
 <constraint check time> [[NOT] DEFERRABLE]
   | [NOT] DEFERRABLE [<constraint check time>]
<constraint check time> ::= INITIALLY DEFERRED | INITIALLY
IMMEDIATE
```

A deferrable constraint can be "turned off" during a transaction. The initial state tells you whether to enforce it at the start of the transaction or wait until the end of the transaction, before the `COMMIT`. Only certain combinations of these attributes make sense.

1. If INITIALLY DEFERRED is specified, then the constraint has to be DEFERRABLE.

2. If INITIALLY IMMEDIATE is specified or implicit and neither DEFERRABLE nor NOT DEFERRABLE is specified, then NOT DEFERRABLE is implicit.

The transaction statement can then use the following statement to set the constraints as needed.

```
<set constraints mode statement> ::=
 SET CONSTRAINTS <constraint name list> {DEFERRED | IMMEDIATE}
<constraint name list>
  ::= ALL | <constraint name> [{<comma> <constraint name>}...]
```

This feature was new with full SQL-92, and it is not widely implemented in the smaller SQL products. In effect, they use 'NOT DEFERRABLE INITIALLY IMMEDIATE' on all the constraints.

NOT NULL Constraint

The most important column constraint is the NOT NULL, which forbids the use of NULLs in a column. Use this constraint routinely, and remove it only when you have good reason. It will help you avoid the complications of NULL values when you make queries against the data. The other side of the coin is that you should provide a DEFAULT value to replace the NULL that would have been created.

The NULL is a special marker in SQL that belongs to all data types. SQL is the only language that has such a creature; if you can understand how it works, you will have a good grasp of SQL. It is not a value; it is a marker that holds a place where a value might go. But it must be cast to a data type for physical storage.

A NULL means that we have a missing, unknown, miscellaneous, or inapplicable value in the data. It can mean many other things, but just consider those four for now. The problem is which of these four possibilities the NULL indicates depends on how it is used. To clarify this, imagine that I am looking at a carton of Easter eggs and I want to know their colors. If I see an empty hole, I have a missing egg, which I hope will be provided later. If I see a foil-wrapped egg, I have an unknown color value in my set. If I see a multicolored egg, I have a miscellaneous value in my set. If I see a cue ball, I have an inapplicable value in my set. The way you handle each situation is a little different.

When you use NULLs in math calculations, they propagate in the results so that the answer is another NULL. When you use them in logical expressions or comparisons, they return a logical value of UNKNOWN and give SQL its strange three-valued logic. They sort either always high or always low in the collation sequence. They group together for some operations, but not for others. In short, NULLs cause a lot of irregular features in SQL, which we will discuss later. Your best bet is just to memorize the situations and the rules for NULLs when you cannot avoid them.

CHECK() Constraint

The CHECK() constraint tests the rows of the table against a logical expression, which SQL calls a search condition, and rejects rows whose search condition returns FALSE. However, the constraint accepts rows when the search condition returns TRUE or UNKNOWN. This is not the same rule as the WHERE clause, which rejects rows that test UNKNOWN. The reason for this "benefit-of-the-doubt" feature is so that it will be easy to write constraints on NULL-able columns.

The usual technique is to do simple range checking, such as CHECK (rating BETWEEN 1 AND 10), or to verify that a column's value is in an enumerated set, such as CHECK (sex IN (0, 1, 2, 9)), with this constraint. Remember that the sex column could also be set to NULL, unless a NOT NULL constraint is also added to the column's declaration. Although it is optional, it is a really good idea to use a constraint name. Without it, most SQL products will create a huge, ugly, unreadable random string for the name, since they need to have one in the schema tables. If you provide your own, you can drop the constraint more easily and understand the error messages when the constraint is violated.

For example, you can enforce the rule that a firm must not hire anyone younger than 21 years of age for a job that requires a liquor-serving license by using a single check clause to check the applicant's birth date and hire date. However, you cannot put the current system date into the CHECK() clause logic for obvious reasons, it is always changing.

The real power of the CHECK() clause comes from writing complex expressions that verify relationships with other rows, with other tables, or with constants. Before SQL-92, the CHECK() constraint could only reference columns in the table in which it was declared. In Standard SQL, the CHECK() constraint can reference any schema object. As an example of how complex things can get, consider a database of movies.

First, let's enforce the rule that no country can export more than ten titles.

```
CREATE TABLE Exports
(movie_title CHAR(25) NOT NULL,
 country_code CHAR(2) NOT NULL, -- use 2-letter ISO  nation codes
 sales_amt DECIMAL(12, 2) NOT NULL,
 PRIMARY KEY (movie_title, country_code),
 CONSTRAINT National_Quota
 CHECK (-- reference to same table
        10 <= ALL (SELECT COUNT(movie_title)
     FROM Exports AS E1
    GROUP BY E1.country_code))
);
```

When doing a self-join, you must use the base table name and not all correlation names. Let's make sure no movies from different countries have the same title.

```
CREATE TABLE ExportMovies
(movie_title CHAR(25) NOT NULL,
 country_code CHAR(2) NOT NULL,
 sales_amt DECIMAL(12, 2) NOT NULL,
 PRIMARY KEY (movie_title, country_code),
 CONSTRAINT National_Quota
 CHECK (NOT EXISTS  -- self-join
        (SELECT *
   FROM ExportMovies AS E1
  WHERE ExportMovies.movie_title = E1.movie_title
    AND ExportMovies.country_code <> E1.country_code)
);
```

Here is way to enforce the rule that you cannot export a movie to its own country of origin.

```
CREATE TABLE ExportMovies
(movie_title CHAR(25) NOT NULL,
 country_code CHAR(2) NOT NULL,
 sales_amt DECIMAL(12, 2) NOT NULL,
 PRIMARY KEY (movie_title, country_code),
 CONSTRAINT Foreign_film
```

```
CHECK (NOT EXISTS     -- reference to second table
 (SELECT *
    FROM Movies AS M1
   WHERE M1.movie_title = ExportMovies.movie_title
     AND M1.country_of_origin = ExportMovies.country_code)));
```

These table-level constraints often use a `NOT EXISTS()` predicate. Despite the fact that you can often do a lot of work in a single constraint, it is better to write a lot of small constraints, so that you know exactly what went wrong when one of them is violated.

Another important point to remember is that all constraints are true if the table is empty. This is handled by the `CREATE ASSERTION` statement, which we will discuss shortly.

UNIQUE and PRIMARY KEY Constraints

The `UNIQUE` constraint says that no duplicate values are allowed in the column or columns involved.

```
<unique specification> ::= UNIQUE | PRIMARY KEY
```

File system programmers understand the concept of a `PRIMARY KEY`, but for the wrong reasons. They are used to a file, which can have only one key because that key is used to determine the physical order of the records within the file. Tables have no order; the term `PRIMARY KEY` in SQL has to do with defaults in referential actions, which we will discuss later.

There are some subtle differences between `UNIQUE` and `PRIMARY KEY`. A table can have only one `PRIMARY KEY` but many `UNIQUE` constraints. A `PRIMARY KEY` is automatically declared to have a `NOT NULL` constraint on it, but a `UNIQUE` column can have `NULL`s in a row unless you explicitly add a `NOT NULL` constraint. Adding the `NOT NULL` whenever possible is a good idea, as it makes the column into a proper relational key.

There is also a multiple-column form of the `<unique specification>`, which is usually written at the end of the column declarations. It is a list of columns in parentheses after the proper keyword, and it means that the combination of those columns is unique. For example, I might declare `PRIMARY KEY (city, department)` so I can be sure that though I have offices in many cities and many identical departments in those offices, there is only one personnel department in Chicago.

REFERENCES Clause

The <references specification> is the simplest version of a referential constraint definition, which can be quite tricky. For now, let us just consider the simplest case:

```
<references specification> ::=
 [CONSTRAINT <constraint name>]
  REFERENCES <referenced table name>[(<reference column>)]
```

This relates two tables together, so it is different from the other options we have discussed so far. What this says is that the value in this column of the referencing table must appear somewhere in the referenced table's column named in the constraint. Furthermore, the referenced column must be in a UNIQUE constraint. For example, you can set up a rule that the Orders table can have orders only for goods that appear in the Inventory table.

If no <reference column> is given, then the PRIMARY KEY column of the referenced table is assumed to be the target. This is one of those situations where the PRIMARY KEY is important, but you can always play it safe and explicitly name a column. There is no rule to prevent several columns from referencing the same target column. For example, we might have a table of flight crews that has pilot and copilot columns that both reference a table of certified pilots.

A circular reference is a relationship in which one table references a second table, which in turn references the first table. The old gag about "you cannot get a job until you have experience, and you cannot get experience until you have a job!" is the classic version of this.

Notice that the columns in a multicolumn FOREIGN KEY must match to a multicolumn PRIMARY KEY or UNIQUE constraint. The syntax is:

```
 [CONSTRAINT <constraint name>]
FOREIGN KEY (<column list>)
  REFERENCES <referenced table name>[(<reference column list>)]
```

Referential Actions

The REFERENCES clause can have two subclauses that take actions when a database event changes the referenced table. This feature came with Standard SQL and took a while to be implemented in most SQL products. The two database events are updates and deletes, and the subclauses look like this:

```
<referential triggered action> ::=
  <update rule> [<delete rule>] | <delete rule> [<update rule>]

<update rule> ::= ON UPDATE <referential action>
<delete rule> ::= ON DELETE <referential action>

<referential action> ::= CASCADE | SET NULL | SET DEFAULT | NO
ACTION
```

When the referenced table is changed, one of the referential actions is set in motion by the SQL engine.

1. The `CASCADE` option will change the values in the referencing table to the new value in the referenced table. This is a very common method of DDL programming that allows you to set up a single table as the trusted source for an identifier. This way the system can propagate changes automatically.

   This removes one of the arguments for nonrelational system-generated surrogate keys. In early SQL products that were based on a file system for their physical implementation, the values were repeated for both the referenced and referencing tables. Why? The tables were regarded as separate units, like files.

   Later SQL products regarded the schema as a whole. The referenced values appeared once in the referenced table, and the referencing tables obtained them by following pointer chains to that one occurrence in the schema. The results are much faster update cascades, a physically smaller database, faster joins, and faster aggregations.

2. The `SET NULL` option will change the values in the referencing table to a `NULL`. Obviously, the referencing column needs to be `NULL`-able.

3. The `SET DEFAULT` option will change the values in the referencing table to the default value of that column. Obviously, the referencing column needs to have some `DEFAULT` declared for it, but each referencing column can have its own default in its own table.

4. The `NO ACTION` option explains itself. Nothing is changed in the referencing table, and it is possible that some error message about reference violation will be raised. If a referential

constraint does not specify any ON UPDATE or ON DELETE rule in the update rule, then NO ACTION is implicit. You will also see the reserved word RESTRICT in some products instead of NO ACTION.

Standard SQL has more options about how matching is done between the referenced and referencing tables. Most SQL products have not implemented them, so I will not mention them anymore.

Standard SQL has deferrable constraints. This option lets the programmer turn a constraint off during a session, so that the table can be put into a state that would otherwise be illegal. However, at the end of a session, all the constraints are enforced. Many SQL products have implemented these options, and they can be quite handy, but I will not mention them until we get to the section on transaction control.

1.1.4 UNIQUE Constraints versus UNIQUE Indexes

UNIQUE constraints are not the same thing as UNIQUE indexes. Technically speaking, indexes do not even exist in Standard SQL. They were considered too physical to be part of a logical model of a language. In practice, however, virtually all products have some form of "access enhancement" for the DBA to use, and most often, it is an index.

The column referenced by a FOREIGN KEY has to be either a PRIMARY KEY or a column with a UNIQUE constraint; a unique index on the same set of columns cannot be referenced, since the index is on one table and not a relationship between two tables.

Although there is no order to a constraint, an index is ordered, so the unique index might be an aid for sorting. Some products construct special index structures for the declarative referential integrity (DRI) constraints, which in effect "pre-JOIN" the referenced and referencing tables.

All the constraints can be defined as equivalent to some CHECK constraint. For example:

```
PRIMARY KEY = CHECK (UNIQUE (SELECT <key columns> FROM <table>)
     AND (<key columns>) IS NOT NULL)

UNIQUE = CHECK (UNIQUE (SELECT <key columns> FROM <table>))

NOT NULL = CHECK (<column> IS NOT NULL)
```

These predicates can be reworded in terms of other predicates and subquery expressions, and then passed on to the optimizer.

1.1.5 Nested UNIQUE Constraints

One of the basic tricks in SQL is representing a one-to-one or many-to-many relationship with a table that references the two (or more) entity tables involved by their primary keys. This third table has several popular names, such as "junction table" or "join table," but we know that it is a relationship. This type of table needs constraints to ensure that the relationships work properly.

For example, here are two tables:

```
CREATE TABLE Boys
(boy_name VARCHAR(30) NOT NULL PRIMARY KEY
 ...);

CREATE TABLE Girls
(girl_name VARCHAR(30) NOT NULL PRIMARY KEY,
 ...);
```

Yes, I know using names for a key is a bad practice, but it will make my examples easier to read. There are a lot of different relationships that we can make between these two tables. If you don't believe me, just watch the *Jerry Springer Show* sometime. The simplest relationship table looks like this:

```
CREATE TABLE Couples
(boy_name VARCHAR(30) NOT NULL
        REFERENCES Boys (boy_name)
        ON UPDATE CASCADE
        ON DELETE CASCADE,
 girl_name VARCHAR(30) NOT NULL,
        REFERENCES Girls(girl_name)
        ON UPDATE CASCADE
        ON DELETE CASCADE);
```

The Couples table allows us to insert rows like this:

```
('Joe Celko', 'Hilary Duff')
('Joe Celko', 'Lindsay Lohan')
('Toby McGuire', 'Lindsay Lohan')
('Joe Celko', 'Hilary Duff')
```

Oops! I am shown twice with Hilary Duff, because the Couples table does not have its own key. This mistake is easy to make, but the way to fix it is not obvious.

```
CREATE TABLE Orgy
(boy_name VARCHAR(30) NOT NULL
        REFERENCES Boys (boy_name)
        ON DELETE CASCADE
        ON UPDATE CASCADE,
 girl_name VARCHAR(30) NOT NULL,
        REFERENCES Girls(girl_name)
        ON UPDATE CASCADE
        ON DELETE CASCADE,
 PRIMARY KEY (boy_name, girl_name));   -- compound key
```

The Orgy table gets rid of the duplicated rows and makes this a proper table. The primary key for the table is made up of two or more columns and is called a compound key because of that fact. These are valid rows now.

```
('Joe Celko', 'Hilary Duff')
('Joe Celko', 'Lindsay Lohan')
('Toby McGuire', 'Lindsay Lohan')
```

But the only restriction on the couples is that they appear only once. Every boy can be paired with every girl, much to the dismay of the Moral Majority. I think I want to make a rule that guys can have as many gals as they want, but the gals have to stick to one guy.

The way I do this is to use a `NOT NULL UNIQUE` constraint on the girl_name column, which makes it a key. It is a simple key, since it is only one column, but it is also a nested key, because it appears as a subset of the compound `PRIMARY KEY`.

```
CREATE TABLE Playboys
(boy_name VARCHAR(30) NOT NULL
        REFERENCES Boys (boy_name)
        ON UPDATE CASCADE
        ON DELETE CASCADE,
 girl_name VARCHAR(30) NOT NULL UNIQUE, -- nested key
        REFERENCES Girls(girl_name)
        ON UPDATE CASCADE
```

```
        ON DELETE CASCADE,
 PRIMARY KEY (boy_name, girl_name));  -- compound key
```

The Playboys is a proper table, without duplicated results, but it also enforces the condition that I get to play around with one or more ladies.

```
('Joe Celko', 'Hilary Duff')
('Joe Celko', 'Lindsay Lohan')
```

The women might want to go the other way and keep company with a series of men.

```
CREATE TABLE Playgirls
(boy_name VARCHAR(30) NOT NULL UNIQUE -- nested key
        REFERENCES Boys (boy_name)
        ON UPDATE CASCADE
        ON DELETE CASCADE,
 girl_name VARCHAR(30) NOT NULL,
        REFERENCES Girls(girl_name)
        ON UPDATE CASCADE
        ON DELETE CASCADE,
 PRIMARY KEY (boy_name, girl_name));  -- compound key
```

The Playgirls table would permit these rows from our original set.

```
('Joe Celko', 'Lindsay Lohan')
('Toby McGuire', 'Lindsay Lohan')
```

Think about all of these possible keys for a minute. The compound `PRIMARY KEY` is now redundant. If each boy appears only once in the table, or each girl appears only once in the table, then each (boy_name, girl_name) pair can appear only once. However, the redundancy can be useful in searching the table, because it will probably create extra indexes that give us a covering of both names. The query engine then can use just the index and touch the base tables.

The Moral Majority is pretty upset about this Hollywood scandal and would love for us to stop running around and settle down in nice stable couples.

```
CREATE TABLE Marriages
(boy_name VARCHAR(30) NOT NULL UNIQUE   -- nested key
        REFERENCES Boys (boy_name)
```

```
        ON UPDATE CASCADE
        ON DELETE CASCADE,
girl_name VARCHAR(30) NOT NULL UNIQUE   -- nested key,
        REFERENCES Girls(girl_name)
        ON UPDATE CASCADE
        ON DELETE CASCADE,
PRIMARY KEY(boy_name, girl_name));   -- redundant compound key!!
```

Since one of the goals of an RDBMS (relational database management system) is to remove redundancy, why would I have that compound primary key? One reason might be to get a covering index on both columns for performance. But the more likely answer is that this is an error that a smart optimizer will spot. I leave same-sex marriages as an exercise for the reader.

The Couples table allows us to insert these rows from the original set.

```
('Joe Celko', 'Hilary Duff')
('Toby McGuire', 'Lindsay Lohan')
```

However, SQL products and theory do not always match. Many products make the assumption that the PRIMARY KEY is somehow special in the data model and will be the way that they should access the table most of the time.

In fairness, making special provision for the PRIMARY KEY is not a bad assumption, because the REFERENCES clause uses the PRIMARY KEY of the referenced table as the default. Many new SQL programmers are not aware that a FOREIGN KEY constraint can also reference any UNIQUE constraint in the same table or in another table. The following nightmare code will give you an idea of the possibilities. The multiple column versions follow the same syntax.

```
CREATE TABLE Foo
(foo_key INTEGER NOT NULL PRIMARY KEY,
  ...
 self_ref INTEGER NOT NULL
  REFERENCES Foo(fookey),
 outside_ref_1  INTEGER NOT NULL
     REFERENCES Bar(bar_key),
 outside_ref_2 INTEGER NOT NULL
    REFERENCES Bar(other_key),
 ...);
```

```
CREATE TABLE Bar
(bar_key INTEGER NOT NULL PRIMARY KEY,
 other_key INTEGER NOT NULL UNIQUE,
 ...);
```

1.1.6 Overlapping Keys

But let's get back to the nested keys. Just how far can we go with them? My favorite example is a teacher's schedule kept in a table like this [I am leaving out reference clauses and `CHECK()` constraints]:

```
CREATE TABLE Schedule
(teacher_name VARCHAR(15) NOT NULL,
 class_name CHAR(15) NOT NULL,
 room_nbr INTEGER NOT NULL,
 period INTEGER NOT NULL,
 PRIMARY KEY (teacher_name, class_name, room_nbr, period));
```

That choice of a primary key is the most obvious one, use all the columns. Typical rows would look like this:

```
('Mr. Celko', 'Database 101', 222, 6)
```

The rules we want to enforce are:

1. A teacher is in only one room each period.
2. A teacher teaches only one class each period.
3. A room has only one class each period.
4. A room has only one teacher in it each period.

Stop reading and see what you come up with for an answer. Okay, now consider using one constraint for each rule in the list, thus.

```
CREATE TABLE Schedule_1 -- version one, WRONG!
(teacher_name VARCHAR(15) NOT NULL,
 class_name CHAR(15) NOT NULL,
 room_nbr INTEGER NOT NULL,
 period INTEGER NOT NULL,
 UNIQUE (teacher_name, room_nbr, period), -- rule #1
 UNIQUE (teacher_name, class_name, period), -- rule #2
```

```
UNIQUE (class_name, room_nbr, period), -- rule #3
UNIQUE (teacher_name, room_nbr, period), -- rule #4
PRIMARY KEY (teacher_name, class_name, room_nbr, period));
```

We know that there are four ways to pick three things from a set of four things. While column order is important in creating an index, we can ignore it for now and then worry about index tuning later.

I could drop the PRIMARY KEY as redundant if I have all four of these constraints in place. But what happens if I drop the PRIMARY KEY and then one of the constraints?

```
CREATE TABLE Schedule_2  -- still wrong
(teacher_name VARCHAR(15) NOT NULL,
 class_name CHAR(15) NOT NULL,
 room_nbr INTEGER NOT NULL,
 period INTEGER NOT NULL,
 UNIQUE (teacher_name, room_nbr, period), -- rule #1
 UNIQUE (teacher_name, class_name, period), -- rule #2
 UNIQUE (class_name, room_nbr, period));    -- rule #3
```

I can now insert these rows in the second version of the table:

```
('Mr. Celko', 'Database 101', 222, 6)
('Mr. Celko', 'Database 102', 223, 6)
```

This gives me a very tough sixth-period teaching load, because I have to be in two different rooms at the same time. Things can get even worse when another teacher is added to the schedule:

```
('Mr. Celko', 'Database 101', 222, 6)
('Mr. Celko', 'Database 102', 223, 6)
('Ms. Shields', 'Database 101', 223, 6)
```

Ms. Shields and I are both in room 223, trying to teach different classes at the same time. Matthew Burr looked at the constraints and the rules, and he came up with this analysis.

```
CREATE TABLE Schedule_3  -- correct version
(teacher_name VARCHAR(15) NOT NULL,
 class_name CHAR(15) NOT NULL,
 room_nbr INTEGER NOT NULL,
```

```
period INTEGER NOT NULL,
UNIQUE (teacher_name, period), -- rules #1 and #2
UNIQUE (room_nbr, period),
UNIQUE (class_name, period));   -- rules #3 and #4
```

If a teacher is in only one room each period, then given a period and a teacher I should be able to determine only one room; i.e., room is functionally dependent upon the combination of teacher and period. Likewise, if a teacher teaches only one class each period, then class is functionally dependent upon the combination of teacher and period. The same thinking holds for the last two rules: class is functionally dependent upon the combination of room and period, and teacher is functionally dependent upon the combination of room and period.

With the constraints that were provided in the first version, you will find that the rules are not enforced. For example, I could enter the following rows:

```
('Mr. Celko', 'Database 101', 222, 6)
('Mr. Celko', 'Database 102', 223, 6)
```

These rows violate the first and second rules.

However, the unique constraints first provided in Schedule_2 do not capture this violation and will allow the rows to be entered.

The following constraint:

```
UNIQUE (teacher_name, room_nbr, period)
```

checks the complete combination of teacher, room, and period, and since ('Mr. Celko', 222, 6) is different from ('Mr. Celko', 223, 6), the DDL does not find any problem with both rows being entered, even though that means that Mr. Celko is in more than one room during the same period.

The constraint:

```
UNIQUE (teacher_name, class_name, period)
```

does not catch its associated rule either, since ('Mr. Celko', 'Database 101', 6) is different from ('Mr. Celko', 'Database 102', 6). As a result, Mr. Celko is able to teach more than one class during the same period, thus violating rule #2. It seems that we'd also be able to add the following row:

```
('Ms. Shields', 'Database 103', 222, 6)
```

This violates the third and fourth rules.

1.1.7 CREATE ASSERTION Constraints

In Standard SQL, CREATE ASSERTION allows you to apply a constraint on the tables within a schema, but not to attach the constraint to any particular table. The syntax is:

```
<assertion definition> ::=
  CREATE ASSERTION <constraint name> <assertion check>
  [<constraint attributes>]

<assertion check> ::=
  CHECK <left paren> <search condition> <right paren>
```

As you would expect, there is a DROP ASSERTION statement, but no ALTER statement. An assertion can do things that a CHECK() clause attached to a table cannot do, because it is outside of the tables involved. A CHECK() constraint is always TRUE if the table is empty.

For example, it is very hard to make a rule that the total number of employees in the company must be equal to the total number of employees in all the health plan tables.

```
CREATE ASSERTION Total_health_Coverage
CHECK (SELECT COUNT(*) FROM Personnel) =
      + (SELECT COUNT(*) FROM HealthPlan_1)
      + (SELECT COUNT(*) FROM HealthPlan_2)
      + (SELECT COUNT(*) FROM HealthPlan_3);
```

1.1.8 Using VIEWs for Schema Level Constraints

Until you can get CREATE ASSERTION constraints, you have to use procedures and triggers to get the same effects. Consider a schema for a chain of stores that has three tables, thus:

```
CREATE TABLE Stores
(store_nbr INTEGER NOT NULL PRIMARY KEY,
 store_name CHAR(35) NOT NULL,
 ...);
```

```
CREATE TABLE Personnel
(ssn CHAR(9) NOT NULL PRIMARY KEY,
 last_name CHAR(15) NOT NULL,
 first_name CHAR(15) NOT NULL,
 ...);
```

The first two explain themselves. The third table, following, shows the relationship between stores and personnel, namely who is assigned to what job at which store and when this happened. Thus:

```
CREATE TABLE JobAssignments
(store_nbr INTEGER NOT NULL
        REFERENCES Stores (store_nbr)
        ON UPDATE CASCADE
        ON DELETE CASCADE,
 ssn CHAR(9) NOT NULL PRIMARY KEY
        REFERENCES Personnel( ssn)
        ON UPDATE CASCADE
        ON DELETE CASCADE,
 start_date TIMESTAMP DEFAULT CURRENT_TIMESTAMP NOT NULL,
 end_date TIMESTAMP,
 CHECK (start_date <= end_date),
 job_type INTEGER DEFAULT 0 NOT NULL -- unassigned = 0
  CHECK (job_type BETWEEN 0 AND 99),
 PRIMARY KEY (store_nbr, ssn, start_date));
```

Let's invent some job_type codes, such as 0 = 'unassigned', 1 = 'stockboy', etc., until we get to 99 = 'Store Manager'. We have a rule that each store has, at most, one manager. In Standard SQL, you could write a constraint like this:

```
CREATE ASSERTION ManagerVerification
CHECK (1 <= ALL (SELECT COUNT(*)
                  FROM JobAssignments
                 WHERE job_type = 99
                 GROUP BY store_nbr));
```

This is actually a bit subtler than it looks. If you change the <= to =, then the stores must have exactly one manager if it has any employees at all.

But as we said, most SQL products still do not allow CHECK() constraints that apply to the table as a whole, nor do they support the scheme-level CREATE ASSERTION statement.

So, how to do this? You might use a trigger, which will involve proprietary, procedural code. Despite the SQL/PSM Standard, most vendors implement very different trigger models and use their proprietary 4GL language in the body of the trigger.

We need to set TRIGGERs that validate the state of the table after each INSERT and UPDATE operation. If we DELETE an employee, this will not create more than one manager per store. The skeleton for these triggers would be something like this:

```
CREATE TRIGGER CheckManagers
AFTER UPDATE ON JobAssignments -- same for INSERT
IF 1 <= ALL (SELECT COUNT(*)
               FROM JobAssignments
              WHERE job_type = 99
              GROUP BY store_nbr)
THEN ROLLBACK;
ELSE COMMIT;
END IF;
```

But being a fanatic, I want a pure SQL solution that is declarative within the limits of most current SQL products.

Let's create two tables. This first table is a Personnel table for the store managers only and it is keyed on their Social Security numbers. Notice the use of DEFAULT and CHECK() on their job_type to ensure that this is really a "managers only" table.

```
CREATE TABLE Job_99_Assignments
(store_nbr INTEGER NOT NULL PRIMARY KEY
        REFERENCES Stores (store_nbr)
        ON UPDATE CASCADE
        ON DELETE CASCADE,
ssn CHAR(9) NOT NULL
        REFERENCES Personnel (ssn)
        ON UPDATE CASCADE
        ON DELETE CASCADE,
start_date TIMESTAMP DEFAULT CURRENT_TIMESTAMP NOT NULL,
end_date TIMESTAMP,
CHECK (start_date <= end_date),
job_type INTEGER DEFAULT 99 NOT NULL
        CHECK (job_type = 99));
```

This second table is a Personnel table for employees who are not 'store manager' and it is also keyed on Social Security numbers. Notice the use of `DEFAULT` for a starting position of 'unassigned' and `CHECK()` on their job_type to ensure that this is really a "no managers allowed" table.

```
CREATE TABLE Job_not99_Assignments
(store_nbr INTEGER NOT NULL
        REFERENCES Stores (store_nbr)
        ON UPDATE CASCADE
        ON DELETE CASCADE,
ssn CHAR(9) NOT NULL PRIMARY KEY
        REFERENCES Personnel (ssn)
        ON UPDATE CASCADE
        ON DELETE CASCADE,
start_date TIMESTAMP DEFAULT CURRENT_TIMESTAMP NOT NULL,
end_date TIMESTAMP,
CHECK (start_date <= end_date),
job_type INTEGER DEFAULT 0 NOT NULL
        CHECK (job_type BETWEEN 0 AND 98) -- no 99 code
);
```

From these two tables, build this `UNION`ed view of all the job assignments in the entire company and show that to users.

```
CREATE VIEW JobAssignments (store_nbr, ssn, start_date,
end_date, job_type)
AS
(SELECT store_nbr, ssn, start_date, end_date, job_type
   FROM Job_not99_Assignments
  UNION ALL
 SELECT store_nbr, ssn, start_date, end_date, job_type
   FROM Job_99_Assignments)
```

The key and job_type constraints in each table, working together, will guarantee at most manager per store. The next step is to add `INSTEAD OF` triggers to the `VIEW` or write stored procedures, so the users can insert, update, and delete from it easily. A simple stored procedure, without error handling or input validation, would be:

```
CREATE PROCEDURE InsertJobAssignments
```

```
(IN store_nbr INTEGER, IN new_ssn CHAR(9), IN new_start_date
DATE, IN new_end_date DATE, IN new_job_type INTEGER)
LANGUAGE SQL
IF new_job_typ <> 99
THEN INSERT INTO Job_not99_Assignments
     VALUES (store_nbr, new_ssn, new_start_date, new_end_date,
new_job_type);
ELSE INSERT INTO Job_99_Assignments
     VALUES (store_nbr, new_ssn, new_start_date, new_end_date,
new_job_type);
END IF;
```

Likewise, a procedure to terminate an employee:

```
CREATE PROCEDURE FireEmployee (IN new_ssn CHAR(9))
LANGUAGE SQL
IF new_job_typ <> 99
THEN DELETE FROM Job_not99_Assignments
      WHERE ssn = new_ssn;
ELSE DELETE FROM Job_99_Assignments
      WHERE ssn = new_ssn;
END IF;
```

If a developer attempts to change the Job_Assignments VIEW directly with an INSERT, UPDATE, or DELETE, he will get an error message telling him that the VIEW is not updatable because it contains a UNION operation. That is a good thing in one way, because we can force the developer to use only the stored procedures.

Again, this is an exercise in programming a solution within certain limits. The TRIGGER is probably going give better performance than the VIEW.

1.1.9 Using PRIMARY KEYs and ASSERTIONs for Constraints

Let's do another version of the "stores and personnel" problem given in section 1.1.8.

```
CREATE TABLE JobAssignments
(ssn CHAR(9) NOT NULL PRIMARY KEY -- nobody is in two Stores
   REFERENCES Personnel (ssn)
   ON UPDATE CASCADE
```

```
  ON DELETE CASCADE,
store_nbr INTEGER NOT NULL
  REFERENCES Stores (store_nbr)
  ON UPDATE CASCADE
  ON DELETE CASCADE);
```

The key on the Social Security number will ensure that nobody is at two stores, and that a store can have many employees assigned to it. Ideally, you want an SQL-92 constraint to check that each employee does have a branch assignment.

The first attempt is usually something like this.

```
CREATE ASSERTION Nobody_Unassigned
CHECK (NOT EXISTS
       (SELECT *
 FROM Personnel AS P
      LEFT OUTER JOIN
      JobAssignments AS J
      ON P.ssn = J.ssn
        WHERE J.ssn IS NULL
  AND P.ssn
      IN (SELECT ssn FROM JobAssignments
  UNION
  SELECT ssn FROM Personnel)));
```

However, this example is overkill and does not prevent an employee from being at more than one store. There are probably indexes on the Social Security number values in both Personnel and JobAssignments tables, so getting a `COUNT()` function should be cheap. This assertion will also work.

```
CREATE ASSERTION Everyone_assigned_one_store
CHECK ((SELECT COUNT(ssn) FROM JobAssignments)
        = (SELECT COUNT(ssn) FROM Personnel));
```

This is a surprise to people at first, because they expect to see a `JOIN` to do the one-to-one mapping between personnel and job assignments. But the PK-FK (primary key–foreign key) requirement provides that for you. Any unassigned employee will make the Personnel table bigger than the JobAssignments table, and an employee in JobAssignments must have a match in Personnel. Good optimizers extract things like that as predicates and use them, which is why we want declarative referential integrity, instead of triggers and application-side logic.

You will need to have a stored procedure that inserts into both tables as a single transaction. The updates and deletes will cascade and clean up the job assignments.

Let's change the specs a bit and allow employees to work at more than one store. If we want to have employees in multiple Stores, we could change the keys on JobAssignments, thus.

```
CREATE TABLE JobAssignments
(ssn CHAR(9) NOT NULL
    REFERENCES Personnel (ssn)
    ON UPDATE CASCADE
    ON DELETE CASCADE,
store_nbr INTEGER NOT NULL
    REFERENCES Stores (store_nbr)
    ON UPDATE CASCADE
    ON DELETE CASCADE,
 PRIMARY KEY (ssn, store_nbr));
```

Then use a COUNT(DISTINCT ...) in the assertion.

```
CREATE ASSERTION Everyone_assigned_at_least_once
CHECK ((SELECT COUNT(DISTINCT ssn) FROM JobAssignments)
= (SELECT COUNT(ssn) FROM Personnel));
```

You must be aware that the uniqueness constraints and assertions work together; a change in one or both of them can also change this rule.

1.1.10 Avoiding Attribute Splitting

Attribute splitting takes many forms. It occurs when you have a single attribute, but put its values in more than one place in the schema. The most common form of attribute splitting is to create separate tables for each value. Another form of attribute splitting is to create separate rows in the same table for part of each value. These concepts are probably easier to show with examples.

Attribute Split Tables

If I were to create a database with a table for male employees and separate table for female employees, you would immediately see that

they should be one table with a column for a sex code. I would have split a table on sex. This is very obvious, but it can also be subtler.

Consider a subscription database that has both organizational and individual subscribers. There are two tables with the same structure and a third table that holds the split attribute, subscription type.

```
CREATE TABLE OrgSubscriptions
(subscr_id INTEGER NOT NULL PRIMARY KEY
    REFERENCES SubscriptionTypes(subscr_id),
 org_name CHAR(35),
 last_name CHAR(15),
 first_name CHAR(15),
 address1 CHAR(35)NOT NULL,
  ...);

CREATE TABLE IndSubscriptions
(subscr_id INTEGER NOT NULL PRIMARY KEY
        REFERENCES SubscriptionTypes(subscr_id),
 org_name CHAR(35),
 last_name CHAR(15),
 first_name CHAR(15),
 address1 CHAR(35)NOT NULL,
  ...);

CREATE TABLE SubscriptionTypes
(subscr_id INTEGER NOT NULL PRIMARY KEY,
 subscr_type CHAR(1) DEFAULT 'I' NOT NULL
      CHECK (subscr_type IN ('I', 'O'));
```

An organizational subscription can go to just a person (last_name, first_name), or just the organization name (org_name), or both. If an individual subscription has no particular person, it is sent to an organization called {Current Resident} instead.

The original specifications enforce a condition that subscr_id be universally unique in the schema.

The first step is to replace the three tables with one table for all subscriptions and move the subscription type back into a column of its own, since it is an attribute of a subscription. Next, we need to add constraints to deal with the constraints on each subscription.

```
CREATE TABLE Subscriptions
(subscr_id INTEGER NOT NULL PRIMARY KEY
    REFERENCES SubscriptionTypes(subscr_id),
 org_name CHAR(35) DEFAULT '{Current Resident}',
 last_name CHAR(15),
 first_name CHAR(15),
 subscr_type CHAR(1) DEFAULT 'I' NOT NULL
      CHECK (subscr_type IN ('I', 'O'),

 CONSTRAINT known_addressee
 CHECK (COALESCE (org_name, first_name, last_name) IS NOT NULL);

 CONSTRAINT junkmail
 CHECK (CASE WHEN subscr_type = 'I' AND org_name = '{Current
Resident}'
             THEN 1
             WHEN subscr_type = 'O' AND org_name = '{Current
Resident}'
             THEN 0 ELSE 1 END = 1),
 address1 CHAR(35)NOT NULL,
 ...);
```

The known_addressee constraint means that we have to have a line with some addressee for this to be a valid subscription. The junk mail constraint ensures that anything not aimed at a known person is classified as an individual subscription.

Attribute Split Rows

Consider this table, which directly models a sign-in/sign-out sheet.

```
CREATE TABLE RegisterBook
(emp_name CHAR(35) NOT NULL,
 sign_time TIMESTAMP DEFAULT CURRENT_TIMESTAMP NOT NULL,
 sign_action CHAR (3) DEFAULT 'IN' NOT NULL
  CHECK (sign_action IN ('IN', 'OUT')),
 PRIMARY KEY (emp_name, sign_time));
```

To answer any basic query, you need to use two rows in a self-join to get the sign-in and sign-out pairs for each employee. The correction design would have been:

```
CREATE TABLE RegisterBook
(emp_name CHAR(35) NOT NULL,
 sign_in_time TIMESTAMP DEFAULT CURRENT_TIMESTAMP NOT NULL,
 sign_out_time TIMESTAMP, -- null means current
 PRIMARY KEY (emp_name, sign_in_time));
```

The single attribute, duration, has to be modeled as two columns in Standard SQL, but it was split into rows identified by a code to tell which end of the duration each one represented. If this were longitude and latitude, you would immediately see the problem and put the two parts of the one attribute (geographical location) in the same row.

1.1.11 Modeling Class Hierarchies in DDL

The classic scenario in an object-oriented (OO) model calls for a root class with all of the common attributes and then specialized subclasses under it. As an example, let's take the class of Vehicles and find an industry standard identifier (the Vehicle Identification Number, or VIN), and add two mutually exclusive subclasses, sport utility vehicles and sedans ('SUV', 'SED').

```
CREATE TABLE Vehicles
(vin CHAR(17) NOT NULL PRIMARY KEY,
 vehicle_type CHAR(3) NOT NULL
       CHECK(vehicle_type IN ('SUV', 'SED')),
 UNIQUE (vin, vehicle_type),
 ...);
```

Notice the overlapping candidate keys. I then use a compound candidate key (vin, vehicle_type) and a constraint in each subclass table to ensure that the vehicle_type is locked and agrees with the Vehicles table. Add some DRI actions and you are done:

```
CREATE TABLE SUV
(vin CHAR(17) NOT NULL PRIMARY KEY,
 vehicle_type CHAR(3) DEFAULT 'SUV' NOT NULL
       CHECK(vehicle_type = 'SUV'),
 UNIQUE (vin, vehicle_type),
 FOREIGN KEY (vin, vehicle_type)
  REFERENCES Vehicles(vin, vehicle_type)
  ON UPDATE CASCADE
  ON DELETE CASCADE,
```

```
 ...);

CREATE TABLE Sedans
(vin CHAR(17) NOT NULL PRIMARY KEY,
 vehicle_type CHAR(3) DEFAULT 'SED' NOT NULL
       CHECK(vehicle_type = 'SED'),
 UNIQUE (vin, vehicle_type),
 FOREIGN KEY (vin, vehicle_type)
  REFERENCES Vehicles(vin, vehicle_type)
  ON UPDATE CASCADE
  ON DELETE CASCADE,
 ...);
```

I can continue to build a hierarchy like this. For example, if I had a Sedans table that broke down into two-door and four-door sedans, I could build a schema like this:

```
CREATE TABLE Sedans
(vin CHAR(17) NOT NULL PRIMARY KEY,
 vehicle_type CHAR(3) DEFAULT 'SED' NOT NULL
       CHECK(vehicle_type IN ('2DR', '4DR', 'SED')),
 UNIQUE (vin, vehicle_type),
 FOREIGN KEY (vin, vehicle_type)
  REFERENCES Vehicles(vin, vehicle_type)
  ON UPDATE CASCADE
  ON DELETE CASCADE,
 ...);

CREATE TABLE TwoDoor
(vin CHAR(17) NOT NULL PRIMARY KEY,
 vehicle_type CHAR(3) DEFAULT '2DR' NOT NULL
       CHECK(vehicle_type = '2DR'),
 UNIQUE (vin, vehicle_type),
 FOREIGN KEY (vin, vehicle_type)
  REFERENCES Sedans(vin, vehicle_type)
  ON UPDATE CASCADE
  ON DELETE CASCADE,
 ...);

CREATE TABLE FourDoor
(vin CHAR(17) NOT NULL PRIMARY KEY,
```

```
vehicle_type CHAR(3) DEFAULT '4DR' NOT NULL
      CHECK(vehicle_type = '4DR'),
UNIQUE (vin, vehicle_type),
FOREIGN KEY (vin, vehicle_type)
 REFERENCES Sedans (vin, vehicle_type)
 ON UPDATE CASCADE
 ON DELETE CASCADE,
...);
```

The idea is to build a chain of identifiers and types in a UNIQUE() constraint that goes up the tree when you use a REFERENCES constraint. Obviously, you can do variants of this trick to get different class structures.

If an entity doesn't have to be exclusively one subtype, you play with the root of the class hierarchy:

```
CREATE TABLE Vehicles
(vin CHAR(17) NOT NULL,
 vehicle_type CHAR(3) NOT NULL
      CHECK(vehicle_type IN ('SUV', 'SED')),
 PRIMARY KEY (vin, vehicle_type),
 ...);
```

Now, start hiding all this stuff in VIEWs immediately and add an INSTEAD OF trigger to those VIEWs.

1.2 Generating Unique Sequential Numbers for Keys

One common vendor extension is using some method of generating a sequence of integers to use as primary keys. These are very nonrelational extensions that are highly proprietary, and have major disadvantages. They all are based on exposing part of the physical state of the machine during the insertion process, in violation of Dr. E. F. Codd's rules for defining a relational database (i.e., rule 8, physical data independence). Dr. Codd's rules are discussed in Chapter 2.

Early SQL products were built on existing file systems. The data was kept in physically contiguous disk pages, in physically contiguous rows, made up of physically contiguous columns, in short, just like a deck of punch cards or a magnetic tape. Most of these sequence generators are an attempt to regain the physical sequence that SQL took out of its logical model, so we can pretend that we have physically contiguous storage.

But physically contiguous storage is only one way of building a relational database, and it is not always the best one. Aside from that, the whole idea of a relational database is that user is not supposed to know how things are stored at all, much less write code that depends on the particular physical representation in a particular release of a particular product.

The exact method used to generate sequences of integers varies from product to product, but the results are all the same, their behavior is unpredictable.

Another major disadvantage of sequential numbers as keys is that they have no check digits, so there is no way to determine if they are valid or not (for a discussion of check digits, see *Joe Celko's Data and Databases: Concepts in Practice*).

So why do people use them? System-generated values are a fast and easy answer to the problem of obtaining a unique primary key. It requires no research and no real data modeling. Drug abuse is also a fast and easy answer to problems. I do not recommend either.

1.2.1 IDENTITY Columns

The Sybase/SQL Server family allows you to declare an exact numeric column with the property `IDENTITY` in Sybase and DB2 or `AUTOINCREMENT` in SQL Anywhere attached to it. These columns will autoincrement with every row that is inserted into the table. The numbering is totally dependent on the order in which the rows were physically inserted into the table, even if they came into the table as a single statement (i.e., `INSERT INTO Foobar SELECT ...;`).

Since this "feature" is highly proprietary, you can get all kinds of implementations. For example, if the next value to be used causes an overflow, then you might get a wraparound to negative values. This occurs with numbers larger than (2^31 - 1) in SQL Anywhere, while Sybase allows the user to set a `NUMERIC(p, 0)` column to any desired size. Some products increment the internal counter before inserting a row, so a rollback can cause gaps in the sequence. You have to know the current release of your product and never expect your code to port to even consider this "feature" in production code.

Let's look at the logical problems. First, try to create a table with two columns and try to make them both `IDENTITY` columns. If you cannot declare more than one column to be of a certain data type, then that thing is not a data type at all, by definition.

Next, create a table with one column and make it an IDENTITY column. Now try to insert, update, and delete different numbers from it. If you cannot insert, update, and delete rows from a table, then it is not a table by definition.

Finally create a simple table with one IDENTITY column and a few other columns. Use a few statements such as:

```
INSERT INTO Foobar (a, b, c) VALUES ('a1', 'b1', 'c1');
INSERT INTO Foobar (a, b, c) VALUES ('a2', 'b2', 'c2');
INSERT INTO Foobar (a, b, c) VALUES ('a3', 'b3', 'c3');
```

These statements put a few rows into the table. Notice that the IDENTITY column sequentially numbered them in the order they were presented. If you delete a row, the gap in the sequence is not filled, and the sequence continues from the highest number that has ever been used in that column in that particular table.

But now use a statement with a query expression in it, like this:

```
INSERT INTO Foobar (a, b, c)
SELECT x, y, z
  FROM Floob;
```

Since a query result is a table, and a table is a set that has no ordering, what should the IDENTITY numbers be? The whole completed set is presented to Foobar all at once, not a row at a time. There are (*n!*) ways to number (*n*) rows, so which one do you pick? The answer has been to use whatever the physical order of the result set happened to be. There's that nonrelational phrase "physical order" again.

But it is actually worse than that. If the same query is executed again, but with new statistics, or after an index has been dropped or added, the new execution plan could bring the result set back in a different physical order. Can you explain from a logical model why the same rows in the second query get different IDENTITY numbers? In the relational model, they should be treated the same if all the values of all the attributes are identical.

Think about trying to do replication on two databases that differ only by an index, or by cache size, or by something that occasionally gives them different execution plans for the same statements.

Want to try to maintain such a system?

1.2.2 ROWID and Physical Disk Addresses

Oracle has the ability to expose the physical address of a row on the hard drive as a special variable called ROWID. This is the fastest way to locate a row in a table, since the read-write head is positioned to the row immediately. This exposure of the underlying physical storage at the logical level means that Oracle is committed to using contiguous storage for the rows of a table, which in turn means that Oracle cannot use hashing, distributed databases, dynamic bit vectors, or any of several newer techniques for VLDB (Very Large Databases). When the database is moved or reorganized for any reason, the ROWID is changed.

1.2.3 Sequential Numbering in Pure SQL

The proper way to do this operation is to insert one row at a time with this Standard SQL statement:

```
INSERT INTO Foobar (keycol, ...)
VALUES (COALESCE((SELECT MAX(keycol) FROM Foobar), 0) + 1, ..);
```

Notice the use of the COALESCE() function to handle the empty table and to get the numbering started with one. This approach generalizes from a row insertion to a table insertion:

```
INSERT INTO Foobar (keycol, ...)
VALUES (COALESCE((SELECT MAX(keycol) FROM Foobar), 0) + 1, ..),

    (COALESCE((SELECT MAX(keycol) FROM Foobar), 0) + 2, ...),
     ...
    (COALESCE((SELECT MAX(keycol) FROM Foobar), 0) + n, ...);
```

Another approach is to put a TRIGGER on the table. Here is the code for SQL-99 TRIGGERs; actual products may have a slightly different syntax:

```
CREATE TRIGGER Autoincrement
 BEFORE INSERT ON Foobar
 REFERENCING NEW AS N1
 FOR EACH ROW
BEGIN
UPDATE N1
   SET keycol = (SELECT COALESCE(MAX(F1.keycol), 0) + 1
```

```
   FROM Foobar AS F1);
COMMIT; -- put each row into the table as it is processed
END;
```

Notice the use of the COALESCE() function to handle the first row inserted into an empty table.

Umachandar Jayachandran (www.umachandar.com) suggested the following method for generating unique identifiers in SQL. His original note was for SQL Server, but it can be generalized to any product with a random number function. The idea is to first split the counters into several *distinct* ranges:

```
CREATE TABLE Counters
(id_nbr_set INTEGER NOT NULL PRIMARY KEY,
 low_val INTEGER NOT NULL,
 high_val INTEGER NOT NULL,
 CHECK (low_val < high_val), -- properly ordered
 CHECK (NOT EXISTS   -- no overlaps
        (SELECT *
   FROM Counters AS C1
  WHERE Counters.low_val BETWEEN C1.low_val AND C1.high_val
     OR Counters.high_val BETWEEN C1.low_val AND C1.high_val))
);

INSERT INTO Counters VALUES (0, 0000000, 0999999);
INSERT INTO Counters VALUES (1, 1000000, 1999999);
INSERT INTO Counters VALUES (2, 2000000, 2999999);
...
INSERT INTO Counters VALUES (9, 9000000, 9999999);
-- and so on...
```

The ranges can be any size you wish. However, uniform sizes have the advantage of matching the uniform random number generator we will be using in the code. The important thing is that the ranges should not overlap each other. Here is a skeleton procedure body:

```
CREATE PROCEDURE GenerateCounters()
LANGUAGE SQL
IF (SELECT SUM(high_val - low_val) FROM Counters) > 0
THEN BEGIN
     DECLARE new_id_nbr INTEGER;
```

```
        DECLARE random_set INTEGER;
        SET new_id_nbr = NULL;
        WHILE (new_id_nbr IS NULL)
        DO SET random_set = CEILING(RAND() * 10);
          -- This will randomly pick one row
           SET new_id_nbr
               = (SELECT low_val
                    FROM Counters
                   WHERE id_set_nbr = random_set
                     AND low_val < high_val);
          UPDATE Counters
             SET low_val = low_val + 1
           WHERE id_nbr_set = random_set
             AND low_val < high_val;
        END WHILE;
        -- code to create a check digit can go here
        END;
ELSE BEGIN -- you are out of numbers
        -- You can reset the Counters table with an UPDATE.
        -- If you take no action, the new id number will be NULL
        END;
END IF;
```

1.2.4 GUIDs

Global Unique Identifiers (GUIDs) are unique exposed physical locators generated by a combination of UTC time and the network address of the device creating it. Microsoft says that they should be unique for about a century. According to Wikipedia (http://en.wikipedia.org/wiki/GUID):

> "The algorithm used for generating new GUIDs has been widely criticized. At one point, the user's network card MAC address was used as a base for several GUID digits, which meant that, e.g., a document could be tracked back to the computer that created it. After this was discovered, Microsoft changed the algorithm so that it no longer contains the MAC address. This privacy hole was used when locating the creator of the Melissa worm."

Besides the usual problems with exposed physical locators, each GUID requires 16 bytes of storage, while a simple `INTEGER` needs only 4 bytes on most machines.

Indexes and `PRIMARY KEY`s built on GUIDs will have worse performance than shorter key columns. This applies to compound keys of less than 16 bytes, too. I mention this because many newbies justify a GUID key on the grounds that it will improve performance. Besides being false, that level of performance is not a real problem in modern hardware. Computers built on 64-bit hardware are becoming common, and so are faster and faster disk drives.

The real problem is that GUIDs are difficult to interpret, so it becomes difficult to work with them directly and trace them back to their source for validation. In fact, the GUID does not have any sorting sequence, so it is impossible to spot a missing value or use them to order results. All you can do is use a `CHECK()` with a regular expression for string of 36 digits and the letters 'A' to 'F' broken apart by four dashes.

The GUID cannot participate in queries involving aggregate functions; you would first have to cast it as a **`CHAR(36)`** and use the string value. Your first thought might have been to make it into a longer `INTEGER`, but the two data types are not compatible. Other features of this data type are very proprietary and will not port out of a Microsoft environment.

1.2.5 Sequence Generator Functions

`COUNTER(*)`, `NUMBER(*)`, `IDENTITY`, and so on are proprietary features that return a new incremented value each time this function is used in an expression. This is a way to generate unique identifiers. This can be either a function call or a column property, depending on the product. It is also a horrible, nonstandard, nonrelational proprietary extension that should be avoided whenever possible.

We will spend some time later on ways to get sequences and unique numbers inside Standard SQL without resorting to proprietary code or the use of exposed physical locators in the hardware.

1.2.6 Unique Value Generators

The most important property of any usable unique value generator is that it will never generate the same value twice. Sequential integers are the first approach vendors implemented in their product as a substitute for a proper key.

In essence, they are a piece of code inside SQL that looks at the last allocated value and adds one to get the next value. Let's start from scratch and build our own version of such a procedure. First create a table called GeneratorValues with one row and two columns:

```
CREATE TABLE GeneratorValues
(lock CHAR(1) DEFAULT 'X' NOT NULL PRIMARY KEY -- only one row
      CHECK (lock = 'X'),
keyval INTEGER DEFAULT 1 NOT NULL -- positive numbers only
     CHECK (keyval > 0));

 -- let everyone use the table
GRANT SELECT, UPDATE(keyval)
ON TABLE GeneratorValues
TO PUBLIC;
```

Now the table needs a function to get out a value and do the increment.

```
CREATE FUNCTION Generator()
RETURNS INTEGER
LANGUAGE SQL
DETERMINISTIC
BEGIN
 -- SET ISOLATION = SERIALIZABLE;
UPDATE GeneratorValues
  SET keyval = keyval + 1;
RETURN (SELECT keyval FROM GeneratorValues);
COMMIT;
END;
```

This solution looks pretty good, but if there are multiple users, this code fragment is capable of allocating duplicate values to different users. It is important to isolate the execution of the code to one and only one user at a time by using `SET ISOLATION = SERIALIZABLE`. Various SQL products will have slightly different ways of achieving this effect, based on their concurrency control methods.

More bad news is that in pessimistic locking systems, you can get serious performance problems resulting from lock contention when a transaction is in serial isolation. The users are put in a single queue for access to the Generator table.

If the application demands gap-free numbering, then we not only have to guarantee that no two sessions ever get the same value, we must also guarantee that no value is ever wasted. Therefore, the lock on the Generator table must be held until the key value is actually used and the entire transaction is committed. Exactly how to handle this is implementation-defined, so I am not going to comment on it.

1.2.7 Preallocated Values

In the old days of paper forms, the company had a forms control officer whose job was to track the forms. A gap in the sequential numbers on a check, bond, stock certificate, or other form was a serious accounting problem. Paper forms were usually preprinted and issued in blocks of numbers as needed. You can imitate this procedure in a database with a little thought and a few simple stored procedures.

Broadly speaking, there were two types of allocation blocks. In one, the sequence is known (the most common example of this is a checkbook). Gaps in the sequence numbers are not allowed, and a destroyed or damaged check has to be explained with a "void" or other notation. The system needs to record which block went to which user, the date and time, and any other information relevant to the auditors.

```
CREATE TABLE FormsControl
(form_nbr CHAR(7) NOT NULL,
 seq INTEGER NOT NULL CHECK(seq > 0),
 PRIMARY KEY (form_nbr, seq),
 recipient CHAR(25) DEFAULT CURRENT_USER NOT NULL,
 issue_date TIMESTAMP DEFAULT CURRENT_TIMESTAMP NOT NULL,
 ...
);
```

The tables that use the form numbers need to have constraints to verify that the numbers were issued and appear in the FormsControl table. The next sequence number is easy to create, but you probably should restrict access to the base table with a stored procedure designed for one kind of form, along these lines.

```
CREATE FUNCTION NextFlobSeq( )
RETURNS INTEGER
LANGUAGE SQL
DETERMINISTIC
BEGIN
```

```
INSERT INTO FormsControl (form_nbr, seq, ...
VALUES ('Flob-1/R',
       (SELECT MAX(seq)+1
  FROM FormsControl
 WHERE form_nbr = 'Flob-1/R'),
        ...  );
```

You can also use views on the FormsControl table to limit user access. If you might be dealing with an empty table, then use this scalar expression:

```
(SELECT COALESCE(MAX(seq), 0)+1
   FROM FormsControl
  WHERE form_nbr = 'Flob-1/R'),
```

The COALESCE() will return a zero, thus ensuring that the sequence starts with one.

1.2.8 Random Order Values

In many applications, we do not want to issue the sequence numbers in sequence. This pattern can give information that we do not wish to expose. Instead, we want to issue generated values in random order. Do not get confused; we want known values that are supplied in random order, not random numbers. Most random number generators can repeat values, which would defeat the purpose of this drill.

While I usually avoid mentioning physical implementations, one of the advantages of random-order keys is to improve the performance of tree indexes. Tree-structured indexes (such as a B-Tree) that have sequential insertions become unbalanced and have to be reorganized frequently. However, if the same set of keys is presented in a random order, the tree tends to stay balanced and you get much better performance.

The generator shown here is an implementation of the additive congruential method of generating values in pseudo-random order and is due to Roy Hann of Rational Commerce Limited, a CA-Ingres consulting firm. It is based on a shift-register and an XOR-gate, and it has its origins in cryptography. While there are other ways to do this, this code is nice because:

1. The algorithm can be written in C or another low-level language for speed. But the math is fairly simple, even in base ten.
2. The algorithm tends to generate successive values that are (usually) "far apart," which is handy for improving the performance of tree indexes. You will tend to put data on separate physical data pages in storage.
3. The algorithm does not cycle until it has generated every possible value, so we don't have to worry about duplicates. Just count how many calls have been made to the generator.
4. The algorithm produces uniformly distributed values, which is a nice mathematical property to have. It also does not include zero.

Let's walk through all the iterations of the four-bit generator illustrated in Figure 1.1.

Figure 1.1 *Four-bit Generator for Random Order Values.*

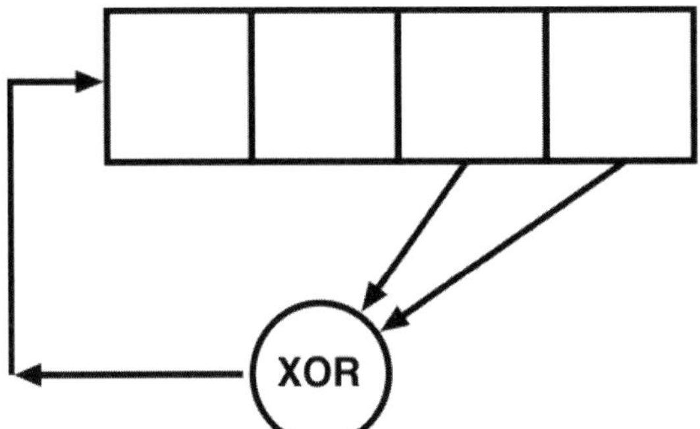

Initially, the shift register contains the value 0001. The two rightmost bits are XORed together, giving 1; the result is fed into the leftmost bit position, and the previous register contents shift one bit right. The iterations of the register are shown in this table, with their base-ten values:

```
iteration 1: 0001 (1)
iteration 2: 1000 (8)
iteration 3: 0100 (4)
iteration 4: 0010 (2)
iteration 5: 1001 (9)
iteration 6: 1100 (12)
```

```
iteration 7: 0110 (6)
iteration 8: 1011 (11)
iteration 9: 0101  (5)
iteration 10:  1010 (10)
iteration 11: 1101 (13)
iteration 12: 1110 (14)
iteration 13: 1111 (15)
iteration 14: 0111 (7)
iteration 15: 0011 (3)
iteration 16: 0001 (1) wrap-around!
```

It might not be obvious that successive values are far apart when we are looking at a tiny four-bit register. But it is clear that the values are generated in no obvious order, all possible values except 0 are eventually produced, and the termination condition is clear, the generator cycles back to 1.

Generalizing the algorithm to arbitrary binary word sizes, and therefore longer number sequences, is not as easy as you might think. Finding the tap positions where bits are extracted for feedback varies according to the word size in an extremely obscure way. Choosing incorrect tap positions results in an incomplete and usually very short cycle, which is unusable. If you want the details and tap positions for words of one to one hundred bits, see E. J. Watson's article in *Mathematics of Computation*, "Primitive Polynomials (Mod 2)" (Watson 1962, pp. 368-369).

The table below shows the tap positions for 8-, 16-, 31-, 32-, and 64-bit words. That should work with any computer hardware you have. The 31-bit word is the one that is probably the most useful, since it gives billions of numbers, uses only two tap positions to make the math easier, and matches most computer hardware. The 32-bit version is not easy to implement on a 32-bit machine, because it will usually generate an overflow error.

Table 1.1 *Tap Positions for Words*

```
Word Length
8 = {0, 2, 3, 4}
16 = {0, 2, 3, 5}
31 = {0, 3}
32 = {0, 1, 2, 3, 5, 7}
64 = {0 1, 3, 4}
```

Using Table 1.1, we can see that we need to tap bits 0 and 3 to construct the 31-bit random-order generated value generator (which is the one most people would want to use in practice):

```
UPDATE Generator31
   SET keyval =
       keyval/2 + MOD(MOD(keyval, 2) + MOD(keyval/8, 2), 2)*2^30;
```

Or if you prefer, the algorithm in C:

```
int Generator31 ()
{static int n = 1;
 n = n >> 1 | ((n^n >> 3) & 1) << 30;
 return n;
}
```

1.3 A Remark on Duplicate Rows

Both of Dr. Codd's relational models do not allow duplicate rows and are based on a set theoretical model. SQL has always allowed duplicate rows and is based on a multiset or bag model.

When the question of duplicates came up in SQL committee, we decided to leave it in the Standard. The example we used internally, and which Len Gallagher used in a reply letter to *Database Programming & Design* magazine and David Beech used in a letter to *Datamation*, was a cash register receipt with multiple occurrences of cans of cat food on it. Because of this example, the literature now refers to this as the "cat food problem."

The fundamental question is: What are you modeling in a table? Dr. Codd and Chris Date's position is that a table is a collection of facts. The other position is that a table can represent an entity, a class, or a relationship among entities. With that approach, a duplicate row means more than one occurrence of an entity. This leads to a more object-oriented view of data, where I have to deal with different fundamental relationships among duplicates, such as:

> *Identity* = "Clark Kent is Superman!" We really have only one entity, but multiple expressions of it. These expression are not substitutable (Clark Kent does not fly until he changes into Superman).

Equality = "Two plus two is four." We really have only one entity with multiple expressions that are always substitutable.

Equivalency = "You use only half as much Concentrated Sudso as your old detergent to get the same cleaning power!" We have two distinct entities, substitutable both ways under all conditions.

Substitutability = "We are out of gin, would you like a vodka martini?" We have two distinct entities, whose replacement for each other is not always in both directions or under all conditions. You might be willing to accept a glass of vodka when there is no wine, but you cannot make a wine sauce with a cup of vodka.

Dr. Codd later added a "degree of duplication" operator to his model as a way of handling duplicates when he realized that there is information in duplication that has to be handled. The degree of duplication is not exactly a `COUNT(*)` or a quantity column in the relation. It does not behave like a numeric column. For example, let us look at table A (let dod means the "degree of duplication" operator for each row):

```
A
x  y
=====
1  a
2  b
3  b
```

When I do a projection on them, I eliminate duplicate rows in Codd's model, but I can reconstruct the original table from the dod function:

```
A
y  dod
======
a   1
b   2
```

See the difference? It is an operator, not a value.

Having said all of this, I try to only use duplicate rows for loading data into an SQL database from legacy sources. Duplicates are very frequent when you get data from the real world, like cash register tapes.

Otherwise, I might leave duplicates in results because using a `SELECT DISTINCT` to remove them will cost too much sorting time, and the sort will force an ordering in the working table, which results in a bad performance hit later.

Dr. Codd mentions this example as "The Supermarket Checkout Problem" in his book, *The Relational Model for Database Management: Version 2* (Codd 1990, pp. 378-379). He critiques the problem and credits it to David Beech in an article entitled "The Need for Duplicate Rows in Tables," *Datamation*, January 1989.

1.4 Other Schema Objects

Let's be picky about definitions. A database is the data that sits under the control of the database management system (DBMS). The DBMS has the schema, rules and operators that apply to the database. The schema contains the definitions of the objects in the database. But we always say "the database," as if it had no parts to it.

In the original SQL-89 language, the only data structure the user could access via SQL was the table, which could be permanent (base tables) or virtual (views). Standard SQL also allows the DBA to define other schema objects, but most of these new features are not yet available in SQL products, or the versions of them that are available are proprietary. Let's take a quick look at these new features, but without spending much time on their details.

1.4.1 Schema Tables

An SQL engine usually keeps the information it needs about the schema by putting it in SQL tables. No two vendors agree on how the schema tables should be named or structured. The SQL Standard defines a set of standard schema information tables. While each vendor will probably keep their own internal schema information tables, many products now have VIEWS that provide standard schema information tables for data exchange and interfaces to external products.

Every SQL product allows users to query the schema tables. User groups have libraries of queries for getting useful information out of the schema tables; you should take the time to get copies of them.

Standard SQL also includes tables for supporting temporal functions, collations, character sets, and so forth, but they might be implemented differently in your actual products.

1.4.2 Temporary Tables

Tables in Standard SQL can be defined as persistent base tables, local temporary tables, or global temporary tables. The complete syntax is:

```
<table definition> ::=
  CREATE [{GLOBAL | LOCAL} TEMPORARY] TABLE <table name>
    <table element list>
    [ON COMMIT {DELETE | PRESERVE} ROWS]
```

A local temporary table belongs to a single user, and a global temporary table is shared by more than one user. When a session using a temporary table is over and the work is COMMITed, the table can be either emptied or saved for the next transaction in the user's session. This is a way of giving the users working storage without giving them CREATE TABLE (and therefore DROP TABLE and ALTER TABLE) privileges.

This has been a serious problem in SQL products for some time. When a programmer can create temporary tables on the fly, the design of the programmer's code quickly becomes a sequential file-processing program, with all the temporary working tapes replaced by temporary working tables. Because the temporary tables are actual tables, they take up physical storage space. If a hundred users call the same procedure, it can allocate tables for a hundred copies of the same data and bring performance down to nothing.

1.4.3 CREATE DOMAIN Statement

The DOMAIN is a new schema element in Standard SQL. It enables you to declare an in-line macro that will allow you to put a commonly used column definition in one place in the schema. You should expect to see this feature in SQL products shortly, since it is easy to implement. The syntax is:

```
<domain definition> ::=
 CREATE DOMAIN <domain name> [AS] <data type>
    [<default clause>]
    [<domain constraint>...]
    [<collate clause>]
```

```
<domain constraint> ::=
  [<constraint name definition>]
  <check constraint definition> [<constraint attributes>]

<alter domain statement> ::=
  ALTER DOMAIN <domain name> <alter domain action>

<alter domain action> ::=
    <set domain default clause>
  | <drop domain default clause>
  | <add domain constraint definition>
  | <drop domain constraint definition>
```

It is important to note that a `DOMAIN` has to be defined with a basic data type and not with other `DOMAIN`s. Once declared, a `DOMAIN` can be used in place of a data type declaration on a column.

The `CHECK()` clause is where you can put the code for validating data items with check digits, ranges, lists, and other conditions. Since the `DOMAIN` is in one place, you can make a good argument for writing the following:

```
CREATE DOMAIN StateCode AS CHAR(2)
     DEFAULT '??'
     CONSTRAINT valid_state_code
     CHECK (VALUE IN ('AL', 'AK', 'AZ', ...));
```

instead of:

```
CREATE DOMAIN StateCode AS CHAR(2)
     DEFAULT '??'
     CONSTRAINT valid_state_code
     CHECK (VALUE IN (SELECT state FROM StateCodeTable));
```

The second method would have been better if you did not have a `DOMAIN` and had to replicate the `CHECK()` clause in multiple tables in the database. This would collect the values and their changes in one place instead of many.

1.4.4 CREATE TRIGGER Statement

A `TRIGGER` is a feature in many versions of SQL that will execute a block of procedural code against the database when a table event occurs. This is not part of Standard SQL, but has been proposed in the SQL3 working document. You can think of a `TRIGGER` as a generalization of the referential actions.

The procedural code is usually written in a proprietary language, but some products let you attach programs in standard procedural languages. A `TRIGGER` could be used to automatically handle discontinued merchandise, for example, by creating a credit slip in place of the original order item data.

There is a Standard syntax for `TRIGGER`s, based on the SQL/PSM Standard, but it is not widely implemented. You should look at what your particular vendor has given you if you want to work with `TRIGGER`s.

The advantages of `TRIGGER`s over declarative referential integrity are that you can do everything that DRI can, and almost anything else, too. The disadvantages are that the optimizer cannot get any data from the procedural code, the `TRIGGER`s take longer to execute, and they are not portable from product to product.

My advice would be to avoid `TRIGGER`s when you can use declarative referential integrity instead. If you do use them, check the code very carefully and keep it simple so that you will not hurt performance.

1.4.5 CREATE PROCEDURE Statement

`CREATE PROCEDURE` allows you to declare and name a module of procedural code written in SQL/PSM or another ANSI X3J programming language. The two major differences in a **`TRIGGER`** and a **`PROCEDURE`** are that a procedure can accept parameters and return values, and that is it is explicitly invoked by a **`CALL`** from a user session and not a database event.

Again, many SQL products have had their own versions of procedure, so you should look at what your particular vendor has given you, check the code very carefully, and keep it simple so you will not hurt performance.

The SQL/PSM (see *Understanding SQL's Stored Procedures* by Jim Melton) for procedural code is an ISO Standard. Still, even with the move to the ISO Standard, existing implementations will still have their own proprietary syntax in many places.

1.4.6 DECLARE CURSOR Statement

I will not spend much time with cursors in this book, but you should understand them at a high level, since you will see them in actual code. Despite a standard syntax, every product has a proprietary version of cursors, because cursors are a low-level construct that works close to the physical implementation in the product.

A CURSOR is a way of converting an SQL result set into a sequential data structure that looks like a simple sequential file. This structure can be handled by the procedural host language, which contains the very statement that executes and creates a structure that looks like a sequential file. In fact, the whole cursor process looks like an old-fashioned magnetic tape system!

You might have noticed that in SQL, the keyword CREATE builds persistent schema objects. The keyword DECLARE builds transient objects that disappear with the end of the session in which they were build. For this reason, you say DECLARE CURSOR, not CREATE CURSOR.

First, you allocate working storage in the host program with a BEGIN DECLARE ... END DECLARE section. This allocation sets up an area where SQL variables can be converted into host language data types, and vice versa. NULLs are handled by declaring INDICATOR variables in the host language BEGIN DECLARE section. The INDICATOR variables are paired with the appropriate host variables. An INDICATOR is an exact numeric data type with a scale of zero, that is, some kind of integer in the host language.

DECLARE CURSOR Statement

The DECLARE CURSOR statement must appear next. The SQL-92 syntax is fairly representative of actual products, but you must read your manual.

```
<declare cursor> ::=
      DECLARE <cursor name> [INSENSITIVE] [SCROLL] CURSOR
        FOR <cursor specification>

<cursor specification> ::=
      <query expression> [<order by clause>]
        [<updatability clause>]

<updatability clause> ::=  FOR {READ ONLY | UPDATE [OF <column
name list>]}

<order by clause> ::=  ORDER BY <sort specification list>

<sort specification list> ::=
```

```
    <sort specification> [{<comma> <sort specification>}...]

<sort specification> ::= <sort key> [<collate clause>]
  [<ordering specification>]

<sort key> ::= <column name>
<ordering specification> ::= ASC | DESC
```

A few things need explaining. First of all, the ORDER BY clause is part of a cursor, not part of a SELECT statement. Because some SQL products, such as SQL Server and Sybase, allow the user to create implicit cursors, many newbies get this wrong. This is easy to implement in products that evolved from sequential file systems and still expose this architecture to the user, in violation of Dr. Codd's rules. Oracle is probably the worst offender as of this writing, but some of the "micro-SQLs" are just as bad.

If either INSENSITIVE, SCROLL, or ORDER BY is specified, or if the working table is a read-only, then an <updatability clause> of READ ONLY is implicit. Otherwise, an <updatability clause> of FOR UPDATE without a <column name list> is implicit.

OPEN Statement

The OPEN <cursor name> statement positions an imaginary read/write head before the first record in the cursor. FETCH statements can then move this imaginary read/write head from record to record. When the read/write head moves past the last record, an exception is raised, like an EOF (end of file) flag in a magnetic tape file system.

Watch out for this model! In some file systems, the read/write head starts on the first record and the EOF flag is set to TRUE when it reads the last record. Simply copying the algorithms from your procedural code into SQL/PSM might not work.

FETCH Statement

```
<fetch statement> ::= FETCH [[<fetch orientation>]
      FROM] <cursor name> INTO <fetch target list>

<fetch orientation> ::=  NEXT | PRIOR | FIRST | LAST
        | {ABSOLUTE | RELATIVE} <simple value specification>
```

The FETCH statement takes one row from the cursor, then converts each SQL data type into a host-language data type and puts result into

the appropriate host variable. If the SQL value was a NULL, the INDICATOR is set to -1; if no indicator was specified, an exception condition is raised.

As you can see, the host program must be sure to check the INDICATORs, because otherwise the value of the parameter will be garbage. If the parameter is passed to the host language without any problems, the INDICATOR is set to zero. If the value being passed to the host program is a non-**NULL** character string and it has an indicator, the indicator is set to the length of the SQL string and can be used to detect string overflows or to set the length of the parameter.

The <fetch orientation> tells the read/write head which way to move. NEXT and PRIOR read one record forward or backward from the current position. FIRST and LAST put the read/write on the first or last records respectively. The ABSOLUTE fetch moves to a given record number. The RELATIVE fetch moves the read/write head forward or backward (*n*) records from the current position. Again, this is a straight imitation of a sequential file system.

CLOSE Statement

The CLOSE <cursor name> statement resets the cursor read/write head to a position before the first row in the cursor. The cursor still exists, but must be reopened before it can be used. This is similar to the CLOSE FILE operations in FORTRAN or COBOL, but with an important difference, the cursor can be recomputed when it is reopened!

DEALLOCATE Statement

The DEALLOCATE CURSOR statement frees up the working storage in the host program. Think of it as dismounting a tape from the tape drive in a sequential file system.

How to Use a CURSOR

The best performance improvement technique for cursors inside the database is not to use them. SQL engines are designed for set processing, and they work better with sets of data than with individual rows. The times when using cursor is unavoidable usually deal with corrections to the database caused by an improper design, or when speed of a cursor is faster because of the physical implementation in the product. For example, a cursor can be used to take redundant duplicates out of a table that does not have a key.

The old argument for cursors in the original Sybase SQL Server training course was this example. You own a bookstore and you want to change prices; all books $25 and over are reduced 10%, and all books under $25 are increased 15%.

```
BEGIN ATOMIC
UPDATE Books
   SET price = price * 0.90
 WHERE price >= $25.00;
UPDATE Books
   SET price = price * 1.15
 WHERE price < $25.00;
END;
```

Oops! Look at a book that was $25.00 ((25.00 * .90) *1.10) = $24.75. So you were told to cursor through the table, and change each row with a cursor.

Today you write:

```
UPDATE Books
   SET price
       = CASE WHEN price < $25.00;
      THEN price * 1.15
      WHEN price >= $25.00
      THEN price * 0.90
      ELSE price END;
```

But Steve Kass pointed out that even back then, it was possible to avoid a cursor:

```
BEGIN ATOMIC
UPDATE Books
   SET price = price * 1.80
WHERE price >= $25.00;
UPDATE Books
   SET price = price * 1.15
WHERE price < $25.00;
UPDATE Books
   SET price = price * 0.50
WHERE price >= $45.00;
END;
```

However, this code makes three passes through the Books table, instead of just one. That could be worse than a cursor!

Limit the number of rows and columns in the cursor's SELECT statement to only those required for the desired result set. This limitation will avoid unnecessary fetching of data, which in turn will require fewer server resources and increase cursor performance.

Use FOR READ ONLY instead of UPDATE cursors, if possible. You will have to watch the transaction isolation level, however.

Opening an INSENSITIVE cursor can cause its rows to be copied to a working table in many products or locked at the table level in others.

Do a CLOSE cursor as soon as you are finished with the result set. This will release any locks on the rows. Always remember to deallocate your CURSORs when you are finished.

Look for your product options. For example, SQL Server has FAST_FORWARD and FORWARD_ONLY cursor options when working with unidirectional, read-only result sets. Using FAST_FORWARD defines a FORWARD_ONLY, READ_ONLY cursor with a number of internal performance optimizations.

Be careful if you are using a CURSOR loop to modify a large number of rows contained within a transaction. Depending on the transaction isolation level, those rows may remain locked until the transaction is committed or rolled back, possibly causing resource contention on the server.

In Standard SQL, there is an SQLSTATE code that tells you if the result set of a GROUP BY has members that excluded NULLs from their aggregate computations. This warning can be raised in the DECLARE CURSOR statement, the OPEN statement, or when the row representing such a grouping is FETCHed. Know how your product handles this situation.

The truth is that the host languages have to use cursors because they are designed for sequential file systems

Positioned UPDATE and DELETE Statements

Obviously, the cursor needs an explicit or implicit <updatability clause> of FOR UPDATE for this to work, and it has to be in the same module as the positioned statements. You get an exception when you try to change a READ ONLY cursor, or if the CURSOR is not positioned on a record.

The clause CURRENT OF <cursor name> refers to the record that the imaginary read/write head is on. This cursor record has to map back to one and only one row in the base table.

```
UPDATE Statement:

<update statement: positioned>
  ::= UPDATE <table name>
 SET <set clause list>
      WHERE CURRENT OF <cursor name>
```

The cursor remains positioned on its current row, even if an exception condition is raised during the update attempt.

```
DELETE FROM Statement:

<delete statement: positioned>
  ::= DELETE FROM <table name>
      WHERE CURRENT OF <cursor name>
```

If, while the cursor is open, another `DELETE FROM` or `UPDATE` statement attempts to modify the current cursor record, then a cursor operation conflict warning is raised. The transaction isolation level then determines what happens. If the `<delete statement: positioned>` deleted the last cursor record, then the position of the cursor is after the last record; otherwise, the position of the cursor is before the next cursor record.

Normalization

THE RELATIONAL MODEL of data, and the normal forms of the relational model, were first defined by Dr. E. F. Codd (Codd 1970), and then extended by other writers after him. Dr. Codd invented the term "normalized relations" by borrowing from the political jargon of the day. The branch of mathematics called relations deals with mappings among sets defined by predicate calculus from formal logic. Just as in an algebraic equation, there are many forms of the same relational statement, but the normal forms of relations are certain formally defined desirable constructions. The goal of normal forms is to avoid certain data anomalies that can occur in unnormalized tables.

Data anomalies are easier to explain with an example, but first please be patient while I define some terms. A predicate is a statement of the form A(X), which means that X has the property A. For example, "John is from Indiana" is a predicate statement; here, "John" is the subject and "is from Indiana" is the predicate. A relation is a predicate with two or more subjects. "John and Bob are brothers" is an example of a relation. The common way of visualizing a set of relational statements is as a table, in which the columns are attributes of the relation, and each row is a specific relational statement.

When Dr. Codd defined the relational model, he gave 0 to 12 rules for the visualization of the relation as a table:

0. *The Foundation Rule*: (Yes, there is a rule zero.) For a system to qualify as a relational database management system, that system must exclusively use its relational facilities to manage the database. SQL is not so pure on this rule, since you can often do procedural things to the data.

1. *The Information Rule*: This rule simply requires that all information in the database be represented in one and only one way, namely, by values in column positions within rows of tables. SQL is good here.

2. *The Guaranteed Access Rule*: This rule is essentially a restatement of the fundamental requirement for primary keys. It states that every individual scalar value in the database must be logically addressable by specifying the name of the containing table, the name of the containing column, and the primary key value of the containing row. SQL follows this rule for tables that have a primary key, but it does not require a table to have a key at all.

3. *Systematic Treatment of NULL Values*: The DBMS is required to support a representation of missing information and inapplicable information that is systematic, distinct from all regular values, and independent of data type. It is also implied that such representations must be manipulated by the DBMS in a systematic way. SQL has a NULL that is used for both missing information and inapplicable information, rather than having two separate tokens as Dr. Codd wished.

4. *Active Online Catalog Based on the Relational Model*: The system is required to support an online, in-line, relational catalog that is accessible to authorized users by means of their regular query language. SQL does this.

5. *The Comprehensive Data Sublanguage Rule*: The system must support at least one relational language that (a) has a linear syntax; (b) can be used both interactively and within application programs; and (c) supports data definition operations (including view definitions), data manipulation operations (update as well as retrieval), security and integrity constraints, and transaction management operations (begin, commit, and rollback).

SQL is pretty good on this point, since all of the operations Codd defined can be written in the DML (Data Manipulation Language).

6. *The View Updating Rule*: All views that are theoretically updatable must be updatable by the system. SQL is weak here, and has elected to standardize on the safest case. View updatability is a very complex problem, now known to be NP-complete. (This is a mathematical term that means that, as the number of elements in a problem increase, the effort to solve it increases so fast and requires so many resources that you cannot find a general answer.) `INSTEAD OF` triggers in SQL allow solutions for particular schemas, even if it is not possible to find a general solution.

7. *High-level Insert, Update, and Delete*: The system must support set-at-a-time `INSERT`, `UPDATE`, and `DELETE` operators. SQL does this.

8. *Physical Data Independence*: This rule is self-explanatory; users are never aware of the physical implementation and deal only with a logical model. Any real product is going to have some physical dependence, but SQL is better than most programming languages on this point.

9. *Logical Data Independence*: This rule is also self-explanatory. SQL is quite good about this point until you start using vendor extensions.

10. *Integrity Independence*: Integrity constraints must be specified separately from application programs and stored in the catalog. It must be possible to change such constraints as and when appropriate without unnecessarily affecting existing applications. SQL has this.

11. *Distribution Independence*: Existing applications should continue to operate successfully (a) when a distributed version of the DBMS is first introduced, and (b) when existing distributed data is redistributed around the system. We are just starting to get distributed versions of SQL, so it is a little early to say whether SQL will meet this criterion or not.

12. *The Nonsubversion Rule*: If the system provides a low-level (record-at-a-time, bit-level) interface, that interface cannot be used to subvert the system (e.g., bypassing a relational security or integrity constraint). SQL is good about this one.

Codd also specified nine structural features, three integrity features, and eighteen manipulative features, all of which are required as well. He later extended the list from 12 rules to 333 in the second version of the relational model. This section is getting too long, and you can look them up for yourself.

Normal forms are an attempt to make sure that you do not destroy true data or create false data in your database. One of the ways of avoiding errors is to represent a fact only once in the database, since if a fact appears more than once, one of the instances of it is likely to be in error—a man with two watches can never be sure what time it is.

This process of table design is called normalization. It is not mysterious, but it can get complex. You can buy CASE tools to help you do it, but you should know a bit about the theory before you use such a tool.

2.1 Functional and Multivalued Dependencies

A normal form is a way of classifying a table based on the functional dependencies (FDs for short) in it. A functional dependency means that if I know the value of one attribute, I can always determine the value of another. The notation used in relational theory is an arrow between the two attributes, for example $A \rightarrow B$, which can be read in English as "A determines B." If I know your employee number, I can determine your name; if I know a part number, I can determine the weight and color of the part; and so forth.

A multivalued dependency (MVD) means that if I know the value of one attribute, I can always determine the values of a set of another attribute. The notation used in relational theory is a double-headed arrow between the two attributes, for instance $A \twoheadrightarrow B$, which can be read in English as "A determines many Bs." If I know a teacher's name, I can determine a list of her students; if I know a part number, I can determine the part numbers of its components; and so forth.

2.2 First Normal Form (1NF)

Consider a requirement to maintain data about class schedules. We are required to keep the course, section, department name, time, room, room size, professor, student, major, and grade. Suppose that we initially set up a Pascal file with records that look like this:

```
Classes = RECORD
          course: ARRAY [1:7] OF CHAR;
```

```
        section: CHAR;
           time: INTEGER;
           room: INTEGER;
       roomsize: INTEGER;
      professor: ARRAY [1:25] OF CHAR;
     dept_name: ARRAY [1:10] OF CHAR;
       students: ARRAY [1:classsize]
                 OF RECORD
                    student ARRAY [1:25] OF CHAR;
                    major ARRAY [1:10] OF CHAR;
                    grade CHAR;
                    END;
         END;
```

This table is not in the most basic normal form of relational databases. First Normal Form (1NF) means that the table has no repeating groups. That is, every column is a scalar (or atomic) value, not an array, or a list, or anything with its own structure.

In SQL, it is impossible not to be in 1NF unless the vendor has added array or other extensions to the language. The Pascal record could be "flattened out" in SQL and the field names changed to data element names to look like this:

```
CREATE TABLE Classes
(course_name CHAR(7) NOT NULL,
 section_id CHAR(1) NOT NULL,
 time_period INTEGER NOT NULL,
 room_nbr INTEGER NOT NULL,
 room_size INTEGER NOT NULL,
 professor_name CHAR(25) NOT NULL,
 dept_name CHAR(10) NOT NULL,
 student_name CHAR (25) NOT NULL,
 major CHAR(10) NOT NULL,
 grade CHAR(1) NOT NULL);
```

This table is acceptable to SQL. In fact, we can locate a row in the table with a combination of (course_name, section_id, student_name), so we have a key. But what we are doing is hiding the Students record array, which has not changed its nature by being flattened.

There are problems.

If Professor 'Jones' of the math department dies, we delete all his rows from the Classes table. This also deletes the information that all his students were taking a math class and maybe not all of them wanted to drop out of the class just yet. I am deleting more than one fact from the database. This is called a deletion anomaly.

If student 'Wilson' decides to change one of his math classes, formerly taught by Professor 'Jones', to English, we will show Professor 'Jones' as an instructor in both the math and the English departments. I could not change a simple fact by itself. This creates false information, and is called an update anomaly.

If the school decides to start a new department, which has no students yet, we cannot put in the data about the professor we just hired until we have classroom and student data to fill out a row. I cannot insert a simple fact by itself. This is called an insertion anomaly.

There are more problems in this table, but you can see the point. Yes, there are some ways to get around these problems without changing the tables. We could permit `NULL`s in the table. We could write routines to check the table for false data. But these are tricks that will only get worse as the data and the relationships become more complex. The solution is to break the table up into other tables, each of which represents one relationship or simple fact.

2.2.1 Note on Repeated Groups

The definition of 1NF is that the table has no repeating groups and that all columns are scalar values. This means a column cannot have arrays, linked lists, tables within tables, or record structures, like those you find in other programming languages. This was very easy to avoid in Standard SQL-92, since the language had no support for them. However, it is no longer true in SQL-99, which introduced several very nonrelational "features." Additionally, several vendors added their own support for arrays, nested tables, and variant data types.

Aside from relational purity, there are good reasons to avoid these SQL-99 features. They are not widely implemented and the vendor-specific extensions will not port. Furthermore, the optimizers cannot easily use them, so they degrade performance.

Old habits are hard to change, so new SQL programmers often try to force their old model of the world into Standard SQL in several ways.

Repeating Columns

One way to "fake it" in SQL is to use a group of columns in which all the members of the group have the same semantic value; that is, they represent the same attribute in the table. Consider the table of an employee and his children:

```
CREATE TABLE Employees
(emp_nbr INTEGER NOT NULL,
 emp_name CHAR(30) NOT NULL,
 ...
 child1 CHAR(30), birthday1 DATE, sex1 CHAR(1),
 child2 CHAR(30), birthday2 DATE, sex2 CHAR(1),
 child3 CHAR(30), birthday3 DATE, sex3 CHAR(1),
 child4 CHAR(30), birthday4 DATE, sex4 CHAR(1));
```

This layout looks like many existing file system records in COBOL and other 3GL languages. The birthday and sex information for each child is part of a repeated group, and therefore violates 1NF. This is faking a four-element array in SQL; the index just happens to be part of the column name!

Suppose I have a table with the quantity of a product sold in each month of a particular year, and I originally built the table to look like this:

```
CREATE TABLE Abnormal
(product CHAR(10) NOT NULL PRIMARY KEY,
 month_01 INTEGER, -- null means no data yet
 month_02 INTEGER,
 ...
 month_12 INTEGER);
```

If I want to flatten it out into a more normalized form, like this:

```
CREATE TABLE Normal
(product CHAR(10) NOT NULL,
 month_nbr INTEGER NOT NULL,
 qty INTEGER NOT NULL,
 PRIMARY KEY (product, month_nbr));
```

I can use the following statement:

```
INSERT INTO Normal (product, month_nbr, qty)
SELECT product, 1, month_01
  FROM Abnormal
 WHERE month_01 IS NOT NULL
UNION ALL
SELECT product, 2, month_02
  FROM Abnormal
 WHERE month_02 IS NOT NULL
...

UNION ALL
SELECT product, 12, month_12
  FROM Abnormal
 WHERE bin_12 IS NOT NULL;
```

While a `UNION ALL` expression is usually slow, this has to be run only once to load the normalized table, and then the original table can be dropped.

Parsing a List in a String

Another popular method is to use a string and fill it with a comma-separated list. The result is a lot of string-handling procedures to work around this kludge. Consider this example:

```
CREATE TABLE InputStrings
(key_col CHAR(10) NOT NULL PRIMARY KEY,
 input_string VARCHAR(255) NOT NULL);

INSERT INTO InputStrings VALUES ('first', '12,34,567,896');
INSERT INTO InputStrings VALUES ('second', '312,534,997,896');
...
```

This will be the table that gets the outputs, in the form of the original key column and one parameter per row.

```
CREATE TABLE Parmlist
(key_col CHAR(5) NOT NULL PRIMARY KEY,
 parm INTEGER NOT NULL);
```

It makes life easier if the lists in the input strings start and end with a comma. You will also need a table called Sequence, which is a set of integers from 1 to (*n*).

```
SELECT key_col,
     CAST (SUBSTRING (',' || I1.input_string || ',', MAX(S1.seq || 1),

                                    (S2.seq - MAX(S1.seq || 1)))
       AS INTEGER),
      COUNT(S2.seq) AS place
  FROM InputStrings AS I1, Sequence AS S1, Sequence AS S2
 WHERE SUBSTRING (',' || I1.input_string || ',', S1.seq, 1) = ','
   AND SUBSTRING (',' || I1.input_string || ',', S2.seq, 1) = ','
   AND S1.seq < S2.seq
   AND S2.seq <= DATALENGTH(I1.input_string) + 1
 GROUP BY I1.key_col, I1.input_string, S2.seq;
```

The S1 and S2 copies of Sequence are used to locate bracketing pairs of commas, and the entire set of substrings located between them is extracted and cast as integers in one nonprocedural step.

The trick is to be sure that the left-hand comma of the bracketing pair is the closest one to the second comma. The place column tells you the relative position of the value in the input string.

Ken Henderson developed a very fast version of this trick. Instead of using a comma to separate the fields within the list, put each value into a fixed-length substring and extract them by using a simple multiplication of the length by the desired array index number. This is a direct imitation of how many compilers handle arrays at the hardware level.

Having said all of this, the right way is to put the list into a single column in a table. This can be done in languages that allow you to pass array elements into SQL parameters, like this:

```
INSERT INTO Parmlist
VALUES (:a[1]), (:a[2]), (:a[3]), ..., (:a[n]);
```

Or, if you want to remove `NULL`s and duplicates:

```
INSERT INTO Parmlist
SELECT DISTINCT x
   FROM VALUES (:a[1]), (:a[2]), (:a[3]), ..., (:a[n]) AS List(x)
WHERE x IS NOT NULL;
```

2.3 Second Normal Form (2NF)

A table is in Second Normal Form (2NF) if it has no partial key dependencies. That is, if X and Y are columns and X is a key, then for any Z that is a proper subset of X, it cannot be the case that $Z \rightarrow Y$. Informally, the table is in 1NF and it has a key that determines all non-key attributes in the table.

In the Pascal example, our users tell us that knowing the student and course is sufficient to determine the section (since students cannot sign up for more than one section of the same course) and the grade. This is the same as saying that (student_name, course_name) → (section_id, grade).

After more analysis, we also discover from our users that (student_name → major)—students have only one major. Since student is part of the (student_name, course_name) key, we have a partial key dependency! This leads us to the following decomposition:

```
CREATE TABLE Classes
(course_name CHAR(7) NOT NULL,
 section_id CHAR(1) NOT NULL,
 time_period INTEGER NOT NULL,
 room_nbr INTEGER NOT NULL,
 room_size INTEGER NOT NULL,
 professor_name CHAR(25) NOT NULL,
PRIMARY KEY (course_name, section_id));

CREATE TABLE Enrollment
(student_name CHAR (25) NOT NULL,
 course_name CHAR(7) NOT NULL,
 section_id CHAR(1) NOT NULL,
 grade CHAR(1) NOT NULL,
PRIMARY KEY (student_name, course_name));

CREATE TABLE Students
(student_name CHAR (25) NOT NULL PRIMARY KEY,
 major CHAR(10) NOT NULL);
```

At this point, we are in 2NF. Every attribute depends on the entire key in its table. Now, if a student changes majors, it can be done in one place. Furthermore, a student cannot sign up for different sections of the same class, because we have changed the key of Enrollment. Unfortunately, we still have problems.

Notice that while room_size depends on the entire key of Classes, it also depends on room_nbr. If the room_nbr is changed for a course_name and section_id, we may also have to change the room_size, and if the room_nbr is modified (we knock down a wall), we may have to change room_size in several rows in Classes for that room.

2.4 Third Normal Form (3NF)

Another normal form can address these problems. A table is in Third Normal Form (3NF) if for all X → Y, where X and Y are columns of a table, X is a key or Y is part of a candidate key. (A candidate key is a unique set of columns that identify each row in a table; you cannot remove a column from the candidate key without destroying its uniqueness.) This implies that the table is in 2NF, since a partial key dependency is a type of transitive dependency. Informally, all the non-key columns are determined by the key, the whole key, and nothing but the key.

The usual way that 3NF is explained is that there are no transitive dependencies. A transitive dependency is a situation where we have a table with columns (A, B, C) and (A → B) and (B → C), so we know that (A → C). In our case, the situation is that (course_name, section_id) → room_nbr, and room_nbr → room_size. This is not a simple transitive dependency, since only part of a key is involved, but the principle still holds. To get our example into 3NF and fix the problem with the room_size column, we make the following decomposition:

```
CREATE TABLE Rooms
(room_nbr INTEGER NOT NULL PRIMARY KEY,
 room_size INTEGER NOT NULL);

CREATE TABLE Classes
(course_name CHAR(7) NOT NULL,
 section_id CHAR(1) NOT NULL,
 PRIMARY KEY (course_name, section_id),
 time_period INTEGER NOT NULL,
 room_nbr INTEGER NOT NULL);

CREATE TABLE Enrollment
(student_name CHAR (25) NOT NULL,
 course_name CHAR(7) NOT NULL,
 PRIMARY KEY (student_name, course_name),
```

```
 section_id CHAR(1) NOT NULL,
 grade CHAR(1) NOT NULL);

CREATE TABLE Students
(student_name CHAR (25) NOT NULL PRIMARY KEY,
 major CHAR(10) NOT NULL);
```

A common misunderstanding about relational theory is that 3NF tables have no transitive dependencies. As indicated above, if X → Y, X does not have to be a key if Y is part of a candidate key. We still have a transitive dependency in the example—(room_nbr, time_period) → (course_name, section_id)—but since the right side of the dependency is a key, it is technically in 3NF. This table structure still has unreasonable behavior, though: several courses can be assigned to the same room at the same time.

Another form of transitive dependency is a computed column. For example:

```
CREATE TABLE Stuff
(width INTEGER NOT NULL,
 length INTEGER NOT NULL,
 height INTEGER NOT NULL,
 volume INTEGER NOT NULL
        CHECK (width * length * height = volume),
 PRIMARY KEY (width, length, height));
```

The volume column is determined by the other three columns, so any change to one of the three columns will require a change to the volume column. You can use a VIEW to create computed columns.

2.5 Elementary Key Normal Form (EKNF)

Elementary Key Normal Form (EKNF) is a subtle enhancement on 3NF. By definition, EKNF tables are also in 3NF. This happens when there is more than one unique composite key and they overlap. Such cases can cause redundant information in the overlapping column(s). For example, in the following table, let's assume that a subject title is also a unique identifier for a given subject in the following table:

```
CREATE TABLE Enrollment
(student_id  INTEGER NOT NULL,
```

```
 course_code CHAR(6) NOT NULL,
 course_name VARCHAR(15) NOT NULL,
 PRIMARY KEY (student_id, course_name)
-- , UNIQUE (student_id, course_name) alternative key
 );
```

```
Enrollment
student_id  course_name  course_name
=======================================
   1        'CS-100'      'ER Diagrams'
   1        'CS-114'      'Database Design'
   2        'CS-114'      'Database Design'
```

This table, although it is in 3NF, violates EKNF. The primary key of the above table is the combination of (student_id, course_name). However, we can also see an alternative key (student_id, course_name) as well. The above schema could result in update and deletion anomalies, because values of both course_name and course_name tend to be repeated for a given subject.

The following schema is a decomposition of the above table to satisfy EKNF:

```
CREATE TABLE Subjects
(course_name CHAR(6) NOT NULL PRIMARY KEY,
 course_name VARCHAR(15) NOT NULL);

CREATE TABLE Enrollment
(student_id  INTEGER NOT NULL,
 course_name CHAR(6) NOT NULL,
 PRIMARY KEY (student_id, course_name));
```

For reasons that will become obvious in the following section, most designers do not ensure a table is in EKNF, as they will move directly on to Boyce-Codd Normal Form after ensuring that a schema is in 3NF. Thus, EKNF is included here only for reasons of historical accuracy and completeness.

2.6 Boyce-Codd Normal Form (BCNF)

A table is in BCNF when for all nontrivial FDs ($X \rightarrow A$), X is a superkey for the whole schema. A superkey is a unique set of columns that

identify each row in a table, but you can remove some columns from it and it will still be a key. Informally, a superkey is carrying extra weight.

BCNF is the normal form that actually removes all transitive dependencies. A table is in BCNF if for all (X → Y), X is a key—period. We can go to this normal form just by adding another key with `UNIQUE` (room, time_period) constraint clause to the table Classes.

There are some other interesting and useful "higher" normal forms, but they are outside of the scope of this discussion. In our example, we have removed all of the important anomalies with BCNF.

3NF was concerned with the relationship between key and nonkey columns. However, a column can often play both roles. Consider a table for computing salesmen's bonus gifts, which has for each salesman his base salary, the number of sales points he has won in a contest, and the bonus gift awarded for that combination of salary range and points. For example, we might give a fountain pen to a beginning salesman with a base pay rate somewhere between $15,000 and $20,000 and 100 sales points, but give a car to a master salesman whose salary is between $30,000 and $60,000 and who has 200 points. The functional dependencies are, therefore:

```
(paystep, points) -> gift
gift -> points
```

Let's start with a table that has all the data in it and normalize it.

```
Gifts
Salary_amt  points gift
===========================
15000       100    'Pencil'
17000       100    'Pen'
30000       200    'Car'
31000       200    'Car'
32000       200    'Car'
```

This schema is in 3NF, but it has problems. You cannot insert a new gift into our offerings and points unless you have a salary to go with it. If you remove any sales points, you lose information about the gifts and salaries (e.g., only people in the $30,000 range can win a car). And, finally, a change in the gifts for a particular point score would have to affect all the rows within the same pay step. This table needs to be broken apart into two tables:

```
PayGifts
Salary_amt  gift
=================
15000       'Pencil'
17000       'Pen'
30000       'Car'
31000       'Car'
32000       'Car'
```

```
GiftsPoints
gift     points
===============
'Pencil'  100
'Pen'     100
'Car'     200
```

2.7 Fourth Normal Form (4NF)

Fourth Normal Form (4NF) makes use of multivalued dependencies. The problem it solves is that the table has too many of them. For example, consider a table of departments, their projects, and the parts they stock. The MVDs in the table would be:

```
dept_name ->> jobs

dept_name ->> parts
```

Assume that dept_name 'd1' works on jobs 'j1' and 'j2' with parts 'p1' and 'p2'; that dept_name 'd2' works on jobs 'j3', 'j4', and 'j5' with parts 'p2' and 'p4'; and that dept_name 'd3' works only on job 'j2' with parts 'p5' and 'p6'. The table would look like this:

```
dept  job   part
=================
'd1'  'j1'  'p1'
'd1'  'j1'  'p2'
'd1'  'j2'  'p1'
'd1'  'j2'  'p2'
'd2'  'j3'  'p2'
'd2'  'j3'  'p4'
'd2'  'j4'  'p2'
```

```
'd2'  'j4'  'p4'
'd2'  'j5'  'p2'
'd2'  'j5'  'p4'
'd3'  'j2'  'p5'
'd3'  'j2'  'p6'
```

If you want to add a part to a dept_name, you must create more than one new row. Likewise, removing a part or a job from a row can destroy information. Updating a part or job name will also require multiple rows to be changed.

The solution is to split this table into two tables, one with (dept_name, jobs) in it and one with (dept_name, parts) in it. The definition of 4NF is that we have no more than one MVD in a table. If a table is in 4NF, it is also in BCNF.

2.8 Fifth Normal Form (5NF)

Fifth Normal Form (5NF), also called the Join-Projection Normal Form or the Projection-Join Normal Form, is based on the idea of a lossless JOIN or the lack of a join-projection anomaly. This problem occurs when you have an *n*-way relationship, where $n > 2$. A quick check for 5NF is to see if the table is in 3NF and all the candidate keys are single columns.

As an example of the problems solved by 5NF, consider a table of house notes that records the buyer, the seller, and the lender:

```
HouseNotes
buyer     seller    lender
==================================
'Smith'   'Jones'     'National Bank'
'Smith'   'Wilson'    'Home Bank'
'Nelson'  'Jones'     'Home Bank'
```

This table is a three-way relationship, but because many CASE tools allow only binary relationships, it might have to be expressed in an E-R (entity-relationship) diagram as three binary relationships, which would generate CREATE TABLE statements leading to these tables:

```
BuyerLender
buyer     lender
=============================
'Smith'       'National Bank'
'Smith'       'Home Bank'
'Nelson'      'Home Bank'

SellerLender
seller    lender
=======================
'Jones'      'National Bank'
'Wilson'     'Home Bank'
'Jones'      'Home Bank'

BuyerSeller
buyer   seller
================
'Smith'   'Jones'
'Smith'   'Wilson'
'Nelson'  'Jones'
```

The trouble is that when you try to assemble the original information by joining pairs of these three tables together as follows:

```
SELECT BS.buyer, SL.seller, BL.lender
  FROM BuyerLender AS BL,
       SellerLender AS SL,
       BuyerSeller AS BS
 WHERE BL.buyer = BS.buyer
   AND BL.lender = SL.lender
   AND SL.seller = BS.seller;
```

you will recreate all the valid rows in the original table, such as ('Smith', 'Jones', 'National Bank'), but there will also be false rows, such as ('Smith', 'Jones', 'Home Bank'), which were not part of the original table. This is called a join-projection anomaly.

There are also strong JPNFs and overstrong JPNFs, which make use of JOIN dependencies (JDs for short). Unfortunately, there is no systematic way to find a JPNF or 4NF schema, because the problem is known to be NP-complete.

As an aside, 3NF is very popular with CASE tools, and most of them can generate a schema where all of the tables are in 3NF. They obtain the FDs from an E-R diagram or from a statistical analysis of the existing data, then put them together into tables and check for normal forms.

The bad news is that it is often possible to derive more than one 3NF schema from a set of FDs. Most CASE tools that produce an E-R diagram will find only one of them, and go no further. However, if you use an ORM (Object Role Model) tool properly, the schema will be in 5NF. I suggest strongly that you get any of the books by Terry Halpin on this technique: *Information Modeling and Relational Databases from Conceptual Analysis to Logical Design*, ISBN 1-55860-672-6; *Database Modeling with Microsoft® Visio for Enterprise Architects*, ISBN 1-55860-919-9.

2.9 Domain-Key Normal Form (DKNF)

Ronald Fagin defined Domain/Key Normal Form (DKNF) in 1981 as a schema that has all of the domain constraints and functional dependencies enforced. There is not yet a general algorithm that will always generate the DKNF solution, given a set of constraints. We can, however, determine DKNF in many special cases, and it is a good guide to writing DDL in the real world.

Let's back up a bit and look at the mathematical model under normalization. An FD has a defined system of axioms that can be used in normalization problems. These six axioms, known as Armstrong's axioms, are given below:

Reflexive: X → X

Augmentation: If X → Y then XZ → Y

Union: If (X → Y and X → Z) then X → YZ

Decomposition: If X → Y and Z a subset of Y, then X → Z

Transitivity: If (X → Y and Y → Z) then X → Z

Pseudotransitivity: If (X → Y and YZ → W) then XZ → W

They make good sense if you just look at them, which is something we like in a set of axioms. In the real world, the FDs are the business rules we are trying to model.

In the normalization algorithm for 3NF (developed by P. A. Berstein, 1976) we use the axioms to get rid of redundant FDs. For example, if we are given:

```
A -> B
A -> C
B -> C
DB -> E
DAF -> E
```

A → C is redundant, because it can be derived from A → B and B → C with transitivity. Also, DAF → E is redundant, because it can be derived from DB → E and A → B with transitivity (which gives us DA → E) and augmentation (which then allows DAF → E). What we would like to find is the smallest set of FDs from which we can generate all of the given rules. This is called a nonredundant cover. For the FDs above, one cover would be:

```
A -> B
B -> C
DB -> E
```

Once we do this, Berstein shows that we can just create a table for each of the FDs where A, B, and DB are the respective keys. We have taken it easy so far, but now it's time for a challenge.

As an example of a schema with multiple 3NF tables, here is a problem that was used in a demonstration by DBStar Corporation (now Evoke Software). The company used it as an example in a demonstration that comes with their CASE tool.

We are given an imaginary and simplified airline that has a database for scheduling flights and pilots. Most of the relationships are obvious things. Flights have only one departure time and one destination. They can get a different pilot and can be assigned to a different gate each day of the week. The FDs for the database are given below:

```
1) flight -> destination
2) flight -> hour
3) (day, flight) -> gate
4) (day, flight) -> pilot
5) (day, hour, pilot) -> gate
6) (day, hour, pilot) -> flight
```

```
7) (day, hour, pilot) -> destination
8) (day, hour, gate) -> pilot
9) (day, hour, gate) -> flight
10) (day, hour, gate) -> destination
```

A purist, looking at this collection of FDs, will be bothered by the redundancies in this list. But in the real world, when you interview people, they do not speak to you in a minimal set; they state things that they know to be true in their situation. In fact, they very often leave out relationships that they consider too obvious to mention.

Your problem is to find 3NF or stronger database schemas in these FDs. You have to be careful! You have to have all of the columns, obviously, but your answer could be in 3NF and still ignore some of the FDs. For example, this will not work:

```
CREATE TABLE PlannedSchedule
(flight, destination, hour, PRIMARY KEY (flight));

CREATE TABLE ActualSchedule
(day, flight, gate, pilot, PRIMARY KEY (day, flight));
```

If we apply the Union axiom to some of the FDs, we get:

```
(day, hour, gate) -> (destination, flight, pilot)
(day, hour, pilot) -> (destination, flight, gate)
```

This example says that the user has required that if we are given a day, an hour, and a gate we should be able to determine a unique flight for that day, hour, and gate. We should also be able to determine a unique flight given a day, hour, and pilot.

Given the PlannedSchedule and ActualSchedule tables, you cannot produce views where either of the two constraints we just mentioned is enforced. If the query "What flight does pilot X have on day Y and hour Z?" gives you more than one answer, it violates the FDs and common sense. Here is an example of a schema that is allowable in this proposed schema, but is undesirable given our constraints:

```
PlannedSchedule
 flight  hour  destination
 =========================
   118  17:00 Dallas
```

```
   123  13:00 Omaha
   155  17:00 Los Angeles
   171  13:00 New York
   666  13:00 Dis

ActualSchedule
 day flight pilot   gate
========================
 Wed    118  Tom     12A
 Wed    155  Tom     13B
 Wed    171  Tom     12A
 Thu    123  John    12A
 Thu    155  John    12A
 Thu    171  John    13B
```

The constraints mean that we should be able to find a unique answer to each of the following questions and not lose any information when inserting and deleting data:

1. Which flight is leaving from gate 12A on Thursdays at 13:00? This question looks fine until you realize that you don't know any further information about flight 666, which was not required to have anything about its day or pilot in the ActualSchedule table. Likewise, I can add a flight to the ActualSchedule table that has no information in the PlannedSchedule table.
2. Which pilot is assigned to the flight that leaves gate 12A on Thursdays at 13:00? This has the same problem as before.
3. What is the destination of the flight in query 1 and 2? This has the same problem as before.
4. What gate is John leaving from on Thursdays at 13:00?
5. Where is Tom flying to on Wednesdays at 17:00?
6. What flight is assigned to Tom on Wednesdays at 17:00?

It might help if we gave an example showing how one of the FDs in the problem can be derived using the axioms of FD calculus, just like you would do a geometry proof:

```
Given:
1) (day, hour, gate) -> pilot
2) (day, hour, pilot) -> flight

prove that:
(day, hour, gate) -> flight.

3) (day, hour) -> (day, hour);          Reflexive
4) (day, hour, gate) -> (day, hour);    Augmentation on 3
5) (day, hour, gate) -> (day, hour, pilot); Union 1 & 4
6) (day, hour, gate) -> flight;  Transitive 2 and 5
Q.E.D.
```

The answer is to start by attempting to derive each of the FDs from the rest of the set. What we get is several short proofs, each requiring different "given" FDs in order to get to the derived FD.

Here is a list of each of the proofs used to derive the ten fragmented FDs in the problem. With each derivation, we include every derivation step and the legal FD calculus operation that allows us to make that step. An additional operation that we include here, which was not included in the axioms we listed earlier, is left reduction. Left reduction says that if XX → Y then X → Y. The reason it was not included is that this is actually a theorem, and not one of the basic axioms (a side problem: can you derive left reduction?).

```
Prove: (day, hour, pilot) -> gate
a) day -> day;                    Reflexive
b) (day, hour, pilot) -> day;          Augmentation (a)
c) (day, hour, pilot) -> (day, flight);   Union (6, b)
d) (day, hour, pilot) -> gate;          Transitive (c, 3)
Q.E.D.

Prove: (day, hour, gate) -> pilot
a) day -> day;                 Reflexive
b) day, hour, gate -> day;       Augmentation (a)
c) day, hour, gate -> (day, flight);  Union (9, b)
d) day, hour, gate -> pilot;      Transitive (c, 4)
Q.E.D.

Prove: (day, flight) -> gate
a) (day, flight, pilot) -> gate;   Pseudotransitivity (2, 5)
```

```
b) (day, flight, day, flight) -> gate; Pseudotransitivity (a, 4)
c) (day, flight) -> gate;      Left reduction (b)
Q.E.D.

Prove:  (day, flight) -> pilot
a) (day, flight, gate) -> pilot;   Pseudotransitivity (2, 8)
b) (day, flight, day, flight) -> pilot; Pseudotransitivity (a,
3)
c) (day, flight) -> pilot;      Left reduction (b)
Q.E.D.

Prove: (day, hour, gate) -> flight
a) (day, hour) -> (day, hour);   Reflexivity
b) (day, hour, gate) -> (day, hour);    Augmentation (a)
c) (day, hour, gate) -> (day, hour, pilot);  Union (b, 8)
d) (day, hour, gate) -> flight;       Transitivity (c, 6)
Q.E.D.

Prove: (day, hour, pilot) -> flight
a) (day, hour) -> (day, hour);  Reflexivity
b) (day, hour, pilot) -> (day, hour); Augmentation (a)
c) (day, hour, pilot) -> day, hour, gate;  Union (b, 5)
d) (day, hour, pilot) -> flight;      Transitivity (c, 9)
Q.E.D.

Prove: (day, hour, gate) -> destination
a) (day, hour, gate) -> destination; Transitivity (9, 1)
Q.E.D.

Prove: (day, hour, pilot) -> destination
a) (day, hour, pilot) -> destination;    Transitivity (6, 1)
Q.E.D.
```

Now that we've shown you how to derive eight of the ten FDs from other FDs, you can try mixing and matching the FDs into sets so that each set meets the following criteria:

1. Each attribute must be represented on either the left or right side of at least one FD in the set.
2. If a given FD is included in the set, then all the FDs needed to derive it cannot also be included.

3. If a given FD is excluded from the set, then the FDs used to derive it must be included.

This produces a set of "nonredundant covers," which can be found through trial and error and common sense. For example, if we exclude (day, hour, gate) → flight, we must then include (day, hour, gate) → pilot, and vice versa, because each is used in the other's derivation. If you want to be sure your search was exhaustive, however, you may want to apply a more mechanical method, which is what the CASE tools do for you.

The algorithm for accomplishing this task is basically to generate all the combinations of sets of the FDs. (flight → destination) and (flight → hour) are excluded in the combination generation because they cannot be derived. This gives us (2^8), or 256, combinations of FDs. Each combination is then tested against the criteria.

Fortunately, a simple spreadsheet does all the tedious work. In this problem, the first criterion eliminates only 15 sets. Then the second criterion eliminates 152 sets, and the third criterion drops another 67. This leaves us with 22 possible covers, 5 of which are the answers we are looking for (we will explain the other 17 later).

These five nonredundant covers are:

```
Set I:
flight -> destination
flight -> hour
(day, hour, gate) -> flight
(day, hour, gate) -> pilot
(day, hour, pilot) -> gate

Set II:
flight -> destination
flight -> hour
(day, hour, gate) -> pilot
(day, hour, pilot) -> flight
(day, hour, pilot) -> gate

Set III:
flight -> destination
flight -> hour
(day, flight) -> gate
(day, flight) -> pilot
(day, hour, gate) -> flight
```

```
Set IV:
flight -> destination
flight -> hour
(day, flight) -> gate
(day, hour, gate) -> pilot
(day, hour, pilot) -> flight

Set V:
flight -> destination
flight -> hour
(day, flight) -> pilot
(day, hour, gate) -> flight
(day, hour, pilot) -> gate
(day, hour, pilot) -> flight
```

At this point, we perform unions on FDs with the same left-hand side and make tables for each grouping with the left-hand side as a key. We can also eliminate symmetrical FD's (defined as $X \rightarrow Y$ and $Y \rightarrow X$, and written with a two headed arrow, $X \leftrightarrow Y$) by collapsing them into the same table.

These possible schemas are at least in 3NF. They are given in shorthand SQL DDL (Data Declaration Language) without data type declarations.

```
Solution 1:
CREATE TABLE R1 (flight, destination, hour,
 PRIMARY KEY (flight));
CREATE TABLE R2 (day, hour, gate, flight, pilot,
  PRIMARY KEY (day, hour, gate),
  UNIQUE (day, hour, pilot),
  UNIQUE (day, flight),
  UNIQUE (flight, hour));

Solution 2:
CREATE TABLE R1 (flight, destination, hour, PRIMARY KEY
(flight));
CREATE TABLE R2 (day, flight, gate, pilot,
  PRIMARY KEY (day, flight));
CREATE TABLE R3 (day, hour, gate, flight,
  PRIMARY KEY (day, hour, gate),
  UNIQUE (day, flight),
```

```
  UNIQUE (flights, hour));
CREATE TABLE R4 (day, hour, pilot, flight,
  PRIMARY KEY (day, hour, pilot));

Solution 3:
CREATE TABLE R1 (flight, destination, hour, flight
  PRIMARY KEY (flight));
CREATE TABLE R2 (day, flight, gate, PRIMARY KEY (day, flight));
CREATE TABLE R3 (day, hour, gate, pilot,
  PRIMARY KEY (day, hour, gate),
  UNIQUE (day, hour, pilot),
  UNIQUE (day, hour, gate));
CREATE TABLE R4 (day, hour, pilot, flight
  PRIMARY KEY (day, hour, pilot),
  UNIQUE(day, flight),
  UNIQUE (flight, hour));

Solution 4:
CREATE TABLE R1 (flight, destination, hour, PRIMARY KEY
(flight));
CREATE TABLE R2 (day, flight, pilot, PRIMARY KEY (day, flight));
CREATE TABLE R3 (day, hour, gate, flight,
  PRIMARY KEY (day, hour, gate),
  UNIQUE (flight, hour));
CREATE TABLE R4 (day, hour, pilot, gate,
  PRIMARY KEY (day, hour, pilot));
```

These solutions are a mess, but they are a 3NF mess! Is there a better answer? Here is one in BCNF and only two tables, proposed by Chris Date (Date 1995, p. 224).

```
CREATE TABLE DailySchedules (flight, destination, hour PRIMARY
KEY (flight));
CREATE TABLE PilotSchedules (day, flight, gate, pilot, PRIMARY
KEY (day, flight));
```

This is a workable schema, but we could expand the constraints to give us better performance and more precise error messages, since schedules are not likely to change:

```
CREATE TABLE DailySchedules
(flight, hour, destination,
```

```
 UNIQUE (flight, hour, destination),
 UNIQUE (flight, hour),
 UNIQUE (flight));

CREATE TABLE PilotSchedules
(day, flight, day, hour, gate, pilot,
 UNIQUE (day, flight, gate),
 UNIQUE (day, flight, pilot),
 UNIQUE (day, flight),
 FOREIGN KEY (flight, hour) REFERENCES R1(flight, hour));
```

2.10 Practical Hints for Normalization

CASE tools implement formal methods for doing normalization. In particular, E-R (entity-relationship) diagrams are very useful for this process. However, a few informal hints can help speed up the process and give you a good start.

Broadly speaking, tables represent either entities or relationships, which is why E-R diagrams work so well as a design tool. Tables that represent entities should have a simple, immediate name suggested by their contents—a table named Students has student data in it, not student data and bowling scores. It is also a good idea to use plural or collective nouns as the names of such tables to remind you that a table is a set of entities; the rows are the single instances of them.

Tables that represent many-to-many relationships should be named by their contents, and should be as minimal as possible. For example, Students are related to Classes by a third (relationship) table for their attendance. These tables might represent a pure relationship, or they might contain attributes that exist within the relationship, such as a grade for the class attended. Since the only way to get a grade is to attend the class, the relationship is going to have a column for it, and will be named "ReportCards," "Grades" or something similar. Avoid naming entities based on many-to-many relationships by combining the two table names. For example, Student_Course is a bad name for the Enrollment entity.

Avoid `NULL`s whenever possible. If a table has too many `NULL`-able columns, it is probably not normalized properly. Try to use a `NULL` only for a value that is missing now, but which will be resolved later. Even better, you can put missing values into the encoding schemes for that column, as discussed in as discussed in Section 5.2 of *SQL Programming Style*, ISBN 0-12-088797-5, on encoding schemes.

A normalized database will tend to have a lot of tables with a small number of columns per table. Don't panic when you see that happen. People who first worked with file systems (particularly on computers that used magnetic tape) tend to design one monster file for an application and do all the work against those records. This made sense in the old days, since there was no reasonable way to JOIN a number of small files together without having the computer operator mount and dismount lots of different tapes. The habit of designing this way carried over to disk systems, since the procedural programming languages were still the same.

The same nonkey attribute in more than one table is probably a normalization problem. This is not a certainty, just a guideline. The key that determines that attribute should be in only one table, and therefore the attribute should be with it.

As a practical matter, you are apt to see the same attribute under different names, and you will need to make the names uniform throughout the entire database. The columns date_of_birth, birthdate, birthday, and dob are very likely the same attribute for an employee.

2.11 Key Types

The logical and physical keys for a table can be classified by their behavior and their source. Table 2.1 is a quick table of my classification system.

Table 2.1 *Classification System for Key Types*

	Natural	Artificial	"Exposed Physical Locator"	Surrogate
Constructed from attributes in the reality of the data model	Y	N	N	Y
Verifiable in reality	Y	N	N	N
Verifiable in itself	Y	Y	N	N
Visible to the user	Y	Y	Y	N

2.11.1 Natural Keys

A natural key is a subset of attributes that occur in a table and act as a unique identifier. The user sees them. You can go to external reality and verify them. Examples of natural keys include the UPC codes on consumer goods (read the package barcode) and coordinates (get a GPS).

Newbies worry about a natural compound key becoming very long. My answer is, "So what?" This is the 21st century; we have much better computers than we did in the 1950s, when key size was a real physical issue. To replace a natural two- or three-integer compound key with a huge GUID that no human being or other system can possibly understand, because they think it will be faster, only cripples the system and makes it more prone to errors. I know how to verify the (longitude, latitude) pair of a location; how do you verify the GUID assigned to it?

A long key is not always a bad thing for performance. For example, if I use (city, state) as my key, I get a free index on just (city) in many systems. I can also add extra columns to the key to make it a super-key, when such a super-key gives me a covering index (i.e., an index that contains all of the columns required for a query, so that the base table does not have to be accessed at all).

2.11.2 Artificial Keys

An artificial key is an extra attribute added to the table that is seen by the user. It does not exist in the external reality, but can be verified for syntax or check digits inside itself. One example of an artificial key is the open codes in the UPC/EAN scheme that a user can assign to his own stuff. The check digits still work, but you have to verify them inside your own enterprise.

Experienced database designers tend toward keys they find in industry standard codes, such as UPC/EAN, VIN, GTIN, ISBN, etc. They know that they need to verify the data against the reality they are modeling. A trusted external source is a good thing to have. I know why this VIN is associated with this car, but why is an auto-number value of 42 associated with this car? Try to verify the relationship in the reality you are modeling. It makes as much sense as locating a car by its parking space number.

2.11.3 Exposed Physical Locators

An exposed physical locator is not based on attributes in the data model and is exposed to the user. There is no way to predict it or verify it. The system obtains a value through some physical process totally unrelated to the logical data model. The user cannot change the locators without destroying the relationships among the data elements.

Examples of exposed physical locators would be physical row locations encoded as a number, string or proprietary data type. If hashing tables were accessible in an SQL product they would qualify, but they are usually hidden from the user.

Many programmers object to putting `IDENTITY` and other auto-numbering devices into this category. To convert the number into a physical location requires a search rather than a hashing table lookup or positioning a read/writer head on a disk drive, but the concept is the same. The hardware gives you a way to go to a physical location that has nothing to do with the logical data model, and that cannot be changed in the physical database or verified externally.

Most of the time, exposed physical locators are used for faking a sequential file's positional record number, so I can reference the physical storage location—a 1960s ISAM file in SQL. You lose all the advantages of an abstract data model and SQL set-oriented programming, because you carry extra data and destroy the portability of code.

The early SQLs were based on preexisting file systems. The data was kept in physically contiguous disk pages, in physically contiguous rows, made up of physically contiguous columns—in short, just like a deck of punch cards or a magnetic tape. Most programmers still carry that mental model, which is why I keep ranting about file versus table, row versus record and column versus field.

But physically contiguous storage is only one way of building a relational database—and it is not the best one. The basic idea of a relational database is that the user is not supposed to know how or where things are stored at all, much less write code that depends on the particular physical representation in a particular release of a particular product on particular hardware at a particular time. This is discussed further in Section 1.2.1, "IDENTITY Columns."

Finally, an appeal to authority, with a quote from Dr. Codd: "Database users may cause the system to generate or delete a surrogate, but they have no control over its value, nor is its value ever displayed to them. . ."

This means that a surrogate ought to act like an index: created by the user, managed by the system, and *never* seen by a user. That means never used in code, DRI, or anything else that a user writes.

Codd also wrote the following:

"There are three difficulties in employing user-controlled keys as permanent surrogates for entities.

1. The actual values of user-controlled keys are determined by users and must therefore be subject to change by them (e.g., if two companies merge, the two employee databases might be combined, with the result that some or all of the serial numbers might be changed).
2. Two relations may have user-controlled keys defined on distinct domains (e.g., one uses Social Security numbers, while the other uses employee serial numbers), and yet the entities denoted are the same.
3. It may be necessary to carry information about an entity either before it has been assigned a user-controlled key value, or after it has ceased to have one (e.g., an applicant for a job and a retiree)."

These difficulties have the important consequence that an equi-join on common key values may not yield the same result as a join on common entities. One solution—proposed in Chapter 4 and more fully in Chapter 14—is to introduce entity domains, which contain system-assigned surrogates. "Database users may cause the system to generate or delete a surrogate, but they have no control over its value, nor is its value ever displayed to them. . ." (Codd 1979).

2.11.4 Practical Hints for Denormalization

The subject of denormalization is a great way to get into religious wars. At one extreme, you will find relational purists who think that the idea of not carrying a database design to at least 3NF is a crime against nature. At the other extreme, you will find people who simply add and move columns all over the database with `ALTER` statements, never keeping the schema stable.

The reason given for denormalization is performance. A fully normalized database requires a lot of `JOIN`s to construct common `VIEW`s of data from its components. `JOIN`s used to be very costly in terms of time and computer resources, so "preconstructing" the `JOIN` in a denormalized table can save quite a bit.

Today, only data warehouses should be denormalized—never a production OLTP system.

Consider this actual problem, which appeared on CompuServe's ORACLE forum some years ago. A pharmaceutical company has an inventory table, and price changes table that look like this:

```
CREATE TABLE Drugs
(drug_nbr INTEGER NOT NULL PRIMARY KEY,
 drug_name CHAR(30) NOT NULL,
 drug_qty INTEGER NOT NULL
          CONSTRAINT positive_quantity
          CHECK(drug_qty >= 0),
 ...);

CREATE TABLE Prices
(drug_nbr INTEGER NOT NULL,
 start_date DATE NOT NULL,
 end_date DATE NOT NULL
          CONSTRAINT started_before_endded
          CHECK(start_date <= end_date),
 price DECIMAL(8,2) NOT NULL,
 PRIMARY KEY (drug_nbr, start_date));
```

Every order has to use the order date to find what the selling price was when the order was placed. The current price will have a value of "eternity" (a dummy date set so high that it will not be reached, such as '9999-12-31'). The `(end_date + INTERVAL '1' DAY)` of one price will be equal to the start_date of the next price for the same drug.

While this is normalized, performance was bad. Every report, invoice or query will have a `JOIN` between Drugs and Prices. The trick might be to add more columns to the Drugs, like this:

```
CREATE TABLE Drugs
(drug_nbr INTEGER PRIMARY KEY,
 drug_name CHAR(30) NOT NULL,
 drug_qty INTEGER NOT NULL
          CONSTRAINT positive_quantity
          CHECK(drug_qty >= 0),
 current_start_date DATE NOT NULL,
 current_end_date DATE NOT NULL,
 CONSTRAINT current_start_before_endded
 CHECK(current_start_date <= current_end_date),
 current_price DECIMAL(8,2) NOT NULL,
```

```
prior_start_date DATE NOT NULL,
prior_end_date DATE NOT NULL,
CONSTRAINT prior_start_before_endded
CHECK(prior_start_date <= prior_end_date),
       AND (current_start_date = prior_end_date + INTERVAL '1'
DAY
 prior_price DECIMAL(8,2) NOT NULL,
 ...);
```

This covered more than 95% of the orders in the actual company, because very few orders have more than two price changes before they are taken out of stock. The odd exception was trapped by a procedural routine.

The other method is to add `CHECK()` constraints that will enforce the rules destroyed by denormalization. We will discuss this later, but the overhead for insertion, updating, and deleting to the table is huge. In fact, in many cases denormalized tables cannot be changed until a complete set of columns is built outside the table. Furthermore, while one set of queries is improved, all others are damaged.

Today, however, only data warehouses should be denormalized. `JOIN`s are far cheaper than they were, and the overhead of handling exceptions with procedural code is far greater than any extra database overhead.

2.11.5 Row Sorting

On May 27, 2001, Fred Block posted a problem on the SQL Server Newsgroup. I will change the problem slightly, but the idea was that he had a table with five character string columns that had to be sorted alphabetically within each row. This "flatten table" denormalization is a very common one that might involve months of the year as columns, or other things that are acting as repeating groups in violation of 1NF.

Let's declare the table and dive into the problem:

```
CREATE TABLE Foobar
(key_col INTEGER NOT NULL PRIMARY KEY,
 c1 VARCHAR(20) NOT NULL,
 c2 VARCHAR(20) NOT NULL,
 c3 VARCHAR(20) NOT NULL,
 c4 VARCHAR(20) NOT NULL,
 c5 VARCHAR(20) NOT NULL);
```

This means that we want this condition to hold:

```
CHECK ((c1 <= c2) AND  (c2 <= c3)
      AND (c3 <= c4) AND (c4 <= c5))
```

Obviously, if he had added this constraint to the table in the first place, we would be fine. Of course, that would have pushed the problem to the front end, and I would not have a topic for this section.

What was interesting was how everyone who read this newsgroup posting immediately envisioned a stored procedure that would take the five values, sort them and return them to their original row in the table. The only way to make this approach work for the whole table was to write an update cursor and loop through all the rows of the table. Itzik Ben-Gan posted a simple procedure that loaded the values into a temporary table, then pulled them out in sorted order, starting with the minimum value, using a loop.

Another trick is the Bose-Nelson sort (Bose-Nelson Sort, *Dr. Dobbs Journal*, September 1985, pp. 282-296), which I had written about in *Dr. Dobb's Journal* back in 1985. This sort is a recursive procedure that takes an integer and then generates swap pairs for a vector of that size. A swap pair is a pair of position numbers from 1 to (*n*) in the vector that need to be exchanged if they are out of order. These swap pairs are also related to Sorting Networks in the literature (see Donald Knuth, *Art of Computer Programming, Volume 3: Sorting and Searching*, 2nd Edition, April 24, 1998, ISBN: 0-201-89685-0).

You are probably thinking that this method is a bit weak, because the results are only good for sorting a fixed number of items. But a table only has a fixed number of columns, so that is not a problem in denormalized SQL.

You can set up a sorting network that will sort five items, with the minimal number of exchanges, nine swaps, like this:

```
Swap(c1, c2);
Swap(c4, c5);
Swap(c3, c5);
Swap(c3, c4);
Swap(c1, c4);
Swap(c1, c3);
Swap(c2, c5);
Swap(c2, c4);
Swap(c2, c3);
```

You might want to deal yourself a hand of five playing cards in one suit to see how it works. Put the cards face down on the table and pick up the pairs, swapping them if required, then turn over the row to see that it is in sorted order when you are done.

In theory, the minimum number of swaps needed to sort (n) items is `CEILING` (log2 (n!)), and as (n) increases, this approaches O(n*log2(n)). Computer science majors will remember this "Big O" expression as the expected performance of the best sorting algorithms, such as Quicksort. The Bose-Nelson method is very good for small values of (n). If (n < 9) then it is perfect, actually. But as things get bigger, Bose-Nelson approaches O(n ^ 1.585). In English, this method is good for a fixed size list of 16 or fewer items, but it goes to Hell after that.

You can write a version of the Bose-Nelson procedure that will output the SQL code for a given value of (n). The obvious direct way to do a `Swap()` is to write a chain of `UPDATE` statements. Remember that in SQL, the `SET` clause assignments happen in parallel, so you can easily write a `SET` clause that exchanges the two items when they are out of order. Using the above swap chain, we get this block of code:

```
BEGIN ATOMIC
-- Swap(c1, c2);
UPDATE Foobar
   SET c1 = c2, c2 = c1
 WHERE c1 > c2;

-- Swap(c4, c5);
UPDATE Foobar
   SET c4 = c5, c5 = c4
 WHERE c4 > c5;

-- Swap(c3, c5);
UPDATE Foobar
SET c3 = c5, c5 = c3
 WHERE c3 > c5;

-- Swap(c3, c4);
UPDATE Foobar
   SET c3 = c4, c4 = c3
 WHERE c3 > c4;

-- Swap(c1, c4);
```

```
UPDATE Foobar
   SET c1 = c4, c4 = c1
 WHERE c1 > c4;

-- Swap(c1, c3);
UPDATE Foobar
   SET c1 = c3, c3 = c1
 WHERE c1 > c3;

-- Swap(c2, c5);
UPDATE Foobar
   SET c2 = c5, c5 = c2
 WHERE c2 > c5;

-- Swap(c2, c4);
UPDATE Foobar
   SET c2 = c4, c4 = c2
 WHERE c2 > c4;

-- Swap(c2, c3);
UPDATE Foobar
   SET c2 = c3, c3 = c2
 WHERE c2 > c3;

END;
```

This is fully portable, Standard SQL code, and it can be machine-generated. But that parallelism is useful. It is worthwhile to combine some of the `UPDATE` statements. But you have to be careful not to change the effective sequence of the swap operations.

If you look at the first two `UPDATE` statements, you can see that they do not overlap. This means you could roll them into one statement like this:

```
-- Swap(c1, c2) AND Swap(c4, c5);
UPDATE Foobar
   SET c1 = CASE WHEN c1 <= c2 THEN c1 ELSE c2 END,
       c2 = CASE WHEN c1 <= c2 THEN c2 ELSE c1 END,
       c4 = CASE WHEN c4 <= c5 THEN c4 ELSE c5 END,
       c5 = CASE WHEN c4 <= c5 THEN c5 ELSE c4 END
 WHERE c4 > c5 OR c1 > c2;
```

The advantage of doing this is that you have to execute only one UPDATE statement, not two. Updating a table, even on nonkey columns, usually locks the table and prevents other users from getting to the data. If you could roll the statements into one single UPDATE, you would have the best of all possible worlds, but I doubt that the code would be easy to read.

We can see this same pattern in the pair of statements:

```
Swap(c1, c3);
Swap(c2, c5);
```

But there are other patterns, so you can write general templates for them. Consider this one:

```
Swap(x, y);
Swap(x, z);
```

Write out all possible triplets and apply these two operations on them, thus:

```
(x, y, z) => (x, y, z)
(x, z, y) => (x, z, y)
(y, x, z) => (x, y, z)
(y, z, x) => (x, z, y)
(z, x, y) => (x, y, z)
(z, y, x) => (x, y, z)
```

The result of this pattern is that *x* is lowest value of the three values, and *y* and *z* either stay in the same relative position to each other or be sorted properly. Properly sorting them would have the advantage of saving exchanges later and also of reducing the set of the subset being operated upon by each UPDATE statement. With a little thought, we can write the following symmetric piece of code.

```
-- Swap(x, y) AND Swap(x, z);
UPDATE Foobar
   SET x = CASE WHEN x BETWEEN y AND z THEN y
                WHEN z BETWEEN y AND x THEN y
                WHEN y BETWEEN z AND x THEN z
                WHEN x BETWEEN z AND y THEN z
                ELSE x END,
```

```
       y = CASE WHEN x BETWEEN y AND z THEN x
                WHEN x BETWEEN z AND y THEN x
                WHEN z BETWEEN x AND y THEN z
                WHEN z BETWEEN y AND x THEN z
                ELSE y END,
       z = CASE WHEN x BETWEEN z AND y THEN y
                WHEN z BETWEEN x AND y THEN y
                WHEN y BETWEEN z AND x THEN x
                WHEN z BETWEEN y AND x THEN x
                ELSE z END
 WHERE x > z OR x > y;
```

While it is very tempting to write more and more of these pattern templates, it might be more trouble than it is worth, because of increased maintenance and readability.

Here is an SQL/PSM program for the Bose-Nelson sort, based on the version given in Frederick Hegeman's "Sorting Networks" article for *The C/C++ User's Journal* (Hegeman 1993). It assumes that you have a procedure called `PRINT()` for output to a text file. You can translate it into the programming language of your choice easily, as long as it supports recursion.

```
CREATE PROCEDURE BoseSort (IN i INTEGER, IN j INTEGER)
LANGUAGE SQL
DETERMINISTIC
BEGIN
DECLARE m INTEGER;
IF j > i
THEN SET m = i + (j-i+1)/2 -1;
     CALL BoseSort(i,m);
     CALL BoseSort(m+1, j);
     CALL BoseMerge(i, m, m+1, j);
END IF;
END;

CREATE PROCEDURE BoseMerge (IN i1 INTEGER, IN i2 INTEGER, IN
'j1' INTEGER, IN 'j2' INTEGER)
LANGUAGE SQL
DETERMINISTIC
BEGIN
DECLARE i_mid INTEGER;
```

```
DECLARE j_mid INTEGER;
IF i2 = i1 AND 'j2' = 'j1'
THEN CALL PRINT('swap', i1, 'j1');
ELSE IF i2 = i1+1 AND 'j2' = 'j1'
     THEN CALL PRINT('swap', i1, 'j1');
          CALL PRINT('swap', i2, 'j1');
     ELSE IF i2 = i1+1 AND 'j2' = 'j1'+1
          THEN CALL PRINT('swap', i1, 'j2');
               CALL PRINT('swap', i1, 'j1');
          ELSE SET i_mid = i1 + (i2-i1+1)/2 - 1;
               IF MOD((i2-i1+1),2) = 0 AND i2-i1 <> 'j2'-'j1'
               THEN SET j_mid = ('j1' + 'j2'-'j1')/2 -1;
                    CALL BoseMerge(i1, i_mid, 'j1', j_mid);
                    CALL BoseMerge(ii_mid+1, i2, j_mid+1, 'j2');
                    CALL BoseMerge(ii_mid+1, i2, 'j1', j_mid);
               END IF;
          END IF;
     END IF;
END IF;
END;
```

Numeric Data in SQL

SQL IS NOT A computational or procedural language; the arithmetic capability of SQL is weaker than that of any other language you have ever used. But there are some tricks that you need to know when working with numbers in SQL and when passing them to a host program. Much of the arithmetic and the functions are defined by implementations, so you should experiment with your particular product and make notes on the defaults, precision, and tools in the math library of your database.

You should also read Chapter 21, which deals with the related topic of aggregate functions. This chapter deals with the arithmetic that you would use across a row, instead of down a column; they are not quite the same.

3.1 Numeric Types

The SQL Standard has a wide range of numeric types. The idea is that any host language can find an SQL numeric type that matches one of its own.

You will also find some vendor extensions in the numeric data types, the most common of which is `MONEY`. This is really a `DECIMAL` or `NUMERIC` data type, which also accepts and displays currency symbols in input and output.

Numbers in SQL are classified as either exact or approximate. An exact numeric value has a precision, *p*, and a scale, *s*. The precision is a positive integer that determines the number of significant digits in a particular radix. The Standard says the radix can be either binary or decimal, so you need to know what your implementation does. The scale is a nonnegative integer that tells you how many decimal places the number has.

Today, there are not that many base-ten platforms, so you probably have a binary machine. However, a number can have one of many binary representations—twos-complement; ones-complement; high-end, or low-end—and various word sizes. The proper mental model of numbers in SQL is not to worry about the "bits and bytes" level of the physical representation, but to think in abstract terms.

The data types `NUMERIC`, `DECIMAL`, `INTEGER`, `BIGINT`, and `SMALLINT` are exact numeric types. An integer has a scale of zero, but the syntax simply uses the word `INTEGER` or the abbreviation `INT`. `SMALLINT` has a scale of zero, but the range of values it can hold is less than or equal to the range that `INTEGER` can hold in the implementation. Likewise, `BIGINT` has a scale of zero, but the range of values it can hold is greater than or equal to the range that `INTEGER` can hold in the implementation. `BIGINT` was added in SQL-99, but had been common in products before then.

`DECIMAL(p,s)` can also be written `DEC(p,s)`. For example, `DECIMAL(8,2)` could be used to hold the number 123456.78, which has eight significant digits and two decimal places.

The difference between `NUMERIC` and `DECIMAL` is subtle. `NUMERIC` specifies the exact precision and scale to be used. `DECIMAL` specifies the exact scale, but the precision is implementation-defined to be equal to or greater than the specified value.

Mainframe COBOL programmers can think of `NUMERIC` as a COBOL `PICTURE` numeric type, whereas `DECIMAL` is like a BCD. Personal computer programmers these days probably have not seen anything like this. You may find that many small-machine SQLs do not support `NUMERIC` or `DECIMAL`, because the programmers do not want to have to have COBOL-style math routines that operate on character strings or an internal decimal representation.

An approximate numeric value consists of a mantissa and an exponent. The mantissa is a signed numeric value; the exponent is a signed integer that specifies the magnitude of the mantissa. An approximate numeric value has a precision. The precision is a positive integer that specifies the number of significant binary digits in the mantissa. The value of an approximate numeric value is the mantissa multiplied by 10 to the exponent. `FLOAT(p)`, `REAL`, and `DOUBLE PRECISION` are the approximate numeric types. There is a subtle difference between `FLOAT(p)`, which has a binary precision equal to or greater than the value given, and `REAL`, which has an implementation-defined precision.

The IEEE Standard 754 for floating point numbers is the most common representation today. It is binary and uses 32 bits for single precision and 64 bits for double precision, which is just right for Intel-based PCs, Macintoshes, and most UNIX platforms. Its math functions are available burned into processor chips, so they will run faster than a software implementation.

The range for single precision numbers is approximately ± 10^-44.85 to 10^38.53, and for double precision, approximately ± 10^-323.3 to 10^308.3. However, there are some special values in the Standard.

Zero cannot be directly represented in this format, so it is modeled as a special value denoted with an exponent field of zero and a fraction field of zero. The sign field can make this either –0 and +0, which are distinct values that compare as equal.

If the exponent is all zeroes, but the fraction is nonzero (else it would be interpreted as zero), then the value is a denormalized number, which is not assumed to have a leading 1 before the binary point. Thus, this represents a number $(-s * 0.f * 2 - 126)$, where s is the sign bit and f is the fraction. For double precision, denormalized numbers are of the form $(-s * 0.f * 2\ -1022)$. You can interpret zero as a special type of denormalized number.

The two values "+infinity" and "–infinity" are denoted with an exponent of all ones and a fraction of all zeroes. The sign bit distinguishes between negative infinity and positive infinity. Being able to denote infinity as a specific value is useful, because it allows operations to continue past overflow situations. Operations with infinite values are well defined in the IEEE floating point.

The value NaN (Not a Number) is used to represent a bit configuration that does not represent a number. NaNs are represented by a bit pattern with an exponent of all ones and a nonzero fraction. There are two categories of NaN: QNaN (Quiet NaN) and SNaN (Signalling NaN).

A QNaN is a NaN with the most significant fraction bit set. QNaNs propagate freely through most arithmetic operations. These values pop out of an operation when the result is not mathematically defined, like division by zero.

An SNaN is a NaN with the most significant fraction bit clear. It is used to signal an exception when used in operations. SNaNs can be handy to assign to uninitialized variables to trap premature usage.

Semantically, QNaNs denote indeterminate operations, while SNaNs denote invalid operations.

SQL has not accepted the IEEE model for mathematics for several reasons. Much of the SQL Standard allows implementation-defined rounding, truncation, and precision to avoid limiting the language to particular hardware platforms. If the IEEE rules for math were allowed in SQL, then we would need type conversion rules for infinite and a way to represent an infinite exact numeric value after the conversion. People have enough trouble with `NULL`s, so let's not go there.

3.1.1 BIT, BYTE, and BOOLEAN Data Types

Machine-level things like a `BIT` or `BYTE` data type have no place in SQL. SQL is a high-level language; it is abstract and defined without regard to *physical* implementation. This basic principle of data modeling is called data abstraction. Bits and bytes are the *lowest* units of hardware-specific physical implementation you can get. Are you on a high-end or low-end machine? Does the machine have 8-, 16-, 32-, 64-, or 128-bit words? Twos-complement or ones-complement math? Hey, the SQL Standard allows decimal machines, so bits do not exist at all!

What about `NULL`s in this data type? To be an SQL data type, you have to have `NULL`s, so what is a `NULL` bit? By definition, a bit is in one of two states, on or off, and has no `NULL`. If your vendor adds `NULL`s to bit, how are the bit-wise operations defined? Oh, what a tangled web we weave when first we mix logical and physical models.

What does the implementation of the host languages do with bits? Did you know that +1, +0, −0 and −1 are all used for `BOOLEAN`s, but not consistently? In C#, Boolean values are 0/1 for `FALSE`/`TRUE`, while VB.NET has Boolean values of 0/-1 for `FALSE`/`TRUE`—and they are proprietary languages from the same vendor. That means *all* the host languages—present, future, and not-yet-defined—can be different.

There are usually two situations in practice. Either the bits are individual attributes, or they are used as a vector to represent a single attribute. In the case of a single attribute, the encoding is limited to two values, which do not port to host languages or other SQLs, cannot be easily understood by an end user, and cannot be expanded.

In the second case, what some newbies, who are still thinking in terms of second- and third-generation programming languages or even punch cards, do is build a vector for a series of "yes/no" status codes, failing to see the status vector as a single attribute. Did you ever play the children's game "20 Questions" when you were young?

Imagine you have six components for a loan approval, so you allocate bits in your second-generation model of the world. You have 64 possible vectors, but only 5 of them are valid (i.e., you cannot be rejected for bankruptcy and still have good credit). For your data integrity, you can:

1. Ignore the problem. This is actually what *most* newbies do.
2. Write elaborate `CHECK()` constraints with user-defined functions or proprietary bit-level library functions that cannot port and that run like cold glue.

Now we add a seventh condition to the vector—which end does it go on? Why? How did you get it in the right place on all the possible hardware that it will ever use? Did all the code that references a bit in a word by its position do it right after the change?

You need to sit down and think about how to design an encoding of the data that is high-level, general enough to expand, abstract, and portable. For example, is that loan approval a hierarchical code? Concatenation code? Vector code? Did you provide codes for unknown, missing, and N/A values? It is not easy to design such things!

3.2 Numeric Type Conversion

There are a few surprises in converting from one numeric type to another. The SQL Standard left it up to the implementation to answer a lot of basic questions, so the programmer has to know his package.

3.2.1 Rounding and Truncating

When an exact or approximate numeric value is assigned to an exact numeric column, it may not fit. SQL says that the database engine will use an approximation that preserves leading significant digits of the original number after rounding or truncating. The choice of whether to truncate or round is implementation-defined, however. This can lead to some surprises when you have to shift data among SQL implementations, or shift storage values from a host language program into an SQL table. It is probably a good idea to create the columns with more decimal places than you think you need.

Truncation is defined as truncation toward zero; this means that 1.5 would truncate to 1, and −1.5 would truncate to −1. This is not true for all programming languages; everyone agrees on truncation toward zero for the positive numbers, but you will find that negative numbers may truncate away from zero (i.e., −1.5 would truncate to −2).

SQL is also indecisive about rounding, leaving the implementation free to determine its method. There are two major types of rounding in programming.

The scientific method looks at the digit to be removed. If this digit is 0, 1, 2, 3, or 4, you drop it and leave the higher-order digit to its left unchanged. If the digit is 5, 6, 7, 8, or 9, you drop it and increment the digit to its left. This method works with a small set of numbers and was popular with FORTRAN programmers because it is what engineers use.

The commercial method looks at the digit to be removed. If this digit is 0, 1, 2, 3, or 4, you drop it and leave the digit to its left unchanged. If the digit is 6, 7, 8, or 9, you drop it and increment the digit to its left. However, when the digit is 5, you want to have a rule that will round up about half the time.

One rule is to look at the digit to the left: if it is odd, then leave it unchanged; if it is even, increment it. There are other versions of the decision rule, but they all try to make the rounding error as small as possible. This method works with a large set of numbers, and it is popular with bankers because it reduces the total rounding error in the system.

Another convention is to round to the nearest even number, so that both 1.5 and 2.5 round to 2, and 3.5 and 4.5 both round to 4. This rule keeps commercial rounding symmetric. The following expression uses the `MOD()` function to determine whether you have an even number or not.

```
ROUND (CAST (amount - .0005 AS DECIMAL (14,4)) -
 (CAST (MOD (CAST (amount*100.0 + .99 AS INTEGER), 2) AS
DECIMAL (14,4))/1000.0), 2);
```

In commercial transactions, you carry money amounts to four or more decimal places, but round them to two decimal places for display. This is a GAAP (Generally Accepted Accounting Practice) in the United States for U.S. dollars and a law in Europe for working with euros.

Here is your first programming exercise for the notes you are making on your SQL.

Generate a table of 5,000 random numbers, both positive and negative, with four decimal places. Round the test data to two decimal places, and total them using both methods.

Notice the difference, and save those results. Now load those same numbers into a table in your SQL, like this:

```
CREATE TABLE RoundTest
(original DECIMAL(10,4) NOT NULL,
 rounded DECIMAL(10,2) NOT NULL);

-- insert the test data
INSERT INTO RoundTest (original) VALUES (2134.5678.  0.00);
 etc.

UPDATE RoundTest SET rounded = original;

-- write a program to use both rounding methods
-- compare those results to this query

SELECT SUM(original), SUM(rounded)
  FROM RoundTest;
```

Compare these results to those from the other two tests. Now you know what your particular SQL is doing. Or, if you got a third answer, there might be other things going on, which we will deal with in Chapter 21 on aggregate functions. We will postpone discussion here, but the order of the rows in a `SUM()` function can make a difference in accumulated floating-point rounding error.

3.2.2 CAST() Function

SQL-92 defines the general `CAST(<cast operand> AS <data type>)` function for all data type conversions, but most implementations use several specific functions of their own for the conversions they support. The SQL-92 `CAST()` function is not only more general, but it also allows the `<cast operand>` to be either a `<column name>`, a `<value expression>`, or a `NULL`.

For numeric-to-numeric conversion, you can do anything you wish, but you have to watch for the rounding errors. The comparison predicates can hide automatic type conversions, so be careful. SQL implementations will also have formatting options in their conversion functions that are not part of the Standard. These functions either use a `PICTURE` string, like COBOL or some versions of BASIC, or return their results in a format set in an environment variable. This is very implementation-dependent.

3.3 Four-Function Arithmetic

SQL is weaker than a pocket calculator. The dyadic arithmetic operators +, −, *, and / stand for addition, subtraction, multiplication, and division, respectively. The multiplication and division operators are of equal precedence and are performed before the dyadic plus and minus operators.

In algebra and in some programming languages, the precedence of arithmetic operators is more restricted. They use the "My Dear Aunt Sally" rule; that is, multiplication is done before division, which is done before addition, which is done before subtraction. This practice can lead to subtle errors.

For example, consider (largenum + largenum − largenum), where largenum is the maximum value that can be represented in its numeric data type. If you group the expression from left to right, you get ((largenum + largenum) − largenum) = overflow error! However, if you group the expression from right to left, you get (largenum + (largenum − largenum)) = largenum.

Because of these differences, an expression that worked one way in the host language may get different results in SQL, and vice versa. SQL could reorder the expressions to optimize them, but in practice, you will find that many implementations will simply parse the expressions from left to right. The best way to be safe is always to make extensive use of parentheses in all expressions, whether they are in the host language or in your SQL.

The monadic plus and minus signs are allowed and you can string as many of them in front of a numeric value of variables as you like. The bad news about this decision is that SQL also uses Ada-style comments, which put the text of a comment line between a double dash and a new line-character. This means that the parser has to figure out whether "--" is two minus signs or the start of a comment. Most versions of SQL also support C-style comment brackets (i.e., `/* comment text */`). Such brackets have been proposed in the SQL3 discussion papers, because some international data transmission standards do not recognize a new line in a transmission, and the double-dash convention will not work.

If both operands are exact numeric, the data type of the result is exact numeric, as you would expect. Likewise, an approximate numeric in a calculation will cast the results to approximate numeric. The kicker is in how the results are assigned in precision and scale.

Let S1 and S2 be the scale of the first and second operands, respectively. The precision of the result of addition and subtraction is implementation-defined, and the scale is the maximum of S1 and S2.

The precision of the result of multiplication is implementation-defined, and the scale is (S1 + S2). The precision and scale of the result of division are implementation-defined, and so are some decisions about rounding or truncating results.

The ANSI X3H2 committee debated about requiring precision and scales in the standard and finally gave up. This means I can start losing high-order digits, especially with a division operation, where it is perfectly legal to make all results single-digit integers.

Nobody does anything that stupid in practice. In the real world, some vendors allow you to adjust the number of decimal places as a system parameter, some default to a few decimal places, and some display as many decimal places as they can, so that you can round off to what you want. You will simply have to learn what your implementation does by experimenting with it.

Most vendors have extended this set of operators with other common mathematical functions. The most common additional functions are modulus, absolute value, power, and square root. But it is also possible to find logarithms to different bases, and to perform exponential, trigonometric, and other scientific, statistical, and mathematical functions.

Precision and scale are implementation-defined for these functions, of course, but they tend to follow the same design decisions as the arithmetic did. The reason is obvious: they are using the same library routines under the covers as the math package in the database engine.

3.4 Arithmetic and NULLs

`NULL`s are probably one of the most formidable database concepts for the beginner. Chapter 6 is devoted to a detailed study of how `NULL`s work in SQL, but this section is concerned with how they act in arithmetic expressions.

The `NULL` in SQL is only one way of handling missing values. The usual description of `NULL`s is that they represent currently unknown values that might be replaced later with real values when we know something. This definition actually covers a lot of territory. The Interim Report 75-02-08 to the ANSI X3 (SPARC Study Group 1975) showed 14 different kinds of incomplete data that could appear as the results of operations or as attribute values. They included such things as arithmetic underflow and overflow, division by zero, string truncation, raising zero to the zeroth power, and other computational errors, as well as missing or unknown values.

The NULL is a global creature, not belonging to any particular data type but able to replace any of their values. This makes arithmetic a bit easier to define. You have to specifically forbid NULLs in a column by declaring the column with a NOT NULL constraint. But in SQL-92, you can use the CAST function to declare a specific data type for a NULL, such as CAST(NULL AS INTEGER). One reason for this convention is completeness; another is to let you pass information about how to create a column to the database engine.

The basic rule for math with NULLs is that they propagate. An arithmetic operation with a NULL will return a NULL. That makes sense; if a NULL is a missing value, then you cannot determine the results of a calculation with it. However, the expression (NULL / 0) looks strange to people. The first thought is that a division by zero should return an error; if NULL is a true missing value, there is no value to which it can resolve and make that expression valid. However, SQL propagates the NULL, while a non-**NULL** value divided by zero will cause a runtime error.

3.5 Converting Values to and from NULL

Since host languages do not support NULLs, the programmer can elect either to replace them with another value that is expressible in the host language or to use indicator variables to signal the host program to take special actions for them.

3.5.1 NULLIF() Function

SQL specifies two functions, NULLIF() and the related COALESCE(), that can be used to replace expressions with NULL, and vice versa. They are part of the CASE expression family.

The NULLIF(V1, V2) function has two parameters. It is equivalent to the following CASE expression:

```
NULLIF(V1, V2) := CASE
                  WHEN (V1 = V2)
                  THEN NULL
                  ELSE V1 END;
```

That is, when the first parameter is equal to the second, the function returns a NULL; otherwise, it returns the first parameter's value. The properties of this function allow you to use it for many purposes. The important properties are these:

1. NULLIF(*x*, *x*) will return NULL for all values of *x*. This includes NULL, since (NULL = NULL) is UNKNOWN, not TRUE.

2. NULLIF(0, (*x* - *x*)) will convert all non-**NULL** values of *x* into NULL.

   But it will convert *x* NULL into *x* zero, since (NULL - NULL) is NULL, and the equality test will fail.

3. NULLIF(1, (*x* - *x* + 1)) will convert all non-**NULL** values of *x* into NULL.

   But it will convert a NULL into a one. This can be generalized for all numeric data types and values.

3.5.2 COALESCE() Function

The COALESCE(<value expression>, ..., <value expression>) function scans the list of <value expression>s from left to right, determines the highest data type in the list, and returns the first non-**NULL** value in the list, casting it to the highest data type. If all the <value expression>s are NULL, the result is NULL.

The most common use of this function is in a SELECT list, where there are columns that have to be added, but one can be a NULL. For example, to create a report of the total pay for each employee, you might write this query:

```
SELECT emp_nbr, emp_name, (salary + commission) AS totalpay
 FROM Employees;
```

But salesmen may work on commission only, or on a mix of salary and commission. The office staff is on salary only. This means an employee could have NULLs in his salary or commission column, which would propagate in the addition and produce a NULL result. A better solution would be:

```
SELECT emp_nbr, emp_name
     (COALESCE(salary, 0) + COALESCE(commission, 0)) AS paycheck
 FROM Employees;
```

A more elaborate use for the COALESCE() function is with aggregate functions. Consider a table of customers' purchases with a category code and the amount of each purchase. You are to construct a query that will

have one row, with one column for each category and one column for the grand total of all customer purchases. The table is declared like this:

```
CREATE TABLE Customers
(cust_nbr INTEGER NOT NULL,
 purchase_nbr INTEGER NOT NULL,
 category CHAR(1)
          CONSTRAINT proper_category
          CHECK (category IN ('A', 'B', 'C'),
 purchase_amt DECIMAL(8, 2) NOT NULL,
 ...  PRIMARY KEY (cust_nbr, purchase_nbr));
```

As an example of the use of COALESCE(), create a table of payments made for each month of a single year. (Yes, this could be done with a column for the months, but bear with me.)

```
CREATE TABLE Payments
(cust_nbr INTEGER NOT NULL,
 jan DECIMAL(8,2),
 feb DECIMAL(8,2),
 mar DECIMAL(8,2),
 apr DECIMAL(8,2),
 may DECIMAL(8,2),
 jun DECIMAL(8,2),
 jul DECIMAL(8,2),
 aug DECIMAL(8,2),
 sep DECIMAL(8,2),
 oct DECIMAL(8,2),
 nov DECIMAL(8,2),
 "dec" DECIMAL(8,2), -- DEC is a reserved word
 PRIMARY KEY cust_nbr);
```

The problem is to write a query that returns the customer and the amount of the last payment he made. Unpaid months are shown with a NULL in them. We could use a COALESCE function like this:

```
SELECT cust_nbr,
       COALESCE ("dec", nov, oct, sep,
                 aug, jul, jun, may, apr, mar, feb, jan)
  FROM Customers;
```

Of course this query is a bit incomplete, since it does not tell you in what month this last payment was made. This can be done with the rather ugly-looking expression that will turn a month's non `NULL` payment into a character string with the name of the month. The general case for a column called "mon," which holds the number of a month within the year, is `NULLIF (COALESCE(NULLIF (0, mon-mon), 'Month' ), 0)` where 'Month' is replaced by the string for the actual name of the particular month. A list of these statements in month order in an `COALESCE` will give us the name of the last month with a payment. The way this expression works is worth working out in detail.

Case 1: mon is a numeric value:

```
NULLIF(COALESCE(NULLIF(0, mon-mon), 'Month'), 0)
NULLIF(COALESCE(NULLIF(0, 0), 'Month'), 0)
NULLIF(COALESCE(NULL, 'Month'), 0)
NULLIF('Month', 0)
('Month')
```

Case 2: mon is *NULL*:

```
NULLIF(COALESCE(NULLIF(0, mon-mon), 'Month'), 0)
NULLIF(COALESCE(NULLIF(0, NULL-NULL), 'Month'), 0)
NULLIF(COALESCE(NULLIF(0, NULL), 'Month'), 0)
NULLIF(COALESCE(0, 'Month'), 0)
NULLIF(0, 0)
(NULL)
```

You can do a lot of work by nesting SQL functions. LISP programmers are used to thinking this way, but most procedural programmers are not. It just takes a little practice and time.

3.6 Vendor Math Functions

All other math functions are vendor extensions, but you can plan on several common ones in most SQL implementations. They are implemented under assorted names, and often with slightly different functionality.

3.6.1 Number Theory Operators

`(x MOD m)` or `MOD(x, m)` is the function that performs modulo or remainder arithmetic. This is tricky when the values of *x* and *m* are not cardinals (i.e., positive, nonzero integers). Experiment and find out how your package handles negative numbers and decimal places.

In September 1996, Len Gallagher proposed an amendment for the `MOD` function in SQL3. Originally, the working draft defined `MOD(x, m)` only for positive values of both *m* and *x*, and left the result to be implementation-dependent when either *m* or *x* is negative.

Negative values of *x* have no required mathematical meaning, and many implementations of `MOD` either don't define them at all or give some result that is the easiest to calculate on a given hardware platform.

However, negative values for *m* do have a very nice mathematical interpretation that we wanted to see preserved in the SQL definition of `MOD`. Len proposed the following:

1. If *x* is positive, then the result is the unique nonnegative exact numeric quantity *r* with scale 0 such that *r* is less than *m* and $x = (m * k) + r$ for some exact numeric quantity *k* with scale 0.
2. Otherwise, the result is an implementation-defined exact numeric quantity *r* with scale 0, which satisfies the requirements that *r* is strictly between *m* and (-*m*) and that $x = (m * k) + r$ for some exact numeric quantity *k* with scale 0, and a completion condition is raised: warning—implementation-defined result.

This definition guarantees that the `MOD` function, for a given positive value of *x*, will be a homomorphism under addition from the mathematical group of all integers, under integer addition, to the modular group of integers {0, 1. . ., *m*-1} under modular addition. This mapping then preserves the following group properties:

1. The additive identity is preserved: `MOD(0, m) = 0`
2. Additive inverse is preserved in the modular group defined by `MOD(-MOD(x, m), m) = m - MOD(x, m)`:

   ```
   MOD(-x, m) = - MOD(x, m)
   ```

3. The addition property is preserved where "⊕" is modular addition defined by `MOD((MOD(m, m) + MOD(x, m)), m)`

```
MOD((m + x), m) = MOD(m, m) ⊕ MOD(x, m)
```

4. Subtraction is preserve under modular subtraction, which is defined as `MOD((MOD(m, m) ⊖ MOD(x, m)), m)`

```
MOD(m-x, m) = MOD(m, m) ⊖ MOD(x, m)
```

From this definition, we would get the following:

```
MOD(12, 5) = 2
MOD(-12, 5) = 3
```

There are some applications where the best result to `MOD(-12, 5)` might be −2 or −3 rather than 3, and that is probably why various implementations of the `MOD` function differ. But the advantages of being able to rely on the above mathematical properties outweigh any other considerations. If a user knows what the SQL result will be, then it is easy to modify the expressions of a particular application to get the desired application result. Table 3.1 is a chart of the differences in SQL implementations.

Table 3.1 *Differences in SQL Implementations*

			Type A	Type B	Type C	Proposal
test	n	m	mod(n, m)	mod(n, m)	mod(n, m)	mod(n, m)
a	12	5	2	2	2	2
b	-12	5	-2	-2	-2	3
c	-12	-5	-2	-2	(-2,3)	(2,-3)
d	-12	-5	2	2	2	-2
e	NULL	5	NULL	NULL	NULL	NULL
f	NULL	NULL	NULL	NULL	NULL	NULL
g	12	NULL	NULL	NULL	NULL	NULL
h	12	0	12	NULL	err	12
i	-12	0	-12	NULL	err	-12
j	0	5	0	0	0	0
k	0	-5	0	0	0	0

```
Type A:
 Oracle 7.0 and Oracle 8.0

Type B:
 DataFlex-ODBC:
 SQL Server 6.5, SP2
 SQLBase Version 6.1 PTF level 4
 Xbase

Type C:
 DB2/400, V3r2:
 DB2/6000 V2.01.1
 Sybase SQL Anywhere 5.5
 Sybase System 11
```

`<data type>(x)` = Converts the number *x* into the `<data type>`. This is the most common form of a conversion function, and it is not as general as the standard `CAST()`.
`ABS(x)` = Returns the absolute value of *x*.
`SIGN(x)` = Returns −1 if *x* is negative, 0 if *x* is zero and +1 if *x* is positive.

3.6.2 Exponential Functions

Exponential functions include:

`POWER(x, n)` = Raises the number *x* to the *n*th power.
`SQRT(x)` = Returns the square root of *x*.
`LOG10(x)` = Returns the base ten logarithm of *x*. See remarks about `LN(x)`.
`LN(x)` or `LOG(x)` = Returns the natural logarithm of *x*. The problem is that logarithms are undefined when ($x <= 0$). Some SQL implementations return an error message, some return a `NULL` and DB2/400; version 3 release 1 returned `*NEGINF` (short for "negative infinity") as its result.
`EXP(x)` = Returns *e* to the *x* power; the inverse of a natural log.

3.6.3 Scaling Functions

Scaling functions include:

`ROUND(x, p)` = Round the number *x* to *p* decimal places.
`TRUNCATE(x, p)` = Truncate the number *x* to *p* decimal places.

Many implementations also allow for the use of external functions written in other programming languages. The SQL/PSM Standard has syntax for a **LANGUAGE** clause in the **CREATE PROCEDURE** statement. The burden of handling NULLs and data type conversion is on the programmer, however.

`FLOOR(x)` = The largest integer less than or equal to *x*.
`CEILING(x)` = The smallest integer greater than or equal to *x*.

The following two functions are in MySQL, Oracle, Mimer, and SQL-2003, but are often mimicked with CASE expressions in actual code.

`LEAST (<expression list>)` = The expressions have to be of the same data type. This function returns the lowest value, whether numeric, temporal or character.
`GREATEST(<expression list>)` = As above, but it returns the highest value.

3.6.4 Converting Numbers to Words

A common function in report writers converts numbers into words so that they can be used to print checks, legal documents, and other reports. This is not a common function in SQL products, nor is it part of the Standard.

A method for converting numbers into words using only Standard SQL by Stu Bloom follows. This was posted on January 2, 2002, on the SQL Server Programming newsgroup. First, create a table:

```
CREATE TABLE NbrWords
(number INTEGER PRIMARY KEY,
 word VARCHAR(30) NOT NULL);
```

Then populate it with the literal strings of NbrWords from 0 to 999. Assuming that your range is 1 to 999,999,999, use the following query; it should be obvious how to extend it for larger numbers and fractional parts.

```
CASE WHEN :num < 1000
     THEN (SELECT word FROM NbrWords
```

```
        WHERE number = :num)
  WHEN :num < 1000000
  THEN (SELECT word FROM NbrWords
        WHERE number = :num / 1000)
       || ' thousand '
       ||  (SELECT word FROM NbrWords
             WHERE MOD (number = :num, 1000))
  WHEN :num < 1000000000
  THEN (SELECT word FROM NbrWords
        WHERE number = :num / 1000000)
      || ' million '
      || (SELECT word FROM NbrWords
            WHERE number = MOD((:num / 1000), 1000))
      || CASE WHEN MOD((:num / 1000), 1000) > 0
              THEN ' thousand '
              ELSE '' END
      || (SELECT word FROM NbrWords
            WHERE number = MOD(:num, 1000))

END;
```

Whether 2,500 is "Twenty-Five Hundred" or "Two Thousand Five Hundred" is a matter of taste and not science. This function can be done with a shorter list of words and a different query, but this is probably the best compromise between code and the size of the table.

Temporal Data Types in SQL

CLIFFORD SIMAK WROTE a science fiction novel entitled *Time Is the Simplest Thing* in 1977. He was wrong. And the problems did not start with the Y2K problems we had in 2000, either. The calendar is irregular, and the only standard unit of time is the second; years, months, weeks, hours, minutes, and so forth are not part of the metric system, but are mentioned in the ISO standards as conventions.

SQL-92 added temporal data to the language, acknowledging what was already in most SQL products by that time. The problem is that each vendor had made an internal trade-off. In Chapter 29, we will get into SQL code, but since this is an area where people do not have a good understanding, it is better to start with foundations.

4.1 Notes on Calendar Standards

Leap years did not exist in the Roman or Egyptian solar calendars prior to the year 708 A.U.C. (*ab urbe condita*, Latin for "from the founding of the City [Rome]").

Unfortunately, the solar year is not an even number of days; there are 365.2422 days in a year, and the fraction adds up over time. The civil and religious solar calendars had drifted with respect to the solar year by approximately one day every four years. For example, the Egyptian calendar drifted completely around approximately every

1,461 years. As a result, it was useless for agriculture, so the Egyptians relied on the stars to predict the flooding of the Nile. Sosigenes of Alexandria knew that the calendar had drifted completely around more than twice since it was first introduced.

To realign the calendar with the seasons, Julius Caesar decreed that the year 708 A.U.C. (that is, the year 46 B.C.E. to us) would have 445 days. Caesar, on the advice of Sosigenes, also introduced leap years (known as bissextile years) at this time. Many Romans simply referred to 708 A.U.C. as the "year of confusion," and thus began the Julian Calendar that was the standard for the world from that point forward.

The Julian calendar added an extra "leap" day every four years and was reasonably accurate in the short or medium range. However, it drifted by approximately three days every 400 years as a result of the 0.0022 fraction of a day adding up.

It had gotten 10 days out of step with the seasons by 1582. (A calendar without a leap year would have drifted completely around slightly more than once between 708 A.U.C. and 2335 A.U.C.—1582 C.E. to us.) The summer solstice, so important to planting crops, no longer had any relationship to June 21. Scientists finally convinced Pope Gregory to realign the calendar by dropping almost two weeks from the month of October in 1582 C.E. The years 800 C.E. and 1200 C.E. were leap years anywhere in the Christian world. But whether or not 1600 C.E. was a leap year depended on where you lived. European countries did not move to the new calendar at the same time or follow the same pattern of adoption.

Note: The abbreviations A.D. (*anno Domini*, Latin for "in the year of Our Lord") and B.C. ("before Christ") have been replaced by C.E. for "common era" and B.C.E. for "before common era" in ISO Standard, to avoid religious references.

The calendar corrections had economic and social ramifications. In Great Britain and its colonies, September 2, 1752, was followed by September 14, 1752. The calendar reform bill of 1751 was entitled "An Act for Regulating the Commencement of the Year and for Correcting the Calendar Now in Use." The bill included provisions to adjust the amount of money owed or collected from rents, leases, mortgages, and similar legal arrangements, so that rents and so forth were prorated by the number of actual elapsed days in the time period affected by the calendar change. Nobody had to pay the full monthly rate for the short month of September in 1752, and nobody had to pay the full yearly rate for the short year.

The serious, widespread, and persistent rioting that followed was not due to the commercial problems that resulted, but to the common belief that each person's days were "numbered"—each person was preordained to be born and die at a divinely ordained time that no human agency could alter in any way. Thus, the removal of 11 days from the month of September shortened the lives of everyone on Earth by 11 days. And there was also the matter of the missing 83 days due to the change of the New Year's Day from March 25 to January 1, which was believed to have a similar effect.

If you think this behavior is insane, consider the number of people today who get upset about the yearly one-hour clock adjustments for daylight saving time.

To complicate matters, the beginning of the year also varied from country to country. Great Britain preferred to begin the year on March 25, while other countries began at Easter, December 25, March 1, and January 1—all of which are important details for historians to keep in mind.

In Great Britain and its colonies, the calendar year 1750 began on March 24 and ended on March 25—that is, the day after March 24, 1750 was March 25, 1751. The leap day was added to the end of the last full month in the year, which was then February. The extra leap day is still added at the end of February, since this part of the calendar structure was not changed.

In Latin, "septem" means seventh, from which we derived September. Likewise, "octem" means eighth, "novem" means ninth and "decem" means tenth. Thus, September should be the seventh month, October should be the eighth, November should be the ninth, and December should be the tenth. So why is September is the ninth month? September was the seventh month until 1752, when the New Year was changed from March 25 to January 1.

Until fairly recently, no one agreed on the proper display format for dates. Every nation seems to have its own commercial conventions. Most of us know that Americans put the month before the day and the British do the reverse, but do you know any other national conventions? National date formats may be confusing when used in an international environment. When it was "12/16/95" in Boston, it was "16/12/95" in London, "16.12.95" in Berlin, and "95-12-16" in Stockholm. Then there are conventions within industries within each country that complicate matters further.

Faced with all of the possibilities, software vendors came up with various general ways of formatting dates for display. The usual ones are some mixtures of a two- or four-digit year, a three-letter or two-digit month and a two-digit day within the month. Slashes, dashes, or spaces can separate the three fields.

At one time, NATO tried to use Roman numerals for the month to avoid language problems among treaty members. The United States Army did a study and found that the four-digit year, three-letter month and two-digit day, format was the least likely to be missorted, misread, or miswritten by English speakers. That is also the reason for 24-hour or military time.

Today, you want to set up a program to convert your data to conform to ISO-8601: "Data Elements and Interchange Formats—Information Interchange—Representation of Dates and Times" as a corporate standard and EDIFACT for EDI messages. This is the "yyyy-mm-dd" format that is part of Standard SQL and will become part of other standard programming languages as they add temporal data types.

The full ISO-8601 timestamp can be either a local time or UTC/GMT time. UTC is the code for "Universal Coordinated Time," which replaced the older GMT, which was the code for "Greenwich Mean Time" (if you listen to CNN, you are used to hearing the term UTC, but if you listen to BBC radio, you are used to the term GMT).

In 1970, the Coordinated Universal Time system was devised by an international advisory group of technical experts within the International Telecommunication Union (ITU). The ITU felt it was best to designate a single abbreviation for use in all languages, in order to minimize confusion. The two alternative original abbreviation proposals for the "Universal Coordinated Time" were CUT (English: Coordinated Universal Time) and TUC (French: *temps universel coordonnè*). UTC was selected both as a compromise between the French and English proposals, and also because the C at the end looks more like an index in UT0, UT1, UT2, and a mathematical-style notation is always the most international approach.

Technically, Universal Coordinated Time is not quite the same thing as Greenwich Mean Time. GMT is a 24-hour astronomical time system based on the local time at Greenwich, England. GMT can be considered equivalent to Universal Coordinated Time when fractions of a second are not important. However, by international agreement, the term UTC is recommended for all general timekeeping applications, and use of the term GMT is discouraged.

Another problem in the United States is that besides having four time zones, we also have "lawful time" to worry about. This is the technical term for time required by law for commerce. Usually, this means whether or not you use daylight saving time.

The need for UTC time in the database and lawful time for display and input has not been generally handled yet. EDI and replicated databases must use UTC time to compare timestamps. A date without a time zone is ambiguous in a distributed system. A transaction created 1995-12-17 in London may be younger than a transaction created 1995-12-16 in Boston.

4.2 SQL Temporal Data Types

Standard SQL has a very complete description of its temporal data types. There are rules for converting from numeric and character strings into these data types, and there is a schema table for global time-zone information that is used to make sure temporal data types are synchronized. It is so complete and elaborate that nobody has implemented it yet—and it will take them years to do so! Because it is an international standard, Standard SQL has to handle time for the whole world, and most of us work with only local time. If you have ever tried to figure out the time in a foreign city before placing a telephone call, you have some idea of what is involved.

The common terms and conventions related to time are also confusing. We talk about "an hour" and use the term to mean a particular point within the cycle of a day ("The train arrives at 13:00") or to mean an interval of time not connected to another unit of measurement ("The train takes three hours to get there"); the number of days in a month is not uniform; the number of days in a year is not uniform; weeks are not related to months; and so on.

All SQL implementations have a `DATE` data type; most have a separate `TIME` and a `TIMESTAMP` data type. These values are drawn from the system clock and are therefore local to the host machine. They are based on what is now called the Common Era calendar, which many people would still call the Gregorian or Christian calendar.

Standard SQL has a set of date and time (`DATE`, `TIME`, and `TIMESTAMP`) and `INTERVAL` (`DAY`, `HOUR`, `MINUTE`, and `SECOND`, with decimal fraction) data types. Both of these groups are temporal data types, but datetimes represent points in the time line, while the interval data types are durations of time. Standard SQL also has a full set of operators for these data types. The full syntax and functionality have not

yet been implemented in any SQL product, but you can use some of the vendor extensions to get around a lot of problems in most existing SQL implementations today.

4.2.1 Tips for Handling Dates, Timestamps, and Times

The syntax and power of date, timestamp, and time features vary so much from product to product that it is impossible to give anything but general advice. This chapter assumes that you have simple date arithmetic in your SQL, but you might find that some library functions will let you do a better job than what you see here. Please continue to check your manuals until the SQL Standard is implemented.

As a general statement, there are two ways of representing temporal data internally. The "UNIX representation" is based on keeping a single long integer, or a word of 64 or more bits, that counts the computer clock ticks from a base starting date and time. The other representation I will call the "COBOL method," since it uses separate fields for year, month, day, hours, minutes and seconds.

The UNIX method is very good for calculations, but the engine must convert from the external ISO-8601 format to the internal format, and vice versa. The COBOL format is the opposite; good for display purposes, but weaker on calculations.

For example, to reduce a `TIMESTAMP` to just a date with the clock set to 00:00 in SQL Server, you can take advantage of their internal representation and write:

```
CAST (FLOOR (CAST (mydate AS FLOAT)) AS DATETIME)
```

Likewise, the following day can be found with this expression:

```
CAST (CEILING (CAST (mydate AS FLOAT)) AS DATETIME)
```

4.2.2 Date Format Standards

The ISO ordinal date formats are described in ISO-2711-1973. Their format is a four-digit year, followed by a digit day within the year (001-366). The year can be truncated to the year within the century. The ANSI date formats are described in ANSI X3.30-1971. Their formats include the ISO Standard, but add a four-digit year, followed by the two-digit month (01-12), followed by the two-digit day within month (01-31). This option is called the calendar date format. Standard SQL uses this all-numeric "yyyy-mm-dd" format to conform to ISO-8601, which had to avoid language-dependent abbreviations. It is fairly easy to write code to handle either format. The ordinal format is better for date arithmetic; the calendar format is better for display purposes.

The Defense Department has now switched to the year, three-letter month, and day format so that documents can be easily sorted by hand or by machine. This is the format I would recommend using for output on reports to be read by people, for just those reasons; otherwise, use the standard calendar format for transmissions.

Many programs still use a year-in-century date format of some kind. This was supposed to save space in the old days when that sort of thing mattered (i.e., when punch cards had only 80 columns). Programmers assumed that they would not need to tell the difference between the years 1900 and 2000 because they were too far apart. Old COBOL programs that did date arithmetic on these formats returned erroneous negative results. If COBOL had a `DATE` data type, instead of making the programmers write their own routines, this would not have happened. Relational database users and 4GL programmers can gloat over this, since they have `DATE` data types built into their products.

4.2.3 Handling Timestamps

`TIMESTAMP(n)` is defined as a timestamp to (*n*) decimal places (e.g., `TIMESTAMP(9)` is nanosecond precision), where the precision is hardware-dependent. The FIPS-127 standard requires at least five decimal places after the second.

`TIMESTAMP`s usually serve two purposes. They can be used as a true timestamp to mark an event connected to the row in which they appear, or they can be used as a sequential number for building a unique key that is not temporal in nature. Some DB2 programs use the microseconds component of a timestamp and invert the numbers to create "random" numbers for keys; of course, this method of generation does not preclude duplicates being generated, but it is a quick and dirty way to create a somewhat random number. It helps to use such a method when using the timestamp itself would generate data "hot spots" in the table space. For example, the date and time when a payment is made on an account are important, and a true timestamp is required for legal reasons. The account number just has to be different from all other account numbers, so we need a unique number, and `TIMESTAMP` is a quick way of getting one.

Remember that a `TIMESTAMP` will read the system clock once and use that same time on all the items involved in a transaction. It does not matter if the actual time it took to complete the transaction was days; a

transaction in SQL is done as a whole unit or is not done at all. This is not usually a problem for small transactions, but it can be for large batched transactions, where very complex updates have to be done.

Using the TIMESTAMP as a source of unique identifiers is fine in most single-user systems, since all transactions are serialized and of short enough duration that the clock will change between transactions—peripherals are slower than CPUs. But in a client/server system, two transactions can occur at the same time on different local workstations. Using the local client machine clock can create duplicates and can add the problem of coordinating all the clients. The coordination problem has two parts:

1. How do you get the clocks to start at the same time? I do not mean simply the technical problem of synchronizing multiple machines to the microsecond, but also the one or two clients who forgot about daylight saving time.
2. How do you make sure the clocks stay the same? Using the server clock to send a timestamp back to the client increases network traffic, yet does not always solve the problem.

Many operating systems, such as those made by Digital Equipment Corporation, represent the system time as a very long integer based on a count of machine cycles since a starting date. One trick is to pull off the least significant digits of this number and use them as a key. But this will not work as transaction volume increases. Adding more decimal places to the timestamp is not a solution either. The real problem lies in statistics.

Open a telephone book (white pages) at random. Mark the last two digits of any 13 consecutive numbers, which will give you a sample of numbers between 00 and 99. What are the odds that you will have a pair of identical numbers? It is not 1 in 100, as you might first think. Start with one number and add a second number to the set; the odds that the second number does not match the first are 99/100. Add a third number to the set; the odds that it matches neither the first nor the second number are 98/100. Continue this line of reasoning and compute (0.99 * 0.98 * . . . * 0.88) = 0.4427 as the odds of not finding a pair. Therefore, the odds that you will find a pair are 0.5572, a bit better than even. By the time you get to 20 numbers, the odds of a match are about 87%; at 30 numbers, the odds exceed a 99% probability of one match. You might want to carry out this model for finding a pair in three-digit numbers and see when you pass the 50% mark.

A good key generator needs to eliminate (or at least minimize) identical keys and give a fairly uniform statistical distribution to avoid excessive index reorganization problems. Most key-generator algorithms are designed to use the system clock on particular hardware or a particular operating system and depend on features with a "near key" field, such as employee name, to create a unique identifier.

The mathematics of such an algorithm is similar to that of a hashing algorithm. Hashing algorithms also try to obtain a uniform distribution of unique values. The difference is that a hashing algorithm must ensure that a hash result is both unique (after collision resolution) and repeatable, so that it can find the stored data. A key generator needs only to ensure that the resulting key is unique in the database, which is why it can use the system clock and a hashing algorithm cannot.

You can often use a random-number generator in the host language to create pseudo-random numbers to insert into the database for these purposes. Most pseudo-random number generators will start with an initial value, called a seed, and use it to create a sequence of numbers. Each call will return the next value in the sequence to the calling program. The sequence will have some of the statistical properties of a real random sequence, but the same seed will produce the same sequence each time, which is why the numbers are called pseudo-random numbers. This also means that if the sequence ever repeats a number, it will begin to cycle. (This is not usually a problem, since the size of the cycle can be hundreds of thousands or even millions of numbers.)

4.2.4 Handling Times

Most databases live and work in one time zone. If you have a database that covers more than one time zone, you might consider storing time in UTC and adding a numeric column to hold the local time-zone offset. The time zones start at UTC, which has an offset of zero. This is how the system-level time-zone table in Standard SQL is defined. There are also ISO-standard three-letter codes for the time zones of the world, such as EST, for Eastern Standard Time, in the United States. The offset is usually a positive or negative number of hours, but there were some odd zones that differed by 15 minutes from the expected pattern; these were removed in 1998.

Now you have to factor in daylight saving time on top of that to get what is called "lawful time," which is the basis for legal agreements. The U.S. government uses DST on federal lands inside states that do not use DST. If the hardware clock in the computer in which the database

resides is the source of the timestamps, you can get a mix of gaps and duplicate times over a year. This is why Standard SQL uses UTC internally.

You should use a 24-hour time format. 24-hour time is less prone to errors than 12-hour (A.M./P.M.) time, since it is less likely to be misread or miswritten. This format can be manually sorted more easily, and is less prone to computational errors. Americans use a colon as a field separator between hours, minutes and seconds; Europeans use a period. (This is not a problem for them, since they also use a comma for a decimal point.) Most databases give you these display options.

One of the major problems with time is that there are three kinds—fixed events ("He arrives at 13:00"), durations ("The trip takes three hours"), and intervals ("The train leaves at 10:00 and arrives at 13:00")—which are all interrelated. Standard SQL introduces an `INTERVAL` data type that does not explicitly exist in most current implementations (Rdb, from Oracle Corporation, is an exception). An `INTERVAL` is a unit of duration of time, rather than a fixed point in time—days, hours, minutes, seconds.

There are two classes of intervals. One class, called year-month intervals, has an express or implied precision that includes no fields other than `YEAR` and `MONTH`, though it is not necessary to use both. The other class, called day-time intervals, has an express or implied interval precision that can include any fields other than `YEAR` or `MONTH`—that is, `DAY`, `HOUR`, `MINUTE`, and `SECOND` (with decimal places).

4.3 Queries with Date Arithmetic

Almost every SQL implementation has a `DATE` data type, but the functions available for them vary quite a bit. The most common ones are a constructor that builds a date from integers or strings; extractors to pull out the month, day, or year; and some display options to format output.

You can assume that your SQL implementation has simple date arithmetic functions, although with different syntax from product to product, such as:

1. A date plus or minus a number of days yields a new date.
2. A date minus a second date yields an integer number of days.

Table 4.1 displays the valid combinations of `<datetime>` and `<interval>` data types in Standard SQL:

Table 4.1 *Valid Combinations of* `<datetime>` *and* `<interval>` *Data Types*

```
<datetime> - <datetime> = <interval>

<datetime> + <interval> = <datetime>

<interval> (* or/) <numeric> = <interval>

<interval> + <datetime> = <datetime>

<interval> + <interval> = <interval>

<numeric> * <interval> = <interval>
```

There are other intuitively obvious rules dealing with time zones and the relative precision of the two operands.

There should also be a function that returns the current date from the system clock. This function has a different name with each vendor: `TODAY`, `SYSDATE`, `CURRENT DATE`, and `getdate()` are some examples. There may also be a function to return the day of the week from a date, which is sometimes called `DOW()` or `WEEKDAY()`. Standard SQL provides for `CURRENT_DATE`, `CURRENT_TIME [ (<time precision>)]` and `CURRENT_TIMESTAMP [ (<timestamp precision>)]` functions, which are self-explanatory.

4.4 The Nature of Temporal Data Models

The rest of this chapter is based on material taken from a five-part series by Richard T. Snodgrass in *Database Programming and Design* (vol. 11, issues 6-10) in 1998. He is one of the experts in this field, and I hope my editing of his material preserves his expertise.

4.4.1 Temporal Duplicates

Temporal data is pervasive. It has been estimated that one of every fifty lines of database application code involves a date or time value. Data warehouses are by definition time-varying; Ralph Kimball states that every data warehouse has a time dimension. Often the time-oriented nature of the data is what lends it value.

DBAs and SQL programmers constantly wrestle with the vagaries of such data. They find that overlaying simple concepts, such as duplicate prevention, on time-varying data can be surprisingly subtle and complex. In honor of the McCaughey children, the world's only known set of living septuplets, this first section will consider duplicates, of which septuplets are just a special case.

Specifically, we examine the ostensibly simple task of preventing duplicate rows via a constraint in a table definition. Preventing duplicates using SQL is thought to be trivial, and truly is when the data is considered to be currently valid. But when history is retained, things get much trickier. In fact, several interesting kinds of duplicates can be defined over such data. And, as is so often the case, the most relevant kind is the hardest to prevent, and requires an aggregate or a complex trigger.

On January 3, 1998, Kenneth Robert McCaughey, the first of the septuplets to be born and the biggest, was released. We consider here a NICUStatus table recording the status of patients in the neonatal intensive care unit at Blank Children's Hospital in Des Moines, Iowa, an excerpt of which is shown in the following table:

```
name              status      from_date     to_date
=======================================================
'Kenneth Robert' 'serious'   '1997-11-19' '1997-11-21'
'Alexis May'     'serious'   '1997-11-19' '1997-11-27'
'Natalie Sue'    'serious'   '1997-11-19' '1997-11-25'
'Kelsey Ann'     'serious'   '1997-11-19' '1997-11-26'
'Brandon James'  'serious'   '1997-11-19' '1997-11-26'
'Nathan Roy'     'serious'   '1997-11-19' '1997-11-28'
'Joel Steven'    'critical'  '1997-11-19' '1997-11-20'
'Joel Steven'    'serious'   '1997-11-20' '1997-11-26'
'Kenneth Robert' 'fair'      '1997-11-21' '1998-01-03'
'Alexis May'     'fair'      '1997-11-27' '1998-01-11'
'Alexis May'     'fair'      '1997-12-02' '9999-12-31'
'Alexis May'     'fair'      '1997-12-02' '9999-12-31'
```

Each row indicating the condition of an infant is timestamped with a pair of dates. The from_date column indicates the day the child first was listed at that status. The to_date column indicates the day the child's condition changed. In concert, these columns specify a period over which the status was valid.

Tables can be timestamped with values other than periods. This representation of the period is termed closed-open, because the starting date is contained in the period but the ending date is not. Periods can also be represented in other ways, though it turns out that the half-open interval representation is highly desirable.

We denote a row that is currently valid with a to_date of "forever" or the "end of time," which in Standard SQL is the actual date '9999-12-31' because of the way that ISO-8601 is defined. This introduces a year-9999 problem with temporal math and will require special handling. The most common alternative approach is to use the `NULL` value as a place marker for the `CURRENT_TIMESTAMP` or for "eternity" without any particular method of resolution. This also will require special handling and will introduce `NULL` problems. When the `NULL` is used for a "still ongoing" marker, the `VIEW`s or queries must use a `COALESCE (end_date, CURRENT_TIMESTAMP)` expression so that you can do the math correctly.

This table design represents the status in reality, termed valid time; there exist other useful kinds of time. Such tables are very common in practice. Often there are many columns, with the timestamp of a row indicating when that combination of values was valid.

A duplicate in the SQL sense is a row that exactly matches, column for column (including `NULL`s), another row. We will term such duplicates nonsequenced duplicates, for reasons that will become clear shortly. The last two rows of the above table are nonsequenced duplicates. However, there are three other kinds of duplicates that are interesting, all present in this table. These variants arise due to the temporal nature of the data.

The last three rows are value-equivalent, in that the values of all the columns except for those of the timestamp are identical. Value equivalence is a particularly weak form of duplication. It does, however, correspond to the traditional notion of duplicate for a nontime-varying snapshot table, e.g., a table with only the two columns, name and status.

The last three rows are also current duplicates. A current duplicate is one present in the current timeslice of the table. As of January 6, 1998, the then-current timeslice of the above table is simply as shown.

Interestingly, whether a table contains current duplicate rows can change over time, even if no modifications are made to the table. In a week, one of these current duplicates will quietly disappear.

```
NICUStatus snapshot (1998-01-06)
name          status
====================
'Alexis May' 'fair'
'Alexis May' 'fair'
'Alexis May' 'fair'
```

The most useful variant is a sequenced duplicate. The adjective sequenced means that the constraint is applied independently at every point in time. The last three rows are sequenced duplicates. These rows each state that Alexis was in fair condition for most of December 1997 and the first eleven days of 1998.

Table 4.2 indicates how these variants interact. Each entry specifies whether rows satisfying the variant in the left column will also satisfy the variant listed across the top. A check mark states that the top variant will be satisfied; an empty entry states that it may not. For example, if two rows are nonsequenced duplicates, they will also be sequenced duplicates, for the entire period of validity. However, two rows that are sequenced duplicates are not necessarily nonsequenced duplicates, as illustrated by the second-to-last and last rows of the example temporal table.

Table 4.2 *Duplicate Interaction*

	sequenced	current	value-equivalent	nonsequenced
sequenced	Y	Y	N	N
current	Y	Y	Y	N
value-equivalent	N	Y	N	N
nonsequenced	Y	Y	Y	Y

The least restrictive form of duplication is value equivalence, as it simply ignores the timestamps. Note from above that this form implies no other. The most restrictive is nonsequenced duplication, as it requires all the column values to match exactly. It implies all but current duplication. The `PRIMARY KEY` or `UNIQUE` constraint prevents value-equivalent rows.

```
CREATE TABLE NICUStatus
(name CHAR(15) NOT NULL,
 status CHAR(8) NOT NULL,
```

```
 from_date DATE NOT NULL,
 to_date DATE NOT NULL,
PRIMARY KEY (name, status));
```

Intuitively, a value-equivalent duplicate constraint states that "once a condition is assigned to a patient, it can never be repeated later," because doing so would result in a value-equivalent row. We can also use a `PRIMARY KEY` or `UNIQUE` constraint to prevent nonsequenced duplicates, by simply including the timestamp columns thus:

```
CREATE TABLE NICUStatus
(...
 PRIMARY KEY (name, status, from_date, to_date));
```

While nonsequenced duplicates are easy to prevent via SQL statements, such constraints are not that useful in practice. The intuitive meaning of the above nonsequenced unique constraint is something like "a patient cannot have a condition twice over identical periods." However, this constraint can be satisfied by simply shifting one of the rows a day earlier or later, so that the periods of validity are not identical; it is still the case that the patient has the same condition at various times. Preventing current duplicates involves just a little more effort:

```
CREATE TABLE NICUStatus
(...
 CHECK (NOT EXISTS
    (SELECT N1.ssn
     FROM NICUStatus AS N1
     WHERE 1 < (SELECT COUNT(name)
            FROM NICUStatus AS N2
            WHERE N1.name = N2.name
             AND N1.status = N2.status
             AND N1.from_date <= CURRENT_DATE
             AND CURRENT_DATE < N1.to_date
             AND N2.from_date <= CURRENT_DATE
             AND CURRENT_DATE < N2.to_date)))
);
```

Here the intuition is that no patient can have two identical status values at the current time.

As mentioned above, the problem with a current uniqueness constraint is that it can be satisfied today, but violated tomorrow, even if there are no changes made to the underlying table.

If we know that the application will never store future data, we can approximate a current uniqueness constraint by simply including the to_date column in a UNIQUE constraint.

```
CREATE TABLE NICUStatus
(...
 UNIQUE (name, status, to_date)
);
```

This works because all current data will have the same to_date value: either the special value DATE '9999-12-31' or a NULL.

Preventing sequenced duplicates is similar to preventing current duplicates. Operationally, two rows are sequenced duplicates if they are value equivalent and their periods of validity overlap. This definition is equivalent to the one given above.

```
CREATE TABLE NICUStatus
(...
CHECK (NOT EXISTS
      (SELECT N1.name
       FROM NICUStatus AS N1
       WHERE 1
         < (SELECT COUNT(name)
           FROM NICUStatus AS N2
           WHERE N1.name = N2.name
            AND N1.status = N2.status
            AND N1.from_date < N2.to_date
            AND N2.from_date < N1.to_date)))
);
```

The tricky subquery states that the periods of validity overlap. The intuition behind a sequenced uniqueness constraint is that at no time can a patient have two identical conditions. This constraint is a natural one. A sequenced constraint is the logical extension of a conventional constraint on a nontemporal table.

The moral of the story is that adding the timestamp columns to the UNIQUE clause will prevent nonsequenced duplicates, value-equivalent duplicates, or some forms of current duplicates, which unfortunately is rarely what is desired. The natural temporal generalization of a conventional duplicate on a snapshot table is a sequenced duplicate. To prevent sequenced duplicates, a rather complex check constraint, or even one or more triggers, is required.

As a challenge, consider specifying in SQL a primary key constraint on a period-stamped valid-time table. Then try specifying a referential integrity constraint between two period-stamped valid-time tables. It is possible, but is certainly not easy.

4.4.2 Temporal Databases

The accepted term for a database that records time-varying information is a "temporal database." The term "time-varying" database is awkward, because even if only the current state is kept in the database (e.g., the current stock, or the current salary and job title of employees), this database will change as reality changes, and so could perhaps be considered a time-varying database. The term "historical database" implies that the database only stores "historical" information, that is, information about the past; a temporal database may store information about the future, e.g., schedules or plans.

The official definition of temporal database is "a database that supports some aspect of time, not counting user-defined time." So, what is user-defined time? This is defined as "an uninterpreted attribute domain of date and time. User-defined time is parallel to domains such as money and integer. It may be used for attributes such as 'birthdate' and 'hiring_date'. The intuition here is that adding a birthdate column to an employee table does not render it temporal, especially since the birthdate of an employee is presumably fixed, and applies to that employee forever. The presence of a `DATE` column will not *a priori* render the database a temporal database; rather, the database must record the time-varying nature of the enterprise it is modeling.

In the summer of 1997, sixteen cases of people falling ill to a lethal strain of the bacterium Escherichia coli, E. coli O157:H7, all in Colorado, were eventually traced back to a processing plant in Columbus, Nebraska. The plant's operator, Hudson Foods, eventually recalled 25 million pounds of frozen hamburger in an attempt to stem this outbreak.

That particular plant presses about 400,000 pounds of hamburger daily. Ironically, this plant received high marks for its cleanliness and adherence to federal food processing standards. What lead to the recall of about one-fifth of the plant's annual output was the lack of data that could link particular patties back to the slaughterhouses that supply

carcasses to the Columbus plant. It is believed that the meat was contaminated in only one of these slaughterhouses, but without such tracking, all were suspect.

Put simply, the lack of an adequate temporal database cost Hudson Foods more than $20 million.

Dr. Brad De Groot is a veterinarian at the University of Nebraska at Lincoln, about 60 miles southeast of Columbus. He is also interested in improving the health maintenance of cows on their way to your freezer. He hopes to establish the temporal relationships between putative risk factor exposure (e.g., a previously healthy cow sharing a pen number with a sick animal) and subsequent health events (e.g., the cow later succumbs to a disease). These relationships can lead to an understanding of how disease is transferred to and among cattle, and ultimately, to better detection and prevention regimes. As input to this epidemiological study, he is massaging data from commercial feed yard record keeping systems to extract the movement of some 55,000 head of cattle through the myriad pens of several large feed yards in Nebraska.

These cattle are grouped into "lots," with subsets of lots moved from pen to pen. One of Brad's tables, the LotLocations table, records how many cattle from each lot are residing in each pen number of each feed yard. The full schema for this table has nine columns, but here is a quick skeleton of the table:

```
LotLocations (feedyard_id, lot_id, pen_id, hd_cnt, from_date,
from_move_order, to_date, to_move_order, record_date)
```

This table is a valid-time state table, in that it records information valid at some time, and it records states, that is, facts that are true over a period of time. The FROM and TO columns delimit the period of validity of the information in the row. The temporal granularity of this table is somewhat finer than a day, in that the move orders are sequential, allowing multiple movements in a day to be ordered in time. The record_date identifies when this information was recorded. For the present purposes, we will omit the from_move_order, to_move_order, and record_date columns, and express our queries on the simplified schema. The first four columns are integer columns; the last two are of type `DATE`.

```
LotLocations
feedyard_id lot_id pen_id  hd_cnt from_date   to_date
=================================================================
        1       137     1     17  '1998-02-07' '1998-02-18'
        1       219     1     43  '1998-02-25' '1998-03-01'
        1       219     1     20  '1998-03-01' '1998-03-14'
        1       219     2     23  '1998-03-01' '1998-03-14'
        1       219     2     43  '1998-03-14' '9999-12-31'
        1       374     1     14  '1998-02-20' '9999-12-31'
```

In the above instance, 17 head of cattle were in pen 1 for 11 days, moving inauspiciously off the feed yard on February 18. Fourteen head of cattle from lot 374 are still in pen 1 (we use '9999-12-31' to denote currently valid rows). Twenty-three head of cattle from lot 219 were moved from pen 1 to pen 2 on March 1, with the remaining 20 head of cattle in that lot moved to pen 2 on March 14, where they still reside.

The previous section discussed three basic kinds of uniqueness assertions: current, sequenced, and nonsequenced. A current uniqueness constraint (of patient and status, on a table recording the status of patients in a neonatal intensive care unit) was exemplified with "each patient has at most one status condition," a sequenced constraint with "at no time can a patient have two identical conditions," and a nonsequenced constraint with "a patient cannot have a condition twice over identical periods." We saw that the sequenced constraint was the most natural analog of the nontemporal constraint, yet was the most challenging to express in SQL. For the LotLocations table, the appropriate uniqueness constraint would be that feedyard_id, lot_id, pen_id are unique at every time, which is a sequenced constraint.

4.4.3 Temporal Projection and Selection

These notions carry over to queries. In fact, for each conventional (nontemporal) query, there exist current, sequenced, and nonsequenced variants over the corresponding valid-time state table. Consider the nontemporal query, "How many head of cattle from lot 219 in feed yard 1 are in each pen?" over the nontemporal table LotLocationsSnapshot(feedyard_id, lot_id, pen_id, hd_cnt). Such a query is easy to write in SQL.

```
SELECT pen_id, hd_cnt
  FROM LotLocations
 WHERE feedyard_id = 1
   AND lot_id = 219;
```

The current analog over the LotLocations valid-time state table is "How many head of cattle from lot 219 in yard 1 are (currently) in each pen?" For such a query, we only are concerned with currently valid rows, and we need only to add a predicate to the "where" clause asking for such rows.

```
SELECT pen_id, hd_cnt
  FROM LotLocations
 WHERE feedyard_id = 1
   AND lot_id = 219
   AND to_date = DATE '9999-12-31';
```

This query returns the following result, stating that all the cattle in the lot are currently in a single pen.

```
Results
pen_id hd_cnt
==============
   2   43
```

The sequenced variant is, "Give the history of how many head of cattle from lot 219 in yard 1 were in each pen." This is also easy to express in SQL. For selection and projection (which is what this query involves), converting to a sequenced query involves merely appending the timestamp columns to the target list of the select statement.

```
SELECT pen_id, hd_cnt, from_date, to_date
  FROM LotLocations
 WHERE feedyard_id = 1
   AND lot_id = 219;
```

The result provides the requested history. We see that lot 219 moved around a bit.

```
Results
pen_id hd_cnt from_date    to_date
=======================================
   1      43  '1998-02-25' '1998-03-01'
   1      20  '1998-03-01' '1998-03-14'
   2      23  '1998-03-01' '1998-03-14'
   2      43  '1998-03-14' '9999-12-31'
```

The nonsequenced variant is "How many head of cattle from lot 219 in yard 1 were, at some time, in each pen?" Here we do not care when the data was valid. Note that the query does not ask for totals; it is interested in whenever a portion of the requested lot was in a pen. The query is simple to express in SQL, as the timestamp columns are simply ignored.

```
SELECT pen_id, hd_cnt
 FROM LotLocations
 WHERE feedyard_id = 1
 AND lot_id = 219;

Results
pen_id hd_cnt
=============
   1   43
   1   20
   2   23
   2   43
```

Nonsequenced queries are often awkward to express in English, but can sometimes be useful.

4.4.4 Temporal Joins

Temporal joins are considerably more involved. Consider the nontemporal query, "Which lots are coresident in a pen?" Such a query could be a first step in determining exposure to putative risks. Indeed, the entire epidemiologic investigation revolves around such queries.

Again, we start by expressing the query on a hypothetical snapshot table, LotLocationSnapshot, as follows. The query involves a self-join on the table, along with projection and selection. The first predicate ensures we do not get identical pairs; the second and third predicates test for coresidency.

```
SELECT L1.lot_id, L2.lot_id, L1.pen_id
  FROM LotLocationSnapshot AS L1,
       LotLocationSnapshot AS L2
 WHERE L1.lot_id< L2.lot_id
   AND L1.feedyard_id = L2.feedyard_id
   AND L1.pen_id = L2.pen_id;
```

The current version of this query on the temporal table is constructed by adding a currency predicate (a to_date of forever) for each correlation name in the FROM clause.

```
SELECT L1.lot_id, L2.lot_id, L1.pen_id
 FROM LotLocations AS L1,
      LotLocations AS L2
 WHERE L1.lot_id< L2.lot_id
  AND L1.feedyard_id = L2.feedyard_id
  AND L1.pen_id = L2.pen_id
  AND L1.to_date = DATE '9999-12-31'
  AND L2.to_date = DATE '9999-12-31';
```

This query will return an empty table on the above data, as none of the lots are currently coresident (lots 219 and 374 are currently in the feed yard, but in different pens).

The nonsequenced variant is "Which lots were in the same pen, perhaps at different times?" As before, nonsequenced joins are easy to specify by ignoring the timestamp columns.

```
SELECT L1.lot_id, L2.lot_id, L1.pen_id
  FROM LotLocations AS L1,
       LotLocations AS L2
 WHERE L1.lot_id< L2.lot_id
   AND L1.feedyard_id = L2.feedyard_id
   AND L1.pen_id = L2.pen_id;
```

The result is the following: all three lots had once been in pen 1.

```
L1    L2  pen_id
================
137   219  1
137   219  1
137   374  1
219   374  1
219   374  1
```

Note, however, that at no time were any cattle from lot 137 coresident with either of the other two lots. To determine coresidency, the sequenced variant is used: "Give the history of lots being coresident in a pen." This requires the cattle to actually be in the pen together, at the same time. The result of this query on the above table is the following.

```
L1  L2  pen_id from_date    to_date
=======================================
219 374 1      '1998-02-25' '1998-03-01'
```

A sequenced join is somewhat challenging to express in SQL. We assume that the underlying table contains no (sequenced) duplicates; that is, a lot can be in a pen number at most once at any time.

The sequenced join query must do a case analysis of how the period of validity of each row L1 of LotLocations overlaps the period of validity of each row L2, also of LotLocations; there are four possible cases.

In the first case, the period associated with the L1 row is entirely contained in the period associated with the L2 row. Since we are interested in those times when both lots are in the same pen, we compute the intersection of the two periods, which in this case is the contained period, that is, the period from L1.from_date to L1.to_date. Below, we illustrate this case, with the right end emphasizing the half-open interval representation.

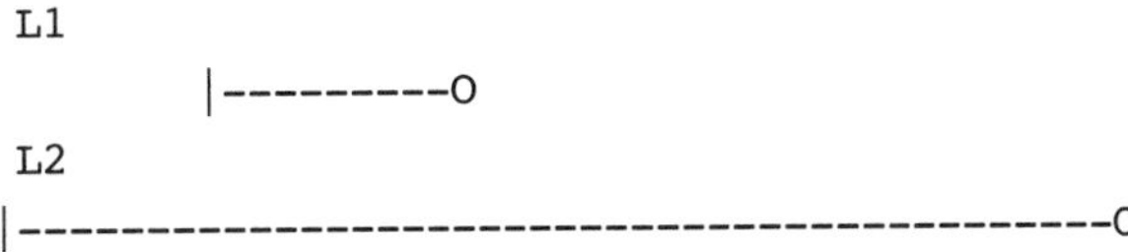

In the second case, neither period contains the other, and the desired period is the intersection of the two periods of validity.

The other cases similarly identify the overlap of the two periods. Each case is translated to a separate select statement, because the target list is different in each case.

```
SELECT L1.lot_id, L2.lot_id, L1.pen_id, L1.from_date, L1.to_date
  FROM LotLocations AS L1,
       LotLocations AS L2
```

```
 WHERE L1.lot_id< L2.lot_id
   AND L1.feedyard_id = L2.feedyard_id
   AND L1.pen_id = L2.pen_id
   AND L2.from_date <= L1.from_date
   AND L1.to_date <= L2.to_date
UNION
SELECT L1.lot_id, L2.lot_id, L1.pen_id, L1.from_date, L2.to_date
  FROM LotLocations AS L1,
       LotLocations AS L2
 WHERE L1.lot_id< L2.lot_id
   AND L1.feedyard_id = L2.feedyard_id
   AND L1.pen_id = L2.pen_id
   AND L1.from_date > L2.from_date
   AND L2.to_date < L1.to_date
   AND L1.from_date < L2.to_date
UNION
SELECT L1.lot_id, L2.lot_id, L1.pen_id, L2.from_date, L1.to_date
  FROM LotLocations AS L1, LotLocations AS L2
 WHERE L1.lot_id< L2.lot_id
   AND L1.feedyard_id = L2.feedyard_id
   AND L1.pen_id = L2.pen_id
   AND L2.from_date > L1.from_date
   AND L1.to_date < L2.to_date
   AND L2.from_date < L1.to_date
UNION
SELECT L1.lot_id, L2.lot_id, L1.pen_id, L2.from_date, L2.to_date
  FROM LotLocations AS L1, LotLocations AS L2
 WHERE L1.lot_id< L2.lot_id
   AND L1.feedyard_id = L2.feedyard_id
   AND L1.pen_id = L2.pen_id
   AND L2.from_date >= L1.from_date
   AND L2.to_date <= L1.to_date;
```

This query requires care to get the fourteen inequalities and the four select target lists correct. The cases where either the start times or the end times match are particularly vexing. The case where the two periods are identical (i.e., `L1.from_date = L2.from_date AND L1.to_date = L2.to_date`) is covered by two of the cases: the first and the last. This introduces an undesired duplicate. However, the `UNION` operator automatically removes duplicates, so the result is correct.

The downside of using UNION is that it does a lot of work to remove these infrequent duplicates generated during the evaluation of the join. We can replace UNION with UNION ALL, which retains duplicates and generally runs faster. If we do that, then we must also add the following to the predicate of the last case.

```
AND NOT (L1.from_date = L2.from_date
         AND L1.to_date = L2.to_date)
```

The result of this query contains two rows.

```
lot_idlot_idpen_id  from_date  to_date
================================================
219     374      1  '1998-02-25' '1998-03-01'
219     374      1  '1998-03-01' '1998-03-14'
```

This result contains no sequenced duplicates (at no time are there two rows with the same values for the columns without timestamps). Converting this result into the equivalent, but shorter, result shown following is a story unto itself.

```
lot_id lot_id pen_id  from_date   to_date
==============================================
219     374      1    '1998-02-25 '1998-03-14'
```

The Standard SQL CASE expression allows this query to be written as a single SELECT statement.

```
SELECT L1.lot_id, L2.lot_id, L1.pen_id,
       CASE WHEN L1.from_date > L2.from_date
            THEN L1.from_date
             ELSE L2.from_date END,
       CASE WHEN L1.to_date > L2.to_date
            THEN L2.to_date
            ELSE L1.to_date END
 FROM LotLocations AS L1,
      LotLocations AS L2
WHERE L1.lot_id< L2.lot_id
  AND L1.feedyard_id = L2.feedyard_id
  AND L1.pen_id = L2.pen_id
  AND (CASE WHEN L1.from_date > L2.from_date
```

```
            THEN L1.from_date
            ELSE L2.from_date END)
      < (CASE WHEN L1.to_date > L2.to_date
              THEN L2.to_date
              ELSE L1.to_date END);
```

The first CASE expression simulates a LastInstant function of two arguments, the second a FirstInstant function of the two arguments. The additional WHERE predicate ensures the period of validity is well formed, that its starting instant occurs before its ending instant. As this version is not based on UNION, it does not introduce extraneous duplicates.

```
SELECT L1.lot_id, L2.lot_id, L1.pen_id,
       GREATEST(L1.from_date, L2.from_date),
      LEAST(L1.to_date, L2.to_date)
  FROM LotLocations AS L1, LotLocations AS L2
 WHERE L1.lot_id< L2.lot_id
   AND L1.feedyard_id = L2.feedyard_id
   AND L1.pen_id = L2.pen_id
   AND GREATEST(L1.from_date, L2.from_date)
       < LEAST(L1.to_date, L2.to_date);
```

In summary, we have investigated current, nonsequenced, and sequenced variants of common types of queries. Current queries are easy: add a currency predicate for each correlation name in the FROM clause. Nonsequenced variants are also straightforward: just ignore the timestamp columns, or treat them as regular columns.

Sequenced queries, of the form "Give the history of . . ." arise frequently. For projections, selections, union, and order by, of which only the first two are exemplified here, the conversion is also easy: just append the timestamp columns to the target list of the select statement. Sequenced temporal joins, however, can be awkward unless a CASE construct or FirstInstant() type of function is available.

All the above approaches assume that the underlying table contains no sequenced duplicates. As a challenge, consider performing in SQL a temporal join on a table possibly containing such duplicates. The result should respect the duplicates of the input table. If that is too easy, try writing in SQL the sequenced query, "Give the history of the number of cattle in pen 1." This would return the following.

```
pen_id hd_cnt from_date    to_date
==========================================
   1     17  '1998-02-07' '1998-02-18'
   1     14  '1998-02-20' '1998-02-25'
   1     57  '1998-02-25' '1998-03-01'
   1     34  '1998-03-01' '1998-03-14'
   1     14  '1998-03-14' '9999-12-31'
```

4.4.5 Modifying Valid-Time State Tables

In the previous section we discussed tracking cattle as they moved from pen to pen in a feed yard. I initially hesitated in discussing this next topic due to its sensitive nature, especially for the animals concerned. But the epidemiological factors convinced me to proceed.

An Aside on Terminology

A *bull* is a male bovine animal (the term also denotes a male moose). A *cow* is a female bovine animal (or a female whale). A *calf* is the young of a cow (or a young elephant). A *heifer* is a cow that has not yet borne a calf (or a young female turtle). *Cattle* are collected bovine animals.

A *steer* is a castrated male of the cattle family. To steer an automobile or a committee is emphatically different from steering a calf. Cows and heifers are not steered, they are spayed or generically neutered, rendering them a *neutered cow*. There is no single term for neutered cow paralleling the term steer, perhaps because spaying is a more invasive surgical procedure than steering, or perhaps because those doing the naming are cowboys.

Bulls are steered to reduce injuries (bulls are quite aggressive animals) as well as to enhance meat quality. Basically, all that fighting reduces glycogen in the muscle fibers, which increases the water content of the meat, which results in less meat per pound—the water boils off during cooking. Heifers are spayed only if they will feed in open fields, because calving in the feed yard is expensive and dangerous to the cow.

Capturing the (time-varying) gender of a lot (a collection of cattle) is important in epidemiological studies, for the gender can affect disease transfer to and between cattle. Hence, Dr. Brad De Groot's feed yard database schema includes the valid-time state table Lots, an excerpt of which is shown in the following table (in this excerpt, we have omitted the feedyard_id, in_weight, owner, and several other columns not relevant to this discussion).

```
Lots
lot_id gender_code from_date     to_date
=============================================
   101    'c'        '1998-01-01' '1998-03-23'
   101    's'        '1998-03-23' '9999-12-31'
   234    'c'        '1998-02-17' '9999-12-31'
   799    's'        '1998-03-12' '9999-12-31'
```

The gender_code is an integer code. For expository purposes, we will use single letters: c = bull calf, h = heifer, and s = steer. The from_date and to_date in concert specify the time period over which the values of all the other columns of the row were valid. In this table, on March 23, 1998, a rather momentous event occurred for the cattle in lot 101: they were steered. Lot 234 consists of calves; a to_date of '9999-12-31' denotes a row that is currently valid. Lot 234 arrived in the feed yard on February 17; lot 799 arrived on March 12.

Brad collects data from the feed yard to populate his database. In doing so he makes a series of modifications to his tables, including the Lots table (modifications comprise insertions, deletions, and updates). We previously presented current, sequenced, and nonsequenced uniqueness constraints and queries. So you have probably already guessed that I'll be discussing here current, sequenced and nonsequenced modifications.

4.4.6 Current Modifications

Consider a new lot of heifers that arrives today. The current insertion would be coded in SQL as follows.

```
INSERT INTO Lots
VALUES (433, 'h', CURRENT_DATE, DATE '9999-12-31')
```

The statement provides a timestamp from "now" to the end of time.

The message from previous case studies is that it is best to initially ignore the timestamp columns, as they generally confound rather than illuminate. Consider lot 101 leaving the feed yard. Ignoring time, this would be expressed as a deletion.

```
DELETE FROM Lots
 WHERE lot_id = 101;
```

A logical current deletion on a valid-time state table is expressed in SQL as an update. Current deletions apply from "now" to "forever."

```
UPDATE Lots
   SET to_date = CURRENT_DATE
 WHERE lot_id = 101
   AND to_date = DATE '9999-12-31';
```

There are two scenarios to consider: the general scenario, where any modification is allowed to the valid-time state table, and the restricted scenario, where only current modifications are performed on the table. The scenarios differentiate the data upon which the modification is performed, and consider whether a noncurrent modification might have been performed in the past. Often we know *a priori* that only current modifications are possible, which tells us something about the data that we can exploit in the (current) modification being performed.

The above statement works only in the restricted scenario. Consider the excerpt of Lots shown in the following table, which is the general scenario. Assume today is July 29. The following table indicates that lot 234 is scheduled to be steered on October 17, though we do not tell that to the calves.

```
Lots
lot_id gender_code from_date    to_date
============================================
 101    'c'         '1998-01-01' '1998-03-23'
 101    's'         '1998-03-23' '9999-12-31'
 234    'c'         '1998-02-17' '1998-10-17'
 234    's'         '1998-10-17' '9999-12-31'
 799    'c'         '1998-03-12' '9999-12-31'
```

A logical current deletion of lot 234 (meaning that the lot left the feed yard today) in the general scenario is implemented as a physical update and a physical delete.

```
UPDATE Lots
  SET to_date = CURRENT_DATE
WHERE lot_id = 234
  AND to_date >= CURRENT_DATE
  AND from_date < CURRENT_DATE
```

```
DELETE FROM Lots
WHERE lot_id = 234
  AND from_date > CURRENT_DATE;
```

These two statements can be done in either order, as the rows they alter are disjoint.

Applying these operations to the original table, we get the following result. All information on lot 234 after today has been deleted.

```
Lots (current deletion)
lot_id gender_code  from_date     to_date
====================================================
101     'c'          '1998-01-01' '1998-03-23'
101     's'          '1998-03-23' '9999-12-31'
234     'c'          '1998-02-17' '1998-07-29'
799     'c'          '1998-03-12' '9999-12-31'
```

Consider steering the cattle in lot 799. On a nontemporal table, this would be stated as:

```
UPDATE Lots
   SET gender_code = 's'
 WHERE lot_id = 799;
```

A logical current update is implemented as a physical delete coupled with a physical insert. This modification on a valid-time state table in the restricted scenario is as follows:

```
INSERT INTO Lots
SELECT DISTINCT 799, 's', CURRENT_DATE, DATE '9999-12-31'
  FROM Lots
 WHERE EXISTS
      (SELECT *
         FROM Lots
         WHERE lot_id = 799
           AND to_date = DATE '9999-12-31');

UPDATE Lots
   SET to_date = CURRENT_DATE
 WHERE lot_id = 799
   AND gender_code <> 's'
   AND to_date = DATE '9999-12-31';
```

The update terminates current values at "now," and the insert adds the new values. The update must occur after the insertion. Alternatively, the portion up to now could be inserted, and the update could change the gender_code to 's' and the from_date to "now."

In the general scenario, a logical current update is more complicated, because there may exist rows that start in the future, as well as rows that end before "forever." For the former, only the gender_code need be changed. For the latter, the to_date must be retained on the inserted row.

The three cases are shown as follows. The period of validity of the row from the table being modified is shown, with time moving left to right and "now" indicated with an X.

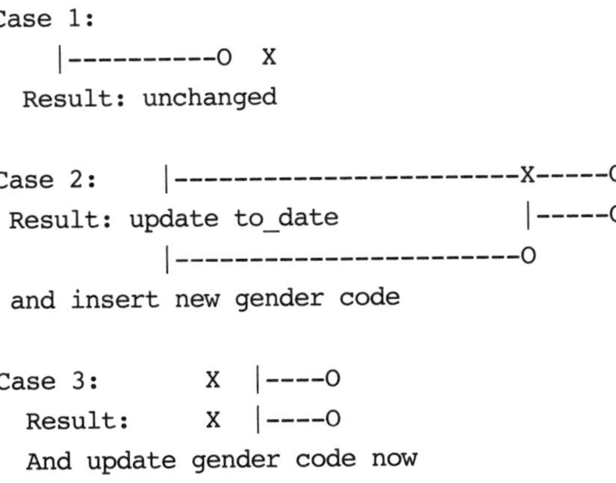

```
Case 1:
    |----------O  X
  Result: unchanged

Case 2:    |-----------------------X-----O
 Result: update to_date           |-----O
           |-----------------------O
 and insert new gender code

Case 3:        X  |----O
  Result:      X  |----O
  And update gender code now
```

In case 1, if a row's period of validity terminates in the past, then the (logical) update will not affect that row. Recall that the logical update applies from "now" to "forever."

In case 2, the row is currently valid. The portion before "now" must be terminated and a new row with an updated gender inserted, with the period of validity starting at "now" and terminating when the original row did.

In case 3, the row starts in the future so the row can be updated as usual. These machinations require two updates and an insertion.

```
INSERT INTO Lots
SELECT lot_id, 's', CURRENT_DATE, to_date
  FROM Lots
 WHERE lot_id = 799
   AND from_date <= CURRENT_DATE
```

```
   AND to_date > CURRENT_DATE;

UPDATE Lots
   SET to_date = CURRENT_DATE
 WHERE lot_id = 799
   AND gender_code <> 's'
   AND from_date < CURRENT_DATE
   AND to_date > CURRENT_DATE;

UPDATE Lots
   SET gender_code = 's'
 WHERE lot_id = 799
   AND from_date >= CURRENT_DATE;
```

The second update can appear anywhere, but the first update must occur after the insertion.

4.4.7 Sequenced Modifications

A current modification applies from "now" to "forever." A sequenced modification generalizes this to apply over a specified period, termed the period of applicability. This period could be in the past or the future, or it could overlap "now."

Most of the previous discussion applies to sequenced modifications, with `CURRENT_DATE` replaced with the start of the period of applicability of the modification, and `DATE '9999-12-31'` replaced with the end of the period of applicability.

In a sequenced insertion, the application provides the period of applicability. As an example, lot 426, a collection of heifers, was on the feed yard from March 26 to April 14.

```
INSERT INTO Lots
VALUES (426, 'h', DATE '1998-03-26', DATE '1998-04-14')
```

Recall that a current deletion in the general scenario is implemented as an update (for those currently valid rows) and a delete (for periods starting in the future). For a sequenced deletion, there are four cases. In each case, the period of validity (PV) of the original tuple is shown above the period of applicability (PA) for the deletion. In case 1, the original row covers the period of applicability, so both the initial and final periods need to be retained. The initial period is retained by setting the to_date to the beginning of the period of applicability; the final period is inserted. In case 2, only the initial portion of the period of validity of the original row is retained. Symmetrically, in case 3, only the final portion of the period need be retained. And in case 4, the entire row should be deleted, as the period of applicability covers it entirely.

```
Case 1:     |----------------------------O

      |---------------O

 Result:    |-------O |-----O


Case 2:     |-----------------------O

      |---------------------O
  Result:    |-------O


Case 3:      |---------------------O
      |-----------------------O
  Result:       |-----O


Case 4:      |---------------O
      |-----------------------------O

  Result: entire row deleted
```

A sequenced deletion requires four physical modifications. We wish to record that lot 234 will be absent from the feed yard for the first three weeks of October, when the steering will take place (as recorded in an earlier table). Hence, the period of applicability is `DATE '1998-10-01'` to `DATE '1998-10-22'` (we're using a to_date of the day after the period ends).

```
INSERT INTO Lots
SELECT lot_id, gender_code, DATE '1998-10-22', to_date
  FROM Lots
 WHERE lot_id = 234
   AND from_date <= DATE '1998-10-01'
   AND to_date > DATE '1998-10-22';
```

```
UPDATE Lots
   SET to_date = DATE '1998-10-01'
 WHERE lot_id = 234
   AND from_date < DATE '1998-10-01'
   AND to_date >= DATE '1998-10-01';

UPDATE Lots
   SET from_date = DATE '1998-10-22'
 WHERE lot_id = 234
   AND from_date < DATE '1998-10-22'
   AND to_date >= DATE '1998-10-22';

DELETE FROM Lots
 WHERE lot_id = 234
   AND from_date >= DATE '1998-10-01'
   AND to_date <= DATE '1998-10-22';
```

Case 1 is reflected in the first two statements; the second statement also covers case 2. The third statement handles case 3, and the fourth, case 4. All four statements must be evaluated in the order shown. They have been carefully designed to cover each case exactly once.

A sequenced update is the temporal analog of a nontemporal update, with a specified period of applicability. Let us again consider steering the cattle in lot 799.

```
UPDATE Lots
   SET gender_code = 's'
 WHERE lot_id = 799;
```

We now convert this to a sequenced update. As with sequenced deletions, there are more cases to consider for sequenced updates, as compared with current updates. The four cases shown below are handled differently in an update. In case 1, the initial and final portions of the period of validity are retained (via two insertions), and the affected portion is updated. In case 2, only the initial portion is retained; in case 3, only the final portion is retained. In case 4, the period of validity is retained, as it is covered by the period of applicability.

In summary, we need to:

1. Insert the old values from the from_date to the beginning of the period of applicability.

2. Insert the old values from the end of the period of applicability to the to_date.
3. Update the explicit columns of rows that overlap the period of applicability
4. Update the from_date to begin at the beginning of the period of applicability of rows that overlap the period of applicability.
5. Update the to_date to end at the end of the period of applicability of rows that overlap the period of applicability.

```
Case 1:      |----------------------------O

       |---------------O

  Old value retained:  |-------O  |-----O

  Updated portion:   |---------------O


Case 2:      |----------------------O

       |---------------------O

  Old value retained:  |-------O

  Updated portion:   |---------------O

Case 3:       |---------------------O

       |----------------------O

  Old value retained:  |-----O

  Updated portion:   |---------------O


Case 4:       |---------------O

       |-----------------------------O

  Result: entire row updated
```

The following is a sequenced update, recording that the lot was steered only for the month of March. (Something magical happened on April 1. The idea here is to show how to implement sequenced updates in general, and not just on cattle.) The period of applicability is thus DATE '1998-03-01' to DATE '1998-04-01'.

The first insert statement handles the initial portions of cases 1 and 2; the second handles the final portions of cases 2 and 3. The first update handles the update for all four cases. The second and third updates adjust the starting dates (for cases 1 and 2) and ending dates (for cases 1 and 3) of the updated portion. Note that the last three update statements will not impact the row(s) inserted by the two insert statements, as the period of validity of those rows lies outside the period of applicability. Again, all five statements must be evaluated in the order shown.

```
INSERT INTO Lots
SELECT lot_id, gender_code, from_date, DATE '1998-03-01'
  FROM Lots
 WHERE lot_id = 799
   AND from_date < DATE '1998-03-01'
   AND to_date > DATE '1998-03-01';

INSERT INTO Lots
SELECT lot_id, gender_code, DATE '1998-04-01', to_date
  FROM Lots
 WHERE lot_id = 799
   AND from_date < DATE '1998-04-01'
   AND to_date > DATE '1998-04-01';

UPDATE Lots
   SET gender_code = 's'
 WHERE lot_id = 799
   AND from_date < DATE '1998-04-01'
   AND to_date > DATE '1998-03-01';

UPDATE Lots
   SET from_date = DATE '1998-03-01'
 WHERE lot_id = 799
   AND from_date < DATE '1998-03-01'
   AND to_date > DATE '1998-03-01';

UPDATE Lots
```

```
  SET to_date = DATE '1998-04-01'
WHERE lot_id = 799
  AND from_date < DATE '1998-04-01'
 AND to_date > DATE '1998-04-01';
```

4.4.8 Nonsequenced Modifications

As with constraints and queries, a nonsequenced modification treats the timestamps identically to the other columns. Consider the modification, "Delete lot 234." The current variant is "Lot 234 has just left the feed yard." A sequenced variant, with a period of applicability, is "Lot 234 will be absent from the feed yard for the first three weeks of June." A nonsequenced deletion mentions the period of validity of the rows to be deleted (for example, "Delete the records of lot 234 that have duration greater than three months.").

```
DELETE FROM Lots
 WHERE lot_id = 234
   AND (to_date - from_date MONTH) > INTERVAL '3' MONTH;
```

The current and sequenced deletes mention what happened in reality, because they model changes. The nonsequenced statement concerns the specific representation (deleting particular records). Conversely, the associated SQL statements for the current and sequenced variants are much more complex than the statement for the nonsequenced delete, for the same reason: the latter is expressed in terms of the representation.

Most modifications will be first expressed as changes to the enterprise being modeled (some fact becomes true, or will be true sometime in the future; some aspect changes, now or in the future; some fact is no longer true). Such modifications are either current or sequenced modifications. Nonsequenced modifications, while generally easier to express in SQL, are rare.

For those who want a challenge, alter the above modification statements to ensure sequenced primary key and referential integrity constraints.

As a final comment, it might be surprising to know that a time-varying gender is relevant outside of cattle databases. I have been told that Pacific Bell's personnel database has a date field associated with gender; more than a dozen of its employees change their gender each month. Only in California . . .

4.4.9 Transaction-Time State Tables

Temporal data is data that varies over time. However, you might be surprised to know that some of the approaches outlined above are applicable even when the enterprise being modeled does *not* vary over time.

Consider astronomical data—specifically, that of stars. While stars coalesce out of galactic dust, heat up, and explode or die out when their fuel is spent, perhaps ending up as black holes, this progression is played out over hundred of millions, or even billions, of years. For all intents and purposes, the position, magnitude (brightness), and spectral type of a star are time-invariant over a comprehensible scale, such as a person's lifetime. This static nature has encouraged the compilation of star catalogues, such as the Smithsonian Astrophysical Observatory J2000 Catalog (http://tdc-www.harvard.edu/software/catalogs) containing almost 300,000 stars, or the Washington Double Star (WDS) Catalog (http://aries.usno.navy.mil/ad/wds/wds.htm), containing some 78,000 double and multiple star systems.

What is time-varying is our knowledge about these stars. For example, the WDS is based on some 451,000 individual observations, by a host of discoverers and observers over the last century. Data is continually being incorporated, to add newly discovered binary systems and to refine the data on known systems, some of which enjoy as many as 100 individual observations.

The challenge in assembling such a catalog lies in correlating the data and winnowing out inconsistent or spurious measurements. As such, it is desirable to capture with each change to the catalog the date that change was made, as well as additional information such as who made the change and the source of the new information. In this way, past versions of the catalog can be reconstructed, and the updates audited, to enable analysis of both the resulting catalog and of its evolution.

We previously considered valid-time state tables, which model time-varying behavior of an enterprise. We now examine transaction-time state tables, which record an evolving understanding of some static system.

A subtle but critical paradigm shift is at play here. A valid-time table models the fluid and continual movement of reality: cattle are transferred from pen to pen; a caterpillar becomes a chrysalis in its cocoon and will later emerge as a butterfly; salaries rise (and sometimes fall) in fits and sputters. A transaction-time table instead captures the succession of states of the stored representation of some (static) fact: a star was thought to have a particular spectral type but is later determined to have somewhat different spectral characteristics; the bond angle within a chemical structure is refined as new X-ray diffraction data becomes available; intermediate configurations within a nuclear transformation are corrected as accelerator data is analyzed.

These two characterizations of time-varying behavior, valid time and transaction time, are orthogonal. We will consider for the most part only transaction time here, bringing it together with valid time in one gloriously expressive structure only at the end.

We consider a subset of the WDS catalog. The WDS bible contains 21 columns; only a few will be used here.

```
_ra_ ra_ ra_ dec_   dec_   discoverer mag_
hour min sec degree minute            first
=============================================
 00  00  08  75     30     'A 1248'    10.5
 05  57  40  00     02     'BU 1190'    6.5
 04  13  20  50     32     'CHR 15'    15.5
 01  23  70 -09     55     'HJ 3433'   10.5
```

RA denotes "right ascension" and dec denotes "declination"; these first five columns place the star's position in the heavens. The discoverer is identified by a one-to-three letter code, along with a discoverer's number. This column provides the primary key for the table. The last column records the magnitude (brightness), or the first component of the dual or multiple star system.

As mentioned previously, this table is constantly updated with new binary stars and with corrections to existing stars. To track these changes, we define a new table, WDS_TT, with two additional columns, trans_start and trans_stop, yielding a transaction-time state table. We term this table an audit log, differentiating it from the original table, which has no timestamps. The trans_start column specifies when the row was inserted into the original table, or when the row was updated (the new contents of the row are recorded here). trans_stop specifies when the row was deleted from the original table or was updated (the old contents of the row are recorded here). Consider the following audit log for the WDS table. We show the timestamps as `DATE`s, but they often are of much finer granularity, such as `TIMESTAMP(6)`, to distinguish multiple transactions occurring in a day, or even within a single second.

```
WDS_TT
ra_  ra_ ra_ dec_   dec_   discoverer mag_  trans_    trans_
hour min sec degree minute            first start     stop
```

```
=================================================================
00  00  00  75   30  'A 1248'   12.0  '1989-03-12' '1992-11-15'
00  00  09  75   30  'A 1248'   12.0  '1992-11-15' '1994-05-18'
00  00  09  75   30  'A 1248'   10.5  '1994-05-18' '1995-07-23'
00  00  08  75   30  'A 1248'   10.5  '1995-07-23' '9999-12-31'
05  57  40  00   02  'BU 1190'   6.5  '1988-11-08' '9999-12-31'
04  13  20  50   32  'CHR 15'   15.5  '1990-02-09' '9999-12-31'
01  23  70 -09   55  'HJ 3433'  10.5  '1991-03-25' '9999-12-31'
02  33  10 -09   25  'LDS3402'  10.6  '1993-12-19' '1996-07-09'
```

A trans_stop time of "forever" ('9999-12-31') indicates that the row is currently in WDS. And as we saw above, WDS currently contains four rows, so four rows of WDS_TT have a trans_stop value of "forever." The binary star 'LDS3402' was inserted the end of 1993, then deleted in July 1996, when it was found to be in error. The binary star 'A 1248' was first inserted in 1989, and was subsequently modified in November 1992 (to correct its ra_sec position), May 1994 (to refine its magnitude), and July 1995 (to refine its position slightly). Note that these changes do not mean that the star is changing, rather that the prior measurements were in error, and have since been corrected. Rows with a past trans_stop date are (now) known to be incorrect.

4.4.10 Maintaining the Audit Log

The audit log can be maintained automatically using triggers defined on the original table. The advantage to doing so is that the applications that maintain the WDS table need not be altered at all when the audit log is defined. Instead, the audit log is maintained purely as a side effect of the modifications applied to the original table.

Using triggers has another advantage: it simplifies specifying the primary key of the audit log. In Chapter 1, we saw that it is challenging to define unique columns or a primary key for a valid-time state table. Not so for a transaction-time state table; all we need to do is append trans_start to the primary key of the original table. Hence, the primary key of WDS_TT is (discoverer, trans_start).

The triggers ensure that the audit log captures all the changes made to the original table. When a row is inserted into the original table, it is also inserted into the audit log, with trans_start initialized to "now" (`CURRENT_DATE`) and trans_stop initialized to "forever." To logically delete a row, the trans_stop of the row is changed to "now" in the audit log. An update is handled as a deletion followed by an insertion.

```
CREATE TRIGGER Insert_WDS
AFTER INSERT ON WDS
REFERENCING NEW AS N
FOR EACH ROW
INSERT INTO WDS_TT(ra_hour, ra_minute, ra_sec,
  dec_degree, dec_minute,
  Discoverer, mag_first,
  trans_start, trans_stop)
VALUES (N.ra_hour, N.ra_minute, N.ra_sec,
  N.dec_degree, N.dec_minute,
  N.discoverer, N.mag_first,
  CURRENT_DATE,
  DATE '9999-12-31');

CREATE TRIGGER Delete_WDS
AFTER DELETE ON WDS
REFERENCING OLD AS O
FOR EACH ROW
UPDATE WDS_TT
   SET stop_time = CURRENT_DATE
 WHERE WDS_TT.discoverer = O.discoverer
  AND WDS_TT.trans_stop = DATE '9999-12-31';

CREATE TRIGGER Update_P
AFTER UPDATE ON WDS
REFERENCING OLD AS O NEW AS N
FOR EACH ROW
BEGIN ATOMIC
  UPDATE WDS_TT
     SET trans_stop = CURRENT_DATE
   WHERE WDS_TT.discoverer = O.discoverer
     AND WDS_TT.trans_stop = DATE '9999-12-31';
  INSERT INTO WDS_TT(ra_hour, ra_minute, ra_sec,
        dec_degree, dec_minute, Discoverer, mag_first,
        trans_start, trans_stop)
  VALUES (N.ra_hour, N.ra_minute, N.ra_sec,
          N.dec_degree, N.dec_minute, N.discoverer, N.mag_first,
          CURRENT_DATE, DATE '9999-12-31');
END;
```

These triggers could be augmented to store other information in the audit log as well, such as CURRENT_USER.

Note that WDS_TT is monotonically increasing in size. The INSERT trigger adds a row to WDS_TT, the DELETE trigger just changes the value of the trans_stop column, and the UPDATE trigger does both, adding one row and updating another. No row is ever deleted from WDS_TT.

4.4.11 Querying the Audit Log

We discussed three variants of queries on valid-time state tables: current, sequenced, and nonsequenced. These variants also apply to transaction-time state tables. To determine the current state of the WDS table, we can either look directly to that table, or get the information from the audit log.

```
SELECT ra_hour, ra_min, ra_sec,
       dec_degree, dec_minute,
        discoverer, mag_first
  FROM WDS_TT
 WHERE trans_stop = DATE '9999-12-31';
```

The utility of an audit log becomes apparent when we wish to *roll back* the WDS table to its state as of a previous point in time. Say we wish to see the WDS table as it existed on April 1, 1994. This reconstruction is best expressed as a view:

```
CREATE VIEW WDS_April_1
AS
SELECT ra_hour, ra_min, ra_sec,
       dec_degree, dec_minute,
        discoverer, mag_first
  FROM WDS_TT
 WHERE trans_start <= DATE '1994-04-01'
   AND DATE '1994-04-01' < trans_stop;
```

The result of this is:

```
WDS_T as of 1994 April 1
ra_  ra_ ra_ dec_   dec_   discoverer mag_
hour min sec degree minute            first
```

```
===========================================
00  00  09  75   30   'A 1248'   12.0
05  57  40  00   02   'BU 1190'   6.5
04  13  20  50   32   'CHR 15'   15.5
01  23  70 -09   55   'HJ 3433'  10.5
02  33  10 -09   25   'LDS3402'  10.6
```

Note that 'LDS3402' is present here (the mistake had not yet been detected), and that 'A1248' has an incorrect magnitude and position (these errors also had not been corrected as of April 1, 1994). What we have done here is roll back time to April 1, 1994 to see what the WDS table looked like at that time. Queries on WDS_April_1 will return the same result as queries on WDS that were presented to the DBMS on that date. So, if we ask, which stars are of magnitude 11 or brighter, as currently known (brighter stars have smaller magnitudes), three double stars would be identified.

```
SELECT Discoverer
  FROM WDS
 WHERE mag_first <= 11.0;

discoverer
==========
'A 1248'
'BU 1190'
'HJ 3433'
```

Asking the same question, as best known on April 1, 1994, yields a different set of stars:

```
SELECT Discoverer
  FROM WDS_April_1
 WHERE mag_first <= 11.0;

discoverer
==========
'BU 1190'
'HJ 3433'
'LDS3402'
```

This is because 'A1248' was thought then (erroneously) to be of magnitude 12, and 'LDS3402' was thought then (also erroneously) to be a double star system, of magnitude 10.6.

Interestingly, the WDS_April_1 can also be defined as a table, instead of as a view. The reason is that no future modifications to the WDS table will alter the state of that table back in April, and so any future query of WDS_April_1, whether a view or a table, will return the same result, independently of when that query is specified. The decision to make WDS_April_1 a view or a table is entirely one of query efficiency versus disk space.

We emphasize that only past states can be so queried. Even though the trans_stop value is "forever" (chosen to make the queries discussed below easier to write), this must be interpreted as "now." We cannot unequivocally state what the WDS table will record in the future; all we know is what is recorded now in that table, and the (erroneous) values that were previously recorded in that table.

Sequenced and nonsequenced queries are also possible on transaction-time state tables. Consider the query, "When was it recorded that 'A1248' had a magnitude other than 10.5?" The first part, "when was it recorded" indicates that we are concerned with transaction time, and thus must use the WDS_TT table. It also implies that if a particular time is returned, the specified relationship should hold during that time. This indicates a sequenced query. In this case, the query is a simple selection and projection.

```
SELECT mag_first, trans_start, trans_stop
  FROM WDS_TT
 WHERE discoverer = 'A 1248'
   AND mag_first <> 10.5;
```

The query results in:

```
mag_   trans_       trans_
first  start         stop
================================
12.0  '1989-03-12' '1992-11-15'
12.0  '1992-11-15' '1994-05-18'
```

This result indicates that for a little more than five years, the magnitude of the first star in this double star system was recorded incorrectly in the database.

We can use all the tricks discussed previously to write sequenced queries on WDS_TT. The query "When was it recorded that a star had a magnitude equal to that of 'A1248'?" The first part again indicates a transaction-time sequenced query; the last part indicates a self-join. This can be expressed in Oracle as:

```
SELECT W1.discoverer,
       GREATEST(W1.trans_start, W2.trans_start),
       LEAST(W1.trans_stop, W2.trans_stop)
  FROM WDS_TT AS W1, WDS_TT AS W2
 WHERE W1.discoverer = 'A 1248'
   AND W2.discoverer <> W1.discoverer
   AND W1.mag_first = W2.mag_first
   AND GREATEST(W1.trans_start, W2.trans_start)
       < LEAST(W1.trans_stop, W2.trans_stop);
```

This results in:

```
discoverer trans_      trans_
           start       stop
=======================================
'HJ 3433'  '1994-05-18' '1995-07-23'
'HJ 3433'  '1995-07-23' '9999-12-31'
```

The results state that in May 1994 it was recorded that HJ3433 had the same magnitude as 'A1248', and this is still thought to be the case.

Nonsequenced queries on transaction-time tables are effective in identifying changes. "When was the ra_sec position of a double star corrected?" A correction is indicated by two rows that meet in transaction time, and that concern the same double star, but have different ra_sec values.

```
SELECT W1.discoverer,
       W1.ra_sec AS old_value, W2.ra_sec AS new_value,
         W1.trans_stop AS when_changed
  FROM WDS_TT AS W1, WDS_TT AS W2
 WHERE W1.discoverer = W2.discoverer
   AND W1.trans_stop = W2.trans_start
   AND W1.ra_sec <> W2.ra_sec;
```

The result indicates that the position of 'A1248' was changed twice, first from 0 to 9, and then to 8:

```
discoverer old_  new_  when_
           value value changed
======================================
'A 1248'  00     09    '1992-11-15'
'A 1248'  09     08    '1995-07-23'
```

4.4.12 Modifying the Audit Log

While queries on transaction-time tables can be current, sequenced, or nonsequenced, the same does *not* hold true for modifications. In fact, the audit log (WDS_TT) should be changed only as a side effect of modifications on the original table (WDS). In the terminology introduced on valid-time state table modifications, the only modifications possible on transaction-time state tables are current modifications affecting the currently stored state. The triggers defined above are very similar to the current modifications described for valid-time tables.

Sequenced and nonsequenced modifications can change the previous state of a valid-time table. But doing so to an audit log violates the semantics of that table. Say we manually insert today into WDS_TT a row with a trans_start value of '1994-04-01'. This implies that the WDS table on that date also contained that same row. But we cannot change the past—specifically, what bits were stored on the magnetic disk. For this reason, manual changes to an audit log should not be permitted; only the triggers should modify the audit log.

4.4.13 Bitemporal Tables

Because valid time and transaction time are orthogonal, it is possible for each to be present or absent independently. When both are supported simultaneously, the table is called a bitemporal table.

While stars are stationary to the eye, sophisticated astronomical instruments can sometimes detect slight motion of some stars. This movement is called "proper motion," to differentiate it from the apparent movement of the stars in the nighttime sky as the earth spins. Star catalogs thus list the star's position as of a particular "epoch," or point in time. The Washington Double Star catalog lists each star system's location as of January 1, 2000—the so-called J2000 epoch. It also indicates the proper motion in units of seconds of arc per 1000 years.

Some star systems are essentially stationary; 'BU733' is highly unusual in that it moves almost an arc second a year, both in ascension and in declination. Stars can sometimes also change magnitude.

We can capture this information in a bitemporal table, WDS_B. Here we show how this table might look:

discoverer	mag_first	trans_start	trans_stop	valid_from	valid_to
'A 1248'	12.0	'1989-03-12'	'1995-11-15'	'1922-05-14'	'9999-12-31'
'A 1248'	12.0	'1995-11-15'	'9999-12-31'	'1922-05-14'	'1994-10-16'
'A 1248'	10.5	'1995-11-15'	'9999-12-31'	'1994-10-16'	'9999-12-31'

This table has two transaction timestamps, and thus records transaction states (the period of time a fact was recorded in the database). The table also has two valid-time timestamps, and thus records valid-time states (the period of time when something was true in reality). While the transaction timestamps should generally be of a finer granularity (e.g., microseconds), the valid time is often much coarser (e.g., day).

Bitemporal tables are initially somewhat challenging to interpret, but such tables can express complex behavior quite naturally. The first photographic plate containing 'A1248' (presumably by discoverer A, R. G. Aitken, who was active in double star sittings for the first four decades of the 20th century) was taken on May 14, 1922. However, this information had to wait almost 70 years before being entered into the database, in March 1989. This row has a valid_to_date date of "forever," meaning that the magnitude was not expected to change. A subsequent plate was taken in October 1994, indicating a slightly brighter magnitude (perhaps the star was transitioning to a supernova), but this information was not entered into the database until November 1995.

This logical update was recorded in the bitemporal table by updating the trans_stop date for the first row to "now," and by inserting two more rows, one indicating that the magnitude of 12 was only for a period of years following June 1922, and indicating that a magnitude of 10.5 was valid after 1994. (Actually, we do not know exactly when the magnitude changed, only that it had changed by the time the October 1994 plate was taken. In other applications, the valid-time from and to dates are generally quite accurately known.)

Modifications to a bitemporal table can specify the valid time, no matter which varieties it is: current, sequenced, or nonsequenced.

However, the transaction time must always be taken from CURRENT_DATE, or better, CURRENT_TIMESTAMP, when the modification was being applied.

Queries can be current, sequenced, or nonsequenced, for both valid and transaction time, in any combination. As one example, consider "What was the history recorded as of January 1, 1994?" "History" implies sequenced in valid time; "recorded as" indicates a transaction timeslice.

```
CREATE VIEW WDS_VT_AS_OF_Jan_1
AS
SELECT discoverer, mag_first, valid_from, valid_to
  FROM WDS_B
 WHERE trans_start <= DATE '1994-01-01'
   AND DATE '1994-01-01' < trans_stop;
```

This returns a valid-time state view, in this case, just the first row of the above table. Valid-time queries can then be applied to this view. This effectively rolls back the database to the state stored on January 1, 1994; valid-time queries on this view will return exactly the same result as valid-time queries actually typed in on that date.

Now consider "List the corrections made on plates taken in the 1920s." "Corrections" implies nonsequenced in transaction time; "taken in the 1920s" indicates sequenced in valid time. This query can be expressed in Oracle as:

```
SELECT B1.discoverer, B1.trans_stop AS When_Changed,
       GREATEST(B1.valid_from_date, B2.valid_from_date) AS
valid_from_date,
       LEAST(B1.valid_to_date, B2.valid_to_date) AS
valid_to_date
  FROM WDS_B B1, WDS_B B2
 WHERE B1.discoverer = B2.discoverer
   AND B1.trans_stop = B2.trans_start
   AND GREATEST(B1.valid_from_date, B2.valid_from_date) < DATE
'1929-12-31'
   AND DATE '1920-01-01' < LEAST(B1.valid_to_date,
B2.valid_to_date)
   AND GREATEST(B1.valid_from_date, B2.valid_from_date)
       < LEAST(B1.valid_to_date, B2.valid_to_date);
```

This query searches for pairs of rows that meet in transaction time, that were valid in the 1920s, and that overlap in valid time. For the above data, one such change is identified.

```
discoverer when_changed valid_from  valid_to
==================================================
'A 1248'   '1995-11-15' '1922-05-14' '1994-10-16'
```

This result indicates that erroneous data concerning information during the period from 1922 to 1994 was corrected in the database in November 1995.

Bitemporal tables record the history of the modeled reality, as well as recording when that history was stored in the database, perhaps erroneously. They are highly useful when the application needs to know both when some fact was true *and* when that fact was known, i.e., when it was stored in the database.

4.4.14 Temporal Support in Standard SQL

SQL-86 and SQL-89 have no notion of time. SQL-92 added datetime and interval data types. The previous sections have shown that expressing integrity constraints, queries, and modifications on time-varying data in SQL is challenging. What is the source of this daunting complexity? While Standard SQL supports time-varying data through the `DATE`, `TIME`, and `TIMESTAMP` data types, the language really has no notion of a time-varying table. SQL also has no concept of current or sequenced constraints, queries, modifications, or views, or of the critical distinction between valid time (modeling the behavior of the enterprise in reality) and transaction time (capturing the evolution of the stored data). In the terminology introduced before, all that SQL supports is nonsequenced operations, which we saw were often the least useful.

Unfortunately, proposals for temporal table support in Standard SQL were not adopted. You have to use fairly complex code for temporal databases. The good news is that SQL code samples for all the case studies, in a variety of dialects, can be found at www.arizona.edu/people.rts/DBPD and other sites that Dr. Snodgrass maintains at www.arizona.edu.

Character Data Types in SQL

SQL-89 DEFINED A `CHARACTER(n)` or `CHAR(n)` data type, which represents a fixed-length string of (*n*) printable characters, where (*n*) is always greater than zero. Some implementations allow the string to contain control characters, but this is not the usual case. The allowable characters are usually drawn from ASCII or EBCDIC character sets and most often use those collation sequences for sorting.

SQL-92 added the `VARYING CHARACTER(n)` or `VARCHAR(n)`, which was already present in many implementations. A `VARCHAR(n)` represents a string that varies in length from 1 to (*n*) printable characters. This is important: SQL does not allow a string column of zero length, but you may find vendors whose products do allow it so that you can store an empty string.

SQL-92 also added `NATIONAL CHARACTER(n)` and `NATIONAL VARYING CHARACTER(n)` data types (or `NCHAR(n)` and `NVARCHAR(n)`, respectively), which are made up of printable characters drawn from ISO-defined Unicode character sets. The literal values use the syntax `N'<string>'` in these data types.

SQL-92 also allows the database administrator to define collation sequences and do other things with the character sets. A Consortium (www.unicode.org/) maintains the Unicode standards and makes them available in book form (*The Unicode Standard, Version 4.0*.

Reading, MA: Addison-Wesley. 2003. ISBN 0-321-18578-1) or on the Web site.

5.1 Problems with SQL Strings

Different programming languages handle strings differently. You simply have to do some unlearning when you get to SQL. Here are the major problem areas for programmers.

In SQL, character strings are printable characters enclosed in single quotation marks. Many older SQL implementations and several programming languages use double quotation marks or have an option that a single quotation mark can be used as an apostrophe. SQL uses two apostrophes together to represent a single apostrophe in a string literal.

Double quotation marks are reserved for column names that have embedded spaces or that are also SQL-reserved words.

Character sets fall into three categories: those defined by national or international standards, those provided by implementations, and those defined by applications. All character sets, however defined, contain the `<space>` character. Character sets defined by applications can be defined to reside in any schema chosen by the application. Character sets defined by standards or by implementations reside in the Information Schema (named `INFORMATION_SCHEMA`) in each catalog, as do collations defined by standards and collations and form-of-use conversions defined by implementations. There is a default collating sequence for each character repertoire, but additional collating sequences can be defined for any character repertoire.

5.1.1 Problems of String Equality

No two languages agree on how to compare character strings as equal unless they are identical in length and match exactly, position for position, character for character.

The first problem is whether uppercase and lowercase versions of a letter compare as equal to each other. Only Latin, Greek, Cyrillic, and Arabic have cases; the first three have upper and lower cases, while Arabic is a connected script that has initial, middle, terminal and stand-alone forms of its letters. Most programming languages, including SQL, ignore case in the program text, but not always in the data. Some SQL implementations allow the DBA to set uppercase and lowercase matching as a system configuration parameter.

Standard SQL has two functions that change the case of a string:

`LOWER(<string expression>)` shifts all letters in the parameter string to corresponding lowercase letters.

`UPPER(<string expression>)` shifts all letters in the string to uppercase.

Most implementations have had these functions (perhaps with different names) as vendor library functions.

Equality between strings of unequal length is calculated by first padding out the shorter string with blanks on the right-hand side until the strings are of the same length. Then they are matched, position for position, for identical values. If one position fails to match, the equality fails.

In contrast, the Xbase languages (FoxPro, dBase, and so on) truncate the longer string to the length of the shorter string and then match them position for position. Other programming languages ignore upper- and lowercase differences.

5.1.2 Problems of String Ordering

SQL-89 was silent on the collating sequence to be used. In practice, almost all SQL implementations use either ASCII or EBCDIC, which are both Roman I character sets in ISO terminology. A few implementations have a Dictionary or Library order option (uppercase and lowercase letters mixed together in alphabetic order: A, a, B, b, C, c, and so on) and many vendors offer a national-language option that is based on the appropriate ISO standard.

National language options can be very complicated. The Nordic languages all share a common ISO character set, but they do not sort the same letters in the same positions. German is sorted differently in Germany and in Austria. Spain only recently decided to quit sorting 'ch' and 'll' as if they were single characters. You need to look at the ISO Unicode implementation for your particular product.

Standard SQL allows the DBA to define a collating sequence for comparisons. The feature is becoming more common as we become more globalized, but you have to see what the vendor of your SQL product actually supports.

5.1.3 Problems of String Grouping

Because the equality test has to pad out the shorter of the two strings, you will often find doing a GROUP BY on a VARCHAR(n) has unpredictable results:

```
CREATE TABLE Foobar (x VARCHAR(5) NOT NULL);
INSERT INTO Foobar VALUES ('a'), ('a '), ('a   '), ('a ');
```

Now, execute the query:

```
SELECT x, CHAR_LENGTH(x)
  FROM Foobar
 GROUP BY x;
```

The value for CHAR_LENGTH(x) will vary for different products. The most common answers are 1, 4, or 5 in this example. A length of 1 is returned because it is the length of the shortest string or because it is the length of the first string physically in the table. A length of 4 is returned because it is the length of the longest string in the table, and a length of 5 because it is the greatest possible length of a string in the table.

You might want to add a constraint that makes sure to trim the trailing blanks to avoid problems.

5.2 Standard String Functions

SQL-92 defines a set of string functions that appear in most products, but with vendor-specific syntax. You will probably find that products will continue to support their own syntax, but will also add the Standard SQL syntax in new releases. String concatenation is shown with the || operator, taken from PL/I.

The SUBSTRING(<string> FROM <start> FOR <length>) function uses three arguments: the source string, the starting position of the substring, and the length of the substring to be extracted. Truncation occurs when the implied starting and ending positions are not both within the given string.

DB2 and other products have a LEFT and a RIGHT function. The LEFT function returns a string consisting of the specified number of leftmost characters of the string expression, and the RIGHT, well, that is kind of obvious.

The fold functions are a pair of functions for converting all the lowercase characters in a given string to uppercase, UPPER(<string>), or all the uppercase ones to lowercase, LOWER(<string>).

TRIM([[<trim specification>] [<trim character>] FROM] <trim source>) produces a result string that is the source string with an unwanted character removed. The <trim source> is the original character value expression. The <trim specification> is either LEADING or TRAILING or BOTH, and the <trim character> is the single character that is to be removed.

The TRIM() function removes the leading and/or trailing occurrences of a character from a string. The default character, if one is not given, is a space. The SQL-92 version is a very general function, but you will find that most SQL implementations have a version that works only with spaces. DB2 instead has two functions: LTRIM for leftmost (leading) blanks and RTRIM for rightmost (trailing) blanks.

A character translation is a function for changing each character of a given string according to some many-to-one or one-to-one mapping between two not necessarily distinct character sets. The syntax TRANSLATE(<string expression> USING <translation>) assumes that a special schema object, called a translation, has already been created to hold the rules for doing all of this.

CHAR_LENGTH(<string>), also written CHARACTER_LENGTH (<string>) determines the length of a given character string, as an integer, in characters. In most current products, this function is usually expressed as LENGTH(), and the next two functions do not exist at all; they assume that the database will only hold ASCII or EBCDIC characters.

BIT_LENGTH(<string>) determines the length of a given character string, as an integer, in bits.

OCTET_LENGTH(<string>) determines the length of a given character string, as an integer, in octets. Octets are units of eight bits that are used by the one and two (Unicode) octet characters sets. This function is the same as TRUNCATE (BIT_LENGTH (<string>)/8).

The POSITION(<search string> IN <source string>) determines the first position, if any, at which the <search string> occurs within the <source string>. If the <search string> is of length zero, then it occurs at position 1 for any value of the <source string>. If the <search string> does not occur in the <source string>, zero is returned. You will also see LOCATE() in DB2 and CHAR_INDEX() in SQL Server.

5.3 Common Vendor Extensions

The original SQL-89 standard did not define any functions for CHAR(n) data types. Standard SQL added the basic functions that have been common to implementations for years. However, there are other common or useful functions, and it is worth knowing how to implement them outside of SQL.

Many vendors also have functions that will format data for display by converting the internal format to a text string. A vendor whose SQL is tied to a 4GL is much more likely to have these extensions, simply because the 4GL can use them. The most common one converts a date and time to a national format.

These functions generally use either a COBOL-style PICTURE parameter or a globally set default format. Some of this conversion work is done with the CAST() function in Standard SQL, but since SQL does not have any output statements, such things will be vendor extensions for some time to come.

Vendor extensions are varied, but there are some that are worth mentioning. The names will be different in different products, but the functionality will be the same:

> SPACE(n) produces a string of (*n*) spaces.
>
> REPLICATE (<string expression>, n) produces a string of (*n*) repetitions of the <string expression>. DB2 calls this one REPEAT(), and you will see other local names for it.
>
> REPLACE (<target string>, <old string>, <new string>) replaces the occurrences of the <old string> with the <new string> in the <target string>.

As an aside, here is a nice trick to reduce several contiguous spaces in a string to a single space to format text:

```
UPDATE Foobar
   SET sentence
       = REPLACE(
          REPLACE(
           REPLACE(sentence, SPACE(1), '<>')
          '><', SPACE(0))
         '<>', SPACE(1));
```

`REVERSE(<string expression>)` reverses the order of the characters in a string to make it easier to search. This function is impossible to write with the standard string operators, because it requires either iteration or recursion.

`FLIP(<string expression>, <pivot>)` will locate the pivot character in the string, then concatenate all the letters to the left of the pivot onto the end of the string and finally erase the pivot character. This is used to change the order of names from military format to civilian format—for example, `FLIP('Smith, John', ',')` yields John Smith. This function can be written with the standard string functions, however.

`NUMTOWORDS(<numeric expression>)` will write out the numeric value as a set of English words to be used on checks or other documents that require both numeric and text versions of the same value.

5.3.1 Phonetic Matching

People's names are a problem for designers of databases. Names are variable-length, can have strange spellings, and are not unique. American names have a diversity of ethnic origins, which give us names pronounced the same way but spelled differently, and vice versa.

Aside from this diversity of names, errors in reading or hearing a name lead to mutations. Anyone who gets junk mail is aware of this. In addition to mail addressed to "Celko," I get mail addressed to "Selco," "Selko," and "Celco," which are phonetic errors. I also get some letters with typing errors, such as "Cellro," "Chelco," and "Chelko" in my mail stack. Such errors result in the mailing of multiple copies of the same item to the same address. To solve this problem, we need phonetic algorithms that can find similar-sounding names.

Soundex Functions

The Soundex family of algorithms is named after the original algorithm. A Soundex algorithm takes a person's name as input and produces a character string that identifies a set of names that are (roughly) phonetically alike.

SQL products often have a Soundex algorithm in their library functions. It is also possible to compute a Soundex in SQL, using string functions and the CASE expression in Standard SQL. Names that sound alike do not always have the same Soundex code. For example, "Lee"

and "Leigh" are pronounced alike, but have different Soundex codes because the silent 'g' in "Leigh" is given a code.

Names that sound alike but start with a different first letter will always have a different Soundex, such as "Carr" and "Karr" will be separate codes.

Finally, Soundex is based on English pronunciation, so European and Asian names may not encode correctly. French surnames like "Beaux" (with a silent 'x') and "Beau" (without it) will result in two different Soundex codes.

Sometimes names that don't sound alike have the same Soundex code. The relatively common names "Powers," "Pierce," "Price," "Perez," and "Park" all have the same Soundex code. Yet "Power," a common way to spell Powers 100 years ago, has a different Soundex code.

The Original Soundex

Margaret O'Dell and Robert C. Russell patented the original Soundex algorithm in 1918. The method is based on the phonetic classification of sounds by how they are made. In case you wanted to know, the six groups are bilabial, labiodental, dental, alveolar, velar, and glottal.

The algorithm is fairly straightforward to code and requires no backtracking or multiple passes over the input word. This should not be too surprising, since it was in use before computers and had to be done by hand by clerks. Here is the algorithm:

1. Capitalize all letters in the word. Pad the word with rightmost blanks as needed during each procedure step.
2. Retain the first letter of the word.
3. Drop all occurrences of the following letters after the first position: A, E, H, I, O, U, W, Y.
4. Change letters from the following sets into the corresponding digits given:

```
1 = B, F, P, V
2 = C, G, J, K, Q, S, X, Z
3 = D, T
4 = L
5 = M, N
6 = R
```

5. Retain only one occurrence of consecutive duplicate digits from the string that resulted after step 4.0.
6. Pad the string that resulted from step 5.0 with trailing zeros and return only the first four positions, which will be of the form `<uppercase letter> <digit> <digit> <digit>`.

An alternative version of the algorithm, due to Russell, changes the letters in step 3.0 to 9s and retains them. Then step 5.0 is replaced by two steps: 5.1, which removes redundant duplicates as before, followed by 5.2, which removes all 9s and closes up the spaces. This allows pairs of duplicate digits to appear in the result string. This version has more granularity and will work better for a larger sample of names.

The problem with Soundex is that it was a manual operation used by the Census Bureau long before computers. The algorithm used was not always applied uniformly from place to place. Surname prefixes, such as "La," "De," "von," or "van," are generally dropped from the last name for Soundex, but not always.

If you are searching for surnames such as "DiCaprio" or "LaBianca," you should try the Soundex codes for both with and without the prefix. Likewise, leading syllables like "Mc," "Mac," and "O" were also dropped.

Then there was a question about dropping H and W along with the vowels. The United States Census Soundex did it both ways, so a name like "Ashcraft" could be converted to "Ascrft" in the first pass, and finally Soundexed to "A261," as it is in the 1920 New York Census. The Soundex code for the 1880, 1900, and 1910 censuses followed both rules. In this case, Ashcraft would be "A226" in some places. The reliability of Soundex is 95.99%, with a selectivity factor of 0.213% for a name inquiry.

Metaphone

Metaphone is another improved Soundex that first appeared in *Computer Language* magazine (Philips 1990). A Pascal version written by Terry Smithwick (Smithwick 1991), based on the original C version by Lawrence Philips, is reproduced with permission here:

```
FUNCTION Metaphone (p : STRING) : STRING;
CONST
VowelSet = ['A', 'E', 'I', 'O', 'U'];
FrontVSet = ['E', 'I', 'Y'];
VarSonSet = ['C', 'S', 'T', 'G'];
```

```
  { variable sound - modified by following 'h' }
FUNCTION SubStr (A : STRING;
 Start, Len : INTEGER) : STRING;
BEGIN
SubStr := Copy (A, Start, Len);
END;
FUNCTION Metaphone (p : STRING) : STRING;
VAR
  i, l, n: BYTE;
  silent, new: BOOLEAN;
  last, this, next, nnext : CHAR;
  m, d: STRING;
BEGIN { Metaphone }
IF (p = '')
THEN BEGIN
  Metaphone := '';
  EXIT;
  END;
{ Remove leading spaces }
FOR i := 1 TO Length (p)
DO p[i] := UpCase (p[i]);
{ Assume all alphas }
{ initial preparation of string }
d := SubStr (p, 1, 2);
IF d IN ('KN', 'GN', 'PN', 'AE', 'WR')
THEN p := SubStr (p, 2, Length (p) - 1);
IF (p[1] = 'X')
THEN p := 'S' + SubStr (p, 2, Length (p) - 1);
IF (d = 'WH')
THEN p := 'W' + SubStr (p, 2, Length (p) - 1);
{ Set up for Case statement }
l := Length (p);
m := '';
      { Initialize the main variable }
new := TRUE;
     { this variable only used next 10 lines!!! }
n := 1;
     { Position counter }
WHILE ((Length (m) < 6) AND (n <> l) )
DO BEGIN { Set up the 'pointers' for this loop-around }
  IF (n > 1)
```

```
THEN last := p[n-1]
ELSE last := #0;
{ use a nul terminated string }
this := p[n];
IF (n < l)
THEN next := p[n+1]
ELSE next := #0;
IF ((n+1) < l)
THEN nnext := p[n+2]
ELSE nnext := #0;
new := (this = 'C') AND (n > 1) AND (last = 'C');
{ 'CC' inside word }
IF (new)
THEN BEGIN
  IF ((this IN VowelSet) AND (n = 1) )
  THEN m := this;
CASE this OF
'B' : IF NOT ((n = l) AND (last = 'M') )
  THEN m := m + 'B';
{ -mb is silent }
'C' : BEGIN     { -sce, i, y = silent }
  IF NOT ((last = 'S') AND (next IN FrontVSet) )
  THEN BEGIN
    IF (next = 'i') AND (nnext = 'A')
    THEN m := m + 'X'{ -cia- }
    ELSE IF (next IN FrontVSet)
      THEN m := m + 'S' { -ce, i, y = 'S' }
      ELSE IF (next = 'H') AND (last = 'S')
        THEN m := m + 'K' { -sch- = 'K' }
        ELSE IF (next = 'H')
          THEN IF (n = 1) AND ((n+2) <= l)
            AND NOT (nnext IN VowelSet)
            THEN m := m + 'K'
            ELSE m := m + 'X';
    END { Else silent }
  END;
{ Case C }
'D' : IF (next = 'G') AND (nnext IN FrontVSet)
    THEN m := m + 'J'
    ELSE m := m + 'T';
'G' : BEGIN
```

```
  silent := (next = 'H') AND (nnext IN VowelSet);

  IF  (n > 1) AND (((n+1) = 1) OR ((next = 'n') AND
    (nnext = 'E') AND (p[n+3] = 'D') AND ((n+3) = 1) )
{ Terminal -gned }
  AND (last = 'i') AND (next = 'n') )
  THEN silent := TRUE;
 { if not start and near -end or -gned.) }
  IF (n > 1) AND (last = 'D'gnuw) AND (next IN FrontVSet)
  THEN { -dge, i, y }
  silent := TRUE;
  IF NOT silent
  THEN IF (next IN FrontVSet)
    THEN m := m + 'J'
    ELSE m := m + 'K';
  END;
'H' : IF NOT ((n = 1) OR (last IN VarSonSet) ) AND (next IN
VowelSet)
    THEN m := m + 'H';
  { else silent (vowel follows) }
'F', 'J', 'L', 'M', 'N', 'R' : m := m + this;
'K' : IF (last <> 'C')
    THEN m := m + 'K';
'P' : IF (next = 'H')
    THEN BEGIN
      m := m + 'F';
      INC (n);

      END  { Skip the 'H' }
    ELSE m := m + 'P';
'Q' : m := m + 'K';
'S' : IF (next = 'H')
    OR ((n > 1) AND (next = 'i') AND (nnext IN ['O', 'A']) )
  THEN m := m + 'X'
  ELSE m := m + 'S';
'T' : IF (n = 1) AND (next = 'H') AND (nnext = 'O')
  THEN m := m + 'T' { Initial Tho- }
  ELSE IF (n > 1) AND (next = 'i') AND (nnext IN ['O', 'A'])
    THEN m := m + 'X'
    ELSE IF (next = 'H')
      THEN m := m + '0'
```

```
     ELSE IF NOT ((next = 'C') AND (nnext = 'H') )
       THEN  m := m + 'T';
 { -tch = silent }
'V' : m := m + 'F';
'W', 'Y' : IF (next IN VowelSet)
    THEN m := m + this;
  { else silent }
'X' : m := m + 'KS';
'Z' : m := m + 'S';
END;
 { Case }
INC (n);
END; { While }
END; { Metaphone }
Metaphone := m
END;
```

NYSIIS Algorithm

The New York State Identification and Intelligence System, or NYSIIS, algorithm is more reliable and selective than Soundex, especially for grouped phonetic sounds. It does not perform well with Y groups, because Y is not translated. NYSIIS yields an alphabetic string key that is filled or rounded to 10 characters.

```
(1) Translate first characters of name:
   MAC => MCC
   KN  => NN
   K => C
   PH  => FF
   PF  => FF
   SCH => SSS
(2) Translate last characters of name:
   EE  => Y
   IE  => Y
   DT,RT,RD,NT,ND => D
(3) The first character of key = first character of name.
(4) Translate remaining characters by following rules,
 scanning one character at a time
   a.  EV => AF else A,E,I,O,U => A
   b.  Q => G   Z => S   M => N
   c.  KN => N  else K => C
```

```
   d.  SCH => SSS  PH => FF
   e.  H => If previous or next character is a consonant use the
previous character.
   f.  W => If previous character is a vowel, use the previous
character.
   Add the current character to result if the current character
is to equal to the last key character.
(5) If last character is S, remove it
(6) If last characters are AY, replace them with Y
(7) If last character is A, remove it
```

The stated reliability of NYSIIS is 98.72%, with a selectivity factor of .164% for a name inquiry. This was taken from Robert L. Taft, "Name Search Techniques," New York State Identification and Intelligence System.

5.4 Cutter Tables

Another encoding scheme for names has been used for libraries for more than 100 years. The catalog number of a book often needs to reduce an author's name to a simple fixed-length code. While the results of a Cutter table look much like those of a Soundex, their goal is different. They attempt to preserve the original alphabetical order of the names in the encodings.

But the librarian cannot just attach the author's name to the classification code. Names are not the same length, nor are they unique within their first letters. For example, "Smith, John A." and "Smith, John B." are not unique until the last letter.

What librarians have done about this problem is to use Cutter tables. These tables map authors' full names into letter-and-digit codes. There are several versions of the Cutter tables. The older tables tended to use a mix of letters (both upper- and lowercase) followed by digits. The three-figure version uses a single letter followed by three digits. For example, using that table:

```
"Adams, J" becomes "A214"
"Adams, M" becomes "A215"
"Arnold" becomes "A752"
"Dana" becomes "D168"
"Sherman" becomes "S553"
"Scanlon" becomes "S283"
```

The distribution of these numbers is based on the actual distribution of names of authors in English-speaking countries. You simply scan down the table until you find the place where your name would fall and use that code.

Cutter tables have two important properties. The first is that they preserve the alphabetical ordering of the original name list, which means that you can do a rough sort on them. The second is that each grouping tends to be of approximately the same size as the set of names gets larger. These properties can be handy for building indexes in a database.

If you would like copies of the Cutter tables, you can find some of them on the Internet. Princeton University Library has posted its rules for names, locations, regions, and other things on its Web site, http://infoshare1.princeton.edu/katmandu/class/cutter.html.

You can also get hard copies from this publisher.

Hargrave House

7312 Firethorn

Littleton, CO 80125

Web site = www.cuttertables.com

NULLs: Missing Data in SQL

A DISCUSSION OF HOW missing data should be handled enters a sensitive area in relational database circles. Dr. E. F. Codd, creator of the relational model, favored two types of missing-value tokens in his book on the second version of the relational model: one for "unknown" (the eye color of a man wearing sunglasses) and one for "not applicable" (the eye color of an automobile). Chris Date, leading author on relational databases, advocates not using any general-purpose tokens for missing values at all. Standard SQL uses one token, based on Dr. Codd's original relational model.

Perhaps Dr. Codd was right—again. In Standard SQL, adding `ROLLUP` and `CUBE` created a need for a function to test `NULL`s to see if they were in fact "real `NULL`s" (i.e., present in the data and therefore assumed to model a missing value) or "created `NULL`s" (i.e., created as place holders for summary rows in the result set).

In their book *A Guide to Sybase and SQL Server*, David McGoveran and C. J. Date said: "It is this writer's opinion than `NULL`s, at least as currently defined and implemented in SQL, are far more trouble than they are worth and should be avoided; they display very strange and inconsistent behavior and can be a rich source of error and confusion. (Please note that these comments and criticisms apply to any system that supports SQL-style `NULL`s, not just to SQL Server specifically.)"

SQL takes the middle ground and has a single general-purpose `NULL` for missing values. Rules for `NULL`s in particular statements appear in the appropriate sections of this book. This section will discuss `NULL`s and missing values in general.

People have trouble with things that are not there. There is no concept of zero in Roman numerals and in other traditional numeral systems. It was centuries before Hindu-Arabic numerals became popular in Europe. In fact, many early Renaissance accounting firms advertised that they did not use the fancy, newfangled notation and kept records in well-understood Roman numerals instead.

Many of the conceptual problems with zero arose from not knowing the difference between ordinal and cardinal numbers. Ordinal numbers measure position; cardinal numbers measure quantity or magnitude. The argument against the zero was this: if there is no quantity or magnitude there, how can you count or measure it? What does it mean to multiply or divide a number by zero? There was considerable linguistic confusion over words that deal with the lack of something.

As the Greek paradox says:

1. No cat has 12 tails.
2. A cat has one more tail than no cat.
3. Therefore, a cat has 13 tails.

Likewise, it was a long time before the idea of an empty set found its way into mathematics. The argument was that if there are no elements, how could you have a set of them? Is the empty set a subset of itself? Is the empty set a subset of all other sets? Is there only one universal empty set or one empty set for each type of set?

Computer science now has its own problem with missing data. The Interim Report 75-02-08 to the ANSI X3 (SPARC Study Group 1975) identified 14 different kinds of incomplete data that could appear as the result of queries or as attribute values. These types included overflows, underflows, errors, and other problems in trying to represent the real world within the limits of a computer.

Instead of discussing the theory for the different models and approaches to missing data, I would rather explain why and how to use `NULL`s in SQL. In the rest of this book, I will be urging you not to use them, which may seem contradictory, but it is not. Think of a `NULL` as a drug; use it properly and it works for you, but abuse it and it can ruin everything. Your best policy is to avoid NULLs when you can and use them properly when you have to.

6.1 Empty and Missing Tables

An empty table or view is a different concept from a missing table. An empty table is one that is defined with columns and constraints, but that has zero rows in it. This can happen when a table or view is created for the first time, or when all the rows are deleted from the table. It is a perfectly good table. By definition, all of its constraints are TRUE.

A missing table has been removed from the database schema with a DROP TABLE statement, or it never existed at all (you probably typed the name wrong). A missing view is a bit different. It, too, can be absent because of a DROP VIEW statement or a typing error. But it can also be absent because a table or view from which it was built has been removed. This means that the view cannot be constructed at runtime, and the database reports a failure. If you used CASCADE behavior when you dropped a table, the view would also be gone; but we'll explore that later.

The behavior of an empty TABLE or VIEW will vary with the way it is used. The reader should look at sections of this book that deal with predicates that use a subquery. In general, an empty table can be treated either as a NULL or as an empty set, depending on context.

6.2 Missing Values in Columns

The usual description of NULLs is that they represent currently unknown values that may be replaced later with real values when we know something. Actually, the NULL covers a lot of territory, since it is the only way of showing any missing values. Going back to basics for a moment, we can define a row in a database as an entity, which has one or more attributes (columns), each of which is drawn from some domain. Let us use the notation E(A) = V to represent the idea that an entity, E, has an attribute, A, which has a value, V. For example, I could write "John(hair) = black" to say that John has black hair.

SQL's general-purpose NULLs do not quite fit this model. If you have defined a domain for hair color and one for car color, then a hair color should not be comparable to a car color, because they are drawn from two different domains. You would need to make their domains comparable with an implicit or explicit casting function. This is now being done in Standard SQL, which has a CREATE DOMAIN statement, but most implementations do not have this feature yet. Trying to find out which employees drive cars that match their hair is a bit weird outside of

Los Angeles, but in the case of NULLs, do we have a hit when a bald-headed man walks to work? Are no hair and no car somehow equal in color? In SQL, we would get an UNKNOWN result, rather than an error, if we compared these two NULLs directly. The domain-specific NULLs are conceptually different from the general NULL, because we know what kind of thing is UNKNOWN. This could be shown in our notation as E(A) = NULL to mean that we know the entity, and we know the attribute, but we do not know the value.

Another flavor of NULL is "Not Applicable" (shown as N/A on forms and spreadsheets and called "I-marks" by Dr. E. F. Codd in his second version of the Relational Model), which we have been using on paper forms and in some spreadsheets for years. For example, a bald man's hair-color attribute is a missing-value NULL drawn from the hair-color domain, but his feather-color attribute is a Not Applicable NULL. The attribute itself is missing, not just the value. This missing-attribute NULL could be written as E(NULL) = NULL in the formula notation.

How could an attribute not belonging to an entity show up in a table? Consolidate medical records and put everyone together for statistical purposes. You should not find any male pregnancies in the result table. The programmer has a choice as to how to handle pregnancies. He can have a column in the consolidated table for "number of pregnancies," put a zero or a NULL in the rows where sex = 'male', and then add some CHECK() clauses to make sure that this integrity rule is enforced.

The other way is to have a column for "medical condition" and one for "number of occurrences" beside it. Another CHECK() clause would make sure male pregnancies do not appear. But what happens when the sex is unknown and all we have is a name like 'Alex Morgan', which could belong to either gender? Can we use the presence of one or more pregnancies to determine that Alex is a woman? What if Alex is a woman who has never borne children? The case where we have NULL(A) = V is a bit strange. It means that we do not know the entity, but we are looking for a known attribute, A, which has a value of V. This is like asking "What things are colored red?"—a perfectly good question, but one that is very hard to ask in an SQL database.

If you want to try writing such a query in SQL, you have to get to the system tables to get the table and column names, then JOIN them to the rows in the tables and come back with the PRIMARY KEY of that row.

For completeness, we could play with all eight possible combinations of known and unknown values in the basic E(A) = V formula. But such combinations are of little use or meaning. For example, NULL(NULL) = V would mean that we know a value, but not the entity or the attribute.

This is like the running joke from *The Hitchhiker's Guide to the Galaxy* (Adams 1979), in which the answer to the question, "What is the meaning of life, the universe, and everything" is 42. Likewise, "total ignorance NULL, shown as NULL(NULL) = NULL, means that we have no information about the entity, even about its existence, its attributes, or their values."

6.3 Context and Missing Values

Create a domain called Tricolor that is limited to the values 'Red', 'White', and 'Blue', and a column in a table drawn from that domain with UNIQUE constraint on it. If my table has a 'Red' and two NULL values in that column, I have some information about the two NULLs. I know they will be either ('White', 'Blue') or ('Blue', 'White') when their rows are resolved. This is what Chris Date calls a "distinguished NULL," which means we have some information in it.

If my table has a 'Red', a 'White', and a NULL value in that column, can I change the last NULL to 'Blue' because it can only be 'Blue' under the rule? Or do I have to wait until I see an actual value for that row? There is no clear way to handle this in SQL. Multiple values cannot be put in a column, nor can the database automatically change values as part of the column declaration.

This idea can be carried farther with marked NULL values. For example, we are given a table of hotel rooms that has columns for check-in date and checkout date. We know the check-in date for each visitor, but we do not know his or her checkout dates. Instead, we know relationships among the NULLs. We can put them into groups—Mr. and Mrs. X will check out on the same day, members of tour group Y will check out on the same day, and so forth. We can also add conditions on them: nobody checks out before his check-in date, tour group Y will leave after January 7, 2005, and so forth. Such rules can be put into SQL database schemas, but it is very hard to do. The usual method is to use procedural code in a host language to handle such things.

David McGoveran has proposed that each column that can have missing data should be paired with a column that encodes the reason for the absence of a value (McGoveran 1993, 1994 January, February, March). The cost is a bit of extra logic, but the extra column makes it easy to write queries that include or exclude values based on the semantics of the situation.

Finally, you might want to look at solutions statisticians have used for missing data. In many kinds of computations, the missing values

are replaced by an average, median or other value constructed from the data set.

6.4 Comparing NULLs

A NULL cannot be compared to another NULL (equal, not equal, less than, greater than, and so forth). This is where we get SQL's three-valued logic instead of two-valued logic. Most programmers do not easily think in three values. But think about it for a minute. Imagine that you are looking at brown paper bags and are asked to compare them without seeing inside of either of them. What can you say about the predicate "Bag A has more tuna fish than Bag B."—is it **TRUE** or **FALSE**? You cannot say one way or the other, so you use a third logical value, **UNKNOWN**.

If I execute `SELECT * FROM SomeTable WHERE SomeColumn = 2;` and then execute `SELECT * FROM SomeTable WHERE SomeColumn <> 2;`, I expect to see all the rows of SomeTable between these two queries. However, I also need to execute `SELECT * FROM SomeTable WHERE SomeColumn IS NULL;` to do that. The `IS [NOT] NULL` predicate will return only TRUE or FALSE.

6.5 NULLs and Logic

George Boole developed two-valued logic and attached his name to Boolean algebra forever (Boole 1854). This is not the only possible system, but it is the one that works best with a binary (two-state) computer and with a lot of mathematics. SQL has three-valued logic: TRUE, FALSE, and UNKNOWN. The UNKNOWN value results from using NULLs in comparisons and other predicates, but UNKNOWN is a logical value and not the same as a NULL, which is a data value marker. That is why you have to say `(x IS [NOT] NULL)` in SQL and not use `(x = NULL)` instead. Table 6.1 shows the tables for the three operators that come with SQL.

Table 6.1 *SQL's Three Operators*

```
 x        NOT
==================
TRUE      FALSE
UNK       UNK
FALSE     TRUE
```

```
AND   |  TRUE   UNK    FALSE
=============================
TRUE  |  TRUE   UNK    FALSE
UNK   |  UNK    UNK    FALSE
FALSE |  FALSE  FALSE  FALSE

 OR   |  TRUE   UNK   FALSE
============================
TRUE  |  TRUE   TRUE  TRUE
UNK   |  TRUE   UNK   UNK
FALSE |  TRUE   UNK   FALSE
```

All other predicates in SQL resolve themselves to chains of these three operators. But that resolution is not immediately clear in all cases, since it is done at run time in the case of predicates that use subqueries.

6.5.1 NULLS in Subquery Predicates

People forget that a subquery often hides a comparison with a NULL. Consider these two tables:

```
CREATE TABLE Table1 (col1 INTEGER);
INSERT Table1 (col1) VALUES (1);
INSERT Table1 (col1) VALUES (2);

CREATE TABLE Table2 (col1 INTEGER);
INSERT Table2 (col1) VALUES (1);
INSERT Table2 (col1) VALUES (2);
INSERT Table2 (col1) VALUES (3);
INSERT Table2 (col1) VALUES (4);
INSERT Table2 (col1) VALUES (5);
```

Notice that the columns are NULL-able. Execute this query:

```
SELECT col1
  FROM Table2
 WHERE col1 NOT IN (SELECT col1 FROM Table1);

Result
col1
======
3
```

```
4
5
```

Now insert a NULL and reexecute the same query:

```
INSERT INTO Table1 (col1) VALUES (NULL);
SELECT col1
  FROM Table2
 WHERE col1 NOT IN (SELECT col1 FROM Table1);
```

The result will be empty. This is counterintuitive, but correct. The NOT IN predicate is defined as:

```
SELECT col1
  FROM Table2
 WHERE NOT (col1 IN (SELECT col1 FROM Table1));
```

The IN predicate is defined as:

```
SELECT col1
  FROM Table2
 WHERE NOT (col1 = ANY (SELECT col1 FROM Table1));
```

This becomes:

```
SELECT col1
  FROM Table2
 WHERE NOT ((col1 = 1)
         OR (col1 = 2)
         OR (col1 = 3)
         OR (col1 = 4)
         OR (col1 = 5)
         OR (col1 = NULL));
```

The last expression is always UNKNOWN, so, applying DeMorgan's laws, the query is really:

```
SELECT col1
  FROM Table2
 WHERE ((col1 <> 1)
         AND (col1 <> 2)
         AND (col1 <> 3)
```

```
AND (coll <> 4)
AND (coll <> 5)
AND UNKNOWN);
```

Look at the truth tables and you will see this always reduces to UNKNOWN, and an UNKNOWN is always rejected in a search condition in a WHERE clause.

6.5.2 Standard SQL Solutions

SQL-92 solved some of the 3VL (three-valued logic) problems by adding a new predicate of the form:

```
<search condition> IS [NOT] TRUE | FALSE | UNKNOWN
```

This predicate will let you map any combination of three-valued logic to two values. For example, ((age < 18) OR (gender = 'Female')) IS NOT FALSE will return TRUE if (age IS NULL) or (gender IS NULL) and the remaining condition does not matter.

6.6 Math and NULLs

NULLs propagate when they appear in arithmetic expressions (+, −, *, /) and return NULL results. See Chapter 3 on numeric data types for more details.

6.7 Functions and NULLs

Most vendors propagate NULLs in the functions they offer as extensions of the standard ones required in SQL. For example, the cosine of a NULL will be NULL. There are two functions that convert NULLs into values:

1. NULLIF (V1, V2) returns a NULL when the first parameter equals the second parameter. The function is equivalent to the following case specification:

```
CASE WHEN (V1 = V2)
   THEN NULL
   ELSE V1 END
```

2. `COALESCE (V1, V2, V3, ..., Vn)` processes the list from left to right and returns the first parameter that is not `NULL`. If all the values are `NULL`, it returns a `NULL`.

6.8 NULLs and Host Languages

This book does not discuss using SQL statements embedded in any particular host language. For that information, you will need to pick up a book for your particular language. However, you should know how `NULL`s are handled when they have to be passed to a host program. No standard host language for which an embedding is defined supports `NULL`s, which is another good reason to avoid using them in your database schema.

Roughly speaking, the programmer mixes SQL statements bracketed by `EXEC SQL` and a language-specific terminator (the semicolon in Pascal and C, `END-EXEC` in COBOL, and so on) into the host program. This mixed-language program is run through an SQL preprocessor that converts the SQL into procedure calls the host language can compile; then the host program is compiled in the usual way.

There is an `EXEC SQL BEGIN DECLARE SECTION`, `EXEC SQL END DECLARE SECTION` pair that brackets declarations for the host parameter variables that will get values from the database via `CURSOR`s. This is the "neutral territory," where the host and the database pass information. SQL knows that it is dealing with a host variable, because these have a colon prefix added to them when they appear in an SQL statement. A `CURSOR` is an SQL query statement that executes and creates a structure that looks like a sequential file. The records in the `CURSOR` are returned, one at a time, to the `BEGIN DECLARE` section of the host program with the `FETCH` statement. This avoids the impedance mismatch between record processing in the host language and SQL's set orientation.

`NULL`s are handled by declaring `INDICATOR` variables in the host language `BEGIN DECLARE` section, which are paired with the host variables. An `INDICATOR` is an exact numeric data type with a scale of zero—that is, some kind of integer in the host language.

The `FETCH` statement takes one row from the cursor, then converts each SQL data type into a host-language data type and puts that result into the appropriate host variable. If the SQL value was a `NULL`, the `INDICATOR` is set to minus one; if no indicator was specified, an exception condition is raised. As you can see, the host program must be sure to check the `INDICATOR`s, because otherwise the value of the parameter will be garbage. If the parameter is passed to the host language without any problems, the INDICATOR is set to zero. If the value being passed to the host program is a non-**NULL** character string and has an indicator, the indicator is set to the length of the SQL string and can be used to detect string overflows or to set the length of the parameter.

Other SQL interfaces such as ODBC, JDBC, and so on have similar mechanisms for telling the host program about NULLs, even though they might not use cursors.

6.9 Design Advice for NULLs

It is a good idea to declare all your base tables with NOT NULL constraints on all columns whenever possible. NULLs confuse people who do not know SQL, and NULLs are expensive. NULLs are usually implemented with an extra bit somewhere in the row where the column appears, rather than in the column itself. They adversely affect storage requirements, indexing, and searching.

NULLs are not permitted in PRIMARY KEY columns. Think about what a PRIMARY KEY that was NULL (or partially NULL) would mean. A NULL in a key means that the data model does not know what makes the entities in that table unique from each other. That in turn says that DBMS cannot decide whether the PRIMARY KEY does or does not duplicate a key that is already in the table.

NULLs should be avoided in FOREIGN KEYs. SQL allows this "benefit of the doubt" relationship, but it can cause a loss of information in queries that involve joins. For example, given a part number code in Inventory that is referenced as a FOREIGN KEY by an Orders table, you will have problems getting a listing of the parts that have a NULL. This is a mandatory relationship; you cannot order a part that does not exist.

An example of an optional foreign key is a Personnel table having a foreign key to a ParoleOfficer table; obviously a NULL here means the person does not (currently) have a parole officer. The NULL can be avoided by forcing the separation of the foreign key into its own table, such that no row exists for a person who has no parole officer. However, this degree of normalization is not always possible, nor would it always be desirable to force the split. There is, too, the issue of what to return if a join of the two tables is required, to return personnel information plus parole officer, if any. There is also finally the issue of whether, when multiple such splits have been made, the retrieval of consolidated information will result in extremely slow queries to produce all the

joined data (and to substitute whatever indicator has been chosen to represent the "missing" data).

NULLs should not be allowed in encoding schemes that are known to be complete. For example, employees are people and people are either male or female. On the other hand, if you are recording the gender of lawful persons (humans, corporations, and other legal entities), you need the ISO sex codes, which use 0 = unknown, 1 = male, 2 = female, 9 = not applicable. No, you have not missed a new gender; code 9 is for legal persons, such as corporations.

The use of all zeros and all nines for "Unknown" and "N/A" is quite common in numeric encoding schemes. This convention is a leftover from the old punch card days, when a missing value was left as a field of blanks (i.e., no punches) that could be punched into the card later. Likewise, a field of all nines would sort to the end of the file, and it was easy to hold the "nine" key down when the keypunch machine was in numeric shift.

However, you have to use NULLs in date fields when a DEFAULT date does not make sense. For example, if you do not know someone's birthdate, a default date does not make sense; if a warranty has no expiration date, then a NULL can act as an "eternity" symbol. Unfortunately, you often know relative times, but it is difficult to express them in a database. For example, a pay raise occurs some time after you have been hired, not before. A convict serving on death row should expect a release date resolved by an event: his termination by execution or by natural causes. This leads to extra columns to hold the status and to control the transition constraints.

There is a proprietary extension to date values in MySQL. If you know the year but not the month, you may enter '1949-00-00'. If you know the year and month, but not the day, you may enter '1949-09-00'. You cannot reliably use date arithmetic on these values, but they do help in some instances, such as sorting people's birthdates or calculating their (approximate) age.

For people's names, you are probably better off using a special dummy string for unknown values rather than the general NULL. In particular, you can build a list of 'John Doe #1', 'John Doe #2', and so forth to differentiate them; and you cannot do that with NULL. Quantities have to use a NULL in some cases. There is a difference between an unknown quantity and a zero quantity; it is the difference between an empty gas tank and not having a car at all. Using negative numbers to represent missing quantities does not work, because it makes accurate calculations too complex.

When programming languages had no `DATE` data types, this could have been handled with a character string of `'9999-99-99 23:59:59.999999'` for "eternity" or "the end of time." When 4GL products with a DATE data type came onto the market, programmers usually inserted the maximum possible date for "eternity." But again, this will show up in calculations and in summary statistics. The best trick was to use two columns, one for the date and one for a flag. But this made for fairly complex code in the 4GL.

6.9.1 Avoiding NULLs from the Host Programs

You can avoid putting `NULL`s into the database from the Host Programs with some programming discipline.

1. *Initialize in the host program*: Initialize all the data elements and displays on the input screen of a client program before inserting data into the database. Exactly how you can make sure that all the programs use the same default values is another problem.

2. *Use automatic defaults*: The database is the final authority on the default values.

3. *Deduce values*: Infer the missing data from the given values. For example, patients reporting a pregnancy are female; patients reporting prostate cancer are male. This technique can also be used to limit choices to valid values for the user.

4. *Track missing data*: Data is tagged as missing, unknown, in error, out-of-date, or whatever other condition makes it missing. This will involve a companion column with special codes.

5. *Determine impact of missing data on programming and reporting*: Numeric columns with `NULL`s are a problem, because queries using aggregate functions can provide misleading results. Aggregate functions drop out the `NULL`s before doing the math, and the programmer has to trap the `SQLSTATE` code for this to make corrections.

6. *Prevent missing data*: Use batch process to scan and validate data elements before it goes into the database. In the early 2000s, there was a sudden concern for data quality as CEOs started going to jail for failing audits. This has lead to a niche in the software trade for data quality tools.

7. *Ensure consistency*: The data types and their NULL-ability constraints have to be consistent across databases (e.g., the chart of account should be defined the same way in both the desktop and enterprise-level databases).

6.10 A Note on Multiple NULL Values

In a discussion on CompuServe in July 1996, Carl C. Federl came up with an interesting idea for multiple missing value tokens in a database.

If you program in embedded SQL, you are used to having to work with an INDICATOR column. This column is used to pass information to the host program, mostly about the NULL or NOT NULL status of the SQL column in the database. What the host program does with the information is up to the programmer. So why not extend this concept a bit and provide an indicator column in SQL? Let's work out a simple example:

```
CREATE TABLE Bob
(keycol INTEGER NOT NULL PRIMARY KEY,
 valcol INTEGER NOT NULL,
 multi_indicator INTEGER NOT NULL
  CHECK (multi_indicator IN (0, -- Known value
                      1, -- Not applicable value
                      2, -- Missing value
                      3  -- Approximate value));
```

Let's set up the rules: when all values are known, we do a regular total. If a value is "not applicable," then the whole total is "not applicable." If we have no "not applicable" values, then "missing value" dominates the total; if we have no "not applicable" and no "missing" values, then we give a warning about approximate values. The general form of the queries will be:

```
SELECT SUM (valcol),
       (CASE WHEN NOT EXISTS (SELECT multi_indicator
                                FROM Bob
                               WHERE multi_indicator > 0)
             THEN 0
             WHEN EXISTS (SELECT *
                            FROM Bob
                           WHERE multi_indicator = 1)
```

```
          THEN 1
          WHEN EXISTS (SELECT *
                         FROM Bob
                        WHERE multi_indicator = 2)
          THEN 2
          WHEN EXISTS (SELECT *
                         FROM Bob
                        WHERE multi_indicator = 3)
          THEN 3
          ELSE NULL END) AS totals_multi_indicator
  FROM Bob;
```

Why would I muck with the valcol total at all? The status is over in the multi_indicator column, just like it was in the original table. Here is an exercise for the reader:

1. Make up a set of rules for multiple missing values and write a query for the `SUM()`, `AVG()`, `MAX()`, `MIN()`, and `COUNT()` functions.
2. Set degrees of approximation (plus or minus five, plus or minus ten, etc.) in the multi_indicator. Assume the valcol is always in the middle. Make the multi_indicator handle the fuzziness of the situation.

```
CREATE TABLE MultiNull
(groupcol INTEGER NOT NULL,
 keycol INTEGER NOT NULL,
 valcol INTEGER NOT NULL CHECK (valcol >= 0),
 valcol_null INTEGER NOT NULL DEFAULT 0,
  CHECK(valcol_null IN
  (0,    -- Known Value
   1,    -- Not applicable
   2,    -- Missing but applicable
   3,    -- Approximate within 1%
   4,    -- Approximate within 5%
   5,    -- Approximate within 25%
   6     -- Approximate over 25% range)),
 PRIMARY KEY (groupcol, keycol),
   CHECK (valcol = 0 AND valcol_null NOT IN (1,2));
```

```
CREATE VIEW Group_MultiNull
(groupcol, valcol_sum, valcol_avg, valcol_max, valcol_min,
row_cnt, notnull_cnt, na_cnt, missing_cnt, approximate_cnt,
appr_1_cnt, approx_5_cnt, approx_25_cnt, approx_big_cnt)
AS
SELECT groupcol, SUM(valcol), AVG(valcol), MAX(valcol),
       MIN(valcol), COUNT(*),
       SUM (CASE WHEN valcol_null = 0 THEN 1 ELSE 0 END)
         AS notnull_cnt,
       SUM (CASE WHEN valcol_null = 1 THEN 1 ELSE 0 END)
         AS na_cnt,
       SUM (CASE WHEN valcol_null = 2 THEN 1 ELSE 0 END)
         AS missing_cnt,
      SUM (CASE WHEN valcol_null IN (3,4,5,6) THEN 1 ELSE 0 END)

         AS approximate_cnt,
       SUM (CASE WHEN valcol_null = 3 THEN 1 ELSE 0 END)
         AS appr_1_cnt,
       SUM (CASE WHEN valcol_null = 4 THEN 1 ELSE 0 END)
         AS approx_5_cnt,
       SUM (CASE WHEN valcol_null = 5 THEN 1 ELSE 0 END)
         AS approx_25_cnt,
       SUM (CASE WHEN valcol_null = 6 THEN 1 ELSE 0 END)
         AS approx_big_cnt
  FROM MultiNull
 GROUP BY groupcol;

SELECT groupcol, valcol_sum, valcol_avg, valcol_max, valcol_min,
       (CASE WHEN row_cnt = notnull_cnt
             THEN 'All are known'
             ELSE 'Not all are known' END) AS warning_message,
      row_cnt, notnull_cnt, na_cnt, missing_cnt,
approximate_cnt,
      appr_1_cnt, approx_5_cnt, approx_25_cnt, approx_big_cnt
 FROM Group_MultiNull;
```

While this is a bit complex for the typical application, it is not a bad idea for a “staging area” database that attempts to scrub the data before it goes to a data warehouse.

Multiple Column Data Elements

THE CONCEPT OF A data element being atomic or scalar is usually taken to mean that it is represented with a single column in a table. This is not always true. A data element is atomic when it cannot be decomposed into independent, meaningful parts. Doing so would result in attribute splitting, a design flaw that we discussed in Section 1.1.11.

Consider an (x, y) coordinate system. A single x or y value identifies a line of points, while the pair has to be taken together to give you a location on the plane. It would be inconvenient to put both coordinates into one column, so we model them in two columns.

7.1 Distance Functions

Since geographical data is important, you might find it handy to locate places by their longitude and latitude, then calculate the distances between two points on the globe. This is not a standard function in any SQL, but it is handy to know.

Assume that we have values (Latitude1, Longitude1, Latitude2, Longitude2) that locate the two points, and that they are in radians, and we have trigonometry functions.

To convert decimal degrees to radians, multiply the number of degrees by pi/180 = 0.017453293 radians/degree, where pi is approximately 3.14159265358979:

```
CREATE FUNCTION Distance
(IN latitude1 REAL, IN longitude1 REAL,
 IN latitude2 REAL, IN longitude2 REAL)
RETURNS REAL
BEGIN
  DECLARE r REAL;
  DECLARE lat REAL;
  DECLARE lon REAL;
  DECLARE a REAL;
  DECLARE c REAL;
  SET r = 6367.00 * 0.6214;

-- calculate the Deltas...
  SET lon = longitude2 - longitude1;
  SET lat = latitude2 - latitude1;

--Intermediate values...
  SET a = SIN(lat / 2) + COS(latitude1)
          * COS(latitude2) * SIN(lon / 2);

--Intermediate result c is the great circle distance in
radians...
  SET c = 2 * ARCSIN(LEAST(1.00, SQRT(a)));

--Multiply the radians by the radius to get the distance
  RETURN (r * c);
END;
```

`LEAST()` function protects against possible round-off errors that could sabotage computation of the `ARCSIN()` if the two points are very nearly antipodal. It exists as a vendor extension in Oracle and MySQL, but can be written with a `CASE` expression in Standard SQL.

7.2 Storing an IP Address in SQL

While not exactly a data type, IP addresses are being used as unique identifiers for people or companies. If you need to verify them, you can send an e-mail or ping them. There are three popular ways to store an IP address: a string, an integer, and a set of four octets.

In a test conducted in SQL Server, all three methods required about the same amount of time, work, and I/O to return data as a string. The latter two have some additional computations, but the overhead was not enough to affect performance very much.

The conclusion was that the octet model with four `TINYINT` columns had two advantages: simpler programming indexes on individual octets, and human readability. But you should look at what happens in your own environment. `TINYINT` is a one-bit integer data type found in SQL Server and other products; `SMALLINT` is the closest thing to it in Standard SQL.

7.2.1 A Single VARCHAR(15) Column

The most obvious way to store IP addresses (for example, '63.246.173.210') is a `VARCHAR(15)` column, with a `CHECK()` constraint that uses a `SIMILAR TO` predicate to be sure that it has the "dots and digits" in the right positions. You have to decide the meaning of leading zeros in an octet and trim them to do string comparisons.

The good points are that programming this is reasonably simple and it is immediately readable by a human. The bad points are that this solution has higher storage costs and requires pattern-matching string functions in searches. It also is harder to pass to some host programs that expect to see the octets to make their IP connections.

To convert the string into octets, you need to use a string procedure. You can write one based on the code given for parsing a comma-separated string into individual integers in Section 22.1, on using the sequence auxiliary table.

7.2.2 One INTEGER Column

This solution has the lowest storage requirements of all the methods, and it keeps the address in one column. Searching and indexing are also minimal.

The bad side is that programming for this solution is much more complex, and you need to write user functions to break it apart into octets. It also has poor human readability. Can you tell me that an `INTEGER` value like '2130706433' represents '127.0.0.1' on sight?

```
CREATE FUNCTION IPIntegerToString (IN ip INTEGER)
RETURNS VARCHAR(15)
LANGUAGE SQL
DETERMINISTIC
BEGIN
DECLARE o1 INTEGER;
```

```
DECLARE o2 INTEGER;
DECLARE o3 INTEGER;
DECLARE o4 INTEGER;

IF ABS(ip) > 2147483647
THEN RETURN '255.255.255.255';
END IF;

SET o1 = ip / 16777216;
IF o1 = 0
THEN SET o1 = 255;
     SET ip = ip + 16777216;
ELSE IF o1 < 0
     THEN IF MOD(ip, 16777216) = 0
  THEN SET o1 = o1 + 256;
  ELSE SET o1 = o1 + 255;
       IF o1 = 128
       THEN SET ip = ip + 2147483648;
       ELSE SET ip = ip + (16777216 * (256 - o1));
       END IF;
  END IF;
     ELSE SET ip = ip - (16777216 * o1);
     END IF;
END IF;

SET ip = MOD(ip, 16777216);
SET o2 = ip / 65536;
SET ip = MOD(ip, 65536);
SET o3 = ip / 256;
SET ip = MOD(ip, 256);
SET o4 = ip;

-- return the string
RETURN
CAST(o1 AS VARCHAR(3)) || '.' ||
CAST(o2 AS VARCHAR(3)) || '.' ||
CAST(o3 AS VARCHAR(3)) || '.' ||
CAST(o4 AS VARCHAR(3));
END;
```

7.2.3 Four SMALLINT Columns

The good points of this solution are that it has a lower storage cost than VARCHAR(15), searching is easy and relatively fast, and you can index on each octet of the address. If you have an SQL with a TINYINT (usually one byte) data type, then you can save even more space.

The bad point is that programming is slightly more complex.

```
CREATE TABLE FourColumnIP
(octet1 SMALLINT NOT NULL
        CHECK (octet1 BETWEEN 0 AND 255),
 octet2 SMALLINT NOT NULL
        CHECK (octet2 BETWEEN 0 AND 255),
 octet3 SMALLINT NOT NULL
        CHECK (octet3 BETWEEN 0 AND 255),
 octet4 SMALLINT NOT NULL
        CHECK (octet4 BETWEEN 0 AND 255),
...);
```

You will need a view for display, but that is straightforward:

```
CREATE VIEW DisplayIP (IP_address_display)
AS
SELECT (CAST(octet1 AS VARCHAR(3))||'.'||
        CAST(octet2 AS VARCHAR(3))||'.'||
        CAST(octet3 AS VARCHAR(3))||'.'||
        CAST(octet4 AS VARCHAR(3))
 FROM FourColumnIP;
```

7.3 Currency and Other Unit Conversions

Currency has to be expressed in both an amount and a unit of currency. The ISO 4217 currency code gives you a standard way of identifying the unit. There are no nondecimal currency systems left on earth, but you will need to talk to the accounting department about the number of decimal places to use in computations. The rules for euros are established by the European Union, and those for U.S. dollars are part of the GAAP (Generally Accepted Accounting Practices).

```
CREATE TABLE InternationalMoney
( ...
currency_code CHAR(3) NOT NULL,
```

```
currency_amt DECIMAL (12,4) NOT NULL,
...);
```

This mixed table is not easy to work with, so it is best to create VIEWs with a single currency for each group of users. This will entail maintaining an exchange rate table to use in the VIEWs.

```
CREATE VIEW EuroMoney (... euro_amt, ...)
AS
SELECT ... (M1.currency_amt * E1.conversion_factor), ...
  FROM InternationalMoney AS M1,
       ExchangeRate AS E1
 WHERE E1.to_currency_code = 'EUR'
   AND E1.from_currency_code = M1.curency_code;
```

But there is a gimmick. There are specific rules about precision and rounding that are mandatory in currency conversion to, from, and through the euro. Conversion between two national currencies must be triangulated; this means that you convert the first currency to euros, then convert the euros to the second currency. Six-figure conversion rates are mandatory, but you should check the status of "Article 235 Regulation" to be sure that nothing has changed since this writing.

7.4 Social Security Numbers

Social Security numbers (SSNs) are so important in the United States that they deserve a separate mention.

You can look up death records using Social Security and the first five digits of the Social Security number, with location and approximate year of issue. The Ancestry.com Web site has a Social Security death search that gives the full nine-digit number of the deceased individual. It does not supply the years or location of issue.

Commercial firms such as Security Software Solutions (Box 30125; Tucson, AZ 85751-0125; phone 800-681-8933; www.veris-ssn.com) will verify Social Security Numbers for living and deceased persons.

The Social Security number is composed of 3 parts, XXX-XX-XXXX, called the Area, Group, and Serial. For the most part, (there are a few exceptions), the Area is determined by where the individual applied for the Social Security Number (before 1972) or resided at time of application (after 1972). The areas are assigned as follows:

```
000 unused
001-003 NH
004-007 ME
008-009 VT
010-034 MA
035-039 RI
040-049 CT
050-134 NY
135-158 NJ
159-211 PA
212-220 MD
221-222 DE
223-231 VA
232-236 WV
237-246 NC
247-251 SC
252-260 GA
261-267 FL
268-302 OH
303-317 IN
318-361 IL
362-386 MI
387-399 WI
400-407 KY
408-415 TN
416-424 AL
425-428 MS
429-432 AR
433-439 LA
440-448 OK
449-467 TX
468-477 MN
478-485 IA
486-500 MO
501-502 ND
503-504 SD
505-508 NE
509-515 KS
516-517 MT
518-519 ID
520 WY
```

```
521-524 CO
525 NM
526-527 AZ
528-529 UT
530 NV
531-539 WA
540-544 OR
545-573 CA
574 AK
575-576 HI
577-579 DC
580 VI Virgin Islands
581-584 PR Puerto Rico
585 NM
586 PI Pacific Islands
       (Northern Mariana Islands, Guam, American Samoa,
        Philippine Islands)
587-588 MS
589-595 FL
596-599 PR Puerto Rico
600-601 AZ
602-626 CA
627-699 unassigned, for future use
700-728 Railroad workers through 1963, then discontinued
729-899 unassigned, for future use

  900-999 not valid Social Security Numbers, but were used for
program purposes when state aid to the aged, blind, and disabled
was converted to a federal program administered by Social
Security Adminstration.
```

As the Areas assigned to a locality are exhausted, new areas from the pool are assigned. This is why some states have noncontiguous groups of Areas.

The Group portion of the Social Security number has no meaning other than to determine whether or not a number has been assigned. Social Security Administration publishes a list every month of the highest Group assigned for each Area. The order of assignment for the Groups is: odd numbers under 10, even numbers over 9, even numbers under 9 except for 00, which is never used, and odd numbers over 10. For example, if the highest group assigned for area 999 is 72, then we know that the number 999-04-1234 is an invalid number because even Groups under 9 have not yet been assigned.

The Serial portion of the Social Security number has no meaning. The Serial is not assigned in strictly numerical order. The Serial 0000 is never assigned.

Before 1973, Social Security cards with preprinted numbers were issued to each local Social Security Administration office. The local office assigned the numbers. In 1973, Social Security number assignment was automated, and outstanding stocks of preprinted cards were destroyed. Computers at headquarters now assign all Social Security numbers. There are rare cases in which the computer system can be forced to accept a manual assignment, such as a person refusing a number with 666 in it.

A pamphlet entitled "The Social Security Number" (Pub. No. 05-10633) provides an explanation of the Social Security number's structure and the method of assigning and validating Social Security numbers.

You can also verify a number with software packages; look at www.searchbug.com/peoplefinder/ssn.aspx.

7.5 Rational Numbers

A rational number is defined as a fraction (a/b) where a and b are both integers. In contrast, an irrational number cannot be defined that way. The classic example of an irrational number is the square root of two. Technically, a binary computer can only represent a subset of the rational numbers. But for some purposes, it is handy to actually model them as (numerator, denominator) pairs. For example, Vadim Tropashko uses rational numbers in the nested interval model for hierarchies in SQL (see *Joe Celko's Trees and Hierarchies in SQL for Smarties*). This means that you need a set of user-defined functions to do basic four-function math and to reduce the fractions.

Elementary school students, when questioned what the sum of 1/2 and 1/4 is, will add the denominators and numerators like this: 1/2 + 1/4 = (1+1)/(2+4) = 2/6 = 1/3. This operation is called the mediant, and it returns the simplest number between the two fractions, if we use smallness of denominator as a measure of simplicity. Indeed, the average of 1/4 and 1/2 has denominator 8, while the mediant has 3.

Table Operations

THERE ARE ONLY FOUR things you can do with a set of rows in an SQL table: insert them into a table, delete them from a table, update the values in them, or query them. The unit of work is a set of whole rows inside a base table.

When you worked with file systems, access was one record at a time, then one field within a record. Since you had repeated groups and other forms of variant records, you could change the structure of each record in the file.

The mental mode in SQL is that you grab a subset as a unit, all at once, in a base table and insert, update, or delete as a unit, all at once. Imagine that you have enough computer power that you can allocate one processor to every row in a table. When you blow your whistle, all the processors do their work in parallel.

8.1 DELETE FROM Statement

The `DELETE FROM` statement in SQL removes zero or more rows of one table. Interactive SQL tools will tell the user how many rows were affected by an update operation, and Standard SQL requires the database engine to raise a completion condition of "no data" if there are zero rows. There are two forms of `DELETE FROM` in SQL: positioned and searched. The positioned deletion is done with cursors;

the searched deletion uses a WHERE clause like the search condition in a SELECT statement.

8.1.1 The DELETE FROM Clause

The syntax for a searched deletion statement is:

```
<delete statement: searched> :: =
  DELETE FROM <table name>
  [WHERE <search condition>]
```

The DELETE FROM clause simply gives the name of the updatable table or view to be changed. Notice that no correlation name is allowed in the DELETE FROM clause. The SQL model for an alias table name is that the engine effectively creates a new table with that new name and populates it with rows identical to the base table or updatable view from which it was built. If you had a correlation name, you would be deleting from this system-created temporary table, and it would vanish at the end of the statement. The base table would never have been touched.

For this discussion, we will assume the user doing the deletion has applicable DELETE privileges for the table. The positioned deletion removes the row in the base table that is the source of the current cursor row. The syntax is:

```
<delete statement: positioned> :: =
  DELETE FROM <table name>
  WHERE CURRENT OF <cursor name>
```

Cursors in SQL are generally more expensive than nonprocedural code and, despite the existence of the Standard, they vary widely in current implementations. If you have a properly designed table with a key, you should be able to avoid them in a DELETE FROM statement.

8.1.2 The WHERE Clause

The most important thing to remember about the WHERE clause is that it is optional. If there is no WHERE clause, all rows in the table are deleted. The table structure still exists, but there are no rows.

Most, but not all, interactive SQL tools will give the user a warning when he or she is about to do this and ask for confirmation. Unless you want to clear out the table, immediately do a ROLLBACK to restore it; if you COMMIT or have set the tool to automatically commit the work, then the data is pretty much gone. The DBA will have to do something to save you. And don't feel badly about doing it at least once while you are learning SQL.

Because we wish to remove a subset of rows all at once, we cannot simply scan the table one row at a time and remove each qualifying row as it is encountered. The way most SQL implementations do a deletion is with two passes on the table. The first pass marks all of the candidate rows that meet the `WHERE` clause condition. This is also when most products check to see if the deletion will violate any constraints. The most common violations involve trying to remove a value that is referenced by a foreign key ("Hey, we still have orders for those pink lawn flamingoes; you cannot drop them from inventory yet!"). But other constraints in `CREATE ASSERTION` statements' `CHECK()` constraints can also cause a `ROLLBACK`.

After the subset is validated, the second pass removes it, either immediately or by marking the rows so that a housekeeping routine can later reclaim the storage space. Then any further housekeeping, such as updating indexes, is done last.

The important point is that while the rows are being marked, the entire table is still available for the `WHERE` condition to use. In many if not most cases, this two-pass method does not make any difference in the results. The `WHERE` clause is usually a fairly simple predicate that references constants or relationships among the columns of a row. For example, we could clear out some Personnel with this deletion:

```
DELETE FROM Personnel
 WHERE iq <= 100;          -- constant in simple predicate
```

or:

```
DELETE FROM Personnel
 WHERE hat_size = iq;    -- uses columns in the same row
```

A good optimizer could recognize that these predicates do not depend on the table as a whole, and would use a single scan for them. The two passes make a difference when the table references itself. Let's fire employees with IQs that are below average for their departments.

```
DELETE FROM Personnel
 WHERE iq < (SELECT AVG(P1.iq)
              FROM Personnel AS P1 -- must have correlation name
```

```
                WHERE Personnel.dept_nbr = P1.dept_nbr);
```

We have the following data:

```
Personnel
emp_nbr   dept_nbr  iq
======================
'Able'     'Acct'   101
'Baker'    'Acct'   105
'Charles'  'Acct'   106
'Henry'    'Mkt'    101
'Celko'    'Mkt'    170
'Popkin'   'HR'     120
 ...
```

If this were done one row at a time, we would first go to Accounting and find the average IQ, (101 + 105 + 106)/3.0 = 104, and fire Able. Then we would move sequentially down the table, and again find the average IQ, (105 + 106)/2.0 = 105.5 and fire Baker. Only Charles would escape the downsizing.

Now sort the table a little differently, so that the rows are visited in reverse alphabetic order. We first read Charles's IQ and compute the average for Accounting (101 + 105 + 106)/3.0 = 104, and retain Charles. Then we would move sequentially down the table, with the average IQ unchanged, so we also retain Baker. Able, however, is downsized when that row comes up.

It might be worth noting that early versions of DB2 would delete rows in the sequential order in which they appear in physical storage. Sybase's SQL Anywhere (*née* WATCOM SQL) has an optional `ORDER BY` clause that sorts the table, then does a sequential deletion on the table. This feature can be used to force a sequential deletion in cases where order does not matter, thus optimizing the statement by saving a second pass over the table. But it also can give the desired results in situations where you would otherwise have to use a cursor and a host language.

Anders Altberg, Johannes Becher, and I tested different versions of a `DELETE` statement whose goal was to remove all but one row of a group. The column dup_cnt is a count of the duplicates of that row in the original table. The three statements tested were:

```
D1:
 DELETE FROM Test
```

```
 WHERE EXISTS (SELECT *
                FROM Test AS T1
               WHERE T1.dup_id = Test.dup_id
                 AND T1.dup_cnt < dup_cnt)
```

```
D2:
DELETE FROM Test
 WHERE dup_cnt > (SELECT MIN(T1.dup_cnt)
                   FROM Test AS T1
                  WHERE T1.dup_id = Test.dup_id);
```

```
D3:
BEGIN ATOMIC
INSERT INTO WorkingTable(dup_id, min_dup_cnt)
SELECT dup_id, MIN(dup_cnt)
  FROM Test
 GROUP BY dup_id;
DELETE FROM Test
 WHERE dup_cnt > (SELECT min_dup_cnt
                  FROM WorkingTable
                 WHERE Working.dup_id = Test.dup_id);
END;
```

Their relative execution speeds in one SQL desktop product were:

```
D1   3.20 seconds
D2  31.22 seconds
D3   0.17 seconds
```

Without seeing the execution plans, I would guess that statement D1 went to an index for the `EXISTS()` test and returned `TRUE` on the first item it found. On the other hand, D2 scanned each subset in the partitioning of Test by dup_id to find the `MIN()` over and over. Finally, the D3 version simply does a `JOIN` on simple scalar columns. With full SQL-92, you could write D3 as:

```
D3-2:
DELETE FROM Test
 WHERE dup_cnt >
      (SELECT min_dup_cnt
         FROM (SELECT dup_id, MIN(dup_cnt)
```

```
                    FROM Test
                   GROUP BY dup_id) AS WorkingTable(dup_id,
min_dup_cnt)
         WHERE Working.dup_id = Test.dup_id);
```

Having said all of this, the faster way to remove redundant duplicates is most often with a CURSOR that does a full table scan.

8.1.3 Deleting Based on Data in a Second Table

The WHERE clause can be as complex as you wish. This means you can have subqueries that use other tables. For example, to remove customers who have paid their bills from the Deadbeats table, you can use a correlated EXISTS predicate, thus:

```
DELETE FROM Deadbeats
 WHERE EXISTS (SELECT *
                FROM Payments AS P1
               WHERE Deadbeats.cust_nbr = P1.cust_nbr
                 AND P1.amtpaid >= Deadbeats.amtdue);
```

The scope rules from SELECT statements also apply to the WHERE clause of a DELETE FROM statement, but it is a good idea to qualify all of the column names.

8.1.4 Deleting within the Same Table

SQL allows a DELETE FROM statement to use columns, constants, and aggregate functions drawn from the table itself. For example, it is perfectly all right to remove everyone who is below average in a class with this statement:

```
DELETE FROM Students
 WHERE grade < (SELECT AVG(grade) FROM Students);
```

But the DELETE FROM clause does not allow for correlation names on the table in the DELETE FROM clause, so not all WHERE clauses that could be written as part of a SELECT statement will work in a DELETE FROM statement. For example, a self-join on the working table in a subquery is impossible.

```
DELETE FROM Personnel AS B1  -- correlation name is INVALID SQL
```

```
WHERE Personnel.boss_nbr = B1.emp_nbr
  AND Personnel.salary > B1.salary);
```

There are ways to work around this. One trick is to build a `VIEW` of the table and use the `VIEW` instead of a correlation name. Consider the problem of finding all employees who are now earning more than their boss and deleting them. The employee table being used has a column for the employee's identification number, emp_nbr, and another column for the boss's employee identification number, boss_nbr.

```
CREATE VIEW Bosses
AS SELECT emp_nbr, salary FROM Personnel;

DELETE FROM Personnel
 WHERE EXISTS (SELECT *
                 FROM Bosses AS B1
                WHERE Personnel.boss_nbr = B1.emp_nbr
                  AND Personnel.salary > B1.salary);
```

Simply using the Personnel table in the subquery will not work. We need an outer reference in the `WHERE` clause to the Personnel table in the subquery, and we cannot get that if the Personnel table is in the subquery. Such views should be as small as possible, so that the SQL engine can materialize them in main storage.

Redundant Duplicates in a Table

Redundant duplicates are unneeded copies of a row in a table. You most often get them because you did not put a `UNIQUE` constraint on the table and then you inserted the same data twice. Removing the extra copies from a table in SQL is much harder than you would think. If fact, if the rows are exact duplicates, you cannot do it with a simple `DELETE FROM` statement. Removing redundant duplicates involves saving one of them while deleting the other(s). But if SQL has no way to tell them apart, it will delete all rows that were qualified by the `WHERE` clause. Another problem is that the deletion of a row from a base table can trigger referential actions, which can have unwanted side effects.

For example, if there is a referential integrity constraint that says a deletion in Table1 will cascade and delete matching rows in Table2, removing redundant duplicates from T1 can leave me with no matching rows in T2. Yet I still have a referential integrity rule that says there must be at least one match in T2 for the single row I preserved in T1. SQL

allows constraints to be deferrable or nondeferrable, so you might be able to suspend the referential actions that the transaction below would cause:

```
BEGIN
INSERT INTO WorkingTable    -- use DISTINCT to kill duplicates
SELECT DISTINCT * FROM MessedUpTable;

DELETE FROM MessedUpTable;  -- clean out messed-up table
INSERT INTO MessedUpTable   -- put working table into it
SELECT * FROM WorkingTable;

DROP TABLE WorkingTable;    -- get rid of working table
END;
```

Removal of Redundant Duplicates with ROWID

Leonard C. Medel came up with several interesting ways to delete redundant duplicate rows from a table in an Oracle database.

Let's assume that we have a table:

```
CREATE TABLE Personnel
(emp_id INTEGER NOT NULL,
 name CHAR(30) NOT NULL,
...);
```

The classic Oracle "delete dups" solution is the statement:

```
DELETE FROM Personnel
 WHERE ROWID < (SELECT MAX(P1.ROWID)
                  FROM Personnel AS P1
                 WHERE P1.dup_id = Personnel.dup_id
                   AND P1.name = Personnel.name);
                   AND ...);
```

The column, or more properly pseudo-column, `ROWID` is based on the physical location of a row in storage. It can change after a user session but not during the session. It is the fastest possible physical access method into an Oracle table, because it goes directly to the physical address of the data. It is also a complete violation of Dr. Codd's rules, which require that the physical representation of the data be hidden from the users.

Doing a quick test on a 100,000-row table, Mr. Medel achieved a nearly tenfold improvement with these two alternatives. In English, the first alternative is to find the highest ROWID for each group of one or more duplicate rows, and then delete every row, except the one with highest ROWID.

```
DELETE FROM Personnel
 WHERE ROWID
       IN (SELECT P2.ROWID
             FROM Personnel AS P2,
                  (SELECT P3.dup_id, P3.name, ...
                          MAX(P3.ROWID) AS max_rowid
                     FROM Personnel AS P3
                    GROUP BY P3.dup_id, P3.name, ...)
                  AS P4
                     WHERE P2.ROWID <> P4.max_rowid
                       AND P2.dup_id = P4.dup_id
                       AND P2.name = P4.name);
```

Notice that the GROUP BY clause needs all the columns in the table.

The second approach is to notice that the set of all rows in the table minus the set of rows we want to keep defines the set of rows to delete. This gives us the following statement:

```
DELETE FROM Personnel
 WHERE ROWID
       IN (SELECT P2.ROWID
             FROM Personnel AS P2
           EXCEPT
           SELECT MAX(P3.ROWID)
             FROM Personnel AS P3
            GROUP BY P3.dup_id, P3.name, ...);
```

Both of these approaches are faster than the short, classic version because they avoid a correlated subquery expression in the WHERE clause.

8.1.5 Deleting in Multiple Tables without Referential Integrity

There is no way to directly delete rows from more than one table in a single DELETE FROM statement. There are two approaches to removing related rows from multiple tables. One is to use a temporary table of the deletion values; the other is to use referential integrity actions. For the purposes of this section, let us assume that we have a database with an Orders table and an Inventory table. Our business rule is that when something is out of stock, we delete it from all the orders.

Assume that no referential integrity constraints have been declared at all. First, create a temporary table of the products to be deleted based on your search criteria, then use that table in a correlated subquery to remove rows from each table involved.

```
CREATE MODULE Foobar
CREATE LOCAL TEMPORARY TABLE Discontinue
(part_nbr INTEGER NOT NULL UNIQUE)
ON COMMIT DELETE ROWS;
 ...
PROCEDURE CleanInventory(...)
BEGIN ATOMIC
INSERT INTO Discontinue
SELECT DISTINCT part_nbr -- pick out the items to be removed
  FROM ...
 WHERE ... ;          -- using whatever criteria you require
DELETE FROM Orders
 WHERE part_nbr IN (SELECT part_nbr FROM Discontinue);
DELETE FROM Inventory
 WHERE part_nbr IN (SELECT part_nbr FROM Discontinue);
COMMIT WORK;
END;
...
END MODULE;
```

In the Standard SQL model, the temporary table is persistent in the schema, but its content is not. TEMPORARY tables are always empty at the start of a session, and they always appear to belong only to the user of the session. The GLOBAL option means that each application gets one copy of the table for all the modules, while LOCAL would limit the scope to the module in which it is declared.

8.2 INSERT INTO Statement

The `INSERT INTO` statement is the only way to get new data into a base table. In practice, there are always other tools for loading large amounts of data into a table, but they are very vendor-dependent.

8.2.1 INSERT INTO Clause

The syntax for `INSERT INTO` is:

```
<insert statement> :: =
  INSERT INTO <table name>
    <insert columns and source>

<insert columns and source> :: =
    [(<insert column list>)]
   <query expression>
  | VALUES <table value constructor list>
  | DEFAULT VALUES

<table value constructor list> :: =
   <row value constructor> [{<comma> <row value
constructor>}...]

<row value constructor> :: =
     <row value constructor element>
   | <left paren> <row value constructor list> <right paren>
   | <row subquery>

<row value constructor list> :: =
   <row value constructor element>
       [{<comma> <row value constructor element>}...]

<row value constructor element> :: =
     <value expression> | NULL |DEFAULT
```

The two basic forms of an `INSERT INTO` are a table constant (usually a single row) insertion and a query insertion. The table constant insertion is done with a `VALUES()` clause. The list of insert values usually consists of constants or explicit `NULL`s, but in theory they could be almost any expression, including scalar `SELECT` subqueries.

The DEFAULT VALUES clause is actually VALUES (DEFAULT, DEFAULT, ..., DEFAULT), so it is just shorthand for a particular single row insertion.

The tabular constant insertion is a simple tool, mostly used in interactive sessions, to put in small amounts of data. A query insertion executes the query and produces a working table, which is inserted into the target table all at once. In both cases, the optional list of columns in the target table has to be union-compatible with the columns in the query or with the values in the VALUES clause. Any column not in the list will be assigned NULL or its explicit DEFAULT value.

8.2.2 The Nature of Inserts

In theory, an insert using a query will place the rows from the query in the target table all at once. The set-oriented nature of an insertion means that a statement like this:

```
INSERT INTO SomeTable (somekey, transaction_time)
SELECT millions, CURRENT_TIMESTAMP
  FROM HugeTable;
```

will have one value for transaction_time in all the rows of the result, no matter how long it takes to load them into SomeTable. Keeping things straight requires a lot of checking behind the scenes. The insertion can fail if just one row violates a constraint on the target table. The usual physical implementation is to put the rows into the target table, but mark the work as uncommitted until the whole transaction has been validated. Once the system knows that the insertion is to be committed, it must rebuild all the indexes. Rebuilding indexes will lock out other users and might require sorting the table, if the table had a clustered index. If you have had experience with a file system, your first thought might be to drop the indexes, insert the new data, sort the table, and reindex it. The utility programs for index creation can actually benefit from having a known ordering. Unfortunately, this trick does not always work in SQL. The indexes maintain the uniqueness and referential integrity constraints, and they cannot be easily dropped and restored. Files stand independently of each other; tables are part of a whole database.

8.2.3 Bulk Load and Unload Utilities

All versions of SQL have a language extension or utility program that will let you read data from an external file directly into a table. There is no standard for this tool, so they are all different. Most of these utilities require the name of the file and the format in which it is written. The simpler versions of the utility just read the file and put it into a single target table. At the other extreme, Oracle uses a miniature language that can do simple editing as each record is read. If you use a simpler tool, it is a good idea to build a working table in which you stage the data for cleanup before loading it into the actual target table. You can apply edit routines, look for duplicates, and put the bad data into another working table for inspection.

The corresponding output utility, which converts a table into a file, usually offers a choice of format options; any computations and selection can be done in SQL. Some of these programs will accept a `SELECT` statement or a `VIEW`; some will only convert a base table. Most tools now have an option to output `INSERT INTO` statements along with the appropriate `CREATE TABLE` and `CREATE INDEX` statements.

8.3 The UPDATE Statement

The function of the `UPDATE` statement in SQL is to change the values in zero or more columns of zero or more of rows of one table. SQL implementations will tell you how many rows were affected by an update operation or, at a minimum, return the `SQLSTATE` value for zero rows affected. There are two forms of `UPDATE` statements: positioned and searched. The positioned `UPDATE` is done with cursors; the searched `UPDATE` uses a `WHERE` that resembles the search condition in a `SELECT` statement.

Positioned `UPDATE`s will not be mentioned in this book, for several reasons. Cursors are used in a host programming language, and we are concerned with pure SQL whenever possible. Secondly, cursors in SQL are different from cursors in SQL-89 and in current implementations, and are not completely available in any implementations at the time of this writing.

8.3.1 The UPDATE Clause

The syntax for a searched update statement is

```
<update statement> :: =
```

```
  UPDATE <table name>
     SET <set clause list>
  [WHERE <search condition>]

<set clause list> :: =
  <set clause> [{, <set clause>}...]

<set clause> :: = <object column> = <update source>

<update source> :: = <value expression> | NULL | DEFAULT

<object column> :: = <column name>
```

The UPDATE clause simply gives the name of the base table or updatable view to be changed.

Notice that no correlation name is allowed in the UPDATE clause. The SQL model for an alias table name is that the engine effectively creates a new table with that new name and populates it with rows identical to the base table or updatable view from which it was built. If you had a correlation name, you would be deleting from this system-created temporary table, and it would vanish at the end of the statement. The base table would never have been touched. Having said this, you will find SQL products that allow the use of a correlation name.

The SET clause is a list of columns to be changed or made; the WHERE clause tells the statement which rows to use. For this discussion, we will assume the user doing the update has applicable UPDATE privileges for each <object column>.

Standard SQL allows a row constructor in the SET clause. The syntax looks like this:

```
UPDATE Foobar
   SET (a, b, c) = (1, 2, 3)
 WHERE x < 12;
```

This is shorthand for the usual syntax, where the row constructor values are matched position for position with the SET clause column list.

8.3.2 The WHERE Clause

As mentioned, the most important thing to remember about the WHERE clause is that it is optional. If there is no WHERE clause, all rows in the table are changed. This is a common error; if you make it, immediately execute a ROLLBACK statement, or call the DBA for help.

All rows that test TRUE for the <search condition> are marked as a subset and not as individual rows. It is also possible that this subset will be empty. This subset is used to construct a new set of rows that will be inserted into the table when the subset is deleted from the table. Note that the empty subset is a valid update that will fire declarative referential actions and triggers.

8.3.3 The SET Clause

Each assignment in the <set clause list> is executed in parallel, and each SET clause changes all the qualified rows at once—or at least that is the theoretical model. In practice, implementations will first mark all of the qualified rows in the table in one pass, using the WHERE clause. If there are no problems, then the SQL engine makes a copy of each marked row in working storage. Each SET clause is executed based on the old row image, and the results are put in the new row image. Finally, the old rows are deleted and the new rows are inserted. If an error occurs during all of this, then system does a ROLLBACK, the table is left unchanged and the errors are reported. This parallelism is not like what you find in a traditional third-generation programming language, so it may be hard to learn. This feature lets you write a statement that will swap the values in two columns, thus:

```
UPDATE MyTable
SET a = b, b = a;

This is not the same thing as

BEGIN ATOMIC
UPDATE MyTable
SET a = b;
UPDATE MyTable
SET b = a;
END;
```

In the first UPDATE, columns a and b will swap values in each row. In the second pair of UPDATEs, column a will get all of the values of column b in each row. In the second UPDATE of the pair, a, which now has the same value as the original value of b, will be written back into column b—no change at all. There are some limits as to what the value

expression can be. The same column cannot appear more than once in a `<set clause list>`—which makes sense, given the parallel nature of the statement. Since both go into effect at the same time, you would not know which `SET` clause to use.

8.3.4 Updating with a Second Table

Most updating is done with simple expressions of the form `SET <column name> = <constant value>`, because `UPDATE`s are done via data-entry programs. It is also possible to have the `<column name>` on both sides of the equal sign! This will not change any values in the table, but it can be used as a way to trigger referential actions that have an `ON UPDATE` condition. However, the `<set clause list>` does not have to contain only simple expressions. It is possible to use one table to post summary data to another. The scope of the `<table name>` is the entire `<update statement>`, so it can be referenced in the `WHERE` clause. This is easier to explain with an example. Assume we have the following tables:

```
CREATE TABLE Customers
(cust_nbr INTEGER NOT NULL PRIMARY KEY,
 acct_amt DECIMAL(8,2) NOT NULL);

CREATE TABLE Payments
(trans_nbr INTEGER NOT NULL PRIMARY KEY,
 cust_nbr INTEGER NOT NULL,
 trans_amt DECIMAL(8,2) NOT NULL);
```

The problem is to post all of the payment amounts to the balance in the Customers table, overwriting the old balance. Such a posting is usually a batch operation, so a searched `UPDATE` statement seems the logical approach. SQL-92 and some—but not all—current implementations allow you use the updated tables' names in a subquery, thus:

```
UPDATE Customers
   SET acct_amt
       = acct_amt
         - (SELECT SUM(amt)
              FROM Payments AS P1
             WHERE Customers.cust_nbr = P1.cust_nbr)
 WHERE EXISTS
```

```
(SELECT *
   FROM Payments AS P2
  WHERE Customers.cust_nbr = P2.cust_nbr);
```

When there is no payment, the scalar query will return an empty set. The `SUM()` of an empty set is always `NULL`. One of the most common programming errors made when using this trick is to write a query that could return more than one row. If you did not think about it, you might have written the last example as:

```
UPDATE Customers
   SET acct_amt
       = acct_amt
         - (SELECT payment_amt
               FROM Payments AS P1
             WHERE Customers.cust_nbr = P1.cust_nbr)
 WHERE EXISTS
       (SELECT *
          FROM Payments AS P2
         WHERE Customers.cust_nbr = P2.cust_nbr);
```

But consider the case where a customer has made more than one payment and we have both of them in the Payments table; the whole transaction will fail. The `UPDATE` statement should return an error message and `ROLLBACK` the entire `UPDATE` statement. In the first example, however, we know that we will get a scalar result because there is only one `SUM(amt)`.

The second common programming error that is made with this kind of `UPDATE` is to use an aggregate function that does not return zero when it is applied to an empty table, such as the `AVG()`. Suppose we wanted to post the average payment amount made by the Customers; we could not just replace `SUM()` with `AVG()` and acct_amt with average balance in the above `UPDATE`. Instead, we would have to add a `WHERE` clause to the `UPDATE` that gives us only those customers who made a payment, thus:

```
UPDATE Customers
   SET payment = (SELECT AVG(P1.amt)
                    FROM Payments AS P1
                   WHERE Customers.cust_nbr = P1.cust_nbr)
 WHERE EXISTS (SELECT *
                 FROM Payments AS P1
                WHERE Customers.cust_nbr = P1.cust_nbr);
```

You can use the WHERE clause to avoid NULLs in cases where a NULL would propagate in a calculation.

Another solution is to use a COALESCE() function to take care of the empty subquery result problem. The general form of this statement is

```
UPDATE T1
   SET c1 = COALESCE ((SELECT c1
                         FROM T2
                        WHERE T1.keycol = T2.keycol), T1.c1),
       c2 = COALESCE ((SELECT c2
                         FROM T2
                        WHERE T1.keycol = T2.keycol), T1.c2),
       ...
 WHERE ... ;
```

This will also leave the unmatched rows alone, but it will do a table scan on T1. Jeremy Rickard improved this by putting the COALESCE() inside the subquery SELECT list. This solution assumes that you have row constructors in your SQL product. For example:

```
UPDATE T2
   SET (c1, c2, ...)
     = (SELECT COALESCE (T1.c1, T2.c1),
               COALESCE (T1.c2, T2.c2),
               ...
          FROM T1
         WHERE T1.keycol = T2.keycol)
 WHERE ... ;
```

8.3.5 Using the CASE Expression in UPDATEs

The CASE expression is very handy for updating a table. The first trick is to realize that you can write SET a = a to do nothing. The statement given above can be rewritten as:

```
UPDATE Customers
   SET payment
     = CASE WHEN EXISTS
                 (SELECT *
                    FROM Payments AS P1
                   WHERE Customers.cust_nbr = P1.cust_nbr)
            THEN (SELECT AVG(P1.amt)
```

```
                FROM Payments AS P1
               WHERE Customers.cust_nbr = P1.cust_nbr)
        ELSE payment END;
```

This statement will scan the entire table since there is no WHERE clause. That might be a bad thing in this example—I would guess that only a small number of customers make a payment on any given day. But very often you were going to do table scans anyway, and this version can be faster.

But the real advantage of the CASE expression is the ability to combine several UPDATE statements into one statement. The execution time will be greatly improved and will save you from having to write a lot of procedural code or really ugly SQL. Consider this example. We have an inventory of books, and we want to first, reduce the books priced $25.00 and up by 10%, and second, increase the price of the books under $25.00 by 15% to make up the difference. The immediate thought is to write:

```
BEGIN ATOMIC -- wrong!
UPDATE Books
   SET price = price * 0.90
 WHERE price >= 25.00;
UPDATE Books
   SET price = price * 1.15
 WHERE price < 25.00;
END;
```

But this does not work. Consider a book priced at exactly $25.00. It goes through the first UPDATE and it is repriced at $22.50; then it goes through the second UPDATE and is repriced $25.88, which is not what we wanted. Flipping the two statements will produce the desired results for this book, but given a book priced at $24.95, we will get $28.69 and then $25.82 as a final price.

```
UPDATE Books
   SET price = CASE WHEN price < 25.00
                    THEN price = price * 1.15
                    ELSE price = price * 0.90 END;
```

This is not only faster, but also correct. However, you have to be careful and be sure that you did not really want a series of functions

applied to the same columns in a particular order. If that is the case, then you need to try to make each assignment expression within the SET clause stand by itself as a complete function instead of one step in a process. Consider this example:

```
BEGIN ATOMIC
UPDATE Foobar
   SET a = x
 WHERE r = 1;
UPDATE Foobar
   SET b = y
 WHERE s = 2;
UPDATE Foobar
   SET c = z
 WHERE t = 3;
UPDATE Foobar
   SET c = z + 1
 WHERE t = 4;
END;
```

This can be replaced by:

```
UPDATE Foobar
   SET a = CASE WHEN r = 1 THEN x ELSE a END,
       b = CASE WHEN s = 2 THEN y ELSE b END,
       c = CASE WHEN t = 3 THEN z
                WHEN t = 4 THEN z + 1
                ELSE c END
 WHERE r = 1
    OR s = 2
    OR t IN (3, 4);
```

The WHERE clause is optional, but might improve performance if the index is right and the candidate set is small. Notice that this approach is driven by the destination of the UPDATE—the columns appear only once in the SET clause. The traditional approach is driven by the source of the changes; first you make updates from one data source, then from the next, and so forth. Think about how you would do this with a set of magnetic tapes applied against a master file.

8.4 A Note on Flaws in a Common Vendor Extension

While I do not like to spend much time discussing nonstandard SQL-like languages, the T-SQL language from Sybase and Microsoft has a horrible flaw in it that users need to be warned about. They have a proprietary syntax that allows a **FROM** clause in the **UPDATE** statement. If the base table being updated is represented more than once in the **FROM** clause, then its rows can be operated on multiple times, in a total violation of relational principles. The correct answer is that when you try to put more than one value into a column, you get a cardinality violation and the **UPDATE** fails. Here is a quick example:

```
CREATE TABLE T1 (x INTEGER NOT NULL);
INSERT INTO T1 VALUES (1), (2), (3), (4);

CREATE TABLE T2 (x INTEGER NOT NULL);
INSERT INTO T2 VALUES (1), (1), (1), (1);
```

Now try to update T1 by doubling all the rows that have a match in T2. The **FROM** clause in the original Sybase version gave you a **CROSS JOIN**.

```
UPDATE T1
   SET T1.x = 2 * T1.x
  FROM T2
 WHERE T1.x = T2.x;
```

```
T1
    x
 ====
   16
    2
    3
    4
```

This is a very simple example, as you can see, but you get the idea. Some of this problem has been fixed in the current version of Sybase, but the syntax is still not standard or portable.

The Microsoft version solved the cardinality problem by simply grabbing one of the values based on the current physical arrangement of the rows in the table. This is a simple example from Adam Machanic:

```
CREATE TABLE Foo
(col_a CHAR(1) NOT NULL,
 col_b INTEGER NOT NULL);

INSERT INTO Foo VALUES ('A', 0),('B', 0),('C', 0);

CREATE TABLE Bar
(col_a CHAR(1) NOT NULL,
 col_b INTEGER NOT NULL);

INSERT INTO Bar
VALUES ('A', 1), ('A', 2),('B', 1), ('C', 1);
```

You run this proprietary UPDATE with a FROM clause:

```
UPDATE Foo
   SET Foo.col_b = Bar.col_b
  FROM Foo INNER JOIN Bar
       ON Foo.col_a = Bar.col_a;
```

The result of the UPDATE cannot be determined. The value of the column will depend upon either order of insertion, (if there are no clustered indexes present), or on order of clustering (but only if the cluster is not fragmented).

8.5 MERGE Statement

SQL-99 added a single statement to mimic a common magnetic tape file system "merge and insert" procedure. The business logic, in a pseudo-code, is like this.

```
FOR EACH row IN the Transactions table
DO IF working row NOT IN Master table
   THEN INSERT working row INTO the Master table;
   ELSE UPDATE Master table
           SET Master table columns to the Transactions table
values
         WHERE they meet a matching criteria;
   END IF;
END FOR;
```

In the 1950s, we would sort the transaction tape(s) and Master tape on the same key, read each one looking for a match, then perform whatever logic is needed. In its simplest form, the MERGE statement looks like this:

```
MERGE INTO <table name> [AS [<correlation name>]]
USING <table reference> ON <search condition>
{WHEN [NOT] MATCHED [AND <search condition>]
 THEN <modification operation>} ...
[ELSE IGNORE]
```

You will notice that use of a correlation name in the MERGE INTO clause is in complete violation of the principle that a correlation name effectively creates a temporary table. There are several other places where SQL 2003 destroyed the original SQL language model, but you do not have to write irregular syntax in all cases.

After a row is matched (or not) to the target table, you can add more <search condition>s in the WHEN clauses. The <modification operation> clause can include insertion, update, or delete operations that follow the same rules as those single statements. This approach can hide complex programming logic in a single statement.

Let's assume that that we have a table of Personnel salary changes at the branch office in a table called PersonnelChanges. Here is a MERGE statement that will take the contents of the PersonnelChanges table and merge them with the Personnel table. Both of them use the emp_nbr as the key. This is a typical, but very simple, use of MERGE INTO.

```
MERGE INTO Personnel
USING (SELECT emp_nbr, salary, bonus, comm
         FROM PersonnelChanges) AS C
  ON Personnel.emp_nbr = C.emp_nbr
WHEN MATCHED
THEN UPDATE
        SET (Personnel.salary, Personnel.bonus, Personnel.comm)
            = (C.salary, C.bonus, C.comm)
WHEN NOT MATCHED
THEN INSERT
     (Personnel.emp_nbr, Personnel.salary, Personnel.bonus,
Personnel.comm)
     VALUES (C.emp_nbr, C.salary, C.bonus, C.comm);
```

Think about it for a minute. If there is a match, then all you can do is update the row. If there is no match, then all you can do is insert the new row.

There are proprietary versions of this statement and other options. In particular, look for the tern "upsert" in the literature. These statements are most often used for adding data to a data warehouse.

If you do not have this statement, you can get the same effect from this pseudocode block of code.

```
BEGIN ATOMIC
UPDATE T1
   SET (a, b, c, ...
       = (SELECT a, b, c, ...
            FROM T2
           WHERE T1.somekey = T2.somekey),
 WHERE EXISTS
       (SELECT *
          FROM T2
         WHERE T1.somekey = T2.somekey);

INSERT INTO T1
SELECT *
  FROM T2
 WHERE NOT EXISTS
       (SELECT *
          FROM T2
         WHERE T1.somekey = T2.somekey);
END;
```

For performance, first do the `UPDATE`, then the `INSERT INTO`. If you `INSERT INTO` first, all rows just inserted will be affected by the `UPDATE` as well.

Comparison or Theta Operators

DR. CODD INTRODUCED THE term "theta operators" in his early papers to refer to what a programmer would have called comparison predicate operators. The large number of data types in SQL makes doing comparisons a little harder than in other programming languages. Values of one data type have to be promoted to values of the other data type before the comparison can be done. The available data types are implementation- and hardware-dependent, so read the manuals for your product.

The comparison operators are overloaded and will work for `<numeric>`, `<character>`, and `<datetime>` data types. The symbols and meanings for comparison operators are shown in table 9.1.

Table 9.1 *Symbols and Meanings for Comparison Operators*

operator	numeric	character	datetime
< :	less than	(collates before)	(earlier than)
= :	equal	(collates equal to)	(same time as)
> :	greater than	(collates after)	(later than)
<= :	at most	(collates before or equals)	(no earlier than)
<> :	not equal	(not the same as)	(not the same time as)
>= :	at least	(collates after or equals)	(no later than)

You will also see != or ~= for "not equal to" in some older SQL implementations. These symbols are borrowed from the C and PL/I programming languages, respectively, and have never been part of standard SQL. It is a bad habit to use them, since it destroys the portability of your code and makes it harder to read.

9.1 Converting Data Types

Numeric data types are all mutually comparable and mutually assignable. If an assignment will result in a loss of the most significant digits, an exception condition is raised. If the least significant digits are lost, the implementation defines what rounding or truncating has occurred and does not report an exception condition. Most often, one value is converted to the same data type as the other, and then the comparison is done in the usual way. The chosen data type is the "higher" of the two, using the following ordering: `SMALLINT`, `INTEGER`, `BIGINT`, `DECIMAL`, `NUMERIC`, `REAL`, `FLOAT`, `DOUBLEPRECISION`.

Floating-point hardware will often affect comparisons for `REAL`, `FLOAT`, and `DOUBLEPRECISION` numbers. There is no good way to avoid this, since it is not always reasonable to use `DECIMAL` or `NUMERIC` in their place. A host language will probably use the same floating-point hardware, so at least errors will be constant across the application.

`CHARACTER` and `CHARACTER VARYING` data types are comparable if and only if they are taken from the same character repertoire. That means that ASCII characters cannot be compared to graphics characters, English cannot be compared to Arabic, and so on. In most implementations, this is not a problem, because the database has only one repertoire.

The comparison takes the shorter of the two strings and pads it with spaces. The strings are compared position by position from left to right, using the collating sequence for the repertoire—ASCII or EBCDIC, in most cases.

Temporal (or `<datetime>`, as they are called in the standard) data types are mutually assignable only if the source and target of the assignment have the same `<datetime>` fields. That is, you cannot compare a date and a time.

The `CAST()` operator can do explicit type conversions before you do a comparison. Table 9.2 shows the valid combinations of source and target data types in Standard SQL . Y means that the combination is syntactically valid without restriction; M indicates that the combination is valid subject to other syntax rules; and N indicates that the combination is not valid. The codes mean yes, maybe, and no in English.

Table 9.2 *Valid Combinations of Source and Target Data Types in Standard SQL*

<value	<cast target>										
expr>	EN	AN	VC	FC	VB	FB	D	T	TS	YM	DT
EN	Y	Y	Y	Y	N	N	N	N	N	M	M
AN	Y	Y	Y	Y	N	N	N	N	N	N	N
C	Y	Y	M	M	Y	Y	Y	Y	Y	Y	Y
B	N	N	Y	Y	Y	Y	N	N	N	N	N
D	N	N	Y	Y	N	N	Y	N	Y	N	N
T	N	N	Y	Y	N	N	N	Y	Y	N	N
TS	N	N	Y	Y	N	N	Y	Y	Y	N	N
YM	M	N	Y	Y	N	N	N	N	N	Y	N
DT	M	N	Y	Y	N	N	N	N	N	N	Y

In Table 9.2,

EN = Exact Numeric

AN = Approximate Numeric

C = Character (Fixed- or Variable-length)

FC = Fixed-length Character

VC = Variable-length Character

B = Bit String (Fixed- or Variable-length)

FB = Fixed-length Bit String

VB = Variable-length Bit String

D = Date

T = Time

TS = Timestamp

YM = Year-Month Interval

DT = Day-Time Interval

9.2 Row Comparisons in SQL

Standard SQL generalized the theta operators so they would work on row expressions and not just on scalars. This feature is not yet popular, but it is very handy for situations where a key is made from more than one column, and so forth. This makes SQL more orthogonal, and it has an intuitive feel to it. Take three row constants:

```
A = (10, 20, 30, 40);

B = (10, NULL, 30, 40);

C = (10, NULL, 30, 100);
```

It seems reasonable to define a row comparison as valid only when the data types of each corresponding column in the rows are union-compatible. If not, the operation is an error and should report a warning. It also seems reasonable to define the results of the comparison to the ANDed results of each corresponding column using the same operator. That is, (A = B) becomes:

```
((10, 20, 30, 40) = (10, NULL, 30, 40));
```

becomes:

```
((10 = 10) AND (20 = NULL) AND (30 = 30) AND (40 = 40))
```

becomes:

```
(TRUE AND UNKNOWN AND TRUE AND TRUE);
```

becomes:

```
(UNKNOWN);
```

This seems to be reasonable and conforms to the idea that a NULL is a missing value that we expect to resolve at a future date, so we cannot draw a conclusion about this comparison just yet. Now consider the comparison (A = C), which becomes:

```
((10, 20, 30, 40) = (10, NULL, 30, 100));
```

becomes:

```
((10 = 10) AND (20 = NULL) AND (30 = 30) AND (40 = 100));
```

becomes:

```
(TRUE AND UNKNOWN AND TRUE AND FALSE);
```

becomes:

```
(FALSE);
```

There is no way to pick a value for column 2 of row C such that the UNKNOWN result will change to TRUE, because the fourth column is always FALSE. This leaves you with a situation that is not very intuitive. The first case can resolve to TRUE or FALSE, but the second case can only go to FALSE.

Standard SQL decided that the theta operators would work as shown in the table below. The expression RX <comp op> RY is shorthand for a row RX compared to a row RY; likewise, RXi means the *i*th column in the row RX. The results are still TRUE, FALSE, or UNKNOWN, if there is no error in type matching. The rules favor solid tests for TRUE or FALSE, using UNKNOWN as a last resort.

The idea of these rules is the same principle that you would use to compare words alphabetically. As you read the columns from left to right, match them by position and compare each one. This is how it would work if you were alphabetizing words.

The rules are

1. RX = RY is TRUE if and only if RXi = RYi for all *i*.
2. RX <> RY is TRUE if and only if RXi <> RYi for some *i*.
3. RX < RY is TRUE if and only if RXi = RYi for all $i < n$ and RXn < RYn for some *n*.
4. RX > RY is TRUE if and only if RXi = RYi for all $i < n$ and RXn > RYn for some *n*.
5. RX <= RY is TRUE if and only if Rx = Ry or Rx < Ry.
6. RX >= RY is TRUE if and only if Rx = Ry or Rx > Ry.
7. RX = RY is FALSE if and only if RX <> RY is TRUE.

8. RX <> RY is FALSE if and only if RX = RY is TRUE.
9. RX < RY is FALSE if and only if RX >= RY is TRUE.
10. RX > RY is FALSE if and only if RX <= RY is TRUE.
11. RX <= RY is FALSE if and only if RX > RY is TRUE.
12. RX >= RY is FALSE if and only if RX < RY is TRUE.
13. RX <comp op> RY is UNKNOWN if and only if RX <comp op> RY is neither TRUE nor FALSE.

The negations are defined so that the NOT operator will still have its usual properties. Notice that a NULL in a row will give an UNKNOWN result in a comparison. Consider this expression:

```
(a, b, c) < (x, y, z)
```

which becomes:

```
((a < x)
  OR ((a = x) AND (b < y))
  OR ((a = x) AND (b = y) AND (c < z)))
```

The standard allows a single-row expression of any sort, including a single-row subquery, on either side of a comparison. Likewise, the BETWEEN predicate can use row expressions in any position in Standard SQL.

Valued Predicates

VALUED PREDICATES IS MY term for a set of related unary Boolean predicates that test for the logical value or NULL value of their operands. IS NULL has always been part of SQL, but the logical IS predicate was new to SQL-92, and is not well implemented at this time.

10.1 IS NULL Predicate

The IS NULL predicate is a test for a NULL value in a column with the syntax:

```
<null predicate> ::= <row value constructor> IS [NOT] NULL
```

It is the only way to test to see if an expression is NULL or not, and it has been in SQL-86 and all later versions of the standard. The SQL-92 standard extended it to accept <row value constructor>, instead of a single column or scalar expression, as we saw in Section 9.2.

This extended version will start showing up in implementations when other row expressions are allowed. If all the values in row R are the NULL value, then R IS NULL is TRUE; otherwise, it is FALSE. If none of the values in R are NULL value, R IS NOT NULL is TRUE; otherwise, it is FALSE. The case where the row is a mix of NULL and

non-**NULL** values is defined by Table 10.1, where Degree means the number of columns in the row expression.

Table 10.1 *Cases Where a Row Is a Mix of NULL and non-**NULL** Values*

Expression	R IS NULL	R IS NOT NULL	NOT R IS NULL	NOT R IS NOT NULL
Degree = 1				
NULL	TRUE	FALSE	FALSE	TRUE
No NULL	FALSE	TRUE	TRUE	FALSE
Degree > 1				
All NULLs	TRUE	FALSE	FALSE	TRUE
Some NULLs	FALSE	FALSE	TRUE	TRUE
No NULLs	FALSE	TRUE	TRUE	FALSE

Note that `R IS NOT NULL` has the same result as `NOT R IS NULL` if and only if R is of degree 1. This is a break in the usual pattern of predicates with a `NOT` option in them. Here are some examples:

```
(1, 2, 3) IS NULL = FALSE
(1, NULL, 3) IS NULL = FALSE
(1, NULL, 3) IS NOT NULL = FALSE
(NULL, NULL, NULL) IS NULL = TRUE
(NULL, NULL, NULL) IS NOT NULL = FALSE
NOT (1, 2, 3) IS NULL = TRUE
NOT (1, NULL, 3) IS NULL = TRUE
NOT (1, NULL, 3) IS NOT NULL = TRUE
NOT (NULL, NULL, NULL) IS NULL = FALSE
NOT (NULL, NULL, NULL) IS NOT NULL = TRUE
```

10.1.1 Sources of NULLs

It is important to remember where `NULL`s can occur. They are more than just a possible value in a column. Aggregate functions on empty sets, `OUTER JOIN`s, arithmetic expressions with `NULL`s, and OLAP operators all return `NULL`s. These constructs often show up as columns in `VIEW`s.

10.2 IS [NOT]{TRUE | FALSE | UNKNOWN} Predicate

This predicate tests a condition that has the truth-value `TRUE`, `FALSE`, or `UNKNOWN`, and returns `TRUE` or `FALSE`. The syntax is:

```
<Boolean test> ::=
    <Boolean primary> [IS [NOT] <truth value>]

<truth value> ::= TRUE | FALSE | UNKNOWN

<Boolean primary> ::=
    <predicate> | <left paren> <search condition> <right paren>
```

As you would expect, the expression `IS NOT <logical value>` is the same as `NOT (IS <logical value>)`, so the predicate can be defined as shown in Table 10.2.

Table 10.2 *Defining the Predicate: True, False, or Unknown*

IS condition	TRUE	FALSE	UNKNOWN
TRUE	TRUE	FALSE	FALSE
FALSE	FALSE	TRUE	FALSE
UNKNOWN	FALSE	FALSE	TRUE

If you are familiar with some of Chris Date's writings, his `MAYBE(x)` predicate is not the same as the ANSI `(x) IS NOT FALSE` predicate, but it is equivalent to the `(x) IS UNKNOWN` predicate. Date's predicate excludes the case where all conditions in the predicate are `TRUE`.

Date points out that it is difficult to ask a conditional question in English. To borrow one of his examples (Date 1990), consider the problem of finding employees who might be programmers born before January 18, 1975 with a salary less than $50,000. The statement of the problem is a bit unclear as to what the "might be" covers—just being a programmer, or all three conditions. Let's assume that we want some doubt on any of the three conditions. With this predicate, the answer is fairly easy to write:

```
SELECT *
  FROM Personnel
 WHERE (job = 'Programmer'
        AND dob < CAST ('1975-01-18' AS DATE)
        AND salary < 50000) IS UNKNOWN;
```

This could be expanded in the old SQL-89 to:

```
SELECT *
  FROM Personnel
 WHERE (job = 'Programmer'
        AND dob < CAST ('1975-01-18' AS DATE)
        AND salary < 50000.00)
    OR (job IS NULL
        AND dob < CAST ('1975-01-18' AS DATE)
        AND salary < 50000.00)
    OR (job = 'Programmer'
        AND dob IS NULL
        AND salary < 50000.00)
    OR (job = 'Programmer'
        AND dob < CAST ('1975-01-18' AS DATE)
        AND salary IS NULL)
    OR (job IS NULL
        AND dob IS NULL
        AND salary < 50000.00)
    OR (job IS NULL
        AND dob < CAST ('1975-01-18' AS DATE)
        AND salary IS NULL)
    OR (job = 'Programmer'
        AND dob IS NULL
        AND salary IS NULL)
    OR (job IS NULL
        AND dob IS NULL
        AND salary IS NULL);
```

The problem is that every possible combination of `NULL`s and non-`NULL`s has to be tested. Since there are three predicates involved, this gives us (3^2) = 8 combinations to check out. The `IS NOT UNKNOWN` predicate does not have to bother with the combinations, only the final logical value.

10.3 IS [NOT] NORMALIZED Predicate

`<string> IS [ NOT] NORMALIZED` determines whether a Unicode string is one of the four normal forms (D, C, KD, or KC). The use of the words "normal form" here are not the same as in a relational context. In the Unicode model, a single character can be built from several other characters. Accent marks can be put on basic Latin letters. Certain combinations of letters can be displayed as ligatures ('æ' becomes 'Ê'). Some languages, such as Hangul (Korean) and Vietnamese, build glyphs from concatenating symbols in two dimensions. Some languages have special forms of one letter that are determined by context, such as the terminal sigma in Greek or accented 'u' in Czech. In short, writing is more complex than just putting one letter after another.

The Unicode standard defines the order of such constructions in their normal forms. You can still produce the same results with different orderings and sometimes with different combinations of symbols. But it is very handy when you are searching such text to know that it is normalized, rather than to try and parse each glyph on the fly. You can find details about normalization and links to free software at www.unicode.org.

CASE Expressions

THE CASE EXPRESSION IS probably the most useful addition in SQL-92. This is a quick overview of how to use the expression, but you will find other tricks spread throughout the book.

The reason it is so important is that:

1. It works with any data type.
2. It allows the programmer to avoid procedural code by replacing `IF-THEN-ELSE` control flow with `CASE` expression inside the query.
3. It makes SQL statements equivalent to primitive recursive functions. You can look up what that means in a book on the theory of computation, but it is a nice mathematical property that guarantees certain kinds of problems can be solved.

11.1 The CASE Expression

The `CASE` expression allows the programmer to pick a value based on a logical expression in his code. ANSI stole the idea and the syntax from the now-defunct Ada programming language. Here is the syntax for a `<case specification>`:

```
<case specification> ::= <simple case> | <searched case>

<simple case> ::=
   CASE <case operand>
     <simple when clause>...
     [<else clause>]
   END

<searched case> ::=
   CASE
     <searched when clause>...
     [<else clause>]
   END

<simple when clause> ::= WHEN <when operand> THEN <result>

<searched when clause> ::= WHEN <search condition> THEN
<result>

<else clause> ::= ELSE <result>

<case operand> ::= <value expression>

<when operand> ::= <value expression>

<result> ::= <result expression> | NULL

<result expression> ::= <value expression>
```

The searched `CASE` expression is probably the most used version of the expression. First, the expression is given a data type by finding the highest data type in its `THEN` clauses. The `WHEN ... THEN ...` clauses are executed in left-to-right order. The first `WHEN` clause that tests `TRUE` returns the value given in its `THEN` clause.

And, yes, you can nest `CASE` expressions inside each other. If no explicit `ELSE` clause is given for the `CASE` expression, then the database will insert an implicit `ELSE NULL` clause. If you wish to return a `NULL` from a `THEN`, however, you should use a `CAST (NULL AS <data type>)` expression to establish the data type for the compiler.

```
--this works
 CASE WHEN 1 = 1
      THEN NULL
      ELSE CAST(NULL AS INTEGER) END

--this works
  CASE WHEN 1 = 1
       THEN CAST(NULL AS INTEGER)
       ELSE NULL END

--this does not work; no <result> to establish a data type
  CASE WHEN 1 = 1
       THEN NULL
       ELSE NULL END

--might or might not work in your SQL
 CAST (CASE WHEN 1 = 1
       THEN NULL
       ELSE NULL END AS INTEGER)
```

I recommend always writing an explicit `ELSE` clause, so that you can change it later when you find a value to return. I would also recommend that you explicitly cast a `NULL` in the `CASE` expression `THEN` clause to the desired data type.

If the `THEN` clauses have results of different data types, the compiler will find the most general one and `CAST()` the others to it. But again, actual implementations might have slightly different ideas about how and when this casting should be done.

The `<simple case expression>` is defined as a searched `CASE` expression in which all the `WHEN` clauses are made into equality comparisons against the `<case operand>`. For example:

```
CASE iso_sex_code
WHEN 0 THEN 'Unknown'
WHEN 1 THEN 'Male'
WHEN 2 THEN 'Female'
WHEN 9 THEN 'N/A'
ELSE NULL END
```

This could also be written as:

```
CASE
WHEN iso_sex_code = 0 THEN 'Unknown'
WHEN iso_sex_code = 1 THEN 'Male'
WHEN iso_sex_code = 2 THEN 'Female'
WHEN iso_sex_code = 9 THEN 'N/A'
ELSE NULL END
```

There is a gimmick in this definition, however. The expression:

```
CASE foo
WHEN 1 THEN 'bar'
WHEN NULL THEN 'no bar'
END
```

becomes:

```
CASE WHEN foo = 1 THEN 'bar'
     WHEN foo = NULL THEN 'no_bar'  -- problem!
     ELSE NULL END
```

The `WHEN foo = NULL` clause is always `UNKNOWN`. This definition can get really weird with a random number generator in the expression. Let's assume that `RANDOM()` uses a seed value and returns a uniformly distributed random floating point number between 0.0000 and 0.99999999 . . . 99 whenever it is called.

This expression will spend most of its time in the `ELSE` clause instead of returning a number word between one and five.

```
SET pick_one = CASE CAST((5.0 * RANDOM()) + 1 AS INTEGER)
               WHEN 1 THEN 'one'
               WHEN 2 THEN 'two'
               WHEN 3 THEN 'three'
               WHEN 4 THEN 'four'
               WHEN 5 THEN 'five'
               ELSE 'This should not happen' END;
```

The expansion will reproduce the `CAST()` expression for each `WHEN` clause, and the `RANDOM()` function will be reevaluated each time. You need to be sure that it is evaluated only once.

```
BEGIN
  DECLARE pick_a_number INTEGER;
  SET pick_a_number = CAST((5.0 * RANDOM()) + 1 AS INTEGER);
  SET pick_one = CASE pick_a_number
                 WHEN 1 THEN 'one'
                 WHEN 2 THEN 'two'
                 WHEN 3 THEN 'three'
                 WHEN 4 THEN 'four'
                 WHEN 5 THEN 'five'
                 ELSE 'This should not happen' END;

END;
```

The variable pick_a_number is also expanded in the WHEN clause, but because it is not a function call, it is not evaluated over and over.

11.1.1 The COALESCE() and NULLIF() Functions

The SQL-92 Standard defines other functions in terms of the CASE expression, which makes the language a bit more compact and easier to implement. For example, the COALESCE() function can be defined for one or two expressions by:

```
1) COALESCE (<value exp #1>) is equivalent to (<value exp #1>)
2) COALESCE (<value exp #1>, <value exp #2>) is equivalent to
   CASE WHEN <value exp #1> IS NOT NULL
        THEN <value exp #1>
        ELSE <value exp #2> END
```

Then we can recursively define it for (*n*) expressions, where (*n* >= 3), in the list by:

```
COALESCE (<value exp #1>, <value exp #2>, ..., n), as equivalent
to:
   CASE WHEN <value exp #1> IS NOT NULL
        THEN <value exp #1>
        ELSE COALESCE (<value exp #2>, ..., n)
   END
```

Likewise,

```
NULLIF (<value exp #1>, <value exp #2>) is equivalent to:
```

```
CASE WHEN <value exp #1> = <value exp #2>
     THEN NULL
     ELSE <value exp #1> END
```

11.1.2 CASE Expressions with GROUP BY

A CASE expression is very useful with a GROUP BY query. For example, to determine how many employees of each gender by department you have in your Personnel table, you can write:

```
SELECT dept_nbr,
       SUM(CASE WHEN gender = 'M' THEN 1 ELSE 0) AS males,
       SUM(CASE WHEN gender = 'F' THEN 1 ELSE 0) AS females
  FROM Personnel
 GROUP BY dept_nbr;
```

or:

```
SELECT dept_nbr,
       COUNT(CASE WHEN gender = 'M' THEN 1 ELSE NULL) AS males,
       COUNT(CASE WHEN gender = 'F' THEN 1 ELSE NULL) AS females
  FROM Personnel
 GROUP BY dept_nbr;
```

I am not sure if there is any general rule as to which form will run faster. Aggregate functions remove NULLs before they perform their operations, so the order of execution might be different in the ELSE 0 and the ELSE NULL versions.

The previous example shows the CASE expression inside the aggregate function; it is possible to put aggregate functions inside a CASE expression. For example, assume you are given a table of employees' skills:

```
CREATE TABLE PersonnelSkills
(emp_id CHAR(11) NOT NULL,
 skill_id CHAR(11) NOT NULL,
 primary_skill_ind CHAR(1) NOT NULL
                   CONSTRAINT primary_skill_given
                   CHECK (primary_skill_ind IN ('Y', 'N'),
PRIMARY KEY (emp_id, skill_id));
```

Each employee has a row in the table for each of his skills. If the employee has multiple skills, she will have multiple rows in the table, and the primary skill indicator will be a 'Y' for her main skill. If she only has one skill (which means one row in the table), the value of primary_skill_ind is indeterminate. The problem is to list each employee once along with her only skill, if she only has one row in the table, or her primary skill, if she has multiple rows in the table.

```
SELECT emp_id,
       CASE WHEN COUNT(*) = 1
            THEN MAX(skill_id)
            ELSE MAX(CASE WHEN primary_skill_ind = 'Y'
                          THEN skill_id END)
                          ELSE NULL END)
       END AS main_skill
  FROM PersonnelSkills
 GROUP BY emp_id;
```

This solution looks at first like a violation of the rule in SQL that prohibits nested aggregate functions, but if you look closely, it is not. The outermost CASE expression resolves to an aggregate function, namely MAX(). The ELSE clause simply has to return an expression inside its MAX() that can be resolved to a single value.

11.1.3 CASE, CHECK() Clauses and Logical Implication

Complicated logical predicates can be put into a CASE expression that returns either 1 (TRUE) or 0 (FALSE):

```
CONSTRAINT implication_example
CHECK (CASE WHEN dept_nbr = 'D1'
            THEN CASE WHEN salary < 44000.00
                      THEN 1 ELSE 0 END
            ELSE 1 END = 1)
```

This is a logical implication operator. It is usually written as an arrow with two stems (⇒), and its definition is usually stated as "a true premise cannot imply a false conclusion" or as "if a then b."

In English, the above condition says "if an employee is in department 'D1', then his salary is less than $44,000.00," which is not the same as saying (dept_nbr = 'D1' AND salary < 44000.00) in the

constraint. In standard Boolean logic, there is a simple transformation called the Smisteru rule (after the engineer who discovered it), which says that `(A ⇒ B)` is equivalent to `(NOT (A) OR B)`.

In SQL, the Data Declaration language (DDL) uses predicates in CHECK() constraints and treats TRUE and UNKNOWN alike. The Data Manipulation Language (DML) uses predicates in the WHERE and ON clauses and treats treats FALSE and UNKNOWN alike. How do you define logical implication with two different rules?

Let's try the Smisteru transform first:

```
CREATE TABLE Foobar_DDL_1
(a CHAR(1) CHECK (a IN ('T', 'F')),
 b CHAR(1) CHECK (b IN ('T', 'F')),
CONSTRAINT implication_example
CHECK (NOT (A ='T') OR (B = 'T')));

INSERT INTO Foobar_DDL_1 VALUES ('T', 'T');
INSERT INTO Foobar_DDL_1 VALUES ('T', 'F'); -- fails
INSERT INTO Foobar_DDL_1 VALUES ('T', NULL);
INSERT INTO Foobar_DDL_1 VALUES ('F', 'T');
INSERT INTO Foobar_DDL_1 VALUES ('F', 'F');
INSERT INTO Foobar_DDL_1 VALUES ('F', NULL);
INSERT INTO Foobar_DDL_1 VALUES (NULL, 'T');
INSERT INTO Foobar_DDL_1 VALUES (NULL, 'F');
INSERT INTO Foobar_DDL_1 VALUES (NULL, NULL);

SELECT * FROM Foobar_DDL_1;

Results
a       b
===========
T        T
T        NULL
F        T
F        F
F        NULL
NULL     T
NULL     F
NULL     NULL
```

Now my original version:

```
CREATE TABLE Foobar_DDL
(a CHAR(1) CHECK (a IN ('T', 'F')),
 b CHAR(1) CHECK (b IN ('T', 'F')),
CONSTRAINT implication_example_2
CHECK(CASE WHEN A = 'T'
           THEN CASE WHEN B = 'T'
                THEN 1 ELSE 0 END
           ELSE 1 END = 1));

INSERT INTO Foobar_DDL
VALUES ('T', 'T')
       ('T', 'F'), -- fails
       ('T', NULL),
       ('F', 'T'), ('F', 'F'), ('F', NULL),
       (NULL, 'T'), (NULL, 'F'), (NULL, NULL);

SELECT * FROM Foobar_DDL;

Results
a       b
===========
T       T
F       T
F       F
F       NULL
NULL    T
NULL    F
NULL    NULL
```

Both agree that a `TRUE` premise cannot lead to a `FALSE` conclusion, but Smisteru allows `('T', NULL)`. Not quite the same implication operators!

Let's now look at the query side of the house:

```
CREATE TABLE Foobar_DML
(a CHAR(1) CHECK (a IN ('T', 'F')),
 b CHAR(1) CHECK (b IN ('T', 'F')));

INSERT INTO Foobar_DML VALUES ('T', 'T');
```

```
INSERT INTO Foobar_DML VALUES ('T', 'F');
INSERT INTO Foobar_DML VALUES ('T', NULL);
INSERT INTO Foobar_DML VALUES ('F', 'T');
INSERT INTO Foobar_DML VALUES ('F', 'F');
INSERT INTO Foobar_DML VALUES ('F', NULL);
INSERT INTO Foobar_DML VALUES (NULL, 'T');
INSERT INTO Foobar_DML VALUES (NULL, 'F');
INSERT INTO Foobar_DML VALUES (NULL, NULL);
```

Using the Smisteru rule as the search condition:

```
SELECT * FROM Foobar_DML WHERE (NOT (A ='T') OR (B = 'T'));

Results
a      b
==========
T      T
F      T
F      F
F      NULL
NULL   T
```

Using the original predicate:

```
SELECT * FROM Foobar_DML
WHERE CASE WHEN A = 'T'
           THEN CASE WHEN B = 'T'
                THEN 1 ELSE 0 END
           ELSE 1 END = 1;

Results
a      b
==========
T      T
F      T
F      F
F      NULL
NULL   T
NULL   F
NULL   NULL
```

This is why I used the CASE expression; it works the same way in both the DDL and DML.

11.1.4 Subquery Expressions and Constants

Subquery expressions are SELECT statements inside of parentheses. Of course, there is more to it than that.

The four flavors of subquery expressions are tabular, columnar, row, and scalar subquery expressions. As you might guess from the names, the tabular or table subquery returns a table as a result, so it has to appear any place that a table is used in SQL-92, which usually means it is in the FROM clause.

The columnar subquery returns a table with a single column in it. This was the important one in the original SQL-86 and SQL-89 standards, because the IN, <comp op> ALL and <comp op> { ANY | SOME} predicates were based on the ability of the language to convert the single column into a list of comparisons connected by ANDs or ORs.

The row subquery returns a single row. It can be used anywhere a row can be used. This sort of query is the basis for the singleton SELECT statement used in the embedded SQL. It is not used too much right now, but with the extension of theta operators to handle row comparisons, it might become more popular.

The scalar subquery returns a single scalar value. It can be used anywhere a scalar value can be used, which usually means it is in the SELECT or WHERE clauses. If a scalar subquery returns an empty result, it is converted to a NULL. If a scalar subquery returns more than one row, you get a cardinality violation.

I will make the *very* general statement now that the performance of scalar subqueries depends largely on the architecture of the hardware upon which your SQL is implemented. A massively parallel machine can allocate a processor to each scalar subquery and get drastic performance improvement.

A table constant of any shape can be constructed using the VALUES() expression. New SQL programmers think that this is only an option in the INSERT INTO statement. However, Standard SQL allows you to use it to build a row as a comma-separated list of scalar expressions, and then build a table as a comma-separated list of those row constructors. Consider this lookup table of ZIP code ranges by state:

```
CREATE VIEW StateZipcodes (state_code, low_zip, high_zip)
AS VALUES ('AK', 99500, 99998),
```

```
 ...
('GA', 30000, 30399),
 ...
('WY', 82000, 83100);
```

This table cannot be changed without dropping the VIEW and rebuilding it. It has no named base table.

11.2 Rozenshtein Characteristic Functions

A characteristic function converts a logical expression into a one if it is TRUE and to a zero if it is FALSE. This is what we have been doing with some of the CASE expressions shown here, but not under that name. The literature uses a lowercase delta (δ) or a capital chi (X) as the symbol for this operator. Programmers first saw this in Ken Iverson's APL programming language, and then later in Donald Knuth's books on programming theory. The name comes from the fact that it is used to define a set by giving a rule for membership in the set.

David Rozenshtein found ways of implementing characteristic functions with algebraic expression on numeric columns in the Sybase T-SQL language (Rozenshtein 1995) before they had a CASE expression in their product. Without going into the details, I will borrow Dr. Rozenshtein's notation and give the major formulas for putting converted numeric comparisons into a computed characteristic function:

```
((a = b) becomes (1 - ABS(SIGN(a - b)))
((a <> b) becomes (ABS(SIGN(a - b)))
((a < b) becomes (1 - SIGN(1 + SIGN(a - b)))
((a <= b) becomes (SIGN(1 - SIGN(a - b)))
((a > b) becomes (1 - SIGN(1 - SIGN(a - b)))
((a >= b) becomes (SIGN(1 + SIGN(a - b)))
```

The basic logical operators can also be put into computed characteristic functions. If we ignore NULLs and use standard Boolean logic, we can write these expressions:

```
 NOT ((a)        becomes (1 - ((a))
(((a) AND ((b)) becomes SIGN(((a) * ((b))
(((a) OR ((b))  becomes SIGN(((a) + ((b))
```

If you remember George Boole's original notation for Boolean Algebra, this will look very familiar. But be aware that if *a* or *b* is a NULL, then the results will be a NULL and not a one or zero—something Mr. Boole never thought about.

Character strings can be handled with the POSITION function, if you are careful.

```
((a = s) becomes POSITION(a IN s)
((a <> s) becomes SIGN (1 - POSITION (a IN s))
```

Rozenshtein's book gives more tricks (Rozenshtein 1995), but many of them depend on Sybase's T-SQL functions and are not portable. Another problem is that the code can become very hard to read, so that what is happening is not obvious to the next programmer to read the code. At this point in time, using the CASE expression is the better choice, since a human being must maintain the code.

LIKE Predicate

THE LIKE PREDICATE IS a string pattern-matching test with the syntax:

```
<like predicate> ::=
    <match value> [NOT] LIKE <pattern>
        [ESCAPE <escape character>]

<match value> ::= <character value expression>
<pattern> ::= <character value expression>
<escape character> ::= <character value expression>
```

The expression `M NOT LIKE P` is equivalent to `NOT (M LIKE P)`, which follows the usual syntax pattern in SQL. Two wildcards are allowed in the `<pattern>` string. They are the '%' and '_' characters. The '_' character represents a single arbitrary character; the '%' character represents an arbitrary substring, possibly of length zero. Notice that there is no way to represent zero or one arbitrary character. This is not the case in many text-search languages, and can lead to problems or very complex predicates.

Any other character in the `<pattern>` represents that character itself. This means that SQL patterns are case-sensitive, but many vendors allow you to set case sensitivity on or off at the database system level.

The <escape character> is used in the <pattern> to specify that the character that follows it is to be interpreted literally rather than as a wildcard. This means that the escape character is followed by the escape character itself, an '_' or a '%'. Old C programmers are used to this convention, where the language defines the escape character as '\', so this is a good choice for SQL programmers, too.

12.1 Tricks with Patterns

The '_' character tests much faster than the '%' character. The reason is obvious: the parser that compares a string to the pattern needs only one operation to match an underscore before it can move to the next character, but has to do some look-ahead parsing to resolve a percentage sign. The wildcards can be inserted in the middle or beginning of a pattern. Thus, 'B%K' will match 'BOOK', 'BLOCK', and 'BK', but it will not match 'BLOCKS'.

The parser would scan each letter and classify it as a wildcard match or an exact match. In the case of 'BLOCKS', the initial 'B' would be an exact match and the parser would continue; 'L', 'O', and 'C' have to be wildcard matches, since they don't appear in the pattern string; 'K' cannot be classified until we read the last letter. The last letter is 'S', so the match fails.

For example, given a column declared to be seven characters long, and a LIKE predicate looking for names that start with 'Mac', you would usually write:

```
SELECT *
  FROM People
 WHERE (name LIKE 'Mac%');
```

However, this might actually run faster:

```
SELECT *
  FROM People
 WHERE (name LIKE 'Mac_   ')
    OR (name LIKE 'Mac__  ')
    OR (name LIKE 'Mac___ ')
    OR (name LIKE 'Mac____');
```

The trailing blanks are also characters that can be matched exactly.

Putting a '%' at the front of a pattern is very time-consuming. For example, you might try to find all names that end in '-son' with this query:

```
SELECT *
  FROM People
 WHERE (name LIKE '%son');
```

The use of underscores instead will make a real difference in most SQL implementations for this query, because most of them always parse from left to right.

```
SELECT *
  FROM People
 WHERE (name LIKE '_son   ')
    OR (name LIKE '__son  ')
    OR (name LIKE '___son ')
    OR (name LIKE '____son');
```

Remember that the '_' character requires a matching character, and the '%' character does not. Thus, this query:

```
SELECT *
  FROM People
 WHERE (name LIKE 'John_%');
```

and this query:

```
SELECT *
  FROM People
 WHERE (name LIKE 'John%');
```

are subtly different. Both will match to 'Johnson' and 'Johns', but the first will not accept 'John' as a match. This is how you get a "one-or-more-characters" pattern match in SQL.

Remember that the <pattern> as well as the <match value> can be constructed with concatenation operators, SUBSTRING(), and other string functions. For example, let's find people whose first names are part of their last names with the query:

```
SELECT *
  FROM People
 WHERE (lastname LIKE '%' || firstname || '%');
```

This will show us people like 'John Johnson', 'Anders Andersen', and 'Bob McBoblin'. This query will also run very slowly. However, this query is case-sensitive and would not work for names such as 'Jon Anjon', so you might want to modify the statement to:

```
SELECT *
  FROM People
 WHERE (UPPER (lastname) LIKE '%' || UPPER (firstname) || '%';
```

12.2 Results with NULL Values and Empty Strings

As you would expect, a NULL in the predicate returns an UNKNOWN result. The NULL can be the escape character, pattern, or match value.

If M and P are both character strings of length zero, M LIKE P defaults to TRUE. If one or both are longer than zero characters, you use the regular rules to test the predicate.

12.3 LIKE Is Not Equality

A very important point that is often missed is that two strings can be equal but not LIKE in SQL. The test of equality first pads the shorter of the two strings with rightmost blanks, then matches the characters in each, one for one. Thus 'Smith' and 'Smith ' (with three trailing blanks) are equal. However, the LIKE predicate does no padding, so 'Smith' LIKE 'Smith   ' tests FALSE because there is nothing to match to the blanks.

A good trick to get around these problems is to use the TRIM() function to remove unwanted blanks from the strings within either or both of the two arguments.

12.4 Avoiding the LIKE Predicate with a Join

Beginners often want to write something similar to <string> IN LIKE (<pattern list>) rather than a string of ORed LIKE predicates. That syntax is illegal, but you can get the same results with a table of patterns and a join.

```
CREATE TABLE Patterns
(template VARCHAR(10) NOT NULL PRIMARY KEY);

INSERT INTO Patterns
VALUES ('Celko%'),
       ('Chelko%'),
       ('Cilko%'),
       ('Selko%),
       ('Silko%');

SELECT A1.lastname
  FROM Patterns AS P1, Authors AS A1
 WHERE A1.lastname LIKE P1.template;
```

This idea can be generalized to find strings that differ from a pattern by one position without actually using a LIKE predicate. First, assume that we have a table of sequential numbers and these following tables with sample data.

```
-- the match patterns
CREATE TABLE MatchList (pattern CHAR(9) NOT NULL PRIMARY KEY);
INSERT INTO MatchList VALUES ('_========');
INSERT INTO MatchList VALUES ('=_=======');
INSERT INTO MatchList VALUES ('==_======');
INSERT INTO MatchList VALUES ('===_=====');
INSERT INTO MatchList VALUES ('====_====');
INSERT INTO MatchList VALUES ('=====_===');
INSERT INTO MatchList VALUES ('======_==');
INSERT INTO MatchList VALUES ('=======_=');
INSERT INTO MatchList VALUES ('========_');

-- the strings to be matched or near-matched
CREATE TABLE Target (nbr CHAR(9) NOT NULL PRIMARY KEY);
INSERT INTO Target VALUES ('123456089'), ('543434344');

-- the strings to be searched for those matches
CREATE TABLE Source (nbr CHAR(9) NOT NULL PRIMARY KEY);
INSERT INTO Source VALUES ('123456089');
INSERT INTO Source VALUES ('123056789');
INSERT INTO Source VALUES ('123456780');
INSERT INTO Source VALUES ('123456789');
```

```
INSERT INTO Source VALUES ('023456789');
INSERT INTO Source VALUES ('023456780');
```

We use an equal sign in the match patterns as a signal to replace it with the appropriate character in the source string and see if they match, but to skip over the underscore.

```
SELECT DISTINCT TR1.nbr
  FROM Sequence AS SE1, Source AS SR1,
       MatchList AS ML1, Target AS TR1
 WHERE NOT EXISTS
      (SELECT *
         FROM Sequence AS SE1, Source AS SR2,
              MatchList AS ML2, Target AS TR2
        WHERE SUBSTRING (ML2.pattern FROM seq FOR 1) = '='
          AND SUBSTRING (SR2.nbr FROM seq FOR 1)
               <> SUBSTRING (TR2.nbr FROM seq FOR 1)
          AND SR2.nbr = SR1.nbr
          AND TR2.nbr = TR1.nbr
          AND ML2.pattern = ML1.pattern
          AND SE1.seq BETWEEN 1 AND (CHARLENGTH (TR2.nbr) -1));
```

This code is due to Jonathan Blitz.

12.5 CASE Expressions and LIKE Predicates

The `CASE` expression in Standard SQL lets the programmer use the `LIKE` predicate in some interesting ways. The simplest example is counting the number of times a particular string appears inside another string. Assume that text_col is `CHAR(25)` and we want the count of a particular string, 'term', within it.

```
SELECT text_col,
       CASE
       WHEN text_col LIKE '%term%term%term%term%term%term%'
       THEN 6
       WHEN text_col LIKE '%term%term%term%term%term%'
       THEN 5
       WHEN text_col LIKE '%term%term%term%term%'
       THEN 4
       WHEN text_col LIKE '%term%term%term%'
```

```
        THEN 3
        WHEN text_col LIKE '%term%term%'
        THEN 2
        WHEN text_col LIKE '%term%'
        THEN 1
        ELSE 0 END AS term_tally
  FROM Foobar
 WHERE text_col LIKE '%term%';
```

This depends on the fact that a `CASE` expression executes the `WHEN` clauses in order of their appearance. We know that the most times a substring can appear is six, because of the length of text_col.

Another use of the `CASE` is to adjust the pattern within the `LIKE` predicate.

```
name LIKE CASE
          WHEN language = 'English'
          THEN 'Red%'
          WHEN language = 'French'
          THEN 'Rouge%'
          ELSE 'R%' END
```

12.6 SIMILAR TO Predicates

As you can see, the `LIKE` predicate is pretty weak, especially if you have used a version of grep(), a utility program from the UNIX operating system. The name is short for "general regular expression parser," and before you ask, a regular expression is a class of formal languages. If you are a computer science major, you have seen them; otherwise, don't worry about it. The bad news is that there are several versions of grep() in the UNIX community, such as egrep(), fgrep(), xgrep(), and a dozen or so others.

The SQL-99 standard added a regular expression predicate of the form `<string expression> SIMILAR TO <pattern>`, which is based on the POSIX version of grep() found in ISO/IEC 9945.

The special symbols in a pattern are:

| means alternation (either of two alternatives)

* means repetition of the previous item zero or more times

+ means repetition of the previous item one or more times

( ), parentheses, may be used to group items into a single unit

[. . .], a bracket expression, specifies a match to any of the characters inside the brackets.

There are abbreviations for lists of commonly used character subsets, taken from POSIX.

`[:ALPHA:]` match any alphabetic character, regardless of case.

`[:UPPER:]` match any upper case alphabetic character

`[:LOWER:]` match any lower case alphabetic character

`[:DIGIT:]` match any numeric digit

`[:ALNUM:]` match any numeric digit or alphabetic character

Examples:

1. The letters 'foo' or 'bar' followed by any string

```
Foobar SIMILAR TO '(foo|bar)%'
```

2. The serial number is a number sign followed by one or more digits

```
serial_nbr SIMILAR TO '#[0-9]+'
serial_nbr SIMILAR TO '#[:DIGIT:]'
```

You should still read your product manual for details, but most grep() functions accept other special symbols for more general searching than the `SIMILAR TO` predicate:

. any character (same as the SQL underscore)

^ start of line (not used in an SQL string)

$ end of line (not used in an SQL string)

\ The next character is a literal and not a special symbol; this is called an `ESCAPE` in SQL

[^] match anything but the characters inside the brackets, after the caret

Regular expressions have a lot of nice properties.

12.7 Tricks with Strings

This is a list of miscellaneous tricks that you might not think about when using strings.

12.7.1 String Character Content

A weird way of providing an edit mask for a varying character column to see if it has only digits in it was proposed by Ken Sheridan on the CompuServe ACCESS forum in October 1999. If the first character is not a zero, then you can check that the `VARCHAR(n)` string is all digits with:

```
CAST (LOG10 (CAST (test_column AS INTEGER) AS INTEGER) = n
```

If the first (*n*) characters are not all digits, then it will not return (*n*). If they are all digits, but the (*n*+1) character is also a digit, it will return (*n*+1), and so forth. If there are nondigit characters in the string, then the innermost `CAST()` function will fail to convert the test_column into a number. If you do have to worry about leading zeros or blanks, then concatenate '1' to the front of the string.

Another trick is to think in terms of whole strings, rather than in a "character-at-a-time" mindset. So how can I tell if a string is all alphabetic, partly alphabetic, or completely nonalphabetic without scanning each character? The answer, from the folks at Ocelot software, is surprisingly easy:

```
CREATE TABLE Foobar
(no_alpha VARCHAR(6) NOT NULL
            CHECK (UPPER(no_alpha) = LOWER(no_alpha)),
 some_alpha VARCHAR(6) NOT NULL
            CHECK (UPPER(some_alpha) <> LOWER(some_alpha)),
 all_alpha VARCHAR(6) NOT NULL
           CHECK (UPPER(all_alpha) <> LOWER(all_alpha)
                 AND LOWER (all_alpha)
                     BETWEEN 'aaaaaa' AND 'zzzzzz'),
  ...);
```

Letters have different upper and lowercase values, but other characters do not. This lets us edit a column for no alphabetic characters, some alphabetic characters, and all alphabetic characters.

12.7.2 Searching versus Declaring a String

You need to be very accurate when you declare a string column in your DDL, but thanks to doing that, you can slack off a bit when you search on those columns in your DML. For example, most credit card numbers are made up of four groups of four digits, and each group has some validation rule, thus:

```
CREATE TABLE CreditCards
(card_nbr CHAR(17) NOT NULL PRIMARY KEY
 CONSTRAINT valid_card_nbr_format
   CHECK (card_nbr SIMILAR TO
          '[0-9][0-9][0-9][0-9]-[0-9][0-9][0-9][0-9]-[0-9][0-
9][0-9][0-9]-[0-9][0-9][0-9][0-9]'),
 CONSTRAINT valid_bank_nbr
   CHECK (SUBSTRING (card_nbr FROM 1 FOR 4)
          IN ('2349', '2345', ...),
 ...);
```

Since we are sure that the credit card number is stored correctly, we can search for it with a simple `LIKE` predicate. For example, to find all the cards with 1234 in the third group, you can use this:

```
SELECT card_nbr
  FROM CreditCards
 WHERE card_nbr LIKE '____-____-1234-____';
```

Or even:

```
SELECT card_nbr
  FROM CreditCards
 WHERE card_nbr LIKE '__________1234_____';
```

The `SIMILAR TO` predicate will build an internal finite-state machine to parse the pattern, while the underscores in the `LIKE` can be optimized so that it can run in parallel down the whole column.

12.7.3 Creating an Index on a String

Many string-encoding techniques have the same prefix, because we read from left to right and tend to put the codes for the largest category to the left. For example, the first group of digits in the credit card numbers is the issuing bank. The syntax might look like this:

```
CREATE INDEX acct_searching
    ON CreditCards
  WITH REVERSE(card_nbr); -- not Standard SQL
```

If your SQL has the ability to define a function in an index, you can reverse or rearrange the string to give faster access. This is very dependent on your vendor, but often the query must explicitly use the same function as the index.

An alternative is to store the rearranged value in the base table and show the actual value in a view. When the view is invoked, the rearranged value will be used for the query without the users knowing it.

BETWEEN and OVERLAPS Predicates

THE BETWEEN AND OVERLAPS predicates both offer a shorthand way of showing that one value lies within a range defined by two other values. The `BETWEEN` predicate works with scalar range limits; the `OVERLAPS` predicate looks at two time periods (defined either by start and end points or by a starting time and an `INTERVAL`) to see if they overlap in time.

13.1 The BETWEEN Predicate

The predicate `<value expression> [ NOT] BETWEEN <low value expression> AND <high value expression>` is a feature of SQL that is used often enough to deserve special attention. It is also just tricky enough to fool beginning programmers. This predicate is actually just shorthand for the expression:

```
((<low value expression> <= <value expression>)
  AND (<value expression> <= <high value expression>))
```

Please note that the end points are included in this definition. This predicate works with any data types that can be compared. Most programmers miss this fact and use it only for numeric values, but it can be used for character strings and temporal data as well. The `<high`

value expression> and <low value expression> can be expressions or constants, but again, programmers tend to use just constants.

13.1.1 Results with NULL Values

The results of this predicate with NULL values for <value expression>, <low value expression>, or <high value expression> follow directly from the definition. If both <low value expression> and <high value expression> are NULL, the result is UNKNOWN for any value of <value expression>. If <low value expression> or <high value expression> is NULL, but not both of them, the result is determined by the value of <value expression> and its comparison with the remaining non-**NULL** term. If <value expression> is NULL, the results are UNKNOWN for any values of <low value expression> and <high value expression>.

13.1.2 Results with Empty Sets

Notice that if <high value expression> is less than <low value expression>, the expression will always be FALSE unless the value is NULL; then it is UNKNOWN. That is a bit confusing, since there is no value to which <value expression> could resolve itself that would produce a TRUE result. But this follows directly from expanding the definition:

```
x BETWEEN 12 AND 15 -- depends on the value of x
x BETWEEN 15 AND 12 -- always FALSE
x BETWEEN NULL AND 15 -- always UNKNOWN
NULL BETWEEN 12 AND 15 -- always UNKNOWN
x BETWEEN 12 AND NULL -- always UNKNOWN
x BETWEEN x AND x -- always TRUE
```

13.1.3 Programming Tips

The BETWEEN range includes the end points, so you have to be careful. Here is an example that deals with changing a percent range on a test into a letter grade:

```
Grades
low_score high_score grade
==========================
    90       100       'A'
```

```
80      90     'B'
70      80     'C'
60      70     'D'
00      60     'F'
```

However, this will not work when a student gets a grade on the borderlines (90, 80, 70, or 60). One way to solve the problem is to change the table by adding 1 to the low scores. Of course, the student who got 90.1 will argue that he should have gotten an 'A' and not a 'B'. If you add 0.01 to the low scores, the student who got 90.001 will argue that he should have gotten an 'A' and not a 'B', and so forth. This is a problem with a continuous variable. A better solution might be to change the predicate to `(score BETWEEN low_score AND high_score) AND (score > low_score)` or simply to `((low_score < score) AND (score <= high_score))`. Neither approach will be much different in this example, since few values will fall on the borders between grades and this table is very, very small.

As a sidebar, the reader might want to look up an introductory book to fuzzy logic. In that model, an entity can have a degree of membership in a set, rather than being strictly in or out of the set. Some experimental databases use fuzzy logic.

However, some indexing schemes might make the `BETWEEN` predicate the better choice for larger tables of this sort. They will keep index values in trees whose nodes hold a range of values (look up a description of the B-Tree family in a computer science book). An optimizer can compare the range of values in the `BETWEEN` predicate to the range of values in the index nodes as a single action. If the `BETWEEN` predicate were presented as two comparisons, it might execute them as separate actions against the database, which would be slower.

13.2 OVERLAPS Predicate

The `OVERLAPS` predicate is a feature not yet available in most SQL implementations, because it requires more of the Standard SQL temporal data features than most implementations have. Many programmers have been faking the functionality of the `INTERVAL` data type with the existing date and time features of their products.

13.2.1 Time Periods and OVERLAPS Predicate

An `INTERVAL` is a measure of temporal duration, expressed in units such as days, hours, minutes, and so forth. This is how you add or

subtract days to or from a date, hours and minutes to or from a time, and so forth. When INTERVALs are more generally available, you will also have an OVERLAPS predicate, which compares two time periods. These time periods are defined as row values with two columns. The first column (the starting time) of the pair is always a <datetime> data type, and the second column (the termination time) is a <datetime> data type that can be used to compute a <datetime> value. If the starting and termination times are the same, this is an instantaneous event.

The result of the <overlaps predicate> is formally defined as the result of the following expression:

```
(S1 > S2 AND NOT (S1 >= T2 AND T1 >= T2))
OR (S2 > S1 AND NOT (S2 >= T1 AND T2 >= T1))
OR (S1 = S2 AND (T1 <> T2 OR T1 = T2))
```

In this expression, S1 and S2 are the starting times of the two time periods, and T1 and T2 are their termination times.

The rules for the OVERLAPS predicate should be intuitive, but they are not. The principles that we wanted in the standard were:

1. A time period includes its starting point, but does not include its end point. The reason for this model is that it follows the ISO convention that there is no 24:00 today; midnight is 00:00 tomorrow. Half-open durations have closure properties that are useful. The concatenation of two half-open durations is a half-open duration.

2. If the time periods are not instantaneous, they overlap when they share a common time period.

3. If the first term of the predicate is an INTERVAL and the second term is an instantaneous event (a <datetime> data type), they overlap when the second term is in the time period (but is not the end point of the time period).

4. If the first and second terms are both instantaneous events, they overlap only when they are equal.

5. If the starting time is NULL and the finishing time is a <datetime> value, the finishing time becomes the starting time and we have an event. If the starting time is NULL and the finishing time is an INTERVAL value, then both the finishing and starting times are NULL.

Please consider how your intuition reacts to these results, when the granularity is at the YEAR-MONTH-DAY level. Remember that a day begins at 00:00.

(today, today) OVERLAPS (today, today) is TRUE

(today, tomorrow) OVERLAPS (today, today) is TRUE

(today, tomorrow) OVERLAPS (tomorrow, tomorrow) is FALSE

(yesterday, today) OVERLAPS (today, tomorrow) is FALSE

Since the OVERLAPS predicate is not yet common in SQL products, let's see what we have to do to handle overlapping times. Consider a table of hotel guests with the days of their stays and a table of special events being held at the hotel. The tables might look like this:

```
CREATE TABLE Guests
(guest_name CHARACTER(30) NOT NULL PRIMARY KEY,
 arrival_date DATE NOT NULL,
 depart_date DATE NOT NULL,
 ...);

 Guests
 guest_name       arrival_date     depart_date
 ===============================================
 'Dorothy Gale'    '2005-02-01'    '2005-11-01'
 'Indiana Jones'   '2005-02-01'    '2005-02-01'
 'Don Quixote'     '2005-01-01'    '2005-10-01'
 'James T. Kirk'   '2005-02-01'    '2005-02-28'
 'Santa Claus'     '2005-12-01'    '2005-12-25'

 CREATE TABLE Celebrations
 (eventname CHARACTER(30) PRIMARY KEY,
  start_date DATE NOT NULL,
  finish_date DATE NOT NULL,
  ...);

 Celebrations
 celeb_name              start_date      finish_date
 ===================================================
 'Apple Month'           '2005-02-01'    '2005-02-28'
 'Christmas Season'      '2005-12-01'    '2005-12-25'
```

```
'Garlic Festival'      '2005-01-15'    '2005-02-15'
'National Pear Week'   '2005-01-01'    '2005-01-07'
'New Year's Day'       '2005-01-01'    '2005-01-01'
'St. Fred's Day'       '2005-02-24'    '2005-02-24'
'Year of the Prune'    '2005-01-01'    '2005-12-31'
```

The BETWEEN operator will work just fine with single dates that fall between the starting and finishing dates of these celebrations, but please remember that the BETWEEN predicate will include the end point of an interval, and the OVERLAPS predicate will not. To find out if a particular date occurs during an event, you can simply write queries like:

```
SELECT guest_name, ' arrived during ', celeb_name
  FROM Guests, Celebrations
 WHERE arrival_date BETWEEN start_date AND finish_date
   AND arrival_date <> finish_date;
```

This query will find the guests who arrived at the hotel during each event. The final predicate can be kept, if you want to conform to the ANSI convention, or dropped, if that makes more sense in your situation. From now on, we will keep both end points to make the queries easier to read.

```
SELECT guest_name, ' arrived during ', celeb_name
  FROM Guests, Celebrations
 WHERE arrival_date BETWEEN start_date AND finish_date;

Results
guest_name       " arrived during "       celeb_name
=========================================================
 'Dorothy Gale'   'arrived during'    'Apple Month'
 'Dorothy Gale'   'arrived during'    'Garlic Festival'
 'Dorothy Gale'   'arrived during'    'Year of the Prune'
 'Indiana Jones'  'arrived during'    'Apple Month'
 'Indiana Jones'  'arrived during'    'Garlic Festival'
 'Indiana Jones'  'arrived during'    'Year of the Prune'
 'Don Quixote'    'arrived during'    'National Pear Week'
 'Don Quixote'    'arrived during'    'New Year's Day'
 'Don Quixote'    'arrived during'    'Year of the Prune'
 'James T. Kirk'  'arrived during'    'Apple Month'
 'James T. Kirk'  'arrived during'    'Garlic Festival'
```

```
'James T. Kirk'  'arrived during'    'Year of the Prune'
'Santa Claus'    'arrived during'    'Christmas Season'
'Santa Claus'    'arrived during'    'Year of the Prune'
```

The obvious question is which guests were at the hotel during each event. A common programming error when trying to find out if two intervals overlap is to write the query with the BETWEEN predicate, thus:

```
SELECT guest_name, ' was here during ', celeb_name
  FROM Guests, Celebrations
 WHERE arrival_date BETWEEN start_date AND finish_date
    OR depart_date BETWEEN start_date AND finish_date;
```

This is wrong, because it does not cover the case where the event began and finished during the guest's visit. Seeing his error, the programmer will sit down and draw a timeline diagram of all four possible overlapping cases, as shown in Figure 13.1.

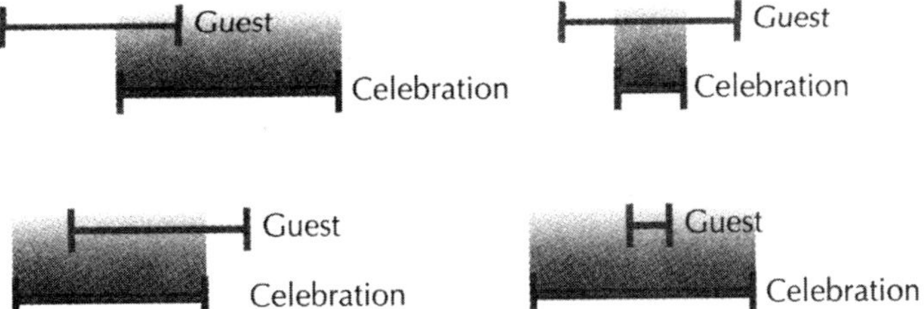

Figure 13.1 *Timeline Diagram of All Possible Overlapping Cases.*

So the programmer adds more predicates, thus:

```
SELECT guest_name, ' was here during ', celeb_name
  FROM Guests, Celebrations
WHERE arrival_date BETWEEN start_date AND finish_date
   OR depart_date BETWEEN start_date AND finish_date
   OR start_date BETWEEN arrival_date AND depart_date
   OR finish_date BETWEEN arrival_date AND depart_date;
```

A thoughtful programmer will notice that the last predicate is not needed and might drop it, but either way, this is a correct query. But it is not the best answer. In the case of the overlapping intervals, there are two cases where a guest's stay at the hotel and an event do not both fall within the same time frame: either the guest checked out before the

event started, or the event ended before the guest arrived. If you want to do the logic, that is what the first predicate will work out to be when you also add the conditions that arrival_date <= depart_date and start_date <= finish_date. But it is easier to see in a timeline diagram, thus:

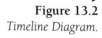

Figure 13.2
Timeline Diagram.

Both cases can be represented in one SQL statement as:

```
SELECT guest_name, celeb_name
  FROM Guests, Celebrations
 WHERE NOT ((depart_date < start_date) OR (arrival_date >
finish_date));

 VIEW GuestsEvents
 guest_name    celeb_name
 ========================================
 'Dorothy Gale'    'Apple Month'
 'Dorothy Gale'    'Garlic Festival'
 'Dorothy Gale'    'St. Fred's Day'
 'Dorothy Gale'    'Year of the Prune'
 'Indiana Jones'    'Apple Month'
 'Indiana Jones'    'Garlic Festival'
 'Indiana Jones'    'Year of the Prune'
 'Don Quixote'      'Apple Month'
 'Don Quixote'      'Garlic Festival'
 'Don Quixote'      'National Pear Week'
 'Don Quixote'      'New Year's Day'
 'Don Quixote'      'St. Fred's Day'
 'Don Quixote'      'Year of the Prune'
 'James T. Kirk'    'Apple Month'
 'James T. Kirk'    'Garlic Festival'
 'James T. Kirk'    'St. Fred's Day'
 'James T. Kirk'    'Year of the Prune'
 'Santa Claus'      'Christmas Season'
 'Santa Claus'      'Year of the Prune'
```

This `VIEW` is handy for other queries. The reason for using the `NOT` in the `WHERE` clause is so that you can add or remove it to reverse the sense of the query. For example, to find out how many celebrations each guest could have seen, you would write:

```
CREATE VIEW GuestCelebrations (guest_name, celeb_name)
AS SELECT guest_name, celeb_name
     FROM Guests, Celebrations
    WHERE NOT ((depart_date < start_date) OR (arrival_date >
finish_date));

SELECT guest_name, COUNT(*) AS celebcount
  FROM GuestCelebrations
 GROUP BY guest_name;

 Results
 guest_name     celebcount
 =========================
 'Dorothy Gale'    4
 'Indiana Jones'   3
 'Don Quixote'     6
 'James T. Kirk'   4
 'Santa Claus'     2
```

Then, to find out how many guests were at the hotel during each celebration, you would write:

```
SELECT celeb_name, COUNT(*) AS guestcount
  FROM GuestCelebrations
 GROUP BY celeb_name;

 Result
 celeb_name           guestcount
 ============================
 'Apple Month'           4
 'Christmas Season'      1
 'Garlic Festival'       4
 'National Pear Week'    1
 'New Year's Day'        1
 'St. Fred's Day'        3
 'Year of the Prune'     5
```

This last query is only part of the story. What the hotel management really wants to know is how many room nights were sold for a

celebration. A little algebra tells you that the length of an event is (Event.finish_date - Event.start_date + INTERVAL '1' DAY) and that the length of a guest's stay is (Guest.depart_date - Guest.arrival_date + INTERVAL '1' DAY). Let's do one of those timeline charts again:

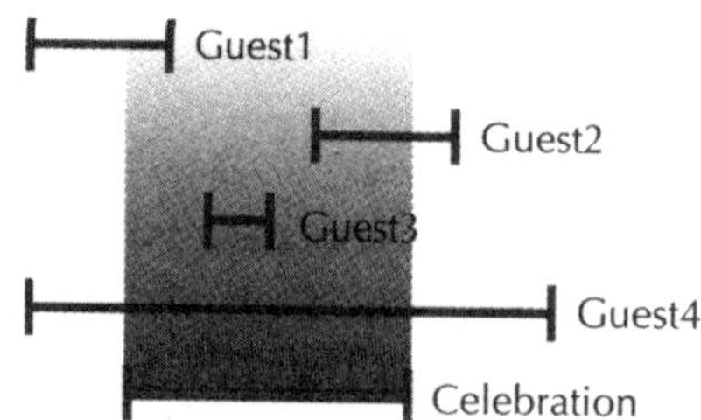

Figure 13.3
Timeline Diagram.

What we want is the part of the Guests interval that is inside the Celebrations interval.

Guests 1 and 2 spent only part of their time at the celebration; Guest 3 spent all of his time at the celebration and Guest 4 stayed even longer than the celebration. That interval is defined by the two points (GREATEST(arrival_date, start_date), LEAST(depart_date, finish_date)).

Instead, you can use the aggregate functions in SQL to build a VIEW on a VIEW, like this:

```
CREATE VIEW Working (guest_name, celeb_name, entered, exited)
AS SELECT GE.guest_name, GE.celeb_name, start_date, finish_date
     FROM GuestCelebrations AS GE, Celebrations AS E1
    WHERE E1.celeb_name = GE.celeb_name
UNION
    SELECT GE.guest_name, GE.celeb_name, arrival_date, depart_date
      FROM GuestCelebrations AS GE, Guests AS G1
     WHERE G1.guest_name = GE.guest_name;
```

```
VIEW Working
 guest_name          celeb_name           entered     exited
 ================================================================
 'Dorothy Gale'  'Apple Month'         '2005-02-01'  '2005-02-28'
 'Dorothy Gale'  'Apple Month'         '2005-02-01'  '2005-11-01'
 'Dorothy Gale'  'Garlic Festival'     '2005-02-01'  '2005-11-01'
 'Dorothy Gale'  'Garlic Festival'     '2005-01-15'  '2005-02-15'
 'Dorothy Gale'  'St. Fred's Day'      '2005-02-01'  '2005-11-01'
```

```
'Dorothy Gale'  'St. Fred's Day'       '2005-02-24'  '2005-02-24'
'Dorothy Gale'  'Year of the Prune'    '2005-02-01'  '2005-11-01'
'Dorothy Gale'  'Year of the Prune'    '2005-01-01'  '2005-12-31'
'Indiana Jones' 'Apple Month'          '2005-02-01'  '2005-02-01'
'Indiana Jones' 'Apple Month'          '2005-02-01'  '2005-02-28'
'Indiana Jones' 'Garlic Festival'      '2005-02-01'  '2005-02-01'
'Indiana Jones' 'Garlic Festival'      '2005-01-15'  '2005-02-15'
'Indiana Jones' 'Year of the Prune'    '2005-02-01'  '2005-02-01'
'Indiana Jones' 'Year of the Prune'    '2005-01-01'  '2005-12-31'
'Don Quixote'   'Apple Month'          '2005-02-01'  '2005-02-28'
'Don Quixote'   'Apple Month'          '2005-01-01'  '2005-10-01'
'Don Quixote'   'Garlic Festival'      '2005-01-01'  '2005-10-01'
'Don Quixote'   'Garlic Festival'      '2005-01-15'  '2005-02-15'
'Don Quixote'   'National Pear Week'   '2005-01-01'  '2005-01-07'
'Don Quixote'   'National Pear Week'   '2005-01-01'  '2005-10-01'
'Don Quixote'   'New Year's Day'       '2005-01-01'  '2005-01-01'
'Don Quixote'   'New Year's Day'       '2005-01-01'  '2005-10-01'
'Don Quixote'   'St. Fred's Day'       '2005-02-24'  '2005-02-24'
'Don Quixote'   'St. Fred's Day'       '2005-01-01'  '2005-10-01'
'Don Quixote'   'Year of the Prune'    '2005-01-01'  '2005-12-31'
'Don Quixote'   'Year of the Prune'    '2005-01-01'  '2005-10-01'
'James T. Kirk' 'Apple Month'          '2005-02-01'  '2005-02-28'
'James T. Kirk' 'Garlic Festival'      '2005-02-01'  '2005-02-28'
'James T. Kirk' 'Garlic Festival'      '2005-01-15'  '2005-02-15'
'James T. Kirk' 'St. Fred's Day'       '2005-02-01'  '2005-02-28'
'James T. Kirk' 'St. Fred's Day'       '2005-02-24'  '2005-02-24'
'James T. Kirk' 'Year of the Prune'    '2005-02-01'  '2005-02-28'
'James T. Kirk' 'Year of the Prune'    '2005-01-01'  '2005-12-31'
'Santa Claus'   'Christmas Season'     '2005-12-01'  '2005-12-25'
'Santa Claus'   'Year of the Prune'    '2005-12-01'  '2005-12-25'
'Santa Claus'   'Year of the Prune'    '2005-01-01'  '2005-12-31'
```

This will put the earliest and latest points in both intervals into one column. Now we can construct a `VIEW` like this:

```
CREATE VIEW Attendees (guest_name, celeb_name, entered, exited)
AS SELECT guest_name, celeb_name, MAX(entered), MIN(exited)
     FROM Working
    GROUP BY guest_name, celeb_name;

VIEW Attendees
```

```
guest_name        celeb_name             entered       exited
=================================================================
'Dorothy Gale'   'Apple Month'          '2005-02-01'  '2005-02-28'
'Dorothy Gale'   'Garlic Festival'      '2005-02-01'  '2005-02-15'
'Dorothy Gale'   'St. Fred's Day'       '2005-02-24'  '2005-02-24'
'Dorothy Gale'   'Year of the Prune'    '2005-02-01'  '2005-11-01'
'Indiana Jones'  'Apple Month'          '2005-02-01'  '2005-02-01'
'Indiana Jones'  'Garlic Festival'      '2005-02-01'  '2005-02-01'
'Indiana Jones'  'Year of the Prune'    '2005-02-01'  '2005-02-01'
'Don Quixote'    'Apple Month'          '2005-02-01'  '2005-02-28'
'Don Quixote'    'Garlic Festival'      '2005-01-15'  '2005-02-15'
'Don Quixote'    'National Pear Week'   '2005-01-01'  '2005-01-07'
'Don Quixote'    'New Year's Day'       '2005-01-01'  '2005-01-01'
'Don Quixote'    'St. Fred's Day'       '2005-02-24'  '2005-02-24'
'Don Quixote'    'Year of the Prune'    '2005-01-01'  '2005-10-01'
'James T. Kirk'  'Apple Month'          '2005-02-01'  '2005-02-28'
'James T. Kirk'  'Garlic Festival'      '2005-02-01'  '2005-02-15'
'James T. Kirk'  'St. Fred's Day'       '2005-02-24'  '2005-02-24'
'James T. Kirk'  'Year of the Prune'    '2005-02-01'  '2005-02-28'
'Santa Claus'    'Christmas Season'     '2005-12-01'  '2005-12-25'
'Santa Claus'    'Year of the Prune'    '2005-12-01'  '2005-12-25'
```

The Attendees VIEW can be used to compute the total number of room days for each celebration. Assume that the difference between two dates will return an integer that is the number of days between them:

```
SELECT celeb_name,
       SUM(exited - entered + INTERVAL '1' DAY) AS roomdays
  FROM Attendees
 GROUP BY celeb_name;

Result
 celeb_name            roomdays
 =============================
 'Apple Month'           85
 'Christmas Season'      25
 'Garlic Festival'       63
 'National Pear Week'     7
 'New Year's Day'         1
 'St. Fred's Day'         3
 'Year of the Prune'    602
```

If you would like to get a count of the room days sold in the month of January, you could use this query, which avoids a BETWEEN or OVERLAPS predicate completely:

```
SELECT SUM(CASE WHEN depart > DATE '2005-01-31'
                THEN DATE '2005-01-31'
                ELSE depart END
            - CASE WHEN arrival_date < DATE '2005-01-01'
                  THEN DATE '2005-01-01'
                  ELSE arrival_date END + INTERVAL '1' DAY) AS
room_days
  FROM Guests
 WHERE depart > DATE '2005-01-01' AND arrival_date <= DATE
'2005-01-31';
```

The [NOT] IN() Predicate

THE IN() PREDICATE IS very natural. It takes a value and sees whether that value is in a list of comparable values. Standard SQL allows value expressions in the list, or for you to use a query to construct the list. The syntax is:

```
<in predicate> ::=
<row value constructor> [NOT] IN <in predicate value>

<in predicate value> ::=
   <table subquery> | (<in value list>)

<in value list> ::=
   <row value expression> { <comma> <row value expression> }...
```

The expression <row value constructor> NOT IN <in predicate value> has the same effect as NOT (<row value constructor> IN <in predicate value>). This pattern for the use of the keyword NOT is found in most of the other predicates.

The expression <row value constructor> IN <in predicate value> has, by definition, the same effect as <row value constructor> = ANY <in predicate value>. Most optimizers will recognize this and execute the same code for both

expressions. This means that if the `<in predicate value>` is empty, such as one you would get from a subquery that returns no rows, the results will be equivalent to `(<row value constructor> = (NULL, ..., NULL))`, which is always evaluated to `UNKNOWN`. Likewise, if the `<in predicate value>` is an explicit list of `NULL`s, the results will be `UNKNOWN`. However, please remember that there is a difference between an empty table and a table with rows of all `NULL`s.

`IN()` predicates with a subquery can sometimes be converted into `EXISTS` predicates, but there are some problems and differences in the predicates. The conversion to an `EXISTS` predicate is often a good way to improve performance, but it will not be as easy to read as the original `IN()` predicate. An `EXISTS` predicate can use indexes to find (or fail to find) a single value that confirms (or denies) the predicate, whereas the `IN()` predicate often has to build the results of the subquery in a working table.

14.1 Optimizing the IN() Predicate

Most database engines have no statistics about the relative frequency of the values in a list of constants, so they will scan them in the order in which they appear in the list. People like to order lists alphabetically or by magnitude, but it would be better to order the list from most frequently occurring values to least frequent. It is also pointless to have duplicate values in the constant list, since the predicate will return TRUE if it matches the first duplicate it finds, and never get to the second occurrence. Likewise, if the predicate is FALSE for that value, it wastes computer time to traverse a needlessly long list.

Many SQL engines perform an `IN()` predicate with a subquery by building the result set of the subquery first as a temporary working table, then scanning that result table from left to right. This can be expensive in many cases; for example, in a query to find employees in a city with a major sport team (we want them to get tickets for us), we could write (assuming that city names are unique):

```
SELECT *
  FROM Personnel
 WHERE city_name
       IN (SELECT city_name _name
             FROM SportTeams);
```

But let us further assume that our personnel are located in (n) cities and the sports teams are in (m) cities, where (m) is much greater than (n). If the matching cities appear near the front of the list generated by the subquery expression, it will perform much faster than if they appear at the end of the list. In the case of a subquery expression, you have no control over how the subquery is presented back in the containing query.

However, you can order the expressions in a list in the order in which they are most likely to occur, such as:

```
SELECT *
  FROM Personnel
 WHERE city_name
       IN ('New York', 'Chicago', 'Atlanta', ..., 'Austin');
```

Incidentally, Standard SQL allows row expression comparisons, so if you have a Standard SQL implementation with separate columns for the city and state, you could write:

```
SELECT *
  FROM Personnel
 WHERE (city_name , state)
       IN (SELECT city_name , state
             FROM SportTeams);
```

Teradata did not get correlated subqueries until 1996, so they often used this syntax as a workaround. I am not sure if you should count them as being ahead or behind the technology for that.

Today, all major versions of SQL remove duplicates in the result table of the subquery, so you do not have to use a `SELECT DISTINCT` in the subquery. You might see this in legacy code. A trick that can work for large lists on some products is to force the engine to construct a list ordered by frequency. This involves first constructing a `VIEW` that has an `ORDER BY` clause; this practice is not part of the SQL standard, which does not allow a `VIEW` to have an `ORDER BY` clause. For example, a paint company wants to find all the products offered by their competitors who use the same color as one of their products. First construct a `VIEW` that orders the colors by frequency of appearance:

```
CREATE VIEW PopColor (color, tally)
AS SELECT color, COUNT(*) AS tally
```

```
  FROM Paints
 GROUP BY color
 ORDER BY tally DESC;
```

Then go to the Competitor data and do a simple column `SELECT` on the `VIEW`, thus:

```
SELECT *
  FROM Competitor
 WHERE color IN (SELECT color FROM PopColor);
```

The `VIEW` is grouped, so it will be materialized in sort order. The subquery will then be executed and (we hope) the sort order will be maintained and passed along to the `IN()` predicate. Another trick is to replace the `IN()` predicate with a `JOIN` operation. For example, you have a table of restaurant telephone numbers and a guidebook, and you want to pick out the four-star places, so you write this query:

```
SELECT restaurant_name, phone_nbr
  FROM Restaurants
 WHERE restaurant_name
       IN (SELECT restaurant_name
             FROM QualityGuide
            WHERE stars = 4);
```

If there is an index on QualityGuide.stars, the SQL engine will probably build a temporary table of the four-star places and pass it on to the outer query. The outer query will then handle it as if it were a list of constants.

However, this is not the sort of column that you would normally index. Without an index on stars, the engine will simply do a sequential search of the QualityGuide table. This query can be replaced with a `JOIN` query, thus:

```
SELECT restaurant_name, phone_nbr
  FROM Restaurants, QualityGuide
 WHERE stars = 4
   AND Restaurants.restaurant_name =
QualityGuide.restaurant_name;
```

This query should run faster, since restaurant_name is a key for both tables and will be indexed to ensure uniqueness. However, this can return duplicate rows in the result table that you can handle with a `SELECT DISTINCT`. Consider a more budget-minded query, where we want places with a meal that costs less than $10, and the menu guidebook lists all the meals. The query looks about the same:

```
SELECT restaurant_name, phone_nbr
  FROM Restaurants
 WHERE restaurant_name
       IN (SELECT restaurant_name
             FROM MenuGuide
            WHERE price <= 10.00);
```

And you would expect to be able to replace it with:

```
SELECT restaurant_name, phone_nbr
  FROM Restaurants, MenuGuide
 WHERE price <= 10.00
   AND Restaurants.restaurant_name = MenuGuide.restaurant_name;
```

Every item in Murphy's Two-Dollar Hash House will get a line in the results of the `JOIN`ed version. However, this can be fixed by changing `SELECT restaurant_name, phone_nbr` to `SELECT DISTINCT restaurant_name, phone_nbr`, but it will cost more time to do a sort to remove the duplicates. There is no good general advice, except to experiment with your particular product.

The `NOT IN()` predicate is probably better replaced with a `NOT EXISTS` predicate. Using the restaurant example again, our friend John has a list of eateries and we want to see those that are not in the guidebook. The natural formation of the query is:

```
SELECT *
  FROM JohnsBook
 WHERE restaurant_name
       NOT IN (SELECT restaurant_name
                 FROM QualityGuide);
```

But you can write the same query with a `NOT EXISTS` predicate and it will probably run faster:

```
SELECT *
  FROM JohnsBook AS J1
 WHERE NOT EXISTS
      (SELECT *
         FROM QualityGuide AS Q1
        WHERE Q1.restaurant_name = J1.restaurant_name);
```

The reason the second version will probably run faster is that it can test for existence using the indexes on both tables. The `NOT IN()` version has to test all the values in the subquery table for inequality. Many SQL implementations will construct a temporary table from the `IN()` predicate subquery, if it has a `WHERE` clause, but the temporary table will not have any indexes. The temporary table can also have duplicates and a random ordering of its rows, so that the SQL engine has to do a full-table scan.

14.2 Replacing ORs with the IN() Predicate

A simple trick that beginning SQL programmers often miss is that an `IN()` predicate can often replace a set of `OR`ed predicates. For example:

```
SELECT *
  FROM QualityControlReport
 WHERE test_1 = 'passed'
    OR test_2 = 'passed'
    OR test_3 = 'passed'
    OR test_4 = 'passed';
```

can be rewritten as:

```
SELECT *
  FROM QualityControlReport
 WHERE 'passed' IN (test_1, test_2, test_3, test_4);
```

The reason this is difficult to see is that programmers get used to thinking of either a subquery or a simple list of constants. They miss the fact that the `IN()` predicate list can be a list of expressions. The optimizer would have handled each of the original predicates separately in the `WHERE` clause, but it has to handle the `IN()` predicate as a single item, which can change the order of evaluation. This might or might not be faster than the list of `OR`ed predicates for a particular query. This formulation might cause the predicate to become nonindexable; you should check the indexability rules of your particular DBMS.

14.3 NULLs and the IN() Predicate

NULLs make some special problems in a NOT IN() predicate with a subquery. Consider these two tables:

```
CREATE TABLE Table1 (x INTEGER);
INSERT INTO Table1 VALUES (1), (2), (3), (4);

CREATE TABLE Table2 (x INTEGER);
INSERT INTO Table2 VALUES (1), (NULL), (2);
```

Now execute the query:

```
SELECT *
 FROM Table1
 WHERE x NOT IN (SELECT x FROM Table2)
```

Let's work it out step by painful step:

1. Do the subquery:

```
SELECT *
  FROM Table1
 WHERE x NOT IN (1, NULL, 2);
```

2. Convert the NOT IN() to its definition:

```
SELECT *
  FROM Table1
 WHERE NOT (x IN (1, NULL, 2));
```

3. Expand IN() predicate:

```
SELECT *
  FROM Table1
 WHERE NOT ((x = 1) OR (x = NULL) OR (x = 2));
```

4. Apply DeMorgan's law:

```
SELECT *
  FROM Table1
```

```
WHERE ((x <> 1) AND (x <> NULL) AND (x <> 2
```

5. Perform the constant logical expression:

```
SELECT *
  FROM Table1
 WHERE ((x <> 1) AND UNKNOWN AND (x <> 2));
```

6. Reduce OR to constant:

```
SELECT *
 FROM Table1
 WHERE UNKNOWN;
```

7. The results are always empty.

Now try this with another set of tables

```
CREATE TABLE Table3 (x INTEGER);
INSERT INTO Table3 VALUES (1), (2), (NULL), (4);

CREATE TABLE Table4 (x INTEGER);
INSERT INTO Table3 VALUES (1), (3), (2);
```

Let's work out the same query step by painful step again.

1. Do the subquery

```
SELECT *
  FROM Table3
 WHERE x NOT IN (1, 3, 2);
```

2. Convert the NOT IN() to Boolean expression

```
SELECT *
  FROM Table3
 WHERE NOT (x IN (1, 3, 2));
```

3. Expand IN() predicate

```
SELECT *
  FROM Table3
```

```
WHERE NOT ((x = 1) OR (x = 3) OR (x = 2));
```

4. Apply DeMorgan's law:

```
SELECT *
  FROM Table3
 WHERE ((x <> 1) AND (x <> 3) AND (x <> 2));
```

5. Compute the result set; I will show it as a UNION with substitutions:

```
 SELECT *
   FROM Table3
  WHERE ((1 <> 1) AND (1 <> 3) AND (1 <> 2)) -- FALSE
UNION ALL
 SELECT *
   FROM Table3
  WHERE ((2 <> 1) AND (2 <> 3) AND (2 <> 2)) -- FALSE
UNION ALL
 SELECT * FROM Table3
  WHERE ((CAST(NULL AS INTEGER) <> 1)
         AND (CAST(NULL AS INTEGER) <> 3)
         AND (CAST(NULL AS INTEGER) <> 2)) -- UNKNOWN
UNION ALL
 SELECT *
   FROM Table3
  WHERE ((4 <> 1) AND (4 <> 3) AND (4 <> 2)); -- TRUE
```

6. The result is one row = (4).

14.4 IN() Predicate and Referential Constraints

One of the most popular uses for the IN() predicate is in a CHECK() clause on a table. The usual form is a list of values that are legal for a column, such as:

```
CREATE TABLE Addresses
(addressee_name CHAR(25) NOT NULL PRIMARY KEY,
 street_loc CHAR(25) NOT NULL,
 city_name CHAR(20) NOT NULL,
 state_code CHAR(2) NOT NULL
       CONSTRAINT valid_state_code
```

```
      CHECK (state_code IN ('AL', 'AK', ...)),
...);
```

This method works fine with a small list of values, but it has problems with a longer list. It is very important to arrange the values in the order that they are most likely to match to the two-letter state_code to speed up the search.

In Standard SQL a constraint can reference other tables, so you could write the same constraint as:

```
CREATE TABLE Addresses
(addressee_name CHAR(25) NOT NULL PRIMARY KEY,
 street_loc CHAR(25) NOT NULL,
 city_name CHAR(20) NOT NULL,
 state_code CHAR(2) NOT NULL,
 CONSTRAINT valid_state_code
 CHECK (state_code
        IN (SELECT state_code
              FROM ZipCodes AS Z1
             WHERE Z1.state_code = Addresses.state_code)),
 ...);
```

The advantage of this is that you can change the ZipCodes table and thereby change the effect of the constraint on the `Addresses` table. This is fine for adding more data in the outer reference (i.e., Quebec joins the United States and gets the code '`QB`'), but it has a bad effect when you try to delete data in the outer reference (i.e., California secedes from the United States and every row with '`CA`' for a state code is now invalid).

As a rule of thumb, use the `IN()` predicate in a `CHECK()` constraint when the list is short, static, and unique to one table. When the list is short, static, but not unique to one table, then use a `CREATE DOMAIN` statement, and put the `IN()` predicate in a `CHECK()` constraint on the domain.

Use a `REFERENCES` clause to a lookup table when the list is long and dynamic, or when several other schema objects (`VIEW`s, stored procedures, etc.) reference the values. A separate table can have an index, and that makes a big difference in searching and doing joins.

14.5 IN() Predicate and Scalar Queries

As mentioned before, the list of an `IN()` predicate can be any scalar expression. This includes scalar subqueries, but most people do not seem to know that this is possible. For example, given tables that model warehouses, trucking centers, and so forth, we can find if we have a product, identified by its UPC code, somewhere in the enterprise.

```
SELECT P.upc
  FROM Picklist AS P
 WHERE P.upc
       IN ((SELECT upc FROM Warehouse AS W WHERE W.upc =
Picklist.upc),
           (SELECT upc FROM TruckCenter AS T WHERE T.upc =
Picklist.upc),
         ...
           (SELECT upc FROM Garbage AS G WHERE G.upc =
Picklist.upc));
```

The empty result sets will become `NULL`s in the list. The alternative to this is usually a chain of `OUTER JOIN`s or an `OR`ed list of `EXISTS()` predicates.

EXISTS() Predicate

THE EXISTS PREDICATE IS very natural. It is a test for a nonempty set. If there are any rows in its subquery, it is `TRUE`; otherwise, it is `FALSE`. This predicate does not give an `UNKNOWN` result. The syntax is:

```
<exists predicate> ::= EXISTS <table subquery>
```

It is worth mentioning that a `<table subquery>` is always inside parentheses to avoid problems in the grammar during parsing.

In SQL-89, the rules stated that the subquery had to have a `SELECT` clause with one column or a `*`. If the `SELECT *` option was used, the database engine would (in theory) pick one column and use it. This fiction was needed because SQL-89 defined subqueries as having only one column.

Some early SQL implementations would work better with `EXISTS(SELECT <column> ...)`, `EXISTS(SELECT <constant> ...)`, or `EXISTS(SELECT * ...)` versions of the predicate. Today, there is no difference in the three forms in the major products, so the `EXISTS(SELECT * ...)` is the preferred form.

Indexes are very useful for `EXISTS()` predicates because they can be searched while the base table is left alone completely. For example, we want to find all employees who were born on the same day as any famous person. The query could be:

```
SELECT P1.emp_name, ' has the same birthday as a famous person!'
  FROM Personnel AS P1
 WHERE EXISTS
       (SELECT *
          FROM Celebrities AS C1
         WHERE P1.birthday = C1.birthday);
```

If the table `Celebrities` has an index on its birthday column, the optimizer will get the current employee's birthday `P1.birthday` and look up that value in the index. If the value is in the index, the predicate is `TRUE` and we do not need to look at the `Celebrities` table at all.

If it is not in the index, the predicate is `FALSE` and there is still no need to look at the `Celebrities` table. This should be fast, since indexes are smaller than their tables and are structured for very fast searching.

However, if `Celebrities` has no index on its birthday column, the query may have to look at every row to see if there is a birthday that matches the current employee's birthday. There are some tricks that a good optimizer can use to speed things up in this situation.

15.1 EXISTS and NULLs

A `NULL` might not be a value, but it does exist in SQL. This is often a problem for a new SQL programmer who is having trouble with `NULL`s and how they behave.

Think of them as being like a brown paper bag—you know that something is inside because you lifted it, but you do not know exactly what that something is. For example, we want to find all the employees who were not born on the same day as a famous person. This can be answered with the negation of the original query, like this:

```
SELECT P1.emp_name, ' was born on a day without a famous person!'
  FROM Personnel AS P1
 WHERE NOT EXISTS
       (SELECT *
          FROM Celebrities AS C1
         WHERE P1.birthday = C1.birthday);
```

But assume that among the celebrities we have a movie star who will not admit her age, shown in the row `('Gloria Glamour', NULL)`. A new SQL programmer might expect that Ms. Glamour would not match to anyone, since we do not know her birthday yet. Actually, she will match to everyone, since there is a chance that they may match when some tabloid newspaper finally gets a copy of her birth certificate. But work out the subquery in the usual way to convince yourself:

```
...
WHERE NOT EXISTS
      (SELECT *
         FROM Celebrities
        WHERE P1.birthday = NULL);
```

becomes:

```
...

WHERE NOT EXISTS
        (SELECT *
           FROM Celebrities
          WHERE UNKNOWN);
```

becomes:

```
...
WHERE TRUE;
```

And you see that the predicate tests to UNKNOWN because of the NULL comparison, and therefore fails whenever we look at Ms. Glamour.

Another problem with NULLs is found when you attempt to convert IN predicates to EXISTS predicates. Using our example of matching our employees to famous people, the query can be rewritten as:

```
SELECT P1.emp_name, ' was born on a day without a famous person!'
  FROM Personnel AS P1
 WHERE P1.birthday NOT IN
                   (SELECT C1.birthday
                      FROM Celebrities AS C1);
```

However, consider a more complex version of the same query, where the celebrity has to have been born in New York City. The IN predicate would be:

```
SELECT P1.emp_name, ' was born on a day without a famous New
Yorker!'
  FROM Personnel AS P1
 WHERE P1.birthday NOT IN
                   (SELECT C1.birthday
                      FROM Celebrities AS C1
                     WHERE C1.birth_city = 'New York');
```

and you would think that the EXISTS version would be:

```
SELECT P1.emp_name, ' was born on a day without a famous New
Yorker!'
  FROM Personnel AS P1
 WHERE NOT EXISTS
       (SELECT *
          FROM Celebrities AS C1
        WHERE C1.birth_city = 'New York'
          AND C1.birthday = P1.birthday);
```

Assume that Gloria Glamour is our only New Yorker and we still do not know her birthday. The subquery will be empty for every employee in the NOT EXISTS predicate version, because her NULL birthday will not test equal to the known employee birthdays.

That means that the NOT EXISTS predicate will return TRUE and we will get every employee to match to Ms. Glamour. But now look at the IN predicate version, which will have a single NULL in the subquery result. This predicate will be equivalent to (Personnel.birthday = NULL), which is always UNKNOWN, and we will get no employees back.

Likewise, you cannot, in general, transform the quantified comparison predicates into EXISTS predicates, because of the possibility of NULL values. Remember that x <> ALL <subquery> is shorthand for x NOT IN <subquery>, and x = ANY <subquery> is shorthand for x IN <subquery>, and it will not surprise you.

In general, the EXISTS predicates will run faster than the IN predicates. The problem is in deciding whether to build the query or the subquery first; the optimal approach depends on the size and distribution of values in each, and that cannot usually be known until runtime.

15.2 EXISTS and INNER JOINs

The [NOT] EXISTS predicate is almost always used with a correlated subquery. Very often the subquery can be "flattened" into a JOIN, which will frequently run faster than the original query. Our sample query can be converted into:

```
SELECT P1.emp_name, ' has the same birthday as a famous person!'
  FROM Personnel AS P1, Celebrities AS C1
 WHERE P1.birthday = C1.birthday;
```

The advantage of the JOIN version is that it allows us to show columns from both tables. We should make the query more informative by rewriting it:

```
SELECT P1.emp_name, ' has the same birthday as ', C1.emp_name
  FROM Personnel AS P1, Celebrities AS C1
 WHERE P1.birthday = C1.birthday;
```

This new query could be written with an EXISTS() predicate, but that is a waste of resources.

```
SELECT P1.emp_name, ' has the same birthday as ', C1.emp_name
  FROM Personnel AS P1, Celebrities AS C1
 WHERE EXISTS
       (SELECT *
          FROM Celebrities AS C2
         WHERE P1.birthday = C2.birthday
           AND C1.emp_name = C2.emp_name);
```

15.3 NOT EXISTS and OUTER JOINs

The NOT EXISTS version of this predicate is almost always used with a correlated subquery. Very often the subquery can be "flattened" into an OUTER JOIN, which will frequently run faster than the original query. Our other sample query was:

```
SELECT P1.emp_name, ' was born on a day without a famous New
Yorker!'
  FROM Personnel AS P1
 WHERE NOT EXISTS
      (SELECT *
         FROM Celebrities AS C1
        WHERE C1.birth_city = 'New York'
          AND C1.birthday = P1.birthday);
```

Which we can replace with:

```
SELECT P1.emp_name, ' was born on a day without a famous New
Yorker!'

  FROM Personnel AS P1
       LEFT OUTER JOIN
       Celebrities AS C1
       ON C1.birth_city = 'New York'
          AND C1.birthday = E2.birthday
  WHERE C1.emp_name IS NULL;
```

This is assuming that we know each and every celebrity name in the Celebrities table. If the column in the WHERE clause could have NULLs in its base table, then we could not prune out the generated NULLs. The test for NULL should always be on (a column of) the primary key, which cannot be NULL. Relating this back to the example, how could a celebrity be a celebrity with an unknown name? Even The Unknown Comic had a name ("The Unknown Comic").

15.4 EXISTS() and Quantifiers

Formal logic makes use of quantifiers that can be applied to propositions. The two forms are "For all*x*, P(*x*)" and "For some*x*, P(*x*)". The first is written as {{inverted uppercase A }} and the second is written as {{reversed uppercase E}}, if you want to look up formulas in a textbook. The quantifiers put into symbols such statements as "all men are mortal" or "some Cretans are liars" so they can be manipulated.

The big question more than 100 years ago was that of existential import in formal logic. Everyone agreed that saying "all men are mortal" implies that "no men are not mortal," but does it also imply that "some men are mortal"—that we have to have at least one man who is mortal?

Existential import lost the battle and the modern convention is that "All men are mortal" has the same meaning as "There are no men who are immortal," but does not imply that any men exist at all. This is the convention followed in the design of SQL. Consider the statement "some salesmen are liars" and the way we would write it with the EXISTS() predicate in SQL:

```
...
EXISTS(SELECT *
```

```
  FROM Personnel AS P1, Liars AS L1
 WHERE P1.job = 'Salesman'
   AND P1.emp_name = L1.emp_name);
```

If we are more cynical about salesmen, we might want to formulate the predicate "all salesmen are liars" with the EXISTS predicate in SQL, using the transform rule just discussed:

```
...
NOT EXISTS(SELECT *
             FROM Personnel AS P1
            WHERE P1.job = 'Salesman'
              AND P1.emp_name
                  NOT IN
                  (SELECT L1.emp_name
                     FROM Liars AS L1));
```

That says, informally, "there are no salesmen who are not liars" in English. In this case, the IN predicate can be changed into JOIN, which should improve performance and be a bit easier to read.

15.5 EXISTS() and Referential Constraints

Standard SQL was designed so that the declarative referential constraints could be expressed as EXISTS() predicates in a CHECK() clause. For example:

```
CREATE TABLE Addresses
(addressee_name CHAR(25) NOT NULL PRIMARY KEY,
 street_loc CHAR(25) NOT NULL,
 city_name CHAR(20) NOT NULL,
 state_code CHAR(2) NOT NULL
            REFERENCES ZipCodeData(state_code),
...);
```

could be written as:

```
CREATE TABLE Addresses
(addressee_name CHAR(25) NOT NULL PRIMARY KEY,
 street_loc CHAR(25) NOT NULL,
```

```
city_name CHAR(20) NOT NULL,
state_code CHAR(2) NOT NULL,
CONSTRAINT valid_state_code
 CHECK (EXISTS(SELECT *
                 FROM ZipCodeData AS Z1
                WHERE Z1.state_code = Addresses.state_code)),
...);
```

There is no advantage to this expression for the DBA, since you cannot attach referential actions with the `CHECK()` constraint. However, an SQL database can use the same mechanisms in the SQL compiler for both constructions.

15.6 EXISTS and Three-Valued Logic

This example is due to an article by Lee Fesperman at FirstSQL. Using Chris Date's "SupplierParts" table with three rows:

```
CREATE TABLE SupplierPart
(sup_nbr CHAR(2) NOT NULL PRIMARY KEY,
 part_nbr CHAR(2) NOT NULL,
 qty INTEGER CHECK (qty > 0));

sup_nbr  part_nbr  qty
======================
'S1'     'P1'      NULL
'S2'     'P1'      200
'S3'     'P1'      1000
```

The row ('S1', 'P1', NULL) means that supplier 'S1' supplies part 'P1' but we do not know what quantity he has.

The query we wish to answer is "Find suppliers of part 'P1', but not in a quantity of 1000 on hand." The correct answer is 'S2'. All suppliers in the table supply 'P1', but we do know 'S3' supplies the part in quantity 1000 and we do not know in what quantity 'S1' supplies the part. The only supplier we eliminate for certain is 'S2'.

An SQL query to retrieve this result would be:

```
SELECT spx.sup_nbr
  FROM SupplierParts AS spx
 WHERE px.part_nbr = 'P1'
```

```
   AND 1000
       NOT IN (SELECT spy.qty
                 FROM SupplierParts AS spy
                WHERE spy.sup_nbr = spx.sup_nbr
                  AND spy.part_nbr = 'P1');
```

According to Standard SQL, this query should return only 'S2', but when we transform the query into an equivalent version, using EXISTS instead, we obtain:

```
SELECT spx.sup_nbr
  FROM SupplierParts AS spx
 WHERE spx.part_nbr = 'P1'
   AND NOT EXISTS
       (SELECT *
          FROM SupplierParts AS spy
         WHERE spy.sup_nbr = spx.sup_nbr
           AND spy.part_nbr = 'P1'
           AND spy.qty = 1000);
```

Which will return ('S1', 'S2'). You can argue that this is the wrong answer because we do not definitely know whether or not 'S1' supplies 'P1' in quantity 1000. The EXISTS() predicate will return TRUE or FALSE, even in situations where a subquery's predicate returns an UNKNOWN (i.e., NULL = 1000).

The solution is to modify the predicate that deals with the quantity in the subquery to explicitly say that you do or not want to give the "benefit of the doubt" to the NULL. You have several alternatives:

1. `(spy.qty = 1000) IS NOT FALSE`

This uses the new predicates in Standard SQL for testing logical values. Frankly, this is confusing to read and worse to maintain.

2. `(spy.qty = 1000 OR spy.qty IS NULL)`

This uses another test predicate, but the optimizer can probably use any index on the qty column.

3.
```
(COALESCE(spy.qty, 1000) = 1000)
```

This is portable and easy to maintain. The only disadvantage is that some SQL products might not be able to use an index on the qty column, because it is in an expression.

The real problem is that the query was formed with a double negative in the form of a `NOT EXISTS` and an implicit `IS NOT FALSE` condition. The problem stems from the fact that the `EXISTS()` predicate is one of the few two-value predicates in SQL, and that `(NOT (NOT UNKNOWN)) = UNKNOWN`.

For another approach based on Dr. Codd's second relational model, visit www.FirstSQL.com and read some of the white papers by Lee Fesperman. He used the two `NULL`s Codd proposed to develop a product.

Quantified Subquery Predicates

A QUANTIFIER IS A logical operator that states the quantity of objects for which a statement is TRUE. This is a logical quantity, not a numeric quantity; it relates a statement to the whole set of possible objects. In everyday life, you see statements like "There is only one mouthwash that stops dinosaur breath," "All doctors drive Mercedes," or "Some people got rich investing in cattle futures," which are quantified.

The first statement, about the mouthwash, is a uniqueness quantifier. If there were two or more products that could save us from dinosaur breath, the statement would be FALSE. The second statement has what is called a universal quantifier, since it deals with all doctors—find one exception and the statement is FALSE. The last statement has an existential quantifier, since it asserts that one or more people exist who got rich on cattle futures—find one example and the statement is TRUE.

SQL has forms of these quantifiers that are not quite like those in formal logic. They are based on extending the use of comparison predicates to allow result sets to be quantified, and they use SQL's three-valued logic, so they do not return just TRUE or FALSE.

16.1 Scalar Subquery Comparisons

Standard SQL allows both scalar and row comparisons, but most queries use only scalar expressions. If a subquery returns a single-row, single-column result table, it is treated as a scalar value in Standard SQL in virtually any place a scalar could appear. For example, to find out if we have any teachers who are more than one year older than the students, I could write:

```
SELECT T1.teacher_name
  FROM Teachers AS T1
 WHERE
   T1.birthday > (SELECT MAX(S1.birthday) - INTERVAL '365' DAY
                    FROM Students AS S1);
```

In this case, the scalar subquery will be run only once and reduced to a constant value by the optimizer before scanning the Teachers table.

A correlated subquery is more complex, because it will have to be executed for each value from the containing query. For example, to find which suppliers have sent us fewer than 100 parts, we would use this query. Notice how the `SUM(quantity)` has to be computed for each supplier number, sup_nbr.

```
SELECT sup_nbr, sup_name
  FROM Suppliers
 WHERE 100 > (SELECT SUM(quantity)
                FROM Shipments
               WHERE Shipments.sup_nbr = Suppliers.sup_nbr);
```

If a scalar subquery returns a `NULL`, we have rules for handling comparison with `NULL`s. But what if it returns an empty result—a supplier that has not shipped us anything? In Standard SQL, the empty result table is converted to a `NULL` of the appropriate data type.

In Standard SQL, you can place scalar or row subqueries on either side of a comparison predicate as long as they return comparable results. But you must be aware of the rules for row comparisons. For example, the following query will find the product manager who has more of his product at the stores than in the warehouse:

```
SELECT manager_name, product_nbr
  FROM Stores AS S1
```

```
WHERE (SELECT SUM(qty)
         FROM Warehouses AS W1
        WHERE S1.product_nbr = W1.product_nbr)
      < (SELECT SUM(qty)
           FROM RetailStores AS R1
          WHERE S1.product_nbr = R1.product_nbr);
```

Here is a programming tip: the main problem with writing these queries is getting a result with more than one row in it. You can guarantee uniqueness in several ways. An aggregate function on an ungrouped table will always be a single value. A JOIN with the containing query based on a key will always be a single value.

16.2 Quantifiers and Missing Data

The quantified predicates are used with subquery expressions to compare a single value to those of the subquery, and take the general form <value expression> <comp op> <quantifier> <subquery>. The predicate "<value expression> <comp op> [ANY|SOME] <table expression>" is equivalent to taking each row, s, (assume that they are numbered from 1 to *n*) of <table expression> and testing "<value expression> <comp op> s" with ORs between the expanded expressions:

```
((<value expression> <comp op> s1)
OR (<value expression> <comp op> s2)
   ...
OR (<value expression> <comp op> sn))
```

When you get a single TRUE result, the whole predicate is TRUE.

As long as <table expression> has cardinality greater than zero and one non-**NULL** value, you will get a result of TRUE or FALSE. The keyword SOME is the same as ANY, and the choice is just a matter of style and readability. Likewise, "<value expression> <comp op> ALL <table expression>" takes each row, s, of <table expression> and tests <value expression> <comp op> s with ANDs between the expanded expressions:

```
((<value expression> <comp op> s1)
AND (<value expression> <comp op> s2)
   ...
AND (<value expression> <comp op> sn))
```

When you get a single FALSE result, the whole predicate is FALSE. As long as <table expression> has cardinality greater than zero and all non-**NULL** values, you will get a result of TRUE or FALSE.

That sounds reasonable so far. Now let EmptyTable be an empty table (no rows, cardinality zero) and NullTable be a table with only NULLs in its rows (cardinality greater than zero). The rules for SQL say that <value expression> <comp op> ALL NullTable always returns UNKNOWN, and likewise <value expression> <comp op> ANY NullTable always returns UNKNOWN. This makes sense, because every row comparison test in the expansion would return UNKNOWN, so the series of OR and AND operators would behave in the usual way.

However, <value expression> <comp op> ALL EmptyTable always returns TRUE, and <value expression> <comp op> ANY EmptyTable always returns FALSE. Most people have no trouble seeing why the ANY predicate works that way; you cannot find a match, so the result is FALSE. But most people have lots of trouble seeing why the ALL predicate is TRUE. This convention is called existential import, and I have just discussed it in Chapter 15. If I were to walk into a bar and announce that I can beat any pink elephant in the bar, that would be a true statement. The fact that there are no pink elephants in the bar merely shows that the problem is reduced to the minimum case.

If this seems unnatural, then convert the ALL and ANY predicates into EXISTS predicates and look at the way that this rule preserves the properties that:

1. $(\forall x\ P(x)) = (\neg \exists x\ (\neg P(x)))$
2. $(\exists x\ P(x)) = \neg (\forall x\ \neg P(x))$

The Table1.x <comp op> ALL (SELECT y FROM Table2 WHERE <search condition>) predicate converts to:

```
... NOT EXISTS
    (SELECT *
       FROM Table1, Table2
      WHERE Table1.x <comp op> Table2.y
        AND NOT <search condition>)...
```

The Table1.x <comp op> ANY (SELECT y FROM Table2 WHERE <search condition>) predicate converts to:

```
... EXISTS
    (SELECT *
```

```
FROM Table1, Table2
WHERE Table1.x <comp op> Table2.y
  AND <search condition>) ...
```

Of the two quantified predicates, the `<comp op> ALL` predicate is used more. The `ANY` predicate is more easily replaced and more naturally written with an `EXISTS()` predicate or an `IN()` predicate. In fact, the standard defines the `IN()` predicate as shorthand for `= ANY` and the `NOT IN()` predicate as shorthand for `<> ANY`, which is how most people would construct them in English.

The `<comp op> ALL` predicate is probably the more useful of the two, since it cannot be written in terms of an `IN()` predicate. The trick with it is to make sure that its subquery defines the set of values in which you are interested. For example, to find the authors whose books all sell for $19.95 or more, you could write:

```
SELECT *
  FROM Authors AS A1
 WHERE 19.95
       < ALL (SELECT price
                FROM Books AS B1
               WHERE A1.author_name = B1.author_name);
```

The best way to think of this is to reverse the usual English sentence "Show me all x that are y" in your mind so that it says "y is the value of all x" instead.

16.3 The ALL Predicate and Extrema Functions

It is counterintuitive at first that these two predicates are not the same in SQL:

```
x >= (SELECT MAX(y) FROM Table1)
x >= ALL (SELECT y FROM Table1)
```

But you have to remember the rules for the extrema functions—they drop out all the `NULL`s before returning the greater or least values. The `ALL` predicate does not drop `NULL`s, so you can get them in the results.

However, if you know that there are no `NULL`s in a column, or are willing to drop the `NULL`s yourself, then you can use the `ALL` predicate to construct single queries to do work that would otherwise be done by two

queries. For example, we could use the table of products and store managers we used earlier in this chapter and find which manager handles the largest number of products. To do this, we would first construct a grouped VIEW and group it again:

```
CREATE VIEW TotalProducts (manager_name, product_tally)
AS SELECT manager_name, COUNT(*)
     FROM Stores
    GROUP BY manager_name;

SELECT manager_name
  FROM TotalProducts
 WHERE product_tally
       = (SELECT MAX(product_tally)
            FROM TotalProducts);
```

But Alex Dorfman found a single query solution instead:

```
SELECT manager_name, COUNT(*)
  FROM Stores
 GROUP BY manager_name
HAVING COUNT(*) + 1
       > ALL (SELECT DISTINCT COUNT(*)
                FROM Stores
               GROUP BY manager_name);
```

The use of the SELECT DISTINCT in the subquery is to guarantee that we do not get duplicate rows when two managers handle the same number of products. You can also add a ... WHERE dept IS NOT NULL clause to the subquery to get the effect of a true MAX() aggregate function.

16.4 The UNIQUE Predicate

The UNIQUE predicate is a test for the absence of duplicate rows in a subquery. The UNIQUE keyword is also used as a table or column. This predicate is used to define the constraint. The UNIQUE column constraint is implemented in many SQL implementations with a CREATE UNIQUE INDEX <indexname> ON <table>(<column list>) statement hidden under the covers. The syntax for this predicate is:

```
<unique predicate> ::= UNIQUE <table subquery>
```

If any two rows in the subquery are equal to each other, the predicate is FALSE. However, the definition in the standard is worded in the negative, so that NULLs get the benefit of the doubt. The query can be written as an EXISTS predicate that counts rows, thus:

```
EXISTS (SELECT <column list>
          FROM <subquery>
        WHERE (<column list>) IS NOT NULL
         GROUP BY <column list>
        HAVING COUNT(*) > 1);
```

An empty subquery is always TRUE, since you cannot find two rows, and therefore duplicates do not exist. This makes sense on the face of it.

NULLs are easier to explain with an example—say a table with only two rows, ('a', 'b') and ('a', NULL). The first columns of each row are non-NULL and are equal to each other, so we have a match so far. The second column in the second row is NULL and cannot compare to anything, so we skip the second column pair and go with what we have, and the test is TRUE. This is giving the NULLs the benefit of the doubt, since the NULL in the second row could become 'b' some day and give us a duplicate row.

Now consider the case where the subquery has two rows, ('a', NULL) and ('a', NULL). The predicate is still TRUE, because the NULLs do not test equal or unequal to each other—not because we are making NULLs equal to each other.

As you can see, it is a good idea to avoid NULLs in UNIQUE constraints.

The SELECT Statement

THE GOOD NEWS ABOUT SQL is that the programmer only needs to learn the SELECT statement to do almost all his work. The bad news is that the statement can have so many nested clauses that it looks like a Victorian novel! The SELECT statement is used to query the database. It combines one or more tables, can do some calculations, and finally puts the results into a result table that can be passed on to the host language.

I have not spent much time on the simple one-table SELECT statements you see in introductory books. I am assuming that the readers are experienced SQL programmers and got enough of those queries when they were learning SQL.

17.1 SELECT and JOINs

There is an order to the execution of the clauses of an SQL SELECT statement that does not seem to be covered in most beginning SQL books. It explains why some things work in SQL and others do not.

17.1.1 One-Level SELECT Statement

The simplest possible SELECT statement is just "SELECT * FROM Sometable;" which returns the entire table as it stands. You can actually write this as "TABLE Sometable" in Standard SQL, but

nobody seems to use that syntax. Though the syntax rules say that all you need are the SELECT and FROM clauses, in practice there is almost always a WHERE clause.

Let's look at the SELECT statement in detail. The syntax for the statement is:

```
SELECT [ALL | DISTINCT] <scalar expression list>
  FROM <table expression>
 [WHERE <search condition>]
 [GROUP BY <grouping column list>]
[HAVING <group condition>];
```

The order of execution is as follows:

1. *Execute the* FROM <table expression> *clause and construct the working result table defined in that clause.* The FROM can have all sorts of other table expressions, but the point is that they return a working table as a result. We will get into the details of those expressions later, with particular attention to the JOIN operators.

   The result table preserves the order of the tables, and the order of the columns within each, in the result. The result table is different from other tables in that each column retains the table name from which it was derived. Thus if table A and table B both have a column named x, there will be a column A.x and a column B.x in the results of the FROM clause. No product actually uses a CROSS JOIN to construct the intermediate table—the working table would get too large too fast. For example, a 1,000-row table and a 1,000-row table would-CROSS JOIN to get a 1,000,000-row working table. This is just the conceptual model we use to describe behavior.

2. *If there is a* WHERE *clause, apply the search condition in it to each row of the* FROM *clause result table.* The rows that test TRUE are retained; the rows that test FALSE or UNKNOWN are deleted from the working set.

   The WHERE clause is where the action is. The predicate can be quite complex and have nested subqueries. The syntax of a subquery is a SELECT statement, which is inside parentheses—failure to use parentheses is a common error for new SQL programmers. Subqueries are where the original SQL got the name

"Structured English Query Language"—the ability to nest SELECT statements was the "structured" part. We will deal with those in another section.

3. *If there is a* GROUP BY <grouping column list> *clause, execute it next.* It uses the FROM and WHERE clause working table and breaks these rows into groups where the columns in the <grouping column list> all have the same value. NULLs are treated as if they were all equal to each other, and form their own group. Each group is then reduced to a single row in a new result table that replaces the old one.

   Each row represents information about its group. Standard SQL does not allow you to use the name of a calculated column such as "(salary + commission) AS total_pay" in the GROUP BY clause, because that column is computed and named in the SELECT clause of this query. It does not exist yet. However, you will find products that allow it because they create a result table first, using names in the SELECT cause, then fill the result table with rows created by the query. There are ways to get the same result by using VIEWs and derived table expressions, which we will discuss later.

   Only four things make sense as group characteristics: the columns that define it, the aggregate functions that summarize group characteristics, function calls and constants, and expressions built from those three things.

4. *If there is a* HAVING *clause, apply it to each of the groups.* The groups that test TRUE are retained; the groups that test FALSE or UNKNOWN are deleted. If there is no GROUP BY clause, the HAVING clause treats the whole table as a single group. It is not true that there must be a GROUP BY clause.

   Standard SQL prohibits correlated queries in a HAVING clause, but there are workarounds that use derived tables.

   The <group condition> must apply to columns in the grouped working table or to group properties, not to the individual rows that originally built the group. Aggregate functions used in the HAVING clause usually appear in the SELECT clause, but that is not part of the standard. Nor does the SELECT clause have to include all the grouping columns.

5. *Finally, apply the* SELECT *clause to the result table.* If a column does not appear in the <expression list>, it is dropped

from the final results. Expressions can be constants or column names, or they can be calculations made from constants, columns, functions, and scalar subqueries.

If the SELECT clause has the DISTINCT option, redundant duplicate rows are deleted from the final result table. The phrase "redundant duplicate" means that one copy of the row is retained. If the SELECT clause has the explicit ALL option or is missing the [ALL | DISTINCT] option, then all duplicate rows are preserved in the final results table. (Frankly, although it is legal syntax, nobody really uses the SELECT ALL option.) Finally, the results are returned.

Let us carry an example out in detail, with a two-table join.

```
SELECT sex, COUNT(*), AVG(age),
       (MAX(age) - MIN(age)) AS
age_range
  FROM Students, Gradebook
 WHERE grade = 'A'
   AND Students.stud_nbr = Gradebook.stud_nbr
 GROUP BY sex
HAVING COUNT(*) > 3;
```

The two starting tables look like this:

```
 CREATE TABLE Students
(stud_nbr INTEGER NOT NULL PRIMARY KEY,
 stud_name CHAR(10) NOT NULL,
 sex CHAR(1) NOT NULL,
 age INTEGER NOT NULL);
```

```
Students
stud_nbr  stud_name  sex    age
================================
 1        'Smith'    'M'    16
 2        'Smyth'    'F'    17
 3        'Smoot'    'F'    16
 4        'Adams'    'F'    17
 5        'Jones'    'M'    16
 6        'Celko'    'M'    17
```

```
7        'Vennor'   'F'    16
8        'Murray'   'M'    18

CREATE TABLE Gradebook
(stud_nbr INTEGER NOT NULL PRIMARY KEY
   REFERENCES Students(stud_nbr),
 grade CHAR(1) NOT NULL);

Gradebook
stud_nbr    grade
=================
  1         'A'
  2         'B'
  3         'C'
  4         'D'
  5         'A'
  6         'A'
  7         'A'
  8         'A'
```

The CROSS JOIN in the FROM clause looks like this:

```
Cross Join working table
Students                                  Gradebook
stud_nbr  stud_name  sex     age  |  stud_nbr     grade
=========================================================
   1       'Smith'    'M'    16   |     1          'A'
   1       'Smith'    'M'    16   |     2          'B'
   1       'Smith'    'M'    16   |     3          'C'
   1       'Smith'    'M'    16   |     4          'D'
   1       'Smith'    'M'    16   |     5          'A'
   1       'Smith'    'M'    16   |     6          'A'
   1       'Smith'    'M'    16   |     7          'A'
   1       'Smith'    'M'    16   |     8          'A'
   2       'Smyth'    'F'    17   |     1          'A'
   2       'Smyth'    'F'    17   |     2          'B'
   2       'Smyth'    'F'    17   |     3          'C'
   2       'Smyth'    'F'    17   |     4          'D'
   2       'Smyth'    'F'    17   |     5          'A'
   2       'Smyth'    'F'    17   |     6          'A'
   2       'Smyth'    'F'    17   |     7          'A'
```

2	'Smyth'	'F'	17	8	'A'
3	'Smoot'	'F'	16	1	'A'
3	'Smoot'	'F'	16	2	'B'
3	'Smoot'	'F'	16	3	'C'
3	'Smoot'	'F'	16	4	'D'
3	'Smoot'	'F'	16	5	'A'
3	'Smoot'	'F'	16	6	'A'
3	'Smoot'	'F'	16	7	'A'
3	'Smoot'	'F'	16	8	'A'
4	'Adams'	'F'	17	1	'A'
4	'Adams'	'F'	17	2	'B'
4	'Adams'	'F'	17	3	'C'
4	'Adams'	'F'	17	4	'D'
4	'Adams'	'F'	17	5	'A'
4	'Adams'	'F'	17	6	'A'
4	'Adams'	'F'	17	7	'A'
4	'Adams'	'F'	17	8	'A'
5	'Jones'	'M'	16	1	'A'
5	'Jones'	'M'	16	2	'B'
5	'Jones'	'M'	16	3	'C'
5	'Jones'	'M'	16	4	'D'
5	'Jones'	'M'	16	5	'A'
5	'Jones'	'M'	16	6	'A'
5	'Jones'	'M'	16	7	'A'
5	'Jones'	'M'	16	8	'A'
6	'Celko'	'M'	17	1	'A'
6	'Celko'	'M'	17	2	'B'
6	'Celko'	'M'	17	3	'C'
6	'Celko'	'M'	17	4	'D'
6	'Celko'	'M'	17	5	'A'
6	'Celko'	'M'	17	6	'A'
6	'Celko'	'M'	17	7	'A'
6	'Celko'	'M'	17	8	'A'
7	'Vennor'	'F'	16	1	'A'
7	'Vennor'	'F'	16	2	'B'
7	'Vennor'	'F'	16	3	'C'
7	'Vennor'	'F'	16	4	'D'
7	'Vennor'	'F'	16	5	'A'
7	'Vennor'	'F'	16	6	'A'
7	'Vennor'	'F'	16	7	'A'
7	'Vennor'	'F'	16	8	'A'

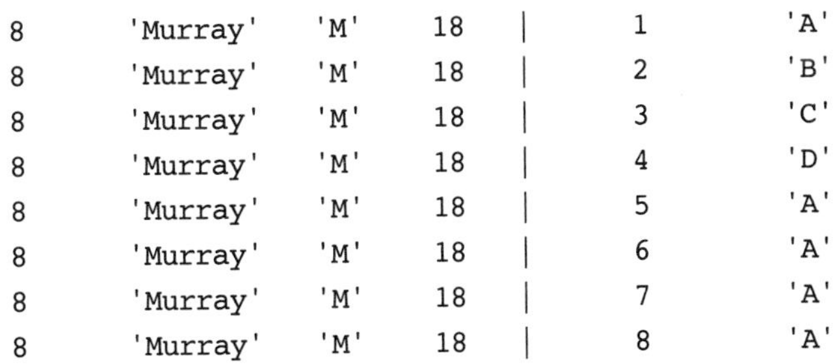

8	'Murray'	'M'	18	1	'A'
8	'Murray'	'M'	18	2	'B'
8	'Murray'	'M'	18	3	'C'
8	'Murray'	'M'	18	4	'D'
8	'Murray'	'M'	18	5	'A'
8	'Murray'	'M'	18	6	'A'
8	'Murray'	'M'	18	7	'A'
8	'Murray'	'M'	18	8	'A'

There are two predicates in the `WHERE`. The first predicate, `grade = 'A'`, needs only the Students table. In fact, an optimizer in a real SQL engine would have removed those rows in the Students table that failed the test before doing the `CROSS JOIN`. The second predicate is `Student.stud_nbr = Gradebook.stud_nbr`, which requires both tables and the constructed row. Predicates that use values from two tables are called `JOIN` conditions for obvious reasons. Now remove the rows that do not meet the conditions. After the `WHERE` clause, the result table looks like this:

```
Cross Join after WHERE clause
Students                               Gradebook
stud_nbr  stud_name  sex    age  |  stud_nbr   grade
=======================================================
  1        'Smith'    'M'    16  |     1        'A'
  5        'Jones'    'M'    16  |     5        'A'
  6        'Celko'    'M'    17  |     6        'A'
  7        'Vennor'   'F'    16  |     7        'A'
  8        'Murray'   'M'    18  |     8        'A'
```

We have a `GROUP BY` clause that will group the working table by sex, thus:

```
by sex
Students                         Gradebook
stud_nbr stud_name sex    age  | stud_nbr  grade
=================================================
  1      'Smith'    'M'    16  | 1          A     sex = 'M' group
  5      'Jones'    'M'    16  | 5          A
  6      'Celko'    'M'    17  | 6          A
  8      'Murray'   'M'    18  | 8          A
----------------------------------------------
  7      'Vennor'   'F'    16  | 7          A     sex = 'F' group
```

And the aggregate functions in the SELECT clause are computed for each group:

```
Aggregate functions
sex    COUNT(*)    AVG(age)    (MAX(age) - MIN(age)) AS age_range
=================================================================
'F'       1          16.00           (16 - 16) = 0
'M'       4          16.75           (18 - 16) = 2
```

The HAVING clause is applied to each group, the SELECT statement is applied last, and we get the final results:

```
Full query with having clause
sex    COUNT(*)    AVG(age)    age_range
========================================
'M'         4          16.75          2
```

Obviously, no real implementation actually produces these intermediate tables; that would be insanely expensive. They are just models to demonstrate how a statement works. The FROM clause can have joins and other operators that create working tables, but the same steps are followed in this order in a nested fashion. Subqueries in the WHERE clause are parsed and expanded the same way.

17.1.2 Correlated Subqueries in a SELECT Statement

A correlated subquery is a subquery that references columns in the tables of its containing query. This is a way to "hide a loop" in SQL. Consider a query to find all the students who are younger than the oldest student of their gender:

```
SELECT *
  FROM Students AS S1
 WHERE age < (SELECT MAX(age)
                FROM Students AS S2
               WHERE S1.sex = S2.sex);
```

1. A copy of the table is made for each correlation name, S1 and S2.Students AS S1:

```
stud_nbr  stud_name   sex    age
==================================
 1         'Smith'    'M'    16
 2         'Smyth'    'F'    17
 3         'Smoot'    'F'    16
 4         'Adams'    'F'    17
 5         'Jones'    'M'    16
 6         'Celko'    'M'    17
 7         'Vennor'   'F'    16
 8         'Murray'   'M'    18
```

2. When you get to the WHERE clause and find the innermost query, you will see that you need to get data from the containing query. The model of execution says that each outer row has the subquery executed on it in parallel with the other rows. Assume we are working on student (1, 'Smith'), who is male. The query in effect becomes:

```
SELECT 1, 'Smith', 'M', 16
  FROM Students AS S1
 WHERE 16 < (SELECT MAX(age)
              FROM Students AS S2
             WHERE 'M' = S2.sex);
```

3. The subquery can now be calculated for male students; the maximum age is 18. When we expand this out for all the other rows, this will give us:

```
SELECT 1, 'Smith', 'M', 16 FROM Students AS S1 WHERE 16 < 18;
SELECT 2, 'Smyth', 'F', 17 FROM Students AS S1 WHERE 17 < 17;
SELECT 3, 'Smoot', 'F', 16 FROM Students AS S1 WHERE 16 < 17;
SELECT 4, 'Adams', 'F', 17 FROM Students AS S1 WHERE 17 < 17;
SELECT 5, 'Jones', 'M', 16 FROM Students AS S1 WHERE 16 < 18;
SELECT 6, 'Celko', 'M', 17 FROM Students AS S1 WHERE 17 < 18;
SELECT 7, 'Vennor', 'F', 16 FROM Students AS S1 WHERE 16 < 17;
SELECT 8, 'Murray', 'M', 18 FROM Students AS S1 WHERE 18 < 18;
```

4. These same steps have been done for each row in the containing query. The model is that all of the subqueries are resolved at once, but again, no implementation really does it that way. The

usual approach is to build procedural loops in the database engine that scan through both tables. The optimizer decides what table is in what loop. The final results are:

```
stud_nbr  stud_name  sex   age
==================================
 1        'Smith'    'M'   16
 3        'Smoot'    'F'   16
 5        'Jones'    'M'   16
 6        'Celko'    'M'   17
 7        'Vennor'   'F'   16
```

Again, no real product works this way, but it has to produce the same results as this process.

17.1.3 SELECT Statement Syntax

SQL-92 added new syntax for JOINs using infixed operators in the FROM clause. The JOIN operators are quite general and flexible, allowing you to do things in a single statement that you could not do in the older notation. The basic syntax is:

```
<joined table> ::=
   <cross join> | <qualified join> | (<joined table>)

<cross join> ::= <table reference> CROSS JOIN <table reference>

<qualified join> ::=
   <table reference> [NATURAL] [<join type>] JOIN
       <table reference> [<join specification>]

<join specification> ::= <join condition> | <named columns join>

<join condition> ::= ON <search condition>

<named columns join> ::= USING (<join column list>)

<join type> ::= INNER | <outer join type> [OUTER] | UNION

<outer join type> ::= LEFT | RIGHT | FULL
```

```
<join column list> ::= <column name list>

<table reference> ::=
   <table name> [[AS] <correlation name>[(<derived column
list>)]]
       | <derived table>
          [AS] <correlation name> [(<derived column list>)]
       | <joined table>

<derived table> ::= <table subquery>

<column name list> ::=
   <column name> [{ <comma> <column name> }...]
```

An INNER JOIN is done by forming the CROSS JOIN and then removing the rows that do not meet the JOIN specification given in the ON clause, as we just demonstrated in the last section. The ON clause can be as elaborate as you want to make it, as long as it refers to tables and columns within its scope. If a <qualified join> is used without a <join type>, INNER is implicit.

However, in the real world, most INNER JOINs are done using equality tests on columns with the same names in different tables, rather than on elaborate predicates. Equi-JOINs are so common that Standard SQL has two shorthand ways of specifying them. The USING (c1, c2, ..., cn) clause takes the column names in the list and replaces them with the clause ON ((T1.c1, T1.c2, ..., T1.cn) = (T2.c1, T2.c2, ..., T2.cn)). Likewise, the NATURAL option is shorthand for a USING() clause that is a list of all the column names that are common to both tables. If NATURAL is specified, a JOIN specification cannot be given; it is already there.

A strong warning: do not use NATURAL JOIN in production code. Any change to the column names will change the join at run time. For the same reason, do not use SELECT * in production code. But the NATURAL JOIN is more dangerous. As Daniel Morgan pointed out, a NATURAL JOIN between two tables with a column named comments can give you a meaningless join on a column containing kilobytes or megabytes of formatted text.

The same sort of warning applies to the USING clause. Neither of these options is widely implemented or used as of 2005.

What's sad about this is that in a properly designed data model, they would work just fine. If you found out that product_id, product_nbr,

and upc were all used for the same data element in your schema, you would do a global change to make sure that one data element has one and only one name. In this case, you would use the better industry standard name upc for this data element.

The UNION JOIN and OUTER JOIN are topics in themselves and will be covered in separate sections.

17.1.4 The ORDER BY Clause

Contrary to popular belief, the ORDER BY clause is not part of the SELECT statement; it is part of a CURSOR declaration. The reason people think it is part of the SELECT statement is that the only way you can get to the result set of a query in a host language is via a cursor. When a vendor tool builds a cursor under the covers for you, they usually allow you to include an ORDER BY clause on the query.

Most optimizers will look at the result set and see from the query whether it is already in sorted order as a result of fetches done with an index, thus avoiding a redundant sorting operation. The bad news is that many programmers have written code that depended on the way that their particular release of a particular brand of SQL product presented the result. When an index is dropped or changed, or when the database is upgraded to a new release or has to be ported to another product, this automatic ordering can disappear.

As part of a cursor, the ORDER BY clause has some properties that you probably did not know existed. Here is the standard syntax.

```
<order by clause> ::=
     ORDER BY <sort specification list>

<sort specification list> ::=
     <sort specification> [{ <comma> <sort specification> }...]

<sort specification> ::=
     <sort key> [<collate clause >] [<ordering specification>]

<sort key> ::= <column name> | <scalar expression>

<ordering specification> ::= ASC | DESC
```

The first things to note is that the sort keys are either column names that must appear in the SELECT clause, or scalar expressions. The use of the positional number of a column is a deprecated feature in Standard SQL. *Deprecation* is a term in the standards world that means this feature will be removed from the next release of the standard; therefore, it should not be used, and your old code must be updated.

These are illegal sorts:

```
SELECT a, (b+c) AS d
  FROM Foobar
 ORDER BY a, b, c; -- illegal!!
```

The columns b and c simply do not exist in the result set of the cursor, so there is no way to sort on them. However, in SQL-99 you were allowed to use a computation in the `ORDER BY`:

```
SELECT a, b, c -- illegal!!
  FROM Foobar
 ORDER BY a, b, (b+c)
```

The correct way to do this is to put the function calls or expressions in the `SELECT` list, name that column, and use the name in the `ORDER BY` clause. This practice lets the user see what values the sorting is done on. Think about it—what good is a report or display when you have no idea how it was sorted?

Furthermore, the sorting columns pass information to middle-tier machines that can sort the data again before distributing it to other front-end clients.

The sort order is based on the collation sequence of the column to which it is attached. The collation can be defined in the schema on character columns, but in most SQL products today collation is either ASCII or EBCDIC. You can expect Unicode to become more popular.

The ORDER BY and NULLs

Whether a sort key value that is `NULL` is considered greater or less than a non-**`NULL`** value is implementation-defined, but all sort key values that are `NULL` shall either be considered greater than all non-**`NULL`** values, or be considered less than all non-**`NULL`** values. There are SQL products that do it either way.

In March 1999, Chris Farrar brought up a question from one of his developers that caused him to examine a part of the SQL Standard that I thought I understood. Chris found some differences between the general understanding and the actual wording of the specification. The situation can be described as follows: a table, Sortable, with two integer

columns, a and b, contains two rows that happen to be in this physical order:

```
Sortable
  a      b
============
 NULL    8
 NULL    4
```

Given the following pseudo-query:

```
SELECT a, b
  FROM Sortable
 ORDER BY a, b;
```

The first question is whether it is legal SQL for the cursor to produce the result sequence:

```
Cursor Result Sequence
    a      b
============
 NULL     8
 NULL     4
```

The problem is that while the SQL Standard set up a rule to make the `NULL`s group together either before or after the known values, we never said that they have to act as if they were equal to each other. What is missing is a statement that says when comparing `NULL` to `NULL`, the result in the context of `ORDER BY` is that `NULL` is equal to `NULL`, just as it is in a `GROUP BY`. This was the intent of the committee, so the expected result should have been:

```
Cursor Result Sequence
  a      b
==========
 NULL   4
 NULL   8
```

Phil Shaw, former IBM representative and one of the oldest members of the committee, dug up the section of the SQL-89 Standard that answered this problem. In SQL-89, the last General Rule of `<comparison predicate>` specified this:

"Although $x = y$" is unknown if both x and y are NULL values, in the context of GROUP BY, ORDER BY, and DISTINCT, a NULL value is identical to or is a duplicate of another NULL value.

That is the rule that causes all NULLs to go into the same group, rather than each in its own group. Apply that rule, and then apply the rules for ORDER BY; the NULL values of column a of the two rows are equal, so you have to order the rows by the columns to the right in the ORDER BY—which is what every SQL product does.

The sort keys are applied from left to right, and a column name can appear only once in the list. But there is no obligation on the part of SQL to use a stable (sequence-preserving) sort. A stable sort on cities, followed by a stable order on states would result in a list with cities sorted within each state, and the states sorted. While stability is a nice property, the nonstable sorts are generally much faster.

You can use computed columns to get specialized sorting orders. For example, construct a table with a character column and an integer column. The goal is to order the results so that it first sorts the integer column descending, but then groups the related character column within the integers. This is much easier to show with an example:

```
CREATE TABLE Foobar
(fruit CHAR(10) NOT NULL,
 score INTEGER NOT NULL,
 PRIMARY KEY (fruit, score));

INSERT INTO Foobar VALUES ('Apples', 2);
INSERT INTO Foobar VALUES ('Apples', 1);
INSERT INTO Foobar VALUES ('Oranges', 5);
INSERT INTO Foobar VALUES ('Apples', 5);
INSERT INTO Foobar VALUES ('Banana', 2);
```

I want to order the results as the following:

```
('Apples', 5)
('Apples', 2)
('Apples', 1)
('Oranges', 5)
('Banana', 2)
```

In the above, the first pass of the sort would have produced this by sorting on the integer column:

```
SELECT F1.fruit, F1.score,
  FROM Foobar AS F1
 ORDER BY F1.score DESC;
```

One outcome might have been any of these:

```
Result #1
('Apples', 5)
('Oranges', 5)
('Apples', 2)
('Banana', 2)
('Apples', 1)

Result #2
('Oranges', 5)
('Apples', 5)
('Apples', 2)
('Banana', 2)
('Apples', 1)

Result #3
('Oranges', 5)
('Apples', 5)
('Banana', 2)
('Apples', 2)
('Apples', 1)

Result #4
('Apples', 5)
('Oranges', 5)
('Banana', 2)
('Apples', 2)
('Apples', 1)
```

If you use:

```
SELECT F1.fruit, F1.score,
  FROM Foobar AS F1
 ORDER BY F1.score DESC, F1.fruit ASC;
Result
('Apples', 5)
('Oranges', 5)
```

```
('Apples', 2)
('Banana', 2)
('Apples', 1)
```

But this is not what we wanted—the order within fruits has been destroyed. Likewise:

```
SELECT F1.fruit, F1.score
  FROM Foobar AS F1
 ORDER BY F1.fruit ASC, F1.score DESC;

Results
('Apples', 5)
('Apples', 2)
('Apples', 1)
('Banana', 2)
('Oranges', 5)
```

But this is still not what we wanted—the order within scores has been destroyed. We need a dummy column to preserve the ordering, thus:

```
SELECT F1.fruit, F1.score,
       (SELECT MAX(score) FROM Foobar AS F2 WHERE F1.fruit =
F2.fruit)
       AS score_preserver
  FROM Foobar AS F1
 ORDER BY score_preserver DESC, F1.fruit ASC, F1.score DESC;
```

Cursors include an `<updatability clause>`, which tells you if the cursor is `FOR READ ONLY` or for `UPDATE [OF <column name list>]` , but this clause in optional. If `ORDER BY` is specified, or if the result table is a read-only table, then the `<updatability clause>` defaults to `FOR READ ONLY`.

The ORDER BY and CASE Expressions

SQL-99 allows you to use a function in an `ORDER BY` clause. While it is now legal, it is still not a good programming practice. Users should see the fields that are used for the sort, so they can use them to read and locate lines of data in reports. The sorting values are usually on the left side of each line, since we read left to right. The most portable method is to use a `CASE` expression that takes an external parameter of the form:

```
SELECT first_name, last_name, dept,
       CASE :flag
       WHEN 'f' THEN first_name
       WHEN 'l' THEN last_name
       WHEN 'd' THEN dept
       ELSE NULL END AS sort_col
  FROM Personnel
 ORDER BY sort_col;
```

Obviously, the expression in the THEN clauses must either be of the same data type or be cast into the same data type. Controlling the direction of the sort is a little trickier and requires two columns, one of which is always set to all NULLs.

```
SELECT last_name,
       CASE :flag
       WHEN 'la' THEN last_name ELSE NULL END AS sort_col1,
       CASE :flag
       WHEN 'ld' THEN last_name ELSE NULL END AS sort_col2
  FROM Personnel
 ORDER BY sort_col1, sort_col2 DESC;
```

You can get a bit fancy with this basic idea:

```
SELECT ...
       CASE :flag_1
              WHEN 'a' THEN CAST (a AS CHAR(n))
              WHEN 'b' THEN CAST (b AS CHAR(n))
              WHEN 'c' THEN CAST (c AS CHAR(n))
              ELSE NULL END AS sort_1,
       CASE :flag_2
              WHEN 'x' THEN CAST (x AS CHAR(n))
              WHEN 'y' THEN CAST (y AS CHAR(n))
              WHEN 'z' THEN CAST (z AS CHAR(n))
              ELSE NULL END AS sort_2,
               ...
       CASE :flag_n
              WHEN 'n1' THEN CAST (n1 AS CHAR(n))
              WHEN 'n2' THEN CAST (n2 AS CHAR(n))
              WHEN 'n3' THEN CAST (n3 AS CHAR(n))
              ELSE NULL END AS sort_2,
```

```
  FROM MyTable
 WHERE ...
ORDER BY sort_1, sort_2, ...;
```

If you have more than one sort column and only a limited set of combinations, use concatenation.

```
CASE :flag_1
       WHEN 'ab'
       THEN CAST(a AS CHAR(n)) ||' ' || CAST(b AS CHAR(n))
       WHEN 'ba'
       THEN CAST(b AS CHAR(n)) ||' ' || CAST(a AS CHAR(n))
       ELSE NULL END AS sort_1,
```

If you need ASC and DESC options, then use a combination of CASE and ORDER BY:

```
CASE :flag_1
       WHEN :flag_1 = 'a' AND :flag_1_ad = 'ASC'
       THEN CAST (a AS CHAR(n))
       WHEN :flag_1 = 'b' AND :flag_1_ad = 'ASC'
       THEN CAST (b AS CHAR(n))
       WHEN :flag_1 = 'c' AND :flag_1_ad = 'ASC'
       THEN CAST (c AS CHAR(n))
       ELSE NULL END AS sort_1_a,
CASE :flag_1
       WHEN :flag_1 = 'a' AND :flag_1_ad = 'DESC'
       THEN CAST (a AS CHAR(n))
       WHEN :flag_1 = 'b' AND :flag_1_ad = 'DESC'
       THEN CAST (b AS CHAR(n))
       WHEN :flag_1 = 'c' AND :flag_1_ad = 'DESC'
       THEN CAST (c AS CHAR(n))
       ELSE NULL END AS sort_1_d
 ..
ORDER BY sort_1_a ASC, sort_1_d DESC
```

I have shown explicit CAST(<exp> AS CHAR(n)), but if the data types of the THEN clause expressions were already the same, there would be no reason to force the conversions. You change the ELSE NULL clause to any constant of the appropriate data type, but it should be

something useful to the reader. A neater way of doing this is to use one column for each sorting option.

```
SELECT MyTable.* ,
       CASE WHEN :flag = 'a' THEN a ELSE NULL END AS sort1,
       CASE WHEN :flag = 'b' THEN b ELSE NULL END AS sort2,
       CASE WHEN :flag = 'c' THEN c ELSE NULL END AS sort3
  FROM Personnel
 WHERE ...
ORDER BY sort1, sort2, sort3;
```

This code is easy to read, and you do not have worry about `CAST()` operations. The trade-off is a larger result set being sent to the cursor.

17.2 OUTER JOINs

`OUTER JOIN`s used to be done with proprietary vendor syntax. Today, the use of the Standard `OUTER JOIN` is universal. An `OUTER JOIN` is a `JOIN` that preserves all the rows in one or both tables, even when they do not have matching rows in the second table. Let's take a real-world situation: I have a table of orders and a table of suppliers that I wish to `JOIN` for a report to tell us how much business we did with each supplier.

With an inner join, the query would be this:

```
SELECT Suppliers.sup_id, sup_name, order_nbr, order_amt
  FROM Suppliers, Orders
 WHERE Suppliers.sup_id = Orders.sup_id;
```

Some suppliers' totals include credits for returned merchandise, and our total business with them works out to zero dollars. Other suppliers never got an order from us at all, so we did zero dollars' worth of business with them, too. But the first case will show up in the query result and be passed on to the report, whereas the second case will disappear in the `INNER JOIN`.

If we had used an `OUTER JOIN`, preserving the Suppliers table, we would have all the suppliers in the results. When a supplier with no orders was found in the Orders table, the order_nbr and order_amt columns would be given a `NULL` value in the result row.

17.2.1 Syntax for OUTER JOINs

In the old SQL-89 standard, there was no OUTER JOIN syntax, so you had to construct it by hand with a messy UNION in products such as earlier versions of DB2 from IBM:

```
SELECT sup_id, sup_name, order_amt   -- regular INNER JOIN
  FROM Suppliers, Orders
 WHERE Suppliers.sup_id = Orders.sup_id
UNION ALL
SELECT sup_id, sup_name, CAST(NULL AS INTEGER) -- preserved rows
of LEFT JOIN
  FROM Suppliers
 WHERE NOT EXISTS
       (SELECT *
          FROM Orders
         WHERE Suppliers.sup_id = Orders.sup_id);
```

You have to use a NULL with the correct data type to make the UNION work, hence the CAST() functions. Some products are smart enough that just NULL by itself will be given the correct data type, but this version is portable and safer.

The other alternative is to insert a constant of some sort to give a more meaningful result. This is easy in the case of a CHARACTER column, where a message like '{{NONE}}' can be quickly understood. It is much harder in the case of a numeric column, where we could have a balance with a supplier that is positive, zero, or negative because of returns and credits. There really is a difference between a vendor we did not use, and a vendor whose returns canceled out its orders.

The most common vendor extensions were for the LEFT OUTER JOIN. These extensions were all different in syntax, or semantics, or both. Today, they are all gone and replaced by the Standard SQL syntax. In the second edition of this book, I described the proprietary extensions in detail; since they are mercifully gone, I am not going to tell you about them in this edition.

The name LEFT OUTER JOIN comes from the fact that the preserved table is on the left side of the operator. Likewise, a RIGHT OUTER JOIN would have the preserved table on the right-hand side, and a FULL OUTER JOIN would preserve both tables.

Here is how OUTER JOINs work in Standard SQL. Assume you are given:

```
Table1      Table2
a  b        a  c
======      ======
1  w        1  r
2  x        2  s
3  y        3  t
4  z
```

and the `OUTER JOIN` expression:

```
Table1
LEFT OUTER JOIN
Table2
ON Table1.a = Table2.a       <== JOIN condition
   AND Table2.c = 't';       <== single table condition
```

We call Table1 the "preserved table" and Table2 the "unpreserved table" in the query. What I am going to give you is a little different, but equivalent to the ANSI/ISO standards.

1. Build the `CROSS JOIN` of the two tables. Scan each row in the result set.
2. If the predicate tests `TRUE` for that row, keep it. You also remove all rows derived from it from the `CROSS JOIN`.
3. If the predicate tests `FALSE` or `UNKNOWN` for that row, then keep the columns from the preserved table, convert all the columns from the unpreserved table to `NULL`s, and remove the duplicates. Let us execute this by hand:

```
 Let @ = passed the first predicate  {{typesetter: pick better
tokens, such as bullets}}
 Let * = passed the second predicate

 Table1 CROSS JOIN Table2
 a  b        a  c
 =========================
 1  w        1  r @
 1  w        2  s
 1  w        3  t *
 2  x        1  r
```

```
2   x      2   s @
2   x      3   t *
3   y      1   r
3   y      2   s
3   y      3   t @* <== the TRUE set
4   z      1   r
4   z      2   s
4   z      3   t *

Table1 LEFT OUTER JOIN Table2
a   b        a   c
=========================
3   y     3      t      <= only TRUE row
-----------------------
1   w     NULL   NULL   Sets of duplicates
1   w     NULL   NULL
1   w     NULL   NULL
-----------------------
2   x     NULL   NULL
2   x     NULL   NULL
2   x     NULL   NULL
3   y     NULL   NULL  <== derived from the TRUE set - Remove
3   y     NULL   NULL
-----------------------
4   z     NULL   NULL
4   z     NULL   NULL
4   z     NULL   NULL
```

The final results are:

```
Table1 LEFT OUTER JOIN Table2
a   b        a   c
=========================
1   w     NULL   NULL
2   x     NULL   NULL
3   y     3      t
4   z     NULL   NULL
```

The basic rule is that every row in the preserved table is represented in the results in at least one result row.

There is a myth among ACCESS programmers that the ON clause can contain only a JOIN condition, and the WHERE can contain only search conditions. This is not true, and the differences in the position of the predicates are important.

Consider the two famous Chris Date tables.

```
Suppliers        SupParts
sup_id           sup_id part_nbr qty
=========        =================
S1               S1     P1      100
S2               S1     P2      250
S3               S2     P1      100
                 S2     P2      250
```

If you write the OUTER JOIN with only the join predicate in the ON clause, like this:

```
SELECT Suppliers.sup_id, SupParts.part_nbr, SupParts.qty
  FROM Suppliers
       LEFT OUTER JOIN
       SupParts
       ON Supplier.sup_id = SupParts.sup_id
 WHERE qty < 200;
```

You get:

```
sup_id part_nbr qty
===================
'S1'    'P1'    100
'S2'    'P1'    100
```

But if you put the search predicate in the ON clause:

```
SELECT Suppliers.sup_id, SupParts.part_nbr, SupParts.qty
  FROM Suppliers
       LEFT OUTER JOIN
       SupParts
       ON Supplier.sup_id = SupParts.sup_id
          AND qty < 200;
```

You get:

```
sup_id part_nbr qty
===================
'S1'    'P1'    100
'S2'    'P1'    100
'S3'    NULL   NULL
```

Another problem is that, in general, the order of execution matters with a chain of `OUTER JOIN`s. That is to say, `((T1 OUTER JOIN T2) OUTER JOIN T3)` does not produce the same results as `(T1 OUTER JOIN (T2 OUTER JOIN T3))`.

I can use any of the options in the `ON` clause of an outer join:

```
SELECT S1.sup_id, S1.sup_name, O1.order_nbr, O1.order_amt
   FROM Suppliers AS S1 LEFT OUTER JOIN Orders AS O1
        ON S1.sup_id = O1.sup_id;
```

or:

```
SELECT S1.sup_id, S1.sup_name, O1.order_nbr, O1.order_amt
  FROM Suppliers AS S1 LEFT OUTER JOIN Orders AS O1
       USING (S1.sup_id);
```

or:

```
SELECT S1.sup_id, S1.sup_name, O1.order_nbr, O1.order_amt
  FROM Suppliers AS S1 NATURAL LEFT OUTER JOIN Orders AS O1;
```

A `SELECT` expression that returns a single row with a single value can be used where a scalar expression can be used. If the result of the scalar query is empty, it is converted to a `NULL`. This will sometimes, but not always, let you write an `OUTER JOIN` as a query within the `SELECT` clause; thus, this query will work only if each supplier has one or zero orders:

```
SELECT sup_id, sup_name, order_nbr,
       (SELECT order_amt
          FROM Orders
         WHERE Suppliers.sup_id = Orders.sup_id)
       AS order_amt
  FROM Suppliers;
```

However, I could write:

```
SELECT sup_id, sup_name,
       (SELECT COUNT(*)
          FROM Orders
         WHERE Suppliers.sup_id = Orders.sup_id)
  FROM Suppliers;
```

instead of writing:

```
SELECT sup_id, sup_name, COUNT(*)
  FROM Suppliers LEFT OUTER JOIN Orders
       ON Suppliers.sup_id = Orders.sup_id
 GROUP BY sup_id, sup_name;
```

17.2.2 NULLs and OUTER JOINs

The NULLs generated by the OUTER JOIN can occur in columns derived from source table columns that have been declared to be NOT NULL. Even if you tried to avoid all the problems with NULLs by making every column in every table of your database schema NOT NULL, they could still occur in OUTER JOIN and OLAP function results. However, a table can have NULLs and still be used in an OUTER JOIN. Consider different JOINs on the following two tables, which have NULLs in the common column:

```
T1              T2
a    x          b    x
========        ===========
1    'r'        7    'r'
2    'v'        8    's'
3    NULL       9    NULL
```

A natural INNER JOIN on column x can only match those values that are equal to each other. But NULLs do not match to anything, even to other NULLs. Thus, there is one row in the result, on the value 'r in column x in both tables.'

```
T1 INNER JOIN T2 ON (T1.x = T2.x)
a    T1.x    b    T2.x
========================
1    'r'     7    'r'
```

Now do a LEFT OUTER JOIN on the tables, which will preserve table T1, and you get:

```
T1 LEFT OUTER JOIN T2 ON (T1.x = T2.x)
a    T1.x    b       T2.x
===========================
1    'r'     7       'r'
2    'v'     NULL    NULL
3    NULL    NULL    NULL
```

Again, there are no surprises. The original INNER JOIN row is still in the results. The other two rows of T1 that were not in the equi-JOIN do show up in the results, and the columns derived from table T2 are filled with NULLs. The RIGHT OUTER JOIN would behave the same way. The problems start with the FULL OUTER JOIN, which looks like this:

```
T1 FULL OUTER JOIN T2 ON (T1.x = T2.x)
a    T1.x    b    T2.x
========================
1    'r'     7    'r'
2    'v'     NULL NULL
3    NULL    NULL NULL
NULL NULL    8    's'
NULL NULL    9    NULL
```

The way this result is constructed is worth explaining in detail.

First do an INNER JOIN on T1 and T2, using the ON clause condition, and put those rows (if any) in the results. Then all rows in T1 that could not be joined are padded out with NULLs in the columns derived from T2 and inserted into the results. Finally, take the rows in T2 that could not be joined, pad them out with NULLs, and insert them into the results. The bad news is that the original tables cannot be reconstructed from an OUTER JOIN. Look at the results of the FULL OUTER JOIN, which we will call R1, and SELECT the first columns from it:

```
SELECT T1.a, T1.x FROM R1
a     x
==========================
1     'r'
2     'v'
3     NULL
NULL  NULL
NULL  NULL
```

The created NULLs remain and cannot be differentiated from the original NULLs. But you cannot throw out those duplicate rows, because they may be in the original table T1.

17.2.3 NATURAL versus Searched OUTER JOINs

It is worth mentioning in passing that Standard SQL has a NATURAL LEFT OUTER JOIN, but it is not implemented in most current versions of SQL. Even those that have the syntax are actually creating an ON clause with equality tests, like the examples we have been using in this chapter.

A NATURAL JOIN has only one copy of the common column pairs in its result. The searched OUTER JOIN has both of the original columns, with their table-qualified names. The NATURAL JOIN has to have a correlation name for the result table to identify the shared columns. We can build a NATURAL LEFT OUTER JOIN by using the COALESCE() function to combine the common column pairs into a single column and put the results into a VIEW where the columns can be properly named, thus:

```
CREATE VIEW NLOJ12 (x, a, b)
AS SELECT COALESCE(T1.x, T2.x), T1.a, T2.b
     FROM T1 LEFT OUTER JOIN T2 ON T1.x = T2.x;
```

```
NLOJ12
x     a    b
==============
'r'    1    7
'v'    2    NULL
NULL   3    NULL
```

Unlike the NATURAL JOINs, the searched OUTER JOIN does not have to use a simple one-column equality as the JOIN search condition.

The search condition can have several predicates, use other comparisons, and so forth. For example,

```
T1 LEFT OUTER JOIN T2 ON (T1.x < T2.x)
a    T1.x    b    T2.x
===================================
1    'r'    8    's'
2    'v'    NULL NULL
3    NULL   NULL NULL
```

as compared to:

```
T1 LEFT OUTER JOIN T2 ON (T1.x > T2.x)
a    T1.x    b    T2.x
=========================================
1    'r'    NULL  NULL
2    'v'    7     'r'
2    'v'    8     's'
3    NULL   NULL  NULL
```

Again, so much of current OUTER JOIN behavior is vendor-specific that the programmer should experiment with his own particular product to see what actually happens.

17.2.4 Self OUTER JOINs

There is no rule that forbids an OUTER JOIN on the same table. In fact, this kind of self-join is a good trick for "flattening" a normalized table into a horizontal report. To illustrate the method, start with a table defined as

```
CREATE TABLE Credits
(student_nbr INTEGER NOT NULL,
 course_name CHAR(8) NOT NULL,
 PRIMARY KEY (student_nbr, course_name));
```

This table represents student IDs and a course name for each class they have taken. However, our rules say that students cannot get credit for CS-102 until they have taken its prerequisite, CS-101; they cannot get credit for CS-103 until they have taken its prerequisite, CS-102; and so forth. Let's first load the table with some sample values.

Notice that student 1 has both courses, student 2 has only the first of the series, and student 3 jumped ahead of sequence and therefore cannot get credit for his CS-102 course until he goes back and takes CS-101 as a prerequisite.

```
Credits
student_nbr  course_name
==========================
    1        'CS-101'
    1        'CS-102'
    2        'CS-101'
    3        'CS-102'
```

What we want is basically a histogram (bar chart) for each student, showing how far he or she has gone in his or her degree programs. Assume that we are only looking at two courses; the result of the desired query might look like this (`NULL` is used to represent a missing value):

```
(1, 'CS-101', 'CS-102')
(2, 'CS-101', NULL)
```

Clearly, this will need a self-`JOIN`, since the last two columns come from the same table, Credits. You have to give correlation names to both uses of the Credits table in the `OUTER JOIN` operator when you construct a self `OUTER JOIN`, just as you would with any other `SELF-JOIN`, thus:

```
SELECT student_nbr, C1.course_name, C2.course_name
 FROM Credits AS C1 LEFT OUTER JOIN Credits AS C2
       ON C1.student_nbr = C2.student_nbr
          AND C1.course_name = 'CS-101'
          AND C2.course_name = 'CS-102';
```

17.2.5 Two or More OUTER JOINs

Some relational purists feel that every operator should have an inverse, and therefore they do not like the `OUTER JOIN`. Others feel that the created `NULL`s are fundamentally different from the explicit `NULL`s in a base table and should have a special token. SQL uses its general-purpose `NULL`s and leaves things at that. Getting away from theory, you will also find that vendors have often done strange things with the ways their products work.

A major problem is that OUTER JOIN operators do not have the same properties as INNER JOIN operators. The order in which FULL OUTER JOINs are executed will change the results (a mathematician would say that they are not associative). To show some of the problems that can come up when you have more than two tables, let us use three very simple two-column tables. Notice that some of the column values match and some do not match, but the three tables have all possible pairs of column names in them.

```
CREATE TABLE T1 (a INTEGER NOT NULL, b INTEGER NOT NULL);
INSERT INTO T1 VALUES (1, 2);

CREATE TABLE T2 (a INTEGER NOT NULL, c INTEGER NOT NULL);
INSERT INTO T2 VALUES (1, 3);

CREATE TABLE T3 (b INTEGER NOT NULL, c INTEGER NOT NULL);
INSERT INTO T3 VALUES (2, 100);
```

Now let's try some of the possible orderings of the three tables in a chain of LEFT OUTER JOINS. The problem is that a table can be preserved or unpreserved in the immediate JOIN and in the opposite state in the containing JOIN.

```
SELECT T1.a, T1.b, T3.c
  FROM ((T1 NATURAL LEFT OUTER JOIN T2)
        NATURAL LEFT OUTER JOIN T3);
 Result
 a  b  c
 ===========
 1  2  NULL

SELECT T1.a, T1.b, T3.c
  FROM ((T1 NATURAL LEFT OUTER JOIN T3)
        NATURAL LEFT OUTER JOIN T2);

 Result
 a  b  c
 ===========
 1  2  100
```

```
SELECT T1.a, T1.b, T3.c
  FROM ((T1 NATURAL LEFT OUTER JOIN T3)
        NATURAL LEFT OUTER JOIN T2);

Result
a    b    c
==============
NULL NULL NULL
```

Even worse, the choice of column in the SELECT list can change the output. Instead of displaying T3.c, use T2.c and you will get:

```
SELECT T1.a, T1.b, T2.c
  FROM ((T2 NATURAL LEFT OUTER JOIN T3)
        NATURAL LEFT OUTER JOIN T1);

Result
a    b    c
===========
NULL NULL 3
```

17.2.6 OUTER JOINs and Aggregate Functions

At the start of this chapter, we had a table of orders and a table of suppliers, which were to be used to build a report to tell us how much business we did with each supplier. The query that will do this is:

```
SELECT Suppliers.sup_id, sup_name, SUM(order_amt)
  FROM Suppliers LEFT OUTER JOIN Orders
       ON Suppliers.sup_id = Orders.sup_id
 GROUP BY sup_id, sup_name;
```

Some suppliers' totals include credits for returned merchandise, so that our total business with them worked out to zero dollars. Each supplier with which we did no business will have a NULL in its order_amt column in the OUTER JOIN. The usual rules for aggregate functions with NULL values apply, so these suppliers will also show a zero total amount. It is also possible to use a function inside an aggregate function, so you could write SUM(COALESCE(T1.x, T2.x)) for the common column pairs.

If you need to tell the difference between a true sum of zero and the result of a NULL in an OUTER JOIN, use the MIN() or MAX() function on the questionable column. These functions both return a NULL result for a NULL input, so an expression inside the MAX() function could be used to print the message MAX(COALESCE(order_amt, 'No Orders')), for example.

Likewise, these functions could be used in a HAVING clause, but that would defeat the purpose of an OUTER JOIN.

17.2.7 FULL OUTER JOIN

The FULL OUTER JOIN is a mix of the LEFT and RIGHT OUTER JOINs, with preserved rows constructed from both tables. The statement takes two tables and puts them in one result table. Again, this is easier to explain with an example than with a formal definition. It is also a way to show how to form a query that will perform the same function. Using Suppliers and Orders again, we find that we have suppliers with whom we have done no business, but we also have orders for which we have not decided on suppliers. To get all orders and all suppliers in one result table, we could use the SQL-89 query:

```
SELECT sup_id, sup_name, order_amt     -- regular INNER JOIN
  FROM Suppliers, Orders
 WHERE Suppliers.sup_id = Orders.sup_id
UNION ALL
SELECT sup_id, sup_name, CAST (NULL AS INTEGER)   -- preserved
rows of LEFT JOIN
  FROM Suppliers
 WHERE NOT EXISTS (SELECT *
                    FROM Orders
                   WHERE Suppliers.sup_id = Orders.sup_id)
UNION ALL
SELECT CAST (NULL AS CHAR(2)), CAST (NULL AS CHAR(10)),
order_amt    -- preserved rows of RIGHT JOIN
  FROM Orders
 WHERE NOT EXISTS (SELECT *
                    FROM Suppliers
                   WHERE Suppliers.sup_id = Orders.sup_id);
```

The same thing in Standard SQL would be:

```
SELECT sup_id, sup_name, order_amt
  FROM Orders FULL OUTER JOIN Suppliers
       ON (Suppliers.sup_id = Orders.sup_id);
```

The FULL OUTER JOIN is not used as much as a LEFT or RIGHT OUTER JOIN. When you are doing a report, it is usually done from a viewpoint that leads to preserving only one side of the JOIN.

That is, you might ask "What suppliers got no business from us?" or ask "What orders have not been assigned a supplier?" but a combination of the two questions is not likely to be in the same report.

17.2.8 WHERE Clause OUTER JOIN Operators

As we have seen, SQL engines that use special operators in the WHERE clause for OUTER JOIN syntax get strange results. But with the Standard SQL syntax for OUTER JOINs, the programmer has to be careful in the WHERE to qualify the JOIN columns of the same name to be sure that he picks up the preserved column. Both of these are legal queries:

```
SELECT *
  FROM T1 LEFT OUTER JOIN T2
       ON T1.a = T2.a
 WHERE T1.a = 15;
```

versus

```
SELECT *
  FROM T1 LEFT OUTER JOIN T2
       ON T1.a = T2.a
 WHERE T2.a = 15;
```

However, the second one will reject the rows with generated NULLs in them. If that is what you wanted, then why bother with an OUTER JOIN in the first place?

There is also a UNION JOIN in the SQL-92 Standard, which returns the results of a FULL OUTER JOIN without the rows that were in the INNER JOIN of the two tables. No product has implemented it as of 2005.

Figure 17.1 shows the various JOINs.

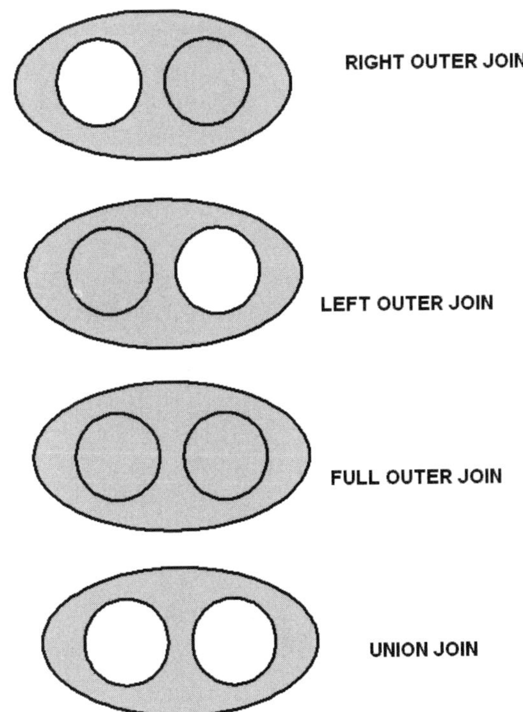

Figure 17.1 *SQL JOIN Functions.*

17.3 Old versus New JOIN Syntax

One of the classics of software engineering is a short paper by the late Edsger Dijkstra entitled "Go To Statement Considered Harmful" (Dijkstra 1968, pp. 147-148). Dijkstra argued for dropping the GOTO statement from programming languages in favor of what we now call structured programming.

One of his observations was that programs that used blocks, WHILE loops, and IF-THEN-ELSE statements were easier to read and maintain. Programs that jumped around via GOTO statements were harder to follow, because the execution path could have arrived at a statement label from anywhere in the code.

With the SQL-92 Standard, we added a set of infixed join operators to SQL, making the syntax closer to the way that relational algebra looks. The infixed OUTER JOIN syntax was meant to replace several different vendor options, which all had different syntax and semantics. It was absolutely needed.

But while we were fixing that problem, we also added a few more options because they were easy to define. Most of them have not been

implemented in actual products yet, and nobody seems to be missing the OUTER UNION or CORRESPONDING clause.

The INNER JOIN operator did get to be popular. This was fairly easy to implement, since vendors only had to extend the parser without having to add more functionality. Additionally, it is a binary operator, and programmers are used to binary operators—add, subtract, multiply, and divide are all binary operators. E-R diagrams use lines between tables to show a relational schema.

But this leads to a linear approach to problem solving that might not be such a good thing in SQL. Consider this statement, which would have been written in the traditional syntax as:

```
SELECT a, b, c
 FROM Foo, Bar, Flub
 WHERE Foo.y BETWEEN Bar.x AND Flub.z;
```

With the infixed syntax, I can write this same statement in any of several ways. For example:

```
SELECT *
 FROM Foo
      INNER JOIN
      Bar ON Foo.y >= Bar.x
      INNER JOIN
      Flub ON Foo.y <= Flub.z;
```

Humans tend to see things that are close together as a unit or as having a relationship. The extra reserved words in the infixed notation tend to work against that perception.

The infixed notation invites a programmer to add one table at a time to the chain of joins. First I built and tested the Foo-Bar join, and when I was happy with the results, I added Flub. "Step-wise" program refinement was one of the mantras of structured programming.

But look at the code; can you see that there is a BETWEEN relationship among the three tables? It is not easy, is it? In effect, you see only pairs of tables and not the whole problem. SQL is an "all-at-once" set-oriented language, not a "step-wise" language.

Technically, the SQL engine is supposed to perform the infixed joins in left to right order as they appear in the FROM clause. It is free to rearrange the order of the joins, if the rearrangement does not change the results. Order of execution does not make a difference with INNER JOINs, but it is very important with OUTER JOINs.

17.4 Scope of Derived Table Names

Another problem is that many SQL programmers do not fully understand the rules for the scope of names. If an infixed join is given a derived table name, then all of the table names inside it are hidden from containing expressions. For example, this will fail:

```
SELECT a, b, c -- wrong!
 FROM (Foo
       INNER JOIN
       Bar ON Foo.y >= Bar.x) AS Foobar (x, y)
      INNER JOIN
      Flub ON Foo.y <= Flub.z;
```

It fails because the table name Foo is not available to the second INNER JOIN. However, this will work:

```
SELECT a, b, c
 FROM (Foo
       INNER JOIN
       Bar ON Foo.y >= Bar.x) AS Foobar (x, y)
      INNER JOIN
      Flub ON Foobar.y <= Flub.z;
```

If you start nesting lots of derived table expressions, you can force an order of execution in the query. It is generally not a good idea to try to outguess the optimizer.

So far, I have shown fully qualified column names. It is a good programming practice, but it is not required. Assume that Foo and Bar both have a column named w. These statements will produce an ambiguous name error:

```
SELECT a, b, c
 FROM Foo
      INNER JOIN
      Bar ON y >= x
      INNER JOIN
      Flub ON y <= w;
```

```
SELECT a, b, c
 FROM Foo, Bar, Flub
 WHERE y BETWEEN x AND w
```

But this statement will work from inside the parentheses first, and then does the outermost INNER JOIN last.

```
SELECT a, b, c
 FROM Foo
      INNER JOIN
      (Bar
      INNER JOIN
      Flub ON y <= w)
      ON y >= x;
```

If Bar did not have a column named w, then the parser would go to the next containing expression, find Foo.w, and use it.

As an aside, there is a myth among new SQL programmers that the join conditions must be in the ON clause, and the search argument predicates (SARGs) must be in the WHERE clause. It is a nice programming style and isolates the search arguments to one location for easy changes. But it is not a requirement.

Am I against infixed joins? No, but they are a bit more complicated than they first appear, and if there are some OUTER JOINs in the mix, things can be very complicated. Just be careful with the new toys, kids.

17.5 JOINs by Function Calls

JOINs can also be done inside functions that relate columns from one or more tables in their parameters. This is easier to explain with an actual example, from John Botibol of Deverill plc in Dorset, U.K. His problem was how to "flatten" legacy data stored in a flat file database into a relational format for a data warehouse. The data included a vast amount of demographic information on people, related to their subjects of interest. The subjects of interest were selected from a list; some subjects required just one answer, and others allowed multiple selections.

The problem was that the data for multiple selections was stored as a string with a one or a zero in positional places to indicate "interested" or "not interested" in that item. The actual list of products was stored in another file as a list. Thus, for one person we might have something like

'101110' together with a list like 1 = Bananas, 2 = Apples, 3 = Bread, 4 = Fish, 5 = Meat, 6 = Butter, if the subject area was foods.

The data was first moved into working tables like this:

```
CREATE TABLE RawSurvey
(rawkey INTEGER NOT NULL PRIMARY KEY,
 rawstring CHAR(20) NOT NULL);

CREATE TABLE SurveyList
(survey_id INTEGER NOT NULL PRIMARY KEY,
 surveytext CHAR(30) NOT NULL);
```

There were always the correct number of ones and zeros for the number of question options in any group (thus, in this case, the answer strings always have six characters) and the list was in the correct order to match the positions in the string. The data had to be ported into SQL, which meant that each survey had to be broken down into a row for each response.

```
CREATE TABLE Surveys
(survey_id INTEGER NOT NULL,
 surveytext CHAR(30) NOT NULL,
 ticked INTEGER NOT NULL
        CONSTRAINT tick_mark
        CHECK (ticked IN (0, 1)) DEFAULT 0,
 PRIMARY KEY (survey_id, surveytext));
```

This table can be loaded with the query:

```
INSERT INTO Surveys(survey_id, surveytext, ticked)
SELECT rawkey, surveytext,
       SUBSTRING(rawstring FROM survey_id FOR 1)
  FROM RawSurvey, SurveyList;
```

The tables are joined in the `SUBSTRING()` function, instead of with a theta operator. The `SUBSTRING()` function returns an empty string if `survey_id` goes beyond the end of the string. The query will always return a number of rows that is equal to or less than the number of characters in `rawstring`. The technique will adjust itself correctly for any number of possible survey answers.

In the real problem, the table SurveyList always contained exactly the right number of entries for the length of the string to be exploded, and the string to be exploded always had exactly the right number of characters, so you did not need a WHERE clause to check for bad data.

17.6 The UNION JOIN

The UNION JOIN was defined in Standard SQL, but I know of no SQL product that has implemented it. As the name implies, it is a cross between a UNION and a FULL OUTER JOIN. The definition followed easily from the other infixed JOIN operators. The syntax has no searched clause:

```
<table expression 1> UNION JOIN <table expression 2>
```

The statement takes two dissimilar tables and puts them into one result table. It preserves all the rows from both tables and does not try to consolidate them. Columns that do not exist in one table are simply padded out with NULLs in the result rows. Columns with the same names in the tables have to be renamed differently in the result. It is equivalent to:

```
<table expression 1>
 FULL OUTER JOIN
 <table expression 2>
 ON 1 = 2;
```

Any searched expression that is always FALSE will work. As an example of this, you might want to combine the medical records of male and female patients into one table with this query:

```
SELECT *
  FROM (SELECT 'male', prostate FROM Males)
       OUTER UNION
       (SELECT 'female', pregnancy FROM Females);
```

to get a result table like this:

```
Result
male  prostate   female  pregnancy
==================================
'male'   no       NULL       NULL
```

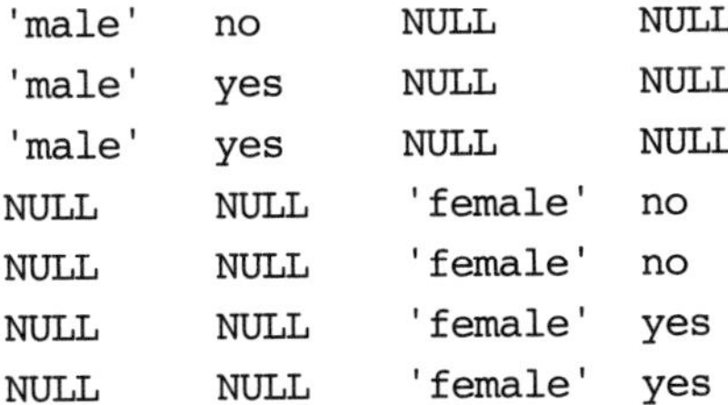

'male'	no	NULL	NULL
'male'	yes	NULL	NULL
'male'	yes	NULL	NULL
NULL	NULL	'female'	no
NULL	NULL	'female'	no
NULL	NULL	'female'	yes
NULL	NULL	'female'	yes

Frédéric Brouard came up with a nice trick for writing a similar join—that is, a join on one table, say a basic table of student data, with either a table of data particular to domestic students or another table of data particular to foreign students, based on the value of a parameter. This differs from a true `UNION JOIN` in that it must have a "root" table to use for the outer joins.

```
CREATE TABLE Students
(student_nbr INTEGER NOT NULL PRIMARY KEY,
 student_type CHAR(1) NOT NULL DEFAULT 'D'
     CHECK (student_type IN ('D', 'F', ...))
 ...);

CREATE TABLE DomesticStudents
(student_nbr INTEGER NOT NULL PRIMARY KEY,
     REFERENCES Students(student_nbr),
 ...);

CREATE TABLE ForeignStudents
(student_nbr INTEGER NOT NULL PRIMARY KEY,
     REFERENCES Students(student_nbr),
 ...);

SELECT Students.*, DomesticStudents.*, ForeignStudents.*
  FROM Students
       LEFT OUTER JOIN
       DomesticStudents
       ON CASE Students.student_type
          WHEN 'D' THEN 1 ELSE NULL END
          = 1
         LEFT OUTER JOIN
         ForeignStudents
         ON CASE Students.student_type
            WHEN 'F'
            THEN 1 ELSE NULL END = 1;
```

17.7 Packing Joins

We can relate two tables together based on quantities in each of them. The simplest example is filling customer orders from our inventories at various stores. To make life easier, let's assume that we have only one product, we process orders in increasing `customer_id` order, and we draw from store inventory by increasing `store_id`.

```
CREATE TABLE Inventory
(store_id INTEGER NOT NULL PRIMARY KEY,
 item_qty INTEGER NOT NULL CHECK (item_qty >= 0));

INSERT INTO Inventory (store_id, item_qty)
VALUES (10, 2),(20, 3), (30, 2);

CREATE TABLE Orders
(customer_id CHAR(5) NOT NULL PRIMARY KEY,
 item_qty INTEGER NOT NULL CHECK (item_qty > 0));

INSERT INTO Orders (customer_id, item_qty)
VALUES ('Bill', 4), ('Fred', 2);
```

What we want to do is fill Bill's order for four units by taking two units from store 1 and two units from store 2. Next we process Fred's order with the one unit left in store 1, and one unit from store 3.

```
SELECT I.store_id, O.customer_id,
       (CASE WHEN O.end_running_qty <= I.end_running_qty
             THEN O.end_running_qty
             ELSE I.end_running_qty END
        - CASE WHEN O.start_running_qty >= I.start_running_qty
               THEN O.start_running_qty
               ELSE I.start_running_qty END)
       AS items_consumed_tally
 FROM (SELECT I1.store_id,
              SUM(I2.item_qty) - I1.item_qty,
              SUM(I2.item_qty)
         FROM Inventory AS I1, Inventory AS I2
        WHERE I2.store_id <= I1.store_id
        GROUP BY I1.store_id, I1.item_qty)
      AS I (store_id, start_running_qty, end_running_qty)
```

```
    INNER JOIN
     (SELECT O1.customer_id,
             SUM(O2.item_qty) - O1.item_qty,
             SUM(O2.item_qty) AS end_running_qty
        FROM Orders AS O1, Orders AS O2
       WHERE O2.customer_id <= O1.customer_id
      GROUP BY O1.customer_id, O1.item_qty)
     AS O (store_id, start_running_qty, end_running_qty)
     ON O.start_running_qty < I.end_running_qty
        AND O.end_running_qty > I.start_running_qty;
-- ORDER BY store_id, customer_id;
```

This can also be done with the new SQL-99 OLAP operators.

17.8 Dr. Codd's T-Join

Dr. E. F. Codd introduced a set of new theta operators, called T-operators, which were based on the idea of a best-fit or approximate equality (Codd 1990). The algorithm for the operators is easier to understand with an example modified from Dr. Codd (Codd 1990).

The problem is to assign the classes to the available classrooms. We want `(class_size < room_size)` to be true after the assignments are made. This will allow us a few empty seats in each room for late students. We can do this in one of two ways. The first way is to sort the tables in ascending order by classroom size and the number of students in a class. We start with the following tables:

```
CREATE TABLE Rooms
(room_nbr CHAR(2) PRIMARY KEY,
 room_size INTEGER NOT NULL);

CREATE TABLE Classes
(class_nbr CHAR(2) PRIMARY KEY,
 class_size INTEGER NOT NULL);
```

These tables have the following rows in them:

```
Classes
class_nbr  class_size
=====================
   'c1'     80
   'c2'     70
```

```
'c3'    65
'c4'    55
'c5'    50
'c6'    40
```

```
Rooms
room_nbr room_size
==================
'r1'     70
'r2'     40
'r3'     50
'r4'     85
'r5'     30
'r6'     65
'r7'     55
```

The goal of the T-Join problem is to assign a class that is smaller than the classroom given it (class_size < room_size). Dr. Codd gives two approaches to the problem.

1. *Ascending Order Algorithm*: Sort both tables into ascending order. Reading from the top of the Rooms table, match each class with the first room that will fit.

```
Classes                     Rooms
class_nbr class_size        room_nbr  room_size
====================        ===================
  'c6'       40               'r5'       30
  'c5'       50               'r2'       40
  'c4'       55               'r3'       50
  'c3'       65               'r7'       55
  'c2'       70               'r6'       65
  'c1'       80               'r1'       70
                              'r4'       85
Results
class_nbr class_size  room_nbr room_size
=========================================
  'c2'        70        'r4'     85
  'c3'        65        'r1'     70
  'c4'        55        'r6'     65
  'c5'        50        'r7'     55
  'c6'        40        'r3'     50
```

2. *Descending Order Algorithm*: Sort both tables into descending order. Reading from the top of the Classes table, match each class with the first room that will fit.

```
Classes                      Rooms
class_nbr  class_size        room_nbr  room_size
======================       ====================
 'c1'        80                'r4'      85
 'c2'        70                'r1'      70
 'c3'        65                'r6'      65
 'c4'        55                'r7'      55
 'c5'        50                'r3'      50
 'c6'        40                'r2'      40
                               'r5'      30

Results
class_nbr  class_size room_nbr  room_size
============================================
 'c1'        80        'r4'       85
 'c3'        65        'r1'       70
 'c4'        55        'r6'       65
 'c5'        50        'r7'       55
 'c6'        40        'r3'       50
```

Notice that the answers are different! Dr. Codd has never given a definition in relational algebra of the T-Join, so I propose that we need one. Informally, for each class, we want the smallest room that will hold it, while maintaining the T-Join condition. Or for each room, we want the largest class that will fill it, while maintaining the T-Join condition. These can be two different things, so you must decide which table is the driver. But either way, I advocate a "best fit" over Codd's "first fit" approach.

In effect, the Swedish and Croatian solutions given later in this section use my definition instead of Dr. Codd's; the Colombian solution is true to the algorithmic approach.

Other theta conditions can be used in place of the "less than" shown here. If "less than or equal" is used, all the classes are assigned to a room in this case, but not in all cases. This is left to the reader as an exercise.

The first attempts in standard SQL are versions grouped by queries. They can, however, produce some rows that would be left out of the answers Dr. Codd was expecting. The first `JOIN` can be written as

```
SELECT class_nbr, class_size, MIN(room_size)
  FROM Rooms, Classes
 WHERE Classes.class_size < Rooms.room_size
 GROUP BY class_nbr, class_size;
```

This will give a result table with the desired room sizes, but not the room numbers. You cannot put the other columns in the SELECT list, since it would conflict with the GROUP BY clause. But also note that the classroom with 85 seats ('r4') is used twice, once by class 'c1' and then by class 'c2':

```
Result
class_nbr  class_size  MIN(room_size)
=====================================
   'c1'         80             85    <== room r4
   'c2'         70             85    <== room r4
   'c3'         65             70
   'c4'         55             65
   'c5'         50             55
   'c6'         40             50
```

Your best bet after this is to use the query in an EXISTS clause.

```
SELECT *
  FROM Rooms, Classes
 WHERE EXISTS (SELECT class_nbr, class_size, MIN(room_size)
                 FROM Rooms, Classes
                WHERE Classes.class_size < Rooms.room_size
                GROUP BY class_nbr, class_size);
```

However, some versions of SQL will not allow a grouped subquery, and others will balk at an aggregate function in an EXISTS predicate. The only way I have found to rectify this is to save the results to a temporary table, then JOIN it back to the Cartesian product of Rooms and Classes. Putting the columns for Rooms into the SELECT list of the same query schema can do the second T-Join:

```
SELECT room_nbr, room_size, MAX(class_size)
  FROM Rooms, Classes
 WHERE Classes.class_size < Rooms.room_size
 GROUP BY room_nbr, room_size;
```

This time, the results are the same as those Dr. Codd got with his procedural algorithm:

```
Result
room_nbr    room_size    MAX(class_size)
========================================
'r4'        85           80
'r1'        70           65
'r6'        65           55
'r7'        55           50
'r3'        50           40
```

If you do a little arithmetic on the data, you find that we have 360 students and 395 seats, 6 classes and 7 rooms. This solution uses the fewest rooms, but note that the 70 students in class 'c2' are left out completely. Room 'r2' is left over, but it has only 40 seats.

As it works out, the best fit of rooms to classes is given by changing the matching rule to "less than or equal." This will leave the smallest room empty and pack the other rooms to capacity, thus:

```
SELECT class_nbr, class_size, MIN(room_size)
  FROM Rooms, Classes
 WHERE Classes.class_size <= Rooms.room_size
 GROUP BY class_nbr, class_size;
```

17.8.1 The Croatian Solution

I published this same problem in an article in *DBMS* magazine (Celko 1992a) and got an answer in QUEL from Miljenko Martinis of Croatia in our Letters column (Miljenko 1992). He then translated it from QUEL into SQL with two views, thus:

```
CREATE VIEW Classrooms -- all possible legal pairs
AS SELECT *
     FROM Classes, Rooms
    WHERE class_size < room_size;

 CREATE VIEW Classrooms1 -- smallest room for the class
AS SELECT *
    FROM Classrooms AS CR1
   WHERE room_size = (SELECT MIN(room_size)
                        FROM Classrooms
                       WHERE class_nbr = CR1.class_nbr);
```

We find the answer with the simple query:

```
SELECT class_nbr, class_size, room_size, room_nbr
  FROM Classrooms1 AS CR1
 WHERE class_size = (SELECT MAX(class_size)
                       FROM Classrooms1
                      WHERE room_nbr = CR1.room_nbr);
```

```
class_nbr  class_size  room_size room_nbr
===========================================
 'c6'          40          50      'r3'
 'c5'          50          55      'r7'
 'c4'          55          65      'r6'
 'c3'          65          70      'r1'
 'c1'          80          85      'r4'
```

17.8.2 The Swedish Solution

I got another solution from Anders Karlsson of Mr. K Software AB in Stockholm, Sweden. Here is a version of that query:

```
SELECT C1.class_nbr, C1.class_size, R1.room_size, R1.room_nbr
  FROM Classes AS C1, Rooms AS R1
 WHERE C1.class_size = (SELECT MAX(C2.class_size)
                          FROM Classes AS C2
                         WHERE R1.room_size > C2.class_size)
   AND NOT EXISTS (SELECT *
                     FROM Rooms AS R2
                    WHERE R2.room_size > C1.class_size
                      AND R2.room_size < R1.room_size);
```

The first predicate says we have the largest class that will go into this room. The second predicate says there is no other room that would fit this class better (i.e., a room that is smaller than the candidate room and still larger than the class at which we are looking).

17.8.3 The Colombian Solution

Francisco Moreno of the Department of Systems Engineering at the University of Antioquia in Colombia came up with another approach and data to demonstrate the problems in the T-Join.

Clean out the existing tables and insert this data:

```
DELETE FROM Classes;
 INSERT INTO Classes
VALUES ('c1', 106),
       ('c2', 105),
       ('c3', 104),
       ('c4', 100),
       ('c5', 99),
       ('c6', 90),
       ('c7', 89),
       ('c8', 88),
       ('c9', 83),
       ('c10', 82),
       ('c11', 81),
       ('c12', 65),
       ('c13', 50),
       ('c14', 49),
       ('c15', 30),
       ('c16', 29),
       ('c17', 28),
       ('c18', 20),
       ('c19', 19);

DELETE FROM Rooms;
 INSERT INTO Rooms
VALUES ('r1', 102),
       ('r2', 101),
       ('r3', 95),
       ('r4', 94),
       ('r5', 85),
       ('r6', 70),
       ('r7', 55),
       ('r8', 54),
       ('r9', 35),
       ('r10', 34),
       ('r11', 25),
       ('r12', 18);
```

Using Codd's T-Join algorithm for descending lists, you would have this mapping:

```
'c1'     106
'c2'     105
'c3'     104
'c4'     100      <--->      'r1'   102
'c5'      99      <--->      'r2'   101
'c6'      90      <--->      'r3'    95
'c7'      89      <--->      'r4'    94
'c8'      88
'c9'      83      <--->      'r5'    85
'c10'     82
'c11'     81
'c12'     65      <--->      'r6'    70
'c13'     50      <--->      'r7'    55
'c14'     49      <--->      'r8'    54
'c15'     30      <--->      'r9'    35
'c16'     29      <--->      'r10'   34
'c17'     28
'c18'     20      <--->      'r11'   25
'c19'     19
                             'r12'   18
```

There are 1,317 students in classes, and 768 seats for them. You can see by inspection that some classes are too large for any room we have. If you started in ascending order, class 'c19' pairs with room 'r11' and you get another result set.

This algorithm is not a best-fit answer, but a first fit answer. This is an important difference. To explain further, the first fit to class 'c4' is room 'r1', which has 102 seats; however, the best fit is room 'r2, which has 101 seats. The algorithm would give us this result table:'

```
Results
class_nbr  class_size  room_size  room_nbr
==========================================
'c4'          100          102       'r1'
'c5'           99          101       'r2'
'c6'           90           95       'r3'
'c7'           89           94       'r4'
'c9'           83           85       'r5'
'c12'          65           70       'r6'
'c13'          50           55       'r7'
'c14'          49           54       'r8'
```

```
'c15'       30        35      'r9'
'c16'       29        34      'r10'
'c18'       20        25      'r11'

704 students served.
```

If you use Swedish or Croatian solution on this data, the answer is:

```
Swedish Result
class_nbr  class_size   room_size  room_nbr
============================================
   'c4'       100         101        'r2'
   'c6'        90          94        'r4'
   'c9'        83          85        'r5'
   'c12'       65          70        'r6'
   'c13'       50          54        'r8'
   'c15'       30          34        'r10'
   'c18'       20          25        'r11'

438 students served.
```

At this point you have a result that is not complete but has the tightest mapping of each class into a room. There is another problem that was not mentioned: we have not had two classes or two rooms of the same size in the data. This will cause some other problems.

Instead of trying to use a single static SQL query, we can use SQL to generate SQL code, then execute it dynamically. This solution is right but, of course, is horrible from a performance viewpoint.

```
-- build a table of possible T-Join pairings
DROP TABLE T-Join;
 CREATE TABLE T-Join AS
SELECT *
  FROM Classes, Rooms
 WHERE room_size > class_size;

-- create a temporary working table
DROP TABLE Ins;
 CREATE TABLE Ins
(class_nbr CHAR(3) NOT NULL,
 class_size INTEGER NOT NULL,
```

```
 room_nbr CHAR(3) NOT NULL,
 room_size INTEGER NOT NULL);

-- create a table with the insertion code for each row
SELECT
'INSERT INTO Ins
SELECT class_nbr, class_size, room_nbr, room_size
  FROM T-Join AS T1
 WHERE room_size
       = (SELECT MAX(room_size)
            FROM T-Join
           WHERE room_size NOT IN (SELECT room_size FROM Ins))
  AND class_size
      = (SELECT MAX(class_size)
           FROM T-Join AS T2
          WHERE class_size NOT IN (SELECT class_size FROM Ins)
            AND T2.class_size < T1.room_size);'
  FROM Rooms
 WHERE room_size > (SELECT MIN(class_size) FROM c);
COMMIT;
```

Now use "`SELECT a, b, c FROM Ins;`" query in a host program with dynamic SQL and execute each statement in the temporary table in order. This will give us the first answer at the start of Section 17.8.3, and it also works for the original data.

Moreno's second solution, which handles duplicates, is more complex, and I will not give it here. It uses the keys of the tables to make rows with duplicate values unique.

VIEWs, Derived Tables, Materialized Tables, and Temporary Tables

VIEWS, DERIVED TABLES, MATERIALIZED tables and temporary tables are ways of putting a query into a named schema object. By that, I mean they hold the query, rather than the results of the query.

A VIEW is also called a virtual table, to distinguish it from temporary and base tables. The definition of a VIEW requires that it act as if an actual physical table is created when its name is invoked. Whether or not the database system actually materializes the results or uses other mechanisms to get the same effect is implementation-defined. The definition of a VIEW is kept in the schema tables to be invoked by name wherever a table could be used. If the VIEW is updatable, then additional rules apply.

The SQL Standard separates administrative (DBA) privileges from user privileges. Table creation is administrative and query execution is a user privilege, so users cannot create their own VIEWs or TEMPORARY TABLEs without having Administrative privileges granted to them.

In the Standard SQL model, a temporary table acts very much like a base table. It is persistent in the schema, but it "cleans itself up" automatically so users do not have to bother, and it can be shared among several users. The temporary table has the same user privileges model as a base table.

However, a user can build a derived table inside a query. This is like building a VIEW on the fly. With the AS operator, we can give names to the results of subquery expressions and use them. The syntax is very simple, but the scoping rules often confuse new users.

```
(<query expression>)
 AS <table name> [(<column list>)]
```

You can think of a VIEW's name being replaced by a derived table expression when it is invoked in a query.

18.1 VIEWs in Queries

The Standard SQL syntax for the VIEW definition is

```
CREATE VIEW <table name> [(<view column list>)]
AS <query expression>
[WITH [<levels clause>] CHECK OPTION]

<levels clause> ::= CASCADED | LOCAL
```

The <levels clause> option in the WITH CHECK OPTION did not exist in SQL-89, and it is still not widely implemented. Section 18.5 of this chapter will discuss this clause in detail. This clause has no effect on queries, but only on UPDATE, INSERT INTO, and DELETE FROM statements.

A VIEW is different from a TEMPORARY TABLE, a derived table, or a base table. You cannot put constraints on a VIEW, as you can with base and TEMPORARY tables. A VIEW has no existence in the database until it is invoked, while a TEMPORARY TABLE is persistent. A derived table exists only in the query in which it is created.

The name of the VIEW must be unique within the database schema, like a table name. The VIEW definition cannot reference itself, since it does not exist yet. Nor can the definition reference only other VIEWs; the nesting of VIEWs must eventually resolve to underlying base tables. This only makes sense if no base tables were involved, what would you be viewing?

18.2 Updatable and Read-Only VIEWs

Unlike base tables, VIEWs are either updatable or read-only, but not both. INSERT, UPDATE, and DELETE operations are allowed on updatable VIEWs and base tables, subject to any other constraints. INSERT, UPDATE, and DELETE are not allowed on read-only VIEWs, but you can change their base tables, as you would expect.

An updatable VIEW is one that can have each of its rows associated with exactly one row in an underlying base table. When the VIEW is changed, the changes pass unambiguously through the VIEW to that underlying base table. Updatable VIEWs in Standard SQL are defined only for queries that meet these criteria:

1. Built on only one table
2. No GROUP BY clause
3. No HAVING clause
4. No aggregate functions
5. No calculated columns
6. No UNION, INTERSECT, or EXCEPT
7. No SELECT DISTINCT clause
8. Any columns excluded from the VIEW must be NULL-able or have a DEFAULT in the base table, so that a whole row can be constructed for insertion

By implication, the VIEW must also contain a key of the table. In short, we are absolutely sure that each row in the VIEW maps back to one and only one row in the base table.

Some updating is handled by the CASCADE option in the referential integrity constraints on the base tables, not by the VIEW declaration.

The definition of updatability in Standard SQL is actually fairly limited, but very safe. The database system could look at information it has in the referential integrity constraints to widen the set of allowed updatable VIEWs. You will find that some implementations are now doing just that, but it is not common yet. The SQL Standard definition of an updatable VIEW is actually a subset of the possible updatable VIEWs, and a very small subset at that. The major advantage of this definition is that it is based on syntax and not semantics. For example, these VIEWs are logically identical:

```
CREATE VIEW Foo1 -- updatable, has a key!
AS SELECT *
     FROM Foobar
    WHERE x IN (1,2);

CREATE VIEW Foo2  -- not updatable!
AS SELECT *
     FROM Foobar
    WHERE x = 1
   UNION ALL
   SELECT *
     FROM Foobar
    WHERE x = 2;
```

But Foo1 is updatable and Foo2 is not. While I know of no formal proof, I suspect that determining whether a complex query resolves to an updatable query for allowed sets of data values possible in the table is an NP-complete problem.

Without going into details, here is a list of types of queries that can yield updatable VIEWs, as taken from "VIEW Update Is Practical" (Goodman 1990):

1. Projection from a single table (Standard SQL)
2. Restriction/projection from a single table (Standard SQL)
3. UNION VIEWs
4. Set difference VIEWs
5. One-to-one joins
6. One-to-one outer joins
7. One-to-many joins
8. One-to-many outer joins
9. Many-to-many joins
10. Translated and coded fields

The CREATE TRIGGER mechanism for tables indicates an action to be performed BEFORE, AFTER, or INSTEAD OF a regular INSERT, UPDATE, or DELETE to that table. It is possible for a user to write INSTEAD OF triggers on VIEWs, which catch the changes and route them to the base tables that make up the VIEW. The database designer has complete control over the way VIEWs are handled.

18.3 Types of VIEWs

The type of SELECT statements and their purpose can classify VIEWs. The strong advantage of a VIEW is that it will produce the correct results when it is invoked, based on the current data. Trying to do the same sort of things with temporary tables or computed columns within a table can be subject to errors and slower to read from disk.

18.3.1 Single-Table Projection and Restriction

In practice, many VIEWs are projections or restrictions on a single base table. This is a common method for obtaining security control by removing rows or columns that a particular group of users is not allowed to see. These VIEWs are usually implemented as in-line macro expansion, since the optimizer can easily fold their code into the final query plan.

18.3.2 Calculated Columns

One common use for a VIEW is to provide summary data across a row. For example, given a table with measurements in metric units, we can construct a VIEW that hides the calculations to convert them into English units.

It is important to be sure that you have no problems with NULL values when constructing a calculated column. For example, given a Personnel table with columns for both salary and commission, you might construct this VIEW:

```
CREATE VIEW Payroll (emp_nbr, paycheck_amt)
AS
SELECT emp_nbr, (salary + COALESCE(commission), 0.00)
  FROM Personnel;
```

Office workers do not get commissions, so the value of their commission column will be NULL. Therefore, we use the COALESCE() function to change the NULLs to zeros.

18.3.3 Translated Columns

Another common use of a VIEW is to translate codes into text or other codes by doing table lookups. This is a special case of a joined VIEW

based on a FOREIGN KEY relationship between two tables. For example, an order table might use a part number that we wish to display with a part name on an order entry screen. This is done with a JOIN between the order table and the inventory table, thus:

```
CREATE VIEW Screen (part_nbr, part_name, ...)
AS SELECT Orders.part_nbr, Inventory.part_name, ...
     FROM Inventory, Orders
    WHERE Inventory.part_nbr = Orders.part_nbr;
```

Sometimes the original code is kept, and sometimes it is dropped from the VIEW. As a general rule, it is a better idea to keep both values, even though they are redundant. The redundancy can be used as a check for users, as well as a hook for nested joins in either of the codes.

The idea of JOIN VIEWs to translate codes can be expanded to show more than just one translated column. The result is often a "star query"—one table in the center joined by FOREIGN KEY relations to many other tables to produce a result that is more readable than the original central table.

Missing values are a problem. If there is no translation for a given code, no row appears in the VIEW or, if an OUTER JOIN was used, a NULL will appear. The programmer should establish a referential integrity constraint to CASCADE changes between the tables to prevent loss of data.

18.3.4 Grouped VIEWs

A grouped VIEW is based on a query with a GROUP BY clause. Since each of the groups may have more than one row in the base from which it was built, these are necessarily read-only VIEWs. Such VIEWs usually have one or more aggregate functions and they are used for reporting purposes. They are also handy for working around weaknesses in SQL. Consider a VIEW that shows the largest sale in each state. The query is straightforward:

```
CREATE VIEW BigSales (state, sales_amt_total)
AS SELECT state_code, MAX(sales_amt)
     FROM Sales
    GROUP BY state_code;
```

SQL does not require that the grouping column(s) appear in the select clause, but it is a good idea in this case.

These VIEWs are also useful for "flattening out" one-to-many relationships. For example, consider a Personnel table, keyed on the employee number (emp_nbr), and a table of dependents, keyed on a combination of the employee number for each dependent's parent (emp_nbr) and the dependent's own serial number (dep_id). The goal is to produce a report of the employees by name with the number of dependents each one has.

```
CREATE VIEW DepTally1 (emp_nbr, dependent_cnt)
AS SELECT emp_nbr, COUNT(*)
     FROM Dependents
    GROUP BY emp_nbr;
```

The report is then simply an OUTER JOIN between this VIEW and the Personnel table.

The OUTER JOIN is needed to account for employees without dependents with a NULL value, like this.

```
SELECT emp_name, dependent_cnt
 FROM Personnel AS P1
      LEFT OUTER JOIN
      DepTally1 AS D1
      ON P1.emp_nbr = D1.emp_nbr;
```

18.3.5 UNIONed VIEWs

Until recently, a VIEW based on a UNION or UNION ALL operation was read-only, because there is no way to map a change onto just one row in one of the base tables. The UNION operator will remove duplicate rows from the results. Both the UNION and UNION ALL operators hide which table the rows came from. Such VIEWs must use a <view column list>, because the columns in a UNION [ALL] have no names of their own. In theory, a UNION of two disjoint tables, neither of which has duplicate rows in itself, should be updatable.

The problem given in Section 18.3.4 on grouped VIEWs could also be done with a UNION query that would assign a count of zero to employees without dependents, thus:

```
CREATE VIEW DepTally2 (emp_nbr, dependent_cnt)
AS (SELECT emp_nbr, COUNT(*)
```

```
       FROM Dependents
      GROUP BY emp_nbr)
     UNION
    (SELECT emp_nbr, 0
       FROM Personnel AS P2
      WHERE NOT EXISTS (SELECT *
                          FROM Dependents AS D2
                         WHERE D2.emp_nbr = P2.emp_nbr));
```

The report is now a simple INNER JOIN between this VIEW and the Personnel table. The zero value, instead of a NULL value, will account for employees without dependents. The report query looks like this.

```
SELECT empart_name, dependent_cnt
  FROM Personnel, DepTally2
 WHERE DepTally2.emp_nbr = Personnel.emp_nbr;
```

Releases of some of the major databases, such as Oracle and DB2, support inserts, updates, and deletes from such views. Under the covers, each partition is a separate table, with a rule for its contents. One of the most common partitions is temporal, so each partition might be based on a date range. The goal is to improve query performance by allowing parallel access to each partition member. However, the trade-off is a heavy overhead with the UNIONed VIEW partitioning. For example, DB2 attempts to insert any given row into each of the tables underlying the UNION ALL view. It then counts how many tables accepted the row. It has to process the entire view, one table at a time, and collect the results.

1. If exactly one table accepts the row, the insert is accepted.
2. If no table accepts the row, a "no target" error is raised.
3. If more than one table accepts the row, then an "ambiguous target" error is raised.

The use of INSTEAD OF triggers gives the user the effect of a single table, but there can still be surprises. Think about three tables: A, B, and C. Table C is disjoint from the other two. Tables A and B overlap. So I can always insert into C, and may or may not be able to insert into A and B if I hit overlapping rows.

Going back to my Y2K consulting days, I ran into a version of such a partition by calendar periods. Their Table C was set up on fiscal quarters, and it got leap year wrong because one of the fiscal quarters ended on the last day of February.

Another approach somewhat like this is to declare explicit partitioning rules in the DDL with a proprietary syntax. The system will handle the housekeeping and the user sees only one table. In the Oracle model, the goal is to put parts of the logical table to different physical tablespaces. Using standard data types, the Oracle syntax looks like this:

```
CREATE TABLE Sales
(invoice_nbr INTEGER NOT NULL PRIMARY KEY,
 sale_year INTEGER NOT NULL,
 sale_month INTEGER NOT NULL,
 sale_day  INTEGER NOT NULL)
PARTITION BY RANGE (sale_year, sale_month, sale_day)
(PARTITION sales_q1 VALUES LESS THAN (1994, 04, 01) TABLESPACE
tsa,
 PARTITION sales_q2 VALUES LESS THAN (1994, 07, 01) TABLESPACE
tsb,
 PARTITION sales_q3 VALUES LESS THAN (1994, 10, 01) TABLESPACE
tsc,
 PARTITION sales q4 VALUES LESS THAN (1995, 01, 01) TABLESPACE
tsd);
```

Again, this will depend on your product, since this has to do with the physical database and not the logical model.

18.3.6 JOINs in VIEWs

A `VIEW` whose query expression is a joined table is not usually updatable, even in theory.

One of the major purposes of a joined view is to "flatten out" a one-to-many or many-to-many relationship. Such relationships cannot map one row in the `VIEW` back to one row in the underlying tables on the "many" side of the `JOIN`. Anything said about a `JOIN` query could be said about a joined view, so they will not be dealt with here; you can refer back to Chapter 17 for a full discussion.

18.3.7 Nested VIEWs

A point that is often missed, even by experienced SQL programmers, is that a `VIEW` can be built on other `VIEW`s. The only restrictions are that

circular references within the query expressions of the VIEWs are illegal, and that a VIEW must ultimately be built on base tables. One problem with nested VIEWs is that different updatable VIEWs can reference the same base table at the same time. If these VIEWs then appear in another VIEW, it becomes hard to determine what has happened when the highest-level VIEW is changed. As an example, consider a table with two keys:

```
CREATE TABLE Canada
(english INTEGER NOT NULL UNIQUE,
 french INTEGER NOT NULL UNIQUE,
 engword CHAR(30),
 frenword CHAR(30));

INSERT INTO Canada
VALUES (1, 2, 'muffins', 'croissants'),
       (2, 1, 'bait', 'escargots');

CREATE VIEW EnglishWords
AS SELECT english, engword
     FROM Canada
    WHERE engword IS NOT NULL;

CREATE VIEW FrenchWords
AS SELECT french, frenword
     FROM Canada
    WHERE frenword IS NOT NULL);
```

We have now tried the *escargots* and decided that we wish to change our opinion of them:

```
UPDATE EnglishWords
   SET engword = 'appetizer'
 WHERE english = 2;
```

Our French user has just tried haggis and decided to insert a new row for his experience:

```
UPDATE FrenchWords
   SET frenword = 'Le swill'
 WHERE french = 3;
```

The row that is created is (NULL, 3, NULL, 'Le swill'), since there is no way for VIEW FrenchWords to get to the VIEW EnglishWords columns. Likewise, the English VIEW user can construct a row to record his translation, (3, NULL, 'Haggis', NULL). But neither of them can consolidate the two rows into a meaningful piece of data.

To delete a row is also to destroy data; the French-speaker who drops 'croissants' from the table also drops 'muffins' from the VIEW EnglishWords.

18.4 How VIEWs Are Handled in the Database System

Standard SQL requires a system schema table with the text of the VIEW declarations in it. What would be handy, but is not easily done in all SQL implementations, is to trace the VIEWs down to their base tables by printing out a tree diagram of the nested structure. Check your user library and see if it has such a utility program (for example, FINDVIEW in the SPARC library for SQL/DS). There are several ways to handle VIEWs, and systems will often use a mixture of them. The major categories of algorithms are materialization and in-line text expansion.

18.4.1 View Column List

The <view column list> is optional; when it is not given, the VIEW will inherit the column names from the query. The number of column names in the <view column list> has to be the same as the degree of the query expression. If any two columns in the query have the same column name, you must have a <view column list> to resolve the ambiguity. The same column name cannot be specified more than once in the <view column list>.

18.4.2 VIEW Materialization

Materialization means that whenever you use the name of the VIEW, the database engine finds its definition in the schema information tables and creates a working table with that name that has the appropriate column names with the appropriate data types. Finally, this new table is filled with the results of the SELECT statement in the body of the VIEW definition.

The decision to materialize a VIEW as an actual physical table is implementation-defined in Standard SQL, but the VIEW must act as if it were a table when accessed for a query. If the VIEW is not updatable, this approach automatically protects the base tables from any improper

changes and is guaranteed to be correct. It uses existing internal procedures in the database engine (create table, insert from query), so this is easy for the database to do.

The downside of this approach is that it is not very fast for large VIEWs, uses extra storage space, cannot take advantage of indexes already existing on the base tables, usually cannot create indexes on the new table, and cannot be optimized as easily as other approaches. However, materialization is the best approach for certain VIEWs. A VIEW whose construction has a hidden sort is usually materialized. Queries with SELECT DISTINCT, UNION, GROUP BY, and HAVING clauses are usually implemented by sorting to remove duplicate rows or to build groups. As each row of the VIEW is built, it has to be saved to compare it to the other rows, so it makes sense to materialize it.

Some products also give you the option of controlling the materializations yourself. The vendor terms vary. A "snapshot" means materializing a table that also includes a timestamp. A "result set" is a materialized table that is passed to a front-end application program for display. Check your particular product.

18.4.3 In-Line Text Expansion

Another approach is to store the text of the CREATE VIEW statement and work it into the parse tree of the SELECT, INSERT, UPDATE, or DELETE statements that use it. This allows the optimizer to blend the VIEW definition into the final query plan. For example, you can create a VIEW based on a particular department, thus:

```
CREATE VIEW SalesDept (dept_name, city_name, ...)
AS SELECT 'Sales', city_name, ...
     FROM Departments
    WHERE dept_name = 'Sales';
```

Then use it as a query, thus:

```
SELECT *
  FROM SalesDept
 WHERE city_name = 'New York';
```

The parser expands the VIEW into text (or an intermediate tokenized form) within the FROM clause. The query would become, in effect,

```
SELECT *
  FROM (SELECT 'Sales', city_name, ...
          FROM Departments
         WHERE dept_name = 'Sales')
       AS SalesDept (dept_name, city_name, ...)
 WHERE city_name = 'New York';
```

The query optimizer would then "flatten it out" into:

```
SELECT *
  FROM Departments
 WHERE (dept_name = 'Sales')
   AND (city_name = 'New York');
```

Though this sounds like a nice approach, it had problems in early systems, where the in-line expansion did not result in proper SQL. An earlier version of DB2 was one such system. To illustrate the problem, imagine that you are given a DB2 table that has a long identification number and some figures in each row. The long identification number is like those 40-digit monsters they give you on a utility bill—they are unique only in the first few characters, but the utility company prints the whole thing out anyway. Your task is to create a report that is grouped according to the first six characters of the long identification number. The immediate naïve query uses the substring operator:

```
SELECT SUBSTRING(long_id FROM 1 TO 6), SUM(amt1), SUM(amt2), ...
  FROM TableA
 GROUP BY id;
```

This does not work; it is incorrect SQL, since the `SELECT` and `GROUP BY` lists do not agree. Other common attempts include `GROUP BY SUBSTRING(long_id FROM 1 TO 6)`, which will fail because you cannot use a function, and `GROUP BY 1`, which will fail because you can use a column position only in a `UNION` statement (column position is now deprecated in Standard SQL) and in the `ORDER BY` in some products.

The `GROUP BY` has to have a list of simple column names drawn from the tables of the `FROM` clause. The next attempt is to build a `VIEW`:

```
CREATE VIEW BadTry (short_id, amt1, amt2, ...)
AS SELECT SUBSTRING(long_id FROM 1 TO 6), amt1, amt2, ...
     FROM TableA;
```

Then do a grouped select on it. This is correct SQL, but it does not work in the old DB2. The compiler apparently tried to insert the `VIEW` into the `FROM` clause, as we have seen, but when it expands it out, the results are the same as those of the incorrect first query attempt with a function call in the `GROUP BY` clause. The trick is to force DB2 to materialize the `VIEW` so that you can name the column constructed with the `SUBSTRING()` function. Anything that causes a sort will do this—the `SELECT DISTINCT`, `UNION`, `GROUP BY`, and `HAVING` clauses, for example.

Since we know that the short identification number is a key, we can use this `VIEW`:

```
CREATE VIEW Shorty (short_id, amt1, amt2, ...)
AS SELECT DISTINCT SUBSTRING(long_id FROM 1 TO 6), amt1, amt2,
...
     FROM TableA;
```

Then the report query is:

```
SELECT short_id, SUM(amt1), SUM(amt2), ...
  FROM Shorty
 GROUP BY short_id;
```

This works fine in DB2. I am indebted to Susan Vombrack of Loral Aerospace for this example. Incidentally, this can be written in Standard SQL as:

```
SELECT *
  FROM (SELECT SUBSTRING(long_id FROM 1 TO 6) AS short_id,
               SUM(amt1), SUM(amt2), ...
           FROM TableA
          GROUP BY long_id)
 GROUP BY short_id;
```

The name on the substring result column in the subquery expression makes it recognizable to the parser.

18.4.4 Pointer Structures

Finally, the system can handle `VIEW`s with special data structures for the `VIEW`. These structures are usually an array of pointers into a base table constructed from the VIEW definition. This is a good way to handle updatable VIEWs in Standard SQL, since the target row in the base table is at the end of a pointer chain in the VIEW structure. Access will be as fast as possible.

The pointer structure approach cannot easily use existing indexes on the base tables. But the pointer structure can be implemented as an index with restrictions. Furthermore, multitable VIEWs can be constructed as pointer structures that allow direct access to the related rows in the table involved in the JOIN. This is very product-dependent, so you cannot make any general assumptions.

18.4.5 Indexing and Views

Note that VIEWs cannot have their own indexes. However, VIEWs can inherit the indexing on their base tables in some implementations. Like tables, VIEWs have no inherent ordering, but a programmer who knows his particular SQL implementation will often write code that takes advantage of the quirks of that product. In particular, some implementations allow you to use an ORDER BY clause in a VIEW (they are allowed only on cursors in standard SQL). This will force a sort and could materialize the VIEW as a working table. When the SQL engine has to do a sequential read of the entire table, the sort might help or hinder a particular query. There is no way to predict the results.

18.5 WITH CHECK OPTION Clause

If WITH CHECK OPTION is specified, the viewed table has to be updatable. This is actually a fast way to check how your particular SQL implementation handles updatable VIEWs. Try to create a version of the VIEW in question using the WITH CHECK OPTION, and see if your product will allow you to create it. The WITH CHECK OPTION is part of the SQL-89 standard, which was extended in Standard SQL by adding an optional <levels clause>. CASCADED is implicit if an explicit LEVEL clause is not given. Consider a VIEW defined as

```
CREATE VIEW V1
AS SELECT *
     FROM Foobar
    WHERE col1 = 'A';
```

and now UPDATE it with

```
UPDATE V1 SET col1 = 'B';
```

The UPDATE will take place without any trouble, but the rows that were previously seen now disappear when we use V1 again. They no longer meet the WHERE clause condition! Likewise, an INSERT INTO statement with VALUES (col1 = 'B') would insert just fine, but its rows would never be seen again in this VIEW. VIEWs created this way will always have all the rows that meet the criteria, and that can be handy. For example, you can set up a VIEW of rows with a status code of 'to be done', work on them, and change a status code to 'finished', and they will disappear from your view. The important point is that the WHERE clause condition was checked only at the time when the VIEW was invoked.

The WITH CHECK OPTION makes the system check the WHERE clause condition for an INSERT or UPDATE. If the new or changed row fails the test, the change is rejected and the VIEW remains the same. Thus, the previous UPDATE statement would get an error message and you could not change certain columns in certain ways. For example, consider a VIEW of salaries under $30,000 defined with a WITH CHECK OPTION to prevent anyone from giving a raise above that ceiling.

The WITH CHECK OPTION clause does not work like a CHECK constraint.

```
CREATE TABLE Foobar (col_a INTEGER);

CREATE VIEW TestView (col_a)
AS
SELECT col_a FROM Foobar WHERE col_a > 0
WITH CHECK OPTION;

INSERT INTO TestView VALUES (NULL); -- This fails!

CREATE TABLE Foobar_2 (col_a INTEGER CHECK (col_a > 0));
INSERT INTO Foobar_2(col_a)
VALUES (NULL); -- This succeeds!
```

The WITH CHECK OPTION must be TRUE, while the CHECK constraint can be either TRUE or UNKNOWN. Once more, you need to watch out for NULLs.

Standard SQL has introduced an optional <levels clause>, which can be either CASCADED or LOCAL. If no <levels clause> is given, a <levels clause> of CASCADED is implicit. The idea of a CASCADED check is that the system checks all the underlying levels that built the VIEW, as well as the WHERE clause condition in the VIEW itself.

If anything causes a row to disappear from the VIEW, the UPDATE is rejected. The idea of a WITH LOCAL check option is that only the local WHERE clause is checked. The underlying VIEWs or tables from which this VIEW is built might also be affected, but we do not test for those effects. Consider two VIEWs built on each other from the salary table:

```
CREATE VIEW Lowpay
AS SELECT *
     FROM Personnel
    WHERE salary <= 250;

CREATE VIEW Mediumpay
AS SELECT *
     FROM Lowpay
    WHERE salary >= 100;
```

If neither VIEW has a WITH CHECK OPTION, the effect of updating Mediumpay by increasing every salary by $1,000 will be passed without any check to Lowpay. Lowpay will pass the changes to the underlying Personnel table. The next time Mediumpay is used, Lowpay will be rebuilt in its own right and Mediumpay rebuilt from it, and all the employees will disappear from Mediumpay.

If only Mediumpay has a WITH CASCADED CHECK OPTION on it, the UPDATE will fail. Mediumpay has no problem with such a large salary, but it would cause a row in Lowpay to disappear, so Mediumpay will reject it. However, if only Mediumpay has a WITH LOCAL CHECK OPTION on it, the UPDATE will succeed. Mediumpay has no problem with such a large salary, so it passes the change along to Lowpay. Lowpay, in turn, passes the change to the Personnel table and the UPDATE occurs. If both VIEWs have a WITH CASCADED CHECK OPTION, the effect is a set of conditions, all of which have to be met. The Personnel table can accept UPDATEs or INSERTs only where the salary is between $100 and $250.

This can become very complex. Consider an example from an ANSI X3H2 paper by Nelson Mattos of IBM (Celko 1993). Let us build a five-layer set of VIEWs, using xx and yy as placeholders for CASCADED or LOCAL, on a base table T1 with columns c1, c2, c3, c4, and c5, all set to a value of 10, thus:

```
CREATE VIEW V1 AS SELECT * FROM T1 WHERE (c1 > 5);
```

```
CREATE VIEW V2 AS SELECT * FROM V1 WHERE (c2 > 5)
       WITH xx CHECK OPTION;

CREATE VIEW V3 AS SELECT * FROM V2 WHERE (c3 > 5);

CREATE VIEW V4 AS SELECT * FROM V3 WHERE (c4 > 5)
       WITH yy CHECK OPTION;

CREATE VIEW V5 AS SELECT * FROM V4 WHERE (c5 > 5);
```

When we set each one of the columns to zero, we get different results, which can be shown in this chart, where S means success and F means failure:

```
 xx/yy             c1   c2   c3   c4   c5
==========================================
cascade/cascade    F    F    F    F    S
local/cascade      F    F    F    F    S
local/local        S    F    S    F    S
cascade/local      F    F    S    F    S
```

To understand the chart, look at the last line. If `xx = CASCADED` and `yy = LOCAL`, updating column c1 to zero via V5 will fail, whereas updating c5 will succeed. Remember that a successful `UPDATE` means the row(s) disappear from V5.

Follow the action for

```
UPDATE V5 SET c1 = 0;
```

`VIEW` V5 has no with check options, so the changed rows are immediately sent to V4 without any testing. `VIEW` V4 does have a `WITH LOCAL CHECK OPTION`, but column `c1` is not involved, so V4 passes the rows to V3. `VIEW` V3 has no with check options, so the changed rows are immediately sent to V2. `VIEW` V2 does have a `WITH CASCADED CHECK OPTION`, so V2 passes the rows to V1 and awaits results. `VIEW` V1 is built on the original base table and has the condition c1 > 5, which is violated by this `UPDATE`. `VIEW` V1 then rejects the `UPDATE` to the base table, so the rows remain in V5 when it is rebuilt.

Now follow the action for:

```
UPDATE V5 SET c3 = 0;
```

VIEW V5 has no with check options, so the changed rows are immediately sent to V4, as before. VIEW V4 does have a WITH LOCAL CHECK OPTION, but column c3 is not involved, so V4 passes the rows to V3 without awaiting the results. VIEW V3 is involved with column c3 and has no with check options, so the rows can be changed and passed down to V2 and V1, where they UPDATE the base table. The rows are not seen again when V5 is invoked, because they will fail to get past VIEW V3. The real problem comes with UPDATE statements that change more than one column at a time. For example, the following command:

```
UPDATE V5 SET c1 = 0, c2 = 0, c3 = 0, c4 = 0, c5 = 0;
```

will fail for all possible combinations of <levels clause>s in the example schema.

Standard SQL defines the idea of a set of conditions that are inherited by the levels of nesting. In our sample schema, these implied tests would be added to each VIEW definition:

```
local/local
V1 = none
V2 = (c2 > 5)
V3 = (c2 > 5)
V4 = (c2 > 5) AND (c4 > 5)
V5 = (c2 > 5) AND (c4 > 5)

cascade/cascade
V1 = none
V2 = (c1 > 5) AND (c2 > 5)
V3 = (c1 > 5) AND (c2 > 5)
V4 = (c1 > 5) AND (c2 > 5) AND (c3 > 5) AND (c4 > 5)
V5 = (c1 > 5) AND (c2 > 5) AND (c3 > 5) AND (c4 > 5)

local/cascade
V1 = none
V2 = (c2 > 5)
V3 = (c2 > 5)
V4 = (c1 > 5) AND (c2 > 5) AND (c4 > 5)
V5 = (c1 > 5) AND (c2 > 5) AND (c4 > 5)

cascade/local
V1 = none
```

```
V2 = (c1 > 5) AND (c2 > 5)
V3 = (c1 > 5) AND (c2 > 5)
V4 = (c1 > 5) AND (c2 > 5) AND (c4 > 5)
V5 = (c1 > 5) AND (c2 > 5) AND (c4 > 5)
```

18.5.1 WITH CHECK OPTION as CHECK() Clause

Lothar Flatz, an instructor for Oracle Software Switzerland, made the observation that while Oracle cannot put subqueries into `CHECK()` constraints, and triggers would not be possible because of the mutating table problem, you can use a `VIEW` that has a `WITH CHECK OPTION` to enforce subquery constraints.

For example, consider a hotel registry that needs to have a rule that you cannot add a guest to a room that another is or will be occupying. Instead of writing the constraint directly, like this:

```
CREATE TABLE Hotel
(room_nbr INTEGER NOT NULL,
 arrival_date DATE NOT NULL,
 departure_date DATE NOT NULL,
 guest_name CHAR(30) NOT NULL,
 CONSTRAINT schedule_right
 CHECK (H1.arrival_date <= H1.departure_date),
 CONSTRAINT no_double_booking
 CHECK (NOT EXISTS
        (SELECT *
           FROM Hotel AS H1, Hotel AS H2
          WHERE H1.room_nbr = H2.room_nbr
            AND H2.arrival_date < H1.arrival_date
            AND H1.arrival_date < H2.departure_date)));
```

The schedule_right constraint is fine, since it has no subquery, but many products will choke on the no_double_booking constraint. Leaving the no_double_booking constraint off the table, we can construct a `VIEW` on all the rows and columns of the Hotel base table and add a `WHERE` clause that will be enforced by the `WITH CHECK OPTION`:

```
CREATE VIEW Hotel_V (room_nbr, arrival_date, departure_date,
guest_name)
AS SELECT H1.room_nbr, H1.arrival_date, H1.departure_date,
H1.guest_name
```

```
 FROM Hotel AS H1
WHERE NOT EXISTS
      (SELECT *
         FROM Hotel AS H2
        WHERE H1.room_nbr = H2.room_nbr
          AND H2.arrival_date < H1.arrival_date
          AND H1.arrival_date < H2.departure_date)
  AND H1.arrival_date <= H1.departure_date
WITH CHECK OPTION;
```

For example,

```
INSERT INTO Hotel_V
VALUES (1, '2006-01-01', '2006-01-03', 'Ron Coe');
COMMIT;
INSERT INTO Hotel_V
VALUES (1, '2006-01-03', '2006-01-05', 'John Doe');
```

will give a WITH CHECK OPTION clause violation on the second INSERT INTO statement, as we wanted.

18.6 Dropping VIEWs

VIEWs, like tables, can be dropped from the schema. The Standard SQL syntax for the statement is:

```
DROP VIEW <table name> <drop behavior>

<drop behavior> ::= [CASCADE | RESTRICT]
```

The <drop behavior> clause did not exist in SQL-86, so vendors had different behaviors in their implementation. The usual way of storing VIEWs was in a schema-level table with the VIEW name, the text of the VIEW, and other information. When you dropped a VIEW, the engine usually removed the appropriate row from the schema tables. You found out about dependencies when you tried to use VIEWs built on other VIEWs that no longer existed. Likewise, dropping a base table could cause the same problem when the VIEW was accessed.

The CASCADE option will find all other VIEWs that use the dropped VIEW and remove them also. If RESTRICT is specified, the VIEW cannot be dropped if there is anything that is dependent on it. This implies a

structure for the schema tables that is different from just a simple single table.

The bad news is that some older products will let you drop the table(s) from which the view is built, but will not drop the view itself.

```
CREATE TABLE Foobar (col_a INTEGER);
CREATE VIEW TestView
AS SELECT col_a
     FROM Foobar;

DROP TABLE Foobar;  -- drop the base table
```

Unless you also cascaded the DROP TABLE statement, the text of the view definition was still in the system. Thus, when you reuse the table and column names, they are resolved at run-time with the view definition.

```
CREATE TABLE Foobar
(foo_key CHAR(5) NOT NULL PRIMARY KEY,
 col_a REAL NOT NULL);
INSERT INTO Foobar VALUES ('Celko', 3.14159);
```

This is a potential security flaw and a violation of the SQL Standard, but be aware that it exists. Notice that the data type of TestView.col_a changed from INTEGER to REAL along with the new version of the table.

18.7 TEMPORARY TABLE Declarations

The temporary table can be used with SQL/PSM code to hold intermediate results rather than requerying or recalculating them over and over. The syntax for creating a TEMPORARY TABLE is:

```
CREATE [GLOBAL | LOCAL] TEMP[ORARY] TABLE <table name>
 (<table element list>)
ON COMMIT [PRESERVE | DELETE] ROWS;
```

This is just like the usual CREATE TABLE statement, with the addition of two pieces of syntax. The <table element>s can be column declarations, constraints, or declarative referential integrity clauses, just as if this were a base table. The differences come from the additional clauses.

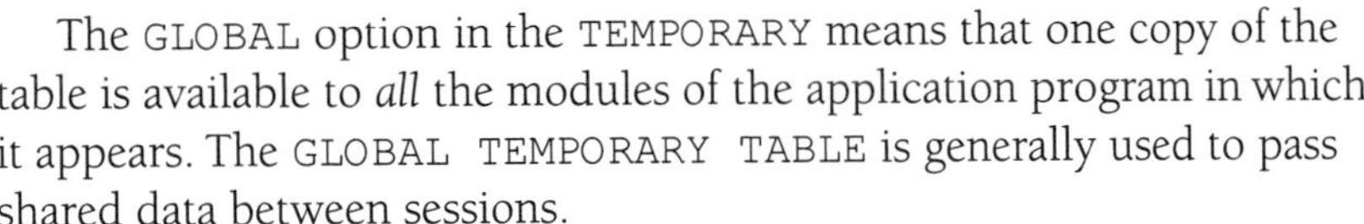

The GLOBAL option in the TEMPORARY means that one copy of the table is available to *all* the modules of the application program in which it appears. The GLOBAL TEMPORARY TABLE is generally used to pass shared data between sessions.

The LOCAL option means that one copy of the table is available to *each* module of the application program in which the temporary table appears. The LOCAL TEMPORARY TABLE is generally used as a "scratch table" within a single module. If more than one user accesses the same LOCAL TEMPORARY TABLE, they each get a copy of the table, initially empty, for their session, or within the scope of the module that uses it.

If you have trouble imagining multiple tables in the schema with the same name (a violation of a basic rule of SQL about uniqueness of schema objects), then imagine a single table created as declared, but with an extra phantom column that contains a user identifier. What the users are then seeing is an updatable VIEW on the LOCAL TEMPORARY TABLE, which shows them only the rows where this phantom column is equal to their user identifier, but not the phantom column itself. New rows are added to the LOCAL TEMPORARY TABLE with the DEFAULT of CURRENT USER.

The concept of modules in SQL is discussed in detail in Jim Melton's *Understanding SQL's Stored Procedure* (Melton 1998), but you can think of them as programs, procedures, functions, subroutines, or blocks of code, depending on the procedural language that you use.

Since this is a table in the schema, you can get rid of it with a DROP TABLE <table name> statement, and you can change it with the usual INSERT INTO, DELETE FROM, and UPDATE statements. The differences are at the start and end of a session or module.

The ON COMMIT [PRESERVE | DELETE] ROWS clause describes the action taken when a COMMIT statement is executed successfully. The PRESERVE option means that the next time this table is used, the rows will still be there and will be deleted only at the end of the session. The DELETE option means that the rows will be deleted whenever a COMMIT statement is executed during the session. In both cases, the table will be cleared out at the end of the session or module.

18.8 Hints on Using VIEWs and TEMPORARY TABLEs

Sometimes this decision is very easy for a programmer. In the Standard SQL model, the user cannot create either a VIEW or a TEMPORARY TABLE. The creation of any schema object belongs to the DBA, so the

user has to use what he is given. However, you should know how to use each structure and which one is best for which situation.

18.8.1 Using VIEWs

Do not nest VIEWs too deeply; the overhead of building several levels eats up execution time, and the extra storage for materialized VIEWs can be expensive. Complex nesting is also hard to maintain. One way to figure out what VIEWs you should have is to inspect the existing queries for repeated subqueries or expressions. These are good candidates for VIEWs.

One of the major uses of VIEWs is security. The DBA can choose to hide certain columns from certain classes of users through a combination of security authorizations and VIEWs. Standard SQL has provisions for restricting access to tables at the column level, but most implementations do not have that feature yet.

Another security trick is to add a column with a special user or security-level identifier to a table. The VIEW hides this column and displays to the user only what he is supposed to see. One possible problem is that a user could try to change something in the VIEW that violates other table constraints; when his attempt returns an error message, he gets some information about the security system that we would rather have hidden from him.

The best way to approach VIEWs is to think of how a user wants to see the database, and then give him a set of VIEWs that make it look as if the database had been designed just for his applications.

18.8.2 Using TEMPORARY TABLEs

The GLOBAL TEMPORARY TABLE can be used to pass data among users, which is something that a VIEW cannot do. The LOCAL TEMPORARY TABLE has two major advantages. The user can load it with the results of a complex, time-consuming query once and use that result set over and over in his session, greatly improving performance. This also prevents the system from locking out other users from the base tables from which the complex query was built.

Dr. Codd discussed the idea of a snapshot, which is an image of a table at a particular moment in time. But it is important to know just what that moment was. You can use a temporary table to hold such a snapshot by adding a column with the DEFAULT of the CURRENT TIMESTAMP.

The Standard SQL model of temporary tables I have just described is not yet common in most implementations. In fact, many SQL products do not have the concept of a temporary table at all, while other products allow users to create temporary tables on the fly. Such tables might last only for their session and are visible only to their creator. These tables may or may not have indexes, constraints, VIEWs, referential integrity, or much of anything else declared on them; they are a pure "scratch table" for the user. Some products allow a user to create a global temporary table that can be accessed by other users. But, again, this is not the ANSI/ISO model.

18.8.3 Flattening a Table with a VIEW

We have a table with the monthly sales data shown as an attribute (the monthly amounts have to be NULL-able to hold missing values for the future):

```
CREATE TABLE AnnualSales1
(salesman CHAR(15) NOT NULL PRIMARY KEY,
 jan DECIMAL(5,2),
 feb DECIMAL(5,2),
 mar DECIMAL(5,2),
 apr DECIMAL(5,2),
 may DECIMAL(5,2),
 jun DECIMAL(5,2),
 jul DECIMAL(5,2),
 aug DECIMAL(5,2),
 sep DECIMAL(5,2),
 oct DECIMAL(5,2),
 nov DECIMAL(5,2),
 "dec" DECIMAL(5,2) -- reserved word!
);
```

The goal is to "flatten" it out so that it looks like this:

```
CREATE TABLE AnnualSales2
(salesman CHAR(15) NOT NULL PRIMARY KEY,
 month_name CHAR(3) NOT NULL
       CONSTRAINT valid_month_abbrev
       CHECK (month_name IN ('Jan', 'Feb', 'Mar', 'Apr',
                          'May', 'Jun', 'Jul', 'Aug',
                          'Sep', 'Oct', 'Nov', 'Dec')),
```

```
 sales_amount DECIMAL(5,2) NOT NULL,
 PRIMARY KEY(salesman, month_name));
```

The trick is to build a VIEW of the original table with a number beside each month:

```
CREATE VIEW NumberedSales
AS SELECT salesman,
        1 AS M01, jan,
        2 AS M02, feb,
        3 AS M03, mar,
        4 AS M04, apr,
        5 AS M05, may,
        6 AS M06, jun,
        7 AS M07, jul,
        8 AS M08, aug,
        9 AS M09, sep,
       10 AS M10, oct,
       11 AS M11, nov,
       12 AS M12, "dec"
  FROM AnnualSales1;
```

Now you can use the auxiliary table of sequential numbers, or you can use a VALUES table constructor to build one. The flattened VIEW is:

```
CREATE VIEW AnnualSales2 (salesman, month, sales_amt)
AS SELECT S1.salesman,
     (CASE WHEN A.nbr = M01 THEN 'Jan'
           WHEN A.nbr = M02 THEN 'Feb'
           WHEN A.nbr = M03 THEN 'Mar'
           WHEN A.nbr = M04 THEN 'Apr'
           WHEN A.nbr = M05 THEN 'May'
           WHEN A.nbr = M06 THEN 'Jun'
           WHEN A.nbr = M07 THEN 'Jul'
           WHEN A.nbr = M08 THEN 'Aug'
           WHEN A.nbr = M09 THEN 'Sep'
           WHEN A.nbr = M10 THEN 'Oct'
           WHEN A.nbr = M11 THEN 'Nov'
           WHEN A.nbr = M12 THEN 'Dec'
           ELSE NULL END),
     (CASE WHEN A.nbr = M01 THEN jan
```

```
          WHEN A.nbr = M02 THEN feb
          WHEN A.nbr = M03 THEN mar
          WHEN A.nbr = M04 THEN apr
          WHEN A.nbr = M05 THEN may
          WHEN A.nbr = M06 THEN jun
          WHEN A.nbr = M07 THEN jul
          WHEN A.nbr = M08 THEN aug
          WHEN A.nbr = M09 THEN sep
          WHEN A.nbr = M10 THEN oct
          WHEN A.nbr = M11 THEN nov
          WHEN A.nbr = M12 THEN "dec"
          ELSE NULL END)
FROM AnnualSales AS S1
     CROSS JOIN
     (VALUES (1), (2), (3), (4), (5), (6),
             (7), (8), (9), (10), (11), (12)) AS A(nbr);
```

If your SQL product has derived tables, this can be written as a single VIEW query.

This technique lets you convert an attribute into a value, which is highly nonrelational, but very handy for a report. The advantage of using a VIEW over using a temporary table to hold the crosstabs query given in another chapter is that the VIEW will change automatically when the underlying base table is changed.

18.9 Using Derived Tables

A derived table can be built in the FROM clause or in a WITH [RECURSIVE] clause. The latter is new to SQL-99. Essentially, a derived table is like an in-line VIEW created by the programmer, rather than by the DBA. The WITH clause allows the query to use the same result set in several places, which was not possible with the original derived table syntax.

18.9.1 Derived Tables in the FROM clause

You have already seen the syntax and some of the uses of derived tables. Most parts of the expression are optional, but it is a very good idea to use them.

```
(<query expression>) [[AS] <table name> [(<column list>)]]
```

The tricky part is in the scoping rules for the subquery expressions. Consider this set of expressions:

```
SELECT *  -- wrong
  FROM (Foo
        LEFT OUTER JOIN
        Bar
        ON Foo.x = Bar.x)
       INNER JOIN Floob
       ON Floob.y = x;
```

Foo, Bar, and Floob are exposed to the outermost query, so x is an ambiguous column name. Change this slightly:

```
SELECT *  -- wrong
  FROM (Foo AS F1
        LEFT OUTER JOIN
        Bar AS B1
        ON F1.x = B1.x)
       INNER JOIN Floob
       ON Floob.y = Foo.x;
```

The aliases F1 and B1 hide the base tables from the outermost query, so Foo.x is an ambiguous column name. One solution is to create an alias for the whole query expression and rename the ambiguous columns.

```
SELECT *
  FROM ((SELECT x FROM Foo)
         LEFT OUTER JOIN
        (SELECT x FROM Bar)
        ON Foo.x = Bar.x)
       AS Foobar(x1, x2)
       INNER JOIN Floob
       ON Floob.y = x1;
```

The outermost query sees only Foobar and cannot reference either Foo or Bar.

The order of execution of the infixed `JOIN` operators is from left to right. It does not make any difference with `INNER JOIN`s and `CROSS`

JOINs, but it very important when you have OUTER JOINs. I strongly recommend that you qualify all the column names.

18.9.2 Derived Tables with a VALUES Constructor

SQL-99 freed the VALUES constructor from the INSERT INTO statement, allowing it to build tables, not just rows. You can see an example of this in Section 18.8.3 for a single column table.

This can be generalized to construct rows, such as

```
VALUES ('John', 7), ('Mark', 8), ('Fred', 10), ('Sam', 7)
```

However, such a table cannot have constraints, nor does it have a name until you add an AS clause. Think of it as a "table constant," rather than as a proper table that can be modified, have constraints, and so forth. Obviously, all the rows must be union-compatible, but the system will pick the default data types. One way around this is to explicitly cast the columns to the desired data types. Doing this for one row is usually enough to force the other rows to follow that pattern.

The columns can contain any scalar expression:

```
(VALUES ((SELECT MAX(x) FROM Foo),  42),
                  ((SELECT MAX(y) FROM Bar),  (12+2)),
                   (12, 3))
 AS Weird (a, b)
```

Since this is a new feature in SQL, you should test your product to see if it has limitations.

18.10 Derived Tables in the WITH Clause

A derived table built with a WITH clause is also called a "Common Table Expression" (CTE) and can be thought of as a named table within an SQL statement that exists only for the duration of that statement. There can be many CTEs in a single SQL statement. Each must have a unique name and be declared at front of a single query using the WITH clause.

The WITH clause is new to SQL-99 and the syntax is:

```
WITH [RECURSIVE]
<subquery expression> AS <table name> [(<column list>)]
<query expression>
```

As a simple example, consider a report that tells us the item(s) that had the highest sales volume, measured in dollars. First, build a query in the WITH clause to total each item by its UPC code. Then using this, find the item with the highest total sales.

```
WITH ItemSummary (upc, price_tot)
AS
(SELECT upc, SUM(price)
   FROM OrderDetails
  GROUP BY upc)
-- main query
SELECT P1.upc, P1.price_tot
  FROM ItemSummary AS P1
 WHERE P1.price_tot
       = (SELECT MAX(P1.price_tot)
            FROM ItemSummary AS P2);
```

Without this feature, the ItemSummary query would have been either repeated in two places or put into a VIEW. A programmer cannot create a view, so that leaves no option. While not so bad in this case, imagine if we had a complex expression to replicate.

There is also a recursive option. Let's make a simple adjacency list model of a bill of materials.

```
CREATE TABLE BillOfMaterials
(part_name CHAR(20) NOT NULL PRIMARY KEY,
 assembly_nbr INTEGER,
 subassembly_nbr INTEGER NOT NULL);
```

The assembly_nbr for the finished product row is set to NULL to show that it is not part of another assembly. The following recursive SQL using a CTE will do the trick (note that we have named our common table expression "Explosion"):

```
WITH RECURSION Explosion (assembly_nbr, subassembly_nbr,
part_name)
AS
(SELECT BOM.assembly_nbr, BOM.subassembly_nbr, BOM.part_name
   FROM BillOfMaterials AS BOM
  WHERE BOM.subassembly_nbr = 12  -- traversal starting point
UNION
```

```
SELECT Child.assembly_nbr, Child.subassembly_nbr,
Child.part_name
  FROM Explosion AS Parent, BillOfMaterials AS Child
 WHERE Parent.subassembly_nbr = Child.assembly_nbr)
-- main select statement
SELECT assembly_nbr, subassembly_nbr, part_name
  FROM Explosion;
```

This will find all of the parts that make up subassembly 12. It begins by pulling a starting set from the BillOfMaterials table, then doing a `UNION` with itself. The original BillOfMaterials table is now hidden inside the expression. Standard SQL requires the use of the keyword `RECURSION` to signal the compiler to keep running until no more rows are added to the Explosion table. The main `SELECT` statement can now use Explosion like any other table.

Partitioning Data in Queries

THIS SECTION IS CONCERNED with how to break the data in SQL into meaningful subsets that can then be presented to the user or passed along for further reduction.

19.1 Coverings and Partitions

We need to define some basic set operations. A *covering* is a collection of subsets, drawn from a set, whose union is the original set. A *partition* is a covering whose subsets do not intersect each other. Cutting up a pizza is a partitioning; smothering it in two layers of pepperoni slices is a covering.

Partitions are the basis for most reports. The property that makes partitions useful for reports is aggregation: the whole is the sum of its parts. For example, a company budget is broken into divisions, divisions are broken into departments, and so forth. Each division budget is the sum of its department's budgets, and the sum of the division budgets is the total for the whole company again. We would not be sure what to do if a department belonged to two different divisions, because that would be a covering and not a partition.

19.1.1 Partitioning by Ranges

A common problem in data processing is classifying things by the way they fall into a range on a numeric or alphabetic scale. The best approach to translating a code into a value when ranges are involved is to set up a table with the high and the low values for each translated value in it. This is covered in the chapter on auxiliary tables, Chapter 22, in more detail, but here is a quick review.

Any missing values will easily be detected, and the table can be validated for completeness. For example, we could create a table of ZIP code ranges and two-character state abbreviation codes, like this:

```
CREATE TABLE StateZip
(state_code CHAR(2) NOT NULL PRIMARY KEY,
 low_zip CHAR(5) NOT NULL UNIQUE,
 high_zip CHAR(5) NOT NULL UNIQUE,
 CONSTRAINT zip_order_okay CHECK(low_zip < high_zip),
 ...  );
```

Here is a query that looks up the city name and state code from the ZIP code in the AddressBook table to complete a mailing label with a simple JOIN that looks like this:

```
SELECT A1.name, A1.street, SZ.city, SZ.state_code, A1.zip
  FROM StateZip AS SZ, AddressBook AS A1
 WHERE A1.zip BETWEEN SZ.low_zip AND SZ.high_zip;
```

You must be careful with this predicate. If one of the three columns involved has a NULL in it, the BETWEEN predicate becomes UNKNOWN and will not be recognized by the WHERE clause. If you design the table of range values with the high value in one row equal to or greater than the low value in another row, both of those rows will be returned when the test value falls on the overlap.

Single-Column Range Tables

If you know that you have a partitioning in the range value tables, you can write a query in SQL that will let you use a table with only the high value and the translation code. The grading system table would have ((100%, 'A'), (89%, 'B'), (79%, 'C'), (69%, 'D'), and (59%,'F')) as its rows. Likewise, a table of the state code and the highest ZIP code in that state could do the same job as the BETWEEN predicate in the previous query.

```
CREATE TABLE StateZip2
(high_zip CHAR(5) NOT NULL,
 state CHAR(2) NOT NULL,
 PRIMARY KEY (high_zip, state));
```

We want to write a query to give us the greatest lower bound or least upper bound on those values. The greatest lower bound (glb) operator finds the largest number in one column that is less than or equal to the target value in the other column. The least upper bound (lub) operator finds the smallest number greater than or equal to the target number. Unfortunately, this is not a good trade-off, because the subquery is fairly complex and slow. The "high and low" columns are a better solution in most cases. Here is a second version of the AddressBook query, using only the high_zip column from the StateZip2 table:

```
SELECT name, street, city, state, zip
  FROM StateZip2, AddressBook
 WHERE state =
       (SELECT state
          FROM StateZip2
         WHERE high_zip =
              (SELECT MIN(high_zip)
                 FROM StateZip2
                WHERE Address.zip <= StateZip2.high_zip));
```

If you want to allow for multiple-row matches by not requiring that the lookup table have unique values, the equality subquery predicate should be converted to an `IN()` predicate.

19.1.2 Partition by Functions

It is also possible to use a function that will partition the table into subsets that share a particular property. Consider the cases where you have to add a column with the function result to the table, because the function is too complex to be reasonably written in SQL.

One common example of this technique is the Soundex function, where it is not a vendor extension; the Soundex family assigns codes to names that are phonetically alike. The complex calculations in engineering and scientific databases that involve functions SQL does not have are another example of this technique.

SQL was never meant to be a computational language. However, many vendors allow a query to access functions in the libraries of other programming languages. You must know the cost in execution time for your product before doing this. One version of SQL uses a threaded-code approach to carry parameters over to the other language's libraries and return the results on each row—the execution time is horrible. Some versions of SQL can compile and link another language's library into the SQL.

Although this is a generalization, the safest technique is to unload the parameter values to a file in a standard format that can be read by the other language. Then use that file in a program to find the function results and create `INSERT INTO` statements that will load a table in the database with the parameters and the results. You can then use this working table to load the result column in the original table.

19.1.3 Partition by Sequences

We are looking for patterns over a history that has a sequential ordering to it. This ordering could be temporal, or via sequence numbering. For example, given a payment history, we want to break it into groupings of behavior—say, whether or not the payments were on time or late.

```
CREATE TABLE PaymentHistory
(payment_nbr INTEGER NOT NULL PRIMARY KEY,
 paid_on_time CHAR(1) DEFAULT 'Y' NOT NULL
     CHECK(paid_on_time IN ('Y', 'N')));

INSERT INTO PaymentHistory
VALUES (1006, 'Y'),
(1005, 'Y'),
(1004, 'N'),
(1003, 'Y'),
(1002, 'Y'),
(1001, 'Y'),
(1000, 'N');
```

The results we want assign a grouping number to each run of on-time/late payments, thus

```
grp payment_nbr paid_on_time
===============================
1         1006          'Y'
1         1005          'Y'
2         1004          'N'
```

```
3        1003        'Y'
3        1002        'Y'
3        1001        'Y'
4        1000        'N'
```

The following solution from Hugo Kornelis depends on the payments always being numbered consecutively.

```
SELECT (SELECT COUNT(*)
          FROM PaymentHistory AS H2,
               PaymentHistory AS H3
         WHERE H3.payment_nbr = H2.payment_nbr + 1
           AND H3.paid_on_time <> H2.paid_on_time
           AND H2.payment_nbr >= H1.payment_nbr) + 1 AS grp,
      payment_nbr, paid_on_time
 FROM PaymentHistory AS H1;
```

This is very useful when looking for patterns in a history. A more complex version of the same problem would involve more than two categories. Consider a table with a sequential numbering and a list of products that have been received.

What we want is the average quality score value for a sequential grouping of the same Product. For example, I need an average of Entries 1, 2, and 3, because this is the first grouping of the same product type, but I do not want that average to include entry 8, which is also Product A, but in a different "group."

```
CREATE TABLE ProductTests
(batch_nbr INTEGER NOT NULL PRIMARY KEY,
 prod_code CHAR(1) NOT NULL,
 prod_quality DECIMAL(8.4) NOT NULL);

INSERT INTO ProductTests (batch_nbr, prod_code, prod_quality)
VALUES (1, 'A', 80),
       (2, 'A', 70),
       (3, 'A', 80),
       (4, 'B', 60),
       (5, 'B', 90),
       (6, 'C', 80),
       (7, 'D', 80),
       (8, 'A', 50),
       (9, 'C', 70);
```

The query then becomes:

```
SELECT X.prod_code, MIN(X.batch_nbr) AS start_batch_nbr,
end_batch_nbr,
       AVG(B4.prod_quality) AS avg_prod_quality
  FROM (SELECT B1.prod_code, B1.batch_nbr,
               MAX(B2.batch_nbr) AS end_batch_nbr
          FROM ProductTests AS B1, ProductTests AS B2
         WHERE B1.batch_nbr <= B2.batch_nbr
           AND B1.prod_code = B2.prod_code
           AND B1.prod_code
               = ALL (SELECT prod_code
                        FROM ProductTests AS B3
                     WHERE B3.batch_nbr BETWEEN B1.batch_nbr AND
B2.batch_nbr)
        GROUP BY B1.prod_code, B1.batch_nbr) AS X
        INNER JOIN
        ProductTests AS B4 -- join to get the quality
measurements
        ON B4.batch_nbr BETWEEN X.batch_nbr AND X.end_batch_nbr
  GROUP BY X.prod_code, X.end_batch_nbr;

Results
prod_code start_batch_nbr end_batch_nbr avg_prod_quality
==========================================================
'A'          1              3              76.6666
'B'          4              5              75.0000
'C'          6              6              80.0000
'D'          7              7              80.0000
'A'          8              8              50.0000
'C'          9              9              70.0000
```

19.2 Relational Division

Relational division is one of the eight basic operations in Codd's relational algebra. The idea is that a divisor table is used to partition a dividend table and produce a quotient or results table. The quotient table is made up of those values of one column for which a second column had all of the values in the divisor.

This is easier to explain with an example. We have a table of pilots and the planes they can fly (dividend); we have a table of planes in the hangar (divisor); we want the names of the pilots who can fly every plane (quotient) in the hangar. To get this result, we divide the PilotSkills table by the planes in the hangar.

```
CREATE TABLE PilotSkills
(pilot CHAR(15) NOT NULL,
 plane CHAR(15) NOT NULL,
 PRIMARY KEY (pilot, plane));

PilotSkills
pilot      plane
=========================
'Celko'    'Piper Cub'
'Higgins'  'B-52 Bomber'
'Higgins'  'F-14 Fighter'
'Higgins'  'Piper Cub'
'Jones'    'B-52 Bomber'
'Jones'    'F-14 Fighter'
'Smith'    'B-1 Bomber'
'Smith'    'B-52 Bomber'
'Smith'    'F-14 Fighter'
'Wilson'   'B-1 Bomber'
'Wilson'   'B-52 Bomber'
'Wilson'   'F-14 Fighter'
'Wilson'   'F-17 Fighter'

CREATE TABLE Hangar
(plane CHAR(15) NOT NULL PRIMARY KEY);

Hangar
plane
=============
'B-1 Bomber'
'B-52 Bomber'
'F-14 Fighter'

PilotSkills DIVIDED BY Hangar
pilot
=============================
'Smith'
'Wilson'
```

In this example, Smith and Wilson are the two pilots who can fly everything in the hangar. Notice that Higgins and Celko know how to fly a Piper Cub, but we don't have one right now. In Codd's original definition of relational division, having more rows than are called for is not a problem.

The important characteristic of a relational division is that the CROSS JOIN of the divisor and the quotient produces a valid subset of rows from the dividend. This is where the name comes from, since the CROSS JOIN acts like a multiplication operator.

19.2.1 Division with a Remainder

There are two kinds of relational division. Division with a remainder allows the dividend table to have more values than the divisor, which was Dr. Codd's original definition. For example, if a pilot can fly more planes than just those we have in the hangar, this is fine with us. The query can be written as

```
SELECT DISTINCT pilot
  FROM PilotSkills AS PS1
 WHERE NOT EXISTS
       (SELECT *
          FROM Hangar
         WHERE NOT EXISTS
               (SELECT *
                  FROM PilotSkills AS PS2
                 WHERE (PS1.pilot = PS2.pilot)
                   AND (PS2.plane = Hangar.plane)));
```

The quickest way to explain what is happening in this query is to imagine a World War II movie, where a cocky pilot has just walked into the hangar, looked over the fleet, and announced, "There ain't no plane in this hangar that I can't fly!" We want to find the pilots for whom there does not exist a plane in the hangar for which they have no skills. The use of the NOT EXISTS() predicates is for speed. Most SQL implementations will look up a value in an index rather than scan the whole table.

This query for relational division was made popular by Chris Date in his textbooks, but it is neither the only method nor always the fastest. Another version of the division can be written so as to avoid three levels of nesting. While it didn't originate with me, I have made it popular in my books.

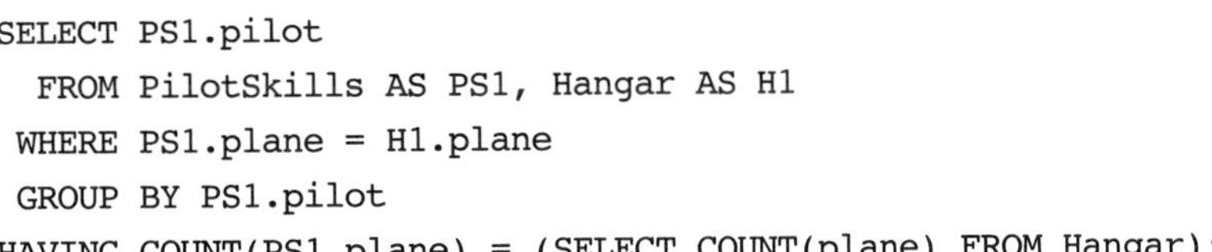

```
SELECT PS1.pilot
  FROM PilotSkills AS PS1, Hangar AS H1
 WHERE PS1.plane = H1.plane
 GROUP BY PS1.pilot
HAVING COUNT(PS1.plane) = (SELECT COUNT(plane) FROM Hangar);
```

There is a serious difference in the two methods. Burn down the hangar, so that the divisor is empty. Because of the `NOT EXISTS()` predicates in Date's query, all pilots are returned from a division by an empty set. Because of the `COUNT()` functions in my query, no pilots are returned from a division by an empty set.

In the sixth edition of his book, *Introduction to Database Systems* (Date 1995), Chris Date defined another operator (`DIVIDEBY ... PER`), which produces the same results as my query, but with more complexity.

19.2.2 Exact Division

The second kind of relational division is exact relational division. The dividend table must match exactly to the values of the divisor without any extra values.

```
SELECT PS1.pilot
  FROM PilotSkills AS PS1
       LEFT OUTER JOIN
       Hangar AS H1
       ON PS1.plane = H1.plane
 GROUP BY PS1.pilot
HAVING COUNT(PS1.plane) = (SELECT COUNT(plane) FROM Hangar)
   AND COUNT(H1.plane) = (SELECT COUNT(plane) FROM Hangar);
```

This query stipulates that a pilot must have the same number of certificates as there are planes in the hangar, and that these certificates all match to a plane in the hangar, not something else. The "something else" is shown by a created `NULL` from the `LEFT OUTER JOIN`.

Please do not make the mistake of trying to reduce the `HAVING` clause with a little algebra to:

```
HAVING COUNT(PS1.plane) = COUNT(H1.plane)
```

It does not work; it will tell you that the hangar has (*n*) planes in it and the pilot is certified for (*n*) planes, but not that those two sets of planes are equal to each other.

19.2.3 Note on Performance

The nested `EXISTS()` predicates version of relational division was made popular by Chris Date's textbooks, while the author is associated with popularizing the COUNT(*) version of relational division. The Winter 1996 edition of *DB2 Magazine* had an article entitled "Powerful SQL: Beyond the Basics" by Sheryl Larsen (www.db2mag.com/db_area/archives/1996/q4/9601lar.shtml), which gave the results of testing both methods. Her conclusion for DB2 was that the nested `EXISTS()` version is better when the quotient has less than 25% of the dividend table's rows, and the `COUNT(*)` version is better when the quotient is more than 25% of the dividend table.

On the other hand, Matthew W. Spaulding at SnapOn Tools reported his test on SQL Server 2000 with the opposite results. He had a table with two million rows for the dividend and around 1,000 rows in the divisor, yielding a quotient of around 1,000 rows as well. The `COUNT` method completed in well under one second, where as the nested `NOT EXISTS` query took roughly five seconds to run.

The moral to the story is to test both methods on your particular product.

19.2.4 Todd's Division

A relational division operator proposed by Stephen Todd is defined on two tables with common columns that are joined together, dropping the `JOIN` column and retaining only those non`JOIN` columns that meet a criterion.

We are given a table, JobParts(job_nbr, part_nbr), and another table, SupParts(sup_nbr, part_nbr), of suppliers and the parts that they provide. We want to get the supplier-and-job pairs such that supplier *sn* supplies all of the parts needed for job *jn*. This is not quite the same thing as getting the supplier-and-job pairs such that job *jn* requires all of the parts provided by supplier *sn*.

You want to divide the JobParts table by the SupParts table. A rule of thumb: the remainder comes from the dividend, but all values in the divisor are present.

```
JobParts          SupParts          Result = JobSups
job pno           sno   pno         job sno
========          =============     ============
'j1'  'p1'        's1'   'p1'         'j1'  's1'
'j1'  'p2'        's1'   'p2'         'j1'  's2'
'j2'  'p2'        's1'   'p3'         'j2'  's1'
'j2'  'p4'        's1'   'p4'         'j2'  's4'
'j2'  'p5'        's1'   'p5'         'j3'  's1'
'j3'  'p2'        's1'   'p6'         'j3'  's2'
                  's2'   'p1'         'j3'  's3'
                  's2'   'p2'         'j3'  's4'
                  's3'   'p2'
                  's4'   'p2'
                  's4'   'p4'
                  's4'   'p5'
```

Pierre Mullin submitted the following query to carry out the Todd division:

```
SELECT DISTINCT JP1.job, SP1.supplier
  FROM JobParts AS JP1, SupParts AS SP1
 WHERE NOT EXISTS
       (SELECT *
          FROM JobParts AS JP2
         WHERE JP2.job = JP1.job
           AND JP2.part
               NOT IN (SELECT SP2.part
                         FROM SupParts AS SP2
                        WHERE SP2.supplier = SP1.supplier));
```

This is really a modification of the query for Codd's division, extended to use a `JOIN` on both tables in the outermost `SELECT` statement. The `IN` predicate for the second subquery can be replaced with a `NOT EXISTS` predicate; it might run a bit faster, depending on the optimizer.

Another related query is finding the pairs of suppliers who sell the same parts. In this data, that would be the pairs (s1, p2), (s3, p1), (s4, p1), (s5, p1):

```
SELECT S1.sup, S2.sup
  FROM SupParts AS S1, SupParts AS S2
```

```
 WHERE S1.sup < S2.sup     -- different suppliers
   AND S1.part = S2.part   -- same parts
 GROUP BY S1.sup, S2.sup
HAVING COUNT(*) = (SELECT COUNT (*)  -- same count of parts
                     FROM SupParts AS S3
                    WHERE S3.sup = S1.sup)
   AND COUNT(*) = (SELECT COUNT (*)
                     FROM SupParts AS S4
                    WHERE S4.sup = S2.sup);
```

This can be modified into Todd's division easily by adding the restriction that the parts must also belong to a common job.

Steve Kass came up with a specialized version that depends on using a numeric code. Assume we have a table that tells us which players are on which teams.

```
CREATE TABLE TeamAssignments
(player_id INTEGER NOT NULL
     REFERENCES Players(player_id)
     ON DELETE CASCADE
     ON UPDATE CASCADE,
 team_id CHAR(5) NOT NULL
     REFERENCES Teams(team_id)
     ON DELETE CASCADE
     ON UPDATE CASCADE,
 PRIMARY KEY (player_id, team_id));
```

To get pairs of players on the same team:

```
SELECT P1.player_id, P2.player_id
  FROM Players AS P1, Players AS P2
WHERE P1.player_id < P2.player_id
 GROUP BY P1.player_id, P2.player_id
HAVING P1.player_id + P2.player_id
     = ALL (SELECT SUM(P3.player_id)
              FROM TeamAssignments AS P3
             WHERE P3.player_id IN (P1.player_id, P2.player_id)
             GROUP BY P3.team_id);
```

19.2.5 Division with JOINs

Standard SQL has several JOIN operators that can be used to perform a relational division. To find the pilots who can fly the same planes as Higgins, use this query:

```
SELECT SP1.Pilot
  FROM (((SELECT plane FROM Hangar) AS H1
         INNER JOIN
         (SELECT pilot, plane FROM PilotSkills) AS SP1
         ON H1.plane = SP1.plane)
       INNER JOIN (SELECT *
                    FROM PilotSkills
                   WHERE pilot = 'Higgins') AS H2
       ON H2.plane = H1.plane)
 GROUP BY Pilot
HAVING COUNT(*) >= (SELECT COUNT(*)
                     FROM PilotSkills
                    WHERE pilot = 'Higgins');
```

The first JOIN finds all of the planes in the hangar for which we have a pilot. The next JOIN takes that set and finds which of those match up with (SELECT * FROM PilotSkills WHERE pilot = 'Higgins') skills. The GROUP BY clause will then see that the intersection we have formed with the joins has at least as many elements as Higgins has planes. The GROUP BY also means that the SELECT DISTINCT can be replaced with a simple SELECT. If the theta operator in the GROUP BY clause is changed from >= to =, the query finds an exact division. If the theta operator in the GROUP BY clause is changed from >= to <= or <, the query finds those pilots whose skills are a superset or a strict superset of the planes that Higgins flies.

It might be a good idea to put the divisor into a VIEW for readability in this query and as a clue to the optimizer to calculate it once. Some products will execute this form of the division query faster than the nested subquery version, because they will use the PRIMARY KEY information to precompute the joins between tables.

19.2.6 Division with Set Operators

The Standard SQL set difference operator, EXCEPT, can be used to write a very compact version of Dr. Codd's relational division. The EXCEPT operator removes the divisor set from the dividend set. If the result is

empty, we have a match; if there is anything left over, it has failed. Using the pilots-and-hangar-tables example, we would write:

```
SELECT DISTINCT Pilot
  FROM PilotSkills AS P1
 WHERE (SELECT plane FROM Hangar
        EXCEPT
        SELECT plane
          FROM PilotSkills AS P2
         WHERE P1.pilot = P2.pilot) IS NULL;
```

Again, informally, you can imagine that we got a skill list from each pilot, walked over to the hangar, and crossed off each plane he could fly. If we marked off all the planes in the hangar, we would keep this guy. Another trick is that an empty subquery expression returns a `NULL`, which is how we can test for an empty set. The `WHERE` clause could just as well have used a `NOT EXISTS()` predicate instead of the `IS NULL` predicate.

19.3 Romley's Division

This somewhat complicated relational division is due to Richard Romley at Salomon Smith Barney. The original problem deals with two tables. The first table has a list of managers and the projects they can manage. The second table has a list of Personnel, their departments, and the projects to which they are assigned. Each employee is assigned to one and only one department, and each employee works on one and only one project at a time. But a department can have several different projects at the same time, and a single project can span several departments.

```
CREATE TABLE MgrProjects
(mgr_name CHAR(10) NOT NULL,
 project_id CHAR(2) NOT NULL,
 PRIMARY KEY(mgr_name, project_id));

INSERT INTO Mgr_Project
VALUES ('M1', 'P1'), ('M1', 'P3'),
       ('M2', 'P2'), ('M2', 'P3'),
       ('M3', 'P2'),
       ('M4', 'P1'), ('M4', 'P2'), ('M4', 'P3');
```

```
CREATE TABLE Personnel
(emp_id CHAR(10) NOT NULL,
 dept CHAR(2) NOT NULL,
 project_id CHAR(2) NOT NULL,
 UNIQUE (emp_id, project_id),
 UNIQUE (emp_id, dept),
 PRIMARY KEY (emp_id, dept, project_id));

-- load department #1 data
INSERT INTO Personnel
VALUES ('Al', 'D1', 'P1'),
       ('Bob', 'D1', 'P1'),
       ('Carl', 'D1', 'P1'),
       ('Don', 'D1', 'P2'),
       ('Ed', 'D1', 'P2'),
       ('Frank', 'D1', 'P2'),
       ('George', 'D1', 'P2');

-- load department #2 data
INSERT INTO Personnel
VALUES ('Harry', 'D2', 'P2'),
       ('Jack', 'D2', 'P2'),
       ('Larry', 'D2', 'P2'),
       ('Mike', 'D2', 'P2'),
       ('Nat', 'D2', 'P2');

-- load department #3 data
INSERT INTO Personnel
VALUES ('Oscar', 'D3', 'P2'),
       ('Pat', 'D3', 'P2'),
       ('Rich', 'D3', 'P3');
```

The problem is to generate a report showing for each manager of each department whether is he qualified to manage none, some, or all of the projects being worked on within the department. To find who can manage some, but not all, of the projects, use a version of relational division:

```
SELECT M1.mgr_name, P1.dept_name
  FROM MgrProjects AS M1
       CROSS JOIN
```

```
        Personnel AS P1
  WHERE M1.project_id = P1.project_id
  GROUP BY M1.mgr_name, P1.dept_name
HAVING COUNT(*) <> (SELECT COUNT(emp_id)
                      FROM Personnel AS P2
                     WHERE P2.dept_name = P1.dept_name);
```

The query is simply a relational division with <> instead of = in the HAVING clause. Richard came back with a modification of my answer that uses a characteristic function inside a single aggregate function.

```
SELECT DISTINCT M1.mgr_name, P1.dept_name
  FROM (MgrProjects AS M1
        INNER JOIN
        Personnel AS P1
        ON M1.project_id = P1.project_id)
         INNER JOIN
         Personnel AS P2
         ON P1.dept_name = P2.dept_name
 GROUP BY M1.mgr_name, P1.dept_name, P2.project_id
HAVING MAX (CASE WHEN M1.project_id = P2.project_id
               THEN 1 ELSE 0 END) = 0;
```

This query uses a characteristic function while my original version compares a count of Personnel under each manager to a count of Personnel under each project_id. The use of GROUP BY M1.mgr_name, P1.dept_name, P2.project_id with the SELECT DISTINCT M1.mgr_name, P1.dept_name is really the tricky part in this new query. What we have is a three-dimensional space with the (x, y, z) axis representing (mgr_name, dept_name, project_id), and then we reduce it to two dimensions (mgr_name, dept) by seeing if Personnel on shared project_ids cover the department or not.

That observation leads to the next changes. We can build a table that shows each combination of manager, department, and the level of authority they have over the projects they have in common. That is the derived table T1 in the following query; authority = 1 means the manager is not on the project and authority = 2 means that he is on the project_id.

```
SELECT T1.mgr_name, T1.dept_name,
       CASE SUM(T1.authority)
       WHEN 1 THEN 'None'
       WHEN 2 THEN 'All'
       WHEN 3 THEN 'Some'
       ELSE NULL END AS power
  FROM (SELECT DISTINCT M1.mgr_name, P1.dept_name,
               MAX (CASE WHEN M1.project_id = P1.project_id
                         THEN 2 ELSE 1 END) AS authority
          FROM MgrProjects AS M1
               CROSS JOIN
               Personnel AS P1
         GROUP BY m.mgr_name, P1.dept_name, P1.project_id) AS T1
 GROUP BY T1.mgr_name, T1.dept_name;
```

Another version, using the airplane hangar example:

```
SELECT PS1.pilot,
       CASE WHEN COUNT(PS1.plane) >
            (SELECT COUNT(plane) FROM Hanger)
                 AND COUNT(H1.plane) =
                     (SELECT COUNT(plane)FROM Hanger)
            THEN 'more than all'
            WHEN COUNT(PS1.plane) =
                 (SELECT COUNT(plane) FROM Hanger)
                 AND COUNT(H1.plane) =
                     (SELECT COUNT(plane) FROM Hanger)
            THEN 'exactly all  '
            WHEN MIN(H1.plane) IS NULL
            THEN 'none         '
            ELSE 'some         ' END AS skill_level
  FROM PilotSkills AS PS1
       LEFT OUTER JOIN
       Hanger AS H1
       ON PS1.plane = H1.plane
 GROUP BY PS1.pilot;
```

We can now sum the authority numbers for all the projects within a department to determine the power this manager has over the department as a whole. If he had a total of one, he has no authority over Personnel on any project in the department. If he had a total of two, he

has power over all Personnel on all projects in the department. If he had a total of three, he has both a one and a two authority total on some projects within the department. Here is the final answer.

```
Results
mgr_name dept power
M1  D1   Some
M1  D2   None
M1  D3   Some
M2  D1   Some
M2  D2   All
M2  D3   All
M3  D1   Some
M3  D2   All
M3  D3   Some
M4  D1   All
M4  D2   All
M4  D3   All
```

19.4 Boolean Expressions in an RDBMS

Given the usual "hangar and pilots" schema, we want to create and store queries that involve Boolean expressions such as "Find the pilots who can fly a Piper Cub and also an F-14 or F-17 Fighter." The trick is to put the expression into the disjunctive canonical form. In English that means a bunch of ANDed predicates that are then ORed together. Any Boolean function can be expressed this way. This form is canonical when each Boolean variable appears exactly once in each term. When all variables are not required to appear in every term, the form is called a disjunctive normal form. The algorithm to convert any Boolean expression into disjunctive canonical form is a bit complicated, but can be found in a good book on circuit design. Our simple example would convert to this predicate.

```
('Piper Cub' AND 'F-14 Fighter') OR ('Piper Cub' AND 'F-17
Fighter')
```

We then load the predicate into this table:

```
CREATE TABLE BooleanExpressions
(and_grp INTEGER NOT NULL,
```

```
 skill CHAR(10) NOT NULL,
 PRIMARY KEY (and_grp, skill));

INSERT INTO BooleanExpressions VALUES (1, 'Piper Cub');
INSERT INTO BooleanExpressions VALUES (1, 'F-14 Fighter');
INSERT INTO BooleanExpressions VALUES (2, 'Piper Cub');
INSERT INTO BooleanExpressions VALUES (2, 'F-17 Fighter');
```

Assume we have a table of job candidates:

```
CREATE TABLE Candidates
(candidate_name CHAR(15) NOT NULL,
 skill CHAR(10) NOT NULL,
 PRIMARY KEY (candidate_name, skill));

INSERT INTO Candidates VALUES ('John', 'Piper Cub'); --winner
INSERT INTO Candidates VALUES ('John', 'B-52 Bomber');
INSERT INTO Candidates VALUES ('Mary', 'Piper Cub'); --winner
INSERT INTO Candidates VALUES ('Mary', 'F-17 Fighter');
INSERT INTO Candidates VALUES ('Larry', 'F-14 Fighter'); --winner
INSERT INTO Candidates VALUES ('Larry', 'F-17 Fighter');
INSERT INTO Candidates VALUES ('Moe', 'F-14 Fighter'); --winner
INSERT INTO Candidates VALUES ('Moe', 'F-17 Fighter');
INSERT INTO Candidates VALUES ('Moe', 'Piper Cub');
INSERT INTO Candidates VALUES ('Celko', 'Piper Cub'); -- loser
INSERT INTO Candidates VALUES ('Celko', 'Blimp');
INSERT INTO Candidates VALUES ('Smith', 'Kite');  -- loser
INSERT INTO Candidates VALUES ('Smith', 'Blimp');
```

The query is simple now:

```
SELECT DISTINCT C1.candidate_name
  FROM Candidates AS C1, BooleanExpressions AS Q1
 WHERE C1.skill = Q1.skill
 GROUP BY Q1.and_grp, C1.candidate_name
HAVING COUNT(C1.skill)
       = (SELECT COUNT(*)
            FROM BooleanExpressions AS Q2
           WHERE Q1.and_grp = Q2.and_grp);
```

You can retain the COUNT() information to rank candidates. For example, Moe meets both qualifications, while other candidates meet only one of the two.

19.5 FIFO and LIFO Subsets

This will be easier to explain with an example for readers who have not worked with an Inventory system before. Imagine that we have a warehouse of one product to which we add stock once a day.

```
CREATE TABLE InventoryReceipts
(receipt_nbr INTEGER PRIMARY KEY,
 purchase_date DATETIME NOT NULL,
 qty_on_hand INTEGER NOT NULL
   CHECK (qty_on_hand >= 0),
 unit_price DECIMAL (12,4) NOT NULL);
```

Let's use this sample data for discussion.

```
InventoryReceipts
receipt_nbr purchase_date qty_on_hand unit_price
=========================================
 1          '2006-01-01'   15      10.00
 2          '2006-01-02'   25      12.00
 3          '2006-01-03'   40      13.00
 4          '2006-01-04'   35      12.00
 5          '2006-01-05'   45      10.00
```

The business now sells 100 units on 2006-01-05. How do you calculate the value of the stock sold? There is not one right answer, but here are some options:

1. Use the current replacement cost, which is $10.00 per unit as of January 5, 2006. That would mean the sale cost us $1,000.00 because of a recent price break.
2. Use the current average price per unit. We have a total of 160 units, for which we paid a total of $1,840.00, and that gives us an average cost of $11.50 per unit, or $1,150.00 in total inventory costs.

3. LIFO, which stands for "Last In, First Out." We start by looking at the most recent purchases and work backwards through time.

```
2006-01-05: 45 * $10.00 = $450.00 and 45 units
2006-01-04: 35 * $12.00 = $420.00 and 80 units
2006-01-03: 20 * $13.00 = $260.00 and 100 with 20 units left over
```

for a total of $1,130.00 in inventory costs.

4. FIFO, which stands for "First In, First Out." We start by looking at the earliest purchases and work forward through time.

```
2006-01-01: 15 * $10.00 = $150.00 and 15 units
2006-01-02: 25 * $12.00 = $300.00 and 40 units
2006-01-03: 40 * $13.00 = $520.00 and 80 units
2006-01-04: 20 * $12.00 = $240.00 with 15 units left over
```

for a total of $1,210.00 in inventory costs.

The first two scenarios are trivial to program. The LIFO and FIFO are more interesting because they involve matching the order against blocks of inventory in a particular order. Consider this view:

```
CREATE VIEW LIFO (stock_date, unit_price, tot_qty_on_hand,
tot_cost)
AS
SELECT R1.purchase_date, R1.unit_price, SUM(R2.qty_on_hand),
SUM(R2.qty_on_hand *
R2.unit_price)
 FROM InventoryReceipts AS R1,
       InventoryReceipts AS R2
 WHERE R2.purchase_date >= R1.purchase_date
 GROUP BY R1.purchase_date, R1.unit_price;
```

A row in this view tells us the total quantity on hand, the total cost of the goods in inventory, and what we were paying for items on each date. The quantity on hand is a running total. We can get the LIFO cost with this query:

```
SELECT (tot_cost - ((tot_qty_on_hand - :order_qty_on_hand) *
unit_price)) AS cost
  FROM LIFO AS L1
 WHERE stock_date
       = (SELECT MAX(stock_date)
            FROM LIFO AS L2
           WHERE tot_qty_on_hand >= :order_qty_on_hand);
```

This is straight algebra and a little logic. Find the most recent date that we had enough (or more) quantity on hand to meet the order. If, by dumb blind luck, there is a day when the quantity on hand exactly matched the order, return the total cost as the answer. If the order was for more than we have in stock, then return nothing. If we go back to a day when we had more in stock than the order was for, then look at the unit price on that day, multiply by the overage and subtract it.

Alternatively, you can use a derived table and a `CASE` expression. The `CASE` expression computes the cost of units that have a running total quantity less than the :order_qty_on_hand, and then it does algebra on the final block of inventory, which would put the running total over the limit. The outer query does a sum on these blocks.

```
SELECT SUM(R3.v) AS cost
  FROM (SELECT R1.unit_price
            * CASE WHEN SUM(R2.qty_on_hand) <=
:order_qty_on_hand
                   THEN R1.qty_on_hand
                   ELSE :order_qty_on_hand
                        - (SUM(R2.qty_on_hand) -
R1.qty_on_hand) END
          FROM InventoryReceipts AS R1,
               InventoryReceipts AS R2
         WHERE R1.purchase_date <= R2.purchase_date
        GROUP BY R1.purchase_date, R1.qty_on_hand, R1.unit_price
        HAVING (SUM(R2.qty_on_hand) - R1.qty_on_hand) <=
:order_qty_on_hand)
       AS R3(v);
```

`FIFO` can be done with a similar `VIEW` or derived table:

```
CREATE VIEW FIFO (stock_date, unit_price, tot_qty_on_hand,
tot_cost)
AS
```

```
SELECT R1.purchase_date, R1.unit_price,
       SUM(R2.qty_on_hand), SUM(R2.qty_on_hand *
R2.unit_price)
 FROM InventoryReceipts AS R1,
       InventoryReceipts AS R2
 WHERE R2.purchase_date <= R1.purchase_date
 GROUP BY R1.purchase_date, R1.unit_price;
```

With the corresponding query:

```
SELECT (tot_cost - ((tot_qty_on_hand - :order_qty_on_hand) *
unit_price)) AS cost
  FROM FIFO AS F1
 WHERE stock_date
       = (SELECT MIN (stock_date)
            FROM FIFO AS F2
           WHERE tot_qty_on_hand >= :order_qty_on_hand);
```

Grouping Operations

I AM SEPARATING THE partitions and grouping operations based on the idea that a group has *group* properties that we are trying to find, so we get an answer back for each group. A partition is simply a way of subsetting the original table so that we get a table back as a result.

20.1 GROUP BY Clause

The `GROUP BY` clause is based on simple partitions. A partition of a set divides the set into subsets such that the union of the subsets returns the original set, and the intersection of the subsets is empty. Think of it as cutting up a pizza pie—each piece of pepperoni belongs to one and only one slice of pizza. When you get to the section on SQL-99 OLAP extensions, you will see "variations on a theme" in the `ROLLUP` and `CUBE` operators, but this is where it all starts.

The `GROUP BY` clause takes the result of the `FROM` and `WHERE` clauses, then puts the rows into groups defined as having the same values for the columns listed in the `GROUP BY` clause. Each group is reduced to a single row in the result table. This result table is called a grouped table, and all operations are now defined on groups rather than on rows.

By convention, the `NULL`s are treated as one group. The order of the grouping columns in the `GROUP BY` clause does not matter, but since all or some of the column names have to appear in the SELECT list, you should probably use the same order in both lists for readability.

Please note the SELECT column names might be a subset of the GROUP BY clause column names, but never the other way around. Let us construct a sample table called Villes to explain in detail how this works. The table is declared as:

```
CREATE TABLE Villes
 (state_code CHAR(2) NOT NULL, -- usps codes
  city_name CHAR(25) NOT NULL,
  PRIMARY KEY (city_name, state_code));
```

We populate it with the names of cities that end in "-ville" in each state. The first problem is to find a count of the number of such cities by state_code. The immediate naïve query might be:

```
SELECT state_code, city_name, COUNT(*)
  FROM Villes
 GROUP BY state_code;
```

The groups for Tennessee would have the rows ('TN', 'Nashville') and ('TN', 'Knoxville'). The first position in the result is the grouping column, which has to be constant within the group. The third column in the SELECT clause is the COUNT(*) for the group, which is clearly two. The city_name column is a problem. Since the table is grouped by states, there can be at most 50 groups, one for each state_code. The COUNT(*) is clearly a single value, and it applies to the group as a whole. But what possible single value could I output for a city_name in each group? Pick a typical city_name and use it? If all the cities have the same name, use that name; otherwise, output a NULL? The worst possible choice would be to output both rows with the COUNT(*) of 2, since each row would imply that there are two cities named Nashville and two cities named Knoxville in Tennessee.

Each row represents a single group, so anything in it must be a characteristic of the group, not of a single row in the group. This is why there is a rule that the SELECT list must be made up only of grouping columns with optional aggregate function expressions.

20.1.1 NULLs and Groups

SQL puts the NULLs into a single group, as if they were all equal. The other option, which was used in some of the first SQL implementations before the standard, was to put each NULL into a group by itself. That is not an unreasonable choice. But to make a meaningful choice between the two options, you would have to know the semantics of the data you are trying to model. SQL is a language based on syntax, not semantics.

For example, if a NULL is being used for a missing diagnosis in a medical record, you know that each patient will probably have a different disease when the NULLs are resolved. Putting the NULLs in one group would make sense if you wanted to consider unprocessed diagnosis reports as one group in a summary. Putting each NULL in its own group would make sense if you wanted to consider each unprocessed diagnosis report as an action item for treatment of the relevant class of diseases. Another example was a traffic ticket database that used NULL for a missing auto tag. Obviously, there is more than one car without a tag in the database. The general scheme for getting separate groups for each NULL is straightforward:

```
SELECT x, ..
  FROM Table1
 WHERE x IS NOT NULL
 GROUP BY x
UNION ALL
SELECT x, ..
  FROM Table1
 WHERE x IS NULL;
```

There will also be cases, such as the traffic tickets, where you can use another GROUP BY clause to form groups where the principal grouping columns are NULL. For example, the VIN (Vehicle Identification Number) is taken when the car is missing a tag, and it would provide a grouping column.

20.2 GROUP BY and HAVING

One of the biggest problems in working with the GROUP BY clause lies in not understanding how the WHERE and HAVING clauses work. Consider this query to find all departments with fewer than five programmers:

```
SELECT dept_nbr
  FROM Personnel
 WHERE job_title = 'Programmer'
 GROUP BY dept_nbr
HAVING COUNT(*) < 5;
```

The result of this query does not have a row for any departments with no programmers. The order of execution of the clauses does `WHERE` first, so those employees whose jobs are not equal to `'Programmer'` are never passed to the `GROUP BY` clause. You have missed data that you might want to trap.

The next query will also pick up those departments that have no programmers, because the `COUNT(DISTINCT x)` function will return a zero for an empty set.

```
SELECT DISTINCT dept_nbr
  FROM Personnel AS P1
 WHERE 5 > (SELECT COUNT(DISTINCT P2.emp_nbr)
             FROM Personnel AS P2
            WHERE P1.dept_nbr = P2.  dept_nbr
              AND P2.job_title = 'Programmer');
```

If there is no `GROUP BY` clause, the `HAVING` clause will treat the entire table as a single group. Many early implementations of SQL required that the `HAVING` clause belong to a `GROUP BY` clause, so you might see old code written under that assumption.

Since the `HAVING` clause applies only to the rows of a grouped table, it can reference only the grouping columns and aggregate functions that apply to the group. That is why this query would fail:

```
SELECT dept_nbr          -- Invalid Query!
  FROM Personnel
 GROUP BY dept_nbr
HAVING COUNT(*) < 5
   AND job_title = 'Programmer';
```

When the `HAVING` clause is executed, job is not in the grouped table as a column—it is a property of a row, not of a group. Likewise, this query would fail for much the same reason:

```
SELECT dept_nbr          -- Invalid Query!
  FROM Personnel
 WHERE COUNT(*) < 5
   AND job_title = 'Programmer'
 GROUP BY dept_nbr;
```

The COUNT(*) does not exist until after the departmental groups are formed.

20.2.1 Group Characteristics and the HAVING Clause

You can use the aggregate functions and the HAVING clause to determine certain characteristics of the groups formed by the GROUP BY clause. For example, given a simple grouped table with three columns:

```
SELECT col1, col2
  FROM Foobar
 GROUP BY col1, col2
HAVING ...  ;
```

You can determine the following properties of the groups with these HAVING clauses:

HAVING COUNT (DISTINCT col_x) = COUNT (col_x)
col_x has all distinct values

HAVING COUNT(*) = COUNT(col_x);
there are no NULLs in the column

HAVING MIN(col_x - <const>) = -MAX(col_x - <const>)
col_x deviates above and below const by the same amount

HAVING MIN(col_x) * MAX(col_x) < 0
either MIN or MAX is negative, not both

HAVING MIN(col_x) * MAX(col_x) > 0
col_x is either all positive or all negative

HAVING MIN(SIGN(col_x)) = MAX(SIGN(col_x))
col_x is all positive, all negative or all zero

HAVING MIN(ABS(col_x)) = 0;
col_x has at least one zero

HAVING MIN(ABS(col_x)) = MIN(col_x)
col_x >= 0 (although the where clause can handle this, too)

HAVING MIN(col_x) = -MAX(col_x)
col_x deviates above and below zero by the same amount

HAVING MIN(col_x) * MAX(col_x) = 0
either one or both of MIN or MAX is zero

HAVING MIN(col_x) < MAX(col_x)
col_x has more than one value (may be faster than count (*) > 1)

HAVING MIN(col_x) = MAX(col_x)
col_x has one value or NULLs

HAVING (MAX(seq) - MIN(seq)+1) = COUNT(seq)
the sequential numbers in seq have no gaps

Tom Moreau contributed most of these suggestions.

Let me remind you again that if there is no GROUP BY clause, the HAVING clause will treat the entire table as a single group. This means that if you wish to apply one of the tests given above to the whole table, you will need to use a constant in the SELECT list.

This will be easier to see with an example. You are given a table with a column of unique sequential numbers that start at 1. When you go to insert a new row, you must use a sequence number that is not currently in the column—that is, fill the gaps. If there are no gaps, then and only then can you use the next highest integer in the sequence.

```
CREATE TABLE Foobar
(seq_nbr INTEGER NOT NULL PRIMARY KEY
         CHECK (seq > 0),
 junk CHAR(5) NOT NULL);

INSERT INTO Foobar
VALUES (1, 'Tom'), (2, 'Dick'), (4, 'Harry'), (5, 'Moe');
```

How do I find if I have any gaps?

```
EXISTS (SELECT 'gap'
          FROM Foobar
        HAVING COUNT(*) = MAX(seq_nbr))
```

You could not use "`SELECT seq_nbr`" because the column values will not be identical within the single group made from the table, so the subquery fails with a cardinality violation. Likewise, "`SELECT *`" fails because the asterisk is converted into a column name picked by the SQL engine. Here is the insertion statement:

```
INSERT INTO Foobar (seq_nbr, junk)
VALUES (CASE WHEN EXISTS      -- no gaps
                  (SELECT 'no gaps'
                     FROM Foobar
                   HAVING COUNT(*) = MAX(seq_nbr))
             THEN (SELECT MAX(seq_nbr) FROM Foobar) + 1
             ELSE (SELECT MIN(seq_nbr) -- gaps
                     FROM Foobar
                    WHERE (seq_nbr - 1)
                          NOT IN (SELECT seq_nbr FROM Foobar)
                      AND seq_nbr > 0) - 1,
      'Celko');
```

The `ELSE` clause has to handle a special situation when 1 is in the seq_nbr column, so that it does not return an illegal zero. The only tricky part is waiting for the entire scalar subquery expression to compute before subtracting one; writing "`MIN(seq_nbr -1)`" or "`MIN(seq_nbr) -1`" in the `SELECT` list could disable the use of indexes in many SQL products.

20.3 Multiple Aggregation Levels

The rule in SQL is that you cannot nest aggregate functions, such as

```
SELECT department, MIN(COUNT(items))  -- illegal syntax!
  FROM Foobar
 GROUP BY department;
```

The usual intent of this is to get multiple levels of aggregation; this example probably wanted the smallest count of items within each department. But this makes no sense, because a department (i.e., a

group) can have only one count, one minimum, one maximum, one average, and so forth for any expression. The nature of descriptive statistics is that they reduce a group characteristic to a scalar value.

20.3.1 Grouped VIEWs for Multiple Aggregation Levels

Business reports are usually based on a hierarchy of nested levels of aggregation. This type of report is so common that there are tools that perform only this sort of task. For example, sales are grouped under the salesmen who made them, then salesmen's departments are grouped into districts, districts are grouped into regions, and so on until we have summary information at the company level. Each level is a partition of the level above it. The summary information can be constructed from the level immediately beneath it in the hierarchy.

Look at Chapter 28 on the Nested Sets model for hierarchies. Frankly, using a report writer will be faster and more powerful than writing SQL code to do the job.

One trick is to use `VIEWs` with `GROUP BY` clauses to build the reporting levels. Using a Sales report example, the following `UNION`ed query will get a report for each level, from the lowest, most detailed level (salesman), through districts and regions, to the highest level (the company).

```
SELECT region, district, salesman, SUM(sales_sales_amt)
  FROM Sales
 GROUP BY region, district, salesman
UNION
SELECT region, district, '{SALESMEN}', SUM(sales_amt)
  FROM Sales
 GROUP BY region, district
UNION
SELECT region, '{OFFICE}', '{SALESMEN}', SUM(sales_amt)
  FROM Sales
 GROUP BY region
UNION
SELECT '{REGION}', '{OFFICE}', '{SALESMEN}', SUM(sales_amt)
  FROM Sales;
```

The constant strings inside the curly brackets will sort below any alphabetic strings in ASCII, and thus will appear on the end of each grouping in the hierarchy. Now that I've shown you this trick, I need to point out its flaws.

20.3.2 Subquery Expressions for Multiple Aggregation Levels

Standard SQL permits you to use a table subquery in a FROM clause and a scalar subquery anywhere that you would use an expression. This lets us do some multilevel aggregation in a single query. For example, to find how each salesman did in his sales district, you can write.

```
SELECT salesman, region, district, SUM(sales_amt) AS
salesman_tot,
      (SELECT SUM(sales_amt)
         FROM Sales AS S1
        WHERE S1.region = S2.region
          AND S1.district = S2.district)
      AS district_tot
  FROM Sales AS S2
 GROUP BY salesman, region, district, district_tot;
```

This query will work because the subquery is a constant for each group. The subquery could also be used in an expression to give the percentage of the district total each salesman contributed.

A trickier query is to find aggregates of aggregates—something like the average of the total sales of the districts for each region. Beginning SQL programmers would try to write queries like this:

```
SELECT region, AVG(SUM(sales_amt)) AS region_average  -- Invalid
SQL
  FROM Sales
 GROUP BY district, region;
```

The parser would gag on AVG(SUM(sales_amt)) and return an error message about nesting aggregate functions. Standard SQL will let you get the desired effect with a little more work. You need a subquery that will compute the sum of the sales for each district within a region.

This table then needs to be averaged for each region, thus:

```
SELECT T1.region, AVG(T1.district_total) AS region_average
    FROM (SELECT region, district, SUM(sales_amt)
            FROM Sales
        GROUP BY region, district) AS T1 (region, district,
district_total)
GROUP BY T1.region;
```

This is a simple derived table, which can be implemented in many ways. However, the best guess would be that the subquery would be constructed once as a materialized table, then used by the SELECT statement in the usual way. Do not think that Standard SQL would let you write:

```
SELECT region,
       AVG(SELECT SUM(sales_amt)    -- Invalid SQL
             FROM Sales AS S1
            WHERE S1.region = S2.region
           GROUP BY district) AS region_average
  FROM Sales AS S2
 GROUP BY region;
```

The parameter for an aggregate function still cannot be another aggregate function or a subquery. The reason for this prohibition is that although this particular subquery is scalar, other subqueries might have multiple rows and/or multiple columns and not be able to return a single value.

20.3.3 CASE Expressions for Multiple Aggregation Levels

Another trick is to replace the nesting of aggregate functions with expressions that return a characteristic of a subset of the group. Given a table that includes movie names and a numeric rating assigned to them by our reviewers, for each movie we might want to know:

1. What was the worst rating, and how many times did it occur?
2. What was the best rating, and how many times did it occur?

This can be done with this query.

```
SELECT movie_name,
       MIN(rating) AS worst_rating,
       COUNT(CASE WHEN NOT EXISTS
                       (SELECT *
                          FROM Reviews AS R2
                         WHERE R2.movie_name = R1.movie_name
                           AND R2.rating < R1.rating)
```

```
                    THEN 1 ELSE NULL END) AS worst_tally,
        MAX(rating) AS best_rating,
        COUNT(CASE WHEN NOT EXISTS
                         (SELECT *
                            FROM Reviews AS R3
                           WHERE R3.movie_name = R1.movie_name
                             AND R3.rating > R1.rating)
                    THEN 1 ELSE NULL END) AS best_tally
  FROM Reviews AS R1
 GROUP BY movie_name;
```

The subquery expression in each of the NOT EXISTS() predicates is building a subset within each movie's reviews such that they are the highest (or lowest). This subset of identical values is then counted in the outermost query. This avoids using a nested aggregate function.

20.4 Grouping on Computed Columns

SQL-99 allows queries that are grouped on the result of a computed column. For example, to do a report by months on sales, you would write:

```
SELECT EXTRACT(MONTH FROM sale_date) AS rpt_month,
SUM(sales_amt)
  FROM Sales
 GROUP BY rpt_month;
```

This is a departure from the SQL processing model in previous standards, which allowed only column names. In the original model, the SELECT statement computes the expressions in the SELECT clause last, so the computed columns do not exist until after the grouping is done, so there should be no way to group them.

However, you can fake it in older versions of SQL by using a subquery expression in the FROM clause to build a working table with the computation in it.

```
SELECT salesmonth, SUM(sales_amt)
  FROM (SELECT EXTRACT(MONTH FROM sale_date) AS salesmonth,
               sales_amt
          FROM Sales)
 GROUP BY salesmonth;
```

Or you can use a correlated subquery expression in the `SELECT` clause.

```
SELECT DISTINCT EXTRACT(MONTH FROM S1.sale_date),
       (SELECT SUM(S2.sales_amt)
          FROM Sales AS S2
         WHERE EXTRACT(MONTH FROM S2.sale_date)
               = EXTRACT(MONTH FROM S1.sale_date))
 FROM Sales AS S1;
```

The first version will probably run faster, since it does not have as many computations in it.

20.5 Grouping into Pairs

The idea is easier to show than to say: you are given a table of people and want to generate a list that has pairs of men and women for a dinner party.

```
CREATE TABLE People
(name VARCHAR(15) NOT NULL,
 gender INTEGER DEFAULT 1 NOT NULL -- iso gender codes
      CHECK (gender IN (1, 2));

INSERT INTO People
VALUES ('Bob', 1), ('Ed', 1), ('Joe', 1), ('Dave', 1);

INSERT INTO People
VALUES ('Sue', 2), ('Joan', 2), ('Kate', 2),
       ('Mary', 2), ('Petra', 2), ('Nancy', 2);
```

A solution from Steve Kass:

```
SELECT A.name, A.gender, COUNT(*) AS rank
  FROM People AS A, People AS B
 WHERE B.name <= A.name
   AND B.gender = A.gender
 GROUP BY A.name, A.gender;
```

For each name, `COUNT(*)` is the alphabetical "rank" of the name in the table, counting only names of the same gender. The join makes this happen, because `COUNT(*)` counts the number of rows in the table that have the same gender as `name` and that come before or equal to `name` in alphabetical order. The results are ordered by this "rank" value first, then by gender, to order the names with matching rank.

While on the right track, the single fact of a dinner couple is split across two rows. You cannot look at one row and answer the question, "Do you have a date?" with this query result. But the basic idea is good, and you can get your pairs on one line:

```
SELECT M1.name AS male, F1.name AS female, COALESCE (M1.rank,
F1.rank)
  FROM (SELECT P1.name, COUNT(P2.name)
          FROM People AS P1, People AS P2
         WHERE P2.name <= P1.name
           AND P1.gender = 1
           AND P2.gender = 1
        GROUP BY P1.name) AS M1(name, rank)
       FULL OUTER JOIN
       (SELECT P1.name, COUNT(P2.name)
          FROM People AS P1, People AS P2
         WHERE P2.name <= P1.name
           AND P1.gender = 2
           AND P2.gender = 2
        GROUP BY P1.name) AS F1(name, rank)
       ON M1.rank = F1.rank;
```

I assume that alphabetical ordering of the two subsets makes the pairs for matching. This query ought to handle the case where there are different numbers of males and females by padding with `NULL`s. It also returns proper pairings without the use of an `ORDER BY`, thus avoiding an actual or hidden `CURSOR`.

20.6 Sorting and GROUP BY

Though it is not required by the standard, most implementations will automatically sort the results of a grouped query. Internally, the groups were built by first sorting the table on the grouping columns and then aggregating them. The `NULL` group can sort either high or low, depending on the vendor.

An `ORDER BY` clause whose columns are not in the same order as those in the `GROUP BY` clause can be expensive to execute if the optimizer does not ignore the extra sort request. It is also possible to sort

a grouped table on an aggregate or calculated column. For example, to show the Sales regions in order of total Sales, you would write:

```
SELECT region, district, SUM(sales_amt) AS district_sales_amt
FROM Sales
GROUP BY region, district
ORDER BY district_sales_amt DESC, region, district;
```

Since it is possible that two or more regions could have the same Sales volume, it is always a good idea to sort by the region column, then by the district column. The extra sorting is cheap to execute and requires no extra storage. It is very likely that your SQL implementation is using a nonstable sort.

A stable sort preserves the original order of the rows with equal-valued sort keys. For example, I am given a deck of playing cards to sort by rank and suit. If I first sort by rank, assuming aces high, I would get a deck with all the deuces, followed by all the treys, and so forth until I got to the aces. Within each of these groups, the suits could be in any order.

If I then sorted the deck on the suits of the cards, I would get (assuming bridge sorting order) deuces of clubs, diamonds, hearts, and finally spades, as the highest rank, followed by treys of clubs, diamonds, hearts, and spades, and so forth up to the aces.

If the second sort were a nonstable sort, it could destroy the ordering of the suits. A second sort that was a stable sort would keep the ordering in the suits.

Stable sorts are almost always slower than nonstable sorts, so nonstable sorts are preferred by most database systems. However, a smart optimizer can see an existing order in the intermediate working table and replace the usual nonstable sort with a stable sort, thereby avoiding extra work. The optimizer can also use clustered indexes and other sources of preexisting ordering in the data.

However, you should never depend on the default ordering of a particular SQL product, since this will not be portable. If ordering is important, use an `ORDER BY` clause with all of the desired columns explicitly given in it. In Standard SQL, you will have to use an `AS` clause on each of the aggregate functions to give it a name that can be used in the `ORDER BY` clause.

A common vendor extension is to permit an integer specifying the ordinal position of the expression in the `SELECT` clause in an `ORDER BY`. The problem with this is that a change to the `SELECT` clause can trash the results.

Aggregate Functions

ONE OF THE MAJOR purposes of a database system is to turn data into information. This usually means doing some statistical summary from that data. Descriptive statistics measure some property of an existing data set and express it as a single number. Though there are very sophisticated measures, most applications require only basic, well-understood statistics. The most common summary functions are the count (or tally), the average (or arithmetic mean), and the sum (or total). This minimal set of descriptive statistical operators is built into the SQL language, and vendors often extend these options with others. These functions are called set functions in the ANSI/ISO SQL standard, but vendors, textbook writers, and everyone else usually call them aggregate functions, so I will use that term.

Aggregate functions first construct a column of values as defined by the parameter. The parameter is usually a single column name, but it can be an arithmetic expression with scalar functions and calculations. Pretty much the only things that cannot be parameters are other aggregate functions (e.g., `SUM(AVG(x))` is illegal) and subqueries (e.g., `AVG(SELECT col1 FROM SomeTable WHERE ...)` is illegal). A subquery could return more than one value, so it would not fit into a column, and an aggregate function would have to try to build a column within a column.

Once the working column is constructed, all the NULLs are removed and the function performs its operation. As you learn the definitions I am about to give, stress the words' known values to remind yourself that the NULLs have been dropped.

There are two options, ALL and DISTINCT, that are shown as keywords inside the parameter list. The keyword ALL is optional and is never really used in practice. It says that all the rows in the working column are retained for the final calculation. The keyword DISTINCT is not optional in these functions. It removes all redundant duplicates values from a working column before the final calculation. Let's look at the particulars of each aggregate function.

21.1 COUNT() Functions

There are two forms of the COUNT() function: cardinality and expression counting.

COUNT(*) returns the number of rows in a table (called the cardinality of the table, in relational terms); it is the only standard aggregate function that uses an asterisk as a parameter. This function is very useful and usually runs quite fast, since it can use system information about the table size. Remember that NULL values are also counted, because this function deals with entire rows and not column values. There is no such thing as "NULL row"—a row exists or it does not, without regard to contents.

An empty table has a COUNT(*) of zero, which makes sense. However, all of the other aggregate functions we will discuss in this section will return an empty set as the result of being given an empty set to operate on—"*ab nilo, ex nilo*." The cardinality is a property of the set as a whole. Summation, average, and so forth are computations done on the elements of the set; if that set is empty, they have no elements from which to build an answer. While it is too late to change SQL, we would have been better off with syntax that uses a table expression in a parameter for cardinality, much like the EXISTS() predicate.

You would think that using the COUNT(*) would be easy, but there are a lot of subtle tricks to it. Think of a database of the presidencies of the United States, with columns for the first name, middle initial(s), and last name of each U. S. President, along with his political party and his terms in office. It might look like this:

```
CREATE TABLE Parties
(party_code CHAR(2) NOT NULL PRIMARY KEY,
```

```
 party_name CHAR(25) NOT NULL);

INSERT INTO Parties
VALUES ('D', 'Democratic'),
       ('DR', 'Democratic Republican'),
       ('R', 'Republican'),
       ('F', 'Federalist'),
       ('W', 'Whig');

CREATE TABLE Presidents
(first_name CHAR(11) NOT NULL,
 initial VARCHAR(4) DEFAULT ' ' NOT NULL, -- one space
 last_name CHAR(11) NOT NULL,
 party_code CHAR(2) NOT NULL
    REFERENCES Parties(party_code)
 start_term INTEGER NOT NULL UNIQUE,
 end_term INTEGER); -- null means current

Presidents
first_name    initial    last_name    party  start_term end_term
==================================================================
'George'       ' '       'Washington'  'F'    1789       1797
'John'         ' '       'Adams'       'F'    1797       1801
'Thomas'       ' '       'Jefferson'   'DR'   1801       1809
'James'        ' '       'Madison'     'DR'   1809       1817
'James'        ' '       'Monroe'      'DR'   1817       1825
'John'         'Q'       'Adams'       'DR'   1825       1829
'Andrew'       ' '       'Jackson'     'D'    1829       1837
'Martin'       ' '       'Van Buren'   'D'    1837       1841
'William'      'H.'      'Harrison'    'W'    1841       1841
'John'         ' '       'Tyler'       'W'    1841       1845
'James'        'K.'      'Polk'        'D'    1845       1849
'Zachary'      ' '       'Taylor'      'W'    1849       1850
'Millard'      ' '       'Fillmore'    'W'    1850       1853
'Franklin'     ' '       'Pierce'      'D'    1853       1857
'James'        ' '       'Buchanan'    'D'    1857       1861
'Abraham'      ' '       'Lincoln'     'R'    1861       1865
'Andrew'       ' '       'Johnson'     'R'    1865       1869
'Ulysses'      'S.'      'Grant'       'R'    1869       1877
'Rutherford'   'B.'      'Hayes'       'R'    1877       1881
'James'        'A.'      'Garfield'    'R'    1881       1881
```

```
'Chester'    'A.'    'Arthur'      'R'  1881  1885
'Grover'     ' '     'Cleveland'   'D'  1885  1889
'Benjamin'   ' '     'Harrison'    'R'  1889  1893
'Grover'     ' '     'Cleveland'   'D'  1893  1897
'William'    ' '     'McKinley'    'R'  1897  1901
'Theodore'   ' '     'Roosevelt'   'R'  1901  1909
'William'    'H.'    'Taft'        'R'  1909  1913
'Woodrow'    ' '     'Wilson'      'D'  1913  1921
'Warren'     'G.'    'Harding'     'R'  1921  1923
'Calvin'     ' '     'Coolidge'    'R'  1923  1929
'Herbert'    'C.'    'Hoover'      'R'  1929  1933
'Franklin'   'D.'    'Roosevelt'   'D'  1933  1945
'Harry'      'S.'    'Truman'      'D'  1945  1953
'Dwight'     'D.'    'Eisenhower'  'R'  1953  1961
'John'       'F.'    'Kennedy'     'D'  1961  1963
'Lyndon'     'B.'    'Johnson'     'D'  1963  1969
'Richard'    'M.'    'Nixon'       'R'  1969  1974
'Gerald'     'R.'    'Ford'        'R'  1974  1977
'James'      'E.'    'Carter'      'D'  1977  1981
'Ronald'     'W.'    'Reagan'      'R'  1981  1989
'George'     'H.W.'  'Bush'        'R'  1989  1993
'William'    'J.'    'Clinton'     'D'  1993  2001
'George'     'W.  '  'Bush'        'R'  2001  NULL
```

Your civics teacher has just asked you to tell her how many people have been President of the United States. So you write the query as `SELECT COUNT(*) FROM` Presidents; and get the wrong answer. For those of you who have been out of high school too long, more than one Adams, more than one John, and more than one Roosevelt have served as president. Many people have had more than one term in office, and Grover Cleveland served two discontinuous terms. In short, this database is not a simple one-row, one-person system. What you really want is not `COUNT(*)`, but something that is able to look at unique combinations of multiple columns. You cannot do this in one column, so you need to construct an expression that is unique. The point is that you need to be very sure that the expression you are using as a parameter is really what you wanted to count.

The `COUNT([ALL] <value expression>)` returns the number of members in the `<value expression>` set. The `NULL`s were thrown away before the counting took place, and an empty set returns zero. The best way to read this is: "Count the number of known values in this expression," with stress on the word known. In this example you might use `COUNT(first_name || ' ' || initial || ' ' || last_name)`.

The `COUNT(DISTINCT <value expression>)` returns the number of unique members in the `<value expression>` set. The `NULL`s were thrown away before the counting took place, and then all redundant duplicates are removed (i.e., we keep one copy). Again, an empty set returns a zero, just as with the other counting functions. Applying this function to a key or a unique column is the same as using the `COUNT(*)` function, but the optimizer may not be smart enough to spot it.

Notice that the use of the keywords `ALL` and `DISTINCT` follows the same pattern here as they did in the [`ALL` | `DISTINCT`] options in the `SELECT` clause of the query expressions.

21.2 SUM() Functions

This function works only with numeric values. You should also consult your particular product's manuals to find out the precision of the results for exact and approximate numeric data types.

`SUM([ALL] <value expression>)` returns the numeric total of all known values. The `NULL`s are removed before the summation takes place. An empty set returns an empty result set, not a zero. If there are other columns in the `SELECT` list, then that empty set will be converted into a `NULL`.

`SUM(DISTINCT <value expression>)` returns the numeric total of all known, unique values. The `NULL`s and all redundant duplicates were removed before the summation took place. Again, an empty set returns an empty result set, not a zero.

That last rule is hard for people to understand. If there are other columns in the `SELECT` list, then that empty result set will be converted into a `NULL`. This is true for the rest of the Standard aggregate functions:

```
-- no rows
SELECT SUM(x)
  FROM EmptyTable;

--one row with (0, NULL) in it
SELECT COUNT(*), SUM(x)
  FROM EmptyTable;
```

The summation of a set of numbers looks as though it should be easy, but it is not. Make two tables with the same set of positive and negative approximate numeric values, but put one in random order and have the other sorted by absolute value. The sorted table will give more accurate results. The reason is simple: positive and negative values of the same magnitude will be added together and will get a chance to cancel each other out. There is also less chance of an overflow or underflow error during calculations. Most PC SQL implementations and a lot of mainframe implementations do not bother with this trick, because it would require a sort for every `SUM()` statement, which would take a long time.

Whenever an exact or approximate numeric value is assigned to exact numeric, it may not fit into the storage allowed for it. SQL says that the database engine will use an approximation that preserves leading significant digits of the original number after rounding or truncating. The choice of whether to truncate or round is implementation-defined, however. This can lead to some surprises when you have to shift data among SQL implementations, or move storage values from a host language program into an SQL table. It is probably a good idea to create the columns with one more decimal place than you think you need.

Truncation is defined as truncation toward zero; this means that 1.5 would truncate to 1, and −1.5 would truncate to −1. This is not true for all programming languages; everyone agrees on truncation toward zero for the positive numbers, but you will find that negative numbers may truncate away from zero (e.g., −1.5 would truncate to −2). SQL is also wishy-washy on rounding, leaving the implementation free to determine its method. There are two major types of rounding, the scientific method and the commercial method, which are discussed in Section 3.2.1 on rounding and truncation math in SQL.

21.3 AVG() Functions

`AVG([ ALL] <value expression>)` returns the average of the values in the value expression set. An empty set returns an empty result set. A set of all `NULL`s will become an empty set. Remember that in general, `AVG(x)` is not the same as `(SUM(x)/COUNT(*))`; the `SUM(x)` function has thrown away the `NULL`s, but the `COUNT(*)` has not.

Likewise, `AVG(DISTINCT <value expression>)` returns the average of the distinct known values in the `<value expression>` set. Applying this function to a key or a unique column is the same as the using `AVG(<value expression>)` function.

Remember that in general `AVG(DISTINCT x)` is not the same as `AVG(x)` or `(SUM(DISTINCT x)/COUNT(*))`. The `SUM(DISTINCT x)` function has thrown away the duplicate values and `NULL`s, but the `COUNT(*)` has not. An empty set returns an empty result set.

The SQL engine is probably using the same code for the totaling in the `AVG()` that it used in the `SUM()` function. This leads to the same problems with rounding and truncation, so you should experiment a little with your particular product to find out what happens.

But even more troublesome than those problems is the problem with the average itself, because it does not really measure central tendency and can be very misleading. Consider the chart below, from Darrell Huff's superlative little book, *How to Lie with Statistics* (Huff 1954). The Sample Company has 25 employees, earning the following salaries:

```
Number of
Employees Salary    Statistic
====================================
   12     $2,000    Mode, Minimum
    1     $3,000    Median
    4     $3,700
    3     $5,000
    1     $5,700    Average
    2     $10,000
    1     $15,000
    1     $45,000    Maximum
```

The average salary (or, more properly, the arithmetic mean) is $5,700. When the boss is trying to look good to the unions, he uses this figure. When the unions are trying to look impoverished, they use the mode, which is the most frequently occurring value, to show that the exploited workers are making $2,000 (which is also the minimum salary in this case).

A better measure in this case is the median, which will be discussed later; that is, the employee with just as many cases above him as below him. That gives us $3,000. The rule for calculating the median is that if there is no actual entity with that value, you fake it.

Most people take an average of the two values on either side of where the median would be; others jump to the higher or lower value. The mode also has a problem, because not every distribution of values has one mode. Imagine a country in which there are as many very poor people as there are very rich people, and there is nobody in between.

This would be a bimodal distribution. If there were sharp classes of incomes, that would be a multimodal distribution.

Some SQL products have median and mode aggregate functions as extensions, but they are not part of the standard. We will discuss in detail how to write them in pure SQL in Chapter 23.

21.3.1 Averages with Empty Groups

The query used here is a bit tricky, so this section can be skipped on your first reading. Sometimes you need to count an empty set as part of the population when computing an average.

This is easier to explain with an example that was posted on CompuServe. A fish and game warden is sampling different bodies of water for fish populations. Each sample falls into one or more groups (muddy bottoms, clear water, still water, and so on) and she is trying to find the average of something that is not there. This is neither quite as strange as it first sounds, nor quite as simple, either. She is collecting sample data on fish in a table like this:

```
CREATE TABLE Samples
(sample_id INTEGER NOT NULL,
 fish CHAR(20) NOT NULL,
 found_cnt INTEGER NOT NULL,
 PRIMARY KEY (sample_id, fish));

CREATE TABLE SampleGroups
(group_id INTEGER NOT NULL,
 sample_id INTEGER NOT NULL,
 PRIMARY KEY (group_id, sample_id);
```

Assume some of the data looks like this:

```
Samples
sample_id    fish      found_cnt
============================
1           'Seabass'    14
1           'Minnow'     18
2           'Seabass'    19
```

```
SampleGroups
group_id   sample_id
=====================
     1          1
     1          2
     2          2
```

She needs to get the average number of each species of fish in the sample groups. For example, using sample group 1 as shown, which has samples 1 and 2, we could use the parameters `:my_fish = 'Minnow'` and `:my_group = 1` to find the average number of minnows in sample group 1, thus:

```
SELECT fish, AVG(found_cnt)
  FROM Samples
 WHERE sample_id
       IN (SELECT sample_id
             FROM SampleGroups
            WHERE group_id = :my_group)
   AND fish = :my_fish
 GROUP BY fish;
```

But this query will give us an average of 18 minnows, which is wrong. There were no minnows for sample_id = 2, so the average is ((18 + 0)/2) = 9. The other way is to do several steps to get the correct answer—first use a `SELECT` statement to get the number of samples involved, then another `SELECT` to get the sum, and then manually calculate the average.

The obvious answer is to enter a count of zero for each animal under each sample_id, instead of letting it be missing, so you can use the original query. You can create the missing rows with:

```
INSERT INTO Samples
SELECT M1.sample_id, M2.fish, 0
  FROM Samples AS M1, Samples AS M2
 WHERE NOT EXISTS (SELECT *
                     FROM Samples AS M3
                    WHERE M1.sample_id = M3.sample_id
                      AND M2.fish = M3.fish);
```

Unfortunately, it turns out that we have over 100,000 different species of fish and thousands of samples. This trick will fill up more disk space than we have on the machine. The best trick is to use this statement:

```
SELECT fish, SUM(found_cnt)/
       (SELECT COUNT(sample_id)
          FROM SampleGroups
         WHERE group_id = :my_group)
  FROM Samples
 WHERE fish = :my_fish
 GROUP BY fish;
```

This query is using the rule that the average is the sum of values divided by the count of the set. Another way to do this would be to use an OUTER JOIN and preserve all the group IDs, but that would create NULLs for the fish that are not in some of the sample groups, and you would have to handle them.

21.3.2 Averages across Columns

The sum of several columns can be done with COALESCE() function to effectively remove the NULLs by replacing them with zeros:

```
SELECT (COALESCE(c1, 0.0)
        + COALESCE(c2, 0.0)
        + COALESCE(c3, 0.0)) AS c_total
  FROM Foobar;
```

Likewise, the minimum and maximum values of several columns can be done with a CASE expression, or the GREATEST() and LEAST() functions.

Taking an average across several columns is easy if none of the columns are NULL. You simply add the values and divide by the number of columns. However, getting rid of NULLs is a bit harder. The first trick is to count the NULLs:

```
SELECT (COALESCE(c1-c1, 1)
        + COALESCE(c2-c2, 1)
        + COALESCE(c3-c3, 1)) AS null_cnt
  FROM Foobar;
```

The trick is to watch out for a row with all NULLs in it. This could lead to a division by zero error.

```
SELECT CASE WHEN COALESCE(c1, c2, c3) IS NULL
       THEN NULL
       ELSE (COALESCE(c1, 0.0)
             + COALESCE(c2, 0.0)
             + COALESCE(c3, 0.0))
            / (3 - (COALESCE(c1-c1, 1)
                   + COALESCE(c2-c2, 1)
                    + COALESCE(c3-c3, 1))
       END AS hortizonal_avg
  FROM Foobar;
```

21.4 Extrema Functions

The MIN() and MAX() functions are known as extrema functions in mathematics. They assume that the elements of the set have an ordering, so it makes sense to select a first or last element based on its value. SQL provides two simple extrema functions, and you can write queries to generalize these to (n) elements.

21.4.1 Simple Extrema Functions

MAX([ALL | DISTINCT] <value expression>) returns the greatest known value in the <value expression> set. This function will work on character and temporal values, as well as numeric values. An empty set returns an empty result set. Technically, you can write MAX(DISTINCT <value expression>), but it is the same as MAX(<value expression>); this form exists only for completeness, and nobody ever uses it.

MIN([ALL | DISTINCT] <value expression>) returns the smallest known value in the <value expression> set. This function will also work on character and temporal values, as well as numeric values. An empty set returns a NULL. Likewise, MIN(DISTINCT <value expression>) exists, but it is defined only for completeness and nobody ever uses it.

The MAX() for a set of numeric values is the largest. The MAX() for a set of temporal data types is the one closest to 9999-12-31, which is the final data in the ISO-8601 Standard. The MAX() for a set of character strings is the last one in the ascending sort order. Likewise, the MIN() for a set of numeric values is the smallest. The MIN() for a set of temporal data types is the one furthest from 9999-12-31. The MIN() for a set of character strings is the first one in the ascending sort order, but you have to know the collation used.

People have a hard time understanding the MAX() and MIN() aggregate functions when they are applied to temporal data types. They seem to expect the MAX() to return the date closest to the current date. Likewise, if the set has no dates before the current date, they seem to expect the MIN() function to return the date closest to the current date. Human psychology wants to use the current time as an origin point for temporal reasoning.

Consider the predicate "billing_date < (CURRENT_DATE - INTERVAL '90' DAY)" as an example. Most people have to stop and figure out that this is looking for billings that are over 90 days past due. This same thing happens with MIN() and MAX() functions.

SQL also has funny rules about comparing VARCHAR strings, which can cause problems. When two strings are compared for equality, the shortest one is right-padded with blanks; then they are compared position for position. Thus, the strings 'John' and 'John   ' are equal. You will have to check your implementation of SQL to see which string is returned as the MAX() and which as the MIN(), or whether there is any pattern to it at all.

There are some tricks with extrema functions in subqueries that differ from product to product. For example, to find the current employee status in a table of Salary Histories, the obvious query is:

```
SELECT *
  FROM SalaryHistory AS S0
 WHERE S0.change_date
       = (SELECT MAX(S1.change_date)
            FROM SalaryHistory AS S1
           WHERE S0.emp_id = S1.emp_id);
```

But you can also write the query as:

```
SELECT *
  FROM SalaryHistory AS S0
 WHERE NOT EXISTS
       (SELECT *
          FROM SalaryHistory AS S1
         WHERE S0.emp_id = S1.emp_id
           AND S0.change_date < S1.change_date);
```

The correlated subquery with a `MAX()` will be implemented by going to the subquery and building a working table, which is grouped by emp_id. Then for each group you will keep track of the maximum and save it for the final result.

However, the `NOT EXISTS` version will find the first row that meets the criteria and, when found, return `TRUE`. Therefore, the `NOT EXISTS()` predicate might run faster.

21.4.2 Generalized Extrema Functions

This is known as the Top (or Bottom) (*n*) values problem, and it originally appeared in *Explain* magazine; it was submitted by Jim Wankowski of Hawthorne, CA (Wankowski n.d.). You are given a table of Personnel and their salaries. Write a single SQL query that will display the three highest salaries from that table. It is easy to find the maximum salary with the simple query `SELECT MAX(salary) FROM Personnel;` but SQL does not have a maximum function that will return a group of high values from a column. The trouble with this query is that the specification is bad, for several reasons.

1. How do we define "best salary" in terms of an ordering? Is it base pay or does it include commissions? For the rest of this section, assume that we are using a simple table with a column that has the salary for each employee.
2. What if we have three or fewer personnel in the company? Do we report all the personnel we do have? Or do we return a `NULL`, empty result set or error message? This is the equivalent of calling the contest for lack of entries.
3. How do we handle two personnel who tied? Include them all and allow the result set to be bigger than three? Pick an arbitrary subset and exclude someone? Or do we return a `NULL`, empty result set, or error message?

To make these problems more explicit, consider this table:

```
Personnel
emp_name    salary
==================
'Able'     1000.00
'Baker'     900.00
```

```
'Charles'   900.00
'Delta'     800.00
'Eddy'      700.00
'Fred'      700.00
'George'    700.00
```

Able, Baker, and Charles are the three highest paid personnel, but \$1,000.00, \$900.00, and \$800.00 are the three highest salaries. The highest salaries belong to Able, Baker, Charles and Delta—a set with four elements.

The way that most new SQL programmers do this in other SQL products is produce a result with an `ORDER BY` clause, then read the first so many rows from that cursor result. In Standard SQL, cursors have an `ORDER BY` clause but no way to return a fixed number of rows. However, most SQL products have propriety syntax to clip the result set at exactly some number of rows. Oh, yes, did I mention that the whole table has to be sorted, and that this can take some time if the table is large?

The best algorithm for this problem is the Partition algorithm by C. A. R. Hoare. This is the procedure in QuickSort that splits a set of values into three partitions—those greater than a pivot value, those less than the pivot and those values equal to the pivot. The expected run time is only $(2*n)$ operations.

In practice, it is a good idea to start with a pivot at or near the *k*th position you seek, because real data tends to have some ordering already in it. If the file is already in sorted order, this trick will return an answer in one pass. Here is the algorithm in Pascal.

```
CONST
    list_length = { some large number };
    ...
TYPE
    LIST = ARRAY [1...list_length] OF REAL;
    ...
PROCEDURE FindTopK (Kth INTEGER, records : LIST);
VAR pivot, left, right, start, finish: INTEGER;
BEGIN
start := 1;
finish := list_length;
WHILE start < finish
DO BEGIN
```

```
  pivot := records[Kth];
  left := start;
  right := finish;
  REPEAT
       WHILE (records[left] > pivot) DO left := left + 1;
       WHILE (records[right] < pivot) DO right := right - 1;
       IF (left >= right)
       THEN BEGIN  { swap right and left elements }
            Swap (records[left], records[right]);
            left := left + 1;
            right := right - 1;
            END;
   UNTIL (left < right);
   IF (right < Kth) THEN start := left;
   IF (left > Kth) THEN finish := right;
   END;

{ the first k numbers are in positions 1 through kth, in no
particular order except that the kth highest number is in
position kth }
END.
```

The original articles in *Explain* magazine gave several solutions (Murchison n.d.; Wankowski n.d.).

One involved `UNION` operations on nested subqueries. The first result table was the maximum for the whole table; the second result table was the maximum for the table entries less than the first maximum; and so forth. The pattern is extensible. It looked like this:

```
SELECT MAX(salary)
  FROM Personnel
 UNION
SELECT MAX(salary)
  FROM Personnel
 WHERE salary < (SELECT MAX(salary)
                   FROM Personnel)
 UNION
SELECT MAX(salary)
  FROM Personnel
 WHERE salary < (SELECT MAX(salary)
                   FROM Personnel
                  WHERE salary
                       < (SELECT MAX(salary) FROM Personnel));
```

This answer can give you a pretty serious performance problem because of the subquery nesting and the UNION operations. Every UNION will trigger a sort to remove duplicate rows from the results, since salary is not a UNIQUE column.

A special case of the use of the scalar subquery with the MAX() function is finding the last two values in a set to look for a change. This is most often done with date values for time series work. For example, to get the last two reviews for an employee:

```
SELECT :search_name, MAX(P1.review_date), P2.review_date
  FROM Personnel AS P1, Personnel AS P2
 WHERE P1.review_date < P2.review_date
   AND P1.emp_name = :search_name
   AND P2.review_date = (SELECT MAX(review_date) FROM
Personnel)
 GROUP BY P2.review_date;
```

The scalar subquery is not correlated, so it should run pretty fast and be executed only once.

An improvement on the UNION approach was to find the third highest salary with a subquery, then return all the records with salaries that were equal or higher; this would handle ties. It looked like this:

```
SELECT DISTINCT salary
  FROM Personnel
 WHERE salary >=
       (SELECT MAX(salary)
          FROM Personnel
          WHERE salary < (SELECT MAX(salary)
                            FROM Personnel
                           WHERE salary <
                (SELECT MAX(salary) FROM Personnel)));
```

Another answer was to use correlation names and return a single-row result table. This pattern is more easily extensible to larger groups; it also presents the results in sorted order without requiring the use of an ORDER BY clause. The disadvantage of this answer is that it will return a single row, not a column result. That might make it unusable for joining to other queries. It looked like this:

```
SELECT MAX(P1.salary_amt), MAX(P2.salary_amt),
MAX(P3.salary_amt)
  FROM Personnel AS P1, Personnel AS P2, Personnel AS P3
 WHERE P1.salary_amt > P2.salary_amt
   AND P2.salary_amt > P3.salary_amt;
```

This approach will return the three highest salaries.

The best variation on the single row approach is done with the scalar subquery expressions in SQL. The query becomes:

```
SELECT (SELECT MAX (salary)
          FROM Personnel) AS s1,
       (SELECT MAX (salary)
          FROM Personnel
         WHERE salary NOT IN (s1)) AS s2,
       (SELECT MAX (salary)
          FROM Personnel
         WHERE salary NOT IN (s1, s2)) AS s3,
       ...
       (SELECT MAX (salary)
          FROM Personnel
         WHERE salary NOT IN (s1, s2, ...  s[n-1])) AS sn,
  FROM Dummy;
```

In this case, the table Dummy is anything, even an empty table.

There are single column answers based on the fact that SQL is a set-oriented language, so we ought to use a set-oriented specification. We want to get a subset of salary values that has a count of (n), has the greatest value from the original set as an element, and includes all values greater than its least element.

The idea is to take each salary and build a group of other salaries that are greater than or equal to it—this value is the boundary of the subset. The groups with three or fewer rows are what we want to see. The third element of an ordered list is also the maximum or minimum element of a set of three unique elements, depending on the ordering. Think of concentric sets, nested inside each other. This query gives a columnar answer, and the query can be extended to other numbers by changing the constant in the `HAVING` clause.

```
SELECT MIN(P1.salary_amt)    -- the element on the boundary
  FROM Personnel AS P1, -- P2 gives the elements of the subset
```

```
       Personnel AS P2   -- P1 gives the boundary of the subset
 WHERE P1.salary_amt >= P2.salary_amt
 GROUP BY P2.salary_amt
HAVING COUNT(DISTINCT P1.salary_amt) <= 3;
```

This can also be written as:

```
SELECT P1.salary_amt
  FROM Personnel AS P1
 WHERE (SELECT COUNT(*)
          FROM Personnel AS P2
         WHERE P2.salary_amt >= P1.salary_amt) <= 3;
```

However, the correlated subquery might be more expensive than the GROUP BY clause.

If you would like to know how many ties you have for each value, the query can be modified to this:

```
SELECT MIN(P1.salary_amt) AS top,
       COUNT (CASE WHEN P1.salary_amt = P2.salary_amt
                   THEN 1 ELSE NULL END) / 2 AS ties
  FROM Personnel AS P1, Personnel AS P2
 WHERE P1.salary_amt >= P2.salary_amt
 GROUP BY P2.salary_amt
HAVING COUNT(DISTINCT P1.salary_amt) <= 3;
```

If the salary is unique, the ties column will return a zero; otherwise, you will get the number of occurrences of that value on each row of the result table.

Or if you would like to see the ranking next to the employees, here is another version using a GROUP BY:

```
SELECT P1.emp_name,
       SUM (CASE WHEN (P1.salary_amt || P1.emp_name)
                      < (P2.salary_amt || P1.emp_name)
                 THEN 1 ELSE 0 END) + 1 AS rank
  FROM Personnel AS P1, Personnel AS P2
 WHERE P1.emp_name <> P2.emp_name
 GROUP BY P1.emp_name
HAVING (CASE WHEN (P1.salary_amt || P1.emp_name)
                  < (P2.salary_amt || P1.emp_name)
             THEN 1 ELSE 0 END) <= (:n - 1);
```

The concatenation is to make ties in salary different by adding the key to a string conversion. This query assumes automatic data type conversion, but you can use an explicit `CAST()` function. This also assumes that the collation has a particular ordering of digits and letters—the old "ASCII versus EBCDIC" problem. You can use nested `CASE` expressions to get around.

```
SELECT P1.emp_name,
       SUM (CASE WHEN P1.salary_amt < P2.salary_amt THEN 1
                 WHEN P1.salary_amt > P2.salary_amt THEN 0
                 ELSE CASE WHEN P1.emp_name < P2.emp_name
                           THEN 1 ELSE 0 END
            END) + 1 AS rank
 FROM ...
```

Here is another version that will produce the ties on separate lines with the names of the personnel who made the cut. This answer is due to Pierre Boutquin.

```
SELECT P1.emp_name, P1.salary_amt
  FROM Personnel AS P1, Personnel AS P2
 WHERE P1.salary_amt >= P2.salary_amt
 GROUP BY P1.emp_name, P1.salary_amt
HAVING (SELECT COUNT(*) FROM Personnel) - COUNT(*) + 1 <= :n;
```

The idea is to use a little algebra. If we want to find (n of k) things, then the rejected subset of the set is of size (k-n). Using the sample data, we would get this result.

```
Results
name        salary
==================
'Able'     1000.00
'Baker'     900.00
'Charles'   900.00
```

If we add a new employee at $900, we would also get him, but we would not get a new employee at $800 or less. In many ways, this is the most satisfying answer.

Here are two more versions of the solution:

```
SELECT P1.emp_name, P1.salary_amt
  FROM Personnel AS P1, Personnel AS P2
 GROUP BY P1.emp_name, P1.salary_amt
HAVING COUNT(CASE WHEN P1.salary_amt < P2.salary_amt
                  THEN 1
                  ELSE NULL END) + 1 <= :n;

SELECT P1.emp_name, P1.salary_amt
  FROM Personnel AS P1
       LEFT OUTER JOIN
       Personnel AS P2
       ON P1.salary_amt < P2.salary_amt
 GROUP BY P1.emp_name, P1.salary_amt
HAVING COUNT(P2.salary_amt) + 1 <= :n;
```

The subquery is unnecessary and can be eliminated with either of the above solutions.

As an aside, if you were awake during your college set theory course, you will remember that John von Neumann's definition of ordinal numbers is based on nested sets. You can get a lot of ideas for self-joins from set theory theorems. John von Neumann was one of the greatest mathematicians of this century; he was the inventor of the modern stored program computer and Game Theory. Know your nerd heritage!

It should be obvious that any number can replace three in the query. A subtle point is that the predicate "`P1.salary_amt <= P2.salary_amt`" will include the boundary value, and therefore implies that if we have three or fewer personnel, then we still have a result. If you want to call off the competition for lack of a quorum, then change the predicate to "`P1.salary_amt < P2.salary_amt`" instead.

Another way to express the query would be:

```
SELECT Elements.name, Elements.salary_amt
  FROM Personnel AS Elements
 WHERE (SELECT COUNT(*)
          FROM Personnel AS Boundary
         WHERE Elements.salary_amt < Boundary.salary_amt) < 3;
```

Likewise, the `COUNT(*)` and comparisons in the scalar subquery expression can be changed to give slightly different results.

You might want to test each version to see which one runs faster on your particular SQL product. If you want to swap the subquery and the constant for readability, you may do so in SQL, but not in SQL-89.

What if I want to allow ties? Then just change `COUNT()` to a `COUNT(DISTINCT)` function of the `HAVING` clause, thus:

```
SELECT Elements.name, Elements.salary_amt
  FROM Personnel AS Elements, Personnel AS Boundary
 WHERE Elements.salary_amt <= Boundary.salary_amt
 GROUP BY Elements.name, Elements.salary_amt
HAVING COUNT(DISTINCT Boundary.salary_amt) <= 3;
```

This says that I want to count the values of salary, not the salespersons, so that if two or more of the crew hit the same total, I will include them in the report as tied for a particular position. This also means that the results can be more than three rows, because I can have ties. As you can see, it is easy to get a subtle change in the results with just a few simple changes in predicates.

Notice that you can change the comparisons from "<=" to "<" and the "`COUNT(*)`" to "`COUNT(DISTINCT P2.salary_amt)`" to change the specification.

Ken Henderson came up with another version that uses derived tables and scalar subquery expressions in SQL:

```
SELECT P2.salary_amt
  FROM (SELECT (SELECT COUNT(DISTINCT P1.salary_amt)
                  FROM Personnel AS P1
                 WHERE P3.salary_amt >= P1.salary_amt) AS
ranking,
               P3.salary_amt
          FROM Personnel AS P3) AS P2
 WHERE P2.ranking <= 3;
```

You can get other aggregate functions by using this query with the `IN` predicate. Assume that I have a SalaryHistory table from which I wish to determine the average pay for the three most recent pay changes of each employee. I am going to further assume that if you had three or fewer old salaries, you would still want to average the first, second, or third values you have on record.

```
SELECT S0.emp, AVG(S0.last_salary)
  FROM SalaryHistory AS S0
 WHERE S0.change_date
       IN (SELECT P1.change_date
             FROM SalaryHistory AS P1, SalaryHistory AS P2
            WHERE P1.change_date <= P2.change_date
            GROUP BY P1.change_date
           HAVING COUNT(*) <= 3)
 GROUP BY S0.emp_nbr;
```

21.4.3 Multiple Criteria Extrema Functions

Since the generalized extrema functions are based on sorting the data, it stands to reason that you could further generalize them to use multiple columns in a table. This can be done by changing the `WHERE` search condition. For example, to locate the top (*n*) tall and heavy employees for the basketball team, we could write:

```
SELECT P1.emp_id
  FROM Personnel AS P1, Personnel AS P2
 WHERE P2.height >= P1.height -- major sort term
    OR (P2.height = P1.height -- next sort term
        AND P2.weight >= P1.weight)
 GROUP BY P1.emp_id
HAVING COUNT(*) <= :n;
```

Procedural programmers will recognize this predicate, because it is what they used to write to do a sort on more than one field in a file system. Now it is very important to look at the predicates at each level of nesting to be sure that you have the right theta operator. The ordering of the predicates is also critical—there is a difference between ordering by height within weight or by weight within height.

One improvement would be to use row comparisons:

```
SELECT P1.emp_id
  FROM Personnel AS P1, Personnel AS P2
 WHERE (P2.height, P2.weight) <= (P1.height, P1.weight)
 GROUP BY P1.emp_id
HAVING COUNT(*) <= 4;
```

The down side of this approach is that you cannot easily mix ascending and descending comparisons in the same comparison predicate. The trick is to make numeric columns negative to reverse the sense of the theta operator.

Before you attempt it, here is the scalar subquery version of the multiple extrema problems:

```
SELECT
  (SELECT MAX(P0.height)
     FROM Personnel AS P0
    WHERE P0.weight = (SELECT MAX(weight)
                         FROM Personnel AS P1)) AS s1,
  (SELECT MAX(P0.height)
     FROM Personnel AS P0
    WHERE height NOT IN (s1)
      AND P0.weight = (SELECT MAX(weight)
                         FROM Personnel AS P1
                        WHERE height NOT IN (s1))) AS s2,
  (SELECT MAX(P0.height)
     FROM Personnel AS P0
    WHERE height NOT IN (s1, s2)
      AND P0.weight = (SELECT MAX(weight)
                         FROM Personnel AS P1
                        WHERE height NOT IN (s1, s2))) AS s3
 FROM Dummy;
```

Again, multiple criteria and their ordering would be expressed as multiple levels of subquery nesting. This picks the tallest people and decides ties with the greatest weight within that subset of personnel. While this looks awful and is hard to read, it does run fairly fast, because the predicates are repeated and can be factored out by the optimizer.

Another form of multiple criteria is finding the generalized extrema functions within groupings; for example, finding the top three salaries in each department. Adding the grouping constraints to the subquery expressions gives us an answer.

```
SELECT dept_nbr, salary_amt
  FROM Personnel AS P1
 WHERE (SELECT COUNT(*)
          FROM Personnel AS P2
         WHERE P2.dept_nbr = P1.dept_nbr
           AND P2.salary_amt < P1.salary_amt) < :n;
```

or:

```
SELECT P2.dept_nbr, MIN(P1.salary_amt)
  FROM Personnel AS P1, Personnel AS P2
 WHERE P1.dept_nbr = P2.dept_nbr
   AND P1.salary_amt >= P2.salary_amt
 GROUP BY P2.dept_nbr, P2.salary_amt
HAVING COUNT(DISTINCT P1.salary_amt) <= 3;
```

21.4.4 GREATEST() and LEAST() Functions

Oracle has a proprietary pair of functions that return greatest and least values, respectively—a sort of "horizontal" `MAX()` and `MIN()`. The syntax is `GREATEST (<list of values>)` and `LEAST (<list of values>)`. Awkwardly, DB2 allows `MIN` and `MAX` as synonyms for `LEAST` and `GREATEST`.

If you have `NULL`s, then you have to decide if they sort high or low, if they will be excluded or will propagate the `NULL`, so that you can define this function several ways.

If you don't have `NULL`s in the data:

```
CASE WHEN col1 > col2
  THEN col1 ELSE col2 END
```

If you want the highest non-**NULL** value:

```
CASE WHEN col1 > col2
  THEN col1 ELSE COALESCE(col2, col1) END
```

If you want to return `NULL` where one of the cols is `NULL`:

```
CASE WHEN col1 > col2 OR col1 IS NULL
     THEN col1 ELSE col2 END
```

But for the rest of this section, let's assume (`a < b`) and `NULL` is high:

```
GREATEST (a, b) = b
GREATEST (a, NULL) = NULL
GREATEST (NULL, b) = NULL
GREATEST (NULL, NULL) = NULL
```

We can write this as:

```
GREATEST(x, y) ::= CASE WHEN (COALESCE (x, y) > COALESCE (y, x))
                        THEN x
                        ELSE y END
```

The rules for `LEAST()` are:

```
LEAST (a, b) = a
LEAST (a, NULL) = a
LEAST (NULL, b) = b
LEAST (NULL, NULL) = NULL
```

This is written:

```
LEAST(x, y) ::= CASE WHEN (COALESCE (x, y) <= COALESCE (y, x))
                     THEN COALESCE (x, y)
                     ELSE COALESCE (y, x) END
```

This can be done in Standard SQL, but takes a little bit of work. Let's assume that we have a table that holds the scores for a player in a series of five games and we want to get his best score from all five games.

```
CREATE TABLE Games
(player CHAR(10) NOT NULL PRIMARY KEY,
 score_1 INTEGER NOT NULL DEFAULT 0,
 score_2 INTEGER NOT NULL DEFAULT 0,
 score_3 INTEGER NOT NULL DEFAULT 0,
 score_4 INTEGER NOT NULL DEFAULT 0,
 score_5 INTEGER NOT NULL DEFAULT 0);
```

and we want to find the `GREATEST (score_1, score_2, score_3, score_4, score_5)`.

```
SELECT player, MAX(CASE X.seq_nbr
                   WHEN 1 THEN score_1
       WHEN 2 THEN score_2
             WHEN 3 THEN score_3
                   WHEN 4 THEN score_4
                   WHEN 5 THEN score_5
                   ELSE NULL END) AS best_score
```

```
  FROM Games
       CROSS JOIN
       (VALUES (1), (2), (3), (4), (5)) AS X(seq_nbr)
GROUP BY player;
```

Another approach is to use a pure CASE expression:

```
CASE
WHEN score_1 <= score_2 AND score_1 <= score_3
     AND score_1 <= score_4 AND score_1 <= score_5
THEN score_1
WHEN score_2 <= score_3 AND score_2 <= score_4
     AND score_2 <= score_5
THEN score_2
WHEN score_3 <= score_4 AND score_3 <= score_5
THEN score_3
WHEN score_4 <= score_5
THEN score_4
ELSE score_5
END
```

A final trick is to use a bit of algebra. You can define:

```
GREATEST(a, b) ::= (a + b + ABS(a - b)) / 2
LEAST(a, b) ::= (a + b - ABS(a - b)) / 2
```

Then iterate on it as a recurrence relation on numeric values. For example, for three items, you can use GREATEST (a, GREATEST(b, c)), which expands to:

```
((a + b) + ABS(a - b)
   + 2 * c + ABS((a + b) + ABS(a - b)
   - 2 * c))/4
```

You need to watch for possible overflow errors if the numbers are large and NULLs propagate in the math functions. Here is the answer for five scores.

```
(score_1 + score_2 + 2*score_3 + 4*score_4 + 8*score_5
 + ABS(score_1 - score_2) + ABS((score_1 + score_2) +
ABS(score_1 - score_2) - 2*score_3)
```

```
 + ABS(score_1 + score_2 + 2*score_3 - 4*score_4 + ABS(score_1 -
score_2) + ABS((score_1 + score_2 - 2*score_3) + ABS(score_1 -
score_2)))
 + ABS(score_1 + score_2 + 2*score_3 + 4*score_4 - 8*score_5
 + ABS(score_1 - score_2) + ABS((score_1 + score_2) +
ABS(score_1 - score_2) - 2*score_3)
 + ABS(score_1 + score_2 + 2*score_3 - 4*score_4 + ABS(score_1 -
score_2) + ABS((score_1 + score_2 - 2*score_3) + ABS(score_1 -
score_2))) )) / 16
```

21.5 The LIST() Aggregate Function

The `LIST([ DISTINCT] <string expression>)` is part of Sybase's SQL Anywhere (formerly WATCOM SQL). It is the only aggregate function to work on character strings. It takes a column of strings, removes the `NULL`s and merges them into a single result string with commas between each of the original strings. The `DISTINCT` option removes duplicates as well as `NULL`s before concatenating the strings. This function is a generalized version of concatenation, just as `SUM()` is a generalized version of addition.

MySQL 4.1 extended this function into the `GROUP_CONCAT()` function, which does the same thing but adds options for `ORDER BY` and `SEPARATOR`.

This is handy when you use SQL to write SQL queries. As one simple example, you can apply it against the schema tables and obtain the names of all the columns in a table, then use that list to expand a `SELECT *` into the current column list.

One nonproprietary way of doing this query is with scalar subquery expressions. Assume we have these two tables:

```
CREATE TABLE People
(person_id INTEGER NOT NULL PRIMARY KEY,
 name CHAR(10) NOT NULL);

 INSERT INTO People
 VALUES (1, 'John'), (2, 'Mary'), (3, 'Fred'), (4, 'Jane');

CREATE TABLE Clothes
(person_id INTEGER NOT NULL,
 seq_nbr INTEGER NOT NULL,
 item_name CHAR(10) NOT NULL,
 worn_flag CHAR(1) NOT NULL
```

```
     CONSTRAINT worn_flag_yes_no
     CHECK (worn_flag IN ('Y', 'N')),
PRIMARY KEY (id, seq_nbr));

INSERT INTO Clothes
VALUES (1, 1, 'Hat', 'Y'),
       (1, 2, 'Coat', 'N'),
       (1, 3, 'Glove', 'Y'),
       (2, 1, 'Hat', 'Y'),
       (2, 2, 'Coat', 'Y'),
       (3, 1, 'Shoes', 'N'),
       (4, 1, 'Pants', 'N'),
       (4, 2, 'Socks', 'Y');
```

Using the `LIST()` function, we could get an output of the outfits of the people with the simple query:

```
SELECT P0.person_id, P0.person_name, LIST(item_name) AS fashion
  FROM People AS P0, Clothes AS C0
 WHERE P0.person_id = C0.clothes_id
  AND C0.worn_flag = 'Y'
 GROUP BY P0.person_id, P0.person_name;
```

```
Result
id  name    fashion
========================
 1  'John'  'Hat, Glove'
 2  'Mary'  'Hat, Coat'
 4  'Jane'  'Socks'
```

21.5.1 The LIST() Function with a Procedure

To do this without an aggregate function, you must first know the highest sequence number, so you can create the query. In this case, the query is a simple "`SELECT MAX(seq_nbr) FROM Clothes`" statement, but you might have to use a `COUNT(*)` for other tables.

```
SELECT DISTINCT P0.person_id, P0.person_name,
   SUBSTRING ((SELECT CASE WHEN C1.worn_flag = 'Y'
                      THEN (', ' || item_name) ELSE '' END
            FROM Clothes AS C1
           WHERE C1.clothes_id = C0.clothes_id
```

```
          AND C1.seq_nbr = 1)  ||
     (SELECT CASE WHEN C2.worn_flag = 'Y'
                  THEN (', ' || item_name) ELSE '' END
         FROM Clothes AS C2
        WHERE C2.id = C0.clothes_id
          AND C2.seq_nbr = 2) ||
     (SELECT CASE WHEN C3.worn_flag = 'Y'
                  THEN (', ' || item_name) ELSE '' END
         FROM Clothes AS C3
        WHERE C3.clothes_id = C0.clothes_id
          AND C3.seq_nbr = 3) FROM 3) AS list
  FROM People AS P0, Clothes AS C0
 WHERE P0.person_id = C0.clothes_id;
```

```
id name       list
============================
1 John        Hat, Glove
2 Mary        Hat, Coat
3 Fred
4 Jane        Socks
```

Again, the CASE expression on worn_flag can be replaced with an IS NULL to replace NULLs with an empty string. If you don't want to see that Fred is naked—has an empty string of clothing—then change the outermost WHERE clause to read:

```
   ...
 WHERE P0.person_id = C0.clothes_id AND C0.worn_flag = 'Y';
```

Since you don't want to see a leading comma, remember to TRIM() it off or to use the SUBSTRING() function to remove the first two characters. I opted for the SUBSTRING(), because the TRIM() function requires a scan of the string.

21.5.2 The LIST() Function by Crosstabs

Carl Federl used this to get a similar result:

```
CREATE TABLE Crosstabs
(seq_nbr INTEGER NOT NULL PRIMARY KEY,
 seq_nbr_1 INTEGER NOT NULL,
 seq_nbr_2 INTEGER NOT NULL,
```

```
 seq_nbr_3 INTEGER NOT NULL,
 seq_nbr_4 INTEGER NOT NULL,
 seq_nbr_5 INTEGER NOT NULL);

INSERT INTO Crosstabs
VALUES (1, 1, 0, 0, 0, 0),
       (2, 0, 1, 0, 0, 0),
       (3, 0, 0, 1, 0, 0),
       (4, 0, 0, 0, 1, 0),
       (5, 0, 0, 0, 0, 1);

SELECT Clothes.id,
    TRIM (MAX(SUBSTRING(item_name FROM 1 FOR seq_nbr_1 * 10))
 || ' ' ||  MAX(SUBSTRING(item_name FROM 1 FOR seq_nbr_2 * 10))
 || ' ' ||  MAX(SUBSTRING(item_name FROM 1 FOR seq_nbr_3 * 10))
 || ' ' ||  MAX(SUBSTRING(item_name FROM 1 FOR seq_nbr_4 * 10))
 || ' ' ||  MAX(SUBSTRING(item_name FROM 1 FOR seq_nbr_5 * 10)))
  FROM Clothes, Crosstabs
 WHERE Clothes.seq_nbr = Crosstabs.seq_nbr
   AND Clothes.worn_flag = 'Y'
 GROUP BY Clothes.id;
```

21.6 The PRD() Aggregate Function

Bob McGowan sent me a message on CompuServe asking for help with a problem. His client, a financial institution, tracks investment performance with a table something like this:

```
CREATE TABLE Performance
(portfolio_id CHAR(7) NOT NULL,
 execute_date DATE NOT NULL,
 rate_of_return DECIMAL(13,7) NOT NULL);
```

To calculate a rate of return over a date range, you use the formula:

```
 (1 + rate_of_return [day_1])
* (1 + rate_of_return [day_2])
* (1 + rate_of_return [day_3])
* (1 + rate_of_return [day_4])
 ...
* (1 + rate_of_return [day_N])
```

How would you construct a query that would return one row for each portfolio's return over the date range? What Mr. McGowan really wants is an aggregate function in the `SELECT` clause to return a columnar product, like the `SUM()` returns a columnar total.

If you were a math major, you would write these functions as capital Sigma (Σ) for summation and capital Pi for product (π). If such an aggregate function existed in SQL, the syntax for it would look something like:

```
PRD ([DISTINCT] <expression>)
```

While I am not sure that there is any use for the `DISTINCT` option, the new aggregate function would let us write his problem simply as:

```
SELECT portfolio_id, PRD(1.00 + rate_of_return)
  FROM Performance
 WHERE execute_date BETWEEN start_date AND end_date
 GROUP BY portfolio_id;
```

21.6.1 PRD() Function by Expressions

There is a trick to doing this, but you need a second table that looks like this and covers a period of five days:

```
CREATE TABLE BigPi
(execute_date DATE NOT NULL,
 day_1 INTEGER NOT NULL,
 day_2 INTEGER NOT NULL,
 day_3 INTEGER NOT NULL,
 day_4 INTEGER NOT NULL,
 day_5 INTEGER NOT NULL);
```

Let's assume we wanted to look at January 6 to 10, so we need to update the execute_date column to that range, thus:

```
INSERT INTO BigPi
VALUES ('2006-01-06', 1, 0, 0, 0, 0),
       ('2006-01-07', 0, 1, 0, 0, 0),
       ('2006-01-08', 0, 0, 1, 0, 0),
       ('2006-01-09', 0, 0, 0, 1, 0),
       ('2006-01-10', 0, 0, 0, 0, 1);
```

The idea is that there is a one in the column when BigPi.execute_date is equal to the *n*th date in the range, and a zero otherwise. The query for this problem is:

```
SELECT portfolio_id,
       (SUM((1.00 + P1.rate_of_return) * M1.day_1) *
        SUM((1.00 + P1.rate_of_return) * M1.day_2) *
        SUM((1.00 + P1.rate_of_return) * M1.day_3) *
        SUM((1.00 + P1.rate_of_return) * M1.day_4) *
        SUM((1.00 + P1.rate_of_return) * M1.day_5)) AS product
  FROM Performance AS P1, BigPi AS M1
 WHERE M1.execute_date = P1.execute_date
   AND P1.execute_date BETWEEN '2006-01-06' AND '2006-01-10'
 GROUP BY portfolio_id;
```

If anyone is missing a rate_of_return entry on a date in that range, his or her product will be zero. That might be fine, but if you needed to get a NULL when you have missing data, then replace each SUM() expression with a CASE expression like this:

```
CASE WHEN SUM((1.00 + P1.rate_of_return) * M1.day_N) = 0.00

     THEN CAST (NULL AS DECIMAL(6, 4))
     ELSE SUM((1.00 + P1.rate_of_return) * M1.day_N)
END
```

Alternately, if your SQL has the full SQL set of expressions, use this version:

```
COALESCE (SUM((1.00 + P1.rate_of_return) * M1.day_N), 0.00)
```

21.6.2 The PRD() Aggregate Function by Logarithms

Roy Harvey, another SQL guru who answered questions on CompuServe, found a different solution—one that could only come from someone old enough to remember slide rules and multiplication by adding logs. The nice part of this solution is that you can also use the DISTINCT option in the SUM() function.

But there are a lot of warnings about this approach. Some older SQL implementation might have trouble with using an aggregate function result as a parameter. This has always been part of the standard, but some SQL products use very different mechanisms for the aggregate functions.

Another, more fundamental problem is that a log of zero or less is undefined, so your SQL might return a `NULL` or an error message. You will also see some SQL products that use `LN()` for the natural log and `LOG10()` for the logarithm base ten, and some SQLs that use `LOG(<parameter>, <base>)` for a general logarithm function.

Given all those warnings, the expression for the product of a column from logarithm and exponential functions is:

```
SELECT ((EXP (SUM (LN (CASE WHEN nbr = 0.00
                            THEN CAST (NULL AS FLOAT)
                            ELSE ABS(nbr) END))))
  * (CASE WHEN MIN (ABS (nbr)) = 0.00
          THEN 0.00
          ELSE 1.00 END)
  * (CASE WHEN MOD (SUM (CASE WHEN SIGN(nbr) = -1
                              THEN 1
                              ELSE 0 END), 2) = 1
          THEN -1.00
          ELSE 1.00 END) AS big_pi
 FROM NumberTable;
```

The nice part of this is that you can also use the `SUM (DISTINCT <expression>)` option to get the equivalent of `PRD (DISTINCT <expression>)`.

You should watch the data type of the column involved and use either integer 0 and 1 or decimal 0.00 and 1.00 as is appropriate in the `CASE` statements. It is worth studying the three `CASE` expressions that make up the terms of the Prod calculation.

The first `CASE` expression is to ensure that all zeros and negative numbers are converted to a nonnegative or `NULL` for the `SUM()` function, just in case your SQL raises an exception.

The second `CASE` expression will return zero as the answer if there is a zero in the nbr column of any selected row. The `MIN(ABS(nbr))` trick is handy for detecting the existence of a zero in a list of both positive and negative numbers with an aggregate function.

The third `CASE` expression will return −1 if there is an odd number of negative numbers in the nbr column. The innermost `CASE` expression uses a `SIGN()` function, which returns + 1 for a positive number, −1 for a negative number and 0 for a zero. The `SUM()` counts the −1 results, then the MOD() functions determines whether the count was odd or even.

I present this version of the query first, because this is how I developed the answer. We can do a much better job with a little algebra and logic:

```
SELECT CASE MIN (SIGN (nbr))
       WHEN 1 THEN EXP (SUM (LN (nbr))) -- all positive numbers
       WHEN 0 THEN 0.00                 -- some zeros
       WHEN -1                          -- some negative numbers
       THEN (EXP (SUM (LN (ABS(nbr))))
             * (CASE WHEN
                    MOD (SUM (ABS (SIGN(nbr)-1/ 2)), 2) = 1
                    THEN -1.00 ELSE 1.00 END))
       ELSE CAST (NULL AS FLOAT) END AS big_pi
 FROM NumberTable;
```

For this solution, you will need to have the logarithm, exponential, mod, and sign functions in your SQL product. They are not standards, but they are very common. You might also have problems with data types. The SIGN() function should return an INTEGER, but might return the same data type as its parameter. The LN() function should cast nbr to FLOAT, but again, beware.

The idea is that there are three special cases—all positive numbers, one or more zeros, and some negative numbers in the set. You can find out what your situation is with a quick test on the SIGN() of the minimum value in the set.

Within the case where you have negative numbers, there are two subcases: (1) an even number of negatives, or (2) an odd number of negatives. You then need to apply some high school algebra to determine the sign of the final result.

Itzik Ben-Gan had problems implementing this in SQL Server, and these issues are worth passing along in case your SQL product also has them. The query as written returns a domain error in SQL Server. It should not have done so if the result expressions in the CASE expression had been evaluated *after* the conditional flow had performed a short circuit evaluation. Examining the execution plan of the above query, it looks like the optimizer evaluates all of the possible result expressions in a step prior to handling the flow of the CASE expression.

This means that in the expression after WHEN 1 ... the LN() function is also invoked in an intermediate phase for zeros and negative numbers, and in the expression after `WHEN -1 ...` the `LN(ABS())` is also invoked in an intermediate phase for zeros. This explains the domain error.

To handle this, I had to use the `ABS()` and `NULLIF()` functions in the positive numbers when `CLAUSE`, and the `NULLIF()` function in the negative numbers when `CLAUSE`:

```
...
WHEN 1 THEN EXP(SUM(LN(ABS(NULLIF(result, 0.00)))))
```

and

```
...
WHEN -1
THEN EXP(SUM(LN(ABS(NULLIF(result, 0.00)))))
      * CASE ...
```

If you are sure you will have only positive values in the column being computed, then you can use:

```
PRD(<exp>) = EXP(SUM(LN (<exp>)))
```

or:

```
PRD(<exp>) = POWER(CAST (10.00 AS FLOAT), SUM(LOG10(<exp>)))
```

This depends on your vendor functions. This last version assumes that 10.00 would need to be cast as a `FLOAT` to work with `LOG10()`, but you should read the manual to see what the assumed data types are.

As an aside, the book *Bypasses: A Simple Approach to Complexity* (Melzak 1983), is a short mathematical book on the general principle of conjugacy, the method of using a transform and its inverse to reduce the complexity of a calculation.

21.7 Bitwise Aggregate Functions

A bitwise aggregate function is not a recommended practice, since it will destroy First Normal Form (1NF) by overloading a column with a vector whose components have individual meanings. But it is common enough that I have to mention it. Instead of giving each attribute in the data model its own column, bad programmers will assign a meaning to each bit in the binary representation of an `INTEGER` or `SMALLINT`. Some products will actually expose the physical model for the data types and

have proprietary bitwise AND and OR operators. Most products do not implement bitwise aggregate Boolean operators, however. But I feel like a furniture maker who is telling you what are the best rocks with which to drive screws into wood.

To reiterate, an aggregate function must:

1. Drop all the NULLs
2. Drop all redundant duplicates if DISTINCT is in the parameter list
3. Retain all redundant duplicates if ALL or no other keyword is in the parameter list
4. Perform the required calculation on the remaining values in the expression
5. Return a NULL result for an empty set or for a set of all NULLs [which would be empty after application of (1)]

Notice that rules 2 and 3 do not apply to bitwise operators, since a OR a = a, and a AND a = a.

21.7.1 Bitwise OR Aggregate Function

Let's create a simple table that holds the columns of bits as an integer. The CHECK() constraint prevents negative numbers and bit strings of different lengths.

```
CREATE Table Foobar
(bits INTEGER -- nullable for testing
      CHECK(bits BETWEEN 0 AND 15));
```

What we want is a bitwise OR on the bits column.

```
SELECT MAX (CASE WHEN MOD (bits/1, 2) = 1
                      AND bits IS NOT NULL
                 THEN 1 ELSE 0 END)
       + MAX (CASE WHEN MOD (bits/2, 2) = 1
                        AND bits IS NOT NULL
                   THEN 2 ELSE 0 END)
       + MAX (CASE WHEN MOD (bits/4, 2) = 1
                        AND bits IS NOT NULL
                   THEN 4 ELSE 0 END)
```

```
    + MAX (CASE WHEN MOD (bits/8, 2) = 1
                     AND bits IS NOT NULL
               THEN 8 ELSE 0 END)
FROM Foobar;
```

The "bits/1" is redundant, but I used it to show the pattern for the construction of this expression. The hope is that a good optimizer will the use of a CASE expression inside the MAX() function. This immediately tells the optimizer that the set of possible answers is limited (in these expressions, limited to {0, 2^*n*}), so that once any row has returned the highest possible value, the evaluation can stop. The bad news with this expression is that a NULL in the bits column will return 0000. This can be corrected by adding:

```
SIGN(MAX(bits)) * (<bitwise OR expression>)
```

If Foobar is all zeros, then the SIGN() function will return a zero and an optimizer can spot this shortcut evaluation. If the table is empty, or the bits column is all NULLs, the SIGN() will get a NULL from MAX(bits) and propagate it. If bits are declared NOT NULL, then do not use this factor.

21.7.2 Bitwise AND Aggregate Function

This code is obvious from the previous discussion. The MAX() now becomes a MIN(), since a single zero can set a bit in the aggregate to zero. The trick with the SIGN() function stays the same as before.

```
SELECT SIGN(MAX(bits)) *
       MIN (CASE WHEN MOD (bits/1, 2) = 1
                      AND bits IS NOT NULL
                 THEN 1 ELSE 0 END)
     + MIN (CASE WHEN MOD (bits/2, 2) = 1
                      AND bits IS NOT NULL
                 THEN 2 ELSE 0 END)
     + MIN (CASE WHEN MOD (bits/4, 2) = 1
                      AND bits IS NOT NULL
                 THEN 4 ELSE 0 END)
     + MIN (CASE WHEN MOD (bits/8, 2) = 1
                      AND bits IS NOT NULL
               THEN 8 ELSE 0 END)
FROM Foobar;
```

Auxiliary Tables

AUXILIARY TABLES ARE A way of building functions and lookup tables that would be difficult, if not impossible, to do with the limited computational power of SQL. What SQL is good at is working with tables. Auxiliary tables are not really a part of the data model, but serve as adjuncts to do queries via joins rather than computations.

Auxiliary tables are usually very static and are constructed from an outside data source. Thus they do not require the same constraint checking that dynamic tables do. As a general statement, they need to have a primary key declared so that it will create an index for searching and joining the auxiliary table to other tables in the schema, not to protect the data from redundancy.

The most important auxiliary table is a Calendar, because the Common Era calendar is too irregular for easy computations. Holidays fall on lunar and solar cycles, there are hundreds of fiscal calendars, and so forth. The discussion of Calendar tables will be given in the section on temporal queries. This chapter will examine various kinds of numeric auxiliary tables.

22.1 The Sequence Table

The Sequence table is a simple list of integers from 1 to (*n*) that is used in place of looping constructs in a procedural language. Rather than

incrementing a counter value, we try to work in parallel with a complete set of values.

Unfortunately, SEQUENCE is a reserved word for a proposed construct in Standard SQL that builds a sequence of numbers, but handles them as if they were a list or file rather than a set. The same reserved word is found in Oracle, but not widely used in other products.

This table has the general declaration:

```
CREATE TABLE Sequence
(seq INTEGER NOT NULL PRIMARY KEY
     CONSTRAINT non_negative_nbr
     CHECK (seq > 0)
-- cardinal VARCHAR(25) NOT NULL,
-- ordinal VARCHAR(25) NOT NULL,
 ...
 CONSTRAINT numbers_are_complete
 CHECK ((SELECT COUNT(*) FROM Sequence) =
        (SELECT MAX(seq) FROM Sequence));
```

It includes data such as:

```
seq  cardinal                 ordinal  ...
=========================================
 1    'one'                    'first'
 2    'two'                    'second'
 3    'three'                  'third'
...    ...                      ...
101   'One hundred and one'    'One hundred and first'
...    ...                      ...
```

This table is a list of all the integers from 1 to some value (n). The ordinal and cardinal columns are simply examples of handy things that you might want to do with an integer, such as turn it into English words, which would be difficult in a procedural language or pure SQL.

I have found that is it a bad idea to start with zero, though that seems more natural to computer programmers. The reason for omitting zero is that this auxiliary table is often used to provide row numbering by being CROSS JOINed to another table, and the zero would throw off the one-to-one mapping.

The syntax of the sequence constructor I mentioned at the start of this section looks something like this—each product's syntax will vary, but should have the same parameters:

```
CREATE SEQUENCE <seqname> AS <data type>
START WITH <value>
INCREMENT BY <value>
[MAXVALUE <value>]
[MINALUE <value>]
[[NO] CYCLE];
```

To get a value from it, this expression is used wherever it is a legal data type:

```
NEXT VALUE FOR <seq name>
```

If a sequence needs to be reset, you can use this statement to change the optional clauses or to restart the cycle:

```
ALTER SEQUENCE <seq name>
RESTART WITH <value>; -- begin over
```

To remove the sequence, use the obvious statement:

```
DROP SEQUENCE <seq name>;
```

Even when this feature becomes widely available, it should be avoided. It is a nonrelational extension that behaves like a sequential file or procedural function, rather than in a set-oriented manner. You can currently find it in Oracle, Postgres, and Mimer products.

22.1.1 Enumerating a List

Given a table in a data warehouse for a report that uses the monthly sales data shown as an attribute (the monthly amounts have to be NULL-able to hold missing values for the future):

```
CREATE TABLE AnnualSales1
(salesman CHAR(15) NOT NULL PRIMARY KEY,
 jan DECIMAL(5,2),
 feb DECIMAL(5,2),
```

```
mar DECIMAL(5,2),
apr DECIMAL(5,2),
may DECIMAL(5,2),
jun DECIMAL(5,2),
jul DECIMAL(5,2),
aug DECIMAL(5,2),
sep DECIMAL(5,2),
oct DECIMAL(5,2),
nov DECIMAL(5,2),
"dec" DECIMAL(5,2)); -- DEC is a reserved word
```

The goal is to "flatten" it out so that it looks like this:

```
CREATE TABLE AnnualSales2
(salesman_name CHAR(15) NOT NULL PRIMARY KEY,
 sales_month CHAR(3) NOT NULL
       CONSTRAINT valid_month_code
       CHECK (sales_month
              IN ('Jan', 'Feb', 'Mar', 'Apr',
                  'May', 'Jun', 'Jul', 'Aug',
                  'Sep', 'Oct', 'Nov', 'Dec'),
 sales_amt DECIMAL(5, 2) NOT NULL,
 PRIMARY KEY(salesman, sales_month));
```

The trick is to build a `VIEW` of the original table with a number beside each month.

```
CREATE VIEW NumberedSales
AS SELECT salesman,
          1 AS M01, jan,
          2 AS M02, feb,
          3 AS M03, mar,
          4 AS M04, apr,
          5 AS M05, may,
          6 AS M06, jun,
          7 AS M07, jul,
          8 AS M08, aug,
          9 AS M09, sep,
         10 AS M10, oct,
         11 AS M11, nov,
         12 AS M12, "dec" -- reserved word
   FROM AnnualSales1;
```

Now you can use the auxiliary table of sequential numbers, or you can use a VALUES table constructor to build one. The flattened VIEW is:

```
CREATE VIEW AnnualSales2 (salesman, sales_month, sales_amt)
AS SELECT S1.salesman_name,
       (CASE WHEN A.nbr = M01 THEN 'Jan'
             WHEN A.nbr = M02 THEN 'Feb'
             WHEN A.nbr = M03 THEN 'Mar'
             WHEN A.nbr = M04 THEN 'Apr'
             WHEN A.nbr = M05 THEN 'May'
             WHEN A.nbr = M06 THEN 'Jun'
             WHEN A.nbr = M07 THEN 'Jul'
             WHEN A.nbr = M08 THEN 'Aug'
             WHEN A.nbr = M09 THEN 'Sep'
             WHEN A.nbr = M10 THEN 'Oct'
             WHEN A.nbr = M11 THEN 'Nov'
             WHEN A.nbr = M12 THEN 'Dec'
             ELSE NULL END),
       (CASE WHEN A.nbr = M01 THEN jan
             WHEN A.nbr = M02 THEN feb
             WHEN A.nbr = M03 THEN mar
             WHEN A.nbr = M04 THEN apr
             WHEN A.nbr = M05 THEN may
             WHEN A.nbr = M06 THEN jun
             WHEN A.nbr = M07 THEN jul
             WHEN A.nbr = M08 THEN aug
             WHEN A.nbr = M09 THEN sep
             WHEN A.nbr = M10 THEN oct
             WHEN A.nbr = M11 THEN nov
             WHEN A.nbr = M12 THEN "dec" -- reserved word
             ELSE NULL END)
  FROM NumberedSales AS S1
       CROSS JOIN
       (SELECT seq FROM Sequence WHERE seq <= 12) AS A(month_nbr);
```

If your SQL product has derived tables, this can be written as a single VIEW query.

22.1.2 Mapping a Sequence into a Cycle

It is sometimes handy to map a sequence of numbers to a cycle. The general formula is:

```
SELECT seq, MOD (((seq + (:n-1))/ :n), :n)
  FROM Sequence;
```

As an example, consider the following problem in which we want to display an output with what is called "snaking" in a report. Each ID has several descriptions, and we want to see them in cycles of four (n=4); when a department has more than four job descriptions, we want to start a new row with an incremented position for each subset of four or fewer job descriptions.

```
CREATE TABLE Company
(dept_nbr INTEGER NOT NULL,
 job_nbr INTEGER NOT NULL, -- sequence within department
 job_descr CHAR(6) NOT NULL,
 PRIMARY KEY (dept_nbr, job_nbr));

INSERT INTO Company
VALUES (1, 1, 'desc1'),
       (1, 2, 'desc2'),
       (1, 3, 'desc3');

INSERT INTO Company
VALUES (2, 1, 'desc4'),
       (2, 2, 'desc5'),
       (2, 3, 'desc6'),
       (2, 4, 'desc7'),
       (2, 5, 'desc8'),
       (2, 6, 'desc9');

INSERT INTO Company
VALUES (3, 1, 'desc10'),
       (3, 2, 'desc11'),
       (3, 3, 'desc12');
```

I am going to use a `VIEW` rather than a derived table to make the logic in the intermediate step easier to see.

```
CREATE VIEW Foo2 (dept_nbr, row_grp, d1, d2, d3, d4)
AS
SELECT dept_nbr, (MOD((job_nbr + 3)/4), 4),
       MAX(CASE WHEN MOD(job_nbr, 4) = 1
```

```
                THEN job_descr ELSE '          ' END) AS d1,
      MAX(CASE WHEN MOD(job_nbr, 4) = 2
                THEN job_descr ELSE '          ' END) AS d2,
      MAX(CASE WHEN MOD(job_nbr, 4) = 3
                THEN job_descr ELSE '          ' END) AS d3,
      MAX(CASE WHEN MOD(job_nbr, 4) = 0
                THEN job_descr ELSE '          ' END) AS d4
  FROM Company AS F1
 GROUP BY dept_nbr, job_nbr;

SELECT dept_nbr, row_grp,
       MAX(d1) AS d1, MAX(d2) AS d2, MAX(d3) AS d3, MAX(d4) AS d4
  FROM Foo2
 GROUP BY dept_nbr, row_grp
 ORDER BY dept_nbr, row_grp;

Results
dept_nbr row_grp   d1      d2      d3      d4
===============================================
     1       1     desc1   desc2   desc3
     2       1     desc4   desc5   desc6   desc7
     2       2     desc8   desc9
     3       1     desc10  desc11  desc12
```

This is bad coding practice. Display is a function of the front end, and should not be done in the database.

22.1.3 Replacing an Iterative Loop

While is not recommended as a technique, and it will vary from SQL dialect to dialect, replacing an iterative loop is a good exercise in learning to think in sets. You are given a quoted string made up of integers separated by commas, and your goal is to break each of the integers out as a row in a table.

The obvious approach is to write procedural code that will loop over the input string and cut off all characters from the beginning up to, but not including, the first comma, cast the substring as an integer and then iterate through the rest of the string.

```
CREATE PROCEDURE ParseList (IN inputstring VARCHAR(1000))
LANGUAGE SQL
BEGIN DECLARE i INTEGER;
```

```
SET i = 1;  -- iteration control variable
-- add sentinel comma to end of input string
SET inputstring = TRIM (BOTH '' FROM inputstring || ', ');
WHILE i < CHAR_LENGTH(inputstring)
   DO WHILE SUBSTRING(inputstring, i, 1) <> ', '
      DO SET i = i + 1;
      END WHILE;
 SET outputstring = SUBSTRING(inputstring, 1, i-1);
 INSERT INTO Outputs VALUES (CAST (outputstring AS INTEGER));
 SET inputstring = SUBSTRING(inputstring, i+1);
 END WHILE;
END;
```

Alternately, you can do this with an auxiliary table of sequential numbers and this strange-looking query written in Core SQL-99.

```
CREATE PROCEDURE ParseList (IN inputstring VARCHAR(1000))
LANGUAGE SQL
INSERT INTO ParmList (parmeter_position, param)
 SELECT S1.i,
        CAST (SUBSTRING ((', ' || inputstring ||', ')
                   FROM (S1.i + 1)
                    FOR (S2.i - S1.i - 1))
              AS INTEGER)
   FROM Sequence AS S1,
        Sequence AS S2
  WHERE SUBSTRING((', ' || inputstring ||', ') FROM S1.i FOR 1) = ', '
    AND SUBSTRING((', ' || inputstring ||', ') FROM S2.i FOR 1) = ', '
    AND S2.i
    = (SELECT MIN(S3.i)
             FROM Sequence AS S3
            WHERE S1.i < S3.i
              AND SUBSTRING((', ' || inputstring ||', ')
                       FROM S3.i
                        FOR 1) = ', ')
    AND S1.i < CHAR_LENGTH (inputstring+ 1)
    AND S2.i < CHAR_LENGTH (inputstring+ 2);
```

The trick here is to concatenate commas on the left and right sides of the input string. To be honest, you would probably want to trim blanks and perhaps do other tests on the string, such as seeing that

`LOWER(:instring) = UPPER(:instring)` to avoid alphabetic characters and so forth. That edited result string would be kept in a local variable and used in the `INSERT INTO` statement.

The integer substrings are located between the *i-th* and ((*i*+1)-th comma pairs. In effect, the sequence table replaces the loop counter. The sequence table has to have enough numbers to cover the entire string, but unless you really like to type in long parameter lists, this should not be a problem. The last two predicates are to avoid a Cartesian product with the sequence table.

22.2 Lookup Auxiliary Tables

In the old days, when engineers used slide rules, other people went to the back of their math and financial book to use printed tables of functions. Here you could find trigonometry, or compound interest, or statistical functions. Today, you would more likely calculate the function, because computing power is so cheap. Pocket calculators that sold for hundreds of dollars in the 1960s are now on spikes in the checkout line at office supply stores.

In the days of keypunch data entry, there would be loose-leaf notebooks of the encoding schemes to use sitting next to the incoming paper forms. Today, you would more likely see a WIMP (Windows, Icons, Menus, and Pulldowns) interface.

While the physical mechanisms have changed, the idea of building a table (in the nonrelational sense) is still valid. An auxiliary table holds a static or relatively static set of data. The users do not change the data. Updating one of these tables is a job for the DBA or the data repository administrator, if your shop is that sophisticated. One of the problems with even a simple lookup table change was that the existing data often had to be changed to the new encoding scheme, and this required administrative privileges.

The primary key of an auxiliary table is never an identifier; an identifier is unique in the schema and refers to one entity anywhere it appears. Lookup tables work with values and are not entities by definition. Monstrosities likes "value_id" are absurd.

This is a short list of postfixes that can be used as the name of the key column in auxiliary tables. There is a more complete list of postfixes in my book on *SQL Programming Style* (ISBN: 0-12-088797-5).

- *"_nbr" or "_num"* This is a tag number, a string of digits that names something. Do not use "_no" because it looks like the Boolean yes/

no value. I prefer "nbr" to "num," since it is used as a common abbreviation in several European languages.

- *"_name" or "_nm"* This is an alphabetic name and it explains itself. It is also called a nominal scale.
- *"_code" or "_cd"* A code is a standard maintained by a trusted source, usually outside of the enterprise. For example, the ZIP code is maintained by the United States Postal Service. A code is well understood in its context, so you might not have to translate it for humans.
- *"_cat"* Category is an encoding with an external source that has very distinct groups of entities. There should be strong formal criteria for establishing the category. The classification of Kingdom in biology is an example.
- *"_class"* This is an internal encoding without an external source that reflects a subclassification of the entity. There should be strong formal criteria for the classification. The classification of plants in biology is an example.
- *"_type"* This is an encoding that has a common meaning both internally and externally. A type is usually less formal than a class and might overlap. For example a driver's license might be motorcycle, automobile, taxi, truck, and so forth.

The differences among type, class, and category are an increasing strength of the algorithm for assigning the type, class, or category.

A category is very distinct; you will not often have to guess if something is "animal, vegetable, or mineral" to put it in one of those categories.

A class is a set of things that have some commonality; there are rules for classifying an animal as a mammal or a reptile. You may have some cases where it is harder to apply the rules, such as the egg-laying mammal in Australia, but the exceptions tend to become their own classification—monotremes, in this example.

A type is the weakest of the three, and it might call for a judgment. For example, in some states a three-wheeled motorcycle is licensed as a motorcycle. In other states, it is licensed as an automobile. And in some states, it is licensed as an automobile only if it has a reverse gear.

The three terms are often mixed in actual usage. Stick with the industry standard, even if violates the definitions given above.

- *"_status"* An internal encoding that reflects a state of being which can be the result of many factors. For example, ìcredit_statusî might be computed from several sources.
- *"_addr" or "_loc"* An address or location for an entity. There can be a subtle difference between an address and location.
- *"_date" or "_dt"* This represents the date or temporal dimension. More specifically, it is the date *of* something—employment, birth, termination, and so forth. There is no such column name as just a date by itself.

22.2.1 Simple Translation Auxiliary Tables

The most common form of lookup has two columns: one for the value to be looked up and one for the translation of that value into something the user needs. A simple example would be the two-letter ISO-3166 country codes in a table like this:

```
CREATE TABLE CountryCodes
(country_code CHAR(2) NOT NULL PRIMARY KEY, -- iso-3166
 country_name VARCHAR(20) NOT NULL);
```

You can add a unique constraint on the descriptive column, but most programmers do not bother, because these tables do not change much. When they do change, it is done with data provided by a trusted source. This makes OLTP database programmers a bit uneasy, but data warehouse database programmers understand it.

22.2.2 Multiple Translation Auxiliary Tables

While we want the encoding value to stay the same, we often need to have multiple translations. There can be a short description, a long description, or just a different one, depending on who was looking at the data. For example, consider displaying error messages in various languages in a single table:

```
CREATE TABLE ErrorMessages
(err_msg_code CHAR(5) NOT NULL PRIMARY KEY,
 english_err_msg CHAR(25) NOT NULL ...
 french_err_msg NCHAR(25) NOT NULL ...
 ...
 esperanto NCHAR (25) NOT NULL);
```

Yes, adding a new language does require a structure change. However, since the data is static, the convenience of having all the related translations in one place is probably worth it. This inherently forces you to have all the languages for each error code, while a strict First Normal Form (1NF) table does not.

Your first thought is that an application using this table would be full of code such as:

```
SELECT CASE :my_language
       WHEN 'English' THEN english_err
       WHEN 'French' THEN french_err
        ...  END AS err_msg
  FROM ErrorMessages
 WHERE err_msg_code = '42';
```

This is not usually the case. You have another table that finds the language preferences of the `CURRENT_USER` and presents a `VIEW` to him in the language he desires.

You don't invent or add languages very often. However, I do know of one product that was adding Klingon to its error messages. Seriously, it was for a demo at a trade show to show off the internationalization features. ("Unknown error = Die in ignorance!!" It was a user-surly interface instead of user-friendly.)

22.2.3 Multiple Parameter Auxiliary Tables

This type of auxiliary table has two or more parameters that it uses to seek a value. The classic example from college freshman statistics courses is the Student's *t*-Distribution for small samples. The value of (*r*) is the size of the sample minus one, and the percentages are the confidence intervals. Loosely speaking, the Student's *t*-Distribution is the best guess at the population distribution that we can make without knowing the standard deviation with a certain level of confidence.

r	90%	95%	97.5%	99.5%
1	3.07766	6.31371	12.7062	63.65600
2	1.88562	2.91999	4.30265	9.92482
3	1.63774	2.35336	3.18243	5.84089
4	1.53321	2.13185	2.77644	4.60393
5	1.47588	2.01505	2.57058	4.03212
10	1.37218	1.81246	2.22814	3.16922

```
 30 1.31042  1.69726   2.04227  2.74999
100 1.29007  1.66023   1.98397  2.62589
... 1.28156  1.64487   1.95999  2.57584
```

William Gosset created this statistic in 1908. His employer, Guinness Breweries, required him to publish under a pseudonym, so he chose "Student" and that name stuck.

22.2.4 Range Auxiliary Tables

In a range auxiliary table, there is one parameter, but it must fall inside a range of values. The most common example would be reporting periods or ranges. There is no rule that prevents these ranges from overlapping. For example, "Swimsuit Season" and "BBQ Grill Sale" might have a large number of days in common at a department store. However, it is usually a good idea not to have disjoint ranges.

```
CREATE TABLE ReportPeriods
(period_name CHAR(15) NOT NULL,
 start_date DATE NOT NULL,
 end_date DATE NOT NULL,
 CHECK(start_date < end_date),
 PRIMARY KEY (start_date, end_date));
```

The searching is done with a `BETWEEN` predicate. A `NULL` can be useful as a marker for an open-ended range. Consider a table for grades in a school. The `CHECK()` constraint is not needed because of the static nature of the data, but it gives the optimizer extra information about the two columns and might help improve performance.

```
CREATE TABLE LetterGrades
(letter_grade CHAR(1) NOT NULL PRIMARY KEY,
 low_score DECIMAL(6,3) NOT NULL,
 high_score DECIMAL(6,3));

INSERT INTO LetterGrades
VALUES ('F',  0.000, 60.000),
       ('D', 60.999, 70.000),
       ('C', 70.999, 80.000),
       ('B', 80.999, 90.000),
       ('A', 90.999, NULL);
```

If we had made the last range `('A', 90.999, 100.000)`, then a student who did extra work and got a total score over 100.000 would not have gotten a grade. The alternatives are to use a dummy value, such as `('A', 90.999, 999.999)`, or to use a `NULL` and add the predicate.

```
SELECT ...
  FROM ...
 WHERE Exams.score
       BETWEEN LetterGrades.low_score
           AND COALESCE (LetterGrades.high_score, Exams.score);
```

The choice of using a dummy value or a `NULL` will depend on the nature of the data.

22.2.5 Hierarchical Auxiliary Tables

In a hierarchical auxiliary table, there is one parameter, but it must fall inside one or more ranges of values, and those ranges must be nested inside each other. We want to get an entire path of categories back as a result.

A common example would be the Dewey Decimal Classification system, which we might encode as:

```
CREATE TABLE DeweyDecimalClassification
(category_name CHAR(35) NOT NULL,
 low_dewey INTEGER NOT NULL,
 high_dewey INTEGER NOT NULL,
 CHECK (low_dewey <= high_dewey),
 PRIMARY KEY (low_dewey, high_dewey));

INSERT INTO DeweyDecimalClassification
VALUES ('Natural Sciences & Mathematics', 500, 599),
       ('Mathematics', 510, 519),
       ('General Topics', 511, 511),
       ('Algebra & Number Theory', 512, 512),
         ...,
       ('Probabilities & Applied Mathematics', 519, 519);
```

Thus, a search on 511 returns three rows in the lookup table. The leaf nodes of the hierarchy always have `(low_dewey = high_dewey)`, and the relative nesting level can be determined by (high_dewey - low_dewey) or by the range values themselves.

You can add constraints to prevent overlapping ranges and other things, but these constraints are often left off because the table is "read-only" and the constraints can be verified at load time. This is not a good idea because the CHECK() constraints and PRIMARY KEY delcaration can pass along information to the optimizer to improve performance.

22.2.6 One True Lookup Table

I think that Paul Keister was the first person to coin the term OTLT (One True Lookup Table) for a common SQL programming technique popular with newbies. Later, D. C. Peterson called it a MUCK (Massively Unified Code-Key) table. The technique crops up time and time again, but I'll give Keister credit as the first guy to give it a name. Simply put, the idea is to have one table to do all of the code look-ups in the schema. It usually looks like this:

```
CREATE TABLE Lookups
(code_type CHAR(10) NOT NULL,
 code_value VARCHAR(255) NOT NULL,
 code_description VARCHAR(255) NOT NULL,
 PRIMARY KEY (code_value, code_type));
```

So if we have Dewey Decimal Classification (library codes), ICD (International Classification of Diseases), and two-letter ISO-3166 country codes in the schema, we have them all in one honking big table.

Let's start with the problems in the DDL and then look at the awful queries you have to write (or hide in VIEWs). So we need to go back to the original DDL and add a CHECK() constraint on the code_type column. (Otherwise, we might "invent" a new encoding system by typographical error.)

The Dewey Decimal and ICD codes are numeric, and the ISO-3166 is alphabetic. Oops, we need another CHECK constraint that will look at the code_type and make sure that the string is in the right format. Now the table looks something like this, if anyone attempted to do it right, which is not usually the case:

```
CREATE TABLE Lookups
(code_type CHAR(10) NOT NULL
       CHECK(code_type IN ('DDC', 'ICD', 'ISO3166', ...),
 code_value VARCHAR(255) NOT NULL,
```

```
        CHECK
         (CASE WHEN code_type = 'DDC'
                    AND code_value
                        SIMILAR TO '[0-9][0-9][0-9].[0-9][0-9][0-
9]'
               THEN 1
               WHEN code_type = 'ICD'
                    AND code_value
                        SIMILAR TO '[0-9][0-9][0-9].[0-9][0-9][0-
9]'
               THEN 1
               WHEN code_type = 'ISO3166'
                    AND code_value
                        SIMILAR TO '[A-Z][A-Z]'
               THEN 1 ELSE 0 END = 1),
 code_description VARCHAR(255) NOT NULL,
 PRIMARY KEY (code_value, code_type));
```

Since the typical application database can have dozens and dozens of codes in it, you just keep extending this pattern for as long as required. Not very pretty, is it? That is why most OTLT programmers do not bother with it, and thus destroy data integrity.

The next thing you notice about this table is that the columns are pretty wide `VARCHAR(n)`, or even worse, that they use `NVARCHAR(n)`. The value of (*n*) is most often the largest one allowed in that particular SQL product.

Since you have no idea what is going to be shoved into the table, there is no way to predict and design with a safe, reasonable maximum size. The size constraint has to be put into the `WHEN` clause of that second `CHECK()` constraint, between code_type and code_value.

These large sizes tend to invite bad data. You give someone a `VARCHAR(n)` column, and you eventually get a string with a lot of white space and a small odd character sitting at the end of it. You give someone an `NVARCHAR(255)` column and eventually it will get a Buddhist sutra in Chinese Unicode. I am sure of this, because I load the Diamond or Heart Sutra when I get called to evaluate a database.

If you make an error in the code_type or code_description among codes with the same structure, it might not be detected. You can turn 500.000 from "Natural Sciences and Mathematics" in Dewey Decimal codes into "Coal Workers Pneumoconiosis" in ICD, and vice versa. This can be really difficult to find when one of the similarly structured schemes had unused codes in it.

Now let's consider the problems with actually using the OTLT in the DML. It is always necessary to add the code_type as well as the value that you are trying to look up.

```
SELECT P1.ssn, P1.lastname, ..., L1.code_description
  FROM Lookups AS L1, Personnel AS P1
 WHERE L1.code_type = 'ICD'
   AND L1.code_value = P1.sickness
   AND ...;
```

In this sample query, I need to know the code_type of the Personnel table sickness column and of every other encoded column in the table. If you get a code_type wrong, you can still get a result.

I also need to allow for some overhead for type conversions. It would be much more natural to use `DECIMAL (6,3)` for Dewey Decimal codes instead of `VARCHAR(n)`, so that is probably how it appears in the Personnel table. But why not use `CHAR(7)` for the code? If I had a separate table for each encoding scheme, then I would have used a `FOREIGN KEY` and matched the data types in the referenced and referencing tables. There is no definitive guide for data type choices in the OTLT approach.

When I go to execute a query, I have to pull in the entire lookup table, even if I only use one code. If one code is at the start of the physical storage, and another is at the end of physical storage, I can do a lot of paging. When I update the lookup table, I have to lock out everyone until I am finished. It is like having to carry an encyclopedia set with you, when all you needed was a magazine article.

I am going to venture a guess that this idea came from OO programmers who think of it as some kind of polymorphism done in SQL. They say to themselves that a table is a class, which it is not, and therefore it ought to have polymorphic behaviors, which it does not.

Maybe there are good reasons for the data-modeling principle that a well-designed table is a set of things of the same kind, instead of a pile of unrelated items.

22.3 Auxiliary Function Tables

SQL is not a computational language like FORTRAN and the specialized math packages. It typically does not have the numerical analysis routines to compensate for floating-point rounding errors, or algebraic reductions in the optimizer. But it is good at joins.

Most auxiliary lookup tables are for simple decoding, but they can be used for more complex functions. Let's consider two financial calculations that you cannot do easily: the Net Present Value (NPV) and its related Internal Rate of Return (IRR). Let me stop and ask: how would you program the NPV and IRR in SQL? The answer posted on most newsgroup replies was to write a procedure directly from the equation in the vendor-specific 4GL language and then call it.

As a quick review, let's start with the net present value (NPV) calculation. Imagine that you just got an e-mail from some poor Nigerian civil servant who wants you to send him a small investment now on the promise that he will send you a series of payments over time from money he is stealing from a government bank account. Obviously, you would want the total of the cash flow to be at least equal to the initial investment, or the money is not worth lending. We can assume that you are making a little profit at the end of investment. But is this a good investment? That is, if I took that cash flow and invested it at a given interest rate, what would the result be? That is called the net present value (NPV), and you will want to do at least as well as this value on your investment.

To make this more concrete, let's show a little code and data for your two investment options.

```
CREATE TABLE CashFlows
(project_id CHAR(15) NOT NULL,
 time_period INTEGER NOT NULL,
  CHECK (time_period >= 0),
 amount DECIMAL(12,4) NOT NULL,
 PRIMARY KEY (project_id, time_period));

INSERT INTO CashFlows
VALUES ('Acme', 0, -1000.0000),  ('Acme', 1, 500.0000), ('Acme',
2,400.0000),
       ('Acme', 3, 200.0000), ('Acme', 4, 200.0000),
       ('Beta', 0, -1000.0000), ('Beta', 1, 100.0000), ('Beta',
2, 200.0000),
       ('Beta', 3, 200.0000), ('Beta', 4, 700.0000);
```

I invest $1,000 at the start of each project; the time period is zero and the amount is always negative. Every year I get a different amount back on my investment, so that at the end of the fourth year, I've received a total of $13,000 on the Acme project, less my initial $1,000, for a profit of $12,000. Likewise, the Beta project returns $15,000 at the end.

Beta looks like a better investment. Let's assume we can get 10% return on an investment and that we put our cash flows into that investment. The Net Present Value function in pseudocode is:

```
FOR t FROM 0 TO n
DO SUM(a[t]/(1.00 + r)^ t))
END FOR;
```

In this case, *a[t]* is the cash flow for time period (*t*) and time period (*t* = 0) is the initial investment (it is always negative) and *r* is the interest rate.

When we run them through the equation, we find that Acme has an NPV of $71.9896 and Beta is worth –$115.4293, so Acme is really the better project. We can get more out of the Acme cash flow than the Beta cash flow.

22.3.1 Inverse Functions with Auxiliary Tables

The IRR depends on the NPV. It finds the interest rate at which your investment would break even if you invested back into the same project. Thus, if you can get a better rate, this is a good investment.

Let's build another table.

```
CREATE TABLE Rates
(rate DECIMAL(6,4) NOT NULL PRIMARY KEY);
```

Now let's populate it with some values. One trick to fill the Rates table with values is to use a `CROSS JOIN` and keep values inside a reasonable range.

```
CREATE TABLE Digits(digit DECIMAL (6,4) PRIMARY KEY);

INSERT INTO Digits
VALUES (0.0000), (0.0001), (0.0002), (0.0003), (0.0004),
       (0.0005), (0.0006), (0.0007), (0.0008), (0.0009);

INSERT INTO Rates (rate)
SELECT DISTINCT (D1.digit *1000) + (D2.digit *100) + (D3.digit
*10) + D4.digit
  FROM Digits AS D1, Digits AS D2, Digits AS D3, Digits AS D4
```

```
 WHERE ((D1.digit *1000) + (D2.digit *100) + (D3.digit *10) +
D4.digit)
   BETWEEN {{lower limit}} AND {{upper limit}}; -- pseudocode
DROP TABLE Digits;
```

We now have two choices. We can build a `VIEW` that uses the cash flow table, thus:

```
CREATE VIEW NPV_by_Rate(project_id, rate, npv)
AS
SELECT CF.project_id, R1.rate,
   SUM(amount / POWER((1.00 + R1.rate), time_period))
FROM CashFlows AS CF, Rates AS R1
GROUP BY R1.rate, CF.project_id;
```

Alternately, we can set the amount in the formula to 1 and store the multiplier for the (rate, time_period) pair in another table:

```
INSERT INTO NPV_Mulipliers (time_period, rate, npv_multiplier)
SELECT S.seq, R1.rate,
   SUM(1.00/(POWER((1.00 + R1.rate), seq)))
 FROM Sequence AS S, Rates AS R1
 WHERE S.seq <= {{ upper limit }} --pseudocode
 GROUP BY S.seq, R1.rate;
```

The sequence table contains integers 1 to (*n*); it is a standard auxiliary table, used to avoid iteration.

Assuming we use the `VIEW`, the IRR is now the single query:

```
SELECT 'Acme', rate AS irr, npv
 FROM NPV_by_Rate
 WHERE ABS(npv)
 = (SELECT MIN(ABS(npv))
     FROM NPV_by_Rate)
 AND project_id = 'Acme';
```

In my sample data, I get an IRR of 13.99% at an NPV of –0.04965 for the Acme project. Assume you have hundreds of projects to consider; would you rather write one query or hundreds of procedure calls?

This Web site has a set of slides that deal with the use of interpolation to find the IRR: www.yorku.ca/adms3530/Interpolation.pdf. Using the method described on the Web site, we can write the interpolation for the Acme example as:

```
SELECT R1.rate + (R1.rate* (R1.npv/(R1.npv - R2.npv))) AS irr
  FROM NPV_by_Rate AS R1, NPV_by_Rate AS R2
 WHERE R1.project_id = 'Acme'
   AND R2.project_id = 'Acme'
   AND R1.rate = 0.1000
   AND R2.rate = 0.2100
   AND R1.npv > 0
   AND R2.npv < 0;
```

The important points are that the NPVs from R1 and R2 have to be on both sides of the zero point, so that you can do a linear interpolation between the two rates with which they are associated.

The trade-off is speed for accuracy. The IRR function is slightly concave and not linear; that means that if you graph it, the shape of the curve buckles toward the origin. Picking good (`R1.rate, R2.rate`) pairs is important, but if you want to round off to the nearest whole percentage, you probably have a larger range than you might think. The answer from the original table lookup method, 0.1399, rounds to 14%, as do all of the following interpolations.

```
RI     R2     IRR
======================
0.1000 0.2100 0.140135
0.1000 0.2000 0.143537
0.0999 0.2000 0.143457
0.0999 0.1999 0.143492
0.0800 0.1700 0.135658
```

The advantages of using an auxiliary function table are:

1. All host programs will be using the same calculations.
2. The formula can be applied to hundreds or thousands of projects at one time, instead of just doing one project as you would with a spreadsheet or financial calculator.

Robert J. Hamilton (bobha@seanet.com) posted proprietary T-SQL functions for the NPV and IRR functions. The NPV function was straightforward, but he pointed out several problems with finding the IRR.

By definition, IRR is the rate at which the NPV of the cash flows equals zero. When IRR is well behaved, the graph of NPV as a function of rate is a curve that crosses the x-axis once and only once. When IRR is not well-behaved, the graph crosses the x-axis many times, which means the IRR is either multivalued or undefined.

At this point, we need to ask what the appropriate domain is for IRR. As it turns out, NPV is defined for all possible rates, both positive and negative, except where NPV approaches an asymptote at a rate of –100%, and the power function blows up. What does a negative rate mean when calculating NPV? What does it mean to have a negative IRR? Well it depends on how you look at it.

If you take a mathematical approach, a negative IRR is just another solution to the equation. If you take an economic approach, a negative IRR means you are losing money on the project. Perhaps if you live in a deflationary economy, then a negative cash flow might be profitable in terms of real money, but that is a very unusual situation, and we can dismiss negative IRRs as unreasonable.

This means that a table lookup approach to the IRR must have a very fine granularity and enough scope to cover a lot of situations for the general case. It also means that the table lookup is probably not the way to go. Expressing rates to 5 or 6 decimal places is common in home mortgage finance (i.e., APR 5.6725%), and this degree of precision using the set-based approach does not scale well. Moreover, this is exacerbated by the requirements of using IRR in hyperinflationary economies, where solutions of 200%, 300%, and higher are meaningful.

Here are Mr. Hamilton's functions written in SQL/PSM; one uses a straight-line algorithm, such as you find in Excel and other spreadsheets, and a bounding box algorithm. The bounding box algorithm has better domain integrity, but can inadvertently "skip over" a solution when widening its search.

```
CREATE TABLE CashFlows
(t INTEGER NOT NULL CHECK (t >= 0),
 amount DECIMAL(12,4) NOT NULL);

CREATE TABLE Rates
(rate DECIMAL(7,5) NOT NULL);
```

```
CREATE TABLE Digits
(digit DECIMAL(6,4));
INSERT INTO Digits
VALUES (0.0000), (0.0001), (0.0002), (0.0003), (0.0004),
       (0.0005), (0.0006), (0.0007), (0.0008), (0.0009);

INSERT INTO Rates
SELECT D1.digit * 1000 + D2.digit * 100 + D3.digit * 10 +
D4.digit FROM Digits AS D1, Digits AS D2, Digits AS D3, Digits AS
D4;

INSERT INTO Rates
SELECT rate-1 FROM Rates WHERE rate >= 0;

INSERT INTO Rates
SELECT rate-2 FROM Rates WHERE rate >= 0;

DROP TABLE Digits;

CREATE FUNCTION NPV (IN my_rate FLOAT)
RETURNS FLOAT
DETERMINISTIC
CONTAINS SQL
RETURN (CASE WHEN -- prevent divide by zero at rate = -100%
             ABS (1.0 + my_rate) >= 1.0e-5
             THEN (SELECT SUM (amount * POWER ((1.0 + my_rate),
-t))
                     FROM CashFlows)
             ELSE NULL END);

CREATE FUNCTION irr_bb (IN guess FLOAT)
RETURNS FLOAT
DETERMINISTIC
CONTAINS SQL
BEGIN
  DECLARE maxtry INTEGER;
  DECLARE x1 FLOAT;
  DECLARE x2 FLOAT;
  DECLARE f1 FLOAT;
  DECLARE f2 FLOAT;
  DECLARE x FLOAT;
  DECLARE dx FLOAT;
```

```
  DECLARE x_mid FLOAT;
  DECLARE f_mid FLOAT;

 -- initial bounding box around guess
  SET x1 = guess - 0.005;
  SET f1 = NPV (x1);
  IF f1 IS NULL THEN RETURN (f1); END IF;

  SET x2 = guess + 0.005;
  SET f2 = NPV (x2);
  IF f2 IS NULL THEN RETURN (f2); END IF;

 -- expand bounding box to include a solution
  SET maxtry = 50;
  WHILE maxtry > 0  -- try until solution is bounded
        AND (SIGN(f1) * SIGN(f2)) <> -1
  DO IF ABS (f1) < ABS (f2)
     THEN -- move lower bound
          SET x1 = x1 + 1.6 * (x1 - x2);
          SET f1 = NPV (x1);
          IF f1 IS NULL -- no irr
          THEN RETURN (f1);
          END IF;
     ELSE -- move upper bound
          SET x2 = x2 + 1.6 * (x2 - x1);
          SET f2 = NPV (x2);
          IF f2 IS NULL -- no irr
          THEN RETURN (f2);
          END IF;
    END IF;
    SET maxtry = maxtry - 1;
    END WHILE;
  IF (SIGN(f1) * SIGN(f2)) <> -1
  THEN RETURN (CAST (NULL AS FLOAT));
  END IF;
END;

  -- now find solution with binary search
  SET x = CASE WHEN f1 < 0
               THEN x1
               ELSE x2 END;
```

```
  SET dx = CASE WHEN f1 < 0
                THEN (x2 - x1)
                ELSE (x1 - x2) END;
  SET maxtry = 50;
  WHILE maxtry > 0
  DO SET dx = dx / 2.0; -- reduce steps by half
     SET x_mid = x + dx;
     SET f_mid = NPV (x_mid);
     IF f_mid IS NULL -- no irr
     THEN RETURN (f_mid);
     ELSE IF ABS (f_mid) < 1.0e-5 -- epsilon for problem
          THEN RETURN (x_mid); -- irr found
          END IF;
     END IF;
     IF f_mid < 0
     THEN SET x = x_mid;
     END IF;
     SET maxtry = maxtry - 1;
  END WHILE;
  RETURN (CAST (NULL AS FLOAT));
END;
```

If you prefer to compute the IRR as a straight line, you can use this function:

```
CREATE FUNCTION irr_sl (IN guess FLOAT)
RETURNS FLOAT
DETERMINISTIC
CONTAINS SQL
BEGIN
  DECLARE maxtry INTEGER;
  DECLARE x1 FLOAT; DECLARE x2 FLOAT;
  DECLARE f1 FLOAT; DECLARE f2 FLOAT;

  SET maxtry = 50; -- iterations
  WHILE maxtry > 0
  DO SET x1 = guess;
     SET f1 = NPV (x1);
     IF f1 IS NULL -- no irr
     THEN RETURN (f1);
     ELSE IF ABS (f1) < 1.0e-5 -- irr within epsilon range
```

```
            THEN RETURN (x1);
            END IF;
      END IF;

      -- try again with new guess using two-point formula
      SET x2 = x1 + 1.0e-5;
      SET f2 = NPV (x2);
      IF f2 IS NULL -- no irr
      THEN RETURN (f2);
      END IF;
      IF ABS (f2 - f1) < 1.0e-5
      THEN RETURN (CAST (NULL AS FLOAT));  -- check for divide by
zero
      END IF;
      SET guess = x1 - f1 * (x2 - x1)/ (f2 - f1);
      SET maxtry = maxtry - 1;
  END WHILE;
END;

-- Test table, holds results of straight line algorithm
CREATE TABLE Test_StraightLine
(rate DECIMAL(7,5) NOT NULL,
 npv FLOAT,
 irr DECIMAL(7,5));

CREATE TABLE Test_BoundedBox
(rate DECIMAL(7,5) NOT NULL,
 npv FLOAT,
 irr DECIMAL(7,5));

-- original scenario
-- try t = 0 cashflow of: - 391, irr undefined;
-- try t = 0 cashflow of: -350, irr multivalued;
--      0, irr single-valued (well-behaved)

DELETE FROM CashFlows
INSERT INTO CashFlows
VALUES (0, -350), (1, 100), (2, 100), (3, 100), (4, 100),
       (5, 100), (6, 100), (7, 100), (8, 100), (9, 100),
       (10, 100), (11, 100), (12, 100), (13, 100), (14, 100),
       (15, -1500);
```

```
-- scenario 1a: single valued irr
DELETE FROM CashFlows
INSERT INTO CashFlows
VALUES (0, -800), (1, 100), (2, 100), (3, 100), (4, 100),
       (5, 100), (6, 100), (7, 100), (8, 100), (9, 100),
       (10, 100);

-- scenario 1b: single valued irr, signs reversed
DELETE FROM CashFlows;
INSERT INTO CashFlows
VALUES (0, 800), (1, -100), (2, -100), (3, -100), (4, -100),
       (5, -100), (6, -100), (7, -100), (8, -100), (9, -100),
       (10, -100);

-- scenario 2: double valued irr
DELETE FROM CashFlows;
INSERT INTO CashFlows
VALUES (0, -300), (1, 100), (2, 100), (3, 100), (4, 100),
       (5, 100), (6, 100),(7, 100), (8, 100), (9, 100),
       (10, -690);

-- scenario 3: double valued irr with solutions very CLOSE
together
DELETE FROM CashFlows;
INSERT INTO CashFlows
VALUES (0, -310), (1, 100), (2, 100), (3, 100), (4, 100),
       (5, 100), (6, 100), (7, 100), (8, 100), (9, 100),
       (10, -690);

-- scenario 4: undefined irr
DELETE FROM CashFlows;
INSERT INTO CashFlows
VALUES (0, -320), (1, 100), (2, 100), (3, 100), (4, 100),
       (5, 100), (6, 100), (7, 100), (8, 100), (9, 100),
       (10, -690);

-- run the test
DELETE FROM Test_StraightLine;
INSERT INTO Test_StraightLine (rate, npv, irr)
SELECT rate, NPV (rate), irr_sl(rate)
  FROM Rates;
```

```
DELETE FROM Test_BoundedBox ;
INSERT INTO Test_BoundedBox (rate, npv, irr)
SELECT rate, NPV (rate), irr_bb(rate)
  FROM Rates;

-- View results of the test
SELECT SL.rate, SL.npv AS npv_sl, SL.irr AS irr_sl,
       BB.npv AS npv_bb,
       BB.irr AS irr_bb
  FROM Test_StraightLine AS SL, Test_BoundedBox
 WHERE BB.rate = SL.rate;
```

A computational version of the IRR, due to Richard Romley, returns approximations that become more and more accurate as you feed estimates back into the formula.

```
CREATE FUNCTION IRR(IN project_id CHAR(15), IN my_i
DECIMAL(12,8))
RETURNS DECIMAL(12,8)
LANGUAGE SQL
DETERMINISTIC
RETURN (SELECT CASE WHEN ROUND(my_i, 4) = ROUND(T.i, 4)
                    THEN 100 * (my_I - 1)
                    ELSE IRR(project_id, T.i) END
        FROM (SELECT SUM((amount * (time_period + 1))
                         /(POWER(my_i, time_period)))
                         / SUM((amount * (time_period))
                         /(POWER(my_i, time_period + 1)))
              FROM CashFlows WHERE project_id = my_project_id));
```

22.3.2 Interpolation with Auxiliary Function Tables

SQL is not a functional programming language, so you often have to depend on vendor extensions providing a good library, or on being able to write the functions with the limited power in standard SQL.

However, SQL is good at handling tables, and often, when the range of the function is relatively small, you can often set up auxiliary tables of the general form:

```
CREATE TABLE SomeFunction
(parameter <data type> NOT NULL,
 result <data type> NOT NULL);
```

Thus, the pseudocode expression:

```
SELECT SomeFunction(T1.x), ...
  FROM TableOne AS T1
 WHERE ...
```

is replaced by:

```
SELECT F1.result,
  FROM TableOne AS T1, SomeFunction AS F1
 WHERE T1.x = F1.parameter
   AND ...
```

However, if the function has a large range, the SomeFunction table can become huge or completely impractical.

A technique that has fallen out of favor since the advent of cheap, fast computers is interpolation. It consists of using two known functional values, a and b, and their results in the functions f(*a*) and f(*b*), to find the result of a value, *x*, between them.

Linear interpolation is the easiest method, and if the table has a high precision, it will work quite well for most applications. It is based on the idea that a straight line drawn between two function values f(*a*) and f(*b*) will approximate the function well enough that you can take a proportional increment of *x* relative to (*a*, *b*) and get a usable answer for f(*x*).

The algebra looks like this:

```
f(x) = f(a) + (x - a) * ((f(b) - f(a))/(b-a))
```

In this formula, `(a <= x <= b)`, and *x* is not in the table. This can be translated into SQL as shown following (where *x* is `:myparameter`, `F1` is related to the variable *a*, and `F2` is related to the variable *b*):

```
SELECT :myparameter AS my_input,
       (F1.answer + (:myparameter - F1.param)
       * ((F2.answer - F1.answer)
          / (CASE WHEN F1.param = F2.param
                  THEN 1.00
                  ELSE F2.param - F1.param END)))
       AS answer
  FROM SomeFunction AS F1, SomeFunction AS F2
 WHERE F1.param   -- establish a and f(a)
```

```
= (SELECT MAX(param)
         FROM SomeFunction
        WHERE param  <= :myparameter)
AND F2.param    -- establish b and f(b)
= (SELECT MIN(param)
         FROM SomeFunction
        WHERE param >= :myparameter);
```

The `CASE` expression in the divisor is to avoid division by zero errors when f(x) is in the table.

The rules for interpolation methods are always expressible in four-function arithmetic, which is good for standard SQL. In the old days, with each parameter and result pair, the function tables gave an extra value called delta squared, which was based on finite differences. Delta squared was similar to a second derivative, and could be used in a formula to improve the accuracy of the approximation.

This is not a book on numerical analysis, so you will have to go to a library to find details—or ask an old engineer.

22.4 Global Constants Tables

When you configure a system, you might want to have a way to set and keep constants in the schema. One method for doing this is to have a one-row table that can be set with default values at the start and then updated only by someone with administrative privileges.

```
CREATE TABLE Constants
(lock CHAR(1) DEFAULT 'X'
      NOT NULL PRIMARY KEY
      CHECK (lock = 'X'),
  pi FLOAT DEFAULT 3.142592653 NOT NULL,
   e FLOAT DEFAULT 2.71828182 NOT NULL,
 phi FLOAT DEFAULT 1.6180339887 NOT NULL,
  ...);
```

To initialize the row, execute this statement:

```
INSERT INTO Constants VALUES DEFAULTS;
```

The lock column ensures that there is only one row, and the default values load the initial values. These defaults can include the current user and current timestamp, as well as numeric and character values.

Another version of this idea—one that does not allow for any updates—is a VIEW defined with a table constructor.

```
CREATE VIEW Constants (pi, e, phi, ...)
AS VALUES (3.142592653), (2.71828182), (1.6180339887), ...;
```

The next step is to put in a formula for the constants so that they can be computed on any platform to which this DDL is moved, using the local math library and hardware precision.

Statistics in SQL

SQL IS NOT A statistical programming language. However, there are some tricks that will let you do simple descriptive statistics. Many vendors also include other descriptive statistics in addition to the required ones. Other sections of this book give portable queries for computing some of the more common statistics. Before using any of these queries, you should check to see if they already exist in your SQL product. Built-in functions will run far faster than these queries, so you should use them if portability is not vital. The most common extensions are the median, the mode, the standard deviation, and the variance.

If you need to do a detailed statistical analysis, then you can extract data with SQL and pass it along to a statistical programming language, such as SAS or SPSS.

However, you can build a lot of standard descriptive statistics using what you do have. First, the basic analysis of a single column can start with this VIEW or query to get cumulative and absolute frequencies and percentages:

```
WITH
SELECT F1.x, COUNT(F1.x)
       CAST(ROUND(100. *
              (COUNT(F1.x)) /
              (SELECT COUNT(*) FROM Foobar),0)
```

```
            AS INTEGER)
 FROM Foobar AS F1
GROUP BY F1.x) AS F2(x, abs_freq, abs_perc)
SELECT F2.x,
       F2.abs_freq,
       (SELECT SUM(F3.abs_freq)
          FROM F2 AS F3
         WHERE F3.x <= F2.x)
       AS cum_freq,
       F2.abs_perc,
       (SELECT SUM(F3.abs_perc)
          FROM F2. AS F3
         WHERE F3.x <= F2.x)
       AS cum_percc
  FROM F2;
```

23.1 The Mode

The mode is the most frequently occurring value in a set. If there are two such values in a set, statisticians call it a bimodal distribution; three such values make it trimodal; and so forth.

Most SQL implementations do not have a mode function, since it is easy to calculate. A simple frequency table can be written as a single query in SQL-92.

This version is from Shepard Towindo, and it will handle multiple modes.

```
SELECT salary, COUNT(*) AS frequency
  FROM Payroll
 GROUP BY salary
HAVING COUNT(*)
       >= ALL (SELECT COUNT(*)
                 FROM Payroll
                GROUP BY salary);
```

As an exercise, here is a version that does not use a `GROUP BY` clause to compute the mode. However, the execution time might be a bit longer than you would like.

```
SELECT DISTINCT salary
  FROM Personnel AS P1
```

```
WHERE NOT EXISTS
      (SELECT *
         FROM Personnel AS P2
        WHERE EXISTS
              (SELECT COUNT(*)
                 FROM Personnel AS P3
                WHERE P1.salary = P3.salary
                   < (SELECT COUNT(*)
                        FROM Personnel AS P4
                       WHERE P2.salary = P4.salary)));
```

For a more accurate picture, you can allow for a 5% difference among frequencies that are near the mode, but would otherwise not technically qualify.

```
SELECT AVG(salary) AS mode
  FROM Payroll
 GROUP BY salary
HAVING COUNT(*)
       >= ALL (SELECT COUNT(*) * 0.95
                 FROM Payroll
                GROUP BY salary);
```

The mode is a weak descriptive statistic, because it can be changed by small amounts of additional data. For example, if we have 100,000 cases where the value of the part_color variable is 'red' and 99,999 cases where the value is 'green', the mode is 'red'. However, when two more 'green' cases are added to the set, the mode switches to 'green'. A better idea is to allow for some variation (k), in the values. In general the best way to compute k is probably as a percentage of the total number of occurrences. Of course, knowledge of the actual situation could change this. For k = 2% error, the query would look like this:

```
SELECT var_col AS mode, occurs
  FROM ModeFinder
 WHERE occurs
       BETWEEN (SELECT MAX(occurs) - (0.02 * SUM(occurs))
                  FROM ModeFinder))
           AND (SELECT MAX(occurs) + (0.02 * SUM(occurs))
                  FROM ModeFinder));
```

This would return the result set ('red', 'green') for the example table, and would not change to ('green') until the ratio of 'red' to 'green' tipped by two percentage points.

Likewise, you can use a derived table to get the mode.

```
WITH (SELECT salary, COUNT(*)
        FROM Payroll
       GROUP BY salary)
     AS P1 (salary, occurs)
SELECT salary
  FROM P1
 WHERE P1.occurs
       = (SELECT MAX(occurs) IN P1);
```

This is probably the best approach, since the `WITH` clause will materialize the P1 table and can locate the `MAX()` while doing so.

23.2 The AVG() Function

One problem is that SQLs likes to maintain the data types, so if *x* is an `INTEGER`, you may get an integer result. You can avoid this by writing `AVG(1.0 * x)` or `AVG(CAST (X AS FLOAT))` or `AVG(CAST (X AS DECIMAL (s,p)))` to be safe. This is implementation-defined, so check your product first.

Newbies tend to forget that the built-in aggregate functions drop the rows with `NULL`s before doing the computations. This means that `(SUM(x)/COUNT(*))` is not the same as `AVG(x)`. Consider `(x * 1.0)/COUNT(*)` versus `AVG(COALESCE(x * 1.0, 0.0))` as versions of the mean that handle `NULL`s differently.

Sample and population means are slightly different. A sample needs to use frequencies to adjust the estimate of the mean. The formula `SUM(x * 1.0 * abs_perc/100) AS mean_p` needs the `VIEW` we had at the start of this section.

The name "mean_p" is to remind us that it is a population mean and not the simple `AVG()` of the sample data in the table.

23.3 The Median

The median is defined as the value for which there are just as many cases with a value below it as above it. If such a value exists in the data set, this value is called the statistical median by some authors. If no such value exists in the data set, the usual method is to divide the data set into two halves of equal size such that all values in one half are lower than any value in the other half. The median is then the average of the highest value in the lower half and the lowest value in the upper half, and is called the financial median by some authors. The financial median is the most common term used for this median, so we will stick to it. Let us use Date's famous Parts table, from several of his textbooks (Date 1983, 1995a), which has a column for weight in it, like this:

```
Parts
part_nbr  part_name part_color  weight  city_name
=================================================
   'p1'  'Nut'       'Red'       '12'   'London'
   'p2'  'Bolt'      'Green'     '17'   'Paris'
   'p3'  'Cam'       'Blue'      '12'   'Paris'
   'p4'  'Screw'     'Red'       '14'   'London'
   'p5'  'Cam'       'Blue'      '12'   'Paris'
   'p6'  'Cog'       'Red'       '19'   'London'
```

First, sort the table by weights and find the three rows in the lower half of the table. The greatest value in the lower half is 12; the smallest value in the upper half is 14; their average, and therefore the median, is 13. If the table had an odd number of rows, we would have looked at only one row after the sorting.

The median is a better measure of central tendency than the average, but it is also harder to calculate without sorting. This is a disadvantage of SQL, compared with procedural languages, and it might be the reason that the median is not a common vendor extension in SQL implementations. The variance and standard deviation are quite common, probably because they require no sorting and are therefore much easier to calculate; however, they are less useful to commercial users.

23.3.1 Date's First Median

Date proposed two different solutions for the median (Date 1992a; Celko and Date 1993). His first solution was based on the fact that if you duplicate every row in a table, the median will stay the same. The duplication will guarantee that you always work with a table that has an even number of rows. The first version that appeared in his column was wrong and drew some mail from me and from others who had different solutions. Here is a corrected version of his first solution:

```
CREATE VIEW Temp1
AS SELECT weight FROM Parts
   UNION ALL
   SELECT weight FROM Parts;

CREATE VIEW Temp2
AS SELECT weight
     FROM Temp1
    WHERE (SELECT COUNT(*) FROM Parts)
            <= (SELECT COUNT(*)
                  FROM Temp1 AS T1
                 WHERE T1.weight >= Temp1.weight)
      AND (SELECT COUNT(*) FROM Parts)
            <= (SELECT COUNT(*)
                  FROM Temp1 AS T2
                 WHERE T2.weight <= Temp1.weight);

SELECT AVG(DISTINCT weight) AS median
  FROM Temp2;
```

This involves the construction of a doubled table of values, which can be expensive in terms of both time and storage space. The use of `AVG(DISTINCT x)` is important, because leaving it out would return the simple average instead of the median. Consider the set of weights (12, 17, 17, 14, 12, 19). The doubled table, Temp1, is then (12, 12, 12, 12, 14, 14, 17, 17, 17, 17, 19, 19). But because of the duplicated values, Temp2 becomes (14, 14, 17, 17, 17, 17), not just (14, 17). The simple average is (96 / 6.0) = 16; it should be (31/2.0) = 15.5 instead.

23.3.2 Celko's First Median

A slight modification of Date's solution will avoid the use of a doubled table, but it depends on a `CEILING()` function.

```
SELECT MIN(weight)    -- smallest value in upper half
  FROM Parts
 WHERE weight
       IN (SELECT P1.weight
             FROM Parts AS P1, Parts AS P2
            WHERE P2.weight >= P1.weight
            GROUP BY P1.weight
          HAVING COUNT(*)
```

```
                <= (SELECT CEILING(COUNT(*) / 2.0)
                      FROM Parts))
UNION
SELECT MAX(weight)    -- largest value in lower half
  FROM Parts
 WHERE weight IN (SELECT P1.weight
                    FROM Parts AS P1, Parts AS P2
                   WHERE P2.weight <= P1.weight
                  HAVING COUNT(*) <=
                         (SELECT CEILING(COUNT(*) / 2.0)
                            FROM Parts));
```

Alternately, using the same idea and a CASE expression:

```
SELECT AVG(DISTINCT CAST(weight AS FLOAT)) AS median
  FROM (SELECT MAX(weight)
          FROM Parts AS B1
        WHERE (SELECT COUNT(*) + 1
                 FROM Parts
                WHERE weight < B1.weight)
             <= (SELECT CEILING (COUNT(*)/2.0)
                   FROM Parts)
       UNION ALL
       SELECT MAX(weight)
         FROM Parts AS B
        WHERE (SELECT COUNT(*) + 1
                 FROM Parts
                WHERE weight < B.weight)
              <= CASE (SELECT MOD (COUNT(*), 2)
                         FROM Parts)
                 WHEN 0
                 THEN (SELECT CEILING (COUNT(*)/2.0) + 1
                         FROM Parts)
                 ELSE (SELECT CEILING (COUNT(*)/2.0)
                         FROM Parts)
                 END) AS Medians(weight);
```

Older versions of SQL allow a HAVING clause only with a GROUP BY; this may not work with your SQL. The CEILING() function is included to be sure that if there is an odd number of rows in Parts, the two halves will overlap on that value. Again, truncation and rounding in division

are implementation-defined, so you will need to experiment with your product.

23.3.3 Date's Second Median

Date's second solution (Date 1995b) was based on Celko's median, folded into one query:

```
SELECT AVG(DISTINCT Parts.weight) AS median
  FROM Parts
 WHERE Parts.weight IN
        (SELECT MIN(weight)
           FROM Parts
          WHERE Parts.weight IN
                (SELECT P2.weight
                   FROM Parts AS P1, Parts AS P2
                  WHERE P2.weight <= P1.weight
                  GROUP BY P2.weight
         HAVING COUNT(*)
                <= (SELECT CEILING(COUNT(*) / 2.0)
                      FROM Parts))
        UNION
        SELECT MAX(weight)
          FROM Parts
         WHERE Parts.weight IN
               (SELECT P2.weight
                  FROM Parts AS P1, Parts AS P2
                 WHERE P2.weight >= P1.weight
                 GROUP BY P2.weight
               HAVING COUNT(*)
                      <= (SELECT CEILING(COUNT(*) / 2.0)
                            FROM Parts)));
```

Date mentions that this solution will return a NULL for an empty table and that it assumes there are no NULLs in the column. If there are NULLs, the WHERE clauses should be modified to remove them.

23.3.4 Murchison's Median

Rory Murchison of the Aetna Institute has a solution that modifies Date's first method by concatenating the key to each value to make sure that every value is seen as a unique entity. Selecting the middle values is then a special case of finding the *n*th item in the table.

```
SELECT AVG(weight)
  FROM Parts AS P1
 WHERE EXISTS
      (SELECT COUNT(*)
         FROM Parts AS P2
        WHERE CAST(weight AS CHAR(5)) || P2.part_nbr >=
              CAST(weight AS CHAR(5)) || P1.part_nbr
       HAVING COUNT(*) = (SELECT FLOOR(COUNT(*) / 2.0)
                            FROM Parts)
          OR COUNT(*) = (SELECT CEILING((COUNT(*) / 2.0)
                            FROM Parts));
```

This method depends on being able to have a `HAVING` clause without a `GROUP BY`, which is part of the ANSI standard but often missed by new programmers.

Another handy trick, if you don't have `FLOOR()` and `CEILING()` functions, is to use `(COUNT(*) + 1) / 2.0` and `COUNT(*) / 2.0 + 1` to handle the odd-and-even-elements problem. Just to work it out, consider the case where the `COUNT(*)` returns 8 for an answer: (8 + 1) / 2.0 = (9 / 2.0) = 4.5 and (8 / 2.0) + 1 = 4 + 1 = 5.

The 4.5 will round to 4 in DB2 and other SQL implementations. The case where the `COUNT(*)` returns 9 would work like this: (9 + 1) / 2.0 = (10 / 2.0) = 5 and (9 / 2.0) + 1 = 4.5 + 1 = 5.5, which will likewise round to 5 in DB2.

23.3.5 Celko's Second Median

This is another method for finding the median that uses a working table with the values, as well as a tally of their occurrences from the original table. This working table should be quite a bit smaller than the original table, and it should be very fast to construct if there is an index on the target column. The Parts table will serve as an example, thus:

```
-- construct Working table of occurrences by weight
CREATE TABLE Working
(weight REAL NOT NULL,
 occurs INTEGER NOT NULL);

INSERT INTO Working (weight, occurs)
```

```
SELECT weight, COUNT(*)
  FROM Parts
 GROUP BY weight;
```

Now that we have this table, we want to use it to construct a summary table that has the number of occurrences of each weight and the total number of data elements before and after we add them to the working table.

```
-- construct table of cumulative tallies
CREATE TABLE Summary
(weight REAL NOT NULL,
 occurs INTEGER NOT NULL, -- number of occurrences
 pre_tally INTEGER NOT NULL, -- cumulative tally before
   post_tally INTEGER NOT NULL);

 -- cumulative tally after
INSERT INTO Summary
SELECT S2.weight, S2.occurs, SUM(S1.occurs) - S2.occurs,
       SUM(S1.occurs)
  FROM Working AS S1, Working AS S2
 WHERE S1.weight <= S2.weight
 GROUP BY S2.weight, S2.occurs;
```

Let (n / 2.0) be the middle position in the table. There are two mutually exclusive situations. In the first case, the median lies in a position between the pre_tally and post_tally of one weight value. In the second case, the median lies on the pre_tally of one row and the post_tally of another. The middle position can be calculated by the scalar subquery `(SELECT MAX(post_tally) / 2.0  FROM Summary)`.

```
SELECT AVG(S3.weight) AS median
  FROM Summary AS S3
 WHERE (S3.post_tally > (SELECT MAX(post_tally) / 2.0 FROM
Summary)
   AND S3.pre_tally < (SELECT MAX(post_tally) / 2.0 FROM
Summary))
    OR S3.pre_tally = (SELECT MAX(post_tally) / 2.0 FROM Summary)
    OR S3.post_tally = (SELECT MAX(post_tally) / 2.0 FROM
Summary);
```

The first predicate, with the AND operator, handles the case where the median falls inside one weight value; the other two predicates handle the case where the median is between two weights. A BETWEEN predicate will not work in this query.

These tables can be used to compute percentiles, deciles, and quartiles simply by changing the scalar subquery. For example, to find the highest tenth (first decile), the subquery would be (SELECT 9 * MAX(post_tally) / 10 FROM Summary); to find the highest two-tenths, (SELECT 8 * MAX(post_tally) / 10 FROM Summary). In general, to find the highest *n*-tenths, (SELECT (10 - n) * MAX(post_tally) / 10 FROM Summary).

23.3.6 Vaughan's Median with VIEWs

Philip Vaughan of San Jose, California proposed a simple median technique based on all of these methods. It derives a VIEW with unique weights and number of occurrences, and then derives a VIEW of the middle set of weights.

```
CREATE VIEW ValueSet(weight, occurs)
AS SELECT weight, COUNT(*)
     FROM Parts
    GROUP BY weight;
```

The MiddleValues VIEW is used to get the median by taking an average. The clever part of this code is the way it handles empty result sets in the outermost WHERE clause that result from having only one value for all weights in the table. Empty sets sum to NULL, because there is no element to map the index.

```
CREATE VIEW MiddleValues(weight)
AS SELECT weight
     FROM ValueSet AS VS1
    WHERE (SELECT SUM(VS2.occurs)/2.0 + 0.25
             FROM ValueSet AS VS2) >
          (SELECT SUM(VS2.occurs)
             FROM ValueSet AS VS2
            WHERE VS1.weight <= VS2.weight) - VS1.occurs
      AND (SELECT SUM(VS2.occurs)/2.0 + 0.25
             FROM ValueSet AS VS2) >
          (SELECT SUM(VS2.occurs)
             FROM ValueSet AS VS2
```

```
            WHERE VS1.weight >= VS2.weight) - VS1.occurs;

SELECT AVG(weight) AS median FROM MiddleValues;
```

23.3.7 Median with Characteristic Function

Anatoly Abramovich, Yelena Alexandrova, and Eugene Birger presented a series of articles in *SQL Forum* magazine on computing the median (*SQL Forum* 1993, 1994). They define a characteristic function, which they call delta, using the Sybase `SIGN()` function. The delta or characteristic function accepts a Boolean expression as an argument, and returns one if it is `TRUE` and zero if it is `FALSE` or `UNKNOWN`. We can construct the delta function easily with a `CASE` expression.

The authors also distinguish between the statistical median, whose value must be a member of the set, and the financial median, whose value is the average of the middle two members of the set. A statistical median exists when the number of items in the set is odd. If the number of items is even, you must decide whether you want to use the highest value in the lower half (they call this the left median) or the lowest value in the upper half (they call this the right median).

The left statistical median of a unique column can be found with this query, if you assume that we have a column called bin that represents the storage location of a part.

```
SELECT P1.bin
  FROM Parts AS P1, Parts AS P2
 GROUP BY P1.bin
HAVING SUM(CASE WHEN (P2.bin <= P1.bin) THEN 1 ELSE 0 END)
         = (COUNT(*) / 2.0);
```

Changing the direction of the theta test in the `HAVING` clause will allow you to pick the right statistical median if a central element does not exist in the set. You will also notice something else about the median of a set of unique values: it is usually meaningless. What does the median bin number mean, anyway? A good rule of thumb is that if it does not make sense as an average, it does not make sense as a median.

The statistical median of a column with duplicate values can be found with a query based on the same ideas, but you have to adjust the `HAVING` clause to allow for overlap; thus, the left statistical median is found by:

```
SELECT P1.weight
  FROM Parts AS P1, Parts AS P2
```

```
 GROUP BY P1.weight
HAVING SUM(CASE WHEN P2.weight <= P1.weight
                 THEN 1 ELSE 0 END)
            >= (COUNT(*) / 2.0)
   AND SUM(CASE WHEN P2.weight >= P1.weight
                THEN 1 ELSE 0 END)
            >= (COUNT(*) / 2.0);
```

Notice that here the left and right medians can be the same, so there is no need to pick one over the other in many of the situations where you have an even number of items. Switching the comparison operators in the two CASE expressions will give you the right statistical median.

The authors' query for the financial median depends on some Sybase features that cannot be found in other products, so I would recommend using a combination of the right and left statistical medians to return a set of values about the center of the data, and then averaging them. Using a derived table, we can write the query as:

```
SELECT AVG(DISTINCT weight)
  FROM (SELECT P1.weight
          FROM Parts AS P1, Parts AS P2
         GROUP BY P1.weight
        HAVING (SUM(CASE WHEN P2.weight <= P1.weight
                         THEN 1 ELSE 0 END)
                >= ((COUNT(*)) / 2.0)
           AND SUM(CASE WHEN P2.weight >= P1.weight
                        THEN 1 ELSE 0 END)
                >= (COUNT(*)/2.0)));
```

In doing this, we can gain some additional control over the calculations.

This version will use one copy of the left and right median to compute the statistical median. However, by simply changing the AVG(DISTINCT weight) to AVG(weight), the median will favor the direction with the most occurrences. This might be easier to see with an example. Assume that we have weights (13, 13, 13, 14) in the Parts table. A pure statistical median would be (13 + 14) /2.0 = 13.5; however, weighting it would give (13 + 13 + 13 + 14) / 4.0 = 13.25, which is more representative of central tendency.

Another version of the financial median, which uses the CASE expression in both of its forms, is:

```
SELECT CASE MOD(COUNT(*),2)
       WHEN 0        -- even sized table
       THEN (P1.weight + MIN(CASE WHEN P1.weight > P2.weight
                                  THEN P1.weight
                                  ELSE NULL END))/2.0
       ELSE P2.weight --odd sized table
       END
  FROM Parts AS P1, Parts AS P2
 GROUP BY P1.weight
HAVING COUNT(CASE WHEN P1.weight >= P2.weight
                  THEN 1
                  ELSE NULL END)
       = (COUNT(*) + 1) / 2;
```

This answer is due to Ken Henderson.

23.3.8 Celko's Third Median

Another approach involves looking at a picture of a line of sorted values and seeing where the median would fall. Every value in the column weight partitions the table into three sections: values that are less than weight, values that are equal to weight, and values that are greater than weight. We can get a profile of each value with a tabular subquery expression.

Now the question is how to define a median in terms of the partitions. Clearly, the definition of a median means that if (lesser = greater) then weight is the median.

Now look at Figure 23.1 for the other situations. If there are more elements in the greater values than half the size of the table, then weight cannot be a median. Likewise, if there are more elements in the lesser values than half the size of the table, then weight cannot be a median.

If (lesser + equal) = greater, then weight is a left-hand median. Likewise, if (greater + equal) = lesser, then weight is a right-hand median. However, if weight is the median, then both lesser and greater must have tallies of less than half the size of the table. That translates into the following SQL:

```
SELECT AVG(DISTINCT weight)
  FROM (SELECT P1.part_nbr, P1.weight,
               SUM(CASE WHEN P2.weight < P1.weight
                        THEN 1 ELSE 0 END),
               SUM(CASE WHEN P2.weight = P1.weight
```

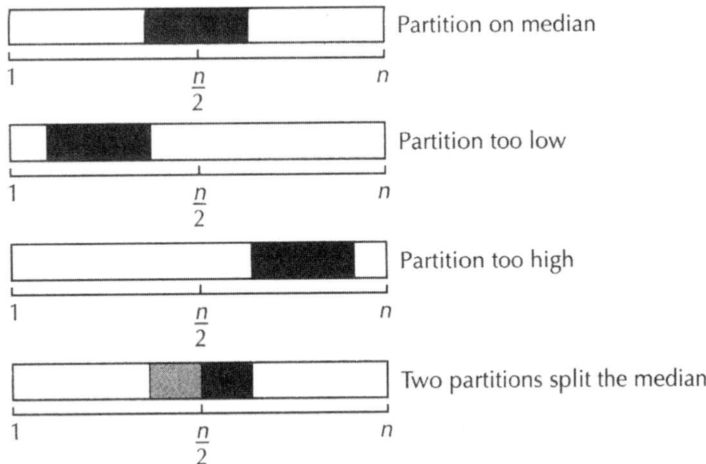

Figure 23.1 *Defining a Median.*

```
                          THEN 1 ELSE 0 END),
                 SUM(CASE WHEN P2.weight > P1.weight
                          THEN 1 ELSE 0 END)
          FROM Parts AS P1, Parts AS P2
         GROUP BY P1.part_nbr, P1.weight)
           AS Partitions (part_nbr, weight, lesser, equal,
greater)
 WHERE lesser = greater
    OR (lesser <= (SELECT COUNT(*) FROM Parts)/2.0
        AND greater <= (SELECT COUNT(*) FROM Parts)/2.0);
```

The reason for not expanding the `VIEW` in the `FROM` clause into a tabular subquery expression is that the table can be used for other partitions of the table, such as quintiles.

It is also worth noting that you can use either `AVG(DISTINCT i)` or `AVG(i)` in the `SELECT` clause. The `AVG(DISTINCT i)` will return the usual median when there are two values. This happens when you have an even number of rows and a partition in the middle, such as, (1, 2, 2, 3, 3, 3) which has (2, 3) in the middle, which gives us 2.5 for the median. The `AVG(i)` will return the weighted median instead. The weighted median looks at the set of middle values and skews in favor of the more common of the two values. The table with (1, 2, 2, 3, 3, 3) would return (2, 2, 3, 3, 3) in the middle, which gives us 2.6 for the weighted median. The weighted median is a more accurate description of the data.

I sent this first attempt to Richard Romley, who invented the method of first working with groups when designing a query. It made it quite a bit simpler, but let me take you through the steps so you can see the reasoning.

Look at the WHERE clause. It could use some algebra, and since it deals only with aggregate functions and scalar subqueries, you could move it into a HAVING clause. Moving things from the WHERE clause into the HAVING clause in a grouped query is important for performance, but it is not always possible.

First, though, let's do some algebra on the expression in the WHERE clause.

```
lesser <= (SELECT COUNT(*) FROM Parts)/2.0
```

Since we already have lesser, equal, and greater for every row in the derived table Partitions, and since the sum of lesser, equal, and greater must always be exactly equal to the total number of rows in the Parts table, we can replace the scalar subquery with this expression:

```
lesser <= (lesser + equal + greater)/2.0
```

But this is the same as:

```
2.0 * lesser <= lesser + equal + greater
```

which becomes:

```
2.0 * lesser - lesser <= equal + greater
```

which becomes:

```
lesser <= equal + greater
```

So the query becomes:

```
SELECT AVG(DISTINCT weight)
  FROM (SELECT P1.part_nbr, P1.weight,
                SUM(CASE WHEN P2.weight < P1.weight
                         THEN 1 ELSE 0 END),
                SUM(CASE WHEN P2.weight = P1.weight
                         THEN 1 ELSE 0 END),
                SUM(CASE WHEN P2.weight > P1.weight
```

```
                              THEN 1 ELSE 0 END)
               FROM Parts AS P1, Parts AS P2
              GROUP BY P1.part_nbr, P1.weight)
                 AS Partitions (part_nbr, weight, lesser, equal,
greater)
 WHERE lesser = greater
    OR (lesser <= equal + greater
         AND greater <= equal + lesser);
```

We can rewrite the WHERE clause with DeMorgan's law.

```
 WHERE lesser = greater
    OR (equal >= lesser - greater
        AND equal >= greater - lesser)
```

But this is the same as:

```
 WHERE lesser = greater
    OR equal >= ABS(lesser - greater)
```

But if the first condition was true (lesser = greater), the second must necessarily also be true (i.e., equal >= 0), so the first clause is redundant and can be eliminated completely.

```
 WHERE equal >= ABS(lesser - greater)
```

So much for algebra. Instead of a WHERE clause operating on the columns of the derived table, why not perform the same test as a HAVING clause on the inner query that derives Partitions? This eliminates all but one column from the derived table, it will run much faster, and it simplifies the query to this:

```
SELECT AVG(DISTINCT weight)
  FROM (SELECT P1.weight
          FROM Parts AS P1, Parts AS P2
         GROUP BY P1.part_nbr, P1.weight
        HAVING SUM(CASE WHEN P2.weight = P1.weight
                        THEN 1 ELSE 0 END)
        >= ABS(SUM(CASE WHEN P2.weight < P1.weight THEN 1
                        WHEN P2.weight > P1.weight THEN -1
                        ELSE 0 END)))
        AS Partitions;
```

If you prefer to use functions instead of a CASE expression, then use this version of the query:

```
SELECT AVG(DISTINCT weight)
  FROM (SELECT P1.weight
          FROM Parts AS P1, Parts AS P2
         GROUP BY P1.part_nbr, P1.weight
        HAVING SUM(ABS(1 - SIGN(P1.weight - P2.weight))
               >= ABS(SUM(SIGN (P1.weight - P2.weight)))
        AS Partitions;
```

23.3.9 Ken Henderson's Median

In many SQL products, the fastest way to find the median is to use a cursor and just go to the middle of the sorted table. Ken Henderson published a version of this solution with a cursor that can be translated in SQL/PSM. Assume that we wish to find the median of column "x" in table Foobar.

```
BEGIN
DECLARE idx INTEGER;
DECLARE median NUMERIC(20,5);
DECLARE median2 NUMERIC(20,5);
DECLARE Median_Cursor CURSOR FOR
 SELECT x
   FROM Foobar
  ORDER BY x
    FOR READ ONLY;

SET idx
    = CASE
      WHEN (MOD(SELECT COUNT(*) FROM Foobar), 2) = 0
      THEN (SELECT COUNT(*) FROM Foobar)/2
      ELSE ((SELECT COUNT(*) FROM Foobar)/2) + 1 END;

OPEN Median_Cursor;
FETCH ABSOLUTE idx FROM Median_Cursor INTO median;
IF MOD(idx, 2) = 0
THEN FETCH Median_Cursor INTO median2;
     SET median = (median + median2)/2;
END IF;
CLOSE Median_Cursor;
END;
```

This might not be true in other products. Some of them have a median function that uses the balanced tree indexes to locate the middle of the distribution.

If the distribution is symmetrical and has only a single peak, then the mode, median, and mean are the same value. If not, then the distribution is somehow skewed. If (mode < median < mean) then the distribution is skewed to the right. If (mode > median > mean) then the distribution is skewed to the left.

23.4 Variance and Standard Deviation

The standard deviation is a measure of how far away from the average the values in a normally distributed population are. It is hard to calculate in SQL, because it involves a square root, and standard SQL has only the basic four arithmetic operators.

Many vendors will allow you to use other math functions, but in all fairness, most SQL databases are in commercial applications and have little or no need for engineering or statistical calculations.

The usual trick is to load the raw data into an appropriate host language, such as FORTRAN, and do the work there. The formula for the standard deviation is:

$$\sqrt{\sum x^2 - ((\sum x^2/n)/(n - 1)))}$$

where (n) is the number of items in the sample set, and the *x*s are the values of the items.

The variance is defined as the standard deviation squared, so we can avoid taking a square root and keep the calculations in pure SQL. The queries look like this:

```
CREATE TABLE Samples (x REAL NOT NULL);
INSERT INTO Samples (x)
VALUES (64.0), (48.0), (55.0), (68.0), (72.0),
       (59.0), (57.0), (61.0), (63.0), (60.0),
       (60.0), (43.0), (67.0), (70.0), (65.0),
       (55.0), (56.0), (64.0), (61.0), (60.0);
SELECT ((COUNT(*) * SUM(x*x)) - (SUM(x) * SUM(x)))
        /(COUNT(*) * (COUNT(*)-1)) AS variance
  FROM Samples;
```

If you want to check this on your own SQL product, the correct answer is 48.9894 . . . or just 49 depending how you handle rounding. If your SQL product has a standard deviation operator, use it instead.

23.5 Average Deviation

If you have a version of SQL with an absolute value function, `ABS()`, you can also compute the average deviation following this pattern:

```
BEGIN
SELECT AVG(x) INTO :average FROM Samples;
SELECT SUM(ABS(x - :average)) / COUNT(x) AS AverDeviation
  FROM Samples;
END;
```

This is a measure of how far data values drift away from the average, without any consideration of the direction of the drift.

23.6 Cumulative Statistics

A cumulative or running statistic looks at each data value and how it is related to the whole data set. The most common examples involve changes in an aggregate value over time or on some other well-ordered dimension. A bank balance, which changes with each deposit or withdrawal, is a running total over time. The total weight of a delivery truck as we add each package is a running total over the set of packages. But since two packages can have the same weight, we need a way to break ties—for example, use the arrival dates of the packages, and if that fails, use the alphabetical order of the last names of the shippers. In SQL, this means that we need a table with a key that we can use to order the rows.

Computer people classify reports as one-pass reports or two-pass reports, a terminology that comes from the number of times the computer used to have to read the data file to produce the desired results. These are really cumulative aggregate statistics.

Most report writers can produce a listing with totals and other aggregated descriptive statistics after each grouping (e.g., "Give me the total amount of sales broken down by salesmen within territories"). Such reports are called banded reports or control-break reports, depending on the vendor. The closest thing to such reports that the SQL language has is the `GROUP BY` clause used with aggregate functions.

The two-pass report involves finding out something about the group as a whole in the first pass, then using that information in the second pass to produce the results for each row in the group. The most common two-pass reports order the groups against each other ("Show me the total sales in each territory, ordered from high to low") or show the cumulative totals or cumulative percentages within a group ("Show me what percentage each customer contributes to total sales").

23.6.1 Running Totals

Running totals keep track of changes, which usually occur over time, but these could be changes on some other well-ordered dimension. A common example we all know is a bank account, for which we record withdrawals and deposits in a checkbook register. The running total is the balance of the account after each transaction. The query for the checkbook register is simply:

```
SELECT B0.transaction, B0.trans_date, SUM(B1.amount) AS balance
  FROM BankAccount AS B0, BankAccount AS B1
 WHERE B1.trans_date <= B0.trans_date
 GROUP BY B0.transaction, B0.trans_date;
```

You can use a scalar subquery instead:

```
SELECT B0.transaction, B0.trans_date,
       (SELECT SUM(B1.amount)
          FROM BankAccount AS B1
         WHERE B1.trans_date <= B0.trans_date) AS balance
 FROM BankAccount AS B0;
```

Which version will work better is dependent on your SQL product. Notice that this query handles both deposits (positive numbers) and withdrawals (negative numbers). There is a problem with running totals when two items occur at the same time. In this example, the transaction code keeps the transactions unique, but it is possible to have a withdrawal and a deposit on the same day that will be aggregated together.

If we showed the withdrawals before the deposits on that day, the balance could fall below zero, which might trigger some actions we don't want. The rule in banking is that deposits are credited before withdrawals on the same day, so simply extend the transaction date to show all

deposits with a time before all withdrawals to fool the query. But remember that not all situations have a clearly defined policy like this.

Here is another version of the cumulative total problem that attempts to reduce the work done in the outermost query. Assume we have a table with data on the amount of sales to customers. We want to see each amount and the cumulative total, in order by the amount, at which the customer gave us more than $500.00 in business.

```
SELECT C1.cust_id, C1.sales_amt, SUM(C2.sales_amt) AS
cumulative_amt
  FROM Customers AS C1
       INNER JOIN
       Customers AS C2
       ON C1.sales_amt <= C2.sales_amt
 WHERE C1.sales_amt
        >= (SELECT MAX(X.sales_amt)
              FROM (SELECT C3.
                      FROM Customers AS C3
                           INNER JOIN
                           Customers AS C4
                           ON C3.sales_amt <= C4.sales_amt
                     GROUP BY C3.cust_id, C3.sales_amt
                    HAVING SUM(C4.sales_amt) >= 500.00) AS
X(sales_amt))
 GROUP BY C1.cust_id, C1.sales_amt;
```

This query limits the processing that must be done in the outer query by first calculating the cutoff point for each customer. This sort of trick is best for larger tables where the self-join is often very slow.

23.6.2 Running Differences

Another kind of statistic, related to running totals, is running differences. In this case, we have the actual amount of something at various points in time and we want to compute the change since the last reading. Here is a quick scenario: we have a clipboard and a paper form on which we record the quantities of a chemical in a tank at different points in time from a gauge. We need to report the time, the gauge reading, and the difference between each reading and the preceding one. Here is some sample result data, showing the calculation we need:

```
tank   reading              quantity  difference
==================================================
'50A'   '2005-02-01-07:30'    300    NULL  --starting data
'50A'   '2005-02-01-07:35'    500    200
'50A'   '2005-02-01-07:45'   1200    700
'50A'   '2005-02-01-07:50'    800    -400
'50A'   '2005-02-01-08:00'   NULL    NULL
'50A'   '2005-02-01-09:00'   1300    500
'51A'   '2005-02-01-07:20'   6000    NULL  -- starting data
'51A'   '2005-02-01-07:22'   8000    2000
'51A'   '2005-02-01-09:30'   NULL    NULL
'51A'   '2005-02-01-00:45'   5000    -3000
'51A'   '2005-02-01-01:00'   2500    -2500
```

The `NULL` values mean that we missed taking a reading. The trick is a correlated subquery expression that computes the difference between the quantity in the current row and the quantity in the row with the largest known time value that is less than the time in the current row on the same date and on the same tank.

```
SELECT tank, time,
      (quantity
       - (SELECT quantity
            FROM Deliveries AS D1
           WHERE D1.tank = D0.tank -- same tank
             AND D1.time
                 = (SELECT (MAX D2.time) -- most recent delivery
                      FROM Deliveries AS D2
                     WHERE D2.tank = D0.tank -- same tank
                      AND D2.time < D0.time))) AS difference
 FROM Deliveries AS D0;
```

This is a modification of the running-totals query, but it is more elaborate, since it cannot use the sum of the prior history.

23.6.3 Cumulative Percentages

Cumulative percentages are a bit more complex than running totals or differences. They show what percentage of the whole set of data values the current subset of data values is. Again, this is easier to show with an example than to say in words. You are given a table of the sales made by your sales force, which looks like this:

```
CREATE TABLE Sales
(salesman CHAR(10),
 client_name CHAR(10),
 sales_amount DECIMAL (9,2) NOT NULL,
PRIMARY KEY (salesman, client_name));
```

The problem is to show each salesman, his client, the amount of that sale, what percentage of his total sales volume that one sale represents, and the cumulative percentage of his total sales we have reached at that point. We will sort the clients from the largest amount to the smallest. This problem is based on a salesman's report originally written for a small commercial printing company. The idea was to show the salesmen where their business was coming from and to persuade them to give up their smaller accounts (defined as the lower 20%) to new salesmen. The report lets the salesman run his finger down the page and see which customers represented the top 80% of his income.

We can use derived tables to build layers of aggregation in the same query.

```
SELECT S0.salesman, S0.client_name, S0.sales_amt,
      ((S0.sales_amt * 100)/ ST.salesman_total)
         AS percent_of_total,
      (SUM(S1.sales_amt)/((S0.sales_amt * 100)/
ST.salesman_total))
         AS cum_percent
  FROM Sales AS S0
       INNER JOIN
       Sales AS S1
       ON (S0.salesman, S0.client_name) <= (S1.salesman,
S1.client_name)
         INNER JOIN
         (SELECT S2.salesman, SUM(S1.sales_amt)
            FROM Sales AS S2
          GROUP BY S2.salesman) AS ST(salesman, salesman_total)
         ON S0.salesman = ST.salesman
 GROUP BY S0.salesman, S0.client_name, S0.sales_amt;
```

However, if your SQL allows subqueries in the `SELECT` clause but not in the `FROM` clause, you can fake it with this query:

```
SELECT S0.salesman, S0.client_name, S0.sales_amt
      (S0.sales_amt * 100.00/ (SELECT SUM(S1.sales_amt)
                                FROM Sales AS S1
                               WHERE S0.salesman = S1.salesman))
      AS percentage_of_total,
      (SELECT SUM(S3.sales_amt)
         FROM Sales AS S3
        WHERE S0.salesman = S3.salesman
          AND (S3.sales_amt > S0.sales_amt
               OR (S3.sales_amt = S0.sales_amt
                   AND S3.client_name >= S0.client_name))) *
100.00
      / (SELECT SUM(S2.sales_amt)
           FROM Sales AS S2
          WHERE S0.salesman = S2.salesman) AS cum_percent
  FROM Sales AS S0;
```

This query will probably run like glue.

23.6.4 Rankings and Related Statistics

Martin Tillinger posted this problem on the MSACCESS forum of CompuServe in early 1995. How do you rank your salesmen in each territory, given a SalesReport table that looks like this?

```
CREATE TABLE SalesReport
(salesman CHAR(20) NOT NULL PRIMARY KEY
      REFERENCES Salesforce(salesman),
 territory INTEGER NOT NULL,
 sales_tot DECIMAL (8,2) NOT NULL);
```

This statistic is called a ranking. A ranking is shown as integers that represent the ordinal values (first, second, third, and so on) of the elements of a set based on one of the values. In this case, sales personnel are ranked by their total sales within a territory. The one with the highest total sales is in first place, the next highest is in second place, and so forth.

The hard question is how to handle ties. The rule is that if two salespersons have the same value, they have the same ranking, and there are no gaps in the rankings. This is the nature of ordinal numbers—there cannot be a third place without a first and a second place. A query that will do this for us is:

```
SELECT S1.salesman, S1.territory, S1.sales_tot,
      (SELECT COUNT(DISTINCT sales_tot)
         FROM SalesReport AS S2
        WHERE S2.sales_tot >= S1.sales_tot
          AND S2.territory = S1.territory) AS rank
 FROM SalesReport AS S1;
```

You might also remember that this is really a version of the generalized extrema functions we already discussed. Another way to write this query is thus:

```
SELECT S1.salesman, S1.territory, MAX(S1.sales_tot),
       SUM (CASE
            WHEN (S1.sales_tot || S1.name)
                <= (S2.sales_tot || S2.name)
            THEN 1 ELSE 0 END) AS rank
 FROM SalesReport AS S2, SalesReport AS S2
WHERE S1.salesman <> S2.salesman
  AND S1.territory = S2.territory
GROUP BY S1.salesman, S1.territory;
```

This query uses the `MAX()` function on the nongrouping columns in the SalesReport to display them so that the aggregation will work.

It is worth looking at the four possible variations on this basic query to see what each change does to the result set.

Version 1: `COUNT(DISTINCT) and >=` yields a ranking.

```
SELECT S1.salesman, S1.territory, S1.sales_tot,
      (SELECT COUNT(DISTINCT sales_tot)
         FROM SalesReport AS S2
        WHERE S2.sales_tot >= S1.sales_tot
          AND S2.territory = S1.territory) AS rank
 FROM SalesReport AS S1;
```

```
salesman    territory sales_tot       rank
=============================================
'Wilson'           1     990.00          1
'Smith'            1     950.00          2
'Richards'         1     800.00          3
'Quinn'            1     700.00          4
'Parker'           1     345.00          5
'Jones'            1     345.00          5
```

```
'Hubbard'           1      345.00            5
'Date'              1      200.00            6
'Codd'              1      200.00            6
'Blake'             1      100.00            7
```

Version 2: `COUNT(DISTINCT)` and > yields a ranking, but it starts at zero.

```
SELECT S1.salesman, S1.territory, S1.sales_tot,
      (SELECT COUNT(DISTINCT sales_tot)
         FROM SalesReport AS S2
        WHERE S2.sales_tot > S1.sales_tot
          AND S2.territory = S1.territory) AS rank
  FROM SalesReport AS S1;
```

```
salesman    territory sales_tot       rank
=============================================
'Wilson'            1      990.00            0
'Smith'             1      950.00            1
'Richard'           1      800.00            2
'Quinn'             1      700.00            3
'Parker'            1      345.00            4
'Jones'             1      345.00            4
'Hubbard'           1      345.00            4
'Date'              1      200.00            5
'Codd'              1      200.00            5
'Blake'             1      100.00            6
```

Version 3: `COUNT(ALL)` and >= yields a standing which starts at one.

```
SELECT S1.salesman, S1.territory, S1.sales_tot,
      (SELECT COUNT(sales_tot)
         FROM SalesReport AS S2
        WHERE S2.sales_tot >= S1.sales_tot
          AND S2.territory = S1.territory) AS standing
  FROM SalesReport AS S1;
```

```
salesman    territory sales_tot   standing
=============================================
'Wilson'            1      990.00            1
'Smith'             1      950.00            2
```

```
'Richard'        1      800.00          3
'Quinn'          1      700.00          4
'Parker'         1      345.00          7
'Jones'          1      345.00          7
'Hubbard'        1      345.00          7
'Date'           1      200.00          9
'Codd'           1      200.00          9
'Blake'          1      100.00         10
```

Version 4: `COUNT(ALL)` and > yields a standing that starts at zero.

```
SELECT S1.salesman, S1.territory, S1.sales_tot,
      (SELECT COUNT(sales_tot)
         FROM SalesReport AS S2
        WHERE S2.sales_tot > S1.sales_tot
          AND S2.territory = S1.territory) AS standing
 FROM SalesReport AS S1;
```

```
salesman    territory sales_tot    standing
===============================================
'Wilson'         1      990.00          0
'Smith'          1      950.00          1
'Richard'        1      800.00          2
'Quinn'          1      700.00          3
'Parker'         1      345.00          4
'Jones'          1      345.00          4
'Hubbard'        1      345.00          4
'Date'           1      200.00          7
'Codd'           1      200.00          7
'Blake'          1      100.00          9
```

Another system, used in some British schools and in horse racing, will also leave gaps in the numbers, but in a different direction. For example given this set of Marks:

```
Marks  class_standing
======================
100          1
 90          2
 90          2
 70          4
```

Both students with 90 were second because only one person had a higher mark. The student with 70 was fourth because there were three people ahead of him. With our data, that would be:

```
SELECT S1.salesman, S1.territory, S1.sales_tot,
      (SELECT COUNT(S2. sales_tot)
         FROM SalesReport AS S2
        WHERE S2.sales_tot > S1.sales_tot
          AND S2.territory = S1.territory) + 1 AS british
  FROM SalesReport AS S1;
```

```
salesman    territory sales_tot      british
=============================================
'Wilson'           1     990.00           1
'Smith'            1     950.00           2
'Richard'          1     800.00           3
'Quinn'            1     700.00           4
'Parker'           1     345.00           5
'Jones'            1     345.00           5
'Hubbard'          1     345.00           5
'Date'             1     200.00           8
'Codd'             1     200.00           8
'Blake'            1     100.00          10
```

As an aside for the mathematicians among the readers, I always use the heuristics that it helps solve an SQL problem to think in terms of sets. What we are looking for in these ranking queries is how to assign an ordinal number to a subset of the SalesReport table. This subset is the rows that have an equal or higher sales volume than the salesman at whom we are looking. Or in other words, one copy of the SalesReport table provides the elements of the subsets, and the other copy provides the boundary of the subsets. This count is really a sequence of nested subsets.

If you happen to have had a good set theory course, you would remember John von Neumann's definition of the *n*th ordinal number; it is the set of all ordinal numbers less than the *n*th number.

23.6.5 Quintiles and Related Statistics

Once you have the ranking, it is fairly easy to classify the data set into percentiles, quintiles, or deciles. These are coarser versions of a ranking that use subsets of roughly equal size. A quintile is 1/5 of the population,

a decile is 1/10 of the population, and a percentile is 1/100 of the population. I will present quintiles here, since whatever we do for them can be generalized to other partitionings. This statistic is popular with schools, so I will use the SAT scores for an imaginary group of students for my example.

```
SELECT T1.student_id, T1.score, T1.rank,
       CASE WHEN T1.rank <= 0.2 * T2.population_size THEN 1
            WHEN T1.rank <= 0.4 * T2.population_size THEN 2
            WHEN T1.rank <= 0.6 * T2.population_size THEN 3
            WHEN T1.rank <= 0.8 * T2.population_size THEN 4
            ELSE 5 END AS quintile
  FROM (SELECT S1.student_id, S1.score,
               (SELECT COUNT(*)
                  FROM SAT_Scores AS S2
                 WHERE S2.score >= S1.score)
          FROM SAT_Scores AS S1) AS T1(student_id, score, rank)
               CROSS JOIN
              (SELECT COUNT(*) FROM SAT_Scores)
               AS T2(population_size);
```

The idea is straightforward: compute the rank for each element and then put it into a bucket whose size is determined by the population size. There are the same problems with ties that we had with rankings, as well as problems about what to do when the population is skewed.

23.7 Cross Tabulations

A cross tabulation, or crosstab for short, is a common statistical report. It can be done in IBM's QMF tool, using the ACROSS summary option, and in many other SQL-based reporting packages. SPSS, SAS, and other statistical packages have library procedures or language constructs for crosstabs. Many spreadsheets can load the results of SQL queries and perform a crosstab within the spreadsheet.

If you can use a reporting package on the server in a client/server system instead of the following method, do so. It will run faster and in less space than the method discussed here.

However, if you have to use the reporting package on the client side, the extra time required to transfer data will make these methods on the server side much faster.

A one-way crosstab "flattens out" a table to display it in a report format. Assume that we have a table of sales by product and the dates the sales were made. We want to print out a report of the sales of products by years for a full decade. The solution is to create a table and populate it to look like an identity matrix (all elements on the diagonal are one, all others zero) with a rightmost column of all ones to give a row total, then `JOIN` the Sales table to it.

```
CREATE TABLE Sales
(product_name CHAR(15) NOT NULL,
 product_price DECIMAL(5,2) NOT NULL,
 qty INTEGER NOT NULL,
 sales_year INTEGER NOT NULL);

CREATE TABLE Crosstabs
(year INTEGER NOT NULL,
 year1 INTEGER NOT NULL,
 year2 INTEGER NOT NULL,
 year3 INTEGER NOT NULL,
 year4 INTEGER NOT NULL,
 year5 INTEGER NOT NULL,
 row_total INTEGER NOT NULL);
```

The table would be populated as follows:

```
Sales_year year1  year2  year3  year4  year5  row_total
=========================================================
1990         1      0      0      0      0      1
1991         0      1      0      0      0      1
1992         0      0      1      0      0      1
1993         0      0      0      1      0      1
1994         0      0      0      0      1      1
```

The query to produce the report table is

```
SELECT S1.product_name,
   SUM(S1.qty * S1.product_price * C1.year1),
   SUM(S1.qty * S1.product_price * C1.year2),
   SUM(S1.qty * S1.product_price * C1.year3),
   SUM(S1.qty * S1.product_price * C1.year4),
   SUM(S1.qty * S1.product_price * C1.year5),
```

```
  SUM(S1.qty * S1.product_price * C1.row_total)
FROM Sales AS S1, Crosstabs AS C1
WHERE S1.year = C1.year
GROUP BY S1.product_name;
```

Obviously, `(S1.product_price * S1.qty)` is the total dollar amount of each product in each year. The year *n* column will be either a one or a zero. If it is a zero, the total dollar amount in the `SUM()` is zero; if it is a one, the total dollar amount in the `SUM()` is unchanged.

This solution lets you adjust the time frame being shown in the report by replacing the values in the year column to whatever consecutive years you wish. A two-way crosstab takes two variables and produces a spreadsheet with all values of one variable on the rows and all values of the other represented by the columns. Each cell in the table holds the `COUNT` of entities that have those values for the two variables. `NULL`s will not fit into a crosstab very well, unless you decide to make them a group of their own or to remove them.

Another trick is to use the `POSITION()` function to convert a string into a one or a zero. For example, assume we have a "day of the week" function that returns a three-letter abbreviation and we want to report the sales of items by day of the week in a horizontal list.

```
CREATE TABLE Weekdays
(day_name CHAR(3) NOT NULL PRIMARY KEY,
 mon INTEGER NOT NULL,
 tue INTEGER NOT NULL,
 wed INTEGER NOT NULL,
 thu INTEGER NOT NULL,
 fri INTEGER NOT NULL,
 sat INTEGER NOT NULL,
 sun INTEGER NOT NULL);

INSERT INTO WeekDays
VALUES ('MON', 1, 0, 0, 0, 0, 0, 0),
       ('TUE', 0, 1, 0, 0, 0, 0, 0),
       ('WED', 0, 0, 1, 0, 0, 0, 0),
       ('THU', 0, 0, 0, 1, 0, 0, 0),
       ('FRI', 0, 0, 0, 0, 1, 0, 0),
       ('SAT', 0, 0, 0, 0, 0, 1, 0),
       ('SUN', 0, 0, 0, 0, 0, 0, 1);
```

```
SELECT item,
      SUM(amt * qty *
          * mon * POSITION('MON' IN DOW(sales_date))) AS mon_tot,
      SUM(amt * qty
          * tue * POSITION('TUE' IN DOW(sales_date))) AS tue_tot,
      SUM(amt * qty
          * wed * POSITION('WED' IN DOW(sales_date))) AS wed_tot,
      SUM(amt * qty
          * thu * POSITION('THU' IN DOW(sales_date))) AS thu_tot,
      SUM(amt * qty
          * fri * POSITION('FRI' IN DOW(sales_date))) AS fri_tot,
      SUM(amt * qty
          * sat * POSITION('SAT' IN DOW(sales_date))) AS sat_tot,
      SUM(amt * qty
          * sun * POSITION('SUN' IN DOW(sales_date))) AS sun_tot
 FROM Weekdays, Sales;
```

There are also totals for each column and each row, as well as a grand total. Crosstabs of (n) variables are defined by building an n-dimensional spreadsheet. But you cannot easily print (n) dimensions on two-dimensional paper. The usual trick is to display the results as a two-dimensional grid with one or both axes as a tree structure. The way the values are nested on the axis is usually under program control; thus, "race within sex" shows sex broken down by race, whereas "sex within race" shows race broken down by sex.

Assume that we have a table, Personnel (emp_nbr, sex, race, job_nbr, salary_amt), keyed on employee number, with no NULLs in any columns. We wish to write a crosstab of employees by sex and race, which would look like this:

```
         asian  black  caucasian   latino   Other TOTALS
==============================================================
Male       3      2        12         5        5   27
Female     1     10        20         2        9   42
TOTAL      4     12        32         7       14   69
```

The first thought is to use a GROUP BY and write a simple query, thus:

```
SELECT sex, race, COUNT(*)
  FROM Personnel
 GROUP BY sex, race;
```

This approach works fine for two variables and would produce a table that could be sent to a report writer program to give a final version. But where are your column and row totals? This means you also need to write these two queries:

```
SELECT race, COUNT(*) FROM Personnel GROUP BY race;
SELECT sex, COUNT(*) FROM Personnel GROUP BY sex;
```

However, what I wanted was a table with a row for males and a row for females, with columns for each of the racial groups, just as I drew it.

But let us assume that we want to get this information broken down within a third variable, such as a job code. I want to see the job_nbr and the total by sex and race within each job code. Our query set starts to get bigger and bigger. A crosstab can also include other summary data, such as total or average salary within each cell of the table.

23.7.1 Crosstabs by Cross Join

A solution proposed by John M. Baird of Datapoint in San Antonio, Texas involves creating a matrix table for each variable in the crosstab, thus:

```
SexMatrix
sex   Male Female
==================
'M'      1   0
'F'      0   1

RaceMatrix
race        asian  black  caucasian     latino   Other
=========================================================
asian         1       0          0          0         0
black         0       1          0          0         0
caucasian     0       0          1          0         0
latino        0       0          0          1         0
Other         0       0          0          0         1
```

The query then constructs the cells by using a `CROSS JOIN` (Cartesian product) and summation for each one, thus:

```
SELECT job_nbr,
     SUM(asian * male) AS AsianMale,
     SUM(asian * female) AS AsianFemale,
     SUM(black * male) AS BlackMale,
     SUM(black * female) AS BlackFemale,
     SUM(cauc * male) AS CaucMale,
     SUM(cauc * female) AS CaucFemale,
     SUM(latino * male) AS LatinoMale,
     SUM(latino * female) AS LatinoFemale,
     SUM(other * male) AS OtherMale,
     SUM(other * female) AS OtherFemale
  FROM Personnel, SexMatrix, RaceMatrix
 WHERE (RaceMatrix.race = Personnel.race)
   AND (SexMatrix.sex = Personnel.sex)
 GROUP BY job_nbr;
```

Numeric summary data can be obtained from this table. For example, the total salary for each cell can be computed by `SUM(<race> * <sex> * salary) AS <cell name>` in place of what we have here.

23.7.2 Crosstabs by Outer Joins

Another method, due to Jim Panttaja, uses a series of temporary tables or `VIEW`s and then combines them with `OUTER JOIN`s.

```
CREATE VIEW Guys (race, maletally)
AS SELECT race, COUNT(*)
     FROM Personnel
    WHERE sex = 'M'
    GROUP BY race;
```

Correspondingly, you could have written:

```
CREATE VIEW Dolls (race, femaletally)
AS SELECT race, COUNT(*)
     FROM Personnel
    WHERE sex = 'F'
    GROUP BY race;
```

But they can be combined for a crosstab, without column and row totals, like this:

```
SELECT Guys.race, maletally, femaletally
  FROM Guys LEFT OUTER JOIN Dolls
       ON Guys.race = Dolls.race;
```

The idea is to build a starting column in the crosstab, then progressively add columns to it. You use the `LEFT OUTER JOIN` to avoid missing-data problems.

23.7.3 Crosstabs by Subquery

Another method takes advantage of the orthogonality of correlated subqueries in SQL-92. Think about what each row or column in the crosstab wants.

```
SELECT DISTINCT race,
       (SELECT COUNT(*)
          FROM Personnel AS P1
         WHERE P0.race = P1.race
           AND sex = 'M') AS MaleTally,
       (SELECT COUNT(*)
          FROM Personnel AS P2
         WHERE P0.race = P2.race
           AND sex = 'F') AS FemaleTally
 FROM Personnel AS P0;
```

An advantage of this approach is that you can attach another column to get the row tally by adding

```
(SELECT COUNT(*)
   FROM Personnel AS P3
  WHERE P0.race = P3.race) AS RaceTally
```

Likewise, to get the column tallies, union the previous query with:

```
SELECT  'Summary',
        (SELECT COUNT(*)
           FROM Personnel
          WHERE sex = 'M') AS GrandMaleTally,
        (SELECT COUNT(*)
           FROM Personnel
          WHERE sex = 'F') AS GrandFemaleTally,
```

```
      (SELECT COUNT(*)
         FROM Personnel) AS GrandTally
  FROM Personnel;
```

23.7.4 Crosstabs by CASE Expression

Probably the best method is to use the `CASE` expression. If you need to get the final row of the traditional crosstab, you can add:

```
SELECT sex,
    SUM(CASE race WHEN 'caucasian' THEN 1 ELSE 0 END) AS
caucasian,
    SUM(CASE race WHEN 'black' THEN 1 ELSE 0 END) AS black,
    SUM(CASE race WHEN 'asian' THEN 1 ELSE 0 END) AS asian,
    SUM(CASE race WHEN 'latino' THEN 1 ELSE 0 END) AS latino,
    SUM(CASE race WHEN 'other' THEN 1 ELSE 0 END) AS other,
    COUNT(*) AS row_total
FROM Personnel
GROUP BY sex
UNION ALL
SELECT '    ',
    SUM(CASE race WHEN 'caucasian' THEN 1 ELSE 0 END),
    SUM(CASE race WHEN 'black' THEN 1 ELSE 0 END),
    SUM(CASE race WHEN 'asian' THEN 1 ELSE 0 END),
    SUM(CASE race WHEN 'latino' THEN 1 ELSE 0 END),
    SUM(CASE race WHEN 'other' THEN 1 ELSE 0 END),
    COUNT(*) AS column_total
FROM Personnel;
```

23.8 Harmonic Mean and Geometric Mean

The harmonic mean is defined as the reciprocal of the arithmetic mean of the reciprocals of the values of a set. It is appropriate when dealing with rates and prices. Of limited use, it is found mostly in averaging rates.

```
SELECT COUNT(*)/SUM(1.0/x) AS harmonic_mean
  FROM Foobar;
```

The geometric mean is the exponential of the mean of the logs of the data items. You can also express it as the nth root of the product of the (n) data items. This second form is more subject to rounding errors than

the first. The geometric mean is sometimes a better measure of central tendency than the simple arithmetic mean when you are analyzing change over time.

```
SELECT EXP (AVG (LOG (nbr))) AS geometric_mean
  FROM NumberTable;
```

If you have negative numbers this will blow up, because the logarithm is not defined for values less than or equal to zero.

23.9 Multivariable Descriptive Statistics in SQL

More and more SQL products are adding more complicated descriptive statistics to their aggregate function library. For example, CA-Ingres comes with a very nice set of such tools.

Many of the single-column aggregate functions for which we just gave code are built-in functions. If you have that advantage, then use them. They will have corrections for floating-point rounding errors and be more accurate.

Descriptive statistics are not all single-column computations. You often want to know relationships among several variables for prediction and description. Let's pick one statistic that is representative of this class of functions and see what problems we have writing our own aggregate function for it.

23.9.1 Covariance

The covariance is defined as a measure of the extent to which two variables move together. Financial analysts use it to determine the degree to which return on two securities is related over time. A high covariance indicates similar movements. This code is due to Steve Kass:

```
CREATE TABLE Samples
(sample_nbr INTEGER NOT NULL PRIMARY KEY,
 x FLOAT NOT NULL,
 y FLOAT NOT NULL);

INSERT INTO Samples
VALUES (1, 3, 9), (2, 2, 7), (3, 4, 12), (4, 5, 15), (5, 6, 17);

SELECT sample_nbr, x, y,
       ((1.0/n) * SUM((x - xbar)*(y - ybar))) AS covariance
```

```
FROM Samples
     CROSS JOIN
     (SELECT COUNT(*), AVG(x), AVG(y) FROM Samples)
     AS A (n, xbar, ybar)
GROUP BY n;
```

23.9.2 Pearson's r

One of the most useful covariants is Pearson's *r*, or the linear correlation coefficient. It measures the strength of the linear association between two variables. In English, given a set of observations (x1, y1), (x2, y2), . . . , (x*n*, y*n*), I want to know: when one variable goes up or down, how well does the other variable follow it?

The correlation coefficient always takes a value between +1 and -1. Positive one means that they match to each other exactly. Negative one means that increasing values in one variable correspond to decreasing values in the other variable. A correlation value close to zero indicates no association between the variables. In the real world, you will not see +1 or −1 very often—this would mean that you are looking at a natural law, and not a statistical relationship. The values in between are much more realistic, with 0.70 or greater being a strong correlation.

The formula translates into SQL in a straightforward manner.

```
CREATE TABLE Samples
(sample_name CHAR(3) NOT NULL PRIMARY KEY,
x REAL, y REAL);
INSERT INTO Samples
VALUES ('a', 1.0, 2.0), ('b', 2.0, 5.0), ('c', 3.0, 6.0);
-- r= 0.9608

SELECT (SUM(x - AVG(x))*(y - AVG(y)))
       / SQRT(SUM((x - AVG(x))^2) * SUM((y - AVG(y))^2))
       AS pearson_r
 FROM Samples;
```

`SQRT()` is the square root function, which is quite common in SQL today, and `^2` is the square of the number. Some products use `POWER(x, n)` instead of the exponent notation. Alternately, or you can use repeated multiplication.

23.9.3 NULLs in Multivariable Descriptive Statistics

If (x, y) = (`NULL`, `NULL`), then the query will drop the pair in the aggregate functions, as per the usual rules of SQL. But what is the correct (or reasonable) behavior if (x, y) has one and only one `NULL` in the pair? We can make several arguments.

1. Drop the pairs that contain any `NULL`s. That is quick and easy with a "`WHERE x IS NOT NULL AND y IS NOT NULL`" clause added to the query. The argument is that if you don't know one or both values, how can you know what their relationship is?
2. Convert `(x, NULL)` to `(x, AVG(y))` and `(NULL, y)` to `(AVG(x), y)`. The idea is to "smooth out" the missing values with a reasonable replacement that is based on the whole set from which known values were drawn. There might be better replacement values in a particular situation, but that idea would still hold.
3. Replace (`NULL`, `NULL`) with (a, a) for some value to say that the `NULL`s are in the same grouping. This kind of "pseudo-equality" is the basis for putting `NULL`s into one group in a `GROUP BY` operation. I am not sure what the correct practice for the `(x, NULL)` and `(y, NULL)` pairs are.
4. First calculate a linear regression with the known pairs, say `y = (a + b* x)`, and then fill in the expected values. If you forgot your high school algebra, that would be `y[ i] = a + b * x[ i]` for the pair `(x[ i], NULL)`, and `x[ i] = (y - a) / b`.
5. Catch the `SQLSTATE` warning code message (found in Standard SQL) to show that an aggregate function has dropped `NULL`s before doing the computations, and use the message to report to the user about the missing data.

I can also use `COUNT(*)` and `COUNT(x+y)` to determine how much data is missing. I think we would all agree that if I have a small subset of non-**`NULL`** pairs, then my correlation is less reliable than if I obtained it from a large subset of non-**`NULL`** pairs.

There is no right answer to this question. You will need to know the nature of your data to make a good decision.

Regions, Runs, Gaps, Sequences, and Series

TABLES DO NOT HAVE an ordering to their rows. Yes, the physical storage of the rows in many SQL products might be ordered if the product is built on an old file system. More modern implementations might not construct and materialize the result set rows until the end of the query execution.

The first rule in a relational database is that all relationships are shown in tables by values in columns. This means that things involving an ordering must have a table with at least two columns. One column, the sequence number, is the primary key; the other column has the value that holds that position in the sequence.

The sequence column has consecutive unique integers, without any gaps in the numbering. Examples of this sort of data would be ticket numbers, time series data taken at fixed intervals, and the like. The ordering of those identifiers carries some information, such as physical or temporal location. A subsequence is a set of consecutive unique identifiers within a larger containing sequence that has some property. This property is usually consecutive numbering.

For example, given the data

```
CREATE TABLE List
(seq_nbr INTEGER NOT NULL UNIQUE,
 val INTEGER NOT NULL UNIQUE);
```

```
INSERT INTO List
VALUES (1, 99), (2, 10), (3, 11), (4, 12), (5, 13), (6, 14), (7,
0);
```

You can find subsequences of size three that follow the rule—(10, 11, 12), (11, 12, 13), and (12, 13, 14)—but the longest sequence is (10, 11, 12, 13, 14), and it is of size five.

A run is like a sequence, but the numbers do not have to be consecutive, just increasing and contiguous. For example, given the run {(1, 1), (2, 2), (3, 12), (4, 15), (5, 23)}, you can find subruns of size three: (1, 2, 12), (2, 12, 15), and (12, 15, 23).

A region is contiguous, and all the values are the same. For example, {(1, 1), (2, 0), (3, 0), (4, 0), (5, 25)} has a region of zeros that is three items long.

In procedural languages, you would simply sort the data and scan it. In SQL, you have to define everything in terms of sets and nested sets. Some of these queries can be done with the OLAP addition to SQL-99, but they are not yet common in SQL products.

24.1 Finding Subregions of Size (n)

This example is adapted from *SQL and Its Applications* (Lorie and Daudenarde 1991). You are given a table of theater seats:

```
CREATE TABLE Theater
(seat_nbr INTEGER NOT NULL PRIMARY KEY, -- sequencing number
 occupancy_status CHAR(1) NOT NULL             -- values
       CONSTRAINT valid_occupancy_status
       CHECK (occupancy_status IN ('A', 'S'));
```

In this table, an occupancy_status code of 'A' means available, and 'S' means sold. Your problem is to write a query that will return the subregions of (*n*) consecutive seats still available. Assume that consecutive seat_nbrs means that the seats are also consecutive for a moment, ignoring rows of seating where seat_nbr(*n*) and seat_nbr((*n*) + 1) might be on different physical theater rows. For (*n*) = 3, we can write a self-JOIN query, thus:

```
SELECT T1.seat_nbr, T2.seat_nbr, T3.seat_nbr
  FROM Theater AT T1, Theater AT T2, Theater AT T3
 WHERE T1.occupancy_status = 'A'
```

```
AND T2.occupancy_status = 'A'
AND T3.occupancy_status = 'A'
AND T2.seat_nbr = T1.seat_nbr + 1
AND T3.seat_nbr = T2.seat_nbr + 1;
```

The trouble with this answer is that it works only for (n = 3). This pattern can be extended for any (n), but what we really want is a generalized query where we can use (n) as a parameter to the query.

The solution given by Lorie and Daudenarde starts with a given seat_nbr and looks at all the available seats between it and ((n) - 1) seats further up. The real trick is switching from the English-language statement "All seats between here and there are available" to the passive-voice version, "Available is the occupancy_status of all the seats between here and there," so that you can see the query.

```
SELECT seat_nbr, ' thru ', (seat_nbr + (:(n) - 1))
  FROM Theater AS T1
 WHERE occupancy_status = 'A'
   AND 'A' = ALL (SELECT occupancy_status
                    FROM Theater AS T2
                   WHERE T2.seat_nbr > T1.seat_nbr
                    AND T2.seat_nbr <=  T1.seat_nbr + (:(n) - 1));
```

Please notice that this returns subregions. That is, if seats (1, 2, 3, 4, 5) are available, this query will return (1, 2, 3), (2, 3, 4), and (3, 4, 5) as its result set.

24.2 Numbering Regions

Instead of looking for a region, we want to number the regions in the order in which they appear. For example, given a view or table with a payment history, we want to break it into groupings of behavior—for example, whether or not the payments were on time or late.

```
CREATE TABLE PaymentHistory
(payment_nbr INTEGER NOT NULL PRIMARY KEY,
 paid_on_time CHAR(1) DEFAULT 'Y' NOT NULL
     CHECK(paid_on_time IN ('Y', 'N')));

INSERT INTO PaymentHistory
VALUES (1006, 'Y'), (1005, 'Y'),
```

```
(1004, 'N'),
(1003, 'Y'), (1002, 'Y'), (1001, 'Y'),
(1000, 'N');
```

The results we want assign a grouping number to each run of on-time/late payments, thus:

```
Results
grping payment_nbr paid_on_time
================================
1         1006          'Y'
1         1005          'Y'
2         1004          'N'
3         1003          'Y'
3         1002          'Y'
3         1001          'Y'
4         1000          'N'
```

A solution by Hugo Kornelis depends on the payments always being numbered consecutively.

```
SELECT (SELECT COUNT(*)
          FROM PaymentHistory AS H2,
               PaymentHistory AS H3
         WHERE H3.payment_nbr = H2.payment_nbr + 1
           AND H3.paid_on_time <> H2.paid_on_time
           AND H2.payment_nbr >= H1.payment_nbr) + 1 AS grping,
      payment_nbr, paid_on_time
 FROM PaymentHistory AS H1;
```

This can be modified for more types of behavior.

24.3 Finding Regions of Maximum Size

A query to find a region, rather than a subregion of a known size, of seats was presented in *SQL Forum* (Rozenshtein, Abramovich, and Birger 1993).

```
SELECT T1.seat_nbr, ' thru ', T2.seat_nbr
  FROM Theater AS T1, Theater AS T2
 WHERE T1.seat_nbr < T2.seat_nbr
```

```
   AND NOT EXISTS
           (SELECT *
              FROM Theater AS T3
             WHERE (T3.seat_nbr BETWEEN T1.seat_nbr AND
T2.seat_nbr
               AND T3.occupancy_status <> 'A')
                OR (T3.seat_nbr = T2.seat_nbr + 1
                    AND T3.occupancy_status = 'A')
                OR (T3.seat_nbr = T1.seat_nbr - 1
                    AND T3.occupancy_status = 'A'));
```

The trick here is to look for the starting and ending seats in the region. The starting seat_nbr of a region is to the right of a sold seat_nbr, and the ending seat_nbr is to the left of a sold seat_nbr. No seat_nbr between the start and the end has been sold.

If you only keep the available seat_nbrs in a table, the solution is a bit easier. It is also a more general problem that applies to any table of sequential, possibly noncontiguous, data:

```
CREATE TABLE AvailableSeating
 (seat_nbr INTEGER NOT NULL
       CONSTRAINT valid_seat_nbr
       CHECK (seat_nbr BETWEEN 001 AND 999));

INSERT INTO Seatings
VALUES (199), (200), (201), (202), (204),
       (210), (211), (212), (214), (218);
```

You need to create a result that will show the start and finish values of each sequence in the table, thus:

```
 Results
 start finish
 ============
  199    202
  204    204
  210    212
  214    214
  218    218
```

This is a common way of finding the missing values in a sequence of tickets sold, unaccounted-for invoices, and so forth. Imagine a number line with closed dots for the numbers that are in the table and open dots for the numbers that are not. What do you see about a sequence? Well, we can start with a fact that anyone who has done inventory knows: the number of elements in a sequence is equal to the ending sequence number minus the starting sequence number plus one. This is a basic property of ordinal numbers:

```
(finish - start + 1) = Length of open seats
```

This tells us that we need to have a self-JOIN with two copies of the table, one for the starting value and one for the ending value of each sequence. Once we have those two items, we can compute the length with our formula and see if it is equal to the count of the items between the start and finish.

```
SELECT S1.seat_nbr, MAX(S2.seat_nbr) -- start and rightmost item
  FROM AvailableSeating AS S1
       INNER JOIN
       AvailableSeating AS S2  -- self-join
       ON S1.seat_nbr <= S2.seat_nbr
          AND (S2.seat_nbr - S1.seat_nbr + 1) -- formula for length
             = (SELECT COUNT(*) -- items in the sequence
                  FROM AvailableSeating AS S3
                 WHERE S3.seat_nbr BETWEEN S1.seat_nbr AND S2.seat_nbr)
                   AND NOT EXISTS (SELECT *
                                     FROM AvailableSeating AS S4
                                    WHERE S1.seat_nbr - 1 = S4.seat_nbr)
 GROUP BY S1.seat_nbr;
```

Finally, we need to be sure that we have the furthest item to the right as the end item. Each sequence of (*n*) items has (*n*) subsequences that all start with the same item. So we finally do a GROUP BY on the starting item and use a MAX() to get the rightmost value.

However, there is a faster version with three tables. This solution is based on another property of the longest possible sequences. If you look to the right of the last item, you do not find anything. Likewise, if you look to the left of the first item, you do not find anything either. These missing items that are "just over the border" define a sequence by framing it. There also cannot be any "gaps"—missing items—inside those borders. That translates into SQL as:

```
SELECT S1.seat_nbr, MIN(S2.seat_nbr) --start and leftmost border
  FROM AvailableSeating AS S1, AvailableSeating AS S2
 WHERE S1.seat_nbr <= S2.seat_nbr
   AND NOT EXISTS  -- border items of the sequence
       (SELECT *
          FROM AvailableSeating AS S3
         WHERE S3.seat_nbr NOT BETWEEN S1.seat_nbr AND
S2.seat_nbr
           AND (S3.seat_nbr = S1.seat_nbr - 1
                OR S3.seat_nbr = S2.seat_nbr + 1))
 GROUP BY S1.seat_nbr;
```

We do not have to worry about getting the rightmost item in the sequence, but we do have to worry about getting the leftmost border. Once we do a `GROUP BY`, we use a `MIN()` to get what we want.

Since the second approach uses only three copies of the original table, it should be a bit faster. Also, the `EXISTS()` predicates can often take advantage of indexing and thus run faster than subquery expressions, which require a table scan.

Michel Walsh came up with two novel ways of getting the range of seat numbers that have been used in the table. He saw that the difference between the value and its rank is a constant for all values in the same consecutive sequence, so we just have to group, and count, on the value minus its rank to get the various consecutive runs (or just keep the maximum). It is so simple, an example will show everything:

```
data = {1, 2, 5, 6, 7, 8, 9, 11, 12, 22}

 data  rank  (data_rank) AS absent
=================================
  1      1      0
  2      2      0
  5      3      2
  6      4      2
  7      5      2
  8      6      2
  9      7      2
 11      8      3
```

```
12       9      3
22      10     12

absent  COUNT(*)
================
  0        2
  2        5
  3        2
 12        1
```

As you can see, the maximum contiguous sequence is 5 (for rows having (data – rank) = 2). Rank is defined as how many values are less than or equal to the actual value, with the assumption of a set of integers without repeated values. This is the query:

```
SELECT X.absent, COUNT(*)
  FROM (SELECT my_data,
               (SELECT COUNT(*)
                  FROM Foobar AS F2
                 WHERE F2.my_data <= F1.my_data),
               (SELECT COUNT(*)
                  FROM Foobar AS F2
                 WHERE F2.my_data <= F1.my_data) - F1.my_data
          FROM Foobar AS F1)
       AS X(my_data, rank, absent);
```

Playing with this basic idea, Mr. Walsh came up with this second query.

```
SELECT MIN(Z.seat_nbr), MAX(Z.seat_nbr)
  FROM (SELECT S1.seat_nbr,
               S1.seat_nbr
               - (SELECT COUNT(*)
                    FROM Seating AS S2
                   WHERE S2.seat_nbr <= S1.seat_nbr)
          FROM Seating AS S1)
       AS Z (seat_nbr, dif_rank)
 GROUP BY Z.dif_rank;
```

The derived table finds the lengths of the blocks of seats to the left of each seat_nbr and uses that length to form groups.

24.4 Bound Queries

Another form of query asks whether there is an overall trend between two points in time bounded by a low value and a high value in the sequence of data. This is easier to show with an example. Let us assume that we have data on the selling prices of a stock in a table. We want to find periods of time when the price was generally increasing.

Consider this data:

```
MyStock
sale_date       price
=====================
'2006-12-01'   10.00
'2006-12-02'   15.00
'2006-12-03'   13.00
'2006-12-04'   12.00
'2006-12-05'   20.00
```

The stock was generally increasing in all the periods that began on December 1 or ended on December 5—that is, it finished higher at the ends of those periods, in spite of the slump in the middle. A query for this problem is:

```
SELECT S1.sale_date AS start_date, S2.sale_date AS finish_date
  FROM MyStock AS S1, MyStock AS S2
 WHERE S1.sale_date < S2.sale_date
   AND NOT EXISTS
        (SELECT *
           FROM MyStock AS S3
          WHERE S3.sale_date BETWEEN S1.sale_date AND
S2.sale_date
            AND S3.price NOT BETWEEN S1.price AND S2.price);
```

24.5 Run and Sequence Queries

Runs are informally defined as sequences with gaps. That is, we have a set of unique numbers whose order has some meaning, but the numbers are not all consecutive. Time series information in which the samples are taken at irregular intervals is an example of this sort of data. Runs can be constructed in the same manner as the sequences by making a minor change in the search condition. Let's do these queries with an abstract table made up of a sequence number and a value:

```
CREATE TABLE Runs
(seq_nbr INTEGER NOT NULL PRIMARY KEY,
 val INTEGER NOT NULL);

 Runs
 seq_nbr    val
 ==========
   1      6
   2     41
   3     12
   4     51
   5     21
   6     70
   7     79
   8     62
   9     30
  10     31
  11     32
  12     34
  13     35
  14     57
  15     19
  16     84
  17     80
  18     90
  19     63
  20     53
  21      3
  22     59
  23     69
  24     27
  25     33
```

One problem is that we do not want to get back all the runs and sequences of length one. Ideally, the length (*n*) of the run should be adjustable. This query will find runs of length (*n*) or greater; if you want runs of exactly (*n*), change the "greater than" sign to an equal sign.

```
SELECT R1.seq_nbr AS start_seq_nbr, R2.seq_nbr AS
end_seq_nbr__nbr
  FROM Runs AS R1, Runs AS R2
```

```
 WHERE R1.seq_nbr < R2.seq_nbr       -- start and end points
   AND (R2.seq_nbr - R1.seq_nbr) > (:(n) - 1) -- length
restrictions
   AND NOT EXISTS     -- ordering within the end points
       (SELECT *
          FROM Runs AS R3, Runs AS R4
         WHERE R4.seq_nbr BETWEEN R1.seq_nbr AND R2.seq_nbr
           AND R3.seq_nbr BETWEEN R1.seq_nbr AND R2.seq_nbr
           AND R3.seq_nbr < R4.seq_nbr
           AND R3.val > R4.val);
```

This query sets up the S1 sequence number as the starting point and the S2 sequence number as the ending point of the run. The monster subquery in the `NOT EXISTS()` predicate is looking for a row in the middle of the run that violates the ordering of the run. If there is none, the run is valid. The best way to understand what is happening is to draw a linear diagram. This shows that as the ordering (seq_nbr) increases, so must the corresponding values (val).

A sequence has the additional restriction that every value increases by one as you scan the run from left to right. This means that in a sequence, the highest value minus the lowest value, plus one, is the length of the sequence.

```
SELECT R1.seq_nbr AS start_seq_nbr, R2.seq_nbr AS
end_seq_nbr__nbr
  FROM Runs AS R1, Runs AS R2
 WHERE R1.seq_nbr < R2.seq_nbr
   AND (R2.seq_nbr - R1.seq_nbr) = (R2.val - R1.val) -- order
condition
   AND (R2.seq_nbr - R1.seq_nbr) > (:(n) - 1) -- length
restrictions
   AND NOT EXISTS
       (SELECT *
            FROM Runs AS R3
         WHERE R3.seq_nbr BETWEEN R1.seq_nbr AND R2.seq_nbr
            AND((R3.seq_nbr - R1.seq_nbr) <> (R3.val - R1.val)
                OR (R2.seq_nbr - R3.seq_nbr) <> (R2.val -
R3.val)));
```

The subquery in the `NOT EXISTS` predicate says that there is no point in between the start and the end of the sequence that violates the ordering condition.

Obviously, any of these queries can be changed from increasing to decreasing, or from strictly increasing to simply increasing or simply decreasing, and so on, by changing the comparison predicates. You can also change the query for finding sequences in a table by altering the size of the step from 1 to *k*, by observing that the difference between the starting position and the ending position should be *k* times the difference between the starting value and the ending value.

24.5.1 Filling in Sequence Numbers

A fair number of SQL programmers want to reuse a sequence of numbers for keys. While I do not approve of the practice of generating a meaningless, unverifiable key after the creation of an entity, the problem of inserting missing numbers is interesting. The usual specifications are:

1. Begin the sequence with one, if it is missing or the table is empty.
2. Reuse the lowest missing number first.
3. Do not exceed some maximum value; if the sequence is full, then give us a warning or a NULL. Another option is to give us `(MAX(seq_nbr) +1)`, so we can add to the high end of the list.

This answer is a good example of thinking in terms of sets rather than doing row-at-a-time processing.

```
SELECT MIN(new_seq_nbr)
  FROM (SELECT CASE
               WHEN (seq_nbr + 1)
                    NOT IN (SELECT seq_nbr FROM List)
               THEN (seq_nbr + 1)
               WHEN (seq_nbr - 1)
                    NOT IN (SELECT seq_nbr FROM List)
               THEN (seq_nbr - 1)
               WHEN 1 NOT IN (SELECT seq_nbr FROM List)
               THEN 1 ELSE NULL END
          FROM List
          WHERE seq_nbr BETWEEN 1 AND
                (SELECT MAX(seq_nbr) FROM List)
          AS P(new_seq_nbr);
```

The idea is to build a table expression of some of the missing values, then pick the minimum one. The starting value, one, is treated as an exception. Since an aggregate function cannot take a query expression as a parameter, we have to use a derived table.

Along the same lines, we can use aggregate functions in a CASE expression:

```
SELECT CASE WHEN MAX(seq_nbr) = COUNT(*)
            THEN CAST(NULL AS INTEGER)
                 -- THEN MAX(seq_nbr) + 1 as other option
            WHEN MIN(seq_nbr) > 1
            THEN 1
            WHEN MAX(seq_nbr) <> COUNT(*)
            THEN (SELECT MIN(seq_nbr)+1
                    FROM List
                   WHERE (seq_nbr)+1
                          NOT IN (SELECT seq_nbr FROM List))
            ELSE NULL END
  FROM List;
```

The first WHEN clause sees whether the table is already full and returns a NULL; the NULL must be cast as an INTEGER to become an expression that can then be used in the THEN clause. However, you might want to increment the list by the next value.

The second WHEN clause looks to see whether the minimum sequence number is one or not. If so, it uses one as the next value

The third WHEN clause handles the situation when there is a gap in the middle of the sequence. It picks the lowest missing number. The ELSE clause is in case of errors and should not be executed.

The order of execution in the CASE expression is important. It is a way of forcing an inspection of the table's values from front to back. Simpler methods based on group characteristics would be:

```
SELECT COALESCE(MIN(L1.seq_nbr) + 1, 1)
  FROM List AS L1
       LEFT OUTER JOIN
       List AS L2
       ON L1.seq_nbr = L2.seq_nbr - 1
 WHERE L2.seq_nbr IS NULL;
```

or:

```
SELECT MIN(F1.seq_nbr + 1)
FROM List AS F1
UNION ALL
VALUE (0)
WHERE (L1.seq_nbr +1)
NOT IN (SELECT seq_nbr FROM List);
```

Finding entire gaps follows from this pattern, and we get this short piece of code.

```
SELECT (s + 1) AS gap_start,
       (e - 1) AS gap_end
  FROM (SELECT L1.seq_nbr, MIN(L2.seq_nbr)
          FROM List AS L1, List AS L2
         WHERE L1.seq_nbr < L2.seq_nbr
         GROUP BY L1.seq_nbr)
       AS G(s, e)
 WHERE (e - 1) > s;
```

Without the derived table we get:

```
SELECT (L1.seq_nbr + 1) AS gap_start,
       (MIN(L2.seq_nbr) - 1) AS gap_end
  FROM List AS L1, List AS L2
 WHERE L1.seq_nbr < L2.seq_nbr
 GROUP BY L1.seq_nbr
HAVING (MIN(L2.seq_nbr) - L1.seq_nbr) > 1;
```

24.6 Summation of a Series

While this topic is a bit more mathematical than most SQL programmers actually have to use in their work, it does demonstrate the power of SQL and a little knowledge of some basic college math.

The summation of a series builds a running total of the values in a table and shows the cumulative total for each value in the series. Let's create a table and some sample data.

```
CREATE TABLE Series
(seq_nbr INTEGER NOT NULL PRIMARY KEY,
```

```
val INTEGER NOT NULL,
answer INTEGER  -- null means not computed yet
);

Sequences
seq_nbr    val  answer
======================
  1          6       6
  2         41      47
  3         12      59
  4         51     110
  5         21     131
  6         70     201
  7         79     280
  8         62     342
  ...
```

This simple summation is not a problem.

```
UPDATE Series
   SET answer = (SELECT SUM(R1.val)
                   FROM Series AS S1
                  WHERE R1.seq_nbr <= Series.seq_nbr)
 WHERE answer IS NULL;
```

This is the form we can use for most problems of this type with only one level of summation. But things can be worse. This problem came from Francisco Moreno, and on the surface it sounds easy. First, create the usual table and populate it.

```
DROP TABLE Series;
CREATE TABLE Series
(seq_nbr INTEGER NOT NULL,
 val REAL NOT NULL,
 answer REAL);

INSERT INTO Series
VALUES (0, 6.0, NULL),
       (1, 6.0, NULL),
       (2, 10.0, NULL),
       (3, 12.0, NULL),
       (4, 14.0, NULL);
```

The goal is to compute the average of the first two terms, then add the third value to the result and average the two of them, and so forth. In this data, we would have:

```
seq_nbr  val   answer
=====================
   0      6.0  NULL
   1      6.0   6.0
   2     10.0   8.0
   3     12.0  10.0
   4     14.0  12.0
```

The first thing we need to do is get rid of the value where (seq_nbr = 0) and change the table to read:

```
seq_nbr  val    answer
======================
 1        12.0  NULL
 2        10.0  NULL
 3        12.0  NULL
 4        14.0  NULL
```

The obvious approach is to do the calculations directly.

```
UPDATE Series
   SET answer = (Series.val
                 + (SELECT R1.answer
                      FROM Series AS S1
                     WHERE R1.seq_nbr = Series.seq_nbr - 1))/2.0
 WHERE answer IS NULL;
```

But there is a problem with this approach. It will only calculate one value at a time. The reason is that this series is much more complex than a simple running total.

What we have is actually a double summation, in which the terms are defined by a continued fraction. Let's work out the first four answers by brute force and see if we can find a pattern.

```
answer1 = (12)/2 = 6
answer2 = ((12)/2 + 10)/2 = 8
answer3 = (((12)/2 + 10)/2 + 12)/2  = 10
answer4 = (((((12)/2 + 10)/2 + 12)/2) + 14)/2 = 12
```

The real trick is to do some algebra and get rid of the nested parentheses.

```
answer1 = (12)/2 = 6
answer2 = (12/4) + (10/2) = 8
answer3 = (12/8) + (10/4) + (12/2) = 10
answer4 = (12/16) + (10/8) + (12/4) + (14/2) = 12
```

When we see powers of 2, we know we can reseq_nbr them with a formula:

```
answer1 = (12)/2^1 = 6
answer2 = (12/(2^2)) + (10/(2^1)) = 8
answer3 = (12/(2^3)) + (10/(2^2)) + (12/(2^1)) = 10
answer4 = (12/2^4) + (10/(2^3)) + (12/(2^2)) + (14/(2^1)) = 12
```

The problem is that you need to "count backwards" from the current value to compute higher powers for the previous terms of the summation. That is simply (current_val - previous_val + 1). Putting it all together, we get this expression:

```
UPDATE Series
   SET answer
       = (SELECT SUM(val
                 * POWER(2,
                         CASE WHEN R1.seq_nbr > 0
                              THEN Series.seq_nbr - R1.seq_nbr + 1
                              ELSE NULL END))
            FROM Series AS S1
           WHERE R1.seq_nbr <= Series.seq_nbr);
```

This assumes that we have a `POWER(base, exponent)` function in our implementation. The reason for the second copy of Series under the name S2 in the `SUM()` expression is that an aggregate function cannot have an outer reference.

24.7 Swapping and Sliding Values in a List

You will often want to manipulate a list of values, changing their sequence position numbers. The simplest such operation is to swap two values in your table.

```
CREATE PROCEDURE SwapValues
(IN low_seq_nbr INTEGER, IN high_seq_nbr INTEGER)
LANGUAGE SQL
BEGIN -- put them in order
SET low_seq_nbr
    = CASE WHEN low_seq_nbr <= high_seq_nbr
           THEN low_seq_nbr ELSE high_seq_nbr;
SET high_seq_nbr
    = CASE WHEN low_seq_nbr <= high_seq_nbr
           THEN high_seq_nbr ELSE low_seq_nbr;
UPDATE Runs -- swap
   SET seq_nbr = low_seq_nbr + ABS(seq_nbr - high_seq_nbr)
 WHERE seq_nbr IN (low_seq_nbr, high_seq_nbr);
END;
```

Inserting a new value into the table is easy:

```
CREATE PROCEDURE InsertValue (IN new_value INTEGER)
LANGUAGE SQL
INSERT INTO Runs (seq_nbr, val)
VALUES ((SELECT MAX(seq_nbr) FROM Runs) + 1, new_value);
```

A bit trickier procedure is to move one value to a new position and slide the remaining values either up or down. This mimics the way a physical queue would act. Here is a solution from Dave Portas.

```
CREATE PROCEDURE SlideValues
(IN old_seq_nbr INTEGER, IN new_seq_nbr INTEGER)
LANGUAGE SQL
UPDATE Runs
   SET seq_nbr
       = CASE
         WHEN seq_nbr = old_seq_nbr THEN new_seq_nbr
        WHEN seq_nbr BETWEEN old_seq_nbr AND new_seq_nbr THEN seq_nbr - 1
        WHEN seq_nbr BETWEEN new_seq_nbr AND old_seq_nbr THEN seq_nbr + 1
         ELSE seq_nbr END
 WHERE seq_nbr BETWEEN old_seq_nbr AND new_seq_nbr
    OR seq_nbr BETWEEN new_seq_nbr AND old_seq_nbr;
```

This handles moving a value to a higher or to a lower position in the table. You can see how calls or slight changes to these procedures could do other related operations.

One of the most useful tricks is to have a calendar table with a Julianized date column. Instead of trying to manipulate temporal data, convert the dates to a sequence of integers and treat the queries as regions, runs, gaps, and so forth.

The sequence can be made up of calendar days or Julianized business days, which do not include holidays and weekends. There are a lot of possible methods.

24.8 Condensing a List of Numbers

The goal is to take a list of numbers and condense them into contiguous ranges. Show the high and low values for each range; if the range has one number, then the high and low values will be the same. This answer is due to Steve Kass.

```
SELECT MIN(i) AS low, MAX(i) AS high
  FROM (SELECT N1.i, COUNT(N2.i) - N1.i
          FROM Numbers AS N1, Numbers AS N2
         WHERE N2.i <= N1.i
         GROUP BY N1.i)
       AS N(i, gp)
 GROUP BY gp;
```

24.9 Folding a List of Numbers

It is possible to use the Sequence table to give columns in the same row, which are related to each other, values with a little math instead of self-joins.

For example, given the numbers 1 to (n), you might want to spread them out across (k) columns. Let ($k = 3$) so we can see the pattern.

```
SELECT seq_nbr,
       CASE WHEN MOD((seq_nbr + 1), 3) = 2
                 AND seq_nbr + 1 <= :n
            THEN (seq_nbr + 1)
            ELSE NULL END AS second,
       CASE WHEN MOD((seq_nbr + 2), 3) = 0
                 AND (seq_nbr + 2) <= :n
            THEN (seq_nbr + 2)
```

```
          ELSE NULL END AS third
  FROM Sequence
 WHERE MOD((seq_nbr + 3), 3) = 1
  AND seq_nbr <= :n;
```

Columns which have no value assigned to them will get a NULL. That is, for ($n = 8$) the incomplete row will be (7, 8, NULL) and for ($n = 7$) it would be (7, NULL, NULL). We never get a row with (NULL, NULL, NULL).

Using math can be fancier. In a golf tournament, the players with the lowest and highest scores are matched together for the next round. Then the players with the second lowest and second highest scores are matched together, and so forth. If the number of players is odd, the player with the middle score sits out that round. These pairs can be built with a simple query.

```
SELECT seq_nbr AS low_score,
       CASE WHEN seq_nbr <= (:n - seq_nbr)
            THEN (:n - seq_nbr) + 1
            ELSE NULL END AS high_score
  FROM Sequence AS S1
 WHERE S1.seq_nbr
       <= CASE WHEN MOD(:n, 2) = 1
               THEN FLOOR(:n/2) + 1
               ELSE (:n/2) END;
```

If you play around with the basic math functions, you can do quite a bit.

24.10 Coverings

Mikito Harakiri proposed the problem of writing the shortest SQL query that would return a minimal cover of a set of intervals. For example, given this table, how do you find the contiguous numbers that are completely covered by the given intervals?

```
CREATE TABLE Intervals
(x INTEGER NOT NULL,
 y INTEGER NOT NULL,
CHECK (x <= y),
PRIMARY KEY (x, y));
```

```
INSERT INTO Intervals VALUES (1, 3);
INSERT INTO Intervals VALUES (2, 5);
INSERT INTO Intervals VALUES (4, 11);
INSERT INTO Intervals VALUES (10, 12);

INSERT INTO Intervals VALUES (20, 21);

INSERT INTO Intervals VALUES (120, 130);
INSERT INTO Intervals VALUES (120, 128);
INSERT INTO Intervals VALUES (120, 122);
INSERT INTO Intervals VALUES (121, 132);
INSERT INTO Intervals VALUES (121, 122);
INSERT INTO Intervals VALUES (121, 124);
INSERT INTO Intervals VALUES (121, 123);
INSERT INTO Intervals VALUES (126, 127);
```

The query should return

```
Results
min_x   MAX(y)
================
  1        12
 20        21
120       132
```

Dieter Nöth found an answer with OLAP functions:

```
SELECT min_x, MAX(y)
  FROM (SELECT x, y,
               MAX(CASE WHEN x <= MAX_Y THEN NULL ELSE x END)
               OVER (ORDER BY x, y
                     ROWS UNBOUNDED PRECEDING) AS min_x
          FROM (SELECT x, y,
                       MAX(y)
                       OVER(ORDER BY x, y
                       ROWS BETWEEN UNBOUNDED PRECEDING
                       AND 1 PRECEDING) AS max_y
                  FROM Intervals)
                AS DT)
       AS DT
 GROUP BY min_x;
```

Here is a query that uses a self-join and three-level, nested correlated subquery that uses the same approach.

```
SELECT I1.x, MAX(I2.y) AS y
  FROM Intervals AS I1
       INNER JOIN
       Intervals AS I2
       ON I2.y > I1.x
 WHERE NOT EXISTS
       (SELECT *
          FROM Intervals AS I3
         WHERE I1.x - 1 BETWEEN I3.x AND I3.y)
           AND NOT EXISTS
              (SELECT *
                 FROM Intervals AS I4
                WHERE I4.y > I1.x
                  AND I4.y < I2.y
                  AND NOT EXISTS
                      (SELECT *
                         FROM Intervals AS I5
                        WHERE I4.y + 1 BETWEEN I5.x AND I5.y))
 GROUP BY I1.x;
```

This is essentially the same format, but converted to use left anti-semi-joins instead of subqueries. I do not think it is shorter, but it might execute better on some platforms, and some people prefer this format to subqueries.

```
SELECT I1.x, MAX(I2.y) AS y
  FROM Intervals AS I1
       INNER JOIN
       Intervals AS I2
       ON I2.y > I1.x
         LEFT OUTER JOIN
         Intervals AS I3
         ON I1.x - 1 BETWEEN I3.x AND I3.y
           LEFT OUTER JOIN
           (Intervals AS I4
            LEFT OUTER JOIN
            Intervals AS I5
            ON I4.y + 1 BETWEEN I5.x AND I5.y)
```

```
ON I4.y > I1.x
   AND I4.y < I2.y
   AND I5.x IS NULL
WHERE I3.x IS NULL
  AND I4.x IS NULL
GROUP BY I1.x;
```

If the table is large, the correlated subqueries (version 1) or the quintuple self-join (version 2) will probably make it slow. But we were asked for a short query, not for a quick one.

Tony Andrews came up with this answer.

```
SELECT Starts.x, Ends.y
  FROM (SELECT x, ROW_NUMBER() OVER(ORDER BY x) AS rn
          FROM (SELECT x, y,
                       LAG(y) OVER(ORDER BY x) AS prev_y
                  FROM Intervals)
         WHERE prev_y IS NULL
            OR prev_y < x) AS Starts,
       (SELECT y, ROW_NUMBER() OVER(ORDER BY y) AS rn
          FROM (SELECT x, y,
                       LEAD(x) OVER(ORDER BY y) AS next_x
                  FROM Intervals)
                 WHERE next_x IS NULL
                    OR y < next_x) AS Ends
WHERE Starts.rn = Ends.rn;
```

John Gilson decided that using recursion is an interesting take on this problem and made this offering:

```
WITH RECURSIVE Cover (x, y, n)
AS (SELECT x, y, (SELECT COUNT(*) FROM Intervals)
     FROM Intervals
    UNION ALL
    SELECT CASE WHEN I3.x <= I.x THEN I3.x ELSE I.x END,
           CASE WHEN I3.y >= I.y THEN I3.y ELSE I.y END,
           I3.n - 1
     FROM Intervals AS I, Cover AS C
    WHERE I.x <= I3.y
      AND I.y >= I3.x
      AND (I.x <> I3.x OR I.y <> I3.y)
```

```
      AND I3.n > 1);

SELECT DISTINCT C1.x, C1.y
  FROM Cover AS C1
 WHERE NOT EXISTS
       (SELECT *
          FROM Cover AS C2
         WHERE C2.x <= C1.x
           AND C2.y >= C1.y
           AND (C1.x <> C2.x OR C1.y <> C2.y))
 ORDER BY C1.x;
```

Finally, try this approach. Assume we have the usual Sequence auxiliary table. Now we find all the holes in the range of the intervals and put them in a `VIEW` or a `WITH` clause–derived table.

```
CREATE VIEW Holes (hole)
AS
SELECT seq_nbr
  FROM Sequence
 WHERE seq_nbr <= (SELECT MAX(y) FROM Intervals)
   AND NOT EXISTS
       (SELECT *
          FROM Intervals
         WHERE seq_nbr BETWEEN x AND y)
UNION VALUES(0)  -- left sentinel value
UNION (SELECT MAX(y) + 1 FROM Intervals); -- right sentinel
value
```

The query picks start and end pairs that are on the edge of a hole and counts the number of holes inside that range. Covering has no holes inside its range.

```
SELECT Starts.x, Ends.y
  FROM Intervals AS Starts,
       Intervals AS Ends,
       Sequence AS S  -- usual auxiliary table
 WHERE S.seq_nbr BETWEEN Starts.x AND Ends.y      -- restrict
seq_nbr numbers
   AND S.seq_nbr < (SELECT MAX(hole) FROM Holes)
   AND S.seq_nbr NOT IN (SELECT hole FROM Holes)    -- not a hole
```

```
   AND Starts.x - 1 IN (SELECT hole FROM Holes) -- on a left cusp
    AND Ends.y + 1 IN (SELECT hole FROM Holes)   -- on a right
cusp
 GROUP BY Starts.x, Ends.y
HAVING COUNT(DISTINCT seq_nbr) = Ends.y - Starts.x + 1; -- no
holes
```

Arrays in SQL

ARRAYS CANNOT BE REPRESENTED directly in SQL-92, but they are a common vendor language extension that became part of SQL-99. Arrays violate the rules of First Normal Form (1NF) required for a relational database, which say that the tables have no repeating groups in any column. A repeating group is a data structure that is not scalar; examples of repeating groups include linked lists, arrays, records, and even tables within a column.

The reason they are not allowed is that a repeating group would have to define a column like a data type. There is no obvious way to JOIN a column that contains an array to other columns, since there are no comparison operators or conversion rules. There is no obvious way to display or transmit a column that contains an array as a result set. Different languages and different compilers for the same language store arrays in column-major or row-major order, so there is no standard. There is no obvious way to write constraints on nonscalar values.

The goal of SQL was to be a database language that would operate with a wide range of host languages. To meet that goal, the scalar data types are as varied as possible to match the host language data types, but as simple in structure as they can be to make the transfer of data to the host language as easy as possible. The extensions after SQL-92 ruin all of these advantages, so it is a good thing they are not widely implemented in products.

25.1 Arrays via Named Columns

An array in other programming languages has a name and subscripts by which the array elements are referenced. The array elements are all of the same data type, and the subscripts are all sequential integers. Some languages start numbering at zero, some start numbering at one, and some let the user set the upper and lower bounds. For example, a Pascal array declaration would look like this:

```
foobar : ARRAY [1..5] OF INTEGER;
```

and would have integer elements foobar[1], foobar[2], foobar[3], foobar[4], and foobar[5]. The same structure is most often mapped into an SQL declaration as:

```
CREATE TABLE Foobar1
(element1 INTEGER NOT NULL,
 element2 INTEGER NOT NULL,
 element3 INTEGER NOT NULL,
 element4 INTEGER NOT NULL,
 element5 INTEGER NOT NULL);
```

The elements cannot be accessed by the use of a subscript in this table, as they can in a true array. That is, to set the array elements equal to zero in Pascal takes one statement with a `FOR` loop in it:

```
FOR i := 1 TO 5 DO foobar[i] := 0;
```

The same action in SQL would be performed with the following statement:

```
UPDATE Foobar1
    SET element1 = 0,
        element2 = 0,
        element3 = 0,
        element4 = 0,
        element5 = 0;
```

This is because there is no subscript that can be iterated in a loop. Any access must be based on column names, not on subscripts. These pseudosubscripts lead to building column names on the fly in dynamic

SQL, giving code that is both slow and dangerous. Even worse, some users will use the same approach in table names, and destroy their logical data model.

Let's assume that we design an Employee table with separate columns for the names of four children, and we start with an empty table and then try to use it.

1. *What happens if we hire a man with fewer than four children?*

   We can fire him immediately or make him have more children. We can restructure the table to allow for fewer children. The usual, and less drastic, solution is to put NULLs in the columns for the nonexistent children. We then have all of the problems associated with NULLs to handle.

2. *What happens if we hire a man with five children?*

   We can fire him immediately or order him to kill one of his children. We can restructure the table to allow five children. We can add a second row to hold the information on children 5 through 8; however, this destroys the uniqueness of the emp_id, so it cannot be used as a key. We can overcome that problem by adding a new column for record number, which will form a two-column key with the emp_id. This leads to needless duplication in the table.

3. *What happens if the employee dies?*

   We will delete all his children's data along with his, even if the company owes benefits to the survivors.

4. *What happens if the child of an employee dies?*

   We can fire him or order him to get another child immediately. We can restructure the table to allow only three children. We can overwrite the child's data with NULLs and get all of the problems associated with NULL values.

   This one is the most common decision. But what if we had used the multiple-row trick and this employee had a fifth child—should that child be brought up into the vacant slot in the current row, and the second row of the set be deleted?

5. *What happens if the employee replaces a dead child with a new one?*

> Should the new child's data overwrite the NULLs in the dead child's data? Should the new child's data be put in the next available slot and overwrite the NULLs in those columns?

Some of these choices involve rebuilding the database. Others are simply absurd attempts to restructure reality to fit the database. The real point is that each insertion or deletion of a child involves a different procedure, depending on the size of the group to which he belongs. File systems had variant records that could change the size of their repeating groups.

Consider, instead a table of employees, and another table for their children:

```
CREATE TABLE Employees
(emp_id INTEGER NOT NULL PRIMARY KEY,
 emp_name CHAR(30) NOT NULL,
 ...);

CREATE TABLE Children
(emp_id INTEGER NOT NULL
        REFERENCES Employees(emp_id)
        ON UPFDATE CASCADE,
 child_name CHAR(30) NOT NULL,
 PRIMARY KEY (emp_id, child_name),
 birthday DATE NOT NULL,
 sex CHAR(1) NOT NULL);
```

To add a child, you insert a row into Children. To remove a child, you delete a row from Children. There is nothing special about the fourth or fifth child that requires the database system to use special procedures. There are no NULLs in either table.

The trade-off is that the number of tables in the database schema increases, but the total amount of storage used will be smaller, because you will keep data only on children who exist, rather than using NULLs to hold space. The goal is to have data in the simplest possible format, so any host program can use it.

Gabrielle Wiorkowski, in her excellent DB2 classes, uses an example of a table for tracking the sales made by salespersons during the past year. That table could be defined as

```
CREATE TABLE AnnualSales1
(salesman CHAR(15) NOT NULL PRIMARY KEY,
 jan DECIMAL(5, 2),
 feb DECIMAL(5, 2),
 mar DECIMAL(5, 2),
 apr DECIMAL(5, 2),
 may DECIMAL(5, 2),
 jun DECIMAL(5, 2),
 jul DECIMAL(5, 2),
 aug DECIMAL(5, 2),
 sep DECIMAL(5, 2),
 oct DECIMAL(5, 2),
 nov DECIMAL(5, 2),
 "dec" DECIMAL(5, 2)  -- DEC[IMAL] is a reserved word
);
```

We have to allow for NULLs in the monthly sales_amts in the first version of the table, but the table is actually quite a bit smaller than it would be if we were to declare it as:

```
CREATE TABLE AnnualSales2
(salesman CHAR(15) NOT NULL PRIMARY KEY,
 sale_month CHAR(3)
      CONSTRAINT valid_month_abbrev
      CHECK (sale_month IN ('Jan', 'Feb', 'Mar', 'Apr',
                            'May', 'Jun', 'Jul', 'Aug',
                            'Sep', 'Oct', 'Nov', 'Dec'),
 sales_amt DECIMAL(5, 2) NOT NULL,
 PRIMARY KEY(salesman, sale_month));
```

In Wiorkowski's actual example in DB2, the break-even point for DASD storage was April; that is, the storage required for AnnualSales1 and AnnualSales2 is about the same in April of the given year.

Queries that deal with individual salespersons will run much faster against the AnnualSales1 table than queries based on the AnnualSales2 table, because all the data is in one row in the AnnualSales1 table. These tables may be a bit messy and they may require function calls to handle possible NULL values, but they are not very complex.

The only reason for using AnnualSales1 is that you have a data warehouse and all you want to see is summary information, grouped into years. This design is not acceptable in an OLTP system.

25.2 Arrays via Subscript Columns

Another approach to faking a multidimensional array is to map arrays into a table with an integer column for each subscript, thus:

```
CREATE TABLE Foobar
(i INTEGER NOT NULL PRIMARY KEY
   CONSTRAINT valid_array_index
   CHECK(i BETWEEN 1 AND 5),
 element REAL NOT NULL);
```

This looks more complex than the first approach, but it is closer to what the original Pascal declaration was doing behind the scenes. Subscripts resolve to unique physical addresses, so it is not possible to have two values for foobar[*i*]; hence, *i* is a key. The Pascal compiler will check to see that the subscripts are within the declared range; hence the `CHECK()` clause.

The first advantage of this approach is that multidimensional arrays are easily handled by adding another column for each subscript. The Pascal declaration:

```
ThreeD : ARRAY [1...3, 1...4, 1...5] OF REAL;
```

is mapped over to:

```
CREATE TABLE ThreeD
(i INTEGER NOT NULL
   CONSTRAINT valid_i
   CHECK(i BETWEEN 1 AND 3),
 j INTEGER NOT NULL
   CONSTRAINT valid_j
   CHECK(j BETWEEN 1 AND 4),
 k INTEGER NOT NULL
   CONSTRAINT valid_k
   CHECK(k BETWEEN 1 AND 5),
 element REAL NOT NULL,
 PRIMARY KEY (i, j, k));
```

Obviously, `SELECT` statements with `GROUP BY` clauses on the subscript columns will produce row and column totals, thus:

```
SELECT i, j, SUM(element) -- sum across the k columns
  FROM ThreeD
 GROUP BY i, j;

SELECT i, SUM(element) -- sum across the j and k columns
  FROM ThreeD
 GROUP BY i;

SELECT SUM(element) -- sum the entire array
  FROM ThreeD;
```

If the original one element/one column approach were used, the table declaration would have 120 columns named element_111 through element_345. There are too many names in this example to handle in any reasonable way; you would not be able to use the `GROUP BY` clauses for array projection, either.

Another advantage of this approach is that the subscripts can be data types other than integers. `DATE` and `TIME` data types are often useful, but `CHARACTER` and approximate numerics have their uses too.

25.3 Matrix Operations in SQL

A matrix is not quite the same thing as an array. Matrices are mathematical structures with particular properties. We cannot take the time to discuss them here; you can find the necessary information in a college freshman algebra book. Though it is possible to do many matrix operations in SQL, it is not a good idea; such queries and operations will eat up resources and run much too long. SQL was never meant to be a language for calculations.

Let us assume that we have two-dimensional arrays that are declared as tables using two columns for subscripts, and that all columns are declared with a `NOT NULL` constraint.

The presence of `NULL`s is not defined in linear algebra, and I have no desire to invent a three-valued linear algebra of my own. Another problem is that a matrix has rows and columns that are not the same as the rows and columns of an SQL table; as you read the rest of this section, be careful not to confuse the two.

```
CREATE TABLE MyMatrix
(element INTEGER NOT NULL, -- could be any numeric data type
 i INTEGER NOT NULL CHECK (i > 0),
```

```
j INTEGER NOT NULL CHECK (j > 0),
CHECK ((SELECT MAX(i) FROM MyMatrix)
        = (SELECT COUNT(i) FROM MyMatrix)),
CHECK ((SELECT MAX(j) FROM MyMatrix)
        = (SELECT COUNT(j) FROM MyMatrix)));
```

The constraints see that the subscripts of each element are within proper range. I am starting my subscripts at one, but a little change in the logic would allow any value.

25.3.1 Matrix Equality

This test for matrix equality is from the article "SQL Matrix Processing" (Mrdalj, Vujovic, and Jovanovic 1996). Two matrices are equal if their cardinalities and the cardinality of the their intersection are all equal.

```
SELECT COUNT(*) FROM MatrixA
UNION
SELECT COUNT(*) FROM MatrixB
UNION
SELECT COUNT(*)
  FROM MatrixA AS A, MatrixB AS B
 WHERE A.i = B.i
   AND A.j = B.j
   AND A.element = B.element;
```

You have to decide how to use this query in your context. If it returns one number, they are the same; otherwise, they are different.

25.3.2 Matrix Addition

Matrix addition and subtraction are possible only between matrices of the same dimensions. The obvious way to do the addition is simply:

```
SELECT A.i, A.j, (A.element + B.element) AS total
  FROM MatrixA AS A, MatrixB AS B
 WHERE A.i = B.i
   AND A.j = B.j;
```

But properly, you ought to add some checking to be sure the matrices match. We can assume that both start numbering subscripts with either one or zero.

```
SELECT A.i, A.j, (A.element + B.element) AS total
  FROM MatrixA AS A, MatrixB AS B
 WHERE A.i = B.i
   AND A.j = B.j
   AND (SELECT COUNT(*) FROM MatrixA) =
       (SELECT COUNT(*) FROM MatrixB)
   AND (SELECT MAX(i) FROM MatrixA) =
       (SELECT MAX(i) FROM MatrixB)
   AND (SELECT MAX(j) FROM MatrixA) =
       (SELECT MAX(j) FROM MatrixB));
```

Likewise, to make the addition permanent, you can use the same basic query in an UPDATE statement:

```
UPDATE MatrixA
  SET element = element + (SELECT element
                              FROM MatrixB
                             WHERE MatrixB.i = MatrixA.i
                               AND MatrixB.j = MatrixA.j)
 WHERE (SELECT COUNT(*) FROM MatrixA)
      =(SELECT COUNT(*) FROM MatrixB)
   AND (SELECT MAX(i) FROM MatrixA)
      = (SELECT MAX(i) FROM MatrixB)
   AND (SELECT MAX(j) FROM MatrixA)
      = (SELECT MAX(j) FROM MatrixB));
```

25.3.3 Matrix Multiplication

Multiplication by a scalar constant is direct and easy:

```
UPDATE MyMatrix
   SET element = element * :constant;
```

Matrix multiplication is not as big a mess as might be expected.

Remember that the first matrix must have the same number of rows as the second matrix has columns. That means A[i, k] * B[k, j] = C[i, j], which we can show with an example:

```
CREATE TABLE MatrixA
(i INTEGER NOT NULL
    CHECK (i BETWEEN 1 AND 10), -- pick your own bounds
 k INTEGER NOT NULL
```

```
   CHECK (k BETWEEN 1 AND 10), -- must match MatrixB.k range
 element INTEGER NOT NULL,
 PRIMARY KEY (i, k));

MatrixA
i    k    element
===================
1    1     2
1    2    -3
1    3     4
2    1    -1
2    2     0
2    3     2

CREATE TABLE MatrixB
(k INTEGER NOT NULL
   CHECK (k BETWEEN 1 AND 10), -- must match MatrixA.k range
 j INTEGER NOT NULL
   CHECK (j BETWEEN 1 AND 4), -- pick your own bounds
 element INTEGER NOT NULL,
 PRIMARY KEY (k, j));

MatrixB
k    j    element
==================
1    1    -1
1    2     2
1    3     3
2    1     0
2    2     1
2    3     7
3    1     1
3    2     1
3    3    -2

CREATE VIEW MatrixC(i, j, element)
AS SELECT i, j, SUM(MatrixA.element * MatrixB.element)
     FROM MatrixA, MatrixB
    WHERE MatrixA.k = MatrixB.k
    GROUP BY i, j;
```

This is taken directly from the definition of multiplication.

25.3.4 Other Matrix Operations

The transposition of a matrix is easy to do:

```
CREATE VIEW TransA (i, j, element)
AS SELECT j, i, element FROM MatrixA;
```

Again, you can make the change permanent with an `UPDATE` statement:

```
UPDATE MatrixA
  SET i = j, j = i;
```

Multiplication by a column or row vector is just a special case of matrix multiplication, but a bit easier. Given the vector V and MatrixA:

```
SELECT i, SUM(A.element * V.element)
  FROM MatrixA AS A, VectorV AS V
 WHERE V.j = A.i
 GROUP BY A.i;
```

Cross tabulations and other statistical functions traditionally use an array to hold data. But you do not need a matrix for them in SQL.

It is possible to do other matrix operations in SQL, but the code becomes so complex, and the execution time so long, that it is simply not worth the effort. If a reader would like to submit queries for eigenvalues and determinants, I will be happy to put them in future editions of this book.

25.4 Flattening a Table into an Array

Reports and data warehouse summary tables often want to see an array laid horizontally across a line. The original one element/one column approach to mapping arrays was based on seeing such reports and duplicating that structure in a table. A subscript is often an enumeration, denoting a month or another time period, rather than an integer.

For example, a row in a "Salesmen" table might have a dozen columns, one for each month of the year, each of which holds the total commission earned in a particular month. The year is really an array, subscripted by the month. The subscripts-and-value approach requires

more work to produce the same results. It is often easier to explain a technique with an example. Let us imagine a company that collects time cards from its truck drivers, each with the driver's name, the week within the year (numbered 0 to 51 or 52, depending on the year), and his total hours. We want to produce a report with one line for each driver and six weeks of his time across the page. The Timecards table looks like this:

```
CREATE TABLE Timecards
(driver_name CHAR(25) NOT NULL,
 week_nbr INTEGER NOT NULL
      CONSTRAINT valid_week_nbr
      CHECK(week BETWEEN 0 AND 52)
 work_hrs INTEGER
       CONSTRAINT zero_or_more_hours
       CHECK(work_hrs >= 0),
 PRIMARY KEY (driver_name, week_nbr));
```

We need to "flatten out" this table to get the desired rows for the report. First, create a working storage table from which the report can be built:

```
CREATE TEMPORARY TABLE TimeReportWork    -- working storage
(driver_name CHAR(25) NOT NULL,
 wk1 INTEGER, -- important that these columns are NULL-able
 wk2 INTEGER,
 wk3 INTEGER,
 wk4 INTEGER,
 wk5 INTEGER,
 wk6 INTEGER);
```

Notice two important points about this table. First, there is no primary key; second, the weekly data columns are NULL-able. This table is then filled with time card values:

```
INSERT INTO TimeReportWork (driver_name, wk1, wk2, wk3, wk4, wk5, wk6)
SELECT driver_name,
       SUM(CASE (week_nbr = :rpt_week_nbr) THEN work_hrs ELSE 0 END) AS wk1,
       SUM(CASE (week_nbr = :rpt_week_nbr - 1) THEN work_hrs ELSE 0 END) AS wk2,
       SUM(CASE (week_nbr = :rpt_week_nbr - 2) THEN work_hrs ELSE 0 END) AS wk3,
       SUM(CASE (week_nbr = :rpt_week_nbr - 3) THEN work_hrs ELSE 0 END) AS wk4,
       SUM(CASE (week_nbr = :rpt_week_nbr - 4) THEN work_hrs ELSE 0 END) AS wk5,
```

```
     SUM(CASE (week_nbr = :rpt_week_nbr - 5) THEN work_hrs ELSE 0 END) AS wk6
  FROM Timecards
 WHERE week_nbr BETWEEN :rpt_week_nbr AND (:rpt_week_nbr - 5);
```

The number of the weeks in the WHERE clauses will vary with the period covered by the report. The parameter :rpt_week_nbr is "week of the report," and it computes backwards for the prior five weeks. If a driver did not work in a particular week, the corresponding weekly column gets a zero hour total. However, if the driver has not worked at all in the last six weeks, we could lose him completely (no time cards, no summary). Depending on the nature of the report, you might consider using an OUTER JOIN to a Personnel table to be sure you have all the drivers' names.

The NULLs are coalesced to zero in this example, but if you drop the ...ELSE 0 clauses, the SUM() will have to deal with a week of all NULLs and return a NULL. This enables you to tell the difference between a driver who was missing for the reporting period and a driver who worked zero hours but turned in a time card for that period. That difference could be important for computing the payroll.

25.5 Comparing Arrays in Table Format

It is often necessary to compare one array or set of values with another when the data is represented in a table. Remember that comparing a set with a set does not involve ordering the elements, whereas an array does. For this discussion, let us create two tables, one for employees and one for their dependents. The children are subscripted in the order of their births—i.e., 1 is the oldest living child, 2 is the second oldest, and so forth.

```
CREATE TABLE Employees
(emp_id INTEGER PRIMARY KEY,
 emp_name CHAR(15) NOT NULL,
 ...  );

CREATE TABLE Dependents
(emp_id INTEGER NOT NULL -- the parent
 kid CHAR(15) NOT NULL, -- the array element
 birthorder INTEGER NOT NULL, -- the array subscript
 PRIMARY KEY (emp_id, kid));
```

The query "Find pairs of employees whose children have the same set of names" is very restrictive, but we can make it more so by requiring that the children be named in the same birth order. Both Mr. X and Mr. Y must have exactly the same number of dependents; both sets of names must match. We can assume that no parent has two children with the same name (George Foreman does not work here) or born at the same time (we will order twins). Let us begin by inserting test data into the Dependents table, thus:

```
Dependents
emp_id kid_name  birthorder
===========================
 1     'Dick'     2
 1     'Harry'    3
 1     'Tom'      1
 2     'Dick'     3
 2     'Harry'    1
 2     'Tom'      2
 3     'Dick'     2
 3     'Harry'    3
 3     'Tom'      1
 4     'Harry'    1
 4     'Tom'      2
 5     'Curly'    2
 5     'Harry'    3
 5     'Moe'      1
```

In this test data, employees 1, 2, and 3 all have dependents named 'Tom', 'Dick', and 'Harry'.

The birth order is the same for the children of employees 1 and 3, but not for employee 2.

For testing purposes, you might consider adding an extra child to the family of employee 3, and so forth, to play with this data.

Though there are many ways to solve this query, this approach will give us some flexibility that others would not. Construct a `VIEW` that gives us the number of dependents for each employee:

```
CREATE VIEW Familysize (emp_id, tally)
AS
SELECT emp_id, COUNT(*)
  FROM Dependents
 GROUP BY emp_id;
```

Create a second VIEW that holds pairs of employees who have families of the same size. (This VIEW is also useful for other statistical work, but that is another topic.)

```
CREATE VIEW Samesize (emp_id1, emp_id2, tally)
AS SELECT F1.emp_id, F2.emp_id, F1.tally
        FROM Familysize AS F1, Familysize AS F2
    WHERE F1.tally = F2.tally
        AND F1.emp_id < F2.emp_id;
```

We will test for set equality by doing a self-JOIN on the dependents of employees with families of the same size. If one set can be mapped onto another with no children left over, and in the same birth order, then the two sets are equal.

```
SELECT D1.emp_id, ' named his ',
       S1.tally, ' kids just like ',
       D2.emp_id
  FROM Dependents AS D1, Dependents AS D2, Samesize AS S1
 WHERE S1.emp_id1 = D1.emp_id
   AND S1.emp_id2 = D2.emp_id
   AND D1.kid = D2.kid
   AND D1.birthorder = D2.birthorder
 GROUP BY D1.emp_id, D2.emp_id, S1.tally
HAVING COUNT(*) = S1.tally;
```

If birth order is not important, then drop the predicate D1.birthorder = D2.birthorder from the query.

This is a form of exact relational division, with a second column equality test as part of the criteria.

Set Operations

BY SET OPERATIONS, I mean union, intersection, and set differences, where the sets in SQL are tables. These are the basic operators used in elementary set theory, which has been taught in the United States public school systems for decades. Since the relational model is based on sets, you would expect that SQL would have had a good variety of set operators from the start. However, this was not the case. Standard SQL has added the basic set operators, but they are still not common in actual products.

There is another problem in SQL that you did not have in high school set theory. SQL tables are multisets (also called bags), which means that, unlike sets, they allow duplicate elements (rows or tuples). Dr. Codd's relational model is stricter and uses only true sets. SQL handles these duplicate rows with an `ALL` or `DISTINCT` modifier in different places in the language; `ALL` preserves duplicates, and `DISTINCT` removes them.

So that we can discuss the result of each operator formally, let R be a row that is a duplicate of some row in TableA, or of some row in TableB, or of both. Let *m* be the number of duplicates of R in TableA and let *n* be the number of duplicates of R in TableB, where ($m >= 0$) and ($n >= 0$). Informally, the engines will pair off the two tables on a row-per-row basis in set operations. We will see how this works for each operator.

For the rest of this discussion, let us create two tables with the same structure, which we can use for examples.

```
CREATE TABLE S1 (a1 CHAR(1));
INSERT INTO S1
VALUES ('a'), ('a'), ('b'), ('b'), ('c');

CREATE TABLE S2 (a2 CHAR(1));
INSERT INTO S2
VALUES ('a'), ('b'), ('b'), ('b'), ('c'), ('d');
```

26.1 UNION and UNION ALL

UNIONs have been supported since SQL-86 with this infixed syntax:

```
<table expression> UNION [ALL] <table expression>
```

The two versions of the UNION statement take two tables and build a result table from them. The two tables must be union-compatible, which means that they have exactly the same number of columns, and that each column in the first table has the same data type (or automatically cast to it) as the column in the same position in the second table. That is, their rows must have the same structure, so they can be put in the same final result table. Most implementations will do some data type conversions to create the result table, but this can depend on your implementation, and you should check it out for yourself.

There are two forms of the UNION statement: the UNION and the UNION ALL. The simple UNION is the same operator you had in high school set theory; it returns the rows that appear in either or both tables and removes redundant duplicates from the result table. The phrase "redundant duplicates" sounds funny, but it means that you leave one copy of the row in the table. The sample tables will yield:

```
(SELECT a1 FROM S1
 UNION
SELECT a2 FROM S2)
============
a
b
c
d
```

In many early SQL implementations, merge-sorting the two tables and discarding duplicates during the sorting did this removal. This had the side effect that the result table was sorted, but you could not depend on that. Later implementations use hashing, indexing, and parallel processing to find the duplicates.

The UNION ALL preserves the duplicates from both tables in the result table. Most early implementations simply appended one table to the other in physical storage. They used file systems based on physically contiguous storage, so this was easy and used the file system code. But, again, you cannot depend on any ordering in the results of either version of the UNION statement. Again, the sample tables will yield:

```
(SELECT a1 FROM S1
 UNION ALL
 SELECT a2 FROM S2)
====
'a'
'a'
'a'
'b'
'b'
'b'
'b'
'b'
'c'
'c'
'd'
```

You can assign names to the columns by using the AS operator to make the result set into a derived table, thus:

```
SELECT rent, utilities, phone
  FROM
(SELECT a, b, c FROM OldLocations WHERE city = 'Boston'
 UNION
 SELECT x, y, z FROM NewLocations WHERE city = 'New York')
 AS Cities (rent, utilities, phone);
```

A few SQL products will attempt to optimize UNIONs if they are made on the same table. Those UNIONs can often be replaced with ORed predicates. For example:

```
SELECT city_name, 'Western'
  FROM Cities
 WHERE market_code = 't'
UNION ALL
SELECT city_name, 'Eastern'
  FROM Cities
 WHERE market_code = 'v';
```

This could be rewritten (probably more efficiently) as:

```
SELECT city_name,
       CASE market_code
       WHEN 't' THEN 'Western'
       WHEN 'v' THEN 'Eastern' END
FROM Cities
WHERE market_code IN ('v', 't');
```

A system architecture based on domains rather than tables is necessary to optimize UNIONs if they are made on different tables.

Doing a UNION to the same table is the same as a SELECT DISTINCT, but the SELECT DISTINCT will probably run faster and preserve the column names too.

26.1.1 Order of Execution

UNION and UNION ALL operators are executed from left to right, unless parentheses change the order of execution. Since the UNION operator is associative and commutative, the order of a chain of UNIONs will not affect the results. However, order and grouping can affect performance. Consider two small tables that have many duplicates between them. If the optimizer does not consider table sizes, use this query:

```
( SELECT * FROM  SmallTable1)
UNION
( SELECT * FROM  BigTable)
UNION
( SELECT * FROM  SmallTable2);
```

It will merge SmallTable1 into BigTable, then merge SmallTable2 into that first result. If the rows of SmallTable1 are spread out in the first result table, locating duplicates from SmallTable2 will take longer than if we had written the query thus:

```
( SELECT * FROM  SmallTable1)
UNION
( SELECT * FROM  SmallTable2)
UNION
( SELECT * FROM  BigTable);
```

Again, optimization of UNIONs is highly product-dependent, so you should experiment with it.

26.1.2 Mixed UNION and UNION ALL Operators

If you know that there are no duplicates, or that duplicates are not a problem in your situation, use UNION ALL, instead of UNION, for speed. For example, if we are sure that BigTable has no duplicates in common with SmallTable1 and SmallTable2, this query will produce the same results as before, but should run much faster:

```
(( SELECT * FROM  SmallTable1)
UNION
( SELECT * FROM  SmallTable2))
UNION ALL
( SELECT * FROM  BigTable);
```

But be careful when mixing UNION and UNION ALL operators. The left-to-right order of execution will cause the last operator in the chain to have an effect on the results.

26.1.3 UNION of Columns from the Same Table

A useful trick for building the union of columns from the same table is to use a CROSS JOIN and a CASE expression:

```
 SELECT CASE WHEN S1.seq_nbr = 1 THEN F1.col1
             WHEN S1.seq_nbr = 2 THEN F1.col2
             ELSE NULL END
   FROM Foobar AS F1
        CROSS JOIN
        Sequence AS S1(seq_nbr)
  WHERE S1.seq_nbr IN (1, 2)
```

This query acts like the UNION ALL statement, but change the SELECT to SELECT DISTINCT and you have a UNION. The advantage of this statement over the more obvious UNION is that it makes only one pass through the table. If you are working with a large table, that can be important for good performance.

26.2 INTERSECT and EXCEPT

Intersection and set difference are part of Standard SQL, but few products have implemented them yet.

The INTERSECT and EXCEPT set operators take two tables and build a new table from them. The two tables must be "union-compatible," which means that they have the same number of columns, and that each column in the first table has the same data type (or automatically casts to it) as the column in the same position in the second table.

That is, their rows have the same structure, so they can be put in the same final result table. Most implementations will do some data type conversions to create the result table, but this is very implementation dependent, and you should check it out for yourself. Like the UNION, the result of an INTERSECT or EXCEPT should use an AS operator if you want to have names for the result table and its columns.

Oracle was the first major vendor to have the EXCEPT operator with the keyword MINUS. The set difference is the rows in the first table, except for those that also appear in the second table. It answers requests like "Give me all the employees except the salesmen" in a natural manner.

Let's take our two multisets and use them to explain the basic model, by making a mapping between them:

```
S1 = {a, a, b, b,    c   }
      |     |  |     |
S2 = {a,    b, b, b, c, d}
```

The INTERSECT and EXCEPT operators remove all duplicates from both sets, so we would have:

```
S1 = {a, b, c   }
      |  |  |
S2 = {a, b, c, d}
```

Therefore,

```
S1 INTERSECT S2 = {a, b, c}
```

and

```
S2 EXCEPT S1 = {d}
S1 EXCEPT S2 = {}
```

When you add the ALL option, things are trickier. The mapped pairs become the unit of work. The INTERSECT ALL keeps each pairing, so that:

```
S1 INTERSECT ALL S2 = {a, b, b, c}
```

The EXCEPT ALL throws them away, retaining what is left in the first set, thus:

```
S2 EXCEPT ALL S1 = {b, d}
```

Trying to write the INTERSECT and EXCEPT with other operators is trickier than it looks. It must be general enough to handle situations where there is no key available and the number of columns is not known.

Standard SQL defines the actions for duplicates in terms of the count of duplicates of matching rows. Let (m) be the number of rows of one kind in S1 and (n) be the number in S2. The UNION ALL will have ($m+n$) copies of the row. The INTERSECT ALL will have LEAST(m, n) copies. EXCEPT ALL will have the greater of either the first table's count minus the second table's count, or zero copies.

The immediate impulse of a programmer is to write the code with EXISTS() predicates. The bad news is that it does not work because of NULLs. This is easier to show with code. Let's redo our two sample tables.

```
CREATE TABLE S1 (a1 CHAR(1));
INSERT INTO S1
VALUES ('a'), ('a'), ('b'), ('b'), ('c'), (NULL), (NULL);

CREATE TABLE S2 (a2 CHAR(1));
INSERT INTO S2
VALUES ('a'), ('b'), ('b'), ('b'), ('c'), ('d'), (NULL);
```

Now build a view to hold the tally of each value in each table.

```
CREATE VIEW DupCounts (a, s1_dup, s2_dup)
AS
SELECT S.a, SUM(s1_dup), SUM(s2_dup)
  FROM (SELECT S1.a1, 1, 0
           FROM S1
         UNION ALL
        SELECT S2.a2, 0, 1
          FROM S2) AS S(a, s1_dup, s2_dup)
 GROUP BY S.a, s1_dup, s2_dup;
```

The `GROUP BY` will put the `NULL`s into a separate group, giving them the right tallies. Now code is a straightforward implementation of the definitions in Standard SQL.

```
-- S1 EXCEPT ALL S2
 SELECT DISTINCT D1.a, (s1_dup - s2_dup) AS dups
   FROM DupCounts AS D1,
        Sequence AS S1
  WHERE S1.seq_nbr <= (s1_dup - s2_dup);

-- S1 INTERSECT ALL S2
 SELECT DISTINCT D1.a,
                 CASE WHEN s1_dup <= s2_dup
                      THEN s1_dup ELSE s2_dup END
                 AS tally
   FROM DupCounts AS D1,
        Sequence AS S1
  WHERE S1.seq_nbr <= CASE WHEN s1_dup <= s2_dup
                           THEN s1_dup ELSE s2_dup END;
```

Notice that we had to use `SELECT DISTINCT`. Without it, the sample data will produce this table.

```
 a   tally
===========
NULL  1
 a    1
 b    2
 b    2   <== redundant row
 c    1
```

The nonduplicated versions are easy to write from the definitions in the Standards. In effect, their duplication tallies are set to one.

```
-- S1 INTERSECT S2
 SELECT D1.a
   FROM DupCounts AS D1
  WHERE s1_dup > 0
    AND s2_dup > 0;

-- S1 EXCEPT S2
 SELECT D1.a
   FROM DupCounts AS D1
  WHERE s1_dup > 0
    AND s2_dup = 0;

-- S2 EXCEPT S1
 SELECT D1.a
   FROM DupCounts AS D1
  WHERE s2_dup > 0
    AND s1_dup = 0;
```

26.2.1 INTERSECT and EXCEPT without NULLs and Duplicates

INTERSECT and EXCEPT are much easier if each of the two tables does not have NULLs and duplicate values in them. Intersection is simply done thus:

```
SELECT *
  FROM S1
 WHERE EXISTS
       (SELECT *
          FROM S2
         WHERE S1.a1 = S2.a2);
```

or

```
SELECT *
  FROM S2
 WHERE EXISTS
       (SELECT *
```

```
          FROM S1
         WHERE S1.a1 = S2.a2);
```

You can also use the following:

```
SELECT DISTINCT S2.*
  FROM (S2 INNER JOIN S1 ON S1.a1 = S2.a2);
```

This is given as a motivation for the next piece of code, but you may find that some SQL engines do joins faster than `EXISTS()` predicates, and vice versa, so it is a good idea to have more than one trick in your bag.

The set difference can be written with an `OUTER JOIN` operator. This code is due to Jim Panttaja.

```
SELECT DISTINCT S2.*
  FROM (S2 LEFT OUTER JOIN S1
        ON S1.a1 = S2.a2)
 WHERE S1.a1 IS NULL;
```

26.2.2 INTERSECT and EXCEPT with NULLs and Duplicates

These versions of `INTERSECT` and `EXCEPT` are due to Itzik Ben-Gan. They make very good use of the `UNION` and `DISTINCT` operators to implement set theory definitions.

```
-- S1 INTERSECT S2
SELECT D.a
FROM (SELECT DISTINCT a1 FROM S1
      UNION ALL
      SELECT DISTINCT a2 FROM S2) AS D(a)
GROUP BY D.a
HAVING COUNT(*) > 1;

-- S1 INTERSECT ALL S2
SELECT D2.a
FROM (SELECT D1.a, MIN(cnt) AS mincnt
      FROM (SELECT a1, COUNT(*)
              FROM S1
             GROUP BY a1
```

```
              UNION ALL
              SELECT a2, COUNT(*)
                FROM S2
               GROUP BY a2) AS D1(a, cnt)
        GROUP BY D1.a
        HAVING COUNT(*) > 1) AS D2
    INNER JOIN
    Sequence
  ON seq_nbr <= mincnt;

-- S1 EXCEPT ALL S2
SELECT D2.a
  FROM (SELECT D1.a, SUM(cnt)
          FROM (SELECT a1, COUNT(*)
                  FROM S1
                 GROUP BY a1
                UNION ALL
                SELECT a2, -COUNT(*)
                  FROM S2
                 GROUP BY a2)
               AS D1(a, cnt)
         GROUP BY D1.a
        HAVING SUM(cnt) > 0)
       AS D2(a, dups)
       INNER JOIN
       Sequence ON seq_nbr <= D2.dups;
```

The Sequence table is discussed in other places in this book. It is a table of integers from 1 to (*n*) that is used to replace iteration and counting in SQL. Obviously, (*n*) must be large enough for these statements to work.

26.3 A Note on ALL and SELECT DISTINCT

Here is a series of observations about the relationship between the `ALL` option in set operations and the `SELECT DISTINCT` options in a query from Beught Gunne.

Given two tables with duplicate values:

```
CREATE TABLE A (i INTEGER NOT NULL);
INSERT INTO A VALUES (1), (1), (2), (2), (4), (4);
```

```
CREATE TABLE B (i INTEGER NOT NULL);
INSERT INTO B VALUES (2), (2), (3), (3);
```

The `UNION` and `INTERSECT` operations have regular behavior in that:

```
(A UNION B) = SELECT DISTINCT (A UNION ALL B) = ((1), (2), (3))
```

and

```
(A INTERSECT B) = SELECT DISTINCT (A INTERSECT ALL B) = (2)
```

However,

```
(A EXCEPT B) <> SELECT DISTINCT (A EXCEPT ALL B)
```

Or, more literally, (1) <> ((1), (2)) for the tables given in the example. Likewise, we have:

```
(B EXCEPT A) = SELECT DISTINCT (B EXCEPT ALL A) = (3)
```

by a coincidence of the particular values used in these tables.

26.4 Equality and Proper Subsets

At one point, when SQL was still in the laboratory at IBM, there was a `CONTAINS` operator that would tell you if one table was a subset of another. It disappeared in later versions of the language and no vendor picked it up. Set equality was never part of SQL as an operator, so you would have to have used the two expressions `((A CONTAINS B) AND (B CONTAINS A))` to find out.

Today, you can use the methods shown in the section on Relational Division to determine containment or equality. However, Itzik Ben-Gan came up with a novel approach for finding containment and equality that is worth a mention.

```
SELECT SUM(DISTINCT match_col)
  FROM (SELECT CASE
               WHEN S1.col
                    IN (SELECT S2.col FROM S2)
               THEN 1 ELSE -1 END
          FROM S1) AS X(match_col)
HAVING SUM(DISTINCT match_col) = :n;
```

You can set (`:n`) to 1, 0, or –1 for each particular test.

When I find a matching row in S1, I get a +1; when I find a mismatched row in S1, get a –1 and they sum together to give me a zero. Therefore, S1 is a proper subset of S2. If they sum to +1, then they are equal. If they sum to –1, they are disjoint.

Subsets

I AM DEFINING SUBSET operations as queries, which extract a particular subset from a given set, as opposed to set operations, which work among sets. The obvious way to extract a subset from a table is just to use a `WHERE` clause, which will pull out the rows that meet that criterion. But not all the subsets we want are easily defined by such a simple predicate. This chapter is a collection of tricks for constructing useful, but not obvious, subsets from a table.

27.1 Every nth Item in a Table

SQL is a set-oriented language, which cannot identify individual rows by their physical positions in a disk file that holds a table. Instead, a unique logical key is detected by logical expressions, and a row is retrieved. If you are given a file of employees in which the ordering of the file is based on their employee numbers, and you want to pick out every *n*th employee record for a survey, the job is easy. You write a procedure that loops through the file and writes every *n*th one to a second file.

The immediate thought of how this should be done in SQL is to simply compute `MOD (emp_nbr, :n)`, where `MOD()` is the modulo function found in most SQL implementations, and save those employee rows where this function is zero. The trouble is that

employees are not issued consecutive identification numbers. The identification numbers are unique.

Vendor extensions often include an exposed physical row locator that gives a sequential numbering to the physical records; this sequential numbering can be used to perform these functions. This practice is a complete violation of Dr. Codd's definition of a relational database, and it requires that the underlying physical implementation use a contiguous sequential record for each row. Such things are highly proprietary, but because these features are so low-level, they will run very fast on that one particular product.

Row numbers have more problems than being nonstandard. If the physical storage is rearranged, then the row numbers have to change. Users logged on and looking at the same base table through different VIEWs may or may not get the same row number for the same physical row. One of the advantages of an RDBMS was supposed to be that the logical view of the data would be consistent, even when the physical storage changed.

You can get similar results with a self-JOIN on the Personnel table to partition it into a nested series of grouped tables, just as we did for the "to top *n*" problem. You then pick out the largest value in each group. There may be an index or a uniqueness constraint on the emp_nbr column to ensure uniqueness, so the EXISTS predicate will get a performance boost.

```
SELECT P1.emp_nbr
  FROM Personnel AS P1
 WHERE EXISTS
       (SELECT MAX(emp_nbr)
          FROM Personnel AS P2
         WHERE P1.emp_nbr >= P2.emp_nbr
        HAVING MOD (COUNT(*), :n) = 0);
```

A nonnested version of the same query looks like this:

```
SELECT P1.emp_nbr
  FROM Personnel AS P1, Personnel AS P2
 WHERE P1.emp_nbr >= P2.emp_nbr
 GROUP BY P1.emp_nbr
HAVING MOD (COUNT(*), :n) = 0;
```

Both queries count the number of P2 rows with a value less than the P1 row.

27.2 Picking Random Rows from a Table

The answer is that, basically, you cannot directly pick a set of random rows from a table in SQL. There is no randomize operator in the standard, and you don't often find the same pseudo-random number generator function in various vendor extensions, either.

Picking random rows from a table for a statistical sample is a handy thing, and you do it in other languages with a pseudo-random number generator. There are two kinds of random drawings from a set, with or without replacement. If SQL had random number functions, I suppose they would be shown as `RANDOM(x)` and `RANDOM(DISTINCT x)`. But there is no such function in SQL, and none is planned. Examples from the real world include dealing a poker hand (a random with no replacement situation) and shooting craps (a random with replacement situation). If two players in a poker game get identical cards, you are using a pinochle deck. In a craps game, each roll of the dice is independent of the previous one and can repeat it.

The problem is that SQL is a set-oriented language, and wants to do an operation "all at once" on a well-defined set of rows. Random sets are defined by a nondeterministic procedure by definition, instead of a deterministic logic expression.

The SQL/PSM language does have an option to declare or create a procedure that is `DETERMINISTIC` or `NOT DETERMINISTIC`. The `DETERMINISTIC` option means that the optimizer can compute this function once for a set of input parameter values and then use that result everywhere in the current SQL statement that a call to the procedure with those parameters appears. The `NOT DETERMINISTIC` option means given the same parameters, you might not get the same results for each call to the procedure within the same SQL statement.

Unfortunately, most SQL products do not have this feature in their proprietary procedural languages. Thus, the random number function in Oracle is nondeterministic and the one in SQL Server is deterministic. For example,

```
CREATE TABLE RandomNbrs
(seq_nbr INTEGER NOT NULL PRIMARY KEY,
 randomizer FLOAT NOT NULL);
```

```
INSERT INTO RandomNbrs
VALUES (1, RANDOM()),
       (2, RANDOM()),
       (3, RANDOM());
```

This query will result in the three rows all getting the same value in the randomizer column in a version of SQL Server, but three different numbers in a version of Oracle.

While subqueries are not allowed in `DEFAULT` clauses, system-related functions such as `CURRENT_TIMESTAMP` and `CURRENT_USER` are allowed. In some SQL implementations, this includes the `RANDOM()` function.

```
CREATE TABLE RandomNbrs2
(seq_nbr INTEGER PRIMARY KEY,
 randomizer FLOAT  -- warning !! not standard SQL
            DEFAULT (
(CASE (CAST(RANDOM() + 0.5 AS INTEGER) * -1)
 WHEN 0.0 THEN 1.0 ELSE -1.0 END)
 * MOD (CAST(RANDOM() * 100000 AS INTEGER), 10000)
 * RANDOM())
 NOT NULL);

INSERT INTO RandomNbrs2
VALUES (1, DEFAULT);
   (2, DEFAULT),
   (3, DEFAULT),
   (4, DEFAULT),
   (5, DEFAULT),
   (6, DEFAULT),
   (7, DEFAULT),
   (8, DEFAULT),
   (9, DEFAULT),
   (10, DEFAULT);
```

Here is a sample output from an SQL Server 7.0 implementation.

```
 seq_nbr   randomizer
============================
   1    -121.89758452446999
   2    -425.61113508053933
```

```
 3    3918.1554683876675
 4    9335.2668286173412
 5      54.463890640027664
 6      -5.0169085346410522
 7   -5430.63417246276
 8     915.9835973796487
 9      28.109161998753301
10     741.79452047043048
```

The best way to do this is to add a column to the table to hold a random number, then use an external language with a good pseudo-random number generator in its function library to load the new column with random values with a cursor in a host language. You have to do it this way, because random number generators work differently from other function calls. They start with an initial value called a "seed" (shown as Random[0] in the rest of this discussion) provided by the user or the system clock. The seed is used to create the first number in the sequence, Random[1]. Then each call, Random [*n*], to the function uses the previous number to generate the next one, Random[*n*+1].

There is no way to do a sequence of actions in SQL without a cursor, so you are in procedural code.

The term "pseudo-random number generator" is often referred to as a just "random number generator," but this is technically wrong. All of the generators will eventually return a value that appeared in the sequence earlier and the procedure will hang in a cycle. Procedures are deterministic, and we are living in a mathematical heresy when we try to use them to produce truly random results. However, if the sequence has a very long cycle and meets some other tests for randomness over the range of the cycle, then we can use it.

There are many kinds of generators. The linear congruence pseudo-random number generator family has generator formulas of the form:

```
Random[n+1] := MOD ((x * Random[n] + y), m);
```

There are restrictions on the relationships among x, y, and m that deal with their relative primality. Knuth gives a proof that if

```
Random[0] is not a multiple of 2 or 5
m = 10^e where (e >= 5)
y = 0
MOD (x, 200) is in the set (3, 11, 13, 19, 21, 27, 29, 37, 53,
```

```
59, 61, 67, 77, 83, 91, 109, 117, 123, 131, 133, 139, 141, 147,
163, 171, 173, 179, 181, 187, 189, 197)
```

then the period will be 5 * 10^(*e*-2).

There are old favorites that many C programmers use from this family, such as:

```
Random(n+1) := (Random(n) * 1103515245) + 12345;
Random(n+1) := MOD ((16807 * Random(n)), ((2^31) - 1));
```

The first formula has the advantage of not requiring a `MOD` function, so it can be written in standard SQL. However, the simplest generator that can be recommended (Park and Miller) uses:

```
Random(n+1) := MOD ((48271 * Random(n)), ((2^31) - 1));
```

Notice that the modulus is a prime number; this is important.

The period of this generator is ((2^31) – 2), which is 2,147,483,646, or more than two billion numbers before this generator repeats. You must determine whether this is long enough for your application.

If you have an `XOR` function in your SQL, then you can also use shift register algorithms. The `XOR` is the bitwise exclusive `OR` that works on an integer as it is stored in the hardware; I would assume 32 bits on most small computers. Some usable shift register algorithms are:

```
Random(n+1) := Random(n-103) XOR Random(n-250);
Random(n+1) := Random(n-1063) XOR Random(n-1279);
```

One method for writing a random number generator on the fly when the vendor's library does not have one is to pick a seed using one or more key columns and a call to the system clock's fractional seconds, such as `RANDOM(keycol + EXTRACT (SECOND FROM CURRENT_TIME)) * 1000`. This avoids problems with patterns in the keys, while the key column values ensure uniqueness of the seed values.

Another method is to use a `PRIMARY KEY` or `UNIQUE` column(s) and apply a hashing algorithm. You can pick one of the random number generator functions already discussed and use the unique value, as if it were the seed, as a quick way to get a hashing function. Hashing algorithms try to be uniformly distributed, so if you can find a good one, you will approach nearly unique random selection. The trick is that the hashing algorithm has to be simple enough to be written in the limited math available in SQL.

Once you have a column of random numbers, you can convert the random numbers into a randomly ordered sequence with this statement:

```
UPDATE RandomNbrs
   SET randomizer = (SELECT COUNT(*)
                       FROM Sequence AS S1
                      WHERE S1.randomizer <= Sequence.seq_nbr);
```

To get one random row from a table, you can use this approach:

```
CREATE VIEW LotteryDrawing (keycol, ..., spin)
AS SELECT LotteryTickets.*,
         (RANDOM(<keycol> + <fractional seconds from clock>))
     FROM LotteryTickets
    GROUP BY spin
   HAVING COUNT(*) = 1;
```

Then simply use this query:

```
SELECT *
  FROM LotteryDrawing
 WHERE spin = (SELECT MAX(spin)
                 FROM LotteryDrawing)
```

The pseudo-random number function is not standard SQL, but it is common enough. Using the keycol as the seed *probably* means that you will get a different value for each row, but we can avoid duplicates with the GROUP BY... HAVING. Adding the fractional seconds will change the result every time, but it might be illegal in some SQL products, which disallow variable elements in VIEW definitions.

Let's assume you have a function called RANDOM() that returns a random number between 0.00 and 1.00. If you just want one random row out of the table, and you have a numeric key column, Tom Moreau proposed that you could find the MAX() and MIN(), then calculate a random number between them.

```
SELECT L1.*
  FROM LotteryDrawing AS L1
 WHERE col_1
```

```
        = (SELECT MIN(keycol)
                + (MAX (keycol) - MIN (keycol) * RANDOM()))
             FROM LotteryDrawing AS L2);
```

Here is a version which uses the COUNT(*) functions and a self-join instead.

```
SELECT L1.*
  FROM LotteryDrawing AS L1
 WHERE CEILING ((SELECT COUNT(*) FROM LotteryDrawing)
                   * RANDOM())
       = (SELECT COUNT(*)
            FROM LotteryDrawing AS L2
           WHERE L1.keycol <= L2.keycol);
```

The rounding away from zero is important, since we are in effect numbering the rows from one. The idea is to use the decimal fraction to hit the row that is far into the table when the rows are ordered by the key.

Having shown you this code, I have to warn you that the pure SQL has a good number of self-joins, and they will be expensive to run.

27.3 The CONTAINS Operators

Set theory has two symbols for subsets. One, $\subset$, means that set A is contained within set B; this is sometimes said to denote a proper subset. The other, $\subseteq$ means "is contained in or equal to," and is sometimes called just a subset or containment operator.

Standard SQL has never had an operator to compare tables against each other for equality or containment. Several college textbooks on relational databases mention a CONTAINS predicate, which does not exist in Standard SQL. This predicate existed in the original System R, IBM's first experimental SQL system, but it was dropped from later SQL implementations because of the expense of running it.

27.3.1 Proper Subset Operators

The IN predicate is a test for membership. For those of you who remember your high school set theory, membership is shown with a stylized epsilon with the containing set on the right side: $a \in A$. Membership is for one element, whereas a subset is itself a set, not just an element. As an example of a subset predicate, consider a query to tell you the names of each employee who works on all of the projects in department 5. Using the System R syntax:

```
SELECT name  -- Not valid SQL!
  FROM Personnel
 WHERE (SELECT project_nbr
          FROM WorksOn
         WHERE Personnel.emp_nbr = WorksOn.emp_nbr)
       CONTAINS
        (SELECT project_nbr
           FROM Projects
         WHERE dept_nbr = 5);
```

In the second SELECT statement of the CONTAINS predicate, we build a table of all the projects in department 5. In the first SELECT statement of the CONTAINS predicate, we have a correlated subquery that will build a table of all the projects each employee works on. If the table of the employee's projects is equal to or a superset of the department 5 table, the predicate is TRUE.

You must first decide what you are going to do about duplicate rows in either or both tables. That is, does the set { a, b, c } contain the multiset { a, b, b } or not? Some SQL set operations, such as SELECT and UNION, have options to remove or keep duplicates from the results (e.g., UNION ALL and SELECT DISTINCT).

I would argue that duplicates should be ignored, and that the multiset is a subset of the other. For our example, let us use a table of employees and another table with the names of the company bowling team members, which should be a proper subset of the Personnel table. For the bowling team to be contained in the set of employees, each bowler must be an employee; or, to put it another way, there must be no bowler who is not an employee.

```
NOT EXISTS (SELECT *
    FROM Bowling AS B1
        WHERE B1.emp_nbr NOT IN (SELECT emp_nbr FROM Personnel))
```

27.3.2 Table Equality

How can I find out if two tables are equal to each other? This is a common programming problem, and the specification sounds obvious.

When two sets, A and B, are equal, then we know that:

1. Both have the same number of elements
2. No elements in A are not in B
3. No elements in B are not in A
4. Set A is equal to the intersection of A and B
5. Set B is equal to the intersection of A and B
6. Set B is a subset of A
7. Set A is a subset of B

as well as probably a few other things vaguely remembered from an old math class. But equality is not as easy as it sounds in SQL, because the language is based on multisets or bags, which allow duplicate elements, and the language has NULLs. Given this list of multisets, which pairs are equal to each other?

```
S0 = {a, b, c}
S1 = {a, b, NULL}
S2 = {a, b, b, c, c}
S3 = {a, b, NULL}
S4 = {a, b, c}
S5 = {x, y, z}
```

Everyone will agree that S0 = S4, because they are identical.

Everyone will agree that S5 is not equal to any other set because it has no elements in common with any of them. How do you handle redundant duplicates? If you ignore them, then S0 = S2. Should NULLs be given the benefit of the doubt and matched to any known value or not? If so, then S0 = S1 and S0 = S3. But then do you want to say that S1 = S3 because we can pair up the NULLs with each other?

To make matters even worse: are two rows equal if they match on just their keys, on a particular subset of their columns, or on all their columns? The reason this question comes up in practice is that you often have to match up data from two sources that have slightly different versions of the same information (i.e., "Joe F. Celko" and "Joseph Frank Celko" are probably the same person).

The good part about matching things on the keys is that you do have a true set—keys are unique and cannot have NULLs. If you go back to the list of set equality tests that I gave at the start of this article, you can see some possible ways to code a solution.

If you use facts 2 and 3 in the list, then you might use `NOT EXISTS()` predicates.

```
...
WHERE NOT EXISTS (SELECT *
                   FROM A
                  WHERE A.keycol
                    NOT IN (SELECT keycol
                              FROM B
                             WHERE A.keycol = B.keycol))
  AND NOT EXISTS (SELECT *
                   FROM B
                  WHERE B.keycol
                    NOT IN (SELECT keycol
                              FROM A
                             WHERE A.keycol = B.keycol))
```

This query can also be written as:

```
WHERE NOT EXISTS
          (SELECT *
             FROM A
                  EXCEPT [ALL]
                  SELECT *
                    FROM B
                   WHERE A.keycol = B.keycol)
           UNION
           SELECT *
             FROM B
                  EXCEPT [ALL]
                  SELECT *
                    FROM A
                   WHERE A.keycol = B.keycol))
```

The use of the optional `EXCEPT ALL` operators will determine how duplicates are handled.

However, if you look at 1, 4, and 5, you might come up with this answer:

```
...
WHERE (SELECT COUNT(*)FROM A)
```

```
       = (SELECT COUNT(*)
            FROM A INNER JOIN B
                 ON A.keycol = B.keycol)
   AND (SELECT COUNT(*)FROM B)
       = (SELECT COUNT(*)
             FROM A INNER JOIN B
                  ON A.keycol = B.keycol)
```

This query will produce a list of the unmatched values; you might want to keep them in two columns instead of coalescing them as I have shown here.

```
SELECT DISTINCT COALESCE(A.keycol, B.keycol) AS non_matched_key
   FROM A
        FULL OUTER JOIN
        B
        ON A.keycol = B.keycol
  WHERE A.keycol IS NULL
        OR B.keycol IS NULL;
```

Eventually, you will be able to handle this with the INTERSECT [ALL] and UNION [ALL] operators in Standard SQL and tune the query to whatever definition of equality you wish to use.

Unfortunately, these examples are for just comparing the keys. What do we do if we have tables without keys, or if we want to compare all the columns?

GROUP BY, DISTINCT, and a few other things in SQL treat NULLs as if they were equal to each other. This is probably the definition of equality we would like to use.

Remember that if one table has more columns or more rows than the other, we can stop right there, since they cannot possibly be equal under that definition. We have to assume that the tables have the same number of columns, of the same type, and in the same positions. But row counts look useful. Imagine that there are two children, each with a bag of candy. To determine that both bags are identical, the first children can start by pulling a piece of candy out and asking the other, "How many red ones do you have?" If the two counts disagree, we know that the bags are different. Now ask about the green pieces. We do not have to match each particular piece of candy in one bag with a particular piece of candy in the other bag. The counts are enough information, only if they differ. If the counts are the same, more work needs to be done. We could each have one brown piece of candy, but mine could be an M&M, and yours could be a malted milk ball.

Now, generalize that idea. Let's combine the two tables into one big table, with an extra column, x0, to show from where each row originally came.

Now form groups based on all the original columns. Within each group, count the number of rows from one table and the number of rows from the second table. If the counts are different, there are unmatched rows.

This will handle redundant duplicate rows within one table. This query does not require that the tables have keys. The assumption in a GROUP BY clause is that all NULLs are treated as if they were equals. Here is the final query.

```
SELECT x1, x2, ..., xn,
       COUNT(CASE WHEN x0 = 'A'
                  THEN 1 ELSE 0 END) AS a_tally,
       COUNT(CASE WHEN x0 = 'B'
                  THEN 1 ELSE 0 END) AS b_tally
  FROM (SELECT 'A', A.* FROM A
        UNION ALL
        SELECT 'B', B.* FROM B) AS X (x0, x1, x2, ..., xn)
 GROUP BY x1, x2, x3, x4, ... xn
HAVING COUNT(CASE WHEN x0 = 'A' THEN 1 ELSE 0 END)
      <> COUNT(CASE WHEN x0 = 'B' THEN 1 ELSE 0 END);
```

You might want to think about the differences that changing the expression for the derived table X can make. If you use a UNION instead of a UNION ALL, then the row count for each group in both tables will be one. If you use a SELECT DISTINCT instead of a SELECT, then the row count in just that table will be one for each group.

Subset Equality

A surprisingly usable version of set equality is finding identical subsets within the same table. These identical subsets can build partitions that are known as equivalence classes in set theory. Let's use Chris Date's suppliers-and-parts table to find pairs of suppliers who provide exactly the same parts—that is, the set of parts from one supplier is equal to the set of parts from the other supplier.

```
CREATE TABLE SupParts
(sup_nbr CHAR(2) NOT NULL,
 part_nbr CHAR(2) NOT NULL,
 PRIMARY KEY (sup_nbr, part_nbr));
```

The usual way of proving that two sets are equal is to show that set A contains set B and set B contains set A.

Any of the methods given above can be modified to handle two copies of the same table under aliases. Instead, consider another approach. First JOIN one supplier to another on their common parts, eliminating the situation where the first supplier is also the second supplier, so that you have the intersection of the two subsets. If the intersection has the same number of pairs as each of the two subsets has elements, the two subsets are equal.

```
SELECT SP1.sup_nbr, SP2.sup_nbr, COUNT(*) AS part_count
  FROM SupParts AS SP1
       INNER JOIN
       SupParts AS SP2
        ON SP1.part_nbr = SP2.part_nbr
           AND SP1.sup_nbr < SP2.sup_nbr
 GROUP BY SP1.sup_nbr, SP2.sup_nbr
HAVING COUNT(*) = (SELECT COUNT(*)
                     FROM SupParts AS SP3
                    WHERE SP3.sup_nbr = SP1.sup_nbr)
   AND COUNT(*) = (SELECT COUNT(*)
                     FROM SupParts AS SP4
                    WHERE SP4.sup_nbr = SP2.sup_nbr);
```

If there is an index on the supplier number in the SupParts table, it can provide the counts directly, as well as helping with the JOIN operation. The only problem with this answer is that it is hard to see the groups of suppliers among the pairs. The part_count column helps a bit, but it does not assign a grouping identifier to the rows.

27.4 Picking a Representative Subset

This problem and solution for it are due to Ross Presser. The problem is to find a subset of rows such that each value in each of two columns appears in at least one row. The purpose is to produce a set of samples from a large table. The table has a club_name column and an ifc column;

I want a set of samples that contains at least one of each club_name and at least one of each ifc, but no more than necessary.

```
CREATE TABLE Memberships
(member_id INTEGER NOT NULL PRIMARY KEY,
 club_name CHAR(7) NOT NULL,
 ifc CHAR(4) NOT NULL);

CREATE TABLE Samples
(member_id INTEGER NOT NULL PRIMARY KEY,
 club_name CHAR(7) NOT NULL,
 ifc CHAR(4) NOT NULL);

INSERT INTO Memberships
VALUES (6401715, 'aarprat', 'ic17'),
        (1058337, 'aarprat', 'ic17'),
        (459443, 'aarpprt', 'ic25'),
        (4018210, 'aarpbas', 'ig21'),
        (2430656, 'aarpbas', 'ig21'),
        (6802081, 'aarpprd', 'ig29'),
        (4236511, 'aarpprd', 'ig29'),
        (2162104, 'aarpbas', 'ig21'),
        (2073679, 'aarpprd', 'ig29'),
        (8148891, 'aarpbas', 'ig21'),
        (1868445, 'aarpbas', 'ig21'),
        (6749213, 'aarpbas', 'ig21'),
        (8363621, 'aarppup', 'ig29'),
        (9999, 'aarppup', 'ic17');  -- redundant
```

To help frame the problem better, consider this subset, which has a row with both a redundant club_name value and ifc value.

```
Non-Minimal subset
member_id  club_name      ifc
==========================
9999        aarppup   ic17 <== redundant row
1058337     aarprat   ic17 <== ifc
459443      aarpprt   ic25
1868445     aarpbas   ig21
2073679     aarpprd   ig29
8363621     aarppup   ig29 <== club_name
```

There can be more than one minimal solution. But we would be happy to simply find a near-minimal solution.

David Portas came up with a query that gives a near-minimal solution. This will produce a sample containing at least one row of each value in the two columns. It isn't guaranteed to give the *minimum* subset, but it should contain at most (c + i – 1) rows, where (c) is the number of distinct clubs and (i) the number of distinct ifcs.

```
SELECT member_id, club_name, ifc
  FROM Memberships AS M
 WHERE member_id
       IN
       (SELECT MIN(member_id)
          FROM Memberships
          GROUP BY club_name
       UNION ALL
       SELECT MIN(member_id)
         FROM Memberships AS M2
        GROUP BY ifc
       HAVING NOT EXISTS
             (SELECT *
                FROM Memberships
               WHERE member_id
                    IN (SELECT MIN(member_id)
                          FROM Memberships
                         GROUP BY club_name)
                AND ifc = M2.ifc));
```

I am not sure it's possible to find the minimum subset every time, unless you use an iterative solution. The results are very dependent on the exact data involved.

Ross Presser's iterative solution used the six-step system below, and found that the number of rows resulting depended on both the order of the insert queries and on whether we used `MAX()` or `MIN()`. That said, the resulting row count only varied from 403 to 410 rows on a real run of 52,776 invoices for a set where (c = 325) and (i = 117). Portas's query gave a result of 405 rows, which is worse but not fatally worse.

```
-- first step: unique clubs
INSERT INTO Samples (member_id, club_name, ifc)
SELECT MIN(Randommid), club_name, MIN(ifc)
  FROM Memberships
```

```
 GROUP BY club_name
HAVING COUNT(*) = 1;
-- second step: unique ifcs where club_name not already there
INSERT INTO Samples (member_id, club_name, ifc)
SELECT MIN(Memberships.Member_id), MIN(Memberships.club_name),
       Memberships.ifc
  FROM Memberships
 GROUP BY Memberships.ifc
HAVING MIN(Memberships.club_name)
       NOT IN (SELECT club_name FROM Samples)
       AND COUNT(*) = 1;

-- intermezzo: views for missing ifcs, missing clubs
CREATE VIEW MissingClubs (club_name)
AS
SELECT Memberships.club_name
  FROM Memberships
       LEFT OUTER JOIN
       Samples
       ON Memberships.club_name = Samples.club_name
 WHERE Samples.club_name IS NULL
 GROUP BY Memberships.club_name;

CREATE VIEW MissingIfcs (ifc)
AS
SELECT Memberships.ifc
  FROM Memberships
       LEFT OUTER JOIN
       Samples
       ON Memberships.ifc = Samples.ifc
 WHERE Samples.ifc IS NULL
 GROUP BY Memberships.ifc;

-- third step: distinct missing clubs that are also missing ifcs
INSERT INTO Samples (member_id, club_name, ifc)
SELECT MIN(Memberships.Member_id), Memberships.club_name,
       MIN(Memberships.ifc)
  FROM Memberships, MissingClubs, MissingIfcs
 WHERE Memberships.club_name = MissingClubs.club_name
   AND Memberships.ifc = MissingIfcs.ifc
GROUP BY Memberships.club_name;
```

```
-- fourth step: distinct missing ifcs that are also missing clubs
INSERT INTO Samples (member_id, club_name, ifc)
SELECT MIN(Memberships.member_id), MIN(Memberships.club_name,
       Memberships.ifc
  FROM Memberships, MissingClubs, MissingIfcs
 WHERE Memberships.club_name = MissingClubs.club_name)
   AND Memberships.ifc = MissingIfcs.ifc
GROUP BY Memberships.ifc;

-- fifth step: remaining missing ifcs
INSERT INTO Samples (member_id, club_name, ifc)
SELECT MIN(Memberships.member_id), MIN(memberships.club_name),
       memberships.ifc
  FROM Memberships, MissingIfcs
 WHERE Memberships.ifc = MissingIfcs.ifc
 GROUP BY Memberships.ifc;

-- sixth step: remaining missing clubs
INSERT INTO Samples (Member_id, club_name, ifc)
SELECT MIN(Memberships.Member_id), Memberships.club_name,
       MIN(Memberships.ifc)
  FROM Memberships, MissingClubs
 WHERE Memberships.club_name = MissingClubs.club_name
 GROUP BY Memberships.club_name;
```

We can check the candidate rows for redundancy removal with the two views that were created earlier to be sure.

Trees and Hierarchies in SQL

I HAVE A SEPARATE book (*Joe Celko's Trees and Hierarchies in SQL for Smarties*, 2004) devoted to this topic in great detail, so this chapter will be a very quick discussion of the three major approaches to modeling trees and hierarchies in SQL.

A tree is a special kind of directed graph. Graphs are data structures that are made up of nodes (usually shown as boxes) connected by edges (usually shown as lines with arrowheads). Each edge represents a one-way relationship between the two nodes it connects. In an organizational chart, the nodes are positions that can be filled by employees, and each edge is the "reports to" relationship. In a parts explosion (also called a bill of materials), the nodes are assembly units that eventually resolve down to individual parts from inventory, and each edge is the "is made of" relationship.

The top of the tree is called the root. In an organizational chart, it is the highest authority; in a parts explosion, it is the final assembly. The number of edges coming out of the node is its outdegree, and the number of edges entering it is its indegree. A binary tree is one in which a parent can have at most two children; more generally, an *n*ary tree is one in which a node can have at most outdegree *n*.

The nodes of the tree that have no subtrees beneath them are called the leaf nodes. In a parts explosion, they are the individual parts, which cannot be broken down any further. The descendants, or

children, of a node (the parent) are every node in the subtree that has the parent node as its root.

There are several ways to define a tree: it is a graph with no cycles; it is a graph where all nodes except the root have indegree one and the root has indegree zero. Another defining property is that a path can be found from the root to any other node in the tree by following the edges in their natural direction.

The tree structure and the nodes are very different things and therefore should be modeled in separate tables. But I am going to violate that design rule in this chapter and use an abstract tree in this chapter (see Figure 28.1).

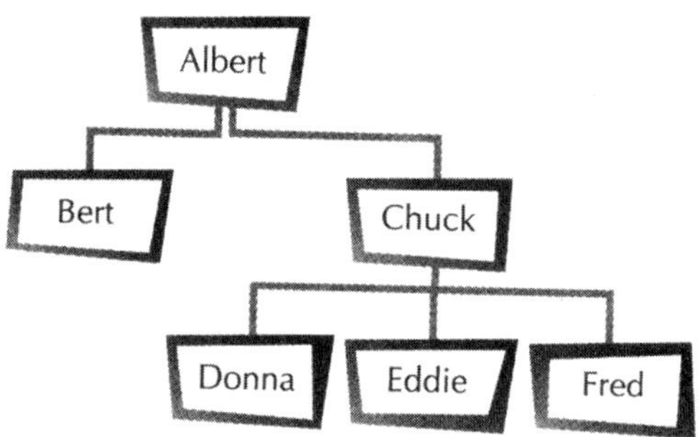

Figure 28.1 *An Abstract Tree Model.*

This little tree is small enough that you can remember what it looks like as you read the rest of this chapter. It will illustrate the various techniques discussed here. I will use the terms "child," "parent," and "node," but you may see other terms used in various books on graphs.

28.1 Adjacency List Model

Most SQL databases use the adjacency list model for two reasons. The first reason is that Dr. Codd came up with it in the early days of the relational model, and nobody thought about it after that. The second reason is that the adjacency list is a way of "faking" pointer chains, the traditional programming method in procedural languages for handling trees. It is a recording of the edges in a "boxes and arrows" diagram, something like this simple table:

```
CREATE TABLE AdjTree
(child CHAR(2) NOT NULL,
 parent CHAR(2),  -- null is root
 PRIMARY KEY (child, parent));
```

```
AdjTree
child  parent
=============
'A'    NULL
'B'    'A'
'C'    'A'
'D'    'C'
'E'    'C'
'F'    'C'
```

The queries for the leaf nodes and root are obvious. The root has a NULL parent, and the left nodes have no subordinates. Each row models two nodes that share an adjacent edge in a directed graph. The adjacency list model is both the most common and the worst possible tree model. On the other hand, it is the best way to model any general graph.

28.1.1 Complex Constraints

The first problem is that the adjacency list model requires complex constraints to maintain any data integrity. In practice, the usual solution is to ignore the problems and hope that nothing bad happens to the structure. But if you care about data integrity, you need to be sure that:

1. There is only one root node.

```
CREATE TABLE AdjTree
(child CHAR(2) NOT NULL,
 parent CHAR(2),  -- null is root
 PRIMARY KEY (child, parent),
 CONSTRAINT one_root
 CHECK((SELECT COUNT(*)
          FROM AdjTree
         WHERE parent IS NULL) = 1)
...);
```

2. There are no cycles. Unfortunately, this cannot be done without a trigger. The trigger code must trace all the paths looking for a cycle. The most obvious constraint to prohibit a single node cycle in the graph would be:

```
CHECK (child <> parent) - cannot be your own father!
```

But that does not detect ($n > 2$) node cycles. We know that the number of edges in a tree is the number of nodes minus one, so this is a connected graph. That constraint looks like this:

```
CHECK ((SELECT COUNT(*) FROM AdjTree) -1  -- edges
       = (SELECT COUNT(parent) FROM AdjTree)) -- nodes
```

The `COUNT(parent)` will drop the `NULL` in the root row. That gives us the effect of having a constraint to check for one `NULL`:

```
CHECK((SELECT COUNT(*) FROM Tree WHERE parent IS NULL) = 1)
```

This is a necessary condition, but it is not a sufficient condition. Consider this data, in which 'D' and 'E' are both in a cycle, and that cycle is not in the tree structure.

```
Cycle
child parent
===========
'A'   NULL
'B'   'A'
'C'   'A'
'D'   'E'
'E'   'D'
```

One approach would be to remove all the leaf nodes and repeat this procedure until the tree is reduced to an empty set. If the tree does not reduce to an empty set, then there is a disconnected cycle.

```
CREATE FUNCTION TreeTest() RETURNS CHAR(6)
LANGUAGE SQL
BEGIN ATOMIC
DECLARE row_count INTEGER;
SET row_count = (SELECT COUNT(DISTINCT parent) + 1 FROM
AdjTree);
-- put a copy in a temporary table
INSERT INTO WorkTree
SELECT emp, parent FROM AdjTree;

WHILE row_count > 0
```

```
DO DELETE FROM WorkTree -- prune leaf nodes
    WHERE Tree.child
        NOT IN (SELECT T2.parent
                  FROM Tree AS T2
                 WHERE T2.parent IS NOT NULL);
   SET row_count = row_count -1;
END WHILE;
IF NOT EXISTS (SELECT * FROM WorkTree)
THEN RETURN ('Tree  ');  --pruned everything
ELSE RETURN ('Cycles');  --cycles were left
END IF;
END;
```

28.1.2 Procedural Traversal for Queries

The second problem is that the adjacency list model requires that you traverse from node to node to answer any interesting questions, such as "Does Mr. King have any authority over Mr. Jones?" or any other aggregations up and down the tree.

```
SELECT P1.child, ' parent to ', C1.child
  FROM AdjTree AS P1, AdjTree AS C1
 WHERE P1.child = C1.parent;
```

But something is missing here. This query gives only the immediate parent of the node. Your parent's parent also has authority over you, and so forth, up the tree until we find someone who has no subordinates. To go two levels deep in the tree, we need to do a more complex self-JOIN, thus:

```
SELECT B1.child, ' parent to ', E2.child
  FROM AdjTree AS B1, AdjTree AS E1, AdjTree AS E2
 WHERE B1.child = E1.parent
   AND E1.child = E2.parent;
```

Unfortunately, you have no idea just how deep the tree is, so you must keep extending this query until you get an empty set back as a result. The practical problem is that most SQL compilers will start having serious problems optimizing queries with a large number of tables.

The other methods are to declare a CURSOR and traverse the tree with procedural code. This is usually painfully slow, but it will work for any depth of tree. It also defeats the purpose of using a nonprocedural language like SQL. With Common Table Expressions in SQL-99, you can also write a query that recursively constructs the transitive closure of the table by hiding the traversal. This feature is not popular yet, and it is still slow compared to the nested sets model.

28.1.3 Altering the Table

Insertion of a new node is the only easy operation in the adjacency list model. You simply do an `INSERT INTO` statement and check to see that the parent already exists in the table.

Deleting an edge in the middle of tree will cause the table to become a forest of separate trees. You need some rule for rearranging the structure. The two usual methods are to promote a subordinate to the vacancy (and cascade the vacancy downward) or to assign all the subordinates to their parent's parent (the orphans go to live with grandparents).

Consider what has to happen when a middle-level node is changed. The change must occur in both the child and parent columns.

```
UPDATE AdjTree
   SET child
       = CASE WHEN child = 'C'
              THEN 'C1',
              ELSE child END,
       parent
       = CASE WHEN parent= 'C'
              THEN 'C1',
              ELSE parent END
 WHERE 'C' IN (parent, child);
```

28.2 The Path Enumeration Model

The next method for representing hierarchies in SQL was first discussed in detail by Stefan Gustafsson on an Internet site for SQL Server users. Later, Tom Moreau and Itzik Ben-Gan developed it in more detail in their book *Advanced Transact-SQL for SQL Server 2000* (Moreau and Ben-Gan first edition was October 2000). This model stores the path from the root to each node as a string at that node.

Of course, we purists might object that this is a denormalized table, since the path is not a scalar value. The worst-case operation you can do in this representation is to alter the root of the tree. We then have to recalculate all the paths in the entire tree. But if the assumption is that structural modifications high in the tree are relatively uncommon, then this might not be a problem. The table for the simple tree we will use for this chapter looks like this:

```
CREATE TABLE PathTree
(node CHAR(2) NOT NULL PRIMARY KEY,
 path VARCHAR (900) NOT NULL);
```

The example tree would get the following representation:

```
 node  path
 ===========
 'A'   'a/'
 'B'   'a/b/'
 'C'   'a/c/'
 'D'   'a/c/d/'
 'E'   'a/c/e/'
 'F'   'a/c/f/'
```

What we have done is concatenate the node names and separate them with a slash. All of the operations will depend on string manipulations, so we'd like to have short node identifiers to keep the paths short. We would prefer, but not require, identifiers of one length to make substrings easier.

You have probably recognized this because I used a slash separator; this is a version of the directory paths used in several operating systems such as the UNIX family and Windows.

28.2.1 Finding Subtrees and Nodes

The major trick in this model is the `LIKE` predicate. The subtree rooted at `:my_node` is found with this query.

```
SELECT node
  FROM PathTree
 WHERE path LIKE '%' || :my_node || '%';
```

Finding the root node is easy, since that is the substring of any node up to the first slash. However, the leaf nodes are harder.

```
 SELECT T1.node
   FROM PathTree AS T1
```

```
WHERE NOT EXISTS
      (SELECT *
         FROM PathTree AS T2
       WHERE T2.path LIKE T1.path || '/_');
```

28.2.2 Finding Levels and Subordinates

The depth of a node is shown by the number of '/' characters in the path string. If you have a `REPLACE()` that can remove the '/' characters, the difference between the length of the part with and without those characters gives you the level.

```
CREATE VIEW DetailedTree (node, path, level)
AS SELECT node, path,
          CHARLENGTH (path)
           - CHARLENGTH (REPLACE (path, '/', ''))
     FROM PathTree;
```

The immediate descendents of a given node can be found with this query, if you know the length of the node identifiers. In this sample data, that length is one character:

```
SELECT :mynode, T2.node
  FROM PathTree AS T1, PathTree AS T2
 WHERE T1.node = :mynode
   AND T2.path LIKE T1.path || '_/';
```

This can be expanded with `OR`ed like predicates that cover the possible lengths of the node identifiers.

28.2.3 Deleting Nodes and Subtrees

This is a bit weird at first, because the removal of a node requires that you first update all the paths. Let us delete node 'B' in the sample tree:

```
BEGIN ATOMIC
UPDATE PathTree
   SET path
       = REPLACE (path, 'b/', '')
 WHERE POSITION ('b/' IN path) > 0;
DELETE FROM PathTree
 WHERE node = 'B';
END;
```

Deleting a subtree rooted at `:my_node` is actually simpler:

```
DELETE FROM PathTree
 WHERE path LIKE (SELECT path
                    FROM PathTree
                   WHERE node = :my_node   ||'%';
```

28.2.4 Integrity Constraints

If a path has the same node in it twice, then there is a cycle in the graph. We can use a `VIEW` with just the node names in it to some advantage here.

```
CHECK (NOT EXISTS
        (SELECT *
           FROM NodeList AS D1, PathTree AS P1
          WHERE CHAR_LENGTH (REPLACE (D1.node, P1.path, ''))
                < (CHAR_LENGTH(P1.path) - CHAR_LENGTH(D1.node))
       ))
```

Unfortunately, a subquery in a constraint is not widely implemented yet.

28.3 Nested Set Model of Hierarchies

Since SQL is a set-oriented language, the nested set model is a better model for the approach discussed here. If you have used HTML, XML or a language with a block structure, then you understand the basic idea of this model. The lft and rgt columns (their names are abbreviations for "left" and "right," which are reserved words in Standard SQL) are the count of the "tags" in an XML representation of a tree.

Imagine circles inside circles without any of them overlapping, the way you would draw a markup language structure. This has some predictable results that we can use for building queries, as shown in Figures 28.2, 28.3, and 28.4.

If that mental model does not work for you, to convert the "boxes and arrows" graph into a nested set model, think of a little worm crawling along the tree. The worm starts at the top, the root, makes a complete trip around the tree. When he comes to a node, he puts a number in the cell on the side that he is visiting and increments his counter. Each node will get two numbers, one for the right side and one for the left.

Figure 28.2

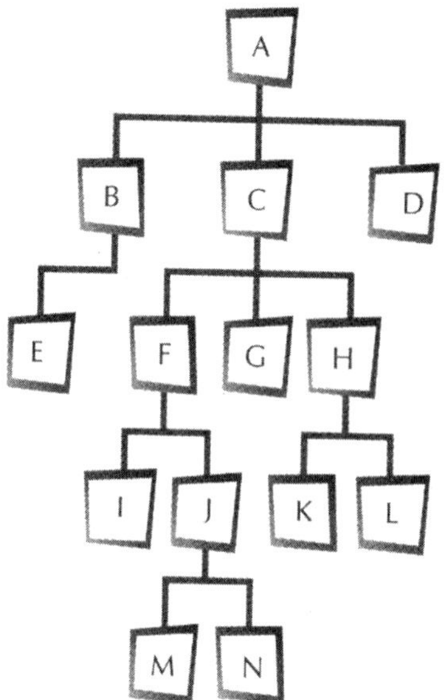

Figure 28.3

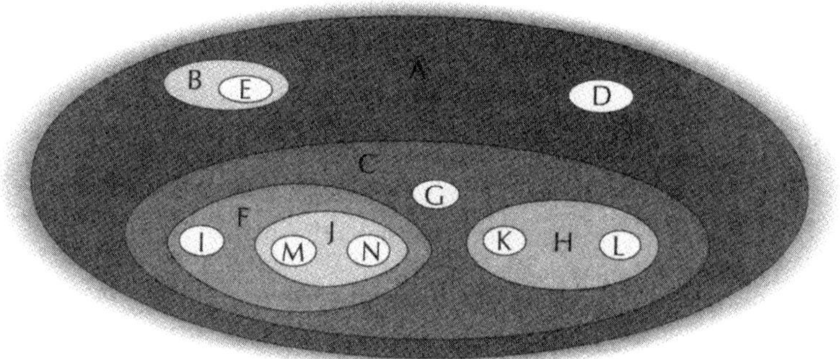

Figure 28.4

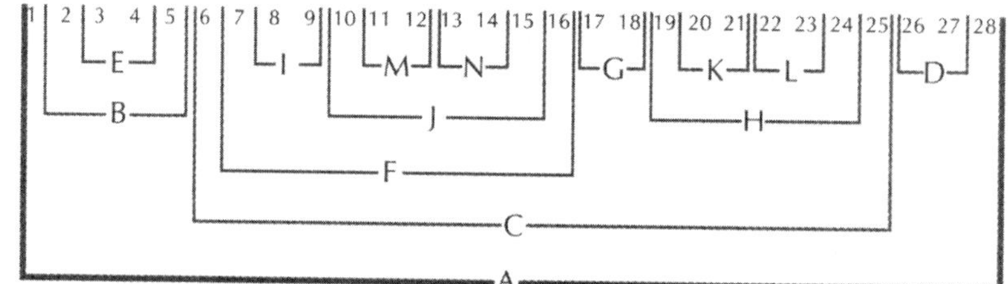

Computer science majors will recognize this as a modified preorder tree traversal algorithm.

```
CREATE TABLE NestTree
(node CHAR(2) NOT NULL PRIMARY KEY,
 lft INTEGER NOT NULL UNIQUE CHECK (lft > 0),
 rgt INTEGER NOT NULL UNIQUE CHECK (rgt > 1),
 CONSTRAINT order_okay CHECK (lft < rgt));
```

```
NestTree
 node lft   rgt
===============
'A'     1    12
'B'     2     3
'C'     4    11
'D'     5     6
'E'     7     8
'F'     9    10
```

Another nice thing is that the name of each node appears once and only once in the table. The path enumeration and adjacency list models used lots of self-references to nodes, which made updating more complex.

28.3.1 The Counting Property

The lft and rgt numbers have a definite meaning and carry information about the location and nature of each subtree. The root is always `(lft, rgt) = (1, 2 * (SELECT COUNT(*) FROM TreeTable))` and leaf nodes always have `(lft + 1 = rgt)`.

```
SELECT node AS root
  FROM NestTree
 WHERE lft = 1;

SELECT node AS leaf
  FROM NestTree
 WHERE lft = (rgt - 1);
```

Another very useful result of the counting property is that any node in the tree is the root of a subtree (the leaf nodes are a degenerate case) of size (rgt - lft +1)/2.

28.3.2 The Containment Property

In the nested set model table, all the descendants of a node can be found by looking for the nodes with a rgt and lft number between the lft and rgt values of their parent node. For example, to find out all the subordinates of each boss in the corporate hierarchy, you would write:

```
SELECT Superiors.node, ' is a boss of ', Subordinates.node
  FROM NestTree AS Superiors, NestTree AS Subordinates
 WHERE Subordinates.lft BETWEEN Superiors.lft AND Superiors.rgt;
```

This would tell you that everyone is also his own boss, so in some situations you would also add the predicate:

```
... AND Subordinates.lft <> Superiors.lft
```

This simple self-JOIN query is the basis for almost everything that follows in the nested set model. The containment property does not depend on the values of lft and rgt having no gaps, but the counting property does.

The level of a node in a tree is the number of edges between the node and the root. The larger the depth number, the farther away the node is from the root. A path is a set of edges that directly connect two nodes.

The nested set model uses the fact that each containing set is "wider" (where width = (rgt - lft)) than the sets it contains.

Obviously, the root will always be the widest row in the table. The level function is the number of edges between two given nodes; it is fairly easy to calculate. For example, to find the level of each subordinate node, you would use

```
SELECT T2.node, (COUNT(T1.node) - 1) AS level
  FROM NestTree AS T1, NestTree AS T2
 WHERE T2.lft BETWEEN T1.lft AND T1.rgt
 GROUP BY T2.node;
```

The reason for using the expression (COUNT(*) - 1) is to remove the duplicate count of the node itself, because a tree starts at level zero. If you prefer to start at one, then drop the extra arithmetic.

28.3.3 Subordinates

The Nested Set Model usually assumes that the subordinates are ranked by age, seniority, or in some other way from left to right among the immediate subordinates of a node. The adjacency model does not have a concept of such rankings, so the following queries are not possible without extra columns to hold the rankings in the adjacency list model.

The most senior subordinate is found by this query:

```
SELECT Subordinates.node, ' is the oldest child of ', :my_node
  FROM NestTree AS Superiors, NestTree AS Subordinates
 WHERE Superiors.node = :my_node
   AND Subordinates.lft - 1 = Superiors.lft; -- leftmost child
```

Most junior subordinate:

```
SELECT Subordinates.node, ' is the youngest child of ', :my_node
  FROM NestTree AS Superiors, NestTree AS Subordinates
 WHERE Superiors.node = :my_node
   AND Subordinates.rgt = Superiors.rgt - 1; -- rightmost child
```

To convert a nested set model into an adjacency list model with the immediate subordinates, use this query in a VIEW.

```
CREATE VIEW AdjTree (parent, child)
AS
SELECT B.node, E.node
  FROM NestTree AS E
       LEFT OUTER JOIN
       NestTree AS B
       ON B.lft
          = (SELECT MAX(lft)
               FROM NestTree AS S
              WHERE E.lft > S.lft
                AND E.lft < S.rgt);
```

28.3.4 Hierarchical Aggregations

To find the level of each node, so you can print the tree as an indented listing. Technically, you should declare a cursor to go with the ORDER BY clause.

```
SELECT COUNT(T2.node) AS indentation, T1.node
  FROM NestTree AS T1, NestTree AS T2
 WHERE T1.lft BETWEEN T2.lft AND T2.rgt
 GROUP BY T1.lft, T1.emp
 ORDER BY T1.lft;
```

This same pattern of grouping will also work with other aggregate functions. Let's assume a second table contains the weight of each of the nodes in the NestTree. A simple hierarchical total of the weights by subtree is a two-table join.

```
SELECT Superiors.node, SUM (Subordinates.weight) AS
subtree_weight
  FROM NestTree AS Superiors, NestTree AS Subordinates
       NodeWeights AS W
 WHERE Subordinates.lft BETWEEN Superiors.lft AND Superiors.rgt
   AND W.node = Subordinates,node;
```

28.3.5 Deleting Nodes and Subtrees

Another interesting property of this representation is that the subtrees must fill from lft to rgt. In other tree representations, it is possible for a parent node to have a rgt child and no lft child. This lets you assign some significance to being the leftmost child of a parent. For example, the node in this position might be the next in line for promotion in a corporate hierarchy.

Deleting a single node in the middle of the tree is conceptually harder than removing whole subtrees. When you remove a node in the middle of the tree, you have to decide how to fill the hole.

There are two ways. The first method is to promote one of the children to the original node's position—Dad dies and the oldest son takes over the business. The second method is to connect the children to the parent of the original node—Mom dies and Grandma adopts the kids. This is the default action in a nested set model because of the containment property; the deletion will destroy the counting property, however.

If you wish to close multiple gaps, you can do this by renumbering the nodes, thus:

```
UPDATE NestTree
   SET lft = (SELECT COUNT(*)
                FROM (SELECT lft FROM NestTree
                       UNION ALL
                      SELECT rgt FROM NestTree) AS LftRgt (seq_nbr)
               WHERE seq_nbr <= lft),
       rgt = (SELECT COUNT(*)
                FROM (SELECT lft FROM NestTree
                       UNION ALL
                      SELECT rgt FROM NestTree) AS LftRgt (seq_nbr)
 WHERE seq_nbr <= rgt);
```

If the derived table LftRgt is a bit slow, you can use a temporary table and index it or use a `VIEW` that will be materialized.

```
CREATE VIEW LftRgt (seq_nbr)
AS SELECT lft FROM NestTree
   UNION
   SELECT rgt FROM NestTree;
```

28.3.6 Converting Adjacency List to Nested Set Model

It would be fairly easy to load an adjacency list model table into a host language program, then use a recursive preorder tree traversal program from a college freshman data structures textbook to build the nested set model. Here is a version with an explicit stack in SQL/PSM.

```
-- Tree holds the adjacency model
CREATE TABLE Tree
(node CHAR(10) NOT NULL,
 parent CHAR(10));

-- Stack starts empty, will holds the nested set model
CREATE TABLE Stack
(stack_top INTEGER NOT NULL,
 node CHAR(10) NOT NULL,
 lft INTEGER,
 rgt INTEGER);
```

```
BEGIN ATOMIC
DECLARE counter INTEGER;
DECLARE max_counter INTEGER;
DECLARE current_top INTEGER;

SET counter = 2;
SET max_counter = 2 * (SELECT COUNT(*) FROM Tree);
SET current_top = 1;

--clear the stack
DELETE FROM Stack;

-- push the root
INSERT INTO Stack
SELECT 1, node, 1, max_counter
  FROM Tree
 WHERE parent IS NULL;

-- delete rows from tree as they are used
DELETE FROM Tree WHERE parent IS NULL;

WHILE counter <= max_counter- 1
  DO IF EXISTS (SELECT *
               FROM Stack AS S1, Tree AS T1
              WHERE S1.node = T1.parent
                AND S1.stack_top = current_top)
     THEN  -- push when top has subordinates and set lft value
       INSERT INTO Stack
      SELECT (current_top + 1), MIN(T1.node), counter, CAST(NULL
AS INTEGER)
        FROM Stack AS S1, Tree AS T1
       WHERE S1.node = T1.parent
         AND S1.stack_top = current_top;

       -- delete rows from tree as they are used
       DELETE FROM Tree
        WHERE node = (SELECT node
                        FROM Stack
                       WHERE stack_top = current_top + 1);
       -- housekeeping of stack pointers and counter
       SET counter = counter + 1;
       SET current_top = current_top + 1;
```

```
      ELSE -- pop the stack and set rgt value
        UPDATE Stack
           SET rgt = counter,
               stack_top = -stack_top -- pops the stack
         WHERE stack_top = current_top;
        SET counter = counter + 1;
        SET current_top = current_top - 1;
      END IF;
    END WHILE;
END;

-- the top column is not needed in the final answer
SELECT node, lft, rgt FROM Stack;
```

This is not the fastest way to do a conversion, but since conversions are probably not going to be frequent tasks, it might be good enough when translated into your SQL product's procedural language.

28.4 Other Models for Trees and Hierarchies

Other models for trees are discussed in a separate book, but these three methods represent the major families of models. You can also use specialized models for specialized trees, such as binary trees. The real point is that you can use SQL for hierarchical structures, but you have to pick the right one for your task. I would classify the choices as:

1. *Frequent node changes and infrequent structure changes*. Example: organizational charts where personnel come and go, but the organization stays much the same.
2. *Infrequent node changes with frequent structure changes*. Example: a message board where the e-mails are the nodes that never change, and the structure is simply extended with each new e-mail.
3. *Infrequent node changes and infrequent structure changes*. Example: historical data in a data warehouse that has a categorical hierarchy in place as a dimension.
4. *Both frequent node changes and frequent structure changes*. Example: a mapping system that attempts to find the best path from a central dispatch to the currently most critical node through a tree that is also changing. Let's make that a bit clearer

with the concrete example of getting a fire truck from the engine house to the worst fire in its service area, based on the traffic at the time.

I am not going to pick any particular tree model for any of those situations. The answer, once again, is "Well, it all depends . . ."

Temporal Queries

TEMPORAL DATA IS THE hardest type of data for people to handle conceptually. Perhaps time is difficult because it is dynamic and all other data types are static, or perhaps it is because time allows multiple parallel events. This is an old puzzle that still catches people. If a hen and a half can lay an egg and a half in a day and a half, then how many hens does it take to lay six eggs in six days? Do not look at the rest of the page; try to answer the question in your head.

The answer is a hen and a half—although you might want to round that up to two hens in the real world. People tend to get tripped up on the rate (eggs per hen per day) because they handle time incorrectly. For example, if a cookbook has a recipe that serves one, and you want to serve 100 guests, you increase the amount of ingredients by 100, but you do not cook it 100 times longer.

The algebra in this problem looks like this, where we want to solve for the rate in terms of "eggs per day," a strange but convenient unit of measurement for summarizing the hen house output:

$$1^{1}/_{2} \text{ hens} * 1^{1}/_{2} \text{ days} * \text{rate} = 1^{1}/_{2} \text{ eggs}$$

The first urge is to multiple both sides by in an attempt to turn every $1^{1}/_{2}$ into a 1. But what you actually get is:

1 hens * $1^{1}/_{2}$ days * rate = 1 egg; multiply by eggs per hen

$1^{1}/_{2}$ days * rate = 1 egg per hen; divide by the number of hens

rate = egg per hen per day; divide by $1^{1}/_{2}$ days

If you still do not get it, draw a graph.

29.1 Temporal Math

Almost every SQL implementation has a `DATE` data type, but the functions available for that data type vary quite a bit. The most common ones are a constructor that builds a date from integers or strings; extractors to pull out the month, day, or year; and some display options to format output.

You can assume that your SQL implementation has simple date arithmetic functions, although with different syntax from product to product, such as:

1. A date plus or minus a number of days yields a new date
2. A date minus a second date yields an integer number of days

Table 29.1 shows the valid combinations of `<datetime>` and `<interval>` data types in Standard SQL:

Table 29.1 *Valid Combinations of Temporal Data Types in Standard SQL*

```
<datetime> - <datetime> = <interval>

<datetime> + <interval> = <datetime>

<interval> (* or/) <numeric> = <interval>

<interval> + <datetime> = <datetime>

<interval> + <interval> = <interval>

<numeric> * <interval> = <interval>
```

Other rules, dealing with time zones and the relative precision of the two operands, are intuitively obvious.

There should also be a function that returns the current date from the system clock. This function has a different name with each vendor: TODAY, SYSDATE, NOW(), CURRENT DATE, and getdate() are some examples. There may also be a function to return the day of the week from a date, which is sometimes called DOW() or WEEKDAY(). Standard SQL provides for CURRENT_ DATE, CURRENT_TIME [(<time precision>)], and CURRENT_TIMESTAMP [(<timestamp precision>)] functions, which are self-explanatory.

29.2 Personal Calendars

One of the most common applications of dates is to build calendars that list upcoming events or actions to be taken by their user. People have no trouble with using a paper calendar to trigger their own actions, but the idea of having an internal calendar as a table in their database is somehow strange. Programmers seem to prefer to write a function that calculates the date and matches it to events.

It is easier to create a table for cyclic data than people initially think. The months and days of the week within a year repeat themselves in a cycle of 28 years. A table of just more than 10,000 rows can hold a complete cycle. The cycle has to repeat itself every 400 years, so today is on the same day of the week that it was on 400 years ago.

As an example, consider the rule that a stockbroker must settle a transaction within three business days after a trade. Business days are defined as excluding Saturdays, Sundays, and certain holidays. The holidays are determined at the start of the year by the New York Stock Exchange, but this can be changed by an act of Congress or presidential decree, or the SEC can order that trading stop in a security. The problem is how to write an SQL query that will return the proper settlement date given a trade date.

There are several tricks in this problem. The real trick is to decide what you want and not to be fooled by what you have. You have a list of holidays, but you want a list of settlement days. Let's start with a table of the given holidays and their names:

```
CREATE TABLE Holidays -- Insert holiday list into this table
(holiday_date DATE NOT NULL PRIMARY KEY,
 holiday_name CHAR(20) NOT NULL);
```

The next step is to build a table of trade and settlement dates for the whole year. Building the `INSERT INTO` statements to load the second table is easily done with a spreadsheet; these always have good date functions.

Let's start by building a simple list of the dates over the range we want use and putting them into a table called Settlements:

```
CREATE TABLE Settlements
(trade_date DATE NOT NULL PRIMARY KEY,
 settle_date DATE NOT NULL);

INSERT INTO Settlements
VALUES ('2005-02-01', '2005-02-01'),
       ('2005-02-02', '2005-02-02'),
       ('2005-02-03', '2005-02-03');
 etc.
```

We know that we cannot trade on a holiday or weekend. You probably could have excluded weekends in the spreadsheet, but if not, use this statement.

```
DELETE FROM Settlements
 WHERE trade_date IN (SELECT holi_date FROM Holidays)
    OR DayOfWeek(trade_date) IN ('Saturday', 'Sunday');
```

This does not handle the holiday settlements, however. The trouble with a holiday is that it can fall on a weekend, in which case we just handled it, it can last only one day, or it can last any number of days. The table of holidays is built on the assumption that each day of a multiday holiday has a row in the table.

We now have to update the table so that the regular settlement days are three business-days forward of the trade date. But we have all the business days in the trade_date column of the Settlements table now.

```
 UPDATE Settlements
    SET settle_date
        = (SELECT trade_date
             FROM Settlements AS S1
            WHERE Settlements.trade_date < S1.trade_date
              AND (SELECT COUNT(*)
                     FROM Settlements AS S2
```

```
                WHERE S2.trade_date
                      BETWEEN Settlements.trade_date
                          AND S1.trade_date) = 3);
```

The final settlement table will be about 250 rows per year and only two columns wide. This is quite small; it will fit into main storage easily on any machine. Finding the settlement day is a straight, simple query; if you had built only the Holiday table, you would have had to provide procedural code.

29.3 Time Series

One of the major problems in the real world is how to handle a series of events that occur in the same time period or in some particular order. The code is tricky and a bit hard to understand, but the basic idea is that you have a table with start and stop times for events, and you want to get information about them as a group.

29.3.1 Gaps in a Time Series

The timeline can be partitioned into intervals, and a set of intervals can be drawn from that partition for reporting. One of the stock questions on an employment form asks the prospective employee to explain any gaps in his record of employment. Most of the time this gap means that you were unemployed. If you are in data processing, you answer that you were consulting, which is a synonym for unemployed.

Given this table, how would you write an SQL query to display the time periods and their durations for each of the candidates? You will have to assume that your version of SQL has DATE functions that can do some simple calendar math.

```
CREATE TABLE JobApps
(candidate CHAR(25) NOT NULL,
 jobtitle CHAR(15) NOT NULL,
 start_date DATE NOT NULL,
 end_date DATE -- null means still employed
         CONSTRAINT started_before_ended
         CHECK(start_date <= end_date)
 ...);
```

Notice that the end date of the current job_code is set to NULL because SQL does not support an "eternity" or "end of time" value for temporal data types. Using '9999-12-31 23:59:59.999999', the highest possible date value that SQL can represent, is not a correct model and can cause problems when you do temporal arithmetic. The NULL can be handled with a COALESCE() function in the code, as I will demonstrate later.

It is obvious that this has to be a self-JOIN query, so you have to do some date arithmetic. The first day of each gap is the last day of an employment period plus one day, and that the last day of each gap is the first day of the next job_code minus one day. This start-point and end-point problem is the reason that SQL defined the OVERLAPS predicate this way.

All versions of SQL support temporal data types and arithmetic. But unfortunately, no two implementations look alike, and few look like the ANSI standard. The first attempt at this query is usually something like the following, which will produce the right results, but with a lot of extra rows that are just plain wrong. Assume that if I add a number of days to a date, or subtract a number of days from it, I get a new date.

```
SELECT J1.candidate,
       (J1.end_date + INTERVAL '1' DAY) AS gap_start,
 (J2.start_date - INTERVAL '1' DAY) AS gap_end,
       (J2.start_date - J1.end_date) AS gaplength
  FROM JobApps AS J1, JobApps AS J2
 WHERE J1.candidate = J2.candidate
   AND (J1.end_date + INTERVAL '1' DAY) < J2.start_date;
```

Here is why this does not work. Imagine that we have a table that includes a candidate named 'Bill Jones' with the following work history:

```
Result
candidate      jobtitle        start_date    end_date
=======================================================
'John Smith'  'Vice Pres'     '1999-01-10'  '1999-12-31'
'John Smith'  'President'     '2000-01-12'  '2001-12-31'
'Bill Jones'  'Scut Worker'   '2000-02-24'  '2000-04-21'
'Bill Jones'  'Manager'       '2001-01-01'  '2001-01-05'
'Bill Jones'  'Grand Poobah'  '2001-04-04'  '2001-05-15'
```

We would get this as a result:

```
Result
candidate      gap_start     gap_end     gaplength
===================================================
'John Smith'  '2000-01-01'  '200001-11'  12
'Bill Jones'  '2000-04-22'  '200012-31'  255
'Bill Jones'  '2001-01-06'  '2001-04-03' 89
'Bill Jones'  '2000-04-22'  '2001-04-03' 348 <=  false data
```

The problem is that the 'John Smith' row looks just fine and can fool you into thinking that you are doing fine. He had two jobs; therefore, there was one gap in between. However, 'Bill Jones' cannot be right—only two gaps separate three jobs, yet the query shows three gaps.

The query does its JOIN on all possible combinations of start and end dates in the original table. This gives false data in the results by counting the end of one job_code, 'Scut Worker' and the start of another, 'Grand Poobah', as a gap. The idea is to use only the most recently ended job_code for the gap. This can be done with a `MIN()` function and a correlated subquery. The final result is this:

```
SELECT J1.candidate, (J1.end_date + INTERVAL '1' DAY) AS
gap_start,
       (J2.start_date - INTERVAL '1' DAY) AS gap_end
  FROM JobApps AS J1, JobApps AS J2
 WHERE J1.candidate = J2.candidate
   AND J2.start_date
       = (SELECT MIN(J3.start_date)
            FROM JobApps AS J3
           WHERE J3.candidate = J1.candidate
             AND J3.start_date > J1.end_date)
   AND (J1.end_date + INTERVAL '1' DAY)
        < (J2.start_date - INTERVAL '1' DAY)
UNION ALL
SELECT J1.candidate, MAX(J1.end_date) + INTERVAL '1' DAY,
       CURRENT_TIMESTAMP
  FROM JobApps AS J1
 GROUP BY J1.candidate
HAVING COUNT(*) = COUNT(DISTINCT J1.end_date);
```

The length of the gap can be determined with simple temporal arithmetic. The purpose of the `UNION ALL` is to add the current period of unemployment, if any, to the final answer.

29.3.2 Continuous Time Periods

Given a series of jobs that can start and stop at any time, how can you be sure that an employee doing all these jobs was really working without any gaps? Let's build a table of timesheets for one employee.

```
CREATE TABLE Timesheets
(job_code CHAR(5) NOT NULL PRIMARY KEY,
 start_date DATE NOT NULL,
 end_date DATE NOT NULL,
 CHECK (start_date <= end_date));

INSERT INTO Timesheets (job_code, start_date, end_date)
VALUES ('j1', '2008-01-01', '2008-01-03');
       ('j2', '2008-01-06', '2008-01-10'),
       ('j3', '2008-01-05', '2008-01-08'),
       ('j4', '2008-01-20', '2008-01-25'),
       ('j5', '2008-01-18', '2008-01-23'),
       ('j6', '2008-02-01', '2008-02-05'),
       ('j7', '2008-02-03', '2008-02-08'),
       ('j8', '2008-02-07', '2008-02-11'),
       ('j9', '2008-02-09', '2008-02-10'),
       ('j10', '2008-02-01', '2008-02-11'),
       ('j11', '2008-03-01', '2008-03-05'),
       ('j12', '2008-03-04', '2008-03-09'),
       ('j13', '2008-03-08', '2008-03-14'),
       ('j14', '2008-03-13', '2008-03-20');
```

The most immediate answer is to build a search condition for all of the characteristics of a continuous time period.

This algorithm is due to Mike Arney, a DBA at BORN Consulting. It uses derived tables to get the extreme start and ending dates of a contiguous run of durations.

```
SELECT Early.start_date, MIN(Latest.end_date)
  FROM (SELECT DISTINCT start_date
          FROM Timesheets AS T1
```

```
          WHERE NOT EXISTS
                (SELECT *
                   FROM Timesheets AS T2
                  WHERE T2.start_date < T1.start_date
                    AND T2.end_date >= T1.start_date)
        ) AS Early (start_date)
        INNER JOIN
        (SELECT DISTINCT end_date
           FROM Timesheets AS T3
          WHERE NOT EXISTS
                (SELECT *
                   FROM Timesheets AS T4
                  WHERE T4.end_date > T3.end_date
                    AND T4.start_date <= T3.end_date)
        ) AS Latest (end_date)
        ON Early.start_date <= Latest.end_date
GROUP BY Early.start_date;

  Result
  start_date     end_date
  ===========================
  '2008-01-01'   '2008-01-03'
  '2008-01-05'   '2008-01-10'
  '2008-01-18'   '2008-01-25'
  '2008-02-01'   '2008-02-11'
  '2008-03-01'   '2008-03-20'
```

However, another way of doing this is a query, which will also tell you which jobs bound the continuous periods.

```
SELECT T2.start_date,
       MAX(T1.end_date) AS finish_date,
       MAX(T1.job_code || ' to ' || T2.job_code) AS job_code_pair
  FROM Timesheets AS T1, Timesheets AS T2
 WHERE T2.job_code <> T1.job_code
   AND T1.start_date BETWEEN T2.start_date AND T2.end_date
   AND T2.end_date BETWEEN T1.start_date AND T1.end_date
 GROUP BY T2.start_date;
```

```
Result
start_date     finish_date  job_code_pair
==========================================
'2008-01-05'  '2008-01-10'  'j2 to J3'
'2008-01-18'  '2008-01-25'  'j4 to J5'
'2008-02-01'  '2008-02-08'  'j7 to J6'
'2008-02-03'  '2008-02-11'  'j8 to J7'

DELETE FROM Results
 WHERE EXISTS
      (SELECT R1.job_code_list
         FROM Results AS R1
        WHERE POSITION (Results.job_code_list
                        IN R1.job_code_list) > 0);
```

A third solution will handle an isolated job_code like 'j1', as well as three or more overlapping jobs, like 'j6', 'j7', and 'j8'.

```
SELECT T1.start_date,
       MIN(T2.end_date) AS finish_date,
       MIN(T2.end_date + INTERVAL '1'  DAY) -
       - MIN(T1.start_date) AS duration   -- find any
(T1.start_date)
  FROM Timesheets AS T1, Timesheets AS T2
 WHERE T2.start_date >= T1.start_date
   AND T2.end_date >= T1.end_date
   AND NOT EXISTS
       (SELECT *
          FROM Timesheets AS T3
         WHERE (T3.start_date <= T2.end_date
                AND T3.end_date > T2.end_date)
           OR (T3.end_date >= T1.start_date
               AND T3.start_date < T1.start_date))
 GROUP BY T1.start_date;
```

You will also want to look at how to consolidate overlapping intervals of integers.

A fourth solution uses the auxiliary Calendar table (see Section 29.9 for details) to find the dates that are and are not covered by any of the durations. The coverage flag and calendar date can then be used directly by other queries that need to look at the status of single days instead of date ranges.

```
SELECT C1.cal_date,
       SUM(DISTINCT
           CASE
          WHEN C1.cal_date BETWEEN T1.start_date AND T1.end_date
           THEN 1 ELSE 0 END) AS covered_date_flag
  FROM Calendar AS C1, Timesheets AS T1
 WHERE C1.cal_date BETWEEN (SELECT MIN(start_date FROM
Timesheets)
                       AND (SELECT MAX(end_date FROM Timesheets)
 GROUP BY C1.cal_date;
```

This is reasonably fast because the WHERE clause uses static scalar queries to set the bounds, and the Calendar table uses cal_date as a primary key, so it will have an index.

A slightly different version of the problem is to group contiguous measurements into durations that have the value of that measurement.

I have the following table:

```
CREATE TABLE Calibrations
(start_time TIMESTAMP DEFAULT CURRENT_TIMESTAMP
            NOT NULL PRIMARY KEY
 end_time TIMESTAMP NOT NULL,
 CHECK (end_time = start_time + INTERVAL '1' MINUTE,
 cal_value INTEGER NOT NULL);
```

The table has this data:

```
Calibrations
start_time                   end_time                   cal_value
=================================================================
'2005-05-11 02:52:00.000'  '2005-05-11 02:53:00.000'    8
'2005-05-11 02:53:00.000'  '2005-05-11 02:54:00.000'    8
'2005-05-11 02:54:00.000'  '2005-05-11 02:55:00.000'    8
'2005-05-11 02:55:00.000'  '2005-05-11 02:56:00.000'    8
'2005-05-11 02:56:00.000'  '2005-05-11 02:57:00.000'    8
'2005-05-11 02:57:00.000'  '2005-05-11 02:58:00.000'    9
'2005-05-11 02:58:00.000'  '2005-05-11 02:59:00.000'    9
'2005-05-11 02:59:00.000'  '2005-05-11 03:00:00.000'    9
```

```
'2005-05-11 03:00:00.000'  '2005-05-11 03:01:00.000'    9
'2005-05-11 03:01:00.000'  '2005-05-11 03:02:00.000'    9
'2005-05-11 03:02:00.000'  '2005-05-11 03:03:00.000'    8
'2005-05-11 03:03:00.000'  '2005-05-11 03:04:00.000'    8
'2005-05-11 03:04:00.000'  '2005-05-11 03:05:00.000'    8
```

I want to be able to group this data so that it looks like this:

```
start_time                 end_time                  cal_value
==============================================================
'2005-05-11 02:52:00.000'  '2005-05-11 02:57:00.000'    8
'2005-05-11 02:57:00.000'  '2005-05-11 03:02:00.000'    9
'2005-05-11 03:02:00.000'  '2005-05-11 03:05:00.000'    8
```

Background

The table being selected from is updated every minute with a new calibration value. The calibration value can change from minute to minute. I want a select statement that will sum up the start of the cal_value and the end of the calibration value before it changes.

```
SELECT MIN(start_time) AS start_time,
       MAX(end_time) AS end_time,
       cal_value
  FROM (SELECT C1.start_time, C1.end_time, C1.cal_value,
               MIN(C2.start_time)
          FROM Calibrations AS C1
               LEFT OUTER JOIN
               Calibrations AS C2
               ON C1.start_time < C2.start_time
                  AND C1.cal_value <> C2.cal_value
         GROUP BY C1.start_time, C1.end_time, C1.cal_value)
       AS T (start_time, end_time, cal_value, x_time))
 GROUP BY cal_value, x_time;
```

29.3.3 Missing Times in Contiguous Events

Consider the following simple table, which we will use to illustrate how to handle missing times in events.

```
CREATE TABLE Events
(event_id CHAR(2) NOT NULL PRIMARY KEY,
 start_date DATE,
```

```
 end_date DATE,
 CHECK(start_date < end_date));

INSERT INTO Events
VALUES
('A', '2003-01-01', '2003-12-31'),
('B', '2004-01-01', '2004-01-31'),
('C', '2004-02-01', '2004-02-29'),
('D', '2004-02-01', '2004-02-29');
```

Due to circumstances beyond our control, the end_date column may contain a NULL instead of a valid date. Imagine that we had ('B', '2004-01-01',NULL) as a row in the table.

One reasonable solution is to populate the missing end_date with the (start_date –1 day) of the next period. This is easy enough.

```
UPDATE Events
   SET end_date
       = (SELECT MIN(E1.start_date) - INTERVAL '1' DAY)
            FROM Events AS E1
           WHERE E1.start_date > Events.start_date)
 WHERE end_date IS NULL;
```

Likewise, due to circumstances beyond our control, the start_date column may contain a NULL instead of a valid date. Imagine that we had ('B ,NULL, '2004-01-31') as a row in the table. Using the same logic, we could take the last known ending date and add one to it to give us a guess at the missing starting value.

```
UPDATE Events
   SET start_date
       = (SELECT MIN(E1.end_date) + INTERVAL '1' DAY)
            FROM Events AS E1
           WHERE E1.end_date < Events.end_date)
 WHERE start_date IS NULL;
```

This has a nice symmetry to it, but it does not cover all possible cases. Consider an event where we know nothing about the times:

```
INSERT INTO Events
VALUES
```

```
('A', '2003-01-01', '2003-12-31'),
('B', NULL, NULL),
('C', '2004-02-01', '2004-02-29'),
('D', '2004-02-01', '2004-02-29');
```

You can run each of the previous UPDATE statements and get the NULLs filled in with values. However, you can combine them into one update:

```
UPDATE Events
   SET end_date
       = CASE WHEN end_date IS NULL
         THEN (SELECT MIN(E1.start_date) - INTERVAL '1' DAY
                 FROM Events AS E1
                WHERE E1.start_date > Events.start_date)
         ELSE end_date END,
       start_date
       = CASE WHEN start_date IS NULL
         THEN (SELECT MIN(E1.end_date) + INTERVAL '1' DAY
                 FROM Events AS E1
                WHERE E1.end_date < Events.end_date)
         ELSE start_date END
 WHERE start_date IS NULL
    OR end_date IS NULL;
```

The real problem is having no boundary dates on contiguous events, like this:

```
INSERT INTO Events
VALUES
('A', '2003-01-01', '2003-12-31'),
('B', '2004-01-01', NULL),
('C', NULL, '2004-02-29'),
('D', '2004-02-01', '2004-02-29');
```

The result of applying the previous update is that we get an error because it will try to set the start_date equal to end_date in both rows.

Given the restriction that each event lasts for at least one day, event 'B' could have finished on any day between '2004-01-02' and '2004-02-27', and likewise, event 'C' could have begun on any day between '2004-01-03' and '2004-02-28'; note the two different durations.

Any rules we make for resolving the NULLs is going to be arbitrary. For example, we could give event 'B' the benefit of the doubt and assume that it lasted until '2004-02-27' or just as well given event 'C' the same benefit. I might make a random choice of a pair of dates *d*, (*d*+1) in the gap between 'B' and 'C' dates. I might pick a middle point.

However, this pairwise approach does not solve the problem of all the possible combinations of NULL dates.

Let me propose these rules and apply them in order

1. If the start_date is NOT NULL, and the end_date is NOT NULL, then leave the row alone.
2. If the table has too many NULLs in a series, then give up. Report too much missing data.
3. If the start_date IS NULL and the end_date IS NOT NULL, then set the start_date to the day before the end_date.

```
UPDATE Events
   SET start_date
       = (SELECT MIN(E1.end_date) + INTERVAL '1' DAY)
            FROM Events AS E1
           WHERE E1.end_date < Events.end_date)
 WHERE start_date IS NULL
   AND end_date IS NOT NULL;
```

4. If the start_date is NOT NULL and the end_date is NULL, then set the end_date to the day before the next known start_date.

```
UPDATE Events
   SET end_date
       = (SELECT MIN(E1.start_date) - INTERVAL '1' DAY)
            FROM Events AS E1
           WHERE E1.start_date > Events.start_date)
 WHERE start_date IS NOT NULL
   AND end_date IS NULL;
```

5. If the start_date and end_date are both NULL, then look at the prior and following events to get the minimal start_date and/or end_date. This will leave a gap in the dates that has to be handled later.

For example:

```
('A', '2003-01-01', '2003-12-31'),
('B', '2004-01-01', NULL),
('C', NULL, '2004-02-29'),
('D', '2004-02-01', '2004-02-29');
```

Becomes:

```
('A', '2003-01-01', '2003-12-31'),
('B', '2004-01-01', NULL),
('C', '2004-02-28', '2004-02-29'), <= rule #2
('D', '2004-02-01', '2004-02-29');
```

Becomes:

```
('A', '2003-01-01', '2003-12-31'),
('B', '2004-01-01', '2004-02-27'), <= rule #3
('C', '2004-02-28', '2004-02-29'),
('D', '2004-02-01', '2004-02-29');
```

Now consider this data:

```
('A', '2003-01-01', '2003-12-31'),
('B', NULL, NULL),
('C', '2004-02-01', '2004-02-29'),
('D', '2004-02-01', '2004-02-29');
```

The data becomes:

```
('A', '2003-01-01', '2003-12-31'),
('B', '2004-01-01', '2004-01-31'), <= rule #4
('C', '2004-02-01', '2004-02-29'),
('D', '2004-02-01', '2004-02-29');
```

Consider this example:

```
('A', '2003-01-01', '2003-12-31'),
('B', NULL, NULL),
('C', NULL, '2004-02-29'),
('D', '2004-02-01', '2004-02-29');
```

29.3.4 Locating Dates

This little problem is sneakier than it sounds. I first saw it in *Explain* magazine, then met the author, Rudy Limeback, at the Database World conference in Boston years ago. The problem is to print a list of the employees whose birthdays will occur in the next 45 days. The employee files have each date of birth. The answer will depend on what date functions you have in your implementation of SQL, but Rudy was working with DB2.

What makes this problem interesting is the number of possible false starts. Most versions of SQL also have a library function, `MAKEDATE(year, month, day)`, or an equivalent, which will construct a date from three numbers representing a year, month, and day, as well as extraction functions to disassemble a date into integers representing the month, day, and year. The SQL standard would do this with the general function `CAST (<string> AS DATE)`, but there is no provision in the standard for using integers without first converting them to strings, either explicitly or implicitly. For example direct use of strings to build a date:

```
CAST ('2005-01-01' AS DATE)
```

Concatenation causes integer to cast to strings:

```
CAST (2005 || '-'|| 01 ||'-' || 01 AS DATE)
```

The first "gotcha" in this problem is trying to use the component pieces of the dates in a search condition. If you were looking for birthdays all within the same month, it would be easy:

```
SELECT name, dob, CURRENT_DATE
 FROM Employees
WHERE EXTRACT(MONTH FROM CURRENT_DATE) = EXTRACT(MONTH FROM
dob);
```

Attempts to extend this approach fall apart, however, since a 45-day period could extend across three months and possibly into the following year; additionally, it might fall in a leap year. Very soon, the number of function calls is too high and the logic is too complex.

The second "gotcha" is trying to write a simple search condition with these functions to construct the birthday in the current year from the date of birth (dob) in the Employee table:

```
SELECT name, dob, CURRENT_DATE
  FROM Employees
```

```
 WHERE MAKEDATE(EXTRACT (YEAR FROM CURRENT_DATE),-- birthday
this year
                EXTRACT (MONTH FROM dob),
                EXTRACT (DAY FROM dob))
      BETWEEN CURRENT_DATE
          AND (CURRENT_DATE + INTERVAL 45 DAYS);
```

But a leap-year date of birth will cause an exception to be raised on an invalid date if this is not also a leap year. There is also another problem. The third "gotcha" comes when the 45-day period wraps into the next year. For example, if the current month is December 1992, we should include January 1993 birthdays, but they are not constructed by the `MAKEDATE()` function. At this point, you can build a messy search condition that also goes into the next year when constructing birthdays.

Rory Murchison of the Aetna Institute pointed out that if you are working with DB2 or some other SQL implementations, you will have an `AGE(date1 [ ,date2] )` function. This returns the difference in years between date1 and date2. If date2 is missing, it defaults to `CURRENT_DATE`. The `AGE()` function can be constructed from other functions in implementations that do not support it. In Standard SQL, the expression would be `(date2 - date1) YEAR`, which would construct an `INTERVAL` value. That makes the answer quite simple:

```
SELECT name, dob, CURRENT_DATE
  FROM Employees
 WHERE INTERVAL (CURRENT_DATE - birthday) YEAR
       < INTERVAL (CURRENT_DATE - birthday + INTERVAL 45 DAYS)
YEAR;
```

In English, this says that if the employee is a year older 45 days from now, he must have had a birthday in the meantime.

29.3.5 Temporal Starting and Ending Points

Dates can be stored in several different ways in a database. Designers of one product might decide that they want to keep things in a COBOL-like field-oriented format, which has a clear, separate area for the year, month, and day of each date. Another product might want to be more UNIX-like and keep the dates as a displacement in some small unit of time from a starting point, then calculate the display format when it is needed. Standard SQL does not say how a date should be stored, but the

"COBOL approach" is easier to display, and the "temporal displacement approach" can do calculations easier.

The result is that there is no best way to calculate either the first day of the month or the last day of the month from a given date. In the COBOL method, you can get the first day of the month easily by using extraction from the date to build the date, with a 1 in the day field.

To return the last day of the previous month, use this expression:

```
CURRENT_TIMESTAMP - INTERVAL (EXTRACT(DAY FROM
CURRENT_TIMESTAMP) DAYS).
```

Obviously, you can get the first day of this month with:

```
CURRENT_TIMESTAMP
 - (EXTRACT (DAY FROM CURRENT_TIMESTAMP)
    + INTERVAL '1' DAY);
```

Another way is with a user-defined function.

```
CREATE FUNCTION LastDayOfMonth (IN my_date DATE)
RETURNS INTEGER
LANGUAGE SQL
DETERMINISTIC
RETURN
CAST (
CASE
WHEN EXTRACT(MONTH FROM my_date) IN (1, 3, 5, 7, 8, 10, 12) THEN 31
THEN EXTRACT(MONTH FROM my_date) IN (4, 6, 9, 11) THEN 30
ELSE CASE WHEN MOD(EXTRACT (YEAR FROM my_date)/100, 4) <> 0 THEN 28
          WHEN MOD(EXTRACT (YEAR FROM my_date)/100, 400) = 0 THEN 29
          WHEN MOD(EXTRACT (YEAR FROM my_date)/100, 100) = 0 THEN 28
          ELSE 29 END
END AS INTEGER);
```

Another problem that you will find in the real world is that people never read the ISO-8601 standards for temporal data; they insist upon writing midnight as '24:00:00' and letting it "leak" into the next day. That is, '2003-01-01 24:01:00' probably should be '2003-01-02 00:01:00' instead. The `EXTRACT()` function would have a really complicated definition, if this was an acceptable format.

The best bet, if you cannot teach people to use the ISO-8601 Standards, is to correct the string at input time. This can be done with a simple auxiliary time that looks like this:

```
CREATE TABLE FixTheClock
(input_date_string CHAR(6) NOT NULL,
 input_time_pattern CHAR(25) NOT NULL PRIMARY KEY,
 correct_time_string CHAR(25) NOT NULL);

INSERT INTO FixTheClock
VALUES ('2003-01-01', '2003-01-01 24:__:__.______', '2003-01-02
00:');
 ...
```

Then use a LIKE predicate to replace the pattern with the corrected time.

```
SELECT CASE WHEN R1.raw_input_timestamp LIKE
F1.input_time_pattern
            THEN F1.correct_time_string
                 || CAST (EXTRACT(TIMEZONE_MINUTE FROM
R1.raw_input_timestamp) AS VARCHAR(10))
            ELSE raw_input_timestamp END, ...
  FROM RawData AS R1, FixTheClock AS F1
 WHERE F1.input_date_string = SUBSTRING (raw_input_timestamp
FROM 1 FOR 6);
```

Notice that this is strictly a string function and that the results will have to be cast to a temporal data type before being stored in the database.

29.3.6 Average Wait Times

A problem Jerry posted in May 26, 2005 to take a simple table of service events and determine the average number of days between services for a group of machines. Dropping the unimportant columns, the table looked like this.

```
CREATE TABLE ServiceLog
(machine_nbr INTEGER NOT NULL,
 service_date DATE DEFAULT CURRENT_DATE NOT NULL,
 PRIMARY KEY (machine_id, service_date));
```

The first attempt posted built all of the waiting periods and then averaged them.

```
SELECT machine_nbr, AVG(wait) AS avg_wait
  FROM (SELECT T1.machine_nbr,
        CAST ((MIN(T2.service_date) - T1.service_date) DAY AS
INTEGER)
          FROM T AS T1, T AS T2
        WHERE T2.machine_nbr = T1.machine_nbr
          AND T2.machine_nbr = T1.machine_nbr
          AND T2.service_date > T1.service_date
        GROUP BY T1.machine_nbr, T1.service_date
       ) AS T (machine_nbr, wait)
 GROUP BY machine_nbr;
```

Instead, use this:

```
SELECT machine_id,
        CAST (MAX(service_date) - MIN(service_date) DAY AS
INTEGER)
       / (1.0 * COUNT(*) -1) AS AVG_gap
  FROM ServiceLog
 GROUP BY machine_id;
```

The first answer posted was caught in the "procedural mindset" trap. Instead think of each machine as a grouping (subset) that has properties as a whole—duration range, and count of events. If the example had been to find the average size of a shot of scotch given a bottle and (*n*) glasses of known sizes, it would have been obvious—average the volume of scotch over the number of glasses! But replace scotch with total time used and glasses with events, and the answer becomes hard to see.

29.4 Julian Dates

All SQL implementations support a DATE data type, but there is no standard defining how they should implement it internally. Some products represent the year, month, and day as parts of a double-word integer; others use Julianized dates; some use ISO ordinal dates; and some store dates as character strings. The programmer does not care as long as the dates work correctly.

There is a technical difference between a Julian date and a Julianized date. A Julian date is an astronomer's term that counts the number of days since January 1, 4713 B.C.E. This count is now well over 2 billion; only astronomers use it. However, computer companies have corrupted the term to mean a count from some point in time from which they can build a date or time. The fixed point is usually the year 1, or 1900, or the start of the Gregorian calendar.

A Julianized, or ordinal, date is the position of the date within its year, so it falls between 1 and 365 or 366. You will see this number printed on the bottom edges of desk calendar pages. The usual way to find the Julianized day within the current year is to use a simple program that stores the number of days in each month as an array and sums them with the day of the month for the date in question. The only difficult part is remembering to add one if the year is a leap year and the month is after February.

Here is a very fast and compact algorithm that computes the Julian date from a Gregorian date and vice versa. These algorithms appeared as Algorithm 199 (ACM 1980) and were first written in ALGOL by Robert Tantzen. Here are SQL translations of the code:

```
CREATE FUNCTION Julianize1
  (greg_day INTEGER, greg_month INTEGER, greg_year INTEGER)
  RETURNS INTEGER
  LANGUAGE SQL
BEGIN
DECLARE century INTEGER;
DECLARE yearincentury INTEGER;
IF (greg_month > 2)
THEN SET greg_month = greg_month - 3;
ELSE SET greg_month = greg_month + 9;
     SET greg_year = greg_year - 1;
END IF;
SET century = greg_year/100;
SET yearincentury = greg_year - 100 * century;
RETURN ((146097 * century)/4
      + (1461 * yearincentury)/4
      +  (153 * greg_month + 2)/5 + greg_day + 1721119);
END;
```

Remember that the division will be integer division, because the variables involved are all integers. Here is a Pascal procedure taken from

Numerical Recipes in Pascal (Press et al. 1990) for converting a Georgian date to a Julian date. First, you need to know the difference between `TRUNCATE()` and `FLOOR()`. The `FLOOR()` function is also called the greatest integer function; it returns the greatest integer less than its argument. The `TRUNCATE()` function returns the integer part of a number. Thus, they behave differently with negative decimals.

```
FLOOR(-2.5) = -3
FLOOR(-2) = -2
FLOOR(2.5) = 2
FLOOR(2) = 2
TRUNCATE(-2.5) = -2
TRUNCATE(-2) = -2
TRUNCATE(2.5) = 2
TRUNCATE(2) = 2
```

Here is an SQL/PSM version of the algorithm.

```
CREATE FUNCTION Julianize (IN greg_year INTEGER, IN greg_month
INTEGER, IN greg_day INTEGER)
RETURNS INTEGER
BEGIN
DECLARE gregorian INTEGER;
DECLARE greg_year INTEGER;
DECLARE jul_leap INTEGER;
DECLARE greg_month INTEGER;

SET gregorian = 588829;

IF greg_year = 0 -- error: no greg_year zero
THEN SIGNAL SQLSTATE 'no year zero'; -- not actual SQL state
code!
END IF;

IF greg_year < 0
THEN SET greg_year = greg_year + 1;
END IF;
IF greg_month > 2
THEN SET greg_year = greg_year;
     SET greg_month = greg_month + 1;
ELSE SET greg_year = greg_year - 1;
     SET greg_month = greg_month + 13;
```

```
     END IF;
SET greg_day = TRUNCATE(365.2522 * greg_year)
     + TRUNCATE(30.6001 * greg_month)
     + greg_day + 1720995;
IF (greg_day + 31 * (greg_month + 12 * greg_year) >= gregorian)
THEN SET jul_leap = TRUNCATE(greg_year * 0.01);
     SET greg_day = greg_day + 2 - jul_leap + TRUNCATE(0.25 *
jul_leap);
END IF;
END;
```

This algorithm to convert a Julian day number into a Gregorian calendar date is due to Peter Meyer. You need to assume that you have `FLOOR()` and `TRUNCATE()` functions.

```
CREATE PROCEDURE JulDate (IN julian INTEGER,
                 OUT greg_year INTEGER,
                 OUT greg_month INTEGER,
                 OUT greg_day INTEGER)
LANGUAGE SQL
DETERMINISTIC
BEGIN
DECLARE z INTEGER;
DECLARE r INTEGER;
DECLARE g INTEGER;
DECLARE a INTEGER;
DECLARE b INTEGER;

SET z = FLOOR(julian - 1721118.5);
SET r = julian - 1721118.5 - z;
SET g = z - 0.25;
SET a = FLOOR(g/36524.25);
SET b = a - FLOOR(a/4.0);
SET greg_year = FLOOR((b + g)/365.25);
SET c = b + z - FLOOR(365.25 * greg_year);
SET greg_month = TRUNCATE((5 * c + 456)/153);
SET greg_day = c - TRUNCATE((153 * greg_month - 457)/5) + r;
IF greg_month > 12
THEN SET greg_year = greg_year + 1;
     SET greg_month = greg_month - 12;
END IF;
END;
```

There are two problems with these algorithms. First, the Julian day the astronomers use starts at noon. If you think about it, it makes sense because they are doing their work at night. The second problem is that the integers involved get large, and you cannot use floating-point numbers to replace them because the rounding errors are too great. You need long integers that can go to 2.5 million.

29.5 Date and Time Extraction Functions

No two SQL products agree on the functions that should be available for use with <datetime> data types. In keeping with the practice of overloading functions, the SQL3 proposal has a function for extracting components from a datetime or interval value. The syntax looks like this:

```
<extract expression> ::=
 EXTRACT (<extract field> FROM <extract source>)

<extract field> ::= <datetime field> | <time zone field>

<time zone field> ::= TIMEZONE_HOUR | TIMEZONE_MINUTE

<extract source> ::= <datetime value expression>
      | <interval value expression>
```

The interesting feature is that this function always returns a numeric value. For example, `EXTRACT (MONTH FROM birthday)` will be an `INTEGER` between 1 and 12. Vendors might also separate functions, such as `YEAR(<date>)`, `MONTH(<date>)`, and `DAY(<date>)`, that extract components from a `<datetime>` data type. Most versions of SQL also have a library function something like `MAKEDATE(<year>, <month>, <day>)`, `DATE(<year>, <month>, <day>)`, or an equivalent, which will construct a date from three numbers representing a year, month, and day. Standard SQL uses the `CAST` function, but the details are not pretty, since it involves assembling a string in the ISO format and then converting it to a date.

Bill Karwin came up with a fairly portable trick for doing extraction in SQL products that do not have this library function. Use the `LIKE` predicate and `CAST()` operator (or whatever the product uses for formatting output) to convert the `DATE` expressions into character string expressions and test them against a template. For example, to find all the rows of data in the month of March:

```
SELECT *
  FROM Table1
 WHERE CAST(datefield AS CHAR(10)) LIKE '%MAR%';
```

Obviously, this technique can be extended to use other string functions to search for parts of a date or time, to look for ranges of dates and so forth.

The best warning is to read your SQL product manual and see what you can do with its library functions.

29.6 Other Temporal Functions

Another common set of functions, which are not represented in standard SQL, deal with weeks. For example, Sybase's SQL Anywhere (*née* WATCOM SQL) has a `DOW(<date>)` that returns a number between 1 and 7 to represent the day of the week (1 = Sunday, 2 = Monday, . . ., 7 = Saturday, following an ISO standard convention). You can also find functions that add or subtract weeks from a date given the number of the date within the year and so on. The function for finding the day of the week for a date is called Zeller's algorithm:

```
CREATE FUNCTION Zeller (IN z_year INTEGER, IN z_month INTEGER,
IN z_day INTEGER)
RETURNS INTEGER
LANGUAGE SQL
DETERMINISTIC
BEGIN
DECLARE m INTEGER;
DECLARE d INTEGER;
DECLARE y INTEGER;
SET y = z_year;
SET m = z_month - 2;
IF (m <= 0)
THEN SET m = m + 12;
   SET y = y - 1;
END IF;
RETURN (MOD((z_day + (13 * m - 1)/5
   + 5 * MOD(y, 100)/4 - 7 * y/400), 7) + 1);
END;
```

DB2 and other SQLs have an `AGE(<date1>, <date2>)` function, which returns the difference in years between `<date1>` and `<date2>`.

The table in Section 9.1 gives a summary of the type conversions involving `<datetimes>` and `<intervals>` in Standard SQL. Arithmetic operations involving `<datetimes>` or `<intervals>` obey the natural rules associated with dates and times and yield valid `<datetime>` or `<interval>` results according to the Common Era calendar.

Operations involving items of type `<datetime>` require that the `<datetime>` items be mutually comparable. Operations involving intervals require that the `<interval>` items be mutually comparable.

Operations involving a `<datetime>` and an `<interval>` preserve the time zone of the `<datetime>` operand. If the `<datetime>` operand does not include a time zone part, then the local time zone is used.

The `OVERLAPS` predicate determines whether two chronological periods overlap in time (see Section 13.2 for details). A chronological period is specified either as a pair of `<datetimes>` (starting and ending) or as a starting `<datetime>` and an `<interval>`.

`EXTRACT (<temporal unit> FROM <temporal expression>)` takes a `<datetime>` or an `<interval>` and returns an exact numeric value representing the value of one component of the `<datetime>` or `<interval>`.

29.7 Weeks

Weeks are not part of the SQL temporal functions, but they are part of ISO-8601 Standards. While it is not as common in the United States as it is in Europe, many commercial and industrial applications use the week within a year as a unit of time.

Week 01 of a year is defined as the first week that has the Thursday in that year, which is equivalent to the week that contains the fourth day of January. In other words, the first week of a New Year is the week that has the majority of its days in the New Year. Week 01 might also contain days from the previous year, so it does not align with the years.

The standard notation uses the letter 'W' to announce that the following two digits are a week number. The week number component of the vector can be separated with a hyphen or not, as required by space.

```
1999-W01 or 1999W01
```

A single digit between 1 and 7 can extend this notation for the day of the week. For example, the day 1996-12-31, which is Tuesday (day 2) of the first week of 1997, can be shown as:

```
1999-W01-2 or 1999W012
```

The ISO standard avoids explicitly stating the possible range of week numbers, but a little thought will show that the range is between 01 and 52 or between 01 and 53, depending on the particular year. There is one exception to the rule that a year has at least 52 weeks: 1753, when the Gregorian calendar was introduced, had less than 365 days and therefore less than 52 weeks.

SQL Server programmers have to be very careful, because their product does not follow ISO Standards for numbering the weeks in its function library. Furthermore, it is not easy to see how to calculate the weeks between two different dates.

Here is an example from Rudy Limeback (SQL Consultant, r937.com) taken from http://searchdatabase.techtarget.com/dateQuestionNResponse/0,289625,sid13_cid517627_tax285649,00.html,

Suppose we have a beginning date of '2003-02-06' and an end date of '2003-02-19'. I would like to see the weeks as two because the 17th is not a Tuesday. There are a number of ways to approach this problem, and the solution depends on what the meaning of the word "week" is. Here is the calendar for that month, just in case you cannot figure it out in your head.

```
Su Mo Tu We Th Fr Sa
                   1
 2  3  4  5  6  7  8
 9 10 11 12 13 14 15
16 17 18 19 20 21 22
23 24 25 26 27 28
```

In this example, we want the number of weeks between February 6th and 19th.

First method: One. One week after the 6th is the 13th. Another week is the 20th. Since we are only as far as the 19th, it is not two weeks yet.
Second method: Two. The number of days is 14, if we count both the 6th and the 19th at the beginning and end of the specified range. Since there are seven days in a week, 14/7 = 2.

Third method: One. We should not count both the beginning and end days. We do not do it for years, for example. How many years are between 1999 and 2007? Most people would say eight, not nine, and they do this by subtracting the earlier from the later. So using days, 19 – 6 = 13. Then 13/7 = 1.857142. . . which truncates to one.
Fourth method: Two. We want a whole number of weeks, so it is okay to round 1.857142 up to 2.
Fifth method: One. Did you mean whole weeks? There's only one whole week in that date range, and it is the week from the 9th to the 15th. In fact, if the starting date were the 3rd and the ending date the 21st, that would be 18 (or 19) days, and there's still only one whole week in there.
Sixth method: Three. February 6th is in week 6 of 2003. February 19th is in week 8. Between them are several days from each of three different weeks.
Seventh method: Two. February 6th is in week 6 of 2003. February 19th is in week 8. Subtract the week numbers to get 2.

This is why Standard SQL prefers to deal with days, a nice unit of time that does not have fractional parts.

29.7.1 Sorting by Weekday Names

This trick is due to Craig S. Mullins. There is a table with a column containing the name of the days of the week, on which an event happened like this:

```
CREATE TABLE Foobar
(...
 day_name CHAR(3) NOT NULL
    CHECK day_name
         IN ('SUN', 'MON', 'TUE', 'WED', 'THU', 'FRI', 'SAT'),
 ...);
```

How do we sort it properly? We'd want Sunday first, followed by Monday, Tuesday, Wednesday, and so on. Well, if we write the first query that comes to mind, the results will obviously be sorted improperly:

```
SELECT day_name, col1, col2, ...
  FROM Foobar
 ORDER BY day_name;
```

The results from this query would be ordered alphabetically; in other words:

```
FRI
MON
SAT
SUN
THU
TUE
WED
```

Of course, one solution would be to design the table with a numeric column that uses Zeller's number. There is another solution that is both elegant and does not require any change to the database.

```
SELECT day_name, col1, cl2, ...,
       POSITION (day_name IN 'SUNMONTUEWEDTHUFRISAT') AS day_nbr
  FROM Foobar
 ORDER BY day_nbr;
```

Of course, you can go one step further if you'd like. Some queries may need to actually return the day of week. You can use the same technique with a twist to return the day of week value, given only the day's name.

```
CAST (POSITION (day_name IN 'SUNMONTUEWEDTHUFRISAT')/3 AS
INTEGER) + 1;
```

Obviously the same trick can be used with the three-letter month abbreviations. This was very handy in the first release of ACCESS, which did sort dates alphabetically.

29.8 Modeling Time in Tables

Since the nature of time is a continuum, and the ISO model is half-open intervals, the best approach is to have (start_time, end_time) pairs for each event in a history. This is a state transition model of data, where the facts represented by the columns in that row were true for the time period given. For this to work, we need the constraint that the (start_time, end_time) pairs do not overlap.

A NULL ending time is the flag for an "unfinished fact," such as a hotel room stay that is still in progress. A history for an entity can clearly have at most one NULL at a time.

```
CREATE TABLE FoobarHistory
(foo_key INTEGER NOT NULL,
 start_date DATE DEFAULT CURRENT_DATE NOT NULL,
 PRIMARY KEY (foo_key, start_date),
 end_date TIMESTAMP, -- null means current
 foo_status INTEGER NOT NULL,
 ...

CONSTRAINT started_before_ended
CHECK(start_date < end_date),

CONSTRAINT end_time_open_interval
CHECK (end_date = CAST(end_date AS DATE)
                  + INTERVAL '23:59:59.999' HOUR),

CONSTRAINT no_date_overlaps
CHECK (NOT EXISTS
        (SELECT *
           FROM FoobarHistory AS H1, Calendar AS C1
          WHERE C1.cal_date BETWEEN H1.start_date
                AND H1.end_date
          GROUP BY foo_key
         HAVING COUNT(*) > 1)),

CONSTRAINT only_one_current_status
 CHECK (NOT EXISTS
        (SELECT *
           FROM FoobarHistory AS H1
          WHERE H1.end_date IS NULL
          GROUP BY foo_key
         HAVING COUNT(*) > 1))
);
```

The Calendar table is explained in a following section. Table level CHECK() constraints are still not common in SQL implementations, so you might have to use a TRIGGER to enforce integrity.

The real trick here is that the start_date is a DATE data type, so it will be at 00:00:00.00 when it is converted to a TIMESTAMP. The end_time is a TIMESTAMP so we can place it almost, but not quite, to the next day. This will let us use BETWEEN predicates, as we will see in the next section. You could also do this in a VIEW, make both columns DATE data types and add the extra hours to end_time.

In practice, this is going to be highly proprietary code and you might consider using triggers to keep the (start_time, end_time) pairs correct.

29.8.1 Using Duration Pairs

If the table did not have (start_time, end_time) pairs, but used a code to identify the start and finish points of durations, then we need to use a self-join to construct the pairs. For example, how would you write a SELECT query for returning all Projects whose current project status is 10, given the following schema?

```
CREATE TABLE Projects
(proj_id INTEGER NOT NULL PRIMARY KEY,
 proj_name CHAR(15) NOT NULL);

CREATE TABLE ProjectStatusHistory
(project_id INTEGER NOT NULL
    REFERENCES Projects(proj_id),
 proj_date DATE DEFAULT CURRENT_DATE NOT NULL,
 proj_status INTEGER NOT NULL,
 PRIMARY KEY (project_id, proj_date));
```

A solution from David Portas, which assumes that the project is still active:

```
SELECT P.proj_id, P.proj_name
  FROM Projects AS P
 WHERE EXISTS
      (SELECT *
         FROM ProjectStatusHistory AS H
        WHERE H.proj_id = P.proj_id
       HAVING MAX(CASE WHEN H.proj_status = 10
                       THEN proj_date END) = MAX(proj_date));
```

But now try to answer the question: Which projects had a status of 10 on a prior date?

```
SELECT X.proj_id
  FROM (SELECT P1.proj_id, P1.proj_date AS start_date,
               MIN(P2.proj_date) AS end_date
          FROM Projects AS P1
               LEFT OUTER JOIN
               Projects AS P2
               ON P1.proj_id = P2.proj_id
                  AND P1.proj_date < P2.proj_date
         WHERE proj_status = 10
         GROUP BY P1.proj_id, P1.proj_date)
       AS X(proj_id, start_date, end_date)
WHERE :my_date BETWEEN X.start_date
                   AND COALESCE (X.end_date, CURRENT_DATE);
```

The X subquery expression is what Projects would have looked like with (start_time, end_time) pairs.

The `COALESCE()` handles the use of `NULL` for an eternity marker. Depending on the circumstances, you might also use this form of the predicate.

```
WHERE :my_date BETWEEN X.start_date
                   AND COALESCE (X.end_date, :my_date)
```

29.9 Calendar Auxiliary Table

Auxiliary tables are a way of building functions that would be difficult if not impossible to do with the limited computational power of SQL. They should not appear on the E-R diagrams for the database, because they are not really a part of the model but serve as adjuncts to all the tables and queries in the database that could use them.

This is very true with the calendar, because it is so irregular that trying to figure out dates via computations is insanely complex. Look up the algorithms for finding Easter, Ramadan, and other lunar holidays, for example.

Consider the Security and Exchange Commission (SEC) rule that a brokerage transaction must close within three business days. A business day does not include Saturdays, Sundays, or holidays declared by the New York Stock Exchange. You can compute the occurrences of

Saturdays and Sundays with a library function in many SQL products, but not the holidays. In fact, the New York Stock Exchange can be closed by a declared national emergency.

This calendar tables has two general forms. The first form maps single dates into some value and has the general declaration:

```
CREATE TABLE Calendar
(cal_date DATE NOT NULL PRIMARY KEY,
 julian_day INTEGER NOT NULL
            CONSTRAINT valid_julian_day
            CHECK (julian_day BETWEEN 1 AND 366),
 business_day INTEGER NOT NULL CHECK (business_day IN (0, 1)),
 three_business_days DATE NOT NULL,
 fiscal_month INTEGER NOT NULL
              CONSTRAINT valid_month_nbr
              CHECK (fiscal_month BETWEEN 1 AND 12),
 fiscal_year INTEGER NOT NULL,
 ...);
```

Since this is probably going to be a static table that you fill with 10 to 20 years' worth of data at once (20 years is about 7,000 rows—a very small table), you might consider dropping the constraints and keeping only the primary key.

The second form maps an `<interval>` into some value and has the general declaration, with the same constraints as we used in the last section:

```
CREATE TABLE EventCalendar
(event VARCHAR(30) NOT NULL PRIMARY KEY,
 start_date DATE NOT NULL,
 end_date TIMESTAMP NOT NULL,
 ...,
CONSTRAINT started_before_ended
CHECK(start_date < end_date),

CONSTRAINT end_time_open_interval
CHECK (end_date = CAST(end_date AS DATE)
                  + INTERVAL '23:59:59.999' HOUR),

CONSTRAINT no_date_overlaps
CHECK (...),
```

```
CONSTRAINT only_one_current_status
 CHECK (...));
```

The data for the calendar table can be built with the help of a good spreadsheet, since spreadsheets usually have more temporal functions than databases. Events tend to be volatile, so the constraints are a good idea.

29.10 Problems with the Year 2000

The special problems with the year 2000 took on a life of their own in the computer community, so they rate a separate section in this book. Yes, I know you thought it was over by now, but it still shows up and you need to think about it. The three major problems with representations of the year 2000 in computer systems are:

1. The year 2000 has a lot of zeros in it.
2. The year 2000 is a leap year.
3. The year 2000 is a millennium year.
4. Many date fields are not really dates.

29.10.1 The Zeros

I like to call the first problem—the zeros in 2000—the "odometer problem," because it is in the hardware or system level. This is not the same as the millennium problem, where date arithmetic is invalid. If you are using a year-in-century format, the year 2000 does a "roll over" like a car odometer that has reached its limit, leaving a year that is assumed to be 1900 (or something else other than 2000) by the application program.

This problem lives where you cannot see it, in hardware and operating systems related to the system clock. Information on such problems is very incomplete, so you will need to keep yourself posted as new releases of your particular products come out.

Another subtle form of "the zero problem" is that some hashing and random number generators use parts of the system date as a parameter. Zero is a perfectly good number until you try to divide by it and your program aborts.

Another problem is in mainframes. For example, the Unisys 2200 system was set to fail on the first day of 1996 because the eighth bit of

the year field—which is a signed integer—will go to one. Fortunately, the vendor had some solutions ready. Do you know what other hardware uses this convention? You might want to look.

The real killer is with older Intel-based PCs. When the odometer wraps around, DOS jumps to 1980 most of the time, and sometimes to 1984, depending on your BIOS chip. Windows 3.1 jumps to 1900 most of the time. Since PCs are now common as stand-alone units and as workstations, you can test this for yourself. Set the date and time to 1999-12-31 at 23:59:30 Hrs and let the clock run. What happens next depends on your BIOS chip and version of DOS.

The results can be that the clock display shows "12:00 AM" and a date display of "01/01/00," so you think you have no problems. However, you will find that you have newly created files dated 1984 or 1980. Surprise!

This problem is passed along to application programs, but not always the way that you would think. Quicken Version 3 for the IBM PC running on MS-DOS 6 is one example. As you expect, directly inputting the date 2000-01-01 results in the year resetting to 1980 or 1984 off the system clock. But strangely enough, if you let the date wrap from 1999-12-31 into the year 2000, Quicken Version 3 interprets the change as 1901-01-01, and not as 1900.

It is worth doing a Google search for information on older software when you have to work with it.

29.10.2 Leap Year

The second problem always seems to shock people. You might remember being told in grade school that there are 365.25 days per year and that the accumulation of the fractional day creates a leap year every four years. Once more, your teachers lied to you; there are really 365.2422 days per year. Every four years, the extra 0.2400 days accumulate and create an additional day; this gives us a leap year. Every 100 years the missing 0.01 days (i.e., 365.25 – 365.2422 rounded up) balances out and we do not have a leap year. However, every 400 years, the extra 0.0022 days accumulate enough to create an additional day and give us this special leap year; 2000 was one of those years. Since most of us are not over 400 years old, we did not have to worry about this until the year 2000.

The correct test for leap years in SQL/PSM is:

```
CREATE FUNCTION leapyear (IN my_year INTEGER)
RETURNS CHAR(3)
LANGUAGE SQL
```

```
DETERMINISTIC
RETURN (CASE WHEN MOD(my_year, 400) = 0
        THEN 'Yes'
        WHEN MOD(my_year, 100) = 0
        THEN 'No'
        ELSE CASE WHEN MOD(my_year, 4) = 0
                  THEN 'Yes' ELSE 'No '
             END
        END);
```

Or if you would like a more compact form, you can use this solution from Phil Alexander, which will fit into in-line code as a search expression:

```
(MOD(year, 400) = 0
 OR (MOD(year, 4) = 0 AND NOT (MOD(year, 100) = 0)))
```

People who did not know this algorithm wrote lots of programs. I do not mean COBOL legacy programs in your organization; I mean packaged programs for which you paid good money. The date functions in the first releases of Lotus, Excel, and Quattro Pro did not handle the day 2000-02-29 correctly. Lotus simply made an error and the others followed suit to maintain "Lotus compatibility" in their products. Microsoft Excel for Windows Version 4 shows correctly that the next day after 2000-02-28 is 2000-02-29. However, it thinks that the next day after 1900-02-28 is also February 29 instead of March 1. Microsoft Excel for Macintosh does not handle the years 1900 through 1903.

Have you checked all of your word processors, spreadsheets, desktop databases, appointment calendars, and other off-the-shelf packages for this problem yet? Just key in the date 2000-02-29, then do some calculations with date arithmetic and see what happens.

With networked systems, this is a real nightmare. All you need is one program on one node in the network to reject leap year day 2000 and the whole network is useless for that day; transactions might not reconcile for some time afterwards. How many nodes do you think there are in the ATM banking networks in North America and Europe?

29.10.3 The Millennium

I saved the third problem for last because it is the one best known in the popular and computer trade press. We programmers have not been keeping *true* dates in data fields for a few decades. Instead, we have been

using one of several year-in-century formats. These would not work in the last year of the previous millennium (the first millennium of the Common Era calendar ends in the year 2000 and the second millennium begins with the year 2001—that is why Arthur C. Clarke used it for the title of his book).

If only we had been good programmers and not tried to save storage space at the expense of accuracy, we would have used ISO standard formats and would not have had to deal with these problems. Since we did not, programs have been doing arithmetic and comparisons based on the year-in-century and not on the year. A thirty-year mortgage taken out in 1992 will be over in the year 2022, but when you subtract the two year-in-centuries, you get:

```
(22 - 92) = -70 years
```

This is a very early payoff of a mortgage!

Inventory retention programs are throwing away good stock, thinking it is outdated—look at the ten-year retention required in the automobile industry. Lifetime product warranties are now being dishonored because the services schedule dates and manufacturing dates cannot be resolved correctly. One hospital sent a geriatric patient to the children's ward because it kept only two digits of the birth year. Imagine your own horror story.

According to Benny Popek of Coopers & Lybrand LLP (Xenakis 1995), "This problem is so big that we will consider these bugs to be out of the scope of our normal software maintenance contracts. For those clients who insist that we should take responsibility, we'll exercise the cancellation clause and terminate the outsourcing contract."

Popek commented, "We've found that a lot of our clients are in denial. We spoke to one CIO who just refused to deal with the problem, since he's going to retire next year."

But the problem is subtler than just looking for date data fields. Timestamps are often buried inside encoding schemes. If the year-in-century is used for the high-order digits of a serial numbering system, then any program that depends on increasing serial numbers will fail. Those of you with magnetic tape libraries might want to look at your tape labels now. The five-digit code is used in many mainframe shops for archives and tape management software also has the convention that if programmers want a tape to be kept indefinitely, they code the label with a retention date of 99365. This method failed at the start of the year 2000, when the retention label had 00001 in it.

29.10.4 Weird Dates in Legacy Data

Some of the problems with dates in legacy data have been discussed in an article by Randall L. Hitchens (Hitchens 1991) and in one by me on the same subject (Celko 1981). The problem is subtler than Hitchens implied in his article, which dealt with nonstandard date formats. Dates hide in other places, not just in date fields. The most common places are serial numbers and computer-generated identifiers.

In the early 1960s, a small insurance company in Atlanta bought out an even smaller company that sold burial insurance policies to poor people in the Deep South. These policies guaranteed the subscriber a funeral in exchange for a weekly or monthly premium of a few dollars, and were often sold by local funeral homes; they are now illegal.

The burial insurance company used a policy number format identical to that of the larger company. The numbers began with the two digits of the year-in-century, followed by a dash, followed by an eight-digit sequential number.

The systems analysts decided that the easiest way to do this was to add 20 years to the first two digits. Their logic was that no customer would keep these cheap policies for twenty years—and the analyst who did this would not be working there in 20 years, so who cared? As the years passed, the company moved from a simple file system to a hierarchical database and was using the policy numbers for unique record keys. The system simply generated new policy numbers on demand, using a global counter in a policy library routine, and no problems occurred for decades.

There were about 100 burial policies left in the database after 20 years. Nobody had written programs to protect against duplicate keys, since the problem had never occurred. Then, one day, they created their first duplicate number. Sometimes the database would crash, but sometimes the child records would get attached to the wrong parent. This second situation was worse, since the company started paying and billing the wrong people.

The company was lucky enough to have someone who recognized the old burial insurance policies when he saw them. It took months to clean up the problem, because they had to search a warehouse to find the original policy documents. If the policies were still valid, there were insurance regulation problems because those policies had been made illegal in the intervening years.

In this case, the date was being used to generate a unique identifier. But consider a situation in which this same scheme was used, starting in the year 1999, for a serial number. Once the company went into the year

2000, it was no longer possible to select the largest serial number in the database and increment it to get the next one.

29.10.5 The Aftermath

The Y2K crisis is over now, and we have some idea of the cost of this conversion. By various estimates, the total expenditure on remediation by governments and businesses ranged from a low of $200 billion to well over half a trillion dollars. As a result of Y2K, many ISO Standards—not just Standard SQL—require that dates be in ISO-8601 format.

The other good side effect was that people actually looked at their data and became aware of their data quality levels. Most companies would not have done such a data audit without the "Y2K Crisis" looming over their heads.

It might be worth mentioning that old COBOL programmers would check to see if the two-digit year was less than 30 (or some other magical number). If itwas less than that pivot value, they added 2000 to it, if it is not less than the pivot value, they added 1900 to it to come up with a four-digit year. A lot of programs will be exploding 20, 30, or 40 years from now, if they are still chugging along.

Graphs in SQL

THE TERMINOLOGY IN GRAPH theory pretty much explains itself; if it does not, you can read some of the graph theory books suggested in the Appendix. Graphs are important because they are a general way to represent many different types of data and their relationships. Here is a quick review of terms.

A graph is a data structure made up of nodes connected by edges. Edges can be directed (permit travel in only one direction) or undirected (permit travel in both directions). The number of edges entering a node is its indegree; likewise, the number of edges leaving a node is its outdegree. A set of edges that allow you to travel from one node to another is called a path. A cycle is a path that comes back to the node from which it started without crossing itself (this means that a big circle is fine but a figure eight is not).

A tree is a type of directed graph that is important enough to have its own terminology. Its special properties and frequent use have made it important enough to be covered in a separate chapter (chapter 29). The following sections will stress other useful kinds of generalized directed graphs. Generalized directed graphs are classified into nonreconvergent and reconvergent graphs. In a reconvergent graph there are multiple paths between at least one pair of nodes. Reconvergent graphs are either cyclic or acyclic.

The most common way to model a graph in SQL is with an adjacency list model. Each edge of the graph is shown as a pair of nodes in which the ordering matters, and then any values associated with that edge are shown in another column.

30.1 Basic Graph Characteristics

The following code is from John Gilson. This code uses an adjacency list model of the graph, with nodes in a separate table. This is the most common method for modeling graphs in SQL.

```
CREATE TABLE Nodes
(node_id INTEGER NOT NULL PRIMARY KEY);

CREATE TABLE AdjacencyListGraph
(begin_node_id INTEGER NOT NULL REFERENCES Nodes (node_id),
 end_node_id INTEGER NOT NULL REFERENCES Nodes (node_id),
 PRIMARY KEY (begin_node_id, end_node_id),
 CHECK (begin_node_id <> end_node_id));
```

It is also possible to load an acyclic directed graph into a nested set model by splitting the nodes.

```
CREATE TABLE NestedSetsGraph
(node_id INTEGER NOT NULL REFERENCES Nodes (node_id),
 lft INTEGER NOT NULL CHECK (lft >= 1) PRIMARY KEY,
 rgt INTEGER NOT NULL UNIQUE,
 CHECK (rgt > lft),
 UNIQUE (node_id, lft));
```

To split nodes, start at the sink nodes and move up the tree. When you come to a node with an indegree greater than one, replace it with that many copies of the node under each of its superiors. Continue to do this until you get to the root. The acyclic graph will become a tree, but with duplicated node values. There are advantages to this model; we will discuss them in Section 30.3.

30.1.1 All Nodes in the Graph

To view all nodes in the graph, use the following:

```
CREATE VIEW GraphNodes (node_id)
AS
SELECT DISTINCT node_id FROM NestedSetsGraph;
```

30.1.2 Path Endpoints

A path through a graph is a traversal of consecutive nodes along a sequence of edges. Clearly, the node at the end of one edge in the sequence must also be the node at the beginning of the next edge in the sequence. The length of the path is the number of edges that are traversed along the path.

Path endpoints are the first and last nodes of each path in the graph. For a path of length zero, the path endpoints are the same node. If there is more than one path between two nodes, each path will be distinguished by its own distinct set of number pairs for the nested-set representation.

If there is only one path, P, between two nodes, but P is a subpath of more than one distinct path, then the endpoints of P will have number pairs for each of these greater paths. As a canonical form, the least-numbered pairs are returned for these endpoints.

```
CREATE VIEW PathEndpoints
(begin_node_id, end_node_id,
 begin_lft, begin_rgt,
 end_lft, end_rgt)
AS
SELECT G1.node_id, G2.node_id,
       G1.lft, G1.rgt, G2.lft, G2.rgt
  FROM (SELECT node_id, MIN(lft), MIN(rgt)
          FROM NestedSetsGraph
         GROUP BY node_id) AS G1 (node_id, lft, rgt)
        INNER JOIN
        NestedSetsGraph AS G2
        ON G2.lft >= G1.lft
           AND G2.lft < G1.rgt;
```

30.1.3 Reachable Nodes

If a node is reachable from another node, then a path exists from the one node to the other. It is assumed that every node is reachable from itself.

```
CREATE VIEW ReachableNodes (begin_node_id, end_node_id)
AS
SELECT DISTINCT begin_node_id, end_node_id
  FROM PathEndpoints;
```

30.1.4 Edges

Edges are pairs of adjacent connected nodes in the graph. If edge E is represented by the pair of nodes (n0, n1), then n1 is reachable from n0 in a single traversal.

```
CREATE VIEW Edges (begin_node_id, end_node_id)
AS
SELECT begin_node_id, end_node_id
  FROM PathEndpoints AS PE
 WHERE begin_node_id <> end_node_id
   AND NOT EXISTS
       (SELECT *
          FROM NestedSetsGraph AS G
         WHERE G.lft > PE.begin_lft
           AND G.lft < PE.end_lft
           AND G.rgt > PE.end_rgt);
```

30.1.5 Indegree and Outdegree

The indegree of a node, n, is the number of distinct edges ending at n. Nodes that have an indegree of zero are not returned. To determine the indegree of all nodes in the graph:

```
CREATE VIEW Indegree (node_id, node_indegree)
AS
SELECT N.node_id, COUNT(E.begin_node_id)
  FROM GraphNodes AS N
       LEFT OUTER JOIN
       Edges AS E
       ON N.node_id = E.end_node_id
 GROUP BY N.node_id;
```

The outdegree of a node, (n), is the number of distinct edges beginning at (n). Nodes that have an outdegree of zero are not returned. To determine the outdegree of all nodes in the graph:

```
CREATE VIEW Outdegree (node_id, node_outdegree)
AS
SELECT N.node_id, COUNT(E.end_node_id)
  FROM GraphNodes AS N
       LEFT OUTER JOIN
       Edges AS E
       ON N.node_id = E.begin_node_id
 GROUP BY N.node_id;
```

30.1.6 Source, Sink, Isolated, and Internal Nodes

A source node of a graph has a positive outdegree but an indegree of zero; that is, it has edges leading from, but not to, the node. This assumes there are no isolated nodes (nodes belonging to no edges).

```
CREATE VIEW SourceNodes (node_id, lft, rgt)
AS
SELECT node_id, lft, rgt
  FROM NestedSetsGraph AS G1
 WHERE NOT EXISTS
      (SELECT *
         FROM NestedSetsGraph AS G
        WHERE G1.lft > G2.lft
          AND G1.lft < G2.rgt);
```

Likewise, a sink node of a graph has positive indegree but an outdegree of zero; that is, it has edges leading to, but not from, the node. This assumes there are no isolated nodes.

```
CREATE VIEW SinkNodes (node_id)
AS
SELECT node_id
  FROM NestedSetsGraph AS G1
 WHERE lft = rgt - 1
   AND NOT EXISTS
       (SELECT *
          FROM NestedSetsGraph AS G2
         WHERE G1.node_id = G2.node_id
           AND G2.lft < G1.lft);
```

An isolated node belongs to no edges; i.e., it has zero indegree and zero outdegree.

```
CREATE VIEW IsolatedNodes (node_id, lft, rgt)
AS
SELECT node_id, lft, rgt
  FROM NestedSetsGraph AS G1
 WHERE lft = rgt - 1
   AND NOT EXISTS
       (SELECT *
          FROM NestedSetsGraph AS G2
         WHERE G1.lft > G2.lft
           AND G1.lft < G2.rgt);
```

An internal node of a graph has an indegree greater than zero and an outdegree greater than zero; that is, it acts as both a source and a sink.

```
CREATE VIEW InternalNodes (node_id)
AS
SELECT node_id
  FROM (SELECT node_id, MIN(lft) AS lft, MIN(rgt) AS rgt
          FROM NestedSetsGraph
         WHERE lft < rgt - 1
        GROUP BY node_id) AS G1
 WHERE EXISTS
       (SELECT *
          FROM NestedSetsGraph AS G2
         WHERE G1.lft > G2.lft
           AND G1.lft < G2.rgt)
```

30.2 Paths in a Graph

Finding a path in a graph is the most important commercial application of graphs. Graphs model transportation networks, electrical and cable systems, process control flow and thousands of other things.

A path, P, of length L from a node n0 to a node nk in the graph is defined as a traversal of $(L + 1)$ contiguous nodes along a sequence of edges, where the first node is node number 0 and the last is node number k.

```
CREATE VIEW Paths
(begin_node_id, end_node_id, this_node_id,
 seq_nbr,
 begin_lft, begin_rgt, end_lft, end_rgt,
```

```
 this_lft, this_rgt)
AS
SELECT PE.begin_node_id, PE.end_node_id, G1.node_id,
       (SELECT COUNT(*)
          FROM NestedSetsGraph AS G2
         WHERE G2.lft > PE.begin_lft
           AND G2.lft <= G1.lft
           AND G2.rgt >= G1.rgt),
       PE.begin_lft, PE.begin_rgt,
       PE.end_lft, PE.end_rgt,
       G1.lft, G1.rgt
  FROM PathEndpoints AS PE
       INNER JOIN
       NestedSetsGraph AS G1
       ON G1.lft BETWEEN PE.begin_lft
                     AND PE.end_lft
          AND G1.rgt >= PE.end_rgt
```

30.2.1 Length of Paths

The length of a path is the number of edges that are traversed along the path. A path of n nodes has a length of $(n - 1)$.

```
CREATE VIEW PathLengths
(begin_node_id, end_node_id,
 path_length,
 begin_lft, begin_rgt,
 end_lft, end_rgt)
AS
SELECT begin_node_id, end_node_id, MAX(seq_nbr),
       begin_lft, begin_rgt, end_lft, end_rgt
  FROM Paths
 GROUP BY begin_lft, end_lft, begin_rgt, end_rgt,
          begin_node_id, end_node_id;
```

30.2.2 Shortest Path

The following code gives the shortest path length between all nodes, but it does not tell you what the actual path is. There are other queries that use the new CTE feature and recursion, which we will discuss in Section 30.3.

```
CREATE VIEW ShortestPathLengths
(begin_node_id, end_node_id, path_length,
 begin_lft, begin_rgt, end_lft, end_rgt)
AS
SELECT PL.begin_node_id, PL.end_node_id,
       PL.path_length,
       PL.begin_lft, PL.begin_rgt,
       PL.end_lft, PL.end_rgt
  FROM (SELECT begin_node_id, end_node_id,
               MIN(path_length) AS path_length
          FROM PathLengths
         GROUP BY begin_node_id, end_node_id) AS MPL
       INNER JOIN
       PathLengths AS PL
       ON MPL.begin_node_id = PL.begin_node_id
          AND MPL.end_node_id = PL.end_node_id
          AND MPL.path_length = PL.path_length;
```

30.2.3 Paths by Iteration

First, let's build a graph that has a cost associated with each edge and put it into an adjacency list model.

```
INSERT INTO Edges (out_node, in_node, cost)
VALUES ('A', 'B', 50),
 ('A', 'C', 30),
 ('A', 'D', 100),
 ('A', 'E', 10),
 ('C', 'B', 5),
 ('D', 'B', 20),
 ('D', 'C', 50),
 ('E', 'D', 10);
```

To find the shortest paths from one node to the other nodes it can reach, we can write this recursive VIEW.

```
CREATE VIEW ShortestPaths (out_node, in_node, path_length)
AS
WITH RECURSIVE Paths (out_node, in_node, path_length)
AS
(SELECT out_node, in_node, 1
   FROM Edges
```

```
UNION ALL
SELECT E1.out_node, P1.in_node, P1.path_length + 1
  FROM Edges AS E1, Paths AS P1
 WHERE E1.in_node = P1.out_node)
SELECT out_node, in_node, MIN(path_length)
  FROM Paths
 GROUP BY out_node, in_node;

out_node in_node path_length
============================
'A'       'B'     1
'A'       'C'     1
'A'       'D'     1
'A'       'E'     1
'C'       'B'     1
'D'       'B'     1
'D'       'C'     1
'E'       'B'     2
'E'       'D'     1
```

To find the shortest paths without recursion, stay in a loop and add one edge at a time to the set of paths defined so far.

```
CREATE PROCEDURE IteratePaths()
LANGUAGE SQL
MODIFIES SQL DATA
BEGIN
DECLARE old_path_tally INTEGER;
SET old_path_tally = 0;
DELETE FROM Paths; -- clean out working table
INSERT INTO Paths
SELECT out_node, in_node, 1
  FROM Edges; -- load the edges
-- add one edge to each path
WHILE old_path_tally < (SELECT COUNT(*) FROM Paths)
DO SET old_path_tally = (SELECT COUNT(*) FROM Paths);
   INSERT INTO Paths (out_node, in_node, lgth)
   SELECT E1.out_node, P1.in_node, (1 + P1.lgth)
     FROM Edges AS E1, Paths AS P1
    WHERE E1.in_node = P1.out_node
      AND NOT EXISTS -- path is not here already
```

```
          (SELECT *
             FROM Paths AS P2
            WHERE E1.out_node = P2.out_node
              AND P1.in_node = P2.in_node);
END WHILE;
END;
```

The least cost path is basically the same algorithm, but instead of a constant of one for the path length, we use the actual costs of the edges.

```
CREATE PROCEDURE IterateCheapPaths ()
LANGUAGE SQL
MODIFIES SQL DATA
BEGIN
DECLARE old_path_cost INTEGER;
SET old_path_cost = 0;
DELETE FROM Paths; -- clean out working table
INSERT INTO Paths
SELECT out_node, in_node, cost
  FROM Edges; -- load the edges
-- add one edge to each path
WHILE old_path_cost < (SELECT COUNT(*) FROM Paths)
DO SET old_path_cost = (SELECT COUNT(*) FROM Paths);
   INSERT INTO Paths (out_node, in_node, cost)
   SELECT E1.out_node, P1.in_node, (E1.cost + P1.cost)
     FROM Edges AS E1
          INNER JOIN
          (SELECT out_node, in_node, MIN(cost)
             FROM Paths
           GROUP BY out_node, in_node)
          AS P1 (out_node, in_node, cost)
          ON E1.in_node = P1.out_node
             AND NOT EXISTS
                 (SELECT *
                    FROM Paths AS P2
                   WHERE E1.out_node = P2.out_node
                     AND P1.in_node = P2.in_node
                     AND P2.cost <= E1.cost + P1.cost);
END WHILE;
END;
```

30.2.4 Listing the Paths

I took the data for this table from the book *Introduction to Algorithms* (Cormen, Leiserson, and Rivest 1990), page 518. This book was very popular in college courses in the United States. I made one decision that will be important later: I added self-traversal edges (i.e., the node is both the out_node and the in_node of an edge) with weights of zero.

```
INSERT INTO Edges VALUES ('s', 's', 0);
INSERT INTO Edges VALUES ('s', 'u', 3);
INSERT INTO Edges VALUES ('s', 'x', 5);
INSERT INTO Edges VALUES ('u', 'u', 0);
INSERT INTO Edges VALUES ('u', 'v', 6);
INSERT INTO Edges VALUES ('u', 'x', 2);
INSERT INTO Edges VALUES ('v', 'v', 0);
INSERT INTO Edges VALUES ('v', 'y', 2);
INSERT INTO Edges VALUES ('x', 'u', 1);
INSERT INTO Edges VALUES ('x', 'v', 4);
INSERT INTO Edges VALUES ('x', 'x', 0);
INSERT INTO Edges VALUES ('x', 'y', 6);
INSERT INTO Edges VALUES ('y', 's', 3);
INSERT INTO Edges VALUES ('y', 'v', 7);
INSERT INTO Edges VALUES ('y', 'y', 0);
```

I am not happy about this approach, because I have to decide the maximum number of edges in a path before I start looking for an answer. But this solution will work, and I know that a path will have no more than the total number of nodes in the graph. Let's create a table to hold the paths:

```
CREATE TABLE Paths
(step1 CHAR(2) NOT NULL,
 step2 CHAR(2) NOT NULL,
 step3 CHAR(2) NOT NULL,
 step4 CHAR(2) NOT NULL,
 step5 CHAR(2) NOT NULL,
 total_cost INTEGER NOT NULL,
 path_length INTEGER NOT NULL,
 PRIMARY KEY (step1, step2, step3, step4, step5));
```

The step1 node is where I begin the path. The other columns are the second step, third step, fourth step, and so forth. The last step column is the end of the journey. The total_cost column is the total cost, based on the sum of the weights of the edges, on this path. The path length column is harder to explain, but for now, let's just say that it is a count of the nodes visited in the path.

To keep things easier, let's look at all the paths from 's' to 'y' in the graph. The INSERT INTO statement for constructing that set looks likes this:

```
INSERT INTO Paths
SELECT G1.out_node, -- it is 's' in this example
       G2.out_node,
       G3.out_node, G4.out_node,
       G4.in_node, -- it is 'y' in this example
       (G1.cost + G2.cost + G3.cost + G4.cost),
       (CASE WHEN G1.out_node NOT IN (G2.out_node, G3.out_node,
G4.out_node)                THEN 1 ELSE 0 END
       + CASE WHEN G2.out_node NOT IN (G1.out_node, G3.out_node,
G4.out_node)              THEN 1 ELSE 0 END
       + CASE WHEN G3.out_node NOT IN (G1.out_node, G2.out_node,
G4.out_node)              THEN 1 ELSE 0 END
       + CASE WHEN G4.out_node NOT IN (G1.out_node, G2.out_node,
G3.out_node)             THEN 1 ELSE 0 END)
  FROM Edges AS G1,
       Edges AS G2,
       Edges AS G3,
       Edges AS G4
 WHERE G1.out_node = 's'
   AND G1.in_node = G2.out_node
   AND G2.in_node = G3.out_node
   AND G3.in_node = G4.out_node
   AND G4.in_node = 'y';
```

I put in 's' and 'y' as the out_node and in_node of the path, and made sure that the in_node of each step in the path was the out_node of the next step in the path. This is a combinatorial explosion, but it is easy to read and understand.

The sum of the weights is the cost of the path, which is easy to understand. The path_length calculation is a bit harder. This sum of CASE expressions looks at each node in the path. If it is unique within the row, it is assigned a value of one; if it is not unique within the row, it is assigned a value of zero.

All paths will have five steps in them, because that is the way the table is declared. But what if a path shorter than five steps exists between the two nodes? That is where the self-traversal rows are used! Consecutive pairs of steps in the same row can be repetitions of the same node.

Here is what the rows of the Paths table look like after this `INSERT INTO` statement, ordered by descending path_length, and then by ascending cost:

```
Paths  step1 step2 step3 step4 step5 total_cost path_length
==========================================================
  s     s     x     x     y     11          0
  s     s     s     x     y     11          1
  s     x     x     x     y     11          1
  s     x     u     x     y     14          2
  s     s     u     v     y     11          2
  s     s     u     x     y     11          2
  s     s     x     v     y     11          2
  s     s     x     y     y     11          2
  s     u     u     v     y     11          2
  s     u     u     x     y     11          2
  s     u     v     v     y     11          2
  s     u     x     x     y     11          2
  s     x     v     v     y     11          2
  s     x     x     v     y     11          2
  s     x     x     y     y     11          2
  s     x     y     y     y     11          2
  s     x     y     v     y     20          4
  s     x     u     v     y     14          4
  s     u     v     y     y     11          4
  s     u     x     v     y     11          4
  s     u     x     y     y     11          4
  s     x     v     y     y     11          4
```

Clearly, all pairs of nodes could be picked from the original Edges table and the same `INSERT INTO` could be run on them with a minor change in the `WHERE` clause. However, this example is big enough for a short magazine article—and it is too big for most applications. It is safe to assume that people really want the cheapest path. In this example, the

total_cost column defines the cost of a path, so we can eliminate some of the paths from the Paths table with this statement.

```
DELETE FROM Paths
 WHERE total_cost
     > (SELECT MIN(total_cost)
          FROM Paths);
```

Again, if you had all the paths for all possible pairs of nodes, the subquery expression would have a WHERE clause to correlate it to the subset of paths for each possible pair.

In this example, it got rid of three out of twenty-two possible paths. It is helpful, and in some situations we might like having all the options. But these are not distinct options.

As one of many examples, consider the following two paths:

```
(s, x, v, v, y, 11, 2)
```

and

```
(s, x, x, v, y, 11, 2)
```

These paths are both really the same path, (s, x, v, y). Before we decide to write a statement to handle these equivalent rows, let's consider another cost factor. People do not like to change airplanes or trains. If they can go from Amsterdam to New York City without changing planes for the same cost, they are happy. This is where that path_length column comes in. It is a quick way to remove the paths that have more edges than they need to get the job done.

```
DELETE FROM Paths
 WHERE path_length
       > (SELECT MIN(path_length)
            FROM Paths);
```

In this case, that last DELETE FROM statement will reduce the table to one row: (s, s, x, x, y, 11, 0) which reduces to (s, x, y). This single remaining row is very convenient for my example, but if you look at the table, you will see that there was also a subset of equivalent rows that had higher path_length numbers:

```
(s, s, s, x, y, 11, 1)
(s, x, x, x, y, 11, 1)
(s, x, x, y, y, 11, 2)
(s, x, y, y, y, 11, 2)
```

Your task is to write code to handle equivalent rows. Hint: the duplicate nodes will always be contiguous across the row.

30.3 Acyclic Graphs as Nested Sets

Let's start with a simple graph in an adjacency list model.

```
INSERT INTO Nodes (node_id)
VALUES ('a'), ('b'), ('c'), ('d'),
       ('e'), ('f'), ('g'), ('h');

INSERT INTO AdjacencyListGraph (begin_node_id, end_node_id)
VALUES ('a', 'b'), ('a', 'c'), ('b', 'd'), ('c', 'd'),
       ('c', 'g'), ('d', 'e'), ('d', 'f'), ('e', 'h'),
       ('g', 'h');
```

We can convert this adjacency list model to the nested sets model (see Figure 30.1) with a simple stack algorithm:

```
-- Stack to keep track of nodes being traversed in depth-first
fashion
CREATE TABLE NodeStack
(node_id INTEGER NOT NULL PRIMARY KEY
    REFERENCES Nodes (node_id),
 distance INTEGER NOT NULL CHECK (distance >= 0),
 lft INTEGER CHECK (lft >= 1),
 rgt INTEGER,
 CHECK (rgt > lft));

CREATE PROCEDURE AdjacencyListsToNestedSetsGraph ()
LANGUAGE SQL
BEGIN
DECLARE path_length INTEGER;
DECLARE current_number INTEGER;
SET path_length = 0;
SET current_number = 0;
```

```
-- Clear the table that will hold the result
DELETE FROM NestedSetsGraph;
-- Initialize stack by inserting all source nodes of graph
INSERT INTO NodeStack (node_id, distance)
SELECT DISTINCT G1.begin_node_id, path_length
  FROM AdjacencyListGraph AS G1
 WHERE NOT EXISTS
       (SELECT *
          FROM AdjacencyListGraph AS G2
         WHERE G2.end_node_id = G1.begin_node_id);

WHILE EXISTS (SELECT * FROM NodeStack)
DO
  SET current_number = current_number + 1;
  IF EXISTS (SELECT * FROM NodeStack WHERE distance =
path_length)
  THEN UPDATE NodeStack
          SET lft = current_number
        WHERE distance = path_length
          AND NOT EXISTS
              (SELECT *
                 FROM NodeStack AS S2
                WHERE distance = path_length
                  AND S2.node_id < NodeStack.node_id);
       INSERT INTO NodeStack (node_id, distance)
       SELECT G.end_node_id, (S.distance + 1)
         FROM NodeStack AS S,
              AdjacencyListGraph AS G
        WHERE S.distance = path_length
          AND S.lft IS NOT NULL
          AND G.begin_node_id = S.node_id;

       SET path_length = (path_length + 1);
  ELSE SET path_length = (path_length - 1);
       UPDATE NodeStack
          SET rgt = current_number
        WHERE lft IS NOT NULL
          AND distance = path_length;

       INSERT INTO NestedSetsGraph (node_id, lft, rgt)
       SELECT node_id, lft, rgt
         FROM NodeStack
```

```
            WHERE lft IS NOT NULL
              AND distance = path_length;
        DELETE FROM NodeStack
         WHERE lft IS NOT NULL
           AND distance = path_length;
  END IF;
END WHILE;
END;
```

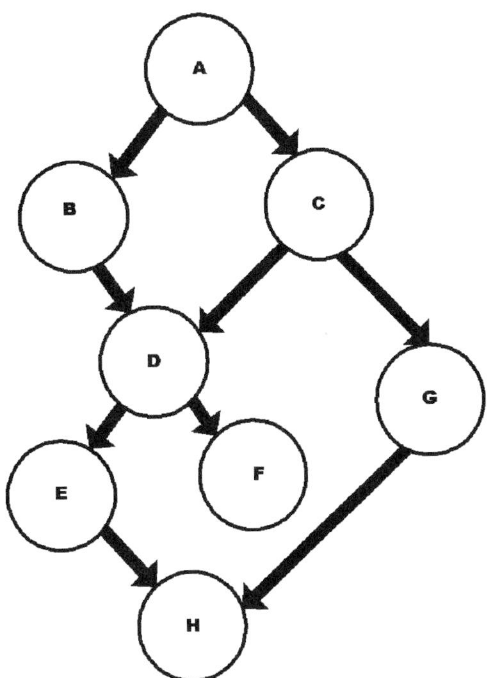

Figure 30.1 *Acyclic Graph as a Nested Set Model.*

You can now use modified versions of the nested set queries you already know on this kind of graph. However, be sure to use DISTINCT options to remove duplicate node references.

30.4 Paths with CTE

The following queries with CTEs are due to Frédéric Brouard of France. The sample data and the narrative are so delightful that I am using his material directly.

Perhaps you never go to France. If this is the case, you may be interested by the fact that there are beautiful girls in Paris, and in

Toulouse you can find a famous dish called *cassoulet* and a small plane construction company named Airbus. You might like to go by car from Paris to Toulouse using the speedway network. I will simplify the trip for you (if you are lost, and do not know how to pronounce your destination, it is simple. Just say "to loose" . . .):

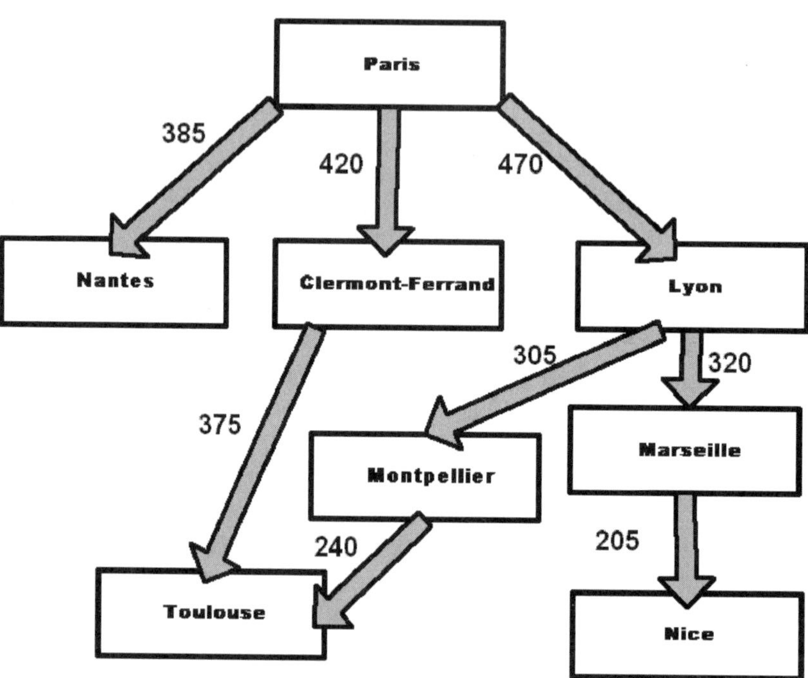

Figure 30.2 *The French Speedway Network.*

```
CREATE TABLE Journeys
(depart_town VARCHAR(32) NOT NULL,
 arrival_town VARCHAR(32) NOT NULL,
CHECK (depart_town <> arrival_town),
PRIMARY KEY (depart_town, arrival_town),
jny_distance INTEGER NOT NULL
      CHECK (jny_distance > 0));

INSERT INTO Journeys
VALUES ('PARIS', 'NANTES', 385),
('PARIS', 'CLERMONT-FERRAND', 420),
('PARIS', 'LYON', 470),
('CLERMONT-FERRAND', 'MONTPELLIER', 335),
('CLERMONT-FERRAND', 'TOULOUSE', 375),
```

```
('LYON', 'MONTPELLIER', 305),
('LYON', 'MARSEILLE', 320),
('MONTPELLIER', 'TOULOUSE', 240),
('MARSEILLE', 'NICE', 205);
```

Now we will try a very simple query, giving all the journeys between towns:

```
WITH RECURSIVE Journeys (arrival_town)
  AS (SELECT DISTINCT depart_town
        FROM Journeys
      UNION ALL
      SELECT arrival_town
        FROM Journeys AS Arrivals,
             Journeys AS Departures
       WHERE Departures.arrival_town = Arrivals.depart_town)
SELECT DISTINCT arrival_town FROM Journeys;

arrival_town
==================
CLERMONT-FERRAND
LYON
MARSEILLE
MONTPELLIER
PARIS
NANTES
TOULOUSE
NICE
```

This query is not very interesting, because we do not know which town we are starting from. We only know the towns where we can go and the fact that we probably could take different routes to get to the same place. Let us see if we can get some more specific information.

First, we want to start from Paris:

```
WITH RECURSIVE Journeys (arrival_town)
  AS (SELECT DISTINCT depart_town
        FROM Journeys
       WHERE depart_town = 'PARIS'
    UNION ALL
    SELECT arrival_town
```

```
       FROM Journeys AS Arrivals
            INNER Journeys AS Departures
                  ON Departures.arrival_town =
Arrivals.depart_town)
SELECT arrival_town FROM Journeys;

arrival_town
=================
PARIS
NANTES
CLERMONT-FERRAND
LYON
MONTPELLIER
MARSEILLE
NICE
TOULOUSE      <= goal
MONTPELLIER
TOULOUSE      <= goal
TOULOUSE      <= goal
```

We probably have three routes to take from Paris to Toulouse. Can we filter the destination? Sure!

```
WITH RECURSIVE Journeys (arrival_town)
  AS (SELECT DISTINCT depart_town
        FROM Journeys
       WHERE depart_town = 'PARIS'
      UNION ALL
      SELECT arrival_town
        FROM Journeys AS Arrivals,
             Journeys AS Departures
       WHERE Departures.arrival_town = Arrivals.depart_town)
SELECT arrival_town
  FROM Journeys
 WHERE arrival_town = 'TOULOUSE';

arrival_town
============
TOULOUSE
TOULOUSE
TOULOUSE
```

We can refine this query by calculating the number of steps involved in the different routes:

```
WITH RECURSIVE Journeys (arrival_town, steps)
  AS (SELECT DISTINCT depart_town, 0
        FROM Journeys
       WHERE depart_town = 'PARIS'
      UNION ALL
      SELECT arrival_town, Departures.steps + 1
        FROM Journeys AS Arrivals,
             Journeys AS Departures
       WHERE Departures.arrival_town = Arrivals.depart_town)
SELECT arrival_town, steps
  FROM Journeys
 WHERE arrival_town = 'TOULOUSE';

arrival_town   Steps
=====================
TOULOUSE       3
TOULOUSE       2
TOULOUSE       3
```

The cherry on the cake is the ability to determine the distances of the different routes:

```
WITH RECURSIVE Journeys (arrival_town, steps, total_distance)
AS
   (SELECT DISTINCT depart_town, 0, 0
     FROM Journeys
     WHERE depart_town = 'PARIS'
     UNION ALL
     SELECT arrival_town, Departures.steps + 1,
            Departures.total_distance + Arrivals.jny_distance
       FROM Journeys AS Arrivals,
            Journeys AS Departures
      WHERE Departures.arrival_town = Arrivals.depart_town)
SELECT arrival_town, steps, total_distance
  FROM Journeys
 WHERE arrival_town = 'TOULOUSE';
```

```
arrival_town  steps total_distance
===================================
TOULOUSE       3          1015
TOULOUSE       2          795
TOULOUSE       3          995
```

The girl hiding in the cake is the ability to determine which different towns we visit by using each of these different routes:

```
WITH RECURSIVE Journeys (arrival_town, steps, total_distance, way)
  AS (SELECT DISTINCT depart_town, 0, 0,
                  CAST('PARIS' AS VARCHAR(MAX))
        FROM Journeys
       WHERE depart_town = 'PARIS'
      UNION ALL
      SELECT arrival_town, Departures.steps + 1,
             Departures.total_distance + Arrivals.jny_distance,
             Departures.way || ', ' ||Arrivals.arrival_town
        FROM Journeys AS Arrivals,
             Journeys AS Departures
       WHERE Departures.arrival_town = Arrivals.depart_town)
SELECT arrival_town, steps, total_distance, way
  FROM Journeys
 WHERE arrival_town = 'TOULOUSE';
```

```
arrival_town steps total_distance   way
======================================================================
TOULOUSE      3     1015             PARIS, LYON, MONTPELLIER, TOULOUSE
TOULOUSE      2     795              PARIS, CLERMONT-FERRAND, TOULOUSE
TOULOUSE      3     995             PARIS, CLERMONT-FERRAND, MONTPELLIER, TOULOUSE
```

And now, ladies and gentleman, the recursive query is proud to present to you the means of solving a very complex problem, called the traveling salesman problem. This is one of the operational research problems for which Edsger Wybe Dijkstra found the first efficient algorithm and received the Turing Award in 1972.

```
WITH RECURSIVE Journey (arrival_town, steps, total_distance, way)
  AS (SELECT DISTINCT depart_town, 0, 0, CAST('PARIS' AS
VARCHAR(MAX))
        FROM Journeys
       WHERE depart_town = 'PARIS'
```

```
    UNION ALL
    SELECT arrival_town, Departures.steps + 1,
           Departures.total_distance + Arrivals.jny_distance,
           Departures.way ||', '||Arrivals.arrival_town
      FROM Journeys AS Arrivals,
           Journeys AS Departures
     WHERE Departures.arrival_town = Arrivals.depart_town),
 ShortestDistance (total_distance)
 AS (SELECT MIN(total_distance)
       FROM Journeys
      WHERE arrival_town = 'TOULOUSE')
SELECT arrival_town, steps, total_distance, way
  FROM Journeys AS J
       ShortestDistance AS S
 WHERE J.total_distance = S.total_distance
   AND arrival_town = 'TOULOUSE';
```

30.4.1 Nonacyclic Graphs

In fact, one thing that is limiting the process in our network of speedways is that we have made routes that only run in a single direction. In other words, we can go from Paris to Lyon, but we are not allowed to go from Lyon to Paris. For that, we need to add the reverse directions in the table, as shown:

```
depart_town  arrival_town  jny_distance
========================================
LYON            PARIS         470
```

This can be done with a very simple query:

```
INSERT INTO Journeys
SELECT arrival_town, depart_town, jny_distance
  FROM Journeys;
```

The only problem is that the previous queries will not work properly:

```
WITH RECURSIVE Journeys (arrival_town)
AS (SELECT DISTINCT depart_town
      FROM Journeys
     WHERE depart_town = 'PARIS'
    UNION ALL
```

```
    SELECT arrival_town
      FROM Journeys AS Arrivals,
           Journeys AS Departures
     WHERE Departures.arrival_town = Arrivals.depart_town)
SELECT arrival_town
  FROM Journeys;
```

This query will give you an error message about the maximum depth of recursion being violated. What happened? The problem is simply that you are trying all routes, including cycling routes like Paris, Lyon, Paris, Lyon, Paris . . . *ad infinitum*. Is there a way to avoid cycling routes? Maybe. In one of our previous queries, we have a column that gives the complete list of stepped towns. Why not use it to avoid cycling? The condition will be: Do not pass through a town that is already in the way. This can be written as:

```
WITH RECURSIVE Journeys (arrival_town, steps, total_distance, way)
  AS (SELECT DISTINCT depart_town, 0, 0, CAST('PARIS' AS VARCHAR(255))
        FROM Journeys
        WHERE depart_town = 'PARIS'
      UNION ALL
      SELECT arrival_town, Departures.steps + 1,
             Departures.total_distance + Arrivals.jny_distance,
             Departures.way ||', '||Arrivals.arrival_town
        FROM Journeys AS Arrivals,
             Journeys AS Departures
       WHERE Departures.arrival_town = Arrivals.depart_town
         AND Departures.way NOT LIKE '%' + Arrivals.arrival_town + '%')
SELECT arrival_town, steps, total_distance, way
  FROM Journeys
WHERE arrival_town = 'TOULOUSE';
```

```
arrival_town  steps total_distance way
==============================================================================
TOULOUSE        3     1015        PARIS, LYON, MONTPELLIER, TOULOUSE
TOULOUSE        4     1485        PARIS, LYON, MONTPELLIER, CLERMONT-FERRAND, TOULOUSE
TOULOUSE        2     795         PARIS, CLERMONT-FERRAND, TOULOUSE
TOULOUSE        3     995         PARIS, CLERMONT-FERRAND, MONTPELLIER, TOULOUSE
```

As you see, a new route is determined. It's the worst so far as distance is concerned, but it is perhaps the most beautiful!

A CTE can simplify the expression of complex queries. Recursive queries must be employed where recursion is needed. Trust your SQL product to terminate a bad query. There is usually an option to set the depth of recursion either in the SQL engine or as an OPTION clause at the end of the CTE clause.

30.5 Adjacency Matrix Model

An adjacency matrix is a square array whose rows are out-nodes and columns are in-nodes of a graph. A one in a cell means that there is edge between the two nodes. Using the graph in Figure 30.1, we would have a array like this:

```
   A B C D E F G H
  ================
A| 1 1 1 0 0 0 0 0
B| 0 1 0 1 0 0 0 0
C| 0 0 1 1 0 0 1 0
D| 0 0 0 1 1 1 0 0
E| 0 0 0 0 1 0 0 1
F| 0 0 0 0 0 1 0 0
G| 0 0 0 0 0 0 1 1
H| 0 0 0 0 0 0 0 1
```

Many graph algorithms are based on the adjacency matrix model and can be translated into SQL. Go back to Chapter 25 for details on modeling matrices in SQL; in particular, review Section 25.3.3, which deals with matrix multiplication in SQL. For example, Dijkstra's algorithm for the shortest distances between each pair of nodes in a graph looks like this in pseudocode:

```
FOR k = 1 TO n
  DO FOR i = 1 TO n
     DO FOR j = 1 TO n
        IF a[i,k] + a[k,j] < a[i,j]
        THEN a[i,j] = a[i,k] + a[k,j]
        END IF;
     END FOR;
  END FOR;
END FOR;
```

You need to be warned that for a graph of n nodes, the table will be of size (n^2). The algorithms often run in (n^3) time. The advantage it has is that once you have completed a table, it can be used for look-ups rather than for recomputing distances over and over.

30.6 Points inside Polygons

Although polygons are not actually part of graph theory, this chapter seemed to be the reasonable place to put this section, since it is also related to spatial queries. A polygon can be described as a set of corner points in an (x, y) coordinate system. The usual query is to tell whether a given point is inside or outside of the polygon.

This algorithm is due to Darel R. Finley. Its main advantage is that it can be done in Standard SQL without trigonometry functions. Its disadvantage is that it does not work for concave polygons. The workaround is to dissect the convex polygons into concave polygons, then add a column for the name of the original area.

```
-- set up polygon, with any ordering of the corners
CREATE TABLE Polygon
(x FLOAT NOT NULL,
 y FLOAT NOT NULL,
 PRIMARY KEY (x, y));

INSERT INTO Polygon
VALUES (2.00, 2.00), (1.00, 4.00),
       (3.00, 6.00), (6.00, 4.00), (5.00, 2.00);

--set up some sample points
CREATE TABLE Points
(xx FLOAT NOT NULL,
 yy FLOAT NOT NULL,
 location VARCHAR(10) NOT NULL,  -- answer the question in
advance!
 PRIMARY KEY (xx, yy));
INSERT INTO Points
VALUES (2.00, 2.00, 'corner'),
       (1.00, 5.00, 'outside'),
       (3.00, 3.00, 'inside'),
       (3.00, 4.00, 'inside'),
       (5.00, 1.00, 'outside'),
       (3.00, 2.00, 'side');
```

```
-- do the query
SELECT P1.xx, P1.yy, p1.location, SIGN(
SUM
 (CASE WHEN (polyY.y < P1.yy AND polyY.x >= P1.yy
           OR polyY.x < P1.yy AND  polyY.y >= P1.yy)
       THEN CASE WHEN polyX.y + (P1.yy - polyY.y)
                     /(polyY.x - polyY.y) * (polyX.x - polyX.y)
< P1.xx
                 THEN 1 ELSE 0 END
       ELSE 0 END))AS flag
  FROM Polygon AS polyY, Polygon AS polyX, Points AS P1
GROUP BY P1.xx, P1.yy, p1.location;
```

When flag = 1, the point is inside; when flag = 0, it is outside.

```
xx   yy  location  flag
========================
1.0  5.0   outside  0
2.0  2.0   corner   0
3.0  3.0   inside   1
3.0  4.0   inside   1
5.0  1.0   outside  0
3.0  2.0   side     1
```

Sides are counted as inside, but if you want to count the corner points as inside, you should start the CASE expression with:

```
CASE WHEN EXISTS
        (SELECT * FROM Polygon
          WHERE x = P1.xx AND y = P1.yy)
     THEN 1 ...".
```

OLAP in SQL

THIS MATERIAL WAS PROVIDED by Michael L. Gonzales from his book, *The IBM Data Warehouse* (Gonzales 2003), as well as his article "The SQL Language of OLAP," (Gonzales 2004).

Most SQL programmers work with OLTP (Online Transaction Processing) databases and have had no exposure to Online Analytic Processing (OLAP) and data warehousing. OLAP is concerned with summarizing and reporting data, so the schema designs and common operations are very different from the usual SQL queries.

As a gross generalization, everything you knew in OLTP is reversed in a data warehouse:

1. OLTP changes data in short, frequent transactions. A data warehouse is bulk-loaded with static data on a schedule, and the data remains constant once it is in place.
2. An OLTP database wants to store only the data needed to do its current work. A data warehouse wants all the historical data it can hold. For example, as of 2005, Wal-Mart had a corporate data warehouse with more than half a petabyte of data online. The definition of a petabyte is 2^50 = 1,125,899,906,842,624 bytes = 1,024 terabytes, or roughly 10^15 bytes.

3. OLTP queries tend to be for simple facts. Data warehouse queries tend to be aggregate relationships that are more complex. For example, an OLTP query might ask, "How much chocolate did Joe Celko buy?" while a data warehouse might ask, "What is the correlation between chocolate purchases, geographic location, and wearing tweed?"
4. OLTP wants to run as fast as possible. A data warehouse is more concerned with the accuracy of computations, and it is willing to wait to get an answer to a complex query.
5. Properly designed OLTP databases are normalized. A data warehouse is usually a Star or Snowflake Schema, which is highly denormalized. The Star Schema is due to Ralph Kimball, and you can get more details about it in his books and articles.

31.1 Star Schema

The Star Schema is a violation of basic normalization rules. There is a large central fact table. This table contains all the facts about an event that you wish to report on, such as sales, in one place. In an OLTP database, the inventory would be in one table, the sales in another table, customers in a third table, and so forth. In the data warehouse, they are all in one huge table.

The dimensions of the values in the fact table are in smaller tables that allow you pick a scale or unit of measurement on that dimension in the fact table. For example, the time dimension for the Sales fact table might be grouped by year, month within year, week within month. Then a weight dimension could give you pounds, kilograms, or stock packaging sizes. A category dimension might classify the stock by department, and so forth. This arrangement lets me ask for my facts aggregated in any granularity of units I wish, and perhaps dropping some of the dimensions.

Until recent changes in SQL, OLAP queries had to be done with special OLAP-centric languages, such as Microsoft's Multidimensional Expressions (MDX). Be assured that the power of OLAP is not found in the wizards or GUIs presented in the vendor demos. The wizards and GUI are often the glitter that lures the uninformed.

Many aspects of OLAP are already integrated with the relational database engine itself. This blending of technology blurs the distinction between an RDBMS and OLAP data management technology, effectively challenging the passive role often relegated to relational databases with regard to dimensional data. The more your RDBMS can address the needs of both traditional relational data and dimensional data, the more you can reduce the cost of OLAP-only technology and get more out of your investment in RDBMS technology, skills, and resources.

31.2 OLAP Functionality

While OLAP systems have the ability to answer "who" and "what" questions, it is their ability to answer "what if" that sets them apart from other BI (business intelligence) tools. Leading RDBMS products, such as DB2 and Oracle, currently offer core OLAP-centric SQL functions, including categories such as ranking, numbering, and grouping. In fact, DB2 added extensions to its optimizer to identify a Star Schema and build a special execution plan for it.

When specifying an OLAP function, a window defines the rows over which the function is applied, and in what order. When used with a column function, the applicable rows can be further refined, relative to the current row, as either a range or a number of rows preceding and following the current row. For example, within a partition by month, an average can be calculated over the previous three-month period.

31.2.1 RANK and DENSE_RANK

So far, we have talked about extending the usual SQL aggregate functions. There are special functions that can be used with the window construct.

`RANK` assigns a sequential rank to a row within a window. The `RANK` of a row is defined as one plus the number of rows that strictly precede the row. Rows that are not distinct within the ordering of the window are assigned equal ranks. If two or more rows are not distinct with respect to the ordering, then there will be one or more gaps in the sequential rank numbering. That is, the results of `RANK` may have gaps in the numbers resulting from duplicate values.

`DENSE_RANK` also assigns a sequential rank to a row in a window. However, a rows `DENSE_RANK` is one plus the number of rows preceding it that are distinct with respect to the ordering. Therefore, there will be no gaps in the sequential rank numbering, with ties being assigned the same rank.

31.2.2 Row Numbering

`ROW_NUMBER` uniquely identifies rows in a resultant set. This function computes the sequential row number of the row within the window

defined by an ordering clause (if one is specified), starting with one for the first row and continuing sequentially to the last row in the window. If an ordering clause, ORDER BY, isn't specified in the window, the row numbers are assigned to the rows in arbitrary order as returned by the subselect.

31.2.3 GROUPING Operators

OLAP functions add the ROLLUP and CUBE extensions to the GROUP BY clause. ROLLUP and CUBE are often referred to as supergroups. They can be written in older Standard SQL using GROUP BY and UNION operators.

GROUP BY GROUPING SET

The GROUPING SET(<column list>) is shorthand in SQL-99 for a series of UNIONed queries that are common in reports. For example, to find the total:

```
SELECT dept_name, CAST(NULL AS CHAR(10)) AS job_title, COUNT(*)
  FROM Personnel
 GROUP BY dept_name
UNION ALL
SELECT CAST(NULL AS CHAR(8)) AS dept_name, job_title, COUNT(*)
  FROM Personnel
 GROUP BY job_title;
```

The above can be rewritten like this.

```
SELECT dept_name, job_title, COUNT(*)
  FROM Personnel
 GROUP BY GROUPING SET (dept_name, job_title);
```

There is a problem with all of the OLAP grouping functions. They will generate NULLs for each dimension at the subtotal levels. How do you tell the difference between a real NULL and a generated NULL? This is a job for the GROUPING() function, which returns zeros for NULLs in the original data, and ones for generated NULLs that indicate a subtotal.

```
SELECT CASE GROUPING(dept_name)
       WHEN 1 THEN 'department total'
       ELSE dept_name END AS dept_name,
```

```
       CASE GROUPING(job_title)
       WHEN 1 THEN 'job total'
       ELSE job_title_name END AS job_title
 FROM Personnel
GROUP BY GROUPING SETS (dept_name, job_title);
```

The grouping set concept can be used to define other OLAP groupings.

ROLLUP

A ROLLUP group, an extension to the GROUP BY clause in SQL-99, produces a result set that contains subtotal rows in addition to the regular grouped rows. Subtotal rows are superaggregate rows that contain further aggregates whose values are derived by applying the same column functions that were used to obtain the grouped rows. A ROLLUP grouping is a series of grouping sets.

```
GROUP BY ROLLUP (a, b, c)
```

is equivalent to:

```
GROUP BY GROUPING SETS
(a, b, c)
(a, b)
(a)
()
```

Notice that the (n) elements of the ROLLUP translate to (n+1) grouping set. Another point to remember is that the order in which the grouping expression is specified is significant for ROLLUP.

The ROLLUP is basically a classic totals and subtotals report, presented as an SQL table.

CUBES

The CUBE supergroup, the other SQL-99 extension to the GROUP BY clause, produces a result set that contains all the subtotal rows of a ROLLUP aggregation and, in addition, contains cross-tabulation rows. Cross-tabulation rows are additional superaggregate rows. As the name implies, they are summaries across columns, representing the data as if it were a spreadsheet. Like ROLLUP, a CUBE group can also be thought of as a series of grouping sets. In the case of a CUBE, all permutations of the

cubed grouping expression are computed along with the grand total. Therefore, the *n* elements of a CUBE translate to 2*n* grouping sets.

```
GROUP BY CUBE (a, b, c)

is equivalent to
GROUP BY GROUPING SETS
(a, b, c) (a, b) (a, c) (b, c) (a) (b) (c) ()
```

Notice that the three elements of the CUBE translate to eight grouping sets. Unlike ROLLUP, the order of specification of elements doesn't matter for CUBE:

```
CUBE (julian_day, sales_person) is the same as CUBE
(sales_person, julian_day).
```

CUBE is an extension of the ROLLUP function. The CUBE function not only provides the column summaries we saw in ROLLUP, but also calculates the row summaries and grand totals for the various dimensions.

Aside from these functions, the ability to define a window is equally important to the OLAP functionality of SQL. You use windows to define a set of rows over which a function is applied and the sequence in which it occurs. Another way to view the concept of a window is to equate it with the concept of a slice. In other words, a window is simply a slice of the overall data domain.

Moreover, when you use an OLAP function with a column function, such as AVG(), SUM(), MIN(),or MAX(), the target rows can be further refined relative to the current row, either as a range or as a number of rows preceding and following the current row. The point is that you can call upon the entire SQL vocabulary to combine with any of your OLAP-centric SQL statements.

31.2.4 The Window Clause

The window clause has three subclauses: partitioning, ordering, and aggregation grouping. The general format is:

```
<aggregate function> OVER (PARTITION BY <column list> ORDER BY
<sort column list> [<aggregation grouping>])
```

A set of column names specifies the partitioning, which is applied to the rows that the preceding FROM, WHERE, GROUP BY, and HAVING clauses produced. If no partitioning is specified, the entire set of rows composes a single partition, and the aggregate function applies to the whole set each time. Though the partitioning looks like a GROUP BY, it is not the same thing. A GROUP BY collapses the rows in a partition into a single row. Partitioning within a window, though, simply organizes the rows into groups without collapsing them.

The ordering within the window clause is like the ORDER BY clause in a CURSOR. It includes a list of sort keys and indicates whether they should be sorted in ascending or descending order. The important thing to understand is that ordering is applied only within each partition.

The <aggregation grouping> defines a set of rows upon which the aggregate function operates for each row in the partition. Thus, in our example, for each month, you specify the set including it and the two preceding rows. This example is from an ANSI paper on the SQL-99 features.

```
SELECT SH.region, SH.month, SH.sales,
       AVG(SH.sales)
       OVER (PARTITION BY SH.region
             ORDER BY SH.month ASC
             ROWS 2 PRECEDING)
       AS moving_average
  FROM SalesHistory AS SH
 ORDER BY SH.month ASC;
```

Here, AVG(SH.sales) OVER (PARTITION BY...) is an OLAP function. The construct inside the OVER() clause defines the window of data to which the aggregate function, AVG() in this example, is applied. In this case, the window clause says to take SalesHistory table and then apply the following operations to it:

1. Partition SalesHistory by region
2. Order the data by month within each region
3. Group each row with the two preceding rows in the same region
4. Compute the moving average on each grouping

The database engine is not required to perform the steps in the order described here, but it must produce the same result set as if they had been carried out that way.

There are two main types of aggregation groups: physical and logical. In physical grouping, you count a specified number of rows that are before or after the current row. The SalesHistory example used physical grouping. In logical grouping, you include all the data in a certain interval, defined in terms of a quantity that can be added to or subtracted from, the current sort key. For instance, you create the same group and can define it as the current month's row plus either:

1. The two preceding rows, as defined by the `ORDER` clause
2. Any row containing a month no less than two months earlier

Physical grouping works well for contiguous data and for programmers who think in terms of sequential files. Physical grouping works for a larger variety of data types than logical grouping, because it does not require operations on values.

Logical grouping works better for data that has gaps or irregularities in the ordering and for programmers who think in SQL predicates. Logical grouping works only if you can do arithmetic on the values (such as numeric quantities and dates).

31.2.5 OLAP Examples of SQL

The following example illustrates advanced OLAP function used in combination with traditional SQL. The result is a valuable SQL statement that epitomizes the power and relevance of BI at the database engine level.

In this example, we want to perform a `ROLLUP` function of sales by region and city.

```
SELECT B.region_type, S.city_id, SUM(S.sales) AS total_sales
  FROM SalesFacts AS S, MarketLookup AS M
 WHERE EXTRACT (YEAR FROM trans_date) = 1999
   AND S.city_id = B.city_id
   AND B.region_type = 6
GROUP BY ROLLUP(B.region_type, S.city_id)
ORDER BY B.region_type, S.city_id;
```

The resultant set is reduced by explicitly querying region 6 and the year 1999. A sample result of the SQL is shown in Table 1, Yearly Sales by city and region. The result shows ROLLUP of two groupings (region, city), returning three totals: region, city, and grand total.

Table 1 Yearly Sales by city and region

region_type_id	city_id	total_sales
6	1	81655
6	2	131512
6	3	58384
...	...	...
...	...	...
...	...	...
6	19	77113
6	20	55520
6	21	63647
6	22	7166
6	23	92230
...	...	...
...	...	...
6	30	1733
6	31	5058
6		1190902
		1190902

31.2.6 Enterprise-Wide Dimensional Layer

The traditional data warehouse architecture includes an atomic layer of granular data, often normalized, that serves as the only source of data for subsequent, subject-specific data marts. Generally, the data marts are implemented as Star Schemas, proprietary MOLAP cubes, or both. Establishing a layer of data marts provides an excellent foundation from which to serve up consistent, multidimensional data on an enterprise scale. But when you couple the current notion of data marts with OLAP-centric SQL functions, it is important that BI architects confirm the value added from proprietary, OLAP-only technology, specifically proprietary multidimensional database servers.

This is especially true when you consider the entire scope of relational technology currently focused on multidimensional data management, including:

- Database kernel support optimized to address multidimensional queries
- RDBMS technology, such as Materialized Query/View Tables used to improve performance
- Metadata capture and management of multidimensional structures, for example, dimensions, supported in the relational environment
- Expanded OLAPcentric SQL vocabulary, standardized for consistent application

Database-resident OLAP functions, coupled with the multidimensional solutions described above, afford the possibility of a single point of truth and efficient management of enterprise-wide traditional relational and multidimensional data requirements. This does not, perhaps, completely eliminate OLAP-only technology, but it certainly minimizes the needed investment to only true value-add.

31.3 A Bit of History

IBM and Oracle jointly proposed these extensions in early 1999, and thanks to ANSI's uncommonly rapid (and praiseworthy) actions, they are part of the SQL-99 Standard. IBM implemented portions of the specifications in DB2 UDB 6.2, which was commercially available in some forms as early as mid-1999. Oracle 8*i* version 2 and DB2 UDB 7.1, both released in late 1999, contain beefed-up implementations.

Other vendors contributed, including database tool vendors Brio, MicroStrategy, and Cognos, and database vendor Informix, among others. A team lead by Dr. Hamid Pirahesh of IBM's Almaden Research Laboratory played a particularly important role. After his team had researched the subject for about a year and come up with an approach to extending SQL in this area, he called Oracle. The companies then learned that each had independently done some significant work. With Andy Witkowski playing a pivotal role at Oracle, the two companies hammered out a joint standards proposal in about two months. Red Brick was actually the first product to implement this functionality before the standard, but in a less complete form. You can find details in the ANSI document "Introduction to OLAP Functions" by Fred Zemke, Krishna Kulkarni, Andy Witkowski, and Bob Lyle.

Transactions and Concurrency Control

IN THE OLD DAYS when we lived in caves and used mainframe computers with batch file systems, transaction processing was easy. You batched up the transactions to be made against the master file into a transaction file. The transaction file was sorted, edited, and ready to go when you ran it against the master file from a tape drive. The output of this process became the new master file, and the old master file and the transaction files were logged to magnetic tape in a huge closet in the basement of the company.

When disk drives, multiuser systems, and databases came along, things got complex—and SQL made them more so. Mercifully, the user does not have to see the details. Well, this chapter is the first layer of the details.

32.1 Sessions

The concept of a user session involves the user first connecting to the database. This is like dialing a phone number, but with a password, to get to the database. The Standard SQL syntax for this statement is:

```
CONNECT TO <connection target>

<connection target> ::=
```

```
<SQL-server name>
  [AS <connection name>]
  [USER <user name>]
| DEFAULT
```

However, you will find many differences in various vendors' SQL products and perhaps in operating system–level login procedures that have to be followed.

Once the connection is established, the user has access to all the parts of the database to which he has been granted privileges. During this session, he can execute zero or more transactions. As one user inserts, updates, and deletes rows in the database, these changes are not made a permanent part of the database until that user issues a `COMMIT WORK` command for that transaction.

However, if the user does not want to make the changes permanent, then he can issue a `ROLLBACK WORK` command, and the database stays as it was before the transaction.

32.2 Transactions and ACID

There is a handy mnemonic for the four characteristics we want in a transaction: the ACID properties. The initials are short for four properties we have to have in a transaction processing system: atomicity, consistency, isolation, and durability.

32.2.1 Atomicity

Atomicity means that either the whole transaction becomes persistent in the database or nothing in the transaction becomes persistent. The data becomes persistent in Standard SQL when a `COMMIT` statement is successfully executed. A `ROLLBACK` statement removes the transaction and the database is restored to its prior (consistent) state before the transaction began.

The `COMMIT` or `ROLLBACK` statement can be explicitly executed by the user or by the database engine when it finds an error. Most SQL engines default to a `ROLLBACK`, unless they are configured to do otherwise.

Atomicity also means that if I were to try to insert one million rows into a table, and one row of that million violated a referential constraint, then the whole set of one million rows would be rejected and the database would do an automatic `ROLLBACK WORK`.

Here is the trade-off. If you do one long transaction, then you are in danger of being screwed by just one tiny little error. However, you do several short transactions in a session, then other users can have access to the database between your transactions and they might change things, much to your surprise.

The solution has been to implement `SAVEPOINT` or `CHECKPOINT` options that act much like a bookmarker. A transaction sets savepoints during its execution, and lets the transaction perform a local rollback to the checkpoint. In our example, we might have been doing savepoints every 1,000 rows. When the 999,999th row inserted has an error that would have caused a `ROLLBACK`, the database engine removes only the work done after the last savepoint was set, and the transaction is restored to the state of uncommitted work (i.e., rows 1 thru 999,000) that existed before the last savepoint.

You will need to look at your particular product to see if it has something like this. The usual alternatives are to break the work into chunks that are run as transactions with a hot program, or to use an ETL tool that scrubs the data completely before loading it into the database.

32.2.2 Consistency

When the transaction starts, the database is in a consistent state; and when it becomes persistent in the database, the database is in a consistent state. The phrase "consistent state" means that all of the data integrity constraints, relational integrity constraints, and any other constraints are true.

However, this does not mean that the database might not go through an inconsistent state during the transaction. Standard SQL has the ability to declare a constraint to be `DEFERRABLE` or `NOT DEFERRABLE` for finer control of a transaction. But the rule is that all constraints have to be true at the end of session. This can be tricky when the transaction has multiple statements, or when it fires triggers that affect other tables.

32.2.3 Isolation

One transaction is isolated from all other transactions. Isolation is also called serializability, because it means that transactions act as if they were executed in isolation of each other. One way to guarantee isolation is to use serial execution, like we had to do in batch systems. In practice, this might not be a good idea, so the system must decide how to interleave the transactions to get the same effect.

Isolation actually becomes more complicated in practice, because one transaction may or may not actually see the data inserted, updated, or deleted by another transaction. This will be dealt with in detail in the section on isolation levels.

32.2.4 Durability

The database is stored on durable media, so that if the database program is destroyed, the database itself persists. Furthermore, the database can be restored to a consistent state when the database system is restored. Log files and backup procedures figure into this property, as well as disk writes done during processing.

This is all well and good if you have just one user accessing the database at a time. But one of the reasons you have a database system is that you also have multiple users who want to access it at the same time in their own sessions. This leads us to concurrency control.

32.3 Concurrency Control

Concurrency control is the part of transaction handling that deals with the way multiple users access the shared database without running into each other—like a traffic light system. One way to avoid any problems is to allow only one user in the database at a time. The only problem with that solution is that the other users are going to get lousy response time. Can you seriously imagine doing that with a bank teller machine system or an airline reservation system, where tens of thousands of users are waiting to get into the system at the same time?

32.3.1 The Five Phenomena

If all you do is execute queries against the database, then the ACID properties hold. The trouble occurs when two or more transactions want to change the database at the same time. In the SQL model, there are five ways that one transaction can affect another:

- *P0 ("Dirty Write")*: Transaction T1 modifies a data item. Another transaction, T2, then further modifies that data item before T1 performs a `COMMIT` or `ROLLBACK`. If T1 or T2 then performs a `ROLLBACK`, it is unclear what the correct data value should be. One reason dirty writes are bad is that they can violate database consistency. Assume there is a constraint between x and y (e.g., $x = y$), and T1 and T2 each maintain the consistency of the constraint if run alone. However, the constraint can easily be violated if the two transactions write *x* and *y* in different orders, which can only happen if there are dirty writes.

- *P1 ("Dirty Read")*: Transaction T1 modifies a row. Transaction T2 then reads that row before T1 performs a `COMMIT WORK`. If T1 then performs a `ROLLBACK WORK`, T2 will have read a row that was never committed, and that may thus be considered to have never existed.
- *P2 ("Nonrepeatable Read")*: Transaction T1 reads a row. Transaction T2 then modifies or deletes that row and performs a `COMMIT WORK`. If T1 then attempts to reread the row, it may receive the modified value or discover that the row has been deleted.
- *P3 ("Phantom")*: Transaction T1 reads the set of rows N that satisfy some `<search condition>`. Transaction T2 then executes statements that generate one or more rows that satisfy the `<search condition>` used by transaction T1. If transaction T1 then repeats the initial read with the same `<search condition>`, it obtains a different collection of rows.)
- *P4 ("Lost Update")*: The lost update anomaly occurs when transaction T1 reads a data item and then T2 updates the data item (possibly based on a previous read), then T1 (based on its earlier read value) updates the data item and `COMMIT`s.

These phenomena are not always bad things. If the database is being used only for queries, without any changes being made during the workday, then none of these problems will occur. The database system will run much faster if you do not have to try to protect yourself from them. They are also acceptable when changes are being made under certain circumstances.

Imagine that I have a table of all the cars in the world. I want to execute a query to find the average age of drivers of red sport cars. This query will take some time to run and during that time, cars will be crashed, bought and sold, new cars will be built, and so forth. But I accept a situation with the five phenomena listed above, because the average age of the information will not change that much from the time I start the query to the time it finishes. Changes after the second decimal place really don't matter.

However, you don't want any of these phenomena to occur in a database where the husband makes a deposit to a joint account and his wife makes a withdrawal. This leads us to the transaction isolation levels.

The original ANSI model included only P1, P2, and P3. The other definitions first appeared in Microsoft Research Technical Report: MSR-TR-95-51 "A Critique of ANSI SQL Isolation Levels" by Hal Berenson, Phil Bernstein, Jim Gray, Jim Melton, Elizabeth O'Neil, and Patrick O'Neil (1995).

32.3.2 The Isolation Levels

In standard SQL, the user gets to set the isolation level of the transactions in his session. The isolation level avoids some of the phenomena we just talked about and gives other information to the database. The syntax for the `<set transaction statement>` is as follows.

```
SET TRANSACTION <transaction mode list>

<transaction mode> ::=
   <isolation level>
 | <transaction access mode>
 | <diagnostics size>

<diagnostics size> ::= DIAGNOSTICS SIZE <number of conditions

<transaction access mode> ::= READ ONLY | READ WRITE

<isolation level> ::= ISOLATION LEVEL <level of isolation>

<level of isolation> ::=
   READ UNCOMMITTED
 | READ COMMITTED
 | REPEATABLE READ
 | SERIALIZABLE
```

The optional `<diagnostics size>` clause tells the database to set up a list for error messages of a given size. This is a Standard SQL feature, so you might not have it in your particular product. The reason is that a single statement can have several errors in it, and the engine is supposed to find them all and report them in the diagnostics area via a `GET DIAGNOSTICS` statement in the host program.

The <transaction access mode> explains itself. The READ ONLY option means that this is a query and lets the SQL engine know that it can relax a bit. The READ WRITE option lets the SQL engine know that rows might be changed, and that it has to watch out for the five phenomena.

The important clause, which is implemented in most current SQL products, is the <isolation level> clause. The isolation level of a transaction defines the degree to which the operations of one transaction are affected by concurrent transactions. The isolation level of a transaction is SERIALIZABLE by default, but the user can explicitly set it in the <set transaction statement>.

The isolation levels each guarantee that each transaction will be executed completely or not at all, and that no updates will be lost. When the SQL engine detects the inability to guarantee the serializability of two or more concurrent transactions or detects unrecoverable errors, it may initiate a ROLLBACK WORK statement on its own.

Let's take a look at a table (Table 32.1) of the isolation levels and the initial three phenomena (P1, P2, and P3). A "Yes" means that the phenomena are possible under that isolation level:

Table 32.1 *Isolation Levels and the Initial Three Phenomena*

```
Isolation Levels and the Three Phenomena
Isolation Level        P1       P2      P3
==========================================
SERIALIZABLE            No       No      No
REPEATABLE READ         No       No     Yes
READ COMMITTED          No      Yes     Yes
READ UNCOMMITTED       Yes      Yes     Yes
```

The SERIALIZABLE isolation level is guaranteed to produce the same results that the concurrent transactions would have, if they had been done in some serial order. A serial execution is one in which each transaction executes to completion before the next transaction begins. The users act as if they are standing in a line waiting to get complete access to the database.

A REPEATABLE READ isolation level is guaranteed to maintain the same image of the database to the user during his session.

A READ COMMITTED isolation level will let transactions in this session see rows that other transactions commit while this session is running.

A READ UNCOMMITTED isolation level will let transactions in this session see rows that other transactions create without necessarily committing while this session is running.

Regardless of the isolation level of the transaction, phenomena P1, P2, and P3 shall not occur during the implied reading of schema definitions performed on behalf of executing a statement, the checking of integrity constraints, and the execution of referential actions associated with referential constraints. We do not want the schema itself changing on users.

32.3.3 CURSOR STABILITY Isolation Level

The CURSOR STABILITY isolation level extends READ COMMITTED locking behavior for SQL cursors by adding a new read action for FETCH from a cursor and requiring that a lock be held on the current item of the cursor. The lock is held until the cursor moves or is closed, possibly by a commit. Naturally, the fetching transaction can update the row, and in that case a write lock will be held on the row until the transaction COMMITs, even after the cursor moves on with a subsequent FETCH. This makes CURSOR STABILITY stronger than READ COMMITTED and weaker than REPEATABLE READ.

CURSOR STABILITY is widely implemented by SQL systems to prevent lost updates for rows read via a cursor. READ COMMITTED, in some systems, is actually the stronger cursor stability. The ANSI standard allows this.

The SQL standards do not say *how* you are to achieve these results. However, there are two basic classes of concurrency control methods—optimistic and pessimistic. Within those two classes, each vendor will have his own implementation.

32.4 Pessimistic Concurrency Control

Pessimistic concurrency control is based on the idea that transactions are expected to conflict with each other, so we need to design a system to avoid the problems before they start.

All pessimistic concurrency control schemes use locks. A lock is a flag placed in the database that gives exclusive access to a schema object to one user. Imagine an airplane toilet door, with its “occupied” sign.

The differences are the level of locking they use; setting those flags on and off costs time and resources. If you lock the whole database, then you will have, in effect, a serial batch processing system, since only one transaction at a time is active. In practice, you would do this only for system maintenance work on the whole database. If you lock at the table level, performance can suffer because users must wait for the most common tables to become available. However, there are transactions that do involve the whole table and this lock level will use only one flag.

If you lock the table at the row level, then other users can get to the rest of the table and you will have the best possible shared access. You will also have a huge number of flags to process, and performance will suffer. This approach is generally not practical.

Page locking is in between table and row locking. This approach puts a lock on subsets of rows within the table that include the desired values. The name comes from the fact that this lock level is usually implemented with pages of physical disk storage. Performance depends on the statistical distribution of data in physical storage, but it is generally a good compromise.

32.5 SNAPSHOT Isolation: Optimistic Concurrency

Optimistic concurrency control is based on the idea that transactions are not very likely to conflict with each other, so we need to design a system to handle the problems as exceptions after they actually occur.

In Snapshot Isolation, each transaction reads data from a snapshot of the (committed) data as of the time the transaction started, called its Start_timestamp. This time may be any time before the transaction's first read. A transaction running in Snapshot Isolation is never blocked attempting a read because it is working on its private copy of the data. But this means that at any time, each data item might have multiple versions, created by active and committed transactions.

When the transaction T1 is ready to commit, it gets a commit_timestamp, which is later than any existing start_timestamp or commit_timestamp. The transaction successfully `COMMIT`s only if no other transaction T2 with a commit_timestamp in T1's execution interval [start_timestamp, commit_timestamp] wrote data that T1 also wrote. Otherwise, T1 will `ROLLBACK`. This "first committer wins" strategy prevents lost updates (phenomenon P4). When T1 `COMMIT`s, its changes become visible to all transactions whose start_timestamps are larger than T1's commit-timestamp.

Snapshot isolation is nonserializable because a transaction's reads come at one instant and the writes at another. We assume we have several transactions working on the same data and a constraint that $(x + y)$ should be positive. Each transaction that writes a new value for x and y is expected to maintain the constraint. While T1 and T2 both act

properly in isolation, the constraint fails to hold when you put them together. The possible problems are:

- *A5 (Data Item Constraint Violation)*: Suppose constraint C is a database constraint between two data items, *x* and *y*, in the database. Here are two anomalies arising from constraint violation:
  - *A5A (Read Skew)*: Suppose transaction T1 reads *x*, and then a second transaction T2 updates *x* and *y* to new values and COMMITs. Now, if T1 reads *y*, it may see an inconsistent state, and therefore produce an inconsistent state as output.
  - *Fuzzy Reads (P2)*: This problem is a degenerate form of Read Skew where $x = y$. More typically, a transaction reads two different but related items (e.g., referential integrity).
- *A5B (Write Skew)*: Suppose T1 reads *x* and *y*, which are consistent with constraint C, and then a T2 reads *x* and *y*, writes *x*, and COMMITs. Then T1 writes *y*. If there were a constraint between *x* and *y*, it might be violated. As an example, consider a constraint at a bank, where account balances are allowed to go negative as long as the sum of commonly held balances remains nonnegative, with an anomaly arising as in history H5.

Clearly, neither A5A nor A5B could arise in histories where P2 is precluded, since both A5A and A5B have T2 write a data item that has been previously read by an uncommitted T1. Thus, phenomena A5A and A5B are only useful for distinguishing isolation levels below REPEATABLE READ in strength.

The ANSI SQL definition of REPEATABLE READ, in its strictest interpretation, captures a degenerate form of row constraints, but misses the general concept. To be specific, locking REPEATABLE READ on Table 2 provides protection from row constraint violations, but the ANSI SQL definition of Table 1, forbidding anomalies A1 and A2, does not.

Snapshot Isolation, however, is surprisingly strong, even stronger than READ COMMITTED.

This approach predates databases by decades. It was implemented manually in the central records department of companies when they started storing data on microfilm. You do not get the actual microfilm; instead, they make a timestamped photocopy for you. You take the copy to your desk, mark it up, and return it to the central records department. The Central Records clerk timestamps your updated document, photographs it and adds it to the end of the roll of microfilm.

But what if user number two also went to the central records department and got a timestamped photocopy of the same document? The Central Records clerk has to look at both timestamps and make a decision. If the first user attempts to put his updates into the database while the second user is still working on his copy, then the clerk has to either hold the first copy or wait for the second copy to show up or to return it to the first user. When both copies are in hand, the clerk stacks the copies on top of each other, holds them up to the light and looks to see if there are any conflicts. If both updates can be made to the database, he does so. If there are conflicts, he must either have rules for resolving the problems or he has to reject both transactions. This is a kind of row-level locking, done after the fact.

32.6 Logical Concurrency Control

Logical concurrency control is based on the idea that the machine can analyze the predicates in the queue of waiting queries and processes on a purely logical level, and then determine which of the statements can be allowed to operate on the database at the same time.

Clearly, all `SELECT` statements can operate at the same time, since they do not change the data. After that, it is tricky to determine which statements conflict with the others. For example, one pair of `UPDATE` statements on two separate tables might be allowed only in a certain order because of `PRIMARY KEY` and `FOREIGN KEY` constraints. Another of pair of `UPDATE` statements on the same tables might be disallowed because they modify the same rows and leave different final states in them.

However, a third pair of `UPDATE` statements on the same tables might be allowed because they modify different rows and have no conflicts with each other.

There is also the problem of having statements waiting too long in the queue to be executed. This is a version of livelock, which we discuss in the next section. The usual solution is to assign a priority number to each waiting transaction and then decrement that priority number when they have been waiting for a certain length of time. Eventually, every transaction will arrive at priority one and be able to go ahead of any other transaction.

This approach also allows you to enter transactions at a higher priority than the transactions in the queue. While it is possible to create a livelock this way, it is not a problem and it lets you bump less important jobs in favor of more important jobs, such as payroll checks.

32.7 Deadlock and Livelocks

It is possible for a user to fail to complete a transaction for reasons other than the hardware failing. A deadlock is a situation where two or more users hold resources that the others need and neither party will surrender the objects to which they have locks. To make this more concrete, imagine that both user A and user B need tables X and Y. User A gets a lock on table X, and User B gets a lock on table Y. They both sit and wait for their missing resource to become available; it never happens. The common solution for a deadlock is for the DBA to kill one or more of the sessions involved and rollback their work.

In a livelock, a user is waiting for a resource, but never gets it because other users keep grabbing it before he gets a chance. None of the other users hold onto the resource permanently, as in a deadlock, but as a group they never free it. To make this more concrete, imagine user A needs all of table X. But a hundred other users are always updating table X, so that user A cannot find a page without a lock on in it the table. He sits and waits for all the pages to become available; it never happens in time.

The DBA can, again, kill one or more of the sessions involved and rollback their work. In some systems, he can raise the priority of the livelocked session so that it can seize the resources as they become available.

None of this is trivial, and each database system will have its own version of transaction processing and concurrency control. This should not be of great concern to the applications programmer, but should be the responsibility of the DBA. But it is nice to know what happens under the covers.

Optimizing SQL

THERE IS NO SET of rules for writing code that will take the best advantage of every query optimizer on every SQL product. The query optimizers depend on the underlying architecture and are simply too different for universal rules; however, we can make some general statements. Just remember that you have to test code. What would improve performance in one SQL implementation might have no effect in another or make the performance worse.

There are two kinds of optimizers: cost-based and rule-based. A rule-based optimizer (such as Oracle before version 7.0) looks at the syntax of the query and plans how to execute the query without considering the size of the tables or the statistical distribution of the data. It will parse a query and execute it in the order in which it was written, perhaps doing some reorganization of the query into an equivalent form using some syntax rules. Basically, it is no optimizer at all.

A cost-based optimizer looks at both the query and the statistical data about the database itself before deciding the best way to execute the query. These decisions involve whether to use indexes, whether to use hashing, which tables to bring into main storage, what sorting technique to use, and so forth. Most of the time (but not all!), it will make better decisions than a human programmer would have, simply because it has more information.

CA-Ingres has one of the best optimizers, which extensively reorders a query before executing it. It is one of the few products that can find most semantically identical queries and reduce them to the same internal form.

Rdb, a DEC product that now belongs to Oracle, uses a searching method taken from an AI (artificial intelligence) game-playing program to inspect the costs of several different approaches before making a decision. DB2 has a system table with a statistical profile of the base tables.

In short, no two products use exactly the same optimization techniques.

The fact that each SQL engine uses a different internal storage scheme and access methods for its data makes some optimizations nonportable. Likewise, some optimizations depend on the hardware configuration, and a technique that was excellent for one product on a single hardware configuration could be a disaster in another product, or on another hardware configuration with the same product.

33.1 Access Methods

For this discussion, let us assume that there are four basic methods of getting to data: table scans or sequential reads of all the rows in the table, access via some kind of index, hashing, and bit vector indexes.

33.1.1 Sequential Access

The table scan is a sequential read of all the data in the order in which it appears in physical storage, grabbing one page of memory at a time. Most databases do not physically remove deleted rows, so a table can use a lot of physical space and yet hold little data. Depending on just how dynamic the database is, you may want to run a utility program to reclaim storage and compress the database. Performance can improve suddenly and drastically after database reorganization.

33.1.2 Indexed Access

Indexed access returns one row at a time. The index is probably going to be a B-Tree of some sort, but it could be a hashed index, inverted file structures, or another format. Obviously, if you do not have an index on a table, then you cannot use indexed access on it.

An index can be clustered or unclustered. A clustered index has a table that is in sorted order in the physical storage. Obviously, there can be only one clustered index on a table. Clustered indexes keep the table in sorted order, so a table scan will often produce results in that order. A clustered index will also tend to put duplicates of the indexed column values on the same page of physical memory, which may speed up aggregate functions. (A side note: "clustered" in this sense is a Sybase/ SQL Server term; Oracle uses the same word to mean a single data page that contains matching rows from multiple tables.)

33.1.3 Hashed Indexes

Writing hashing functions is not easy. The idea is that, given input values, the hashing function will return a physical storage address. If two or more values have the same hash value ("hash clash" or "collision"), then they are put into the same "bucket" in the hash table, or they are run through a second hashing function.

If the index is on a unique column, the ideal situation is a "minimal perfect" hashing function—each value hashes to a unique physical storage address, and there are no empty spaces in the hash table. The next best situation for a unique column is a "perfect" hashing function—every value hashes to one physical storage address without collisions, but there are some empty spaces in the physical hash table storage.

A hashing function for a nonunique column should hash to a bucket small enough to fit into main storage. In the Teradata SQL engine, which is based on hashing, any row can be found in at most two probes, and 90% or more of the accesses require only one probe.

33.1.4 Bit Vector Indexes

The fact that a particular occurrence of an entity has a particular value for a particular attribute is represented as a single bit in a vector or array. Predicates are handled by doing Boolean bit operations on the arrays. These techniques are very fast for large amounts of data and are used by the Nucleus database engine from Sand Technology and Foxpro's Rushmore indexes.

33.2 Expressions and Unnested Queries

Despite the fact that this book is devoted to fancy queries and programming tricks, the truth is that most real work is done with very simple logic. The better the design of the database schema, the easier the queries will be to write.

Here are some tips for keeping your query as simple as possible. Like all general statements, these tips will not be valid for all products in all situations, but they are how the smart money bets. In fairness, most optimizers are smart enough to do many of these things internally today.

33.2.1 Use Simple Expressions

Where possible, avoid JOIN conditions in favor of simple search arguments, called SARGs in the jargon. For example, let's match up students with rides back to Atlanta from a student ride share database.

```
SELECT *
  FROM Students AS S1, Rides AS R1
 WHERE S1.town = R1.town
   AND S1.town = 'Atlanta';
```

Clearly, a little algebra shows you that this is true:

```
SELECT *
  FROM Students AS S1, Rides AS R1
 WHERE R1.town = 'Atlanta'
   AND S1.town = 'Atlanta';
```

However, the second version will guarantee that the two tables involved will be projected to the smallest size, then the CROSS JOIN will be done. Since each of these projections should be fairly small, the JOIN will not be expensive.

Assume that there are ten students out of one hundred going to Atlanta, and five out of one hundred people offering rides to Atlanta. If the JOIN is done first, you would have (100 * 100) = 10,000 rows in the CROSS JOIN to prune with the predicates. This is why no product does the CROSS JOIN first. Instead, many products would do the (S1.town = 'Atlanta') predicate first and get a working table of ten rows to JOIN to the Rides table, which would give us (10 * 100) = 1,000 rows for the CROSS JOIN to prune.

But in the second version, we would have a working table of ten students and another working table of five rides to CROSS JOIN, or merely (5 * 10) rows in the result set.

Another rule of thumb is that, when given a chain of ANDed predicates that test for constant values, the most restrictive ones should be put first. For example,

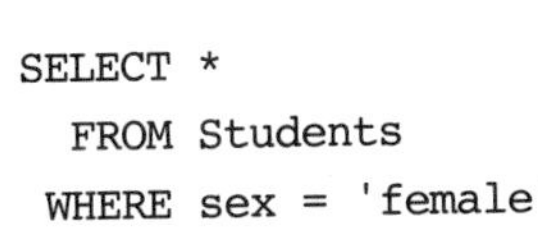

```
SELECT *
  FROM Students
 WHERE sex = 'female'
   AND grade = 'A';
```

That query will probably run slower than the following:

```
SELECT *
  FROM Students
 WHERE grade = 'A'
   AND sex = 'female';
```

because there are fewer 'A' students than number of female students. There are several ways that this query will be executed:

1. Assuming an index on grades, fetch a row from the Students table where grade = 'A'; if sex = 'female' then put it into the final results. The index on grades is called the driving index of the loop through the Students table.
2. Assuming an index on sex, fetch a row from the Students table where sex = 'female'; if grade = 'A' then put it into the final results. The index on sex is now the driving index of the loop through the Students table.
3. Assuming indexing on both, scan the index on sex and put pointers to the rows where sex = 'female' into results working file R1. Scan the index on grades and put pointers to the rows where grade = 'A' into results file R2. Sort and merge R1 and R2, keeping the pointers that appear twice. Use this result to fetch the rows into the final result.

If the hardware can support parallel access, this can be quite fast.

Another application of the same principle is a trick with predicates that involves two columns to force the choice of the index that will be used. Place the table with the smallest number of rows last in the `FROM` clause, and place the expression that uses that table first in the `WHERE` clause. For example, consider two tables, a larger one for orders and a smaller one that translates a code number into English, each with an index on the `JOIN` column:

```
SELECT *
  FROM Orders AS O1, Codes AS C1
 WHERE C1.code = O1.code;
```

This query will probably use a strategy of merging the index values. However, if you add a dummy expression, you can force a loop over the index on the smaller table. For example, assume that all the order type codes are greater than or equal to '00' in our code translation example, so that the first predicate of this query is always `TRUE`:

```
SELECT *
  FROM Orders AS O1, Codes AS C1
 WHERE O1.ordertype >= '00'
   AND C1.somecode = O1.ordertype;
```

The dummy predicate will force the SQL engine to use an index on Orders. This same trick can also be used to force the sorting in an `ORDER BY` clause of a cursor to be done with an index.

Since SQL is not a computational language, implementations do not tend to do even simple algebra:

```
SELECT *
  FROM Sales
 WHERE quantity = 500 + 1/2;
```

This query is the same thing as `quantity = 500.50`, but some dynamic SQLs will take a little extra time to compute and add a half as they check each row of the Sales table. The extra time adds up when the expression involves complex math and/or type conversions. However, this can have another effect that we will discuss in Section 33.8 on expressions that contain indexed columns.

The <> comparison has some unique problems. Most optimizers assume that this comparison will return more rows than it rejects, so they prefer a sequential scan and will not use an index on a column involved in such a comparison. This is not always true, however. For example, to find someone in Ireland who is not a Catholic, you would normally write:

```
SELECT *
  FROM Ireland
 WHERE religion <> 'Catholic';
```

The way around this is to break up the inequality and force the use of an index:

```
SELECT *
  FROM Ireland
 WHERE religion < 'Catholic'
    OR religion > 'Catholic';
```

However, without an index on religion, the ORed version of the predicate could take longer to run.

Another trick is to avoid the x IS NOT NULL predicate and use x >= <minimal constant> instead. The NULLs are kept in different ways in different implementations, but almost never in the same physical storage area as their columns. As a result, the SQL engine has to do extra searching. For example, if we have a CHAR(3) column that holds a NULL or three letters, we could look for missing data with:

```
SELECT *
  FROM Sales
 WHERE alphacode IS NOT NULL;
```

However, it would be better written as:

```
SELECT *
  FROM Sales
 WHERE alphacode >= 'AAA';
```

That syntax avoids the extra reads.

Another trick that often works is to use an index to get a COUNT(), since the index itself may have the number of rows already worked out. For example,

```
SELECT COUNT(*)
  FROM Sales;
```

might not be as fast as:

```
SELECT COUNT(invoice_nbr)
  FROM Sales;
```

where invoice_nbr is the PRIMARY KEY (or any other unique non-**NULL** column) of the Sales table. Being the PRIMARY KEY means that there is a unique index on invoice_nbr. A smart optimizer knows to look for indexed columns automatically when it sees a COUNT(*), but it is worth testing on your product.

33.2.2 String Expressions

Likewise, string expressions can be recalculated each time. A particular problem for strings is that the optimizer will often stop at the '%' or '_' in the pattern of a LIKE predicate, resulting in a string it cannot use with an index. For example, consider this table with a fixed length CHAR(5) column:

```
SELECT *
  FROM Students
 WHERE homeroom LIKE 'A-1__'; -- two underscores in pattern
```

This query may or may not use an index on the homeroom column. However, if we know that the last two positions are always numerals, we can replace this query with:

```
SELECT *
  FROM Students
 WHERE homeroom BETWEEN 'A-100' AND 'A-199';
```

This query can use an index on the homeroom column. Notice that this trick assumes that the homeroom column is CHAR(5), and not a VARCHAR(5) column. If it were VARCHAR(5), then the second query would pick 'A-1', while the original LIKE predicate would not. String equality and BETWEEN predicates pad the shorter string with blanks on the right before comparing them; the LIKE predicate does not pad either the string or the pattern.

33.3 Give Extra Join Information in Queries

Optimizers are not always able to draw conclusions that a human being can draw. The more information contained in the query, the better the chance that the optimizer will be able to find an improved execution plan. For example, to JOIN three tables together on a common column, you might write:

```
SELECT *
  FROM Table1, Table2, Table3
 WHERE Table2.common = Table3.common
   AND Table3.common = Table1.common;
```

Alternately, you might write:

```
SELECT *
  FROM Table1, Table2, Table3
 WHERE Table1.common = Table2.common
   AND Table1.common = Table3.common;
```

Some optimizers will JOIN pairs of tables based on the equi-JOIN conditions in the WHERE clause in the order in which they appear. Let us assume that Table1 is a very small table and that Table2 and Table3 are large. In the first query, doing the Table2–Table3 JOIN first will return a large result set, which is then pruned by the Table1–Table3 JOIN. In the second query, doing the Table1–Table2 JOIN first will return a small result set, which is then matched to the small Table1–Table3 JOIN result set.

The best bet, however, is to provide all the information so that the optimizer can decide when the table sizes change.

This leads to redundancy in the WHERE clause:

```
SELECT *
  FROM Table1, Table2, Table3
 WHERE Table1.common = Table2.common
   AND Table2.common = Table3.common
   AND Table3.common = Table1.common;
```

Do not confuse this redundancy with needless logical expressions that will be recalculated and can be expensive. For example,

```
SELECT *
  FROM Sales
 WHERE alphacode BETWEEN 'AAA' AND 'ZZZ'
   AND alphacode LIKE 'A_C';
```

will redo the BETWEEN predicate for every row. It does not provide any information that can be used for a JOIN, and, very clearly, if the LIKE predicate is TRUE, then the BETWEEN predicate also has to be TRUE.

A final tip, which is not always true, is to order the tables with the fewest rows in the result set last in the FROM clause. This is helpful because as the number of tables increases, many optimizers do not try all the combinations of possible JOIN orderings; the number of combinations is factorial. So the optimizer falls back on the order in the FROM clause.

33.4 Index Tables Carefully

You should create indexes on the tables of your database to optimize your query search time, but do not create any more indexes than are absolutely needed. Indexes have to be updated and possibly reorganized when you INSERT, UPDATE, or DELETE a row in a table.

Too many indexes can result in extra time spent tending indexes that are seldom used. But even worse, the presence of an index can fool the optimizer into using it when it should not. For example, let's look at the following simple query:

```
SELECT *
  FROM Warehouse
 WHERE quantity = 500
   AND color = 'Purply Green';
```

With an index on color, but not on quantity, most optimizers will first search for rows with color = 'Purply Green' via the index, then apply the quantity = 500 test. However, if you were to add an index on quantity, the optimizer would likely take the tests in order, doing the quantity test first. I assume that very few items are 'Purply Green', so it would have been better to test for color first. A smart optimizer with detailed statistics would do this right, but to play it safe, order the predicates from the most restricting (i.e., the smallest number of qualifying rows in the final result) to the least.

An index will not be used if the column is in an expression. If you want to avoid an index, then put the column in a "do nothing" expression, such as the following examples:

```
SELECT *
  FROM Warehouse
 WHERE quantity = 500 + 0
   AND color = 'Purply Green';
```

or

```
SELECT *
  FROM Warehouse
 WHERE quantity + 0 = 500
   AND color = 'Purply Green';
```

This will stop the optimizer from using an index on quantity. Likewise, the expression (`color || = 'Purply Green'`) will avoid the index on color.

Consider an actual example of indexes making trouble, in a database for a small club membership list that was indexed on the members' names as the `PRIMARY KEY`. There was a column in the table that had one of five status codes (paid member, free membership, expired, exchange newsletter, and miscellaneous).

The report query on the number of people by status was:

```
SELECT M1.status, C1.code_text, COUNT(*)
  FROM Members AS M1, Codes AS C1
 WHERE M1.status = C1.status
 GROUP BY M1.status, C1.code_text;
```

In an early PC SQL database product, it ran an order of magnitude slower with an index on the status column than without one. The optimizer saw the index on the Members table and used it to search for each status code text. Without the index, the much smaller Codes table was brought into main storage and five buckets were set up for the `COUNT(*)`; then the Members table was read once in sequence. An index used to ensure uniqueness on a column or set of columns is called a primary index; those used to speed up queries on nonunique column(s) are called secondary. SQL implementations automatically create a primary index on a `PRIMARY KEY` or `UNIQUE` constraint. Implementations may or may not create indexes that link `FOREIGN KEY`s within the table to their targets in the referenced table. This link can be very important, since a lot of `JOIN`s are done from `FOREIGN KEY` to `PRIMARY KEY`.

You also need to know something about the queries to run against the schema. Obviously, if all queries are asked on only one column, then that is all you need to index. The query information is usually given as a statistical model of the expected inputs. For example, you might be told

that 80% of the queries will use the PRIMARY KEY and 20% will use another (near-random) column.

This is pretty much what you would know in a real-world situation, since most of the accessing will be done by production programs with embedded SQL in them; only a small percentage will be *ad hoc* queries.

Without giving you a computer science lecture, a computer problem is called NP-complete if it gets so big, so fast, that it is not practical to solve it for a reasonable-sized set of input values.

Usually this means that you have to try all possible combinations to find the answer. Finding the optimal indexing arrangement is known to be NP-complete (Comer 1978; Paitetsky-Shapiro 1983). This does not mean that you cannot optimize indexing for a particular database schema and set of input queries, but it does mean that you cannot write a program that will do it for all possible relational databases and query sets.

33.5 Watch the IN Predicate

The IN predicate is really shorthand for a series of ORed equality tests. There are two forms: either an explicit list of values is given, or a subquery is used to make such a list of values.

The database engine has no statistics about the relative frequency of the values in a list of constants, so it will assume that the list is in the order in which the values are to be used. People like to order lists alphabetically or by magnitude, but it would be better to order the list from most frequently occurring values to least frequently occurring. It is also pointless to have duplicate values in the constant list, since the predicate will return TRUE if it matches the first duplicate it finds and will never get to the second occurrence. Likewise, if the predicate is FALSE for that value, the program wastes computer time traversing a needlessly long list.

Many SQL engines perform an IN predicate with a subquery by building the result set of the subquery first as a temporary working table, then scanning that result table from left to right. This can be expensive in many cases. For example, the following query:

```
SELECT P1.*
  FROM Personnel AS P1, BowlingTeam AS B1
 WHERE P1.last_name IN (SELECT last_name
                          FROM BowlingTeam AS B1
                         WHERE P1.emp_nbr = B1.emp_nbr)
   AND P1.last_name IN (SELECT last_name
```

```
             FROM BowlingTeam AS B2
            WHERE P1.emp_nbr = B2.emp_nbr);
```

will not run as fast as:

```
SELECT *
  FROM Personnel AS P1
 WHERE first_name || last_name IN
       (SELECT first_name || last_name
          FROM BowlingTeam AS B1
         WHERE P1.emp_nbr = B1.emp_nbr);
```

which can be further simplified to:

```
SELECT P1.*
  FROM Personnel AS P1
 WHERE first_name || last_name IN
       (SELECT first_name || last_name
          FROM BowlingTeam);
```

or, using Standard SQL row constructors, can be simplified to:

```
SELECT P1.*
  FROM Personnel AS P1
 WHERE (first_name, last_name) IN
       (SELECT first_name, last_name
          FROM BowlingTeam);
```

since there can be only one row with a complete name in it.

The first version of the query may make two passes through the Bowling Team table to construct two separate result tables. The second version makes only one pass to construct the concatenation of the names in its result table.

The optimizer is supposed to figure out when two queries are the same, and it will not be fooled by two queries with the same meaning and different syntax. For example, the SQL standard defines the following two queries as identical:

```
SELECT *
  FROM Warehouse AS W1
 WHERE quantity IN (SELECT quantity FROM Sales);
```

```
SELECT *
  FROM Warehouse
 WHERE quantity = ANY (SELECT quantity FROM Sales);
```

However, you will find that some older SQL engines prefer the first version to the second, because they do not convert the expressions into a common internal form. Very often, things like the choice of operators and their order make a large performance difference.

The first query can be converted to this "flattened" JOIN query:

```
SELECT W1.*
  FROM Warehouse AS W1, Sales AS S1
 WHERE W1.qty_on_hand = S1.qty_sold;
```

This form will often be faster if there are indexes to help with the JOIN.

33.6 Avoid UNIONs

A UNION is often implemented by constructing the two result sets, then merge-sorting them together. The optimizer works only within a single SELECT statement or subquery. For example:

```
SELECT *
  FROM Personnel
 WHERE work = 'New York'
UNION
SELECT *
  FROM Personnel
 WHERE home = 'Chicago';
```

is the same as:

```
SELECT DISTINCT *
  FROM Personnel
 WHERE work = 'New York'
    OR home = 'Chicago';
```

The second will run faster.

Another trick is to use UNION ALL in place of UNION whenever duplicates are not a problem. The UNION ALL is implemented as an append operation, without the need for a sort to aid duplicate removal.

33.7 Prefer Joins over Nested Queries

A nested query is hard to optimize. Optimizers try to "flatten" nested queries so they can be expressed as JOINs and the best order of execution can be determined. Consider the database:

```
CREATE TABLE Authors
(author_nbr INTEGER NOT NULL PRIMARY KEY,
 authorname CHAR(50) NOT NULL);

CREATE TABLE Titles
(isbn CHAR(10)NOT NULL PRIMARY KEY,
 title CHAR(50) NOT NULL
 advance_amt DECIMAL(8,2) NOT NULL);

CREATE TABLE TitleAuthors
(author_nbr INTEGER NOT NULL REFERENCES Authors(author_nbr),
 isbn CHAR(10)NOT NULL REFERENCES Titles(isbn),
 royalty_rate DECIMAL(5,4) NOT NULL,
 PRIMARY KEY (author_nbr, isbn));
```

This query finds authors who are getting less than 50% royalties:

```
SELECT author_nbr
  FROM Authors
 WHERE author_nbr
       IN (SELECT author_nbr
             FROM TitleAuthors
             WHERE royalty < 0.50)
```

This query could also be expressed as:

```
SELECT DISTINCT Authors.author_nbr
  FROM Authors, TitleAuthors
 WHERE (Authors.author_nbr = TitleAuthors.author_nbr)
   AND (royalty_rate < 0.50);
```

The SELECT DISTINCT is important. Each author's name will occur only once in the Authors table. Therefore, the IN predicate query should return one occurrence of O'Leary. Assume that O'Leary wrote two books;

with just a SELECT, the second query would return two O'Leary rows, one for each book.

33.8 Avoid Expressions on Indexed Columns

If a column appears in a mathematical or string expression, then the optimizer cannot use its indexes. For example, given a table of tasks and their start and finish dates, to find the tasks that took three days to complete in 1994 we could write:

```
SELECT task_nbr
  FROM Tasks
 WHERE (finish_date - start_date) = INTERVAL '3' DAY
   AND start_date >= CAST ('2005-01-01' AS DATE);
```

But since most of the reports deal with the finish dates, we have an index on that column. This means that the query will run faster if it is rewritten as:

```
SELECT task_nbr
  FROM Tasks
 WHERE finish_date = (start_date + INTERVAL '3' DAY)
  AND start_date >= ('2005-01-01' AS DATE);
```

This same principle applies to columns in string functions and, very often, to LIKE predicates.

However, this can be a good thing for queries with small tables, since it will force those tables to be loaded into main storage instead of being searched by index.

33.9 Avoid Sorting

The SELECT DISTINCT and ORDER BY clauses usually cause a sort in most SQL products, so avoid them unless you really need them. Use them if you need to remove duplicates or if you need to guarantee a particular result set order explicitly. In the case of a small result set, the time to sort it can be longer than the time to process redundant duplicates.

The UNION, INTERSECT, and EXCEPT clauses can do sorts to remove duplicates; the exception is when an index exists that can be used to eliminate the duplicates without sorting. In particular, the UNION ALL will tend to be faster than the plain UNION, so if you have no duplicates or do not mind having them, then use it instead. There are not enough implementations of `INTERSECT ALL` and `EXCEPT ALL` to make a generalization yet.

The `GROUP BY` often uses a sort to cluster groups together, does the aggregate functions, and then reduces each group to a single row based on duplicates in the grouping columns. Each sort will cost you (n*log2(n)) operations. That is a lot of extra computer time that you can save if you do not need to use these clauses.

If a `SELECT DISTINCT` clause includes a set of key columns in it, then all the rows are already known to be unique. Since you can declare a set of columns to be a `PRIMARY KEY` in the table declaration, an optimizer can spot such a query and automatically change `SELECT DISTINCT` to just `SELECT`.

You can often replace a `SELECT DISTINCT` clause with an `EXIST()` subquery, in violation of another rule of thumb that says to prefer unnested queries to nested queries. For example, a query to find the students who are majoring in the sciences would be:

```
SELECT DISTINCT S1.name
  FROM Students AS S1, ScienceDepts AS D1
 WHERE S1.dept = D1.dept;
```

This query can be better replaced with:

```
SELECT S1.name
  FROM Students AS S1
 WHERE EXISTS
       (SELECT *
          FROM ScienceDepts AS D1
         WHERE S1.dept = D1.dept);
```

Another problem is that the DBA might not declare all candidate keys or might declare superkeys instead. Consider a table for a school schedule:

```
CREATE TABLE Schedule
(room_nbr INTEGER NOT NULL,
 course_name CHAR(7) NOT NULL,
 teacher_name CHAR(20) NOT NULL,
 period_nbr INTEGER NOT NULL,
 PRIMARY KEY (room_nbr, period_nbr));
```

This says that if I know the room and the period, I can find a unique teacher and course—"Third-period Freshman English in Room 101 is taught by Ms. Jones." However, I might have also added the constraint `UNIQUE (teacher, period)`, since Ms. Jones can be in only one room and teach only one class during a given period. If the table was not declared with this extra constraint, the optimizer could not use it in parsing a query. Likewise, if the DBA decided to declare `PRIMARY KEY (room_nbr, course_name, teacher_name, period_nbr)`, the optimizer could not break down this superkey into candidate keys.

Avoid using a `HAVING` or a `GROUP BY` clause if the `SELECT` or `WHERE` clause can do all the needed work. One way to avoid grouping is in situations where you know the group criterion in advance and then make it a constant. This example is a bit extreme, but you can convert:

```
SELECT project, AVG(cost)
  FROM Tasks
 GROUP BY project
HAVING project = 'bricklaying';
```

to the simpler and faster:

```
SELECT 'bricklaying', AVG(cost)
  FROM Tasks
 WHERE project = 'bricklaying';
```

Both queries have to scan the entire table to inspect values in the project column. The first query will simply throw each row into a bucket based on its project code, then look at the `HAVING` clause to throw away all but one of the buckets before computing the average. The second query rejects those unneeded rows and arrives at one subset of projects when it scans.

Standard SQL has ways of removing `GROUP BY` clauses, because it can use a subquery in a `SELECT` statement. This is easier to show with an example in which you are now in charge of the Widget-Only Company inventory. You get requisitions that tell how many widgets people are putting into or taking out of the warehouse on a given date. Sometimes that quantity is positive (returns); sometimes it is negative (withdrawals).

The table of requisitions looks like this:

```
CREATE TABLE Requisitions
(req_date DATE NOT NULL,
 rteq_qty INTEGER NOT NULL
     CONSTRAINT non_zero_qty
     CHECK (req_qty <> 0));
```

Your job is to provide a running balance on the quantity on hand with a query. We want something like:

```
RESULT
 req_date     req_qty   qty_on_hand
================================
'2005-07-01'    100     100
'2005-07-02'    120     220
'2005-07-03'   -150      70
'2005-07-04'     50     120
'2005-07-05'    -35      85
```

The classic SQL solution would be:

```
SELECT R1.reqdate, R1.qty, SUM(R2.qty) AS qty_on_hand
  FROM Requisitions AS R1, Requisitions AS R2
 WHERE R2.reqdate <= R1.reqdate
 GROUP BY R1.reqdate, R1.qty;
```

Standard SQL can use a subquery in the SELECT list, even a correlated query. The rule is that the result must be a single value, hence the name scalar subquery; if the query results are an empty table, the result is a NULL.

In this problem, we need to do a summation of all the requisitions posted up to and including the date we are looking at. The query is a nested self-JOIN, thus:

```
SELECT R1.reqdate, R1.qty,
      (SELECT SUM(R2.qty)
         FROM Requisitions AS R2
        WHERE R2.reqdate <= R1.reqdate) AS qty_on_hand
  FROM Requisitions AS R1;
```

Frankly, both solutions are going to run slowly compared to a procedural solution that could build the current quantity on hand from

the previous quantity on hand, using a sorted file of records. Both queries will have to build the subquery from the self-joined table based on dates. However, the first query will also probably sort rows for each group it has to build. The earliest date will have one row to sort, the second earliest date will have two rows, and so forth until the most recent date will sort all the rows. The second query has no grouping, so it just proceeds to the summation without the sorting.

33.10 Avoid CROSS JOINs

Consider a three-table JOIN like this.

```
SELECT P1.paint_color
  FROM Paints AS P1, Warehouse AS W1, Sales AS S1
 WHERE W1.qty_on_hand + S1.qty_sold =
       P1.gallons/2.5;
```

Because all of the columns involved in the JOIN are in a single expression, their indexes cannot be used. The SQL engine will construct the CROSS JOIN of all three tables first and then prune that temporary working table to get the final answer. In Standard SQL, you can first do a subquery with a CROSS JOIN to get one side of the equation:

```
(SELECT (W1.qty_on_hand + S1.qty_sold) AS stuff
  FROM Warehouse AS W1 CROSS JOIN Sales AS S1)
```

and then push it into the WHERE clause, like this:

```
SELECT color
  FROM Paints AS P1
 WHERE EXISTS ((SELECT (W1.qty_on_hand + S1.qty_sold)
                  FROM Warehouse AS W1 CROSS JOIN Sales AS S1)
             = (P1.gallons/2.5));
```

The SQL engine, we hope, will do the two-table CROSS JOIN subquery and put the results into a temporary table. That temporary table will then be filtered using the Paints table, but without generating a three-table CROSS JOIN as the first form of the query did.

With a little algebra, the original equation can be changed around and different versions of this query built with other combinations of tables.

A good rule of thumb is that the `FROM` clause should only have those tables that provide columns to its matching `SELECT` clause.

33.11 Learn to Use Indexes Carefully

By way of review, most indexes are tree structures. They consist of a page or node that has values from the columns of the table from which the index is built, and pointers. The pointers point to other nodes of the tree and eventually point to rows in the table that has been indexed. The idea is that searching the index is much faster than searching the table itself in a sequential fashion (called a table scan).

The index is also ordered on the columns used to construct it; the rows of the table may or may not be in that order. When the index and the table are sorted on the same columns, the index is called a clustered index. The best example of this in the physical world is a large dictionary with a thumb-notch index—the index and the words in the dictionary are both in alphabetical order.

For obvious physical reasons, you can use only one clustered index on a table. The decision as to which columns to use in the index can be important to performance. There is a superstition among older DBAs who have worked with ISAM files and network and hierarchical databases that the primary key must be done with a clustered index. This stems from the fact that in the older file systems, files had to be sorted or hashed on their keys. All searching and navigation was based on this.

This is not true in SQL systems. The primary key's uniqueness will probably be preserved by a unique index, but it does not have to be a clustered unique index. Consider a table of employees keyed by a unique employee identification number. Updates are done with the employee ID number, of course, but very few queries use it. Updating individual rows in a table will actually be about as fast with a clustered or a nonclustered index. Both tree structures will be the same, except for the final physical position to which they point.

However, it might be that the most important corporate unit for reporting purposes is the department, not the employee. A clustered index on the employee ID number would sort the table in employee-ID order. There is no inherent meaning in that ordering; in fact, I would be more likely to sort a list of employees by their last names than by their ID numbers.

However, a clustered index on the (nonunique) department code would sort the table in department order and put employees in the same

department on the same physical page of storage. The result would be that fewer pages would be read to answer queries.

33.12 Order Indexes Carefully

Consider the Personnel table again. There may be a difference among these `CREATE INDEX` statements:

```
1. CREATE INDEX XDeptDiv
   ON Personnel (dept, division);

2. CREATE INDEX XDivDept
   ON Personnel (division, dept);

3. CREATE CLUSTERED INDEX XCDeptDiv
   ON Personnel (dept, division);

4. CREATE CLUSTERED INDEX XCDivDept
   ON Personnel (division, dept);
```

In cases 1 and 2, some products build an index only on the first column and ignore the second column. This is because their SQL engine is based on an older product that allows only single-column indexing, and the parser is throwing out the columns it cannot handle. Other products use the first column to build the index tree structure and the secondary columns in such a way that they are searched much more slowly. Both types of SQL engine are like an alphabetic accordion file. Each pocket of an accordion file locates a letter of the alphabet, but within each pocket you have to do a manual search for a particular paper.

If your implementation suffers from this problem, the best thing to do is to order the columns by their granularity; that is, put the column with the most values first and the column with the fewest values last. In our example, assume that we have a few divisions located in major cities, and within each division we have lots of departments. An indexed search that stops at the division will leave us with a scan over the many departments. An indexed search that stops at the department will leave us with a scan over the few divisions.

Most SQL products will concatenate the columns listed in the `CREATE INDEX` statement. But you have to know in what order they will be concatenated. A telephone book is order by (last_name, first_name), so it is easy to look up someone if you know his or her last name. If you only know the first name, you have to read the whole darn telephone book until you find the right person. You can spot this problem when you have a slow query on a column with an index on it that is using a table scan.

If you are lucky, or have planned things carefully, you can get a covering index for your query. This means that the index has all of the columns needed to answer the query, so the base table upon which it is built never has to be accessed.

In some products, you may find that the ordering will not matter, or that separate nonunique indexes will do as well as or better than a unique compound index. The reason is that they use hashing or bit-map indexes. Foxpro and Nucleus are two examples of products that use different bit-map schemes, but they have some basic features in common. Imagine an array with table row numbers or pointers on its columns, and values for that column on its rows. If a table row has that value in that position, then the bit is set; if not, the bit is zeroed. A search is done by doing bitwise ANDs, ORs, and NOTs on the bit vectors.

This might be easier to explain with an example of the technique. Assume we have a table of Parts, which has columns for the attributes color and weight.

```
Parts
part_nbr part_name  color  weight city
=========================================
'p1'      'Nut'      'Red'     12    'London  -- Physical row # 3
'p2       'Bolt'     'Green'   17    'Paris'  -- Physical row # 4
'p3'      'Cam'      'Blue'    12    'Paris'  -- Physical row # 7
'p4'      'Screw'    'Red'     14    'London' -- Physical row # 9
'p5'      'Cam'      'Blue'    12    'Paris'  -- Physical row # 11
'p6'      'Cog'      'Red'     19    'London' -- Physical row # 10
```

The bit indexes are built by using the physical row and the values of the attributes in an array, thus:

```
INDEX Parts(color)
 Rows   1 2 3 4 5 6 7 8 9  10 11
       ========================
Blue  | 0 0 0 0 0 0 1 0 0  0  1
Green | 0 0 0 1 0 0 0 0 0  0  0
Red   | 0 0 1 0 0 0 0 0 1  1  0
```

```
INDEX Parts(weight)
 Rows  1 2 3 4 5 6 7 8 9 10 11
      ==========================
  12  | 0 0 1 0 0 0 1 0 0  0  1
  17  | 0 0 0 1 0 0 0 0 0  0  0
  14  | 0 0 0 0 0 0 0 0 1  0  0
  19  | 0 0 0 0 0 0 0 0 0  1  0
```

To find a part that weighs 12 units and is colored red, you would perform a bitwise AND, and get a new bit vector as the answer:

```
Red    | 0 0 1 0 0 0 0 0 1 1  0
AND
  12  | 0 0 1 0 0 0 1 0 0  0  1
      ==========================
answer| 0 0 1 0 0 0 0 0 0  0  0
```

To find a part that weighs 12 units or is colored red, you would perform a bitwise OR, and get a new bit vector as the answer:

```
Red   | 0 0 1 0 0 0 0 0 1 1 0
OR
  12  | 0 0 1 0 0 0 1 0 0 0 1
      ========================
answer| 0 0 1 0 0 0 1 0 1 1 0
```

Searches become a combination of bitwise operators on the indexes before any physical access to the table is done.

33.13 Know Your Optimizer

One of the best tricks is to know what your optimizer favors. It is often the case that one query construction will have special code written for it that an equivalent query construction does not. Consider this simple adjacency list model of a tree:

```
CREATE TABLE Tree
(node_id CHAR(2) NOT NULL,
 parent_node_id CHAR(2), -- null is root node
 creation_date DATE DEFAULT CURRENT_TIMESTAMP NOT NULL);
```

Let's try to group all the parent_node_ids and display the creation_date of the most recent subordinate under that parent_node_id. This is a straightforward query that can be done with the following statement:

```
SELECT node_id, T1.parent_node_id, T1.creation_date
  FROM Tree AS T1
 WHERE NOT EXSTS
      (SELECT *
         FROM Tree AS T2
        WHERE T2.parent_node_id = T1.parent_node_id
          AND T2.creation_date > T1.creation_date);
```

The EXISTS() predicate says that there is no sibling younger than the one we picked. Or, as an alternative, you can use an OUTER JOIN to do the same logic.

```
SELECT T1.node_id, T1.parent_node_id, T1.creation_date
  FROM Tree AS T1
       LEFT OUTER JOIN
       Tree AS T2
       ON T2.parent_node_id = T1.parent_node_id
         AND T2.creation_date > T1.creation_date
 WHERE T2.node_id IS NULL;
```

However, this query was run in SQL Server 2000. Lee Tudor pointed out that SQL Server looks for a join to an aggregated self-view on the group condition and aggregate. Performance is far superior to the alternates, due to the query optimizer having a special way of dealing with it.

```
SELECT T1.node_id, T1.parent_node_id, T1.creation_date
  FROM Tree AS T1
       INNER JOIN
       (SELECT parent_node_id, MAX(creation_date)
          FROM Tree
         GROUP BY parent_node_id)
       AS T2 (parent_node_id, creation_date)
       ON T2.parent_node_id = T1.parent_node_id
          AND T2.creation_date = T1.creation_date;
```

The optimizer will change from release to release, but it is a good general statement that once a trick is coded into it, the trick will stay there until there is a major change in the product.

In 1988, Fabian Pascal published an article in *Database Programming and Design* on the PC database systems available at the time (Pascal 1998), in which he wrote seven logically equivalent queries as a test suite. These tests revealed vastly uneven performance for all of the RDBMS products except Ingres. Ingres's timings were approximately the same for all seven queries, and Ingres had the best average time. The other products showed wide variations across the seven queries, with the worst timing more than an order of magnitude longer than the best. In the case of Oracle, the worst timing was more than 600 times the best.

While optimizers have gotten better over the years, there are still "hot spots" in specific optimizers that favor particular constructions.

33.14 Recompile Static SQL after Schema Changes

In most implementations, static SQL is compiled in a host program with a fixed execution plan. If a database schema object is altered, execution plans based on that object have to be changed.

In older SQL implementations, if a schema object was dropped, the programmer had to recompile the queries that referred to it. The SQL engine was not required to do any checking, and most implementations did not. Instead, you could get a runtime error.

Even worse, you could have a scenario like this:

1. Create table A
2. Create view VA on table A
3. Use view VA
4. Drop table A
5. Create a new table A
6. Use view VA

What happens in step 6? That depended on your SQL product, but the results were not good. The worst result was that the entire schema could be hopelessly messed up. The best result was that the VA in step 3 was not the VA in step 6, but was still usable.

Standard SQL added the option of specifying the behavior of any of the `DROP` statements as either `CASCADE` or `RESTRICT`. The `RESTRICT` option is the default in Standard SQL, and it will disallow the dropping of any schema object that is being used to define another object. For example, if RESTRICT is used, you cannot drop a base table that has VIEWs defined on it or is part of a referential integrity constraint. The CASCADE option will drop any of the dependent objects from the schema when the original object is removed.

Be careful with this! The X/Open transaction model assumes a default action of CASCADE, and some products may allow it to be set as a system parameter. The moral to the story is that you should never use an implicit default on statements that can destroy your schema when an explicit clause is available.

Some products will automatically recompile static SQL when an index is dropped; some will not. However, few products automatically recompile static SQL when an index is added. Furthermore, few products automatically recompile static SQL when the statistical distribution within the data has changed. Oracle's Rdb is an exception to this, since it investigates possible execution paths when each query is invoked.

The DBA usually has to update the statistical information explicitly and ask for a recompilation. What usually happens is that one person adds an index and then compiles his program. The new index could either hinder or help other queries when they are recompiled, so it is hard to say whether the new index is a good or a bad thing for the overall performance of the system.

However, it is always bad is when two programmers build indexes that are identical in all but name and never tell each other. Most SQL implementations will not detect this. The duplication will waste both time and space. Whenever one index is updated, the other one will have to be updated also. This is one reason that only the DBA should be allowed to create schema objects.

33.15 Temporary Tables Are Sometimes Handy

Another trick is to use temporary tables to hold intermediate results to avoid CROSS JOINs and excessive recalculations. A materialized VIEW is also a form of temporary table, but you cannot index it. In this problem, we want to find the total amount of the latest balances in all our accounts.

Assume that the Payments table holds the details of each payment and that the payment numbers are increasing over time. The Accounts

table shows the account identification number and the balance after each payment is made. The query might be done like this:

```
SELECT SUM(A1.balance)
  FROM Accounts AS A1, Payments AS P1
 WHERE P1.acct_nbr = A1.acct_nbr
       AND P1.payment_nbr = (SELECT MAX(payment_nbr)
                               FROM Payments AS P2
                              WHERE P2.acct_nbr = A1.acct_nbr);
```

Since this uses a correlated subquery with an aggregate function, it will take a little time to run for each row in the answer. It would be faster to create a temporary working table or VIEW like this:

```
BEGIN
CREATE TABLE LastPayments
(acct INTEGER NOT NULL,
 last_payment_nbr INTEGER NOT NULL,
 payment_amt DECIMAL(8,2) NOT NULL,
 payment_date DATE NOT NULL,
 ...  );

CREATE INDEX LPX ON LastPayment(acct, payment_nbr);

INSERT INTO LastPayments
SELECT acct, payment_nbr, MAX(payment_nbr)
  FROM Payments
 GROUP BY acct, payment_nbr;

SELECT SUM(A1.balance) -- final answer
  FROM Accounts AS A1, LastPayments AS LP1
 WHERE LP1.acct_nbr = A1.acct_nbr
   AND LP1.payment_nbr = A1.payment_nbr;

DROP TABLE LastPayments;

END;
```

Consider this three-table query that creates a list of combinations of items and all the different packages for which the selling price (price and box cost) is 10% of the warranty plan cost. Assume that any item can fit into any box we have and that any item can be put on any warranty plan.

```
SELECT I1.item
  FROM Inventory AS I1, Packages AS P1, Warranty AS W1
 WHERE I1.price + P1.box = W1.plancost * 10;
```

Since all the columns appear in an expression, the engine cannot use indexes, so the query will become a large CROSS JOIN in most SQL implementations. This query can be broken down into a temporary table that has an index on the calculations, thus:

```
BEGIN
CREATE TABLE SellingPrices
(item_name CHAR (15) NOT NULL,
 sell_price DECIMAL (8,2) NOT NULL);

-- optional index on the calculation
CREATE INDEX SPX ON SellingPrices (sell_price);

-- do algebra and get everything on one side of an equation
INSERT INTO SellingPrices (item_name, sell_price)
SELECT DISTINCT I1.item_name, (P1.box + I1.price) * 0.1
  FROM Inventory AS I1, packages AS P1;

-- do the last JOIN
SELECT DISTINCT SP1.item_name
  FROM SellingPrices AS SP1, Warranty AS W1
 WHERE SP1.sell_price = W1.plancost;
END;
```

The Sybase/SQL Server family allows a programmer to create temporary tables on the fly. This is a totally different model of temporary table than the Standard SQL model. The standard model does not allow a user to create any schema objects.

In the Sybase/SQL Server model such *ad hoc* creations have no indexes or constraints, and therefore act like "scratch paper" with its own name. However, they do not give much help to the optimizer. This is a holdover from the days when we allocated scratch tapes in file systems to hold the results from one step to another in a procedural process.

You can often use derived tables in the query in place of these temporary tables. The derived table definition is put into the parse tree, and the execution plan can take advantage of constraints, indexing, and self-joins.

33.16 Update Statistics

This is going to sound obvious, but the optimizer cannot work without valid statistics. Some signs that your statistics need to be updated are:

1. *Two queries with the same basic structure have different execution times*. This usually means that the statistical distribution has changed, so one of the queries is being executed under old assumptions.
2. *You have just loaded a lot of new data*. This is often a good time to do the update to the statistics, because some products can get them as part of the loading operation.
3. *You have just deleted a lot of old data*. Unfortunately, deletion operations do not change statistics like insertions.
4. *You have changed the query mix*. For example, the end-of-the-month reports depend on shared views to aggregate data. In the earlier SQL products, you could put these `VIEW`s into temporary tables and index those tables. This would allow the optimizer to gather statistics. Today, the better SQL products will do the same job under the covers by materializing these `VIEW`s. You need to find out if you need to compute indexes and/or do the statistics.

References

General References

Adams, Douglas. 1980. *The Hitchhiker's Guide to the Galaxy*. New York: Harmony Books (1st U.S. edition). *ISBN 0-517-54209-9.*

Babbage, Charles. *For information, contact the Charles Babbage Institute, University of Minnesota.*

Logic

Bolc, Leonard and Borowik, Piotr. 1992. *Many-Valued Logics*. New York: Springer-Verlag. *ISBN: 3-540-55926-4. This book has a whole chapter devoted to three valued logic systems.*

Boole, George. 1854, 1951. *An Investigation of the Laws of Thought, on Which Are Founded the Mathematical Theories of Logic and Probabilities*. New York: Macmillan and Co., 1854. New York: Dover Books, 1951. *The original is a rare collector's piece, but you can get a reprint of the original 1854 edition (Dover Books, 1951). ISBN 0-486-60028-9*

Celko, Joe. 1992. "SQL Explorer: Voting Systems." *DBMS Magazine* 11.

Mathematical Techniques

Gardner, Martin. 1983. *Wheels, Life, and Other Mathematical Amusements*. New York: W. H. Freeman. *ISBN 0-716-71589-9.*

Huff, Darrell, and Geis, Irving (illustrator). 1993 (reissue). *How to Lie with Statistics*. New York: Norton. *ISBN 0-393-31072-8.*

Melzak, Z. A. 1983. *Bypasses: A Simple Approach to Complexity*. New York: Wiley InterScience. *ISBN 0-471-86854-X.*

Mrdalj, Stevan; Vujovic, Branislav; and Jovanovic, Vladan. 1996. "SQL Matrix Processing." *Database Programming and Design* (August).

Random Numbers

Bays, Carter, and Sharp, W. E. 1992. "Improved Random Numbers for Your Personal Computer or Workstation." *Geobyte* 7(2):25.

Carta, David G. 1990. "Two Fast Implementations of the 'Minimal Standard' Random Number Generator."*Communications of the ACM* 33(1):87.

Chambers, W. G., and Dai, Z. D. 1991. "Simple but Effective Modification to a Multiplicative Congruential Random-number Generator." *IEEE Proceedings: Computers and Digital Technology* 138(3):121.

Chassing, P. 1989. "An Optimal Random Number Generator Zp." *Statistics and Probability Letters* 7(4):307.

Elkins, T. A. 1989. "A Highly Random-number Generator." *Computer Language* 6(12):59.

Hulquist, Paul F. 1991. "A Good Random Number Generator for Microcomputers." *Simulation* 57(4):258.

Kao, Chiang. 1989. "A Random Number Generator for Microcomputers." *OR: The Journal of the Operational Research Society* 40(7):687.

Knuth, Donald. 1981. *The Art of Computer Programming, Volume 2: Seminumeral Algorithms*. (2nd ed.) Reading, MA: Addison-Wesley, p. 29.

———. 1998. *The Art of Computer Programming, Volume 3: Sorting and Searching*. (2nd ed.) Reading, MA: Addison-Wesley Professional.

Komo, John J. 1991. "Decimal Pseudo-random Number Generator." *Simulation* 57(4):228.

Lancaster, Don. 1977. *CMOS Cookbook*. LOC: Sams Publishers, p. 318.

Leva, Joseph L. 1992a. "Algorithm 712: A Normal Random Number Generator." *ACM Transactions on Mathematical Software* 18(4):454.

———. 1992b. "A Fast Normal Random Number Generator."*ACM Transactions on Mathematical Software* 18(4):449.

Macomber, James H., and White, Charles S. 1990. "An N- Dimensional Uniform Random Number Generator Suitible for IBM- Compatible Microcomputers." *Interfaces* 20(3):49.

Maier, W. L. 1991. "A Fast Pseudo Random Number Generator." *Dr. Dobb's Journal* 17(5):152.

Marsaglia, G., Narasimhan, B., and Zaman, A. 1990. "A Random Number Generator for PCs." *Computer Physics Communications* 60:345-349.

Marsaglia, G., and Zaman, A. 1990. "Toward a Univesal Random Number Generator." *Statistics and Probability Letters* 8:35-39.

Morton, Mike. 1985. "A Digital Dissolve for Bit-Mapped Graphics Screens." *Dr. Dobb's Journal* #48.

Park, S. K. and K. W. Miller. 1988. "Random Number Generators: Good Ones are Hard to Find." *CACM* 31(10):1201.

Press, William H. et al. 1989. *Numerical Recipes in Pascal: the Art of Scientific Computing*. (Revised edition.) Cambridge, UK: Cambridge University Press, p. 233. *ISBN 0-52138766-3.*

Sezgin, Fatin. 1990. "On a Fast and Portable Uniform Quasi-random Number Generator." *Simulation Digest* 21(2):30.

Scales and Measurements

Crocker and Algina. 1986. *Introduction to Classical and Modern Test Theory*. Harcourt-Brace. *ISBN 0-030-61634-4.*

Missing Values

Codd, E. F. 1975. "Understanding Relations." *FDT* 7:3-4.

Grahne. 1989. "Horn Tables—an Efficient Tool for Handling Incomplete Information in Databases."*ACM SIGACT/SIGMOD/SIGART Symposium on Principles of Database Systems*, pages 75-82.

Grant. 1977. "Null Values in Relational Databases." *Information Processing Letters* 6:5. North-Holland.

———. 1979. "Partial Values in a Tabular Database Model."*Information Processing Letters* 6:5. North-Holland.

Honeyman. 1980. "Functional Dependencies and the Universal Instance Property in the Relational Model of Database Systems." Doctoral Dissertation, Princeton University.

Lien. 1979. "Multivalued Dependencies with Null Values in Relational Databases." *VLDB V*, Rio De Janeiro. ACM/IEEE.

Lipski. 1981a. "On Semantic Issues Connected with Incomplete Information." *ACM TODS*. pp. 262-296.

———. 1981b. "On Databases with Incomplete Information," *Journal Of the ACM* 28(1):41-47.

McGoveran, David. 1993. "Nothing from Nothing Part I (or, What's Logic Got to Do With It?)."*Database Programming and Design* 6(12):32. *A four part series on missing values which argues against the SQL style NULL in favor of indicators.*

———. 1994a. "Nothing from Nothing Part II: Classical Logic: Nothing Compares 2 U." *Database Programming and Design* 7(1):54.

———. 1994b. "Nothing from Nothing Part III: Can't Lose What You Never Had. *Database Programming and Design* 7(2):42."

———. 1994c. "Nothing from Nothing Part IV: It's in the Way That You Use It. *Database Programming and Design* 7(3):54."

Rozenshtein, David. 1981. "Implementing Null Values in Relations."

———. 1995. *Optimizing Transact SQL*. SQL Forum Press. *ISBN 0-9649812-0-3.*

SPARC Study Group on Database Management Systems. 1975. "Interim Report 75-02-08 to the ANSI X3." *FDT-Bulletin ACM SIGMOD* 7(2).

Vassiliou. 1979. "Null Values in Database Management—A Denotational Semantics Approach."*ACM SIGMOD Conference*, pp. 162-169.

———. 1980. "Functional Dependencies and Incomplete Information."*VLDB VI*, Montreal. ACM/IEEE.

Walker. 1979. "A Universal Table Relational Database Model with Blank Entries."

Zaniolo. 1984. "Database Relations with Null Values." *Journal of Computer and System Sciences* 28(1):142-166.

Regular Expressions

Friedl, Jeffrey E. F. 2002. *Mastering Regular Expressions*. 2nd ed. Cambridge, MA: O'Reilly.

Stubblebine, Tony. 2003. *Regular Expression Pocket Reference*. Cambridge, MA: O'Reilly

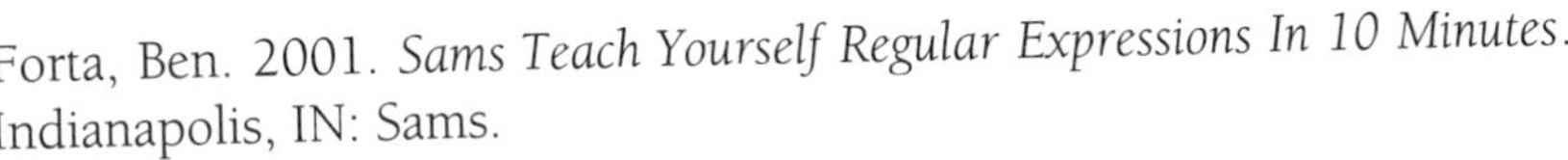

Forta, Ben. 2001. *Sams Teach Yourself Regular Expressions In 10 Minutes*. Indianapolis, IN: Sams.

Good, Nathan A. 2005. *Regular Expression Recipes: A Problem-Solution Approach*. Berkeley, CA: Apress.

Watt, Andrew. 2005. *Beginning Regular Expressions (Programmer to Programmer)*. Indianapolis, IN: Wrox.

Graph Theory

Cormen, Thomas H., Leiserson, Charles E., and Rivest, Ronald L. 1990. *Introduction to Algorithms*. McGraw-Hill Companies. *ISBN 0-262-03141-8.*

Even, Shimon. 1979. *Graph Algorithms*. Rockville, Maryland: Computer Science Press. *ISBN 0-914894-21-8.*

Fulkerson, D. R. (ed.). 1975. *Studies in Graph Theory, vol. I*. American Mathematical Association. *ISBN 0-88358-111-3.*

———. 1975. *Studies in Graph Theory, vol. II*. American Mathematical Association. *ISBN 0-88358-112-3.*

Harary, Frank. 1972. *Graph Theory*. Boston: Addison-Wesley. *ISBN 0-201-02787-9.*

McHugh, James A. 1990. *Algorithmic Graph Theory*. Englewood Cliffs, NJ: Prentice-Hall. *ISBN 0-13-023615-2.*

Ore, Oystein (revised by Robin J. Wilson). 1990. *Graphs and Their Uses*. American Mathematical Association. *ISBN 0-88358-635-2.*

Introductory SQL Books

Atzeni, Paolo, and De Antonellis, Valeria. 1993. *Relational Database Theory*. Redwood City, CA: Benjamin-Cummings. *ISBN 0-8053-0261-1.*

Date, C. J. 1995. *An Introduction to Database Systems*. 6th ed. Reading, MA: Addison-Wesley. *ISBN 0-191-82458-2.*

———. 2003. *An Introduction to Database Systems*. 8th ed. Reading, MA: Addison-Wesley. *ISBN 0-321-19784-4.*

———. 1983. *Database: A Primer*. Boston: Addison-Wesley. *ISBN 0-201-11358-9.*

Groff, James R., and Weinberg; Paul N. 1994. *LAN Times Guide to SQL*. McGraw/Hill. *ISBN 0-07-882026-X.*

Gruber, Martin. 1990. *Understanding SQL*. Sybex. *ISBN 0-89588-644-8.*

Gulutzan, Peter and Pelzer, Trudy. 2002. *SQL Performance Tuning*. Boston, MA: Addison-Wesley. *ISBN 0-201-79169-2.*

Lorie, Raymond and Daudenarde, Jean-Jacques. 1991. *SQL and Its Applications*. Englewood Cliffs, NJ: Prentice-Hall. *ISBN 0-13-837956-4.*

Lusardi, Frank. 1988. *The Database Expert's Guide to SQL*. McGraw-Hill. *ISBN 0-07-039002-9.*

Pascal, Fabian. 1989. *SQL and Relational Basics*. Redwood City, CA: M&T Books. *ISBN 1-55851-063-X. (Out of print.)*

———. 1993. *Understanding Relational Databases*. John Wiley. *ISBN 0-471-58538-6.*

Shasha, Dennis E., and Bonnet, P. 2002. *Database Tuning*. San Francisco, CA: Morgan Kaufmann. *ISBN 1-55860-753-6.*

Stonebraker, Michael. 1988. *Readings in Database Systems*. San Francisco, CA: Morgan Kaufmann. *ISBN 0-934613-65-6.*

Trimble, J. Harvey Jr., and Chappell, David. 1989. *A Visual Introduction to SQL*. John Wiley. *ISBN 0-471-61684-2.*

van der Lans, Rick F. 1989. *The SQL Standard: A Complete Guide Reference*. Hertfordshire, UK: Prentice-Hall International. *ISBN 0-13-840059-8.*

Wellesley Software Group. 1991. *Learning SQL*. Upper Saddle River, NJ: Prentice-Hall. *ISBN 0-13-528704-9.*

Wellesley Software Group. 1992. *Learning Advanced SQL*. Upper Saddle River, NJ: Prentice-Hall. *ISBN 0-13-528712-X.*

Optimizing Queries

Gulutzan, Peter, and Pelzer, Trudy. 1994. *Optimizing SQL: Embedded SQL In C*. R&D Technical Books. *ISBN 0-13-100215-5.*

Shasha, Dennis E. 1992. *Database Tuning: A Principled Approach*. Upper Saddle River, NJ: Prentice-Hall. *ISBN 0-13-205246-6.*

Temporal Data and the Year 2000 Problem

ANSI X3; 30-1985 (R-1991). "Representation for Calendar Date and Ordinal Date for Information Interchange."

ANSI X3; 51-1994. "Information Systems—Representations of Universal Time, Local Time Differentials, and United States Time Zone References for Information Interchange."

Arnold, Dr. Robert S. 1995a. "Millennium Now: Solutions for Century Data Change Impact." *Application Development Trends* (January).

———. 1995b. "Resolving Year 2000 Problems in Legacy Software." Presentation at *Software Quality Week*, San Francisco, CA.

Associated Press. 1995. "Troubled Time." May 25.

Celko, Joe. 1981. "Father Time Software Secrets Allows Updating of Dates." *Information Systems News* (February).

Cini, Al. 1995. "System Bug of the Apocalypse." *Internetwork* (January).

Cohn, Michael B., "No Need to Fear the Year 2000," Computerworld, vol. 28, n. 47, 21 Nov 1994, p. 35.

Fine, Doug. 1995. "Companies Brace for Millennium."*Infoworld* (April 10).

Furman, Jeff Marotta, Albert, and Candiotti, Cliff. 1995. "Party When It's 1999."*Software Magazine* (April).

Hayes, Brian. 1995. "Waiting for 01-01-00." *American Scientist* 83 (January-February).

Hitchens, Randall L. 1991. "Viewpoint." *Computerworld* (January 28).

ISO-8601. 1988. "Data Elements and Interchange Formats—Information Interchange—Representation of Dates and Times."

Murray, Jerome T., and Murray, Marilyn J. 1984. *Computers in Crisis*. Princeton, NJ: Petrocelli Books. *ISBN 0-89433-223-6. A solution, with code, for the Year 2000 problem.*

Ross, Noah. 1995. "The End of the Century Is Nearer Than You Think." *Application Development Trends* (April).

Rubin, Dr. Howard, and Woodward, Jim. "Millenium: A Billion Dollar Software Crisis." videotape by The Computer Channel, Inc.

Sullivan, R. Lee. 1995. "Ghosts in the Machines." *Forbes* (June 19).

Tantzen, Robert G. 1980. "Algorithm 199: Conversion between Calendar Date and Julian Day Number." *Collected Algorithms from the ACM (Association for Computing Machinery)*.

Xenakis; John. 1995. "The Millenium Bug: The *Fine de Siécl* Computer Virus." *CFO Magazine* (July).

Zerubavel, Eviatar. 1985. *The Seven Day Circle*. New York: Free Press. *ISBN 0-02-934680-0. A history of the week in different calendar systems.*

SQL Programming Techniques

Celko, Joe. 1992. "Implementing T-Joins in SQL Queries." *DBMS Magazine* (March).

———. 1993. "Views: More than Meets the Eye."*Database Programming and Design* (September). *Letter citing Nelson Mattos, from an ANSI X3H2 paper.*

———, and Date, C. J. 1993. "Access Path: Lauds and Lectures, Kudos and Critiques."*Database Programming and Design* (September). *Letter to the editor.*

Classics

Bernstein, P. A. 1976. "Synthesizing Third Normal Form Relations from Functional Dependencies." *ACM Transactions on Database Systems* 1(4):277-98.

Codd, E. F. 1970. "A Relational Model of Data for Large Shared Data Banks."*Communications of the ACM* 13(6):377-387. *Association for Computing Machinery.*

Comer, D. 1978. "The Difficulty of Optimum Index Selection." *ACM Transactions on Database Systems* 3(4):440-445.

Damerau, F. J. 1964. "A Technique for Computer Detection of Correction of Spelling Errors." *Communications of the ACM* 7(3).

Date, C. J. 1992. "According to Date: Shedding Some Light." *Database Programming and Design* (February):15-17.

Goodman, Nathan. 1990. "VIEW Update Is Practical." *InfoDB* 5(2).

Information Systems Week (ISW). 1987. "Code Overload Plagues NYC Welfare System." *Information Systems Week* (December).

Limeback, Rudy. Undated publication. "SQL Workshop Challenge." *Explain* (18).

Lorie, Raymond A., and Daudenarde, Jean-Jacques. 1991. *SQL and its Applications*. Englewood Cliffs, NJ: Prentice-Hall.

Martinis, Miljenko. 1992. "Letters column." *DBMS Magazine* (May).

Melton, Jim, and Simon, Alan R. 1993. *Understanding the New SQL: Complete Guide*. San Francisco, CA: Morgan Kaufmann. *ISBN 1-55860-245-3.*

Murchison, Rory. Undated publication. "SQL Workshop Challenge."*Explain* (16).

Paitetsky-Shapiro, G. 1983. "The Optimal Selection of Secondary Indexes in NP-Complete." *SIGMOD Record* 13(2):72-75.

Palmer, Roger. 1994. *The Bar Code Book*. Helmer's Publishing. *ISBN 0-911261-09-5*.

Philips, Lawrence. 1990. "Hanging on the Metaphone (A Phonetic Text-Retrieval Algorithm Better than Soundex)." *Computer Language* 7(12):38.

Rozenshtein, D., Abramovich, Anatoly, and Birger, Eugene. 1993. "Loop-Free SQL Solutions for Finding Continuous Regions." *SQL Forum* 2(6).

Smithwick, Terry. 1991. Pascal version of Lawrence Philips' 1990 "Hanging on the Metaphone (A Phonetic Text-Retrieval Algorithm Better than Soundex)." *Computer Language* 7(12):38.

SQL Forum. 1993, 1994. See articles by Anatoly Abramovich Yelena Alexandrova, and Eugene Birger (July/August 1993, March/April 1994).

Stevens, S. S. 1957. "On the Psychophysical Law," *Psychological Review* 64:153-181.

Tillquist, John, and Kuo, Feng-Yang. 1989. "An Approach to the Recursive Retrieval Problem in the Relational Database." *Communications of the ACM* 32(2):239.

van der Lans, Rick. 1990/1991. "SQL Portability." *The Relational Journal* 2(6).

Verhoeff, J. 1969. "Error Detecting Decimal Codes." *Mathematical Centre Tract #29*, The Mathematical Centre (Amsterdam).

Vicik, Rick. 1993. "Advanced Transact SQL."*SQL* (July/August).

Forum

Wankowski, Jim. Undated publication. "SQL Workshop Solutions."*Explain* (17).

Yozallinas, J. R. 1981. "Letters column." *Tech Specialist* (May).

Updatable Views

Codd, E. F. "RV-6 VIEW Updating." *The Relational Model for Database Management, Version 2. ISBN 0-201-14192-2.*

Date, C. J. 1986. "Updating VIEWs." *Relational Database: Selected Writings*. Reading, MA: Addison-Wesley. *ISBN 0-201-14196-5.*

———. and Darwen, Hugh. 1991. "Role of Functional Dependencies in Query Decomposition."*Relational Database Writings—1989-1991*. Reading, MA: Addison-Wesley. *ISBN 0-201-54303-6*.

Goodman, Nathan. 1990. "VIEW Update Is Practical." *INFODB* 5(2).

Umeshar, Dayal, and Bernstein, P. A. 1982. "On the Correct Translation of Update Operations on Relational VIEWs." *ACM Transactions on Database Systems* 7(3).

Theory, Normalization, and Advanced Database Topics

Bernstein, P. A. 1976. "Synthesizing Third Normal Form Relations from Functional Dependencies." *ACM Transactions on Database Systems* 1(4):277-298.

Codd; E. F. 1990. *The Relational Model for Database Management: Version* 2. Reading, MA: Addison Wesley.

Date, C. J. 1986. *Relational Database Selected Writings*. Reading, MA: Addison-Wesley. *ISBN 0-201-14196-5*.

———. 1990. *Relational Database Writings—1985-1989*. Reading, MA: Addison-Wesley. *ISBN 0-201-50881-8*.

———. 1992. *Relational Database Writings—1989-1991*. Reading, MA: Addison-Wesley. *ISBN 0-201-54303-6*.

———. 1995. *Relational Database Writings—1991-1994*. Reading, MA: Addison-Wesley. *ISBN 0-201-82459-0*.

Dutka, Alan, and Hanson, Howard. 1989. *Fundamentals of Data Normalization*. Reading, MA: Addison-Wesley. *ISBN 0-201-06645-9*.

Fagin, Ron. 1979. "Normal Forms and Relational Database Operators." *Proceedings ACM SIGMOD International Conference on Management of Data. The definitive paper on the five normal forms.*

Fleming, Candace C., and von Halle, Barbara. 1989. *Handbook for Relational Database Design*. Reading, MA: Addison-Wesley. *ISBN 0-201-11434-8*.

Kent, William. 1983. "A Simple Guide to Five Normal Forms in Relational Database Theory." *Communications of the ACM* 26(2).

Maier, David. 1983. *The Theory of Relational Databases*. Redwood City, CA: Computer Science Press. *ISBN 0-914894-42-0*.

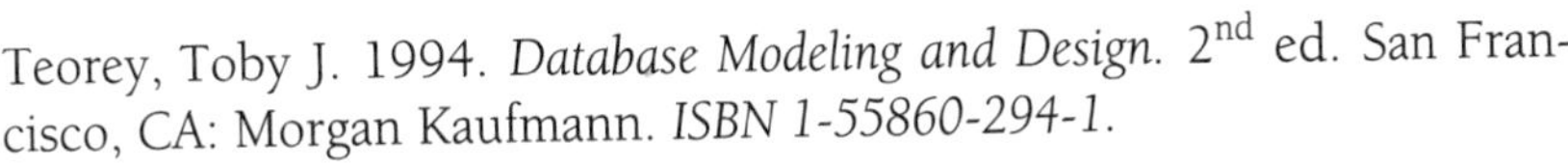

Teorey, Toby J. 1994. *Database Modeling and Design*. 2nd ed. San Francisco, CA: Morgan Kaufmann. *ISBN 1-55860-294-1*.

Books on SQL-92 and SQL-99

Cannan, Stephen, and Otten, Gerard. 1992. *SQL: The Standard Handbook*. McGraw-Hill. *ISBN 0-07-707664-8*.

Date, C. J., and Darwen, Hugh. 1993. *A Guide to the SQL Standard*. LOC: Reading, MA: Addison-Wesley. *ISBN 0-201-55822-X*.

Gruber, Martin. 1990. *Understanding SQL*. Alameda, CA: Sybex. *ISBN 0-89588-644-8*.

Gruber, Martin. 1994. *SQL Instant Reference*. Alameda, CA: Sybex. *ISBN 0-7821-1148-3*.

Gulutzan, Peter, and Pelzer, Trudy. 1999. *SQL-99 Complete, Really*. CMP Books. *ISBN 0-87930568-1*.

Melton, Jim, and Simon, Alan. 1993. *Understanding the New SQL: A Complete Guide*. San Francisco, CA: Morgan Kaufmann. *ISBN 155860-245-3*.

Standards and Related Groups

For ANSI and ISO standards:

American National Standards Institute
1430 Broadway
New York, NY 10018
Phone: (212) 354-3300

Director of Publications
American National Standards Institute
11 West 42nd Street
New York, NY 10036
(212) 642-4900

Copies of the SQL-92 document and other ANSI documents can be purchased from:

Global Engineering Documents Inc
2805 McGaw Avenue
Irvine, CA 92714
Phone: (800) 854-7179

Other consortiums are:

X/Open
1010 El Camino Real #380
Menlo Park, CA 94025
Phone: (415) 323-7992

NOTE: the SQL Access Group is now part of X/Open

NIST
Technology A-266
Gaithersberg, MD 20899

TPC Council
c/o Shanley Public Relations
777 North First Street #600
San Jose, CA 95112-6113
Phone: (408) 295-8894

Object Management Group
492 Old Connecticut Path
Framingham, MA 01701
Phone: (508) 820-4300

Web Sites Related to SQL

The SQL home page is maintained by one of the X3H2 Committee members at:

www.jjc.com/sql_stnd.html

You can also get help with queries and technical stuff at:

www.inquiry.com/techtips/thesqlpro/index.html

Statistics

The American Statistical Association has their material online and you can find many articles on the computation of various statistics.

www.amstat.org/publications/tas/

www.amstat.org/publications/technometrics/

Chan, Tony F., Golub, Gene H., and LeVeque, Randall J. 1983. "Algorithms for Computing the Sample Variance: Analysis and Recommendations. *The American Statistician* 37(3):242-247. "

Welford, B. P. 1962. "Note on a Method for Calculating Corrected Sums of Squares and Products." *Technometrics* 4:419-420.

Temporal Databases

Date, Chris, Darwen, H., and Lorentzos, N.A. 2002. *Temporal Data and the Relational Model*. San Francisco, CA: Morgan Kaufmann. *ISBN 1-55860-855-9.*

Jensen, C. S. Clifford, J., Elmasri, R., Gadia, S. K., Hayes P., and Jajodia, S. (eds). 1994. "A Glossary of Temporal Database Concepts."*ACM SIGMOD Record* 23(1):52-64.

Ozsoyoglu, G., and Snodgrass, R. T. 1995. "Temporal and Real-Time Databases: A Survey." *IEEE Transactions on Knowledge and Data Engineering* 7(4):513-532.

Snodgrass, R. T. (ed.), Ahn, I., Ariav, G., Batory, D., Clifford, J., Dyreson, C.E., Elmasri, R., Grandi F., Jensen C. S., Kaefer W., Kline, N., Kulkarni, K., Leung, T. Y. C., Lorentzos, N., Roddick, J. F., Segev, A., Soo, M. D., and Sripada, S. M. 1995. *The Temporal Query Language TSQL2*. Norwell, MA: Kluwer Academic Publishers.

Snodgrass, R. T., Boehlen, M. H., Jensen, C. S., and Steiner, A. 1996. *Adding Valid Time to SQL/Temporal*. Change proposal, ANSI X3H2-96-501r2, ISO/IEC JTC 1/SC 21/WG 3 DBL-MAD-146r2. *At ftp://ftp.cs.arizona.edu/tsql/tsql2/sql3/mad146.pdf.*

———. 1996. *Adding Transaction Time to SQL/Temporal*. Change proposal, ANSI X3H2-96-502r2, ISO/IEC JTC1/SC21/WG3 DBL MAD-147r2. *At ftp://ftp.cs.arizona.edu/tsql/tsql2/sql3/mad147.pdf.*

Snodgrass, R. T. and Jensen, C. 1999. *Temporal Databases*. San Francisco, CA: Morgan Kaufmann. *ISBN 1-558604-365-9. The book is out of print, but the material is available on the Univerity of Arizona Web site, under the account of Dr. Snodgrass.*

Tansel, A., Clifford, J., Gadia, S. K., Jajodia, S., Segev, A., and Snodgrass, R. T. (eds.). 1993. *Temporal Databases: Theory, Design, and Implementation*. Database Systems and Applications Series. Redwood City, CA: Benjamin/Cummings Pub. Co.

Tsotras, V. J., and Kumar, A. 1996. "Temporal Database Bibliography Update." *ACM SIGMOD Record* 25(1):41-51.

Zaniolo, C. Ceri, S., Faloutsos, C., Snodgrass, R. T., Subrahmanian, V. S., and Zicari, R. 1997. *Advanced Database Systems*. San Francisco, CA: Morgan Kaufmann.

New Citations

Microsoft Research Technical Report: MSR-TR-95-51. 1995. "A Critique of ANSI SQL Isolation Levels" by Hal Berenson, Phil Bernstein, Jim Gray, Jim Melton, Elizabeth O'Neil, and Patrick O'Neil.

Bose, R. C., and R. J. Nelson. A Sorting Problem. *Journal of the ACM*, vol. 9.

Codd, E. F. 1990. *The Relational Model for Database Management: Version 2*. Reading, MA: Addison Wesley.

Codd, E. F. 1979. "Extending the Database Relational Model to Capture More Meaning." *ACM Transactions on Database Systems*. 4(4):397-434

Dijkstra, Edsger. 1968. Go To Statement Considered Harmful. *Communications of the ACM* 11(3):147-148. *Addresses old versus new JOIN syntax.*

Gonzales, Michael L. 2003. *The IBM Data Warehouse*. New York: Wiley.

———. 2004. "The SQL Language of OLAP."*Intelligent Enterprise* (September 18).

Hegeman, Frédérick. 1993. "Sorting Networks,"*The C/C++ User's Journal* (February).

Knuth, Donald. *The Art Of Computer Programming*. vol. 3

Larsen, Sheryl. 1996. "Powerful SQL: Beyond the Basics." *DB2 Magazine* (Winter). *Article may be viewed online at www.db2mag.com/db_area/archives/1996/q4/9601lar.shtml.*

Melton, Jim. 1998. *Understanding SQL's Stored Procedures*. San Francisco, CA: Morgan Kaufmann. *ISBN 1-55860-461-8.*

Moreau, Tom, and Ben-Gan, Itzik. 2001. *Advanced Transact-SQL for SQL Server 2000*. Berkeley, CA: Apress. *ISBN 1-89311-582-8.*

Pascal, Fabian. 1988 OR 1998. "SQL Redundancy and DBMS Performance." *Database Programming and Design* 1(12).

The Unicode Consortium. 2003. *The Unicode Standard, Version 4.0*. Reading, MA: Addison-Wesley. *ISBN 0-321-18578-1.*

Watson, E. J. 1962. "Primitive Polynomials (Mod 2)." *Mathematics of Computation* 16:368-369.

Zemke, Fred, Kulkami, Krishna, Witkowski, Andy, and Lyle, Bob. "Introduction to OLAP Functions." ANSI document.

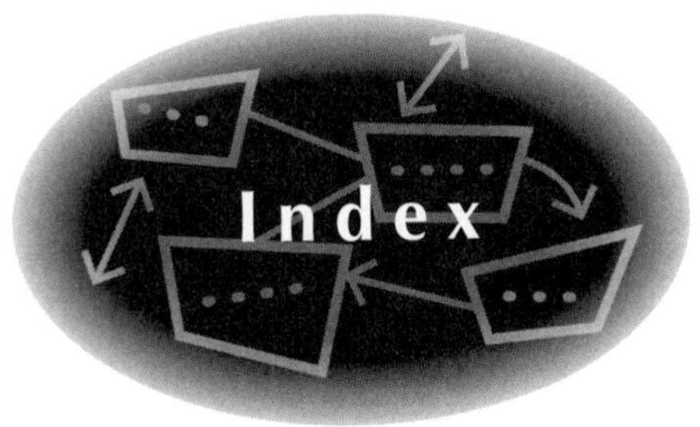

Index

ABOUT THE AUTHOR

Joe Celko is a noted consultant and lecturer, and one of the most-read SQL authors in the world. He is well known for his 10 years of service on the ANSI SQL standards committee, his column in *Intelligent Enterprise* magazine (which won several Reader's Choice Awards), and the war stories he tells to provide real-world insights into SQL programming. His best-selling books include *Joe Celko's SQL for Smarties: Advanced SQL Programming, second edition; Joe Celko's SQL Puzzles and Answers;* and *Joe Celko's Trees and Hierarchies in SQL for Smarties.*